ACC 200

North Carolina State University

2nd Edition

Roby B. Sawyers | Steve Jackson | Greg Jenkins |
Norman H. Godwin | C. Wayne Alderman

 CENGAGE
Learning·

Australia • Brazil • Japan • Korea • Mexico • Singapore • Spain • United Kingdom • United States

CENGAGE
Learning·

ACC 200: North Carolina State University, 2nd Edition

Financial ACCT2, 2nd Edition
includes CengageNOW Printed Access Card
Norman H. Godwin | C. Wayne Alderman

© 2013, 2011 Cengage Learning. All rights reserved.

Managerial ACCT2, 2nd Edition
includes CengageNOW with eBook Printed Access Card
Roby B. Sawyers | Steve Jackson | Greg Jenkins

© 2013, 2011 Cengage Learning. All rights reserved.

Senior Project Development Manager:
Linda deStefano

Market Development Manager:
Heather Kramer

Senior Production/Manufacturing Manager:
Donna M. Brown

Production Editorial Manager:
Kim Fry

Sr. Rights Acquisition Account Manager:
Todd Osborne

For product information and technology assistance, contact us at
Cengage Learning Customer & Sales Support, 1-800-354-9706

For permission to use material from this text or product, submit all requests online at **cengage.com/permissions**
Further permissions questions can be emailed to
permissionrequest@cengage.com

This book contains select works from existing Cengage Learning resources and was produced by Cengage Learning Custom Solutions for collegiate use. As such, those adopting and/or contributing to this work are responsible for editorial content accuracy, continuity and completeness.

Compilation © 2013 Cengage Learning
ISBN-13: 978-1-285-91559-3

ISBN-10: 1-285-91559-3

Cengage Learning
5191 Natorp Boulevard
Mason, Ohio 45040
USA

Cengage Learning is a leading provider of customized learning solutions with office locations around the globe, including Singapore, the United Kingdom, Australia, Mexico, Brazil, and Japan. Locate your local office at: **international.cengage.com/region.**
Cengage Learning products are represented in Canada by Nelson Education, Ltd.
For your lifelong learning solutions, visit **www.cengage.com/custom.**
Visit our corporate website at **www.cengage.com.**

Printed in the United States of America

Brief Contents

Excerpted from:
Financial ACCT2
2nd Edition
Norman H. Godwin | C. Wayne Alderman
9781111530778

Excerpted from:
Managerial ACCT2
2nd Edition
Roby B. Sawyers | Steve Jackson | Greg Jenkins
9781111822606

Financial Accounting

Introduction

Imagine for a moment that you are home for the summer and decide to mow lawns to make some money. With $50 of your own money and $100 borrowed from a relative, you pay $130 to rent a lawn mower and a gas can for June and purchase $20 of gas. During June, you mow 40 lawns at $10 each, buy $175 of additional gasoline, and pay your relative $1 of interest. At the end of June, you have $194 in cash, $10 of gasoline, and $30 due from customers.

Given this information, can you tell what happened to your business in June? Were you profitable? What do you have to show for your efforts? How can you tell? Getting answers to such questions requires accounting.

Accounting is the process of identifying, measuring, and communicating economic information to permit informed judgments and decisions. Put more simply, accounting is the "language of business." When you want to know about the financial results of a business, you must understand and speak accounting. The purpose of this book is to teach you this language.

With this overall purpose in mind, the current chapter introduces the basic terms, principles, and rules that comprise the grammar of the accounting language. It does so by creating the June financial statements of the lawn service scenario described above. At the end of the chapter, you should be familiar with the four main financial statements of accounting. You should also have a working accounting vocabulary that can be built upon in the following chapters.

LO1 Beginning Assumptions

Accounting The process of identifying, measuring, and communicating economic information to permit informed judgments and decisions.

The purpose of accounting is to identify, measure, and communicate economic information about a particular entity to interested users. As a foundation for accomplishing this purpose, accountants make the following four assumptions: economic entity, time period, monetary unit, and going concern.

Accounting, the "language of business," would describe this picture as a guy using an asset (the lawn mower) to generate a revenue (the money he will be paid).

ACCT

Uripos/eStock Photo/Alamy

Economic Entity Assumption

The **economic entity assumption** states that the financial activities of a business can be separated from the financial activities of the business's owner(s). This assumption allows a user to examine a company's accounting information without concern that the information includes the personal affairs of the owner(s). For the lawn service example in the introduction, this means that personal activities such as buying gasoline for your automobile should not be included with the business activities of buying

> **Economic entity assumption** Accountants assume that the financial activities of a business can be separated from the financial activities of the business's owner(s).

After conducting its 2008 audit of General Motors Corporation, the public accounting firm Deloitte & Touche LLP wrote the following in its auditor's report:

"[General Motors'] recurring losses from operations, stockholders' deficit, and inability to generate sufficient cash flow to meet its obligations and sustain its operations raise substantial doubt about its ability to continue as a going concern."

This language is commonly known as a going concern opinion. The auditor uses it to inform the public of its opinion that the company's continued operations are in doubt. Going concern opinions are therefore designed to protect a company's stakeholders and allow them to make decisions with the most accurate information available.

While no company wants to receive a going concern opinion, receiving one does not always mean that the company will cease operations. But, it does mean that there is substantial doubt that the company will continue without significant changes. In the case of General Motors, these significant changes began on June 1, 2009 when the company filed for Chapter 11 bankruptcy protection. With the help of governmental financing, the company then emerged from bankruptcy on July 10, 2009. Since that time, General Motors has improved its financial position and has paid off its debt to the federal government ahead of schedule. As a result, Deloitte and Touch LLP did not include a going concern opinion in its most recent auditor's report for General Motors.

gasoline for the lawn mower. These activities can and should be accounted for separately.

Time Period Assumption

Business owners and other interested parties usually do not want to wait long before they receive information about how a business is doing. They want periodic measurements of the business's success or failure. Accountants therefore assume that economic information can be meaningfully captured and communicated over short periods of time, even if those time periods are somewhat artificial, such as one month or one quarter. This is known as the **time period assumption**.

> **Time period assumption** Accountants assume that economic information can be meaningfully captured and communicated over short periods of time.
>
> **Monetary unit assumption** Accountants assume that the dollar is the most effective means to communicate economic activity.
>
> **Going concern assumption** Accountants assume that a company will continue to operate into the foreseeable future.

Most companies communicate to users on both a quarterly and annual basis. In fact, publicly traded companies such as Starbucks are required by law to file quarterly and annual financial statements with the Securities and Exchange Commission (SEC). For the lawn service example, the time period is the month of June.

Monetary Unit Assumption

The **monetary unit assumption** assumes that the dollar is the most effective means to communicate economic activity. If an economic activity cannot be expressed in dollars, then it is not recorded in the accounting system. It assumes further that the dollar is reasonably stable with respect to inflation and deflation. As a result, accountants do not adjust economic values based on inflation or deflation. A dollar earned in 1982 is the same as a dollar earned in 2012.

Going Concern Assumption

The **going concern assumption** states that a company will continue to operate into the foreseeable future. This assumption enables accountants to use certain techniques that will be described later in the chapter. Unless

On Home Depot's income statement in Appendix C, you can find the following four descriptions: 1) The Home Depot, Inc. and Subsidiaries, 2) amounts in millions, 3) Fiscal Year Ended January 30, 2011. Which assumption does each description best relate?

1) economic entity, 2) monetary unit, 3) time period

there is evidence to the contrary, most companies are assumed to be going concerns. Those that are not going concerns are often in the process of liquidation (that is, selling their resources and paying off their obligations). Because the lawn service will continue through the summer, it is a going concern at the end of June.

LO2 Reporting Profitability: The Income Statement

One of the first questions asked of any business is whether it makes money. Stated differently in "accounting" words, is the business profitable? Does it generate more resources than it uses? Accounting provides answers to these questions with a financial statement called an *income statement*. An income statement reports a company's *revenues* and *expenses*.

Revenues

A **revenue** is an increase in resources resulting from the sale of goods or the provision of services. Receiving $10 for mowing a lawn is an example of a revenue. You have $10 more than you did previously because you provided a service. Other revenue common to businesses is investment income.

Revenues are recorded according to the revenue recognition principle. The **revenue recognition principle** states that a revenue should be recorded when a resource has been earned. A resource is earned when either the sale of the good or the provision of the service is substantially complete and cash collection is reasonably assured.

Given these definitions, total June revenues for the lawn service are as follows. You have only one source of revenue—mowing lawns. Assuming that your customers will pay you, your lawn service creates a revenue each time a lawn is mowed. So, if you mowed 40 lawns at $10 each, revenues total $400 for the month. Note from the previous information that you have yet to collect $30 of that $400. However, revenues are still $400 because cash collection is reasonably assured.

Expenses

An **expense** is a decrease in resources resulting from the sale of goods or provision of services. The gasoline consumed while mowing lawns is an example of an expense. Other expenses common to businesses are wages, taxes, advertising, and utilities.

Expenses are recorded according to the matching principle. The **matching principle** states that expenses should be recorded in the period resources are used to generate revenues. For example, since fuel is used to mow lawns in June, June expenses should include the fuel used.

Given these definitions, total June expenses for the lawn service are as follows. Unlike the revenue side, the lawn service has three sources of expenses. The first is fuel. The amount of fuel used during June can be calculated as follows from the given information:

Amount on hand on June 1	$ 20
+ Amount purchased during June	175
− Amount on hand on June 30	(10)
Amount used during June	$185

Therefore, fuel expense is $185.

> **Revenue** An increase in resources resulting from the sale of goods or the provision of services.
>
> **Revenue recognition principle** The principle that a revenue should be recorded when a resource has been earned.
>
> **Expense** A decrease in resources resulting from the sale of goods or provision of services.
>
> **Matching principle** The principle that expenses should be recorded in the period resources are used to generate revenues.

The second expense relates to your borrowing. You paid your relative $1 at the end of June to compensate her for loaning you $100. Paying for the use of someone else's money is called interest. Therefore, interest expense is $1.

The third expense relates to your use of the rented equipment—the lawn mower and the gas can. You paid $130 for the right to use the equipment during the month. The cost of renting equipment is usually called rent expense. Therefore, rent expense for June is $130.

The Income Statement

Once a company's revenues and expenses are calculated, they are reported on an income statement. An **income statement** is a financial statement that shows a company's revenues and expenses over a specific period of time. Its purpose is to demonstrate the financial success or failure of the company over that specific period of time. When revenues exceed expenses, a company generates net income. When expenses exceed revenues, a company generates a net loss. The basic structure of the statement is as follows:

> Revenues − Expenses = Net Income or Net Loss

Given the revenues and expenses determined previously, the lawn service's June income statement would

Income statement A financial statement that reports a company's revenues and expenses over a specific period of time.

> The income statement's purpose is to demonstrate the financial success or failure of the company over a specific period of time.

appear as Exhibit 1-1. It contains the company name, the statement name, and the time reference, which for this example is the month of June. It also shows that the lawn service generated $84 of net income during June.

Exhibit 1-1 Income Statement for Lawn Service, Inc.

Lawn Service, Inc.
Income Statement
For the Month Ending June 30

Revenues		$400
Expenses:		
Fuel	$185	
Interest	1	
Rent	130	
Total expenses		316
Net income		$ 84

LO3 Reporting Financial Position: The Balance Sheet

Another important issue for any business is its current financial position. What does the business own? What does it owe? Accounting provides answers to these questions with a financial statement called a *balance sheet*. A balance sheet reports a company's *assets*, *liabilities*, and *equity*.

Assets

An asset is a resource of a business. More formally, an **asset** is an economic resource that is objectively measurable, that results from a prior transaction, and that will provide future economic benefit. Cash is a good example of an asset. It can be counted, it is received through a transaction with someone else, and it can be used to buy things in the future. Other common assets include merchandise inventory, equipment, supplies, and investments.

Assets are recorded and reported according to the historical cost principle, which is often shortened to the cost principle. The **cost principle** states that assets should be recorded and reported at the cost paid to acquire them.

Given these definitions, the lawn service has three assets at the end of June—$194 of cash, $10 of remaining fuel, and $30 of receivables from customers. Note that although the lawn service uses a lawnmower and gas can, it rents them from another entity. Therefore, the lawnmower and gas can are assets of the rental company, not the lawn service.

Liabilities

A liability is an obligation of a business. More formally, a **liability** is an obligation of a business that results from a past transaction and will require the sacrifice of economic resources at some future date. Examples of liabilities common to businesses include notes payable to creditors, accounts payable to vendors, salaries payable to employees, and taxes payable to governments. The only liability of the lawn service at the end of June is the $100 borrowed from your relative, who is considered a creditor. As will be explained below, the business does not have a liability for the $50 of your own money that was contributed to the company. You are an owner, not a creditor.

Equity

Equity is the difference between a company's assets and liabilities and represents the share of assets that are claimed by the company's owners. An example of equity with which you may be familiar is home equity.

A homeowner's equity refers to the difference between the value of the home and the amount owed to the bank. Equity in accounting is the same principle except that it refers to the difference between the cost of the business's assets and its liabilities.

A company can generate equity in two ways. The first is through contributed capital. **Contributed capital** is defined as the resources that investors contribute to a business in exchange for an ownership interest. The $50 that you, the owner, put into the lawn service is contributed capital. Note here that contributed capital is not a revenue. The increase of $50 did not result from the lawn service providing a service or selling a product. It came by selling an ownership interest. The most common method that companies use to generate contributed capital is the sale of common stock to investors.

The second way a company generates equity is through profitable operations. When a company generates net income, it can either distribute those profits to owners or retain them in the business to grow the business further. Profits that are distributed to owners are called **dividends**. Note here that dividends are not an expense of a company. They are simply a distribution of company assets to owners. Profits that are retained in the business are called **retained earnings**. A company's retained earnings therefore represent the equity generated and retained from profitable operations. Since the lawn service did not distribute any assets to you, the owner, it retained the entire $84 of June profits.

Asset An economic resource that is objectively measurable, results from a prior transaction, and will provide future economic benefit.

Cost principle The principle that assets should be recorded and reported at the cost paid to acquire them.

Liability An obligation of a business that results from a past transaction and will require the sacrifice of economic resources at some future date.

Equity The difference between a company's assets and liabilities, representing the share of assets that is claimed by the company's owners.

Contributed capital The resources that investors contribute to a business in exchange for ownership interest.

Dividends Profits that are distributed to owners.

Retained earnings Profits that are retained in the business.

Because a balance sheet is reported at a specific point in time, it is often referred to as a snapshot of a business.

The Balance Sheet

A company's assets, liabilities, and equity are reported on a balance sheet. A **balance sheet** is a financial statement that shows a company's assets, liabilities, and equity at a specific point in time. Its purpose is to show, at a given point in time, a company's resources and the claims against those resources. Because a balance sheet is reported at a specific point in time, it is often referred to as a snapshot of a business. The basic structure of the statement is as follows:

Assets = Liabilities + Equity

Given the assets, liabilities, and equity determined previously, the lawn service's balance sheet would appear as Exhibit 1-2. It contains the company name, the statement name, and the time reference, which for this example is June 30.

Notice that total assets equal total liabilities plus total equity. This will always be the case for any

Balance sheet A financial statement that reports a company's assets, liabilities, and equity at a specific point in time.

Statement of retained earnings A financial statement that reports the change in a company's retained earnings over a specific period of time.

Exhibit 1-2 Balance Sheet for Lawn Service, Inc.

Lawn Service, Inc.
Balance Sheet
June 30

Cash	$194	
Accounts receivable	30	
Supplies (fuel)	10	
Total assets		$234
Note payable to relative	$100	
Total liabilities		$100
Contributed capital	$ 50	
Retained earnings	84	
Total equity		134
Total liabilities and equity		$234

business. An entity's assets are always claimed by someone. Either they are owed to someone (in this case, your relative) or claimed by an owner (in this case, you). No asset of any business is ever unclaimed. This relationship between assets, liabilities, and equity is represented by the following equation, known as the fundamental accounting equation: **Assets = Liabilities + Equity**. This fundamental accounting equation is what the balance sheet reports. That is why it is called a *balance* sheet.

LO4 Reporting Equity: The Statement of Retained Earnings

Owners of a business are usually interested in how their equity is growing as a result of profitable operations. They are also interested in how that equity is distributed in the form of dividends. Such information is reported on the statement of retained earnings. A **statement of retained earnings** shows the

HOME DEPOT ANALYSIS

Look at Home Depot's balance sheet in Appendix C. Write out in numbers the company's accounting equation (A = L + E) for the most current year. How many different assets does the company disclose?

1) $40,125 = $21,236 + $18,889 (in millions)
2) Thirteen different assets are listed on the company's balance sheet.

change in a company's retained earnings over a specific period of time. The basic structure of the statement is as follows:

> Retained Earnings, Beginning Balance
> +/– Net Income/Loss
> – Dividends
> = Retained Earnings, Ending Balance

The lawn service's statement of retained earnings would appear as Exhibit 1-3. It contains the company name, the statement name, and the time reference, which for this example is the month of June.

Exhibit 1-3 Statement of Retained Earnings for Lawn Service, Inc.

Lawn Service, Inc.
Statement of Retained Earnings
For the Month Ending June 30

Retained earnings, June 1	$ 0
+ Net income	84
– Dividends	0
Retained earnings, June 30	$ 84

Your business started with no retained earnings but generated net income of $84 in June. Since none of that income was distributed through dividends, the business retained all of those profits. Therefore, retained earnings increased from $0 to $84.

Linking the Income Statement and the Balance Sheet

In addition to showing the change in retained earnings, the statement of retained earnings links the income statement and the balance sheet. A company cannot calculate its retained earnings balance at the end of the period without factoring in the income earned during the period. The statement of retained earnings provides this link by including net income in the calculation of retained earnings, which is then reported on the balance sheet. This means that when preparing financial statements for any business, the income statement must be prepared first, followed by the

> When preparing financial statements, the income statement must be prepared first, followed by the statement of retained earnings and then the balance sheet.

statement of retained earnings and then the balance sheet. A graphical depiction of these links is included in Exhibit 1-4.

Exhibit 1-4 Relationship Among Financial Statements

Income Statement

Revenues	$400
– Expenses	316
Net income	$ 84

Statement of Retained Earnings

Retained earnings, June 1	$ 0
+ Net income	84
– Dividends	0
Retained earnings, June 30	$ 84

Balance Sheet

Total assets	$234
Liabilities	100
Contributed capital	50
Retained earnings	84
Total liabilities and equity	$234

LO5 Reporting Cash Flows: The Statement of Cash Flows

Another important issue for any business is its management of cash. Where does a company get its cash? Where does its cash go? Will there be enough cash to pay bills? Accounting provides answers to these questions with a financial statement called a *statement of cash flows*. A statement of cash flows reports a company's cash inflows and outflows from its *operating*, *investing*, and *financing activities*.

Financing Activities

Most businesses must raise funds to get started. Borrowing money from creditors and receiving contributions from investors are both ways to finance a business's operations. Therefore, generating and repaying cash from creditors and investors are considered *financing activities*. In the lawn service example, you contributed $50 of your own money and borrowed $100 from a relative. Both of these inflows are from financing activities. Therefore, the cash inflow in June from financing activities is $150.

Investing Activities

Once a company has raised sufficient capital from creditors and investors, it usually acquires the revenue-generating assets (for example, equipment) that it needs for operations. The buying and selling of such assets are considered *investing activities*. In the lawn service example, you rented the lawn mower and gas can instead of buying them. Therefore, there were no cash flows from investing activities. The cash flows associated with renting equipment are reported as operating activities.

Statement of cash flows A financial statement that reports a company's sources and uses of cash over a specific period of time.

Operating Activities

After the proper equipment is acquired, a business can begin operations. Operating a business includes activities such as the purchase of supplies, the payment of employees, and the sale of products. These transactions are considered *operating activities*. In the lawn service example, cash flows from operations in the month of June included $370 received from customers for mowing their lawns, $195 ($20 + $175) paid for gasoline to operate the lawn mower, $130 paid for equipment rental, and $1 paid to your relative for the right to use her $100. As a result, the net cash inflow from operating activities for the month was $44 ($370 − $195 − $130 − $1).

The Statement of Cash Flows

The details of a business' cash inflows and outflows are reported on a *statement of cash flows*. The **statement of cash flows** is a financial statement that shows a company's sources and uses of cash over a specific period of time. Its purpose is to inform users about how and why a company's cash changed during the period. The basic structure of the statement is as follows:

> Cash Flows Provided (Used) by Operating Activities
> +/− Cash Flows Provided (Used) by Investing Activities
> +/− Cash Flows Provided (Used) by Financing Activities
> = Net Increase (Decrease) in Cash

Given the cash inflows and outflows described previously, the lawn service's June statement of cash flows

An important issue for any business is its management of cash. Where does a company get its cash? Where does its cash go? Will there be enough cash to pay bills?

would appear as Exhibit 1-5. It contains the company name, the statement name, and the time reference, which for this example is the month of June. It also shows a net change in cash from June 1 to June 30 of $194. Note that

Exhibit 1-5 Statement of Cash Flows for Lawn Service, Inc.

Lawn Service, Inc.
Statement of Cash Flows
For the Month Ending June 30

Operating activities		
Cash received from customers	$ 370	
Cash paid for fuel	(195)	
Cash paid for equipment rental	(130)	
Cash paid for interest	(1)	
Net cash provided by operating activities		$ 44
Investing activities		
Net cash used by investing activities		0
Financing activities		
Cash received from borrowing	$ 100	
Cash received from contributions	50	
Net cash provided by financing activities		150
Net increase in cash		$ 194
Cash balance, June 1		0
Cash balance, June 30		$ 194

the ending cash balance on the statement agrees with the cash balance shown on the balance sheet in Exhibit 1-2.

LO6 Qualitative Characteristics of Accounting Information

Even though accounting is a very quantitative process and the financial statements introduced thus far are full of numbers, accounting information must possess certain qualitative characteristics to be considered useful. The following qualitative characteristics help ensure that accounting information is indeed useful.

Understandability

Accounting information should first and foremost be understandable. **Understandability** refers to the ability of accounting information to "be comprehensible to those who have a reasonable understanding of business . . . and are willing to study the information with reasonable diligence" (SFAC No. 2, par. 40). Notice that this definition puts much of the responsibility on the user of accounting information. Users must be willing to spend a "reasonable" amount of time studying the information. No specifics are given on what is a "reasonable" amount of time, but it is obvious that the more time you spend studying accounting information, the more you will understand.

> **Understandability** The ability of accounting information to "be comprehensible to those who have a reasonable understanding of business . . . and are willing to study the information with reasonable diligence."

HOME DEPOT ANALYSIS

Look at Home Depot's statement of cash flows in Appendix C. How much cash did the company generate or use for operating, investing, and financing activities during the most recent year?

Operating Activities: Generated $4,858 million

Investing Activities: Used $1,012 million

Financing Activities: Used $4,451 million

Relevance

Relevance refers to the capacity of accounting information to make a difference in decisions. Accounting information has this capacity when it possesses feedback value or predictive value. *Feedback value* refers to the ability to assess past performance, while *predictive value* refers to the ability to form expectations of future performance. In the lawn service example, four financial statements were created to demonstrate the financial activities for June. The statements provided feedback on the success of the business, but they also provided the data to generate expectations about July. As a result, the financial statements are relevant to our decision making, which makes them useful.

In addition to having feedback or predictive value, accounting information must be *timely* to be relevant. Information that helps you forecast August revenues is relevant when it is received in July, not when it is received in September. Information is relevant only if it is generated on a timely basis.

Reliability

Reliability refers to the extent to which accounting information can be depended upon to represent what it purports to represent, both in description and in number. To be considered reliable, accounting information

---

Relevance The capacity of accounting information to make a difference in decisions.

Reliability The extent to which accounting information can be depended upon to represent what it purports to represent, both in description and in number.

Comparability The ability to use accounting information to compare or contrast the financial activities of different companies.

---

should be verifiable, should have representational faithfulness, and should be neutral.

Information is *verifiable* if it can be proven to be free from error. One can often prove that accounting information is free from error by comparing the information to an original source document such as an invoice or a contract. For example, the rental cost of the lawn mower in your lawn service is verifiable because you could check the cost against the amount included on the rental agreement. If the two agree, the information is free from error and you can depend on it.

Information has *representational faithfulness* when the description corresponds to the underlying phenomenon. For example, in your lawn service, you purchased fuel to operate the business. In your balance sheet, the remaining fuel was reported as an asset. This reporting was a faithful representation of what the item truly was—a resource.

Information is *neutral* if it is presented in a way that is unbiased toward or against the reporting entity. In other words, neutral information does not portray an entity in a more or less favorable light than the information requires. In the lawn service example, income was reported to be $84, not more or less. The $84 figure was a neutral measure of the activities of the service.

Comparability

Comparability refers to the ability to use accounting information to compare or contrast the financial activities of different companies. Being able to compare information across companies allows an entity to assess its market position within an industry, to gauge its success against a competitor, and/or to set future goals based on industry standards.

As a company gets larger, its materiality threshold usually gets larger as well.

Comparability does not imply uniformity. Accounting rules allow for some discretion in the manner in which accounting is applied to economic phenomenon. As a result, two businesses with the same economic phenomenon could have different accounting information because they use different acceptable accounting methods. Because such differences in accounting methods are a challenge to comparability, accounting rules require that entities disclose the accounting methods that they use so that information can be more easily compared across entities. Usually, such methods are disclosed in the notes to the financial statements, which are discussed in Chapter 2.

Consistency

Consistency refers to the ability to use accounting information to compare or contrast the financial activities of the same entity over time. Consistency is obviously highest when an entity uses the same accounting methods year after year. In such a case, year-to-year comparisons can be very useful because they can reveal trends that help in generating expectations about future performance. However, entities sometimes change the manner in which they account for a particular economic event. Because such changes hinder consistency, accounting rules require that changes be disclosed by the company so that interested parties can assess the effect of the change. Such disclosures are usually found in the notes to the financial statements.

Materiality

Materiality is a concept that is closely related to relevance in that it refers to the threshold at which an item begins to affect decision making. Items meeting or exceeding the threshold are said to be material—that is, they are large enough to possibly affect decision making. Items below the threshold are said to be immaterial—that is, they are small enough that they will not affect decision making. The threshold varies across different companies and across different settings. As a company gets larger, its materiality threshold usually gets larger as well. Often, the materiality threshold is set at some percentage of assets or sales.

To see how materiality is applied, consider the following example from the lawn service. Suppose that an error occurred in the accounting for June transactions such that net income was incorrectly reported as $85 instead of $84. Would such an error affect your decision making about the service? Probably not. In other words, the error is immaterial because $1 is not large enough to affect your decision making.

While materiality is largely quantitative in nature, the materiality threshold is not always solely a function of dollar amounts. For example, an error of $1,000 in a routine transaction may be considered immaterial while a $1,000 error in a nonroutine transaction may be considered material. In addition, transactions that a company may consider immaterial may be considered material by users of the information. Materiality judgments are just that—judgments—and should be made with caution. Furthermore, just because something is immaterial does not mean that errors in accounting should be accepted and condoned. Accounting information must be reliable, so it should be free from error as much as possible.

> **Consistency** The ability to use accounting information to compare or contrast the financial activities of the same entity over time.
>
> **Materiality** The threshold at which a financial item begins to affect decision making.

Conservatism

Conservatism refers to the manner in which accountants deal with uncertainty regarding economic situations. When accountants are faced with uncertainty about how to account for or report a particular transaction or situation, conservatism dictates that they use the accounting that is least likely to overstate the company's assets and revenues or to understate the company's liabilities and expenses. A common example of conservatism in action is the lower-of-cost-or-market rule for inventory. According to this rule, inventory must be recorded and reported at the lower of its cost or its current market value. This ensures that the value of inventory is not overstated. Other applications of conservatism will be discussed in subsequent chapters.

> **Conservatism** The manner in which accountants deal with uncertainty regarding economic situations.
>
> **Conceptual framework of accounting** The collection of concepts that guide the manner in which accounting is practiced.

LO7 The Conceptual Framework

This chapter introduced many of the terms, principles, assumptions, and qualitative characteristics that are necessary to communicate the financial activities and position of a business. While they were initially described as the grammar of the financial accounting language, they are more formally known as components of the conceptual framework of accounting. The **conceptual framework of accounting** is the collection of concepts that guide the manner in which accounting is practiced.

The following tables summarize the elements of this conceptual framework. They will provide a good reference for you as you proceed through the remaining chapters. As you tackle more complex accounting methods and procedures, keep in mind that they are simply extensions of the basic grammar presented in the tables. So, with a good understanding of the conceptual framework, you have the grammar necessary to begin your study of accounting.

Terms Used to Identify and Describe Economic Information

Term	Definition	Reported on the
Asset	A resource of a business	Balance sheet
Liability	An obligation of a business	Balance sheet
Equity	The difference between assets and liabilities	Balance sheet
Contributed capital	Equity resulting from contributions from owners	Balance sheet
Retained earnings	Equity resulting from profitable operations	Balance sheet and statement of retained earnings
Revenue	An increase in assets resulting from selling a good or providing a service	Income statement
Expense	A decrease in assets resulting from selling a good or providing a service	Income statement
Dividend	A distribution of profits to owners	Statement of retained earnings

Principles Used to Measure Economic Information

Principle	Definition	Ramification
Revenue recognition	Revenues are recorded when they are earned.	The receipt of cash is not required to record a revenue.
Matching	Expenses are recorded in the time period when they are incurred to generate revenues.	For many assets, the cost of the asset must be spread over the periods that it is used.
Cost	Assets are recorded and maintained at their historical costs.	Except in a few cases, market values are not used for reporting asset values.

Assumptions Made When Communicating Economic Information

Assumption	Definition	Ramification
Economic entity	The financial activities of a business can be accounted for separately from the business's owners.	We do not have to worry that the financial information of the owner is mixed with the financial information of the business.
Monetary unit	The dollar, unadjusted for inflation, is the best means of communicating accounting information in the United States.	All transactions in foreign currencies are converted to dollars.
Time period	Accounting information can be communicated effectively over short periods of time.	Most businesses prepare quarterly and annual financial statements.
Going concern	The company for which we are accounting will continue its operations indefinitely.	If an entity is not selling its assets, then the cost principle is appropriate.

Qualitative Characteristics that Make Accounting Information Useful

Term	Definition	Ramification
Understandability	Accounting information should be comprehensible by those willing to spend a reasonable amount of time studying it.	Users must spend a reasonable amount of time studying accounting information for it to be understandable.
Relevance	Accounting information should have the capacity to affect decisions.	Information should have predictive or feedback value and should be timely.
Reliability	Accounting information should be dependable to represent what it purports to represent.	Information should be free from error, a faithful representation, and neutral.
Comparability	Accounting information should be comparable across different companies.	Entities must disclose the accounting methods that they use so that comparisons across companies can be made.
Consistency	Accounting information should be comparable across different time periods within a company.	An entity should use the same accounting methods year to year and disclose when they change methods.
Materiality	The threshold over which an item could begin to affect decisions.	Small errors, while not condoned, usually do not affect overall decision making.
Conservatism	When uncertainty exists, accounting information should present the least optimistic alternative.	An entity should choose accounting techniques that guard against overstating revenues or assets.

Financial Statements Used to Communicate Economic Information

Statement	Purpose	Structure	Links to Other Statements
Balance sheet	Shows a company's assets, liabilities, and equity at a specific point in time	Assets = Liabilities + Equity	The balance in retained earnings comes from the statement of retained earnings. The balance in cash should agree with the ending cash balance on the statement of cash flows.
Income statement	Shows a company's revenues and expenses over a specific period of time	Revenue − Expenses = Net Income or Net Loss	Net income goes to the statement of retained earnings to compute retained earnings.
Statement of retained earnings	Shows the changes in a company's retained earnings over a specific period of time	Beginning Retained Earnings +/− Net Income/Loss − Dividends = Ending Retained Earnings	Ending retained earnings goes to the balance sheet.
Statement of cash flows	Shows a company's inflows and outflows of cash over a specific period of time	Operating Cash Flows +/− Investing Cash Flows +/− Financing Cash Flows = Net change in cash	The ending cash balance on the statement of cash flows should agree with the balance in cash on the balance sheet.

Chapter review card

- ➔ Learning Objective and Key Concept Reviews
- ➔ Key Definitions and Formulas

Online (Located at www.cengagebrain.com)

- ➔ Flash Cards and Crossword Puzzles
- ➔ Games and Quizzes
- ➔ E-Lectures
- ➔ Homework Assignments (as directed by your instructor)

CONCEPT QUESTIONS

1. (LO1) What is the definition of accounting?
2. (LO1) What is the going concern assumption of accounting and why is it necessary for accounting?
3. (LO1) What is the economic entity assumption of accounting and why is it important?
4. (LO2) What two terms are used to determine and describe the profitability of an entity?
5. (LO2) When are revenues recognized?
6. (LO2) What does the matching principle state about the recording of revenues and expenses?
7. (LO2, 3) How are revenues different from assets?
8. (LO3) What five terms are used to describe the financial position of an entity?
9. (LO2, 3) How are liabilities different from expenses?
10. (LO3) Explain the difference between contributed capital and equity.
11. (LO2, 3) What are the three principles used in recording revenues, expenses, and assets?
12. (LO3) How are assets recorded?
13. (LO4) How are the balance sheet and income statement linked?
14. (LO2, 3, 4, 5) Explain why the different financial statements are used in accounting, and what purpose each statement serves.
15. (LO6) What are the qualitative characteristics of accounting and why are they necessary to accounting information?
16. (LO6) How are relevance and materiality related?
17. (LO7) What is the conceptual framework of accounting and what purpose does it serve?

MULTIPLE CHOICE

1. (LO1) Which of the following is not included in the definition of accounting?
   a. Identifying economic information
   b. Measuring economic information
   c. Developing economic information
   d. Communicating economic information
2. (LO1) Which assumption states that an economic entity will continue its operations indefinitely?
   a. Monetary unit
   b. Time period
   c. Going concern
   d. Economic entity
3. (LO2) Net income is created in a time period when:
   a. assets exceed liabilities.
   b. revenues exceed expenses.
   c. revenues are less than expenses.
   d. liabilities are greater than assets.
4. (LO2) Which financial statement reports revenues and expenses?
   a. Statement of retained earnings
   b. Balance sheet
   c. Statement of cash flows
   d. Income statement

5. (LO2) The revenue recognition principle states that:
   a. assets are recorded and maintained at their historical costs.
   b. revenues are recorded when they are earned.
   c. the dollar, unadjusted for inflation, is the best means of accounting in the U.S.
   d. revenues are recorded when cash is received.

6. (LO2) During the year, Callie's Bagel Shop had revenues of $125,000. Rent expense was $12,000. Salaries expense was $25,000. Short-term investments were $35,000. Other expenses totaled $40,000. What was Callie's net income?
   a. $85,000
   b. $13,000
   c. $48,000
   d. $60,000

7. (LO2) Which of the following accurately describes the matching principle?
   a. Matches assets and liabilities
   b. Matches income and dividends
   c. Matches retained earnings and income
   d. Matches revenues and expenses

8. (LO3) The basic accounting equation states:
   a. assets and liabilities equal equity.
   b. assets equal liabilities plus equity.
   c. liabilities equal equity plus assets.
   d. revenues minus expenses equals net income.

9. (LO3) Which financial statement reports assets, liabilities, and equity?
   a. Statement of cash flows
   b. Balance sheet
   c. Income statement
   d. Statement of retained earnings

10. (LO3) Retained earnings is defined as:
    a. the difference between assets and liabilities.
    b. equity generated from profitable operations and retained in the business.
    c. a decrease in assets resulting from selling a good or providing a service.
    d. equity resulting from contributions from owners.

11. (LO3) As of December 31, Lurie Company has assets of $18,400 and equity of $6,500. What are the liabilities for Lurie Company as of December 31?
    a. $24,900
    b. $11,900
    c. $14,200
    d. $8,600

12. (LO3) Maker's Company had the following account totals: cash $25,000; inventory $15,000; accounts payable $15,000; retained earnings $25,000; equipment $80,000; investments $10,000; and other assets $40,000. What is Maker's total assets?
    a. $170,000
    b. $190,000
    c. $85,000
    d. $210,000

13. (LO4) The statement of retained earnings links which two financial statements?
    a. The income statement and the balance sheet
    b. The balance sheet and the statement of cash flows
    c. The income statement and the statement of cash flows
    d. The statement of retained earnings does not link any statements

14. (LO4) A company begins a period with a $5,000 retained earnings balance. The company generates $12,000 of revenues and $10,000 of expenses during the period and pays $1,000 of dividends. What is the retained earnings balance at the end of the period?
    a. $7,000
    b. $5,000
    c. $6,000
    d. $1,000

15. (LO5) Which of the following is not one of the sections on the statement of cash flows?
    a. Investing activities
    b. Financing activities
    c. Operating activities
    d. Income activities

16. (LO6) Which of the following is not a qualitative characteristic of accounting?
    a. Understandability
    b. Relevance
    c. Pertinence
    d. Consistency

BRIEF EXERCISES

1. **Calculate Net Income** LO2
   Ted's Typing Service generated $4,000 in revenue in the month of January. Salaries were $1,500 for the month, and supplies used were $200. Additionally, Ted's incurred $50 for advertising during the month.

   Required
   Calculate Ted's net income for the month of January.

2. **Calculate Net Income** LO2
   A manager of a small company has a goal of generating $13,000 in net income. He is confident that his expenses will be approximately $82,500.

   Required
   Calculate the amount of revenue the manager must generate to reach his goal.

3. **Calculate Equity** LO3
   A company reports assets of $10,000 and liabilities of $6,000.

   Required
   Calculate the company's equity.
   Identify which principle relates to each statement.

4. Identify Accounting Principles LO2, 3

Each of the following statements is an application of the revenue recognition principle, the matching principle, or the cost principle.

1. A company records Equipment for the purchase price of $10,000 although the "suggested retail price" was $13,000.
2. A company receives $2,000 for a service to be performed but records only $1,000 as Service Revenue because it earned only half in the current period.
3. A company pays $6,000 for insurance but uses only $4,000 during the period. Therefore, it records only $4,000 as Insurance Expense.

5. Calculate Retained Earnings LO4

At the beginning of the year, a company has retained earnings of $175,000. During the year, the company generates $110,000 of net income and distributes $10,000 in dividends.

Required
Calculate the company's retained earnings at year end.

6. Calculate Cash Flows LO5

A company starts the year with $175,000 in cash. During the year, the company generates $680,000 from operations, uses $516,000 in investing activities, and uses $98,000 in financing activities.

Required
Calculate the company's cash at year end.

7. Identify Accounting Assumptions and Qualitative Characteristics LO1, 6

Consider the following independent scenarios:

1. Luigi's Pizza has been in business for 25 years. All of its operations are profitable, and the accountants believe that the company will operate into the foreseeable future.
2. A bank used the information presented in Tiger Auto's financial statements to determine if it should extend a $300,000 loan to Tiger. The information in the financial statements made a difference in the bank's lending decision.
3. Jim Furio, manager of Martha's Antiques, does not like to change accounting procedures because it hinders his ability to make year-to-year comparisons.
4. Lynn Hagood, owner of Jonesboro Animal Hospital, informs his accountant that he does not want to review any accounting issue that is smaller than 1% of net income.

Required
Identify the accounting assumption or qualitative characteristic that relates to each scenario.

EXERCISES

8. Principles and Assumptions LO1, 3

The following basic accounting principles and assumptions were discussed in the chapter:

- Economic entity   • Going concern
- Monetary unit   • Cost principle
- Time period

_____ 1. Lester Company has a division in Germany. Before preparing the financial statements for the company and the foreign division, Lester translates the financial statements of its Germany division from the euro to U.S. dollars.

_____ 2. Matt enters into a partnership to start a bike shop with a friend. Each partner makes an initial cash investment of $8,000. Matt opens a checking account in the name of the company and transfers $8,000 from his personal account into the new account.

_____ 3. Dreamland Inc. has always prepared financial statements with a year-end of May 31. However, the company is going to sell stock to the public for the first time and is required by the SEC to give quarterly financial reports.

_____ 4. Platt Corp. purchases a fifty acre plot of land to build the world's largest factory. The company recorded the property at the amount of cash given to acquire it.

_____ 5. Lockbox Corp. is in its ninetieth year of business. The owner of the company is going to retire in two months and turn the company over to his son.

Required
Fill in the blank with the appropriate principle or assumption.

9. Identify Income Statement Accounts LO2

The following accounts are taken from a company's financial statements:

1. Rent expense
2. Service revenue
3. Dividends
4. Interest revenue
5. Interest expense
6. Accounts receivable

Required
Indicate whether each account is a revenue (R), expense (E), or neither (N).

10. Accounting Terms   LO3

Consider the following information:
a. Accounts receivable
b. Salaries payable
c. Office supplies
d. Land
e. Contributed capital
f. Notes payable

Required
Indicate whether each of the above items is an asset (A), a liability (L), or part of equity (E).

11. Accounting Terms   LO2, 3

Consider the following information:

Item	Appears On	Classified As
1. Salaries expense	_____	_____
2. Equipment	_____	_____
3. Cash	_____	_____
4. Accounts payable	_____	_____
5. Buildings	_____	_____
6. Contributed capital	_____	_____
7. Retained earnings	_____	_____
8. Interest revenue	_____	_____
9. Advertising expense	_____	_____

Required
Classify each of the items above according to (1) whether it appears on the income statement or balance sheet and (2) whether it is classified as a revenue, expense, asset, liability, or equity.

12. Accounting Terms   LO2, 3, 4

The following items were taken from the financial statements of Tiger Inc.:
a. Income tax expense
b. Interest expense
c. Service revenue
d. Accounts receivable
e. Retained earnings
f. Inventory
g. Accounts payable
h. Contributed capital
i. Dividends

Required
Identify whether each item would appear on the balance sheet, the income statement, or the statement of retained earnings.

13. Classify Cash Flows   LO5

A company entered into the following cash transactions:
1. Cash paid to suppliers
2. Cash received from issuing new common stock
3. Cash paid to purchase new office furniture
4. Cash paid in dividends to owners
5. Cash received from customers

Required
Indicate the section of the statement of cash flows in which each item would appear: operating activities (O), investing activities (I), or financing activities (F).

14. Accounting Terms   LO2, 3, 4, 5

Consider the following information:
a. Revenues during the period
b. Supplies on hand at the end of the year
c. Cash received from borrowings during the year
d. Total liabilities at the end of the period
e. Dividends paid during the year
f. Cash paid for a building
g. Cost of buildings owned at year end

Required
Indicate whether you would find each of the above items on the income statement (IS), the balance sheet (BS), the statement of retained earnings (SRE), or the statement of cash flows (SCF).

15. Financial Statements   LO2, 3, 4, 5

Listed below are questions posed by various users of a company's financial statements.

User	Questions	Financial Statement
Stockholder	How did this year's sales figures compare with last year's sales figures?	_____
Banker	How much in borrowings does the company currently owe?	_____
Supplier	How much does the company owe its suppliers in total?	_____
Stockholder	Did the company have any dividends in the prior year?	_____
Advertising agent	How much advertising did the company incur in order to generate sales?	_____
Banker	What was the company's total interest cost last year?	_____

Required
Fill in the blank with the financial statement(s) (income statement, balance sheet, statement of retained earnings, and/or statement of cash flows) the user would most likely use to find this information.

16. Net Income and Retained Earnings   LO2, 4

Nova Corporation reports the following as of December 31:

Revenues	$10,000
Beginning retained earnings	20,000
Expenses	8,000
Dividends	1,000

Required
Calculate net income and ending retained earnings for the year ending December 31.

17. Balance Sheet Equation   LO3

Consider the following information:

Assets	Liabilities	Equity
50,000	25,000	?
30,000	?	17,000
?	45,000	15,000
68,000	?	13,000
?	14,000	6,000

Required
Use the accounting equation to fill in the missing amounts.

18. Balance Sheet Equation   LO3

Consider the following information:
a. Jenkins Company starts the year with $50,000 in assets and $40,000 in liabilities. Net income for the year is $12,500, and no dividends are paid. How much is Jenkins' equity at the end of the year?
b. McCay Inc. doubles the amount of its assets from the beginning to the end of the year. At the end of the year, liabilities are $50,000, and equity is $30,000. What is the amount of McCay's assets at the beginning of the year?
c. During the year the liabilities of Hudson Corp. triple. At the beginning of the year, assets were $40,000, and equity was $20,000. What is the amount of liabilities at the end of the year?

Required
Use the accounting equation to answer each of the independent questions above.

19. Statement of Retained Earnings   LO4

War Eagle Company's retained earnings on January 1 is $245,800. The following information is available for the first two months of the year:

	January	February
Revenues	$80,000	$102,000
Expenses	85,000	80,000
Dividends	0	7,000

Required
Prepare a statement of retained earnings for the month ending February 28.

20. Statement of Cash Flows   LO5

The following information is for Pasture Corp.:

Cash received from customers	$65,000
Cash received from lenders	20,000
Cash paid to suppliers	20,000
Cash paid for new equipment	50,000
Cash paid for dividends	4,000

Required
Indicate on what section of the statement of cash flows each item would appear and calculate Pasture's net change in cash.

21. Links Between Financial Statements   LO2, 3, 4

Below are incomplete financial statements for Sterling Inc.:

Balance Sheet	
Assets	
Cash	$ 8,000
Inventory	22,000
Building	40,000
Total assets	$70,000
Liabilities	
Accounts payable	$7,000
Equity	
Contributed capital	(a)
Retained earnings	(b)
Total liabilities & equity	$70,000

Income Statement	
Service revenue	$90,000
Salaries expense	(c)
Utilities expense	20,000
Net income	$ (d)

Statement of Retained Earnings	
Retained earnings, beginning balance	$20,000
Net income	(e)
Dividends	10,000
Retained earnings, ending balance	$60,000

Required
Calculate the missing amounts.

22. Complete Financial Statements LO2, 3, 4

The following are incomplete financial statements for Mackabee Inc.:

Balance Sheet

Assets	
Cash	$ 6,000
Inventory	20,000
Building	(a)
Total assets	$64,000
Liabilities	
Accounts payable	$ 7,000
Equity	
Contributed capital	(b)
Retained earnings	(c)
Total liabilities and equity	$64,000

Income Statement

Service revenue	$120,000
Salaries expense	70,000
Administrative expense	30,000
Net income	$ (d)

Statement of Retained Earnings

Beginning retained earnings	$20,000
Net income	(e)
Dividends	(f)
Ending retained earnings	$40,000

Required

Calculate the missing amounts.

23. Qualitative Characteristics LO6

The following qualitative characteristics of accounting were discussed in the chapter:

- Consistency
- Understandability
- Conservatism
- Reliability
- Relevance
- Comparability
- Materiality

_____ 1. The ability of accounting information to be comprehensible to those who have a reasonable understanding of business and are willing to study the information with reasonable diligence.

_____ 2. The capacity to affect business decisions.

_____ 3. The dependability of accounting information.

_____ 4. The ability to compare and contrast the financial activities of the same company over a period of time.

_____ 5. The threshold over which an item begins to affect decision making.

_____ 6. The way in which accountants deal with uncertainty.

_____ 7. The ability to compare and contrast the financial activities of different companies.

Required

Fill in the blank with the appropriate characteristic.

24. Assumptions and Principles LO1, 2, 3

Harbor Corp. had the following situations during the year:

a. Inventory with a cost of $186,400 is reported at its market value of $235,600.

b. Harbor added four additional weeks to its fiscal year so that it could make its income look stronger. Past years were 52 weeks.

c. Harbor's CEO purchased a yacht for personal use and charged it to the company.

d. Revenues of $25,000 earned in the prior year were recorded in the current year.

Required

In each situation, identify the assumption or principle that has been violated and discuss how Harbor should have handled the situation.

PROBLEMS

25. Prepare Financial Statements LO2, 4

This information relates to York Inc. for the year:

Advertising expense	$ 2,400
Dividends paid	7,000
Rent expense	10,400
Retained earnings, January 1	57,000
Salaries expense	28,000
Service revenue	61,000
Utilities expense	1,800

Required

Prepare an income statement and a statement of retained earnings for the year.

26. Prepare Financial Statements LO2, 3, 4

The following items are available from the records of Honky Tonk Records Inc. at the end of the year:

Accounts payable	$27,000
Accounts receivable	21,000
Advertising expense	6,000
Buildings	76,000
Contributed capital	30,000
Cash	6,320
Notes payable	70,000
Salaries expense	9,500
Service revenue	16,820
Equipment	25,000

Required

Prepare Honky Tonk's income statement and statement of retained earnings for the year and its balance sheet at the end of the year.

27. Identify and Correct Income Statement Errors LO2

Muncie Group was organized on January 1. At the end of the year, the company used a first-year accounting student to prepare the following income statement:

Muncie Group Income Statement December 31	
Income from services	$170,000
Accounts receivable	40,000
Total income	$210,000
Less: Expenses	
Salaries	$ 57,000
Advertising	(14,000)
Dividends	10,000
Utilities	22,000
Total expenses	$ 75,000
Net income	$135,000

Required

List all of the deficiencies that you can identify in this income statement and prepare a proper income statement.

28. Identify and Correct Balance Sheet Errors LO3

Bizilia's Inc. was organized on January 1. At the end of the year, an employee with a mathematics degree prepared the following balance sheet:

Bizilia's Inc. Balance Sheet For the Year Ending December 31	
Resources:	
Cash	$ 30,000
Stuff we can sell	40,000
Land	53,000
Retained earnings	17,000
Grand total	$146,000
Debts:	
Money we owe to vendors	$ 43,000
Contributed capital	63,000
Grand total	$106,000

Required

List all of the deficiencies that you can identify in this balance sheet and prepare a proper balance sheet.

29. Errors in Accounting LO1, 2, 3

The Mock Corporation was formed on January 1. At December 31, William Mock, CEO and sole owner, prepared the company's balance sheet as follows:

Mock Corporation Balance Sheet December 31	
Assets	
Cash	$25,000
Accounts receivable	40,000
Inventory	35,000
Building	20,000
Liabilities and Equity	
Accounts payable	$40,000
Building loan	15,000
Retained earnings	37,000

William is not an accountant by trade, and he believes there may be some mistakes in his balance sheet. He has provided you with the following additional information:

1. The building is William's personal beach house. However, he plans on using it for company retreats and for hosting some large clients. He decided to list the asset and the corresponding liability for this reason.
2. The inventory was originally purchased at $12,000, but due to a recent increase in demand, he believes he could sell it for at least $35,000. He thought that $35,000 would best portray the economic reality of his inventory.
3. William included $5,000 in accounts receivable and retained earnings for a service that he will provide next year. Since he is an honest man and will provide the service, he decided to record the amount in this year's balance sheet.

Required

Comment on what accounting assumptions or principles are violated, briefly describe how each item should be accounted for, and prepare a correct balance sheet.

30. Preparing Financial Statements LO2, 3, 4

On June 1 you begin an ocean tour business for the summer by contributing $600 of contributed capital and borrowing $600 from your parents. With your money, you pay $480 in June to rent a boat and supplies consisting of snorkels, fins, masks, and life-jackets. You also purchase advertising in a local paper for $25 and gasoline for $135. You decide to charge $25 per passenger. At the end of the month of June, you have serviced 240 customers and purchased and used an additional $200 in gasoline. Included in those 240 customers were two neighbors who promised future payment which you have not received (totaling $225). You also pay your parents $5 for monthly interest.

Required

Prepare an income statement and a statement of retained earnings for the month ending June 30 and a balance sheet at June 30.

31. Preparing Financial Statements LO2, 3, 4

During the month of April, you conduct art seminars for children. On April 1, you borrow $500 from your parents, buy $400 of supplies, and pay $50 for advertising on the radio and $25 to rent a room in a local recreation center. You charge $20 per child per seminar. At the end of the month, you have held seminars for 80 children, of which you have received payment for 76. You have $30 of supplies remaining, and you pay your parents $5 for the use of their money during the month.

Required

Prepare an income statement and a statement of retained earnings for the month ending April 30 and a balance sheet at April 30.

CASES

32. Read, Locate, and Compare Financial Statements LO2, 3, 5

Access the financial statements in the 2010 annual report for **CVS Caremark Corp.** by clicking on the *Investors* and *Annual Reports* links at www.cvs.com.

Required

a. For CVS Caremark's current year, identify the amounts reported for net revenues, net earnings, total assets, and cash flows from operating activities. Also, identify the date on which the financial statements are prepared.

b. Locate **Walgreens** financial statements for the same year. Identify the same information as in the previous requirement.

c. Compare Walgreens and CVS Caremark. Identify which company is (1) the largest, (2) the most profitable, and (3) the best able to generate cash from its operations.

33. Ethics in Accounting LO1, 2, 6

As the top accountant at Blaire's Costume Jewelry Company, you discover that net income in each of the previous five years has been overstated due to an error in accounting. After much thought, you decide to approach the company president. His response is, "What the public doesn't know won't hurt them. We'll just adjust this year's income to make up for the mistakes. We had a pretty good year, and I think our income for this year can absorb the errors."

Required

Identify the ethical dilemma of this situation, identify the ways that you could respond, and explain the possible consequences of your responses.

34. Written Communication Skills LO2, 3, 4, 5

Your Uncle Ted just won the lottery. He is trying to find companies in which to invest his winnings. However, he is having trouble reading the financial statements because he has no idea what they are saying. Knowing you are in an accounting class, Uncle Ted asks for your advice.

Required

Prepare a written response to your Uncle Ted explaining what information is contained in each financial statement and how it is relevant to investors.

Corporate Financial
Statements

Introduction

Chapter 1 introduced the terms, assumptions, principles, and statements that accounting uses to capture and communicate a company's economic activities. This chapter takes a more detailed look at the accounting information provided by companies, particularly public corporations such as **Bed Bath & Beyond**. Specifically, the chapter introduces the classified balance sheet, the multi-step income statement, and the statement of stockholders' equity. Each of these three financial statements represents a more detailed version of the balance sheet, the income statement, and the statement of retained earnings covered in Chapter 1. The chapter also introduces two analysis techniques, horizontal and vertical analyses, that are simple but powerful tools for generating a more thorough understanding of a company's balance sheet and income statement. At the end of this chapter, you should be comfortable reading through and using the financial statements of almost any company.

LO1 Business Forms

One of the first decisions that any new business faces is the form that it will take. Businesses have the following three basic options:

- Sole proprietorship
- Partnership
- Corporation

A **sole proprietorship** is a business owned by one person and is the most common type of business in the United States. In a sole proprietorship, the owner maintains complete control of the business, bears all the risk of failure, and reaps all the rewards of success. For

Sole proprietorship A business owned by one person.

Inventory is one of the biggest assets for retailers like Bed Bath & Beyond. Because of its importance, it is reported separately on the company's classified balance sheet.

KEVORK DJANSEZIAN/ASSOCIATED PRESS

accounting purposes, a sole proprietorship is accounted for separately from the proprietor's personal affairs. This is an application of the economic entity assumption. For tax purposes, though, a sole proprietor's business is not separated from the proprietor. The income from the business is reported on Schedule C of the owner's personal tax return.

A **partnership** is a business that is formed when two or more proprietors join together to own a business. Partnerships can be established by either a written or oral agreement and can include any number of partners. Partnerships are formed for various reasons, such as joining proprietors with different skills, combining resources, and spreading the financial risk of the business among several people. Like sole proprietorships, a partnership is considered a

Partnership A business that is formed when two or more proprietors join together to own a business.

One of the first decisions that any new business faces is the form that it will take.

separate accounting entity from the individual partners. Also like sole proprietorships, a partner's share of partnership income is reported on the partner's individual tax return.

A **corporation** is a separate legal entity that is established by filing articles of incorporation in a state, usually with the secretary of state's office. Once a corporation is formed, it sells stock to individuals who want to own part of the corporation. This is one of the main reasons that corporations are formed—the ability to raise capital through the sale of ownership interests. It is also why corporation owners are called stockholders. Like a sole proprietorship and a partnership, a corporation is accounted for separately from its owners. However, it is also taxed separately. Income generated by a corporation is taxed on a corporate tax return, not on the stockholders' individual tax returns.

Corporations can be either private or public. A **public corporation** is one in which ownership is available to the public at large. The stock of a public corporation

is usually bought and sold on an open exchange such as the New York Stock Exchange (NYSE) or the National Association of Securities Dealers Automated Quotes (NASDAQ). Such corporations are said to be *publicly traded*. Examples of publicly traded corporations are Microsoft, Kellogg, and Bed Bath & Beyond. From this point forward, this text will focus on the accounting for publicly traded corporations. This will allow you to see accounting issues in companies with which you may be familiar.

LO2 Generally Accepted Accounting Principles

When accounting for their economic activities, public corporations must follow *generally accepted accounting principles*. **Generally accepted accounting principles (GAAP)** are the accounting standards, rules, principles, and procedures that comprise authoritative practice for financial accounting. These principles have been developed over time by several regulatory bodies, the most significant of which are listed as follows.

- Securities and Exchange Commission
- Financial Accounting Standards Board
- American Institute of Certified Public Accountants

The **Securities and Exchange Commission (SEC)** is the federal agency charged to protect investors and maintain the integrity of securities markets. Established by Congress after the 1929 stock market crash, the SEC was given the authority to determine the rules by which publicly traded companies would disclose information to their owners. However, instead of writing all of the rules itself, the SEC delegated much of its accounting

Corporation A separate legal entity that is established by filing articles of incorporation in a state.

Public corporation A separate legal entity in which ownership is available to the public at large.

Generally accepted accounting principles The accounting standards, rules, principles, and procedures that comprise authoritative practice for financial accounting.

Securities and Exchange Commission The federal agency charged to protect investors and maintain the integrity of securities markets.

HOME DEPOT ANALYSIS

Look at the full company name at the top of any of Home Depot's financial statements in Appendix C. Can you tell from the name what form of business the company uses?

The full company name is "The Home Depot, Inc. and Subsidiaries." Inc. stands for incorporated. Thus, Home Depot is a corporation.

rule-making authority to the accounting profession. Today, the accounting organization that sets major accounting standards in the United States is the Financial Accounting Standards Board.

The **Financial Accounting Standards Board (FASB)** is a standard-setting body whose mission is "to establish and improve standards of financial accounting and reporting for the guidance and education of the public, including issuers, auditors, and users of financial information." The FASB usually tackles large issues, such as the accounting for pensions, leases, stock options, and derivatives. It also maintains the conceptual framework discussed in Chapter 1. The Board consists of seven full-time voting members who oversee a standard-setting process of research, deliberation, public input, and board approval. Once the FASB establishes a rule or standard, it is then enforced by the SEC.

While the FASB is accounting's main standard-setting body, the **American Institute of Certified Public Accountants (AICPA)** also plays a role in establishing accounting rules. The AICPA, which is the professional organization of certified public accountants, maintains a board that establishes rules that are often more technical and more specific to certain industries. For example, the AICPA has issued rules for determining profits in the film industry. The rules set by the AICPA are also enforced by the SEC.

Each of these organizations are based in the United States. However, accounting is practiced throughout the world, and there is a movement to develop one set of international accounting standards to be used by all countries. The **International Accounting Standards Board (IASB)** is a board, similar to the FASB, whose mission is to develop a single set of high-quality standards requiring transparent and comparable information. Those standards, which have both similarities to and differences from GAAP, are called **International Financial Reporting**

Standards (IFRS). Because adoption of IFRS is voluntary, the effectiveness of the IASB at accomplishing its mission has been somewhat limited. However, the IASB and the FASB have both agreed to a commitment to the convergence of U.S. and international standards. At some time in the future, the world may very well use one set of global accounting standards set by a global board. But for now, public companies traded on U.S. exchanges must use generally accepted accounting principles.

Financial Accounting Standards Board The standard-setting body whose mission is "to establish and improve standards of financial accounting and reporting for the guidance and education of the public, including issuers, auditors, and users of financial information."

American Institute of Certified Public Accountants The professional organization of certified public accountants whose board establishes rules that are often more technical and more specific to certain industries.

International Accounting Standards Board A board, similar to the FASB, whose mission is to develop a single set of high-quality standards requiring transparent and comparable information.

International Financial Reporting Standards Standards issued by the International Accounting Standards Board.

HOME DEPOT ANALYSIS

Look in Appendix C at the Report of Independent Registered Public Accounting Firm in which the accounting firm is describing its audit of Home Depot's financial statements. According to the auditor, are Home Depot's financial statements prepared in accordance with GAAP?

Yes. As the Report states, the financial information is presented "in conformity with U.S. generally accepted accounting principles."

LO3 The Classified Balance Sheet

Chapter 1 introduced the balance sheet. A balance sheet is a financial statement that summarizes a company's assets, liabilities, and equity at a given point in time. The balance sheet shown in Chapter 1 reported every account of the company. However, most public corporations are much too large to report every account, so they prepare a classified balance sheet instead. A **classified balance sheet** groups together accounts of similar nature and reports them in a few major classifications.

The following sections discuss the various asset, liability, and equity classifications commonly used on classified balance sheets. The February 26, 2011, classified balance sheet of **Bed Bath & Beyond** in Exhibit 2-1 will be used as an illustration. As you review the statement, note that all numbers except per share data are in thousands, meaning that each reported number has three 0's missing. Note also that two years of data are presented, with the most recent year listed first. This is the normal format for most corporate balance sheets. It is also why such statements are often called *comparative* balance sheets.

Assets

An asset is a resource of a business. Assets are generally grouped into five main categories on a classified balance sheet:

- Current assets
- Long-term investments
- Fixed assets
- Intangible assets
- Other assets

Classified balance sheet A type of balance sheet that groups together accounts of similar nature and reports them in a few major classifications.

Current asset Any asset that is reasonably expected to be converted to cash or consumed within one year of the balance sheet date.

Long-term investments The investments in the common stock or debt of another entity that will not be sold within a year.

Fixed assets The tangible resources that are used in a company's operations for more than one year and are not intended for resale.

Current Assets A **current asset** is any asset that is reasonably expected to be converted to cash or consumed within one year of the balance sheet date. Common examples include cash, investments that will mature or be sold within a year, accounts receivable from customers, inventories, and other assets such as prepaid insurance. Current assets are listed in order of their liquidity, which refers to the speed with which a resource can be converted to cash. Cash is listed first, followed by short-term investments, receivables, inventories, and then finally other current assets.

Bed Bath & Beyond reports four current assets totaling over $4 billion on its February 26, 2011, balance sheet. As you might expect from a retailer, the vast majority of those assets (over $1.9 billion) is in *Merchandise inventories*, with a substantial amount also in *Cash and cash equivalents*. The company also reports some *Short-term investment securities* and *Other current assets*.

Long-Term Investments **Long-term investments** are a company's investments in the common stock or debt of another entity that will not be sold within a year. Companies typically list any long-term investments as their first noncurrent asset. Bed Bath & Beyond reports $121 million in *Long-term investment securities*.

Fixed Assets **Fixed assets** are the tangible resources that are used in a company's operations for more than one year and are not intended for resale. Examples include land, buildings, equipment, furniture, and fixtures.

Bed Bath & Beyond reports over $1.1 billion of fixed assets on its February 26, 2011, balance sheet, making them one of the company's largest assets, which makes sense for a retailer. Note, however, that the company uses the term *Property and equipment, net* rather than fixed assets. This is a common name for fixed assets. Note also the word "net" in the description. Most fixed assets are subject to depreciation, which is the process of expensing the cost of an asset over its useful life. Therefore, fixed assets are reported "net" of any depreciation to date. Chapter 8 will discuss depreciation in much more detail.

Exhibit 2-1 Bed Bath & Beyond Classified Balance Sheet

Bed Bath & Beyond Inc. and Subsidiaries
Consolidated Balance Sheets
(in thousands, except per share data)

	February 26, 2011	February 27, 2010
Assets		
Current assets:		
Cash and cash equivalents	$ 1,183,587	$ 1,096,100
Short-term investment securities	605,608	431,476
Merchandise inventories	1,968,907	1,759,703
Other current assets	315,736	276,066
Total current assets	4,073,838	3,563,345
Long-term investment securities	121,446	132,860
Property and equipment, net	1,116,297	1,119,292
Other assets	334,612	336,633
Total assets	$ 5,646,193	$ 5,152,130
Liabilities and Shareholders' Equity		
Current liabilities:		
Accounts payable	$ 709,550	$ 611,163
Accrued expenses and other current liabilities	306,847	281,730
Merchandise credit and gift card liabilities	193,061	172,804
Current income taxes payable	112,982	83,857
Total current liabilities	1,322,440	1,149,554
Deferred rent and other liabilities	292,364	246,273
Income taxes payable	99,730	103,399
Total liabilities	1,714,534	1,499,226
Shareholders' equity:		
Preferred stock—$0.01 par value; authorized 1,000 shares; no shares issued or outstanding	—	—
Common stock—$0.01 par value; authorized 900,000 shares; issued 314,678 and 312,229 shares, respectively;	3,253	3,206
Additional paid-in capital	1,191,123	1,020,515
Retained earnings	5,546,287	4,754,954
Treasury stock, at cost	(2,814,104)	(2,126,499)
Accumulated other comprehensive loss	5,100	728
Total shareholders' equity	3,931,659	3,652,904
Total liabilities and shareholders' equity	$ 5,646,193	$ 5,152,130

Intangible Assets An **intangible asset** is a resource that is used in operations for more than one year, is not intended for resale, and has no physical substance. Examples include trademarks, patents, franchise rights, copyrights, and goodwill. Like fixed assets, intangible assets are subject to depreciation (although it is actually called amortization instead of depreciation) and are reported net of amortization to date. **Bed Bath & Beyond** does not separately report any intangible assets.

Other Assets **Other assets** are those resources that do not fit well into one of the other classifications. The classification can also include those assets that are small enough that they do not warrant separate reporting. Bed Bath & Beyond reports over $334 million in *Other assets*. According to additional information provided by the company, the balance includes the company's intangible assets.

Liabilities

A liability is an obligation of a business. Liabilities are generally classified into two main categories on a classified balance sheet:

- Current liabilities
- Long-term liabilities

> **Intangible asset** A resource that is used in operation for more than one year, is not intended for resale, and has no physical substance.
>
> **Other assets** Resources that do not fit well into one of the other asset classifications or are small enough that they do not warrant separate reporting.

Current Liabilities A **current liability** is an obligation that is reasonably expected to be satisfied within one year. Examples include accounts payable to vendors, salaries payable to employees, and taxes payable to taxing authorities. Even long-term debt, if maturing within one year, is classified as a current liability.

Bed Bath & Beyond reports four current liabilities totaling over $1.3 billion on its February 26, 2011, balance sheet. The largest is over $709 million in *Accounts payable,* which is the amount owed to suppliers. Over $306 million is listed in *Accrued expenses and other current liabilities,* which likely represents obligations relating to employees, advertising, or other operating matters. Also, over $193 million is reported in *Merchandise credit and gift card liabilities.* This represents the value of unredeemed gift cards and other credits. Finally, the company reports almost $113 million of *Current income taxes payable,* which is the amount owed to taxing authorities based on the income earned previously.

Long-Term Liabilities A **long-term liability** is an obligation that is not expected to be satisfied within one year. Examples include notes payable, mortgage payable, and bonds payable. Bed Bath & Beyond has very few long-term liabilities at February 26, 2011. It reports $292 million in *Deferred rent and other liabilities* and over $99 million in *Income taxes payable.*

Equity

Equity is the difference between a company's assets and its liabilities. It is generated from the following two sources:

- Retained earnings
- Contributed capital

Current liability An obligation that is reasonably expected to be satisfied within one year.

Long-term liability An obligation that is not expected to be satisfied within one year.

Retained earnings The amount of equity a company generates by being profitable and retaining those profits in the business.

Contributed capital The amount of equity a company generates through the sale of stock to investors.

Single-step income statement Calculates total revenues and total expenses and then determines net income in one step by subtracting total expenses from total revenues.

Multi-step income statement Calculates income by grouping certain revenues and expenses together and calculating several subtotals of income.

Retained earnings is the amount of equity a company generates by being profitable and retaining those profits in the business. **Contributed capital** is the amount of equity a company generates through the sale of stock to investors. Such equity is often referred to as capital stock. Examples of capital stock include common stock and preferred stock.

Like most publicly traded companies, Bed Bath & Beyond reports its equity accounts in one general section called *Shareholders' equity.* The company reports five balances, the largest of which is $5.5 billion in *Retained earnings.* Such a large balance indicates a very strong record of generating profits in previous years. The other two large balances are *Additional paid-in capital* (over $1.1 billion) and *Treasury stock* (over $2.8 billion). The Additional paid-in capital account represents capital that the company has received through the sale of stock to investors and owners. The Treasury stock account represents capital that the company has paid to owners to buy back the company's stock. Together, these accounts show than Bed Bath & Beyond has paid out more capital than it has received. A more in-depth analysis of treasury stock and equity in general will be left for Chapter 10.

LO4 The Multi-Step Income Statement

Chapter 1 also introduced the income statement. The income statement is a financial statement that summarizes a company's revenues and expenses over a period of time. Companies generally use one of two forms for their income statements—a single-step statement or a multi-step statement.

A **single-step income statement** calculates total revenues and total expenses and then determines net income in one step by subtracting total expenses from total revenues. The income statement prepared in Chapter 1 was a single-step income statement. The major advantage of a single-step statement is its simplicity. However, the disadvantage is that it does not present the information in a manner that is very useful. As a result, most companies prepare multi-step income statements.

A **multi-step income statement** calculates income by grouping certain revenues and expenses together and calculating several subtotals of income. These subtotals provide information on the profitability of various aspects of the company's operations. While most companies prepare multi-step statements, there is some variation in how they are prepared. However, most include either some or all of the following four subtotals of income.

- Gross profit
- Operating profit
- Income before taxes
- Net income

The following sections discuss these subtotals that are commonly used by companies. For illustration purposes, Exhibit 2-2 contains Bed Bath & Beyond's income statement for the fiscal year ended February 26, 2011. Note that the company uses the title, *Consolidated Statements of Earnings,* rather than income statement. Note also that like the balance sheet, the numbers are in thousands. However, unlike the balance sheet, the income statement reports three years of data. The presentation of multiple years of data therefore yields comparative income statements.

Gross Profit

For a retailer like Bed Bath & Beyond, the first line item of a multi-step statement is the revenue generated from sales. **Sales**, which is often labeled net sales, is the resources that a company generates during a period from selling its inventory. Listed next is cost of sales. **Cost of sales**, which is sometimes called cost of goods sold, represents the cost of the inventory that was sold during a period. Subtracting cost of sales from net sales then yields the first subtotal of income, gross profit. **Gross profit**, which is sometimes called gross margin, represents the profit that a company generates when considering only the sales price and the cost of the product

sold. It therefore represents the gross dollar markup that a company is able to achieve when selling its inventory. Note that unlike a retailer, a service company will not report gross profit as a subtotal of income.

For the fiscal period ended February 26, 2011, Bed Bath & Beyond generated over $8.7 billion in *Net sales*. With *Cost of sales* of over $5.1 billion, the company generated a *Gross profit* of over $3.6 billion for the year. Note that with a profit of $3.6 billion on inventory costing $5.1 billion, the average markup on inventory was around 70% of its cost ($3.6 ÷ $5.1). That is, on average, an inventory item costing the company $100 sold for $170.

Operating Profit

After gross profit is reported, operating expenses are listed. **Operating expenses** are the expenses that a company incurs during normal operations. Such expenses are recurring, meaning that they are incurred year after year as the company runs its business. Examples include advertising, salaries, utilities, depreciation, and insurance.

In most multi-step statements, operating expenses are summed together and subtracted from gross profit to yield the second subtotal of income, operating profit.

Sales The resources that a company generates during a period from selling its inventory.

Cost of sales The cost of the inventory sold during a period.

Gross profit The profit that a company generates when considering only the sales price and the cost of the product sold.

Operating expenses Recurring expenses that a company incurs during normal operations.

Exhibit 2-2 Bed Bath & Beyond Multi-step Income Statement

Bed Bath & Beyond Inc. and Subsidiaries
Consolidated Statements of Earnings
(in thousands)

	FISCAL YEAR ENDED		
	February 26, 2011	February 27, 2010	February 28, 2009
Net sales	$8,758,503	$7,828,793	$7,208,340
Cost of sales	5,135,574	4,620,674	4,335,104
Gross profit	3,622,929	3,208,119	2,873,236
Selling, general and administrative expenses	2,334,471	2,227,432	2,199,340
Operating profit	1,288,458	980,687	673,896
Interest income	4,520	4,568	9,412
Earnings before provision for income taxes	1,292,978	985,255	683,308
Provision for income taxes	501,645	385,222	258,185
Net earnings	$ 791,333	$ 600,033	$ 425,123

Albert Lozano/iStockphoto.com

Just like individuals do, corporations must pay taxes on their incomes.

Operating profit represents the profit that a company generates when considering both the cost of the inventory and the normal expenses incurred to operate the business. Other names for operating profit include income from operations or operating income.

Bed Bath & Beyond reports over $2.3 billion of operating expenses in one expense line labeled *Selling, general and administrative expenses*. This is a common description for general operating expenses. Subtracting these operating expenses from gross profit yields an *Operating profit* of over $1.2 billion. So, after considering its two major

> **Operating profit** The profit that a company generates when considering both the cost of the inventory and the normal expenses incurred to operate the business.
>
> **Other revenue and expenses** Revenues and expenses generated outside of normal operations.
>
> **Income before taxes** The profit that a company generates when considering all revenues and expenses except for income taxes.
>
> **Provision for income taxes** The amount of income tax expense for a given period.

expenses—cost of inventory and operating expenses—Bed Bath & Beyond's $8.7 billion in sales yielded about $1.3 billion in profits.

Income Before Taxes

In addition to cost of sales and operating expenses, companies sometimes generate revenues and expenses that are outside of their normal operations. Common examples include interest revenue and interest expense. Such items are listed separately as **other revenues and expenses** and are netted against operating profit to yield the third subtotal of income, income before taxes. **Income before taxes,** also called earnings before income taxes and other similar titles, represents the profit that a company generates when considering all revenues and expenses except for income taxes.

After reporting its operating profit, Bed Bath & Beyond reports *Interest income* of over $4 million. This $4 million, which likely represents the revenues generated from the company's investment portfolios, is added to operating profit to yield *Earnings before provision for income taxes* of $1.3 billion.

Net Income

Like individuals, corporations must pay taxes on their incomes. Usually, the amount of tax in a given period is listed separately on a multi-step statement as provision for income taxes. **Provision for income taxes** is the amount of income tax expense for a given period. When this provision is subtracted from income before taxes,

HOME DEPOT ANALYSIS

Look at Home Depot's income statement in Appendix C. What form of income statement does the company use?

The company uses a multi-step income statement. It shows several subtotals of income, including Gross Profit, Operating Income, Earnings From Continuing Operations Before Provision for Income Taxes, Earnings From Continuing Operations, and Net Earnings.

the final income measure, **net income**, is determined. Bed Bath & Beyond reports a $501 million *Provision for income taxes*. Subtracting that from income before taxes yields *Net earnings* of approximately $791 million.

In summary, Bed Bath & Beyond's multi-step income statement provides a picture of how the company generated its profits in the last period. It generated $3.6 billion in profits due to its inventory markups. Once it subtracted its operating expenses, it had profits of $1.3 billion remaining. After considering other revenues and taxes, $791 million of profits remained from the original sales of $8.7 billion.

LO5 **Horizontal and Vertical Analyses**

The previous sections demonstrate that financial statements communicate economic information about a company to interested parties. For example, investors and creditors learn from Bed Bath & Beyond's income statement that the company earned $791 million of income in the most recent year. This is useful information because it demonstrates that the company was profitable during the year. However, the information can be even more useful if it is compared to something else. For example, is $791 million better or worse than last year? Is it high enough given sales for the period? How does it compare to competitors? Such comparisons provide the necessary context for a more thorough understanding of a company's financial activities. Such context can be easily generated through two techniques called horizontal and vertical analyses.

Horizontal Analysis

Horizontal analysis is a method of analyzing a company's account balances over time. It is normally conducted on both the balance sheet and the income statement. The analysis calculates both the dollar and percentage change in each account balance on a financial statement. As a result, it is very useful in identifying promising or troubling trends in a company. The analysis is called "horizontal" because the calculation compares an account's balance across the columns of yearly data—that is, horizontally across the financial statement.

Horizontal analysis is calculated as follows. First, the dollar change in an account is determined. This is defined as the current-year balance less the prior-year balance. The dollar change is then divided by the prior-year balance to yield a percentage change. These two calculations are shown below.

$$\text{Dollar change in account balance} = \text{Current-year balance} - \text{Prior-year balance}$$

$$\text{Percentage change in account balance} = \frac{\text{Dollar change}}{\text{Prior-year balance}}$$

To illustrate, consider the *Merchandise inventories* balance from Bed Bath & Beyond's balance sheet in Exhibit 2-1:

	February 26, 2011	February 27, 2010
Merchandise inventories	$1,968,907	$1,759,703

The company's inventory increased $209,204 from February 27, 2010, to February 26, 2011. Dividing that increase by the February 27, 2010, balance yields a percentage change of 11.9%. These calculations are shown in the following table. Also shown are similar calculations for a horizontal analysis of *Net earnings* from the company's income statement in Exhibit 2-2.

	Inventories	Net earnings
Current-year balance	$1,968,907	$791,333
− Prior-year balance	− $1,759,703	− $600,033
Dollar change	$ 209,204	$191,300
Dollar change	$209,204	$191,300
Prior-year balance	$1,759,703	$600,033
= Percentage change	= 11.9%	= 31.9%

Net income The final income measure after the provision for income taxes is subtracted from income before taxes.

Horizontal analysis A method of analyzing a company's account balances over time by calculating dollar and percentage changes in each account.

For a full horizontal analysis, both dollar and percentage changes are calculated for each account on both the balance sheet and the income statement. Exhibit 2-3 contains a horizontal analysis of Bed Bath & Beyond's balance sheet and income statement. The column headings show the general calculations, with CY and PY representing current year and prior year, respectively.

An examination of the balance sheet shows overall growth. *Total assets* in the most recent year were $494,063, or 9.6%, higher than the prior year. All of this growth was generated in current assets, with the largest

Exhibit 2-3 Horizontal Analysis of Bed Bath & Beyond's Balance Sheet and Income Statement

Balance Sheet	CY Feb 26, 2011	PY Feb 27, 2010	(CY – PY) $ Change	(CY – PY) PY % Change
Assets				
Current assets:				
Cash and cash equivalents	$1,183,587	$1,096,100	$ 87,487	8.0%
Short-term investment securities	605,608	431,476	174,132	40.4%
Merchandise inventories	1,968,907	1,759,703	209,204	11.9%
Other current assets	315,736	276,066	39,670	14.4%
Total current assets	4,073,838	3,563,345	510,493	14.3%
Long-term investment securities	121,446	132,860	(11,414)	(8.6%)
Property and equipment, net	1,116,297	1,119,292	(2,995)	(0.3%)
Other assets	334,612	336,633	(2,021)	(0.6%)
Total assets	$5,646,193	$5,152,130	$494,063	9.6%
Liabilities and Shareholders' Equity				
Current liabilities:				
Accounts payable	$ 709,550	$ 611,163	$ 98,387	16.1%
Accrued expenses and other current liabilities	306,847	281,730	25,117	8.9%
Merchandise credit and gift card liabilities	193,061	172,804	20,257	11.7%
Current income taxes payable	112,982	83,857	29,125	34.7%
Total current liabilities	1,322,440	1,149,554	172,886	15.0%
Deferred rent and other liabilities	292,364	246,273	46,091	18.7%
Income taxes payable	99,730	103,399	(3,669)	(3.5%)
Total liabilities	1,714,534	1,499,226	$215,308	14.4%
Shareholders' equity:				
Common stock	3,253	3,206	47	1.5%
Additional paid-in capital	1,191,123	1,020,515	170,608	16.7%
Retained earnings	5,546,287	4,754,954	791,333	16.6%
Treasury stock, at cost	(2,814,104)	(2,126,499)	(687,605)	32.3%
Accumulated other comprehensive loss	5,100	728	4,372	600.5%
Total shareholders' equity	3,931,659	3,652,904	278,755	7.6%
Total liabilities and shareholders' equity	$5,646,193	$5,152,130	$494,063	9.6%

Income Statement	Feb 26, 2011	Feb 27, 2010	$ Change	% Change
Net sales	$8,758,503	$7,828,793	$929,710	11.9%
Cost of sales	5,135,574	4,620,674	514,900	11.1%
Gross profit	3,622,929	3,208,119	414,810	12.9%
Selling, general and administrative expenses	2,334,471	2,227,432	107,039	4.8%
Operating profit	1,288,458	980,687	307,771	31.4%
Interest income	4,520	4,568	(48)	(1.1%)
Earnings before provision for income taxes	1,292,978	985,255	307,723	31.2%
Provision for income taxes	501,645	385,222	116,423	30.2%
Net earnings	$ 791,333	$ 600,033	$191,300	31.9%

Common-size statements allow investors and creditors to compare companies of vastly different sizes.

dollar increases in *Short-term investment securities* and *Merchandise inventories*. Overall, the growth in assets was generated through additional liabilities and additional equity. *Total liabilities* increased $215,308, or 14.4%, while *Total shareholders' equity* increased $278,755, or 7.6%. Note that the largest dollar increase in either liabilities or equity was the $791,333 increase to *Retained earnings*. This indicates significant profitability and is a sign of a strong balance sheet.

An examination of the income statement also shows growth. *Net sales* were 11.9% higher than the prior year. With *Cost of sales* increasing slightly less at 11.1%, *Gross profit* was 12.9% higher than the prior year. Moreover, *Selling, general and administrative expenses* increased only 4.8% during the year. This resulted in a $191,300, or 31.9%, increase in *Net earnings* for the year.

In summary, horizontal analysis of the balance sheet and income statement shows that Bed Bath & Beyond is a company that is growing and becoming more profitable over time. Horizontal analysis has provided the context for a more thorough understanding of the financial statements.

Vertical Analysis

Vertical analysis is a method of comparing a company's account balances within one year. It also is normally conducted on both the balance sheet and the income statement. The analysis is calculated by dividing each account balance by a base account, yielding a percentage. The base account is total assets for balance sheet accounts and net sales or revenues for income statement accounts. These two calculations are shown below.

Percentage	For the Balance Sheet	For the Income Statement
	$\dfrac{\text{Account balance}}{\text{Total assets}}$	$\dfrac{\text{Account balance}}{\text{Net sales or Revenue}}$

The product of a vertical analysis is sometimes called a common-size financial statement. A **common-size financial statement** is a statement in which all accounts have been standardized by the overall size of the company. Common-size statements are very useful because they allow investors and creditors to determine the importance of each account to the overall company and to compare that importance to other companies, even those of vastly different sizes.

To illustrate, consider again the *Merchandise inventories* balance from Bed Bath & Beyond's balance sheet in Exhibit 2-1 (see page 29). Also shown are the company's *Total assets*.

	February 26, 2011	February 27, 2010
Merchandise inventories	$1,968,907	$1,759,703
Total assets	$5,646,193	$5,152,130

A vertical analysis divides each inventory balance by total assets for that year. These calculations are shown in the following table. Also shown are similar calculations that would be made for a vertical analysis of *Net earnings* from the company's income statement in Exhibit 2-2. The only difference is that *Net earnings* is divided by *Net sales*, not *Total assets*.

	Current Year	Prior Year
Merchandise inventories	$1,968,907	$1,759,703
Total assets	$5,646,193	$5,152,130
= Percentage of total assets	= 34.9%	= 34.2%
Net earnings	$791,333	$600,033
Net sales	$8,758,503	$7,828,793
= Percentage of net sales	= 9.0%	= 7.7%

For a full vertical analysis, percentages are calculated for every account on each financial statement.

Vertical analysis A method of comparing a company's account balances within one year by dividing each account balance by a base amount to yield a percentage.

Common-size financial statement A statement in which all accounts have been standardized by the overall size of the company.

Exhibit 2-4 contains a vertical analysis of **Bed Bath & Beyond's** balance sheet and income statement. The column headings show the general calculations, with CY and PY representing current year and prior year, respectively.

An examination of the balance sheet shows that the bulk of Bed Bath & Beyond's assets are held in *Merchandise inventories*, *Cash and cash equivalents*, and *Property and equipment*. Together, these three assets make up over 75% of the company's total assets, which makes sense for a retailer like Bed Bath & Beyond. It also shows that the company generated about 30% of its assets through liabilities and about 70% through equity. This shows a relatively low-risk balance sheet.

An examination of the income statement shows that *Cost of sales* was 58.6% of *Net sales* and *Selling,*

Exhibit 2-4 Vertical Analysis of Bed Bath & Beyond's Balance Sheet and Income Statement

Balance Sheet	CY Feb 26, 2011	CY CY Total Assets	PY Feb 27, 2010	PY PY Total Assets
Assets				
Current assets:				
Cash and cash equivalents	$1,183,587	21.0%	$1,096,100	21.3%
Short-term investment securities	605,608	10.7%	431,476	8.4%
Merchandise inventories	1,968,907	34.9%	1,759,703	34.2%
Other current assets	315,736	5.6%	276,066	5.4%
Total current assets	4,073,838	72.2%	3,563,345	69.2%
Long-term investment securities	121,446	2.2%	132,860	2.6%
Property and equipment, net	1,116,297	19.8%	1,119,292	21.7%
Other assets	334,612	5.9%	336,633	6.5%
Total assets	$5,646,193	100.0%	$5,152,130	100.0%
Liabilities and Shareholders' Equity				
Current liabilities:				
Accounts payable	$ 709,550	12.6%	$ 611,163	11.9%
Accrued expenses and other current liabilities	306,847	5.4%	281,730	5.5%
Merchandise credit and gift card liabilities	193,061	3.4%	172,804	3.4%
Current income taxes payable	112,982	2.0%	83,857	1.6%
Total current liabilities	1,322,440	23.4%	1,149,554	22.3%
Deferred rent and other liabilities	292,364	5.2%	246,273	4.8%
Income taxes payable	99,730	1.8%	103,399	2.0%
Total liabilities	1,714,534	30.4%	1,499,226	29.1%
Shareholders' equity:				
Common stock	3,253	0.1%	3,206	0.1%
Additional paid-in capital	1,191,123	21.1%	1,020,515	19.8%
Retained earnings	5,546,287	98.2%	4,754,954	92.3%
Treasury stock, at cost	(2,814,104)	(49.8%)	(2,126,499)	(41.3%)
Accumulated other comprehensive loss	5,100	0.1%	728	0.0%
Total shareholders' equity	3,931,659	69.6%	3,652,904	70.9%
Total liabilities and shareholders' equity	$5,646,193	100.0%	$5,152,130	100.0%

Income Statement	Feb 26, 2011	CY CY Net Sales	Feb 27, 2010	PY PY Net Sales
Net sales	$8,758,503	100.0%	$7,828,793	100.0%
Cost of sales	5,135,574	58.6%	4,620,674	59.0%
Gross profit	3,622,929	41.4%	3,208,119	41.0%
Selling, general and administrative expenses	2,334,471	26.7%	2,227,432	28.5%
Operating profit	1,288,458	14.7%	980,687	12.5%
Interest income	4,520	0.1%	4,568	0.1%
Earnings before provision for income taxes	1,292,978	14.8%	985,255	12.6%
Provision for income taxes	501,645	5.7%	385,222	4.9%
Net earnings	$ 791,333	9.0%	$ 600,033	7.7%

A company's balance sheet often reflects its business model, and a vertical analysis can help you identify one model from another. For example, take the following vertical analyses of selected assets from the 2010 balance sheets of two well-known retailers— Amazon and Wal-Mart. Can you tell which company is which?

	Company A	Company B
Cash and cash equivalents	20.0%	4.6%
Accounts receivable	8.4%	2.4%
Inventories	17.0%	19.4%
Fixed assets, net	12.8%	58.3%

Both Amazon and Wal-Mart are in the business of selling inventory, but their models are different. Wal-Mart is a traditional "bricks and mortar" company that sells its inventory in stores, while Amazon is a dot com company that sells its inventory online. Therefore, Wal-Mart should have a greater percentage of its total assets in fixed assets. Company B has 58.3% of its assets in fixed assets. Therefore, Company B is Wal-Mart.

AP Photo/Paul Sakuma

general and administrative expenses were 26.7%. Taken together, these two major expense categories consumed over 85% of the company's sales revenues. After taxes, the result was that *Net earnings* were 9% of *Net sales*. This means that the company earned 9 cents of profit for every dollar of sales. Note that this percentage is higher than the 7.7% achieved in the prior year. As seen in the horizontal analysis, Bed Bath & Beyond is not only profitable, but its profitability is increasing.

Conduct and interpret horizontal and vertical analyses of Home Depot's inventory and cost of sales found in Appendix C.

Inventory
H/A: ($10,625 − $10,188) / $10,188 = 4.3%
V/A: $10,625 / $40,125 = 26.5%
Cost of Sales
H/A: ($44,693 − $43,764) / $43,764 = 2.1%
V/A: $44,693 / $67,997 = 65.7%

The horizontal analyses indicate that both inventory and cost of sales increased during the year. This reveals that the company is growing. It is selling more and keeping more inventory on hand. As you might expect, the vertical analyses indicate that inventory is a significant part of the company's business. Inventory makes up over one-fourth of total assets. Moreover, for every dollar of sales, the company spends almost 66 cents on the merchandise sold. This leaves only 34 cents to cover all other expenses and generate a profit.

The statement of retained earnings links a company's income statement and balance sheet.

LO6 The Statement of Stockholders' Equity

Chapter 1 introduced the statement of retained earnings. The statement of retained earnings links a company's income statement and balance sheet by showing how net income and dividends change the company's retained earnings balance. All corporations prepare a statement of retained earnings, but most show it as a component of a more comprehensive statement of stockholders' equity.

A **statement of stockholders' equity** is a financial statement that shows how and why each equity account in the company's balance sheet changed from one year to the next. It therefore focuses not only on retained earnings, but also on other equity accounts relating to a company's contributed capital.

For illustration purposes, Exhibit 2-5 contains **Bed Bath & Beyond's** statement of shareholders' equity for the fiscal year ended February 26, 2011. Like the income statement, this statement reports three years of data. However, unlike the income statement, each column reflects the activity in a specific equity account rather than a period of time. The five columns of the statement refer to the five equity accounts from the classified balance sheet. That is, the balances at the bottom of the statement of stockholders' equity are the same balances from

the most recent balance sheet. Note that the numbers are in thousands. Note also that Bed Bath & Beyond uses the word *shareholders'* in the title rather than stockholders'.

The first two accounts, *Common Stock* and *Additional Paid-In Capital,* represent the capital that has been contributed to the company through the issuance of stock. Chapter 10 will discuss in more detail why contributed capital is divided into two accounts. For now, you simply need to add the balances together to yield the total amount received to date. The activity in these accounts for the fiscal year ending February 26, 2011, is located on the bottom third of the statement. The columns of information indicate that the company generated contributed capital during the year primarily through transactions with employees.

The third account, *Retained Earnings,* represents the equity that has been generated through profitable operations and retained in the business. The retained earnings column is in fact Bed Bath & Beyond's statement of retained earnings. In each year presented, net income is added to the beginning retained earnings balance, but no dividends are subtracted. This is because Bed Bath & Beyond elects not to pay dividends.

The fourth account is *Treasury Stock.* Treasury stock is common stock that the company has purchased back from stockholders. Since the purchase of treasury stock is effectively a return of capital to owners, the balance in treasury stock is subtracted from stockholders' equity. The company has been active in repurchasing its stock over the three years. Treasury stock will be covered in more detail in Chapter 10.

The last account, *Accumulated Other Comprehensive Income (Loss),* is beyond the scope of this chapter.

Statement of stockholders' equity A financial statement that shows how and why each equity account in the company's balance sheet changed from one year to the next.

Exhibit 2-5 Bed Bath & Beyond's Statement of Shareholders' Equity

Bed Bath & Beyond Inc. and Subsidiaries
Consolidated Statements of Shareholders' Equity
(in thousands)

	Common Stock		Additional Paid-in Capital	Retained Earnings	Treasury Stock		Accumulated Other Comprehensive Income (Loss)	Total
	Shares	Amount			Shares	Amount		
Balance at March 1, 2008	312,229	$3,122	$ 813,568	$3,729,766	(53,309)	$(1,983,590)	$1,038	$2,561,828
Net earnings				425,123				425,123
Adjustments to comprehensive income							(3,502)	(3,502)
Shares sold under employee stock option plans	1,218	12	19,910					19,922
Issuance of restricted shares	1,224	13	(13)					—
Stock-based compensation			44,906					44,906
Director fees paid in stock	7		197					197
Repurchase of common stock					(1,668)	(48,052)		(48,052)
Change in pension plan				32				32
Balance at February 28, 2009	**314,678**	**3,147**	**878,568**	**4,154,921**	**(54,977)**	**(2,031,642)**	**(4,540)**	**3,000,454**
Net earnings				600,033				600,033
Adjustments to comprehensive income							5,268	5,268
Shares sold under employee stock option plans	4,503	45	96,431					96,476
Issuance of restricted shares	1,369	14	(14)					—
Stock-based compensation			45,411					45,411
Director fees paid in stock	3		119					119
Repurchase of common stock					(2,678)	(94,857)		(94,857)
Balance at February 27, 2010	**320,553**	**3,206**	**1,020,515**	**4,754,954**	**(57,655)**	**(2,126,499)**	**728**	**3,652,904**
Net earnings				791,333				791,333
Adjustments to comprehensive income							4,372	4,372
Shares sold under employee stock option plans	3,804	38	125,058					125,096
Issuance of restricted shares	863	9	(9)					—
Stock-based compensation			45,465					45,465
Director fees paid in stock	2		94					94
Repurchase of common stock					(15,901)	(687,605)		(687,605)
Balance at February 26, 2011	**325,222**	**$3,253**	**$1,191,123**	**$5,546,287**	**(73,556)**	**$(2,814,104)**	**$5,100**	**$3,931,659**

LO7 Information Beyond the Financial Statements

A company's financial statements contain a significant amount of information about the financial activities and position of the company. However, they are not exhaustive, and much information that is useful to creditors and investors is not included on the statements. As a result, companies like Bed Bath & Beyond prepare and report additional information beyond the financial statements. These items are normally included in a company's annual report that is distributed to all shareholders. Three items of significance are the following:

- Notes to the financial statements
- Auditor's report
- Management's Discussion and Analysis

Notes to the Financial Statements

At the bottom of each of Bed Bath & Beyond's financial statements is the following quote: *See accompanying Notes to the Consolidated Financial Statements.* A company's financial statements cannot communicate or disclose to users all the information necessary to adequately understand the financial activities and condition of an entity. Additional information, both quantitative and qualitative, is necessary and can be found in the notes to the financial statements.

The **notes to the financial statements** are the textual and numerical information immediately following the financial statements that (1) disclose the accounting methods used to prepare the financial statements, (2) disclose additional detail and explanation of account balances, and (3) provide information not recognized in the financial statements. Financial statements should not be examined without considering the notes to the financial statements.

Notes to the financial statements The additional textual and numerical information immediately following the financial statements.

Independent auditor's report A report, prepared by a certified public accountant for the public shareholder, stating an opinion on whether the financial statements present fairly, in conformity with GAAP, the company's financial condition and results of operations and cash flows.

The content of the notes to the financial statements varies by company, but there are some similarities across companies. First, the first note of practically all companies summarizes the significant accounting policies used to prepare the financial statements. For example, you can find how a company accounted for its inventory, how the company uses estimates, and how the company recognizes its revenue. This note is especially useful in maintaining the comparability of financial statements across companies. Second, most companies include a note for each of their significant accounts. These notes can vary depending on the type of business, but most companies have notes for significant items such as property and equipment, income taxes, and employee benefit plans, among other things. Exhibit 2-6 contains the titles of the notes to Bed Bath & Beyond's most recent financial statements.

Exhibit 2-6 Bed Bath & Beyond's Notes to the Financial Statements

Bed Bath & Beyond Notes:

1. Summary of significant accounting policies and related matters
2. Property and equipment
3. Lines of credit
4. Fair value measurements
5. Investment securities
6. Provision for income taxes
7. Transactions and balances with related parties
8. Leases
9. Employee benefit plans
10. Commitments and contingencies
11. Supplemental cash flow information
12. Stock-based compensation
13. Summary of quarterly results (unaudited)

Auditor's Report

How do you know if Bed Bath & Beyond's financial statements and notes can be depended upon to be a fair depiction of its financial condition? Since you don't have the ability to determine whether the reported numbers are reliable, you must rely on a third party to provide assurance that the information is reliable. This is why all annual reports contain an *independent auditor's report.*

An **independent auditor's report** is a report, prepared by a certified public accountant for the public shareholder, stating an opinion on whether the financial statements present fairly, in conformity with GAAP, the company's financial condition and results of operations and cash flows. Exhibit 2-7 contains **Bed Bath & Beyond's** most recent auditor's report.

Management's Discussion and Analysis

In addition to financial statements, notes, and the auditor's report, all annual reports contain a section called Management's Discussion and Analysis.

Exhibit 2-7 Bed Bath & Beyond's Auditor's Report

REPORT OF INDEPENDENT REGISTERED PUBLIC ACCOUNTING FIRM

The Board of Directors and Shareholders
Bed Bath & Beyond Inc.:

We have audited the accompanying consolidated balance sheets of Bed Bath & Beyond Inc. and subsidiaries as of February 26, 2011 and February 27, 2010, and the related consolidated statements of earnings, shareholders' equity, and cash flows for each of the fiscal years in the three-year period ended February 26, 2011. In connection with our audits of the consolidated financial statements, we have also audited the financial statement schedule. These consolidated financial statements and financial statement schedule are the responsibility of the Company's management. Our responsibility is to express an opinion on these consolidated financial statements and financial statement schedule based on our audits.

We conducted our audits in accordance with the standards of the Public Company Accounting Oversight Board (United States). Those standards require that we plan and perform the audit to obtain reasonable assurance about whether the financial statements are free of material misstatement. An audit includes examining, on a test basis, evidence supporting the amounts and disclosures in the financial statements. An audit also includes assessing the accounting principles used and significant estimates made by management, as well as evaluating the overall financial statement presentation. We believe that our audits provide a reasonable basis for our opinion.

In our opinion, the consolidated financial statements referred to above present fairly, in all material respects, the financial position of Bed Bath & Beyond Inc. and subsidiaries as of February 26, 2011 and February 27, 2010, and the results of their operations and their cash flows for each of the fiscal years in the three-year period ended February 26, 2011, in conformity with U.S. generally accepted accounting principles. Also in our opinion, the related financial statement schedule, when considered in relation to the basic consolidated financial statements taken as a whole, presents fairly, in all material respects, the information set forth therein.

We also have audited, in accordance with the standards of the Public Company Accounting Oversight Board (United States), the Company's internal control over financial reporting as of February 26, 2011, based on criteria established in Internal Control—Integrated Framework issued by the Committee of Sponsoring Organizations of the Treadway Commission (COSO), and our report dated April 26, 2011 expressed an unqualified opinion on the effectiveness of the Company's internal control over financial reporting.

KPMG LLP

Short Hills, New Jersey
April 26, 2011

As you can see in the above report, **KPMG LLP**, one of the largest public accounting firms in the world, performed the audit. KPMG's opinion is stated in the first sentence of the third paragraph—"the consolidated financial statements . . . present fairly, in all material respects, the financial position of Bed Bath & Beyond Inc. . . . and the results of their operations and their cash flows. . . ." This type of opinion, which is known as an unqualified opinion, is what all companies hope to receive. With this assurance from KPMG, users can consider the financial statements reliable.

Management's Discussion and Analysis (MD&A) is a discussion and analysis of the financial activities of the company by the company's management. The MD&A normally precedes the financial statements in the annual report and contains, among other things, comments on the company's results of operations, its ability to satisfy its current obligations, and its expansion plans.

> **Management's Discussion and Analysis** A discussion and analysis of the financial activities of the company by the company's management.

In some areas, the MD&A is useful in understanding past performance. For example, management usually compares the current year's operating results to the prior year's and explains the reasons for any differences. In other areas, the MD&A is useful in generating expectations for the future. For example, management often discloses how many stores it plans to open or how much in new property and equipment it plans to purchase in the coming year.

Given that the MD&A provides feedback value and predictive value, it is therefore relevant information and should be read along with the financial statements. Exhibit 2-8 contains two excerpts from **Bed Bath & Beyond's** most recent MD&A.

Exhibit 2-8 Excerpts from Bed Bath & Beyond's Management's Discussion and Analysis

Net Sales

Net sales in fiscal 2010 increased $929.7 million to $8.759 billion, representing an increase of 11.9% over $7.829 billion of net sales in fiscal 2009, which increased $620.5 million or 8.6% over the $7.208 billion of net sales in fiscal 2008. For fiscal 2010, approximately 65.2% of the increase in net sales was attributable to an increase in the Company's comparable store sales and the balance of the increase was primarily attributable to an increase in the Company's new store sales. For fiscal 2009, approximately 51.4% of the increase in net sales was attributable to an increase in the Company's new store sales and the balance of the increase was primarily attributable to an increase in the Company's comparable store sales.

Expansion Program

The Company is engaged in an ongoing expansion program involving the opening of new stores in both new and existing markets, the expansion or relocation of existing stores and the continuous review of strategic acquisitions. In the 19-year period from the beginning of fiscal 1992 to the end of fiscal 2010, the chain has grown from 34 to 1,139 stores. Total square footage grew from 0.9 million square feet at the beginning of fiscal 1992 to 35.1 million square feet at the end of fiscal 2010. During fiscal 2010, the Company opened a total of 40 new stores, including 18 BBB stores throughout the United States and Canada, five CTS stores, one Harmon store and 16 buybuy BABY stores, and closed one BBB store, all of which resulted in the aggregate addition of approximately 1.3 million square feet of store space. In May 2008, the Company became a partner in a joint venture which operates two stores in the Mexico City market under the name "Home & More."

The Company plans to continue to expand its operations and invest in its infrastructure to reach its long term objectives. In fiscal 2011, the Company expects to open approximately 45 new stores across all concepts.

STUDY TOOLS

Chapter review card

- Learning Objective and Key Concept Reviews
- Key Definitions and Formulas

Online (Located at www.cengagebrain.com)

- Flash Cards and Crossword Puzzles
- Games and Quizzes
- E-Lectures
- Homework Assignments (as directed by your instructor)

CONCEPT QUESTIONS

1. (LO1) What are the three main forms of business?
2. (LO1) What are the advantages and disadvantages to each form of business?
3. (LO2) To what does the term GAAP refer?
4. (LO2) Who has the authority to determine GAAP?
5. (LO3) How are accounts classified in a classified balance sheet?
6. (LO3) What is the difference between a fixed asset and an intangible asset?
7. (LO3) What are the differences and similarities between the categories of liabilities in the classified balance sheet?
8. (LO3) How is equity classified in a classified balance sheet, and what are the differences in each category?
9. (LO4) Why is a multi-step income statement divided into multiple sections?
10. (LO4) What are the characteristics of each subtotal of income on a multi-step income statement?
11. (LO5) How is horizontal analysis used?
12. (LO5) How is vertical analysis used?
13. (LO5) How is horizontal analysis different from vertical analysis?
14. (LO6) What is shown on the statement of stockholders' equity?
15. (LO6) How is retained earnings calculated? How are retained earnings and stockholders' equity related?
16. (LO7) What information do companies disclose in addition to the financial statements?

MULTIPLE CHOICE

1. (LO1) The form of business in which one individual bears all risk is a:
   a. partnership.
   b. sole proprietorship.
   c. corporation.
   d. none of the above.
2. (LO1) Which form of business issues shares of ownership to the public?
   a. Partnership
   b. Sole proprietorship
   c. Corporation
   d. None of the above
3. (LO2) Which of the following institutions does not play a role in determining GAAP?
   a. Securities and Exchange Commission
   b. Financial Accounting Standards Board

   c. The American Institute of Certified Public Accountants
   d. All of the above play a role in determining GAAP
4. (LO2) GAAP stands for:
   a. Generally Accepted Auditing Procedures.
   b. Governmental Auditing and Accounting Procedures.
   c. Generally Accepted Accounting Principles.
   d. Guidelines for All Accounting Professionals.
5. (LO3) In a classified balance sheet, assets are usually classified as:
   a. current assets, long-term investments, fixed assets, intangible assets, other assets.
   b. current assets, property and equipment, long-term investments, short-term investments, other assets.
   c. short-term assets, long-term assets, tangible assets, intangible assets.
   d. fixed assets, movable assets, long-term assets, short-term assets, other assets.
6. (LO3) Which of the following would not be a current asset?
   a. Inventory
   b. Accounts receivable
   c. Equipment
   d. Supplies
7. (LO4) Which of the following is not included in a calculation of net income?
   a. Operating expenses
   b. Cost of sales
   c. Sales
   d. Goodwill
8. (LO4) Mayer Corporation had sales of $24,000, cost of sales of $10,000, advertising expense of $8,500, and income tax expense of $1,500. What is *gross profit*?
   a. $4,000
   b. $14,000
   c. $5,500
   d. $12,500
9. (LO4) Mayer Corporation had sales of $24,000, cost of goods sales of $10,000, advertising expenses of $8,500, and income tax expense of $1,500. What is *operating profit*?
   a. $4,000
   b. $14,000
   c. $5,500
   d. $12,500
10. (LO5) Horizontal analysis:
    a. states each account balance as a percentage of a base account.
    b. compares account balances within a year.
    c. does not show trends over time.
    d. compares account balances over time.
11. (LO5) The base account for a vertical analysis of the income statement is:
    a. net income.
    b. income before taxes.
    c. net sales.
    d. operating profit.

12. (LO5) A horizontal analysis of inventory yields 5.5%. This means that:
    a. inventory was 5.5% of total assets.
    b. inventory was 5.5% of net sales.
    c. inventory increased 5.5% from the prior year to the current year.
    d. inventory decreased 5.5% from the prior year to the current year.

13. (LO5) A vertical analysis of depreciation expense yields 5.5%. This means that:
    a. depreciation expense was 5.5% of total assets.
    b. depreciation expense was 5.5% of net sales.
    c. depreciation expense increased 5.5% from the prior year to the current year.
    d. depreciation expense decreased 5.5% from the prior year to the current year.

14. (LO5) Last year J&M had assets of $100,000. This year assets are $120,000. A horizontal analysis of assets would yield:
    a. (20.0%).
    b. 16.7%.
    c. 20.0%.
    d. 16.7%.

15. (LO5) Miller Corporation has current assets of $15,000, total assets of $85,000, and net sales of $132,000. A vertical analysis of current assets would yield:
    a. 17.6%.
    b. 11.4%.
    c. 64.4%.
    d. 21.8%.

16. (LO5) McGee Inc. has administrative expenses of $12,000, total assets of $76,000, and net sales of $90,000. A vertical analysis of administrative expenses would yield:
    a. 10.6%.
    b. 15.8%.
    c. 25.1%.
    d. 13.3%.

17. (LO5) Jones Services generated $123,000 in net income in its first year and $115,000 in its second year. A horizontal analysis of net income would yield:
    a. 7.0%.
    b. (6.5%).
    c. 8.7%.
    d. (7.0%).

18. (LO6) Which of the following would not be included on a statement of stockholders' equity?
    a. Common stock
    b. Treasury stock
    c. Retained earnings
    d. Investments in common stock

19. (LO7) Notes to the financial statements do not include:
    a. additional detail and explanation of financial statement account balances.
    b. accounting methods used in the preparation of the financial statements.

c. information such as contingencies and future commitments.
d. discussion and analysis of the company's financial activities by the company's management.

20. (LO7) The auditor's report states an opinion on whether a company's financial statements are:
    a. completely error free.
    b. presented fairly in accordance with GAAP.
    c. better than competitor financial statements.
    d. none of the above.

BRIEF EXERCISES

1. **Miscellaneous Terms** LO1, 7
   The following definitions were discussed in the chapter:
   1. A form of business in which multiple entities join together.
   2. Information following the financial statements that provides additional information and disclosures.
   3. A form of business that is established by filing proper forms in a state.
   4. A report that attests to the fair presentation of a company's financial statements.
   5. The most common form of business.
   6. Analysis of a company's financial activities that focuses on results of operations, ability to pay debts, and expansion plans.

   Required
   Match each definition with one of the following terms: Sole proprietorship; Management's Discussion and Analysis; Notes to the financial statements; Partnership; Auditor's Report; Corporation.

2. **Generally Accepted Accounting Principles** LO2
   The following definitions were discussed in the chapter:
   1. The accounting rules followed by U.S. corporations.
   2. The governmental entity whose mission is to protect investors.
   3. The accounting organization that contributes rules for more technical issues.
   4. The major accounting rule-making body in the United States.
   5. The international accounting rule-making body.

   Required
   Match each definition with one of the following terms: FASB; AICPA; SEC; IASB; GAAP.

3. Classified Balance Sheet LO3

The following accounts were taken from a company's balance sheet:

Supplies	Interest payable
Retained earnings	Equipment
Prepaid insurance	Salaries payable

Required
For each account, indicate whether the account is an asset, a liability, or an equity account. Also indicate the specific asset, liability, or equity classification the account would be reported under on the balance sheet. For example, cash is an asset that would be reported as a current asset.

4. Classified Balance Sheet LO3

The following is a list of accounts taken from Jim's Uniforms:

Accounts receivable	$ 1,200
Sales	18,000
Inventory	3,150
Accounts payable	4,620
Cash	7,330
Prepaid insurance	2,800
Equipment	13,500
Short-term investments	800

Required
Prepare the current asset section of Jim's balance sheet. Make sure to list the accounts in the proper sequence.

5. Calculating Gross Profit LO4

During the month, a retailer generates $15,000 of sales, $2,500 of operating expenses, and $11,500 in cost of sales. At the end of the month, the company had $7,000 of merchandise inventory on hand.

Required
Calculate the company's gross profit for the month.

6. Calculating Operating Profit LO4

Johnson Clothing Supercenter generated a gross profit of $7,750,000 during the year. Also during the year, Johnson incurred advertising expense of $1,500,000, salaries expense of $2,100,000, and income tax expense of $2,000,000.

Required
Calculate the company's operating profit and net income for the year.

7. Horizontal and Vertical Analyses LO5

A company reports the following information from its financial statements:

	Current Year	Prior Year
Inventory	$ 66,540	$ 63,180
Sales	190,405	201,450
Total assets	270,450	240,680

Required
Conduct horizontal and vertical analyses of inventory for the current year. Round percentages to one decimal point (i.e., 10.1%).

8. Horizontal and Vertical Analyses LO5

The following information (in millions) was taken from a recent income statement of The J.M. Smucker Company:

	Current Year	Prior Year
Net sales	$4,605	$3,758
Cost of sales	2,818	2,506
Gross profit	$1,787	$1,252

Required
Conduct horizontal and vertical analyses of gross profit. Was the company more or less profitable in the current year? Do both horizontal and vertical analyses indicate that? For your calculations, round percentages to one decimal point (i.e., 10.1%).

9. Horizontal Analysis LO4, 5

A horizontal analysis of a company's sales resulted in a $1.5 million increase, which equaled a percentage change of 22.8%.

Required
Interpret the dollar change and percentage change and identify which item(s) from the following list would potentially explain the results of the analysis.
a. A sales promotion was highly successful.
b. A manufacturing plant was offline for much of the year due to maintenance.
c. The company opened several new stores.
d. The company lost market share to a new competitor.
e. The company issued $1.5 million of stock during the year.

10. Statement of Stockholders' Equity LO6

A company provides the following account balances for the current year:

Common stock	$ 20,600
Retained earnings, beginning of year	62,496
Additional paid-in capital	100,000
Dividends	9,500
Treasury stock	(22,000)
Net income	22,133

Required
Prepare a statement of stockholders' equity at year-end.

11. Classified Balance Sheet LO3

The following is a list of accounts:
- Mortgage payable, due in 15 years
- Short-term investments
- Cash
- Prepaid rent
- Patents
- Common stock
- Accounts payable
- Buildings
- Notes payable, due in 6 months

Required
Identify each account as a Current asset, Long-term investment, Fixed asset, Intangible asset, Other asset, Current liability, Long-term liability, Contributed capital, or Retained earnings.

12. Classified Balance Sheet LO3

A company reports the following accounts on its classified balance sheet:

Additional paid-in capital	Accounts receivable
Land	Bonds payable, due in 10 years
Treasury stock	Copyrights
Income taxes payable	Dividends payable
Long-term investments	Notes payable, due in 20 months

Required
Identify each account as a Current asset, Long-term investment, Fixed asset, Intangible asset, Other asset, Current liability, Long-term liability, Contributed capital, or Retained earnings.

13. Classified Balance Sheet Terms LO3

The following is a list of balance sheet classifications and descriptions:

a. Current asset
b. Long-term investment
c. Fixed asset
d. Intangible asset
e. Other asset
f. Current liability
g. Long-term liability
h. Capital stock
i. Retained earnings

1. An obligation that is reasonably expected to be satisfied within the normal operations of business.
2. An investment in the common stock or bonds of another entity that the company does not intend to sell within one year.
3. Assets that do not fit into a particular classification of assets (for example, deferred tax liability).
4. An obligation that is not expected to be satisfied within one year.
5. The portion of equity contributed by stockholders through the purchase of stock, which includes common stock and preferred stock.

6. Resources that are reasonably expected to be converted to cash or consumed during the normal operations of business.
7. Tangible resources that are used in the company's operations for more than one year and are not intended for resale.
8. The profits that a company earns over time and retains in the business.
9. Resources to be used in the company's operations for more than one year that have no physical substance.

Required
Match each classification with the appropriate description.

14. Classified Balance Sheet LO3

The following are independent cases:

	Sally's Fish & Chips	Brina's Bar & Grill	Ely's Tanning Salon
ASSETS			
Current assets	3,000	2,500	4,500
Long-term investments	45,500	_____	60,000
Fixed assets	125,750	100,000	150,000
Intangible assets	32,250	55,250	15,000
Other assets	_____	35,500	6,500
Total assets	**220,000**	**225,750**	_____
LIABILITIES			
Current liabilities	15,500	7,000	_____
Long-term liabilities	45,000	_____	65,500
Total liabilities	_____	**75,000**	**69,000**
STOCKHOLDERS' EQUITY			
Capital stock	55,000	_____	67,500
Retained earnings	_____	105,000	_____
Total liabilities and stockholders' equity	**220,000**	_____	_____

Required
Fill in each blank with the appropriate dollar amount.

15. Classified Balance Sheet LO3

The following items were taken from the December 31 balance sheet of Auburn Bowling Lanes:

Buildings, net	$60,200
Accounts receivable	14,520
Prepaid insurance	4,680
Cash	20,840
Equipment, net	63,680
Land	61,200
Mortgage payable	103,040
Common stock	66,000
Retained earnings	40,000
Interest payable	3,600
Accounts payable	12,480

Required

Recreate the company's classified balance sheet, assuming that $13,600 of the mortgage payable balance will be paid within three months of the balance sheet date.

16. Prepare a Classified Balance Sheet   LO3

The following information was taken from the February 26, 2011, balance sheet of **Best Buy**:

(in millions)	
Accounts payable	$ 4,894
Accounts receivable	2,348
Additional paid-in capital	18
Cash	1,103
Short-term investments	22
Common stock	39
Intangible assets	2,587
Long-term liabilities	1,894
Other current assets	1,103
Other current liabilities	3,769
Other equity	863
Other assets	966
Fixed assets	3,823
Retained earnings	6,372
Inventory	5,897

Required

Prepare Best Buy's classified balance sheet at February 26, 2011.

17. Balance Sheet and Income Statement Classifications   LO3, 4

A company uses the following pairs of accounts for its financial statements:
- Sales and Accounts receivable
- Interest payable and Interest expense
- Supplies expense and Supplies
- Inventory and Cost of sales
- Salaries payable and Salaries expense
- Income tax expense and Income tax payable

Required

For each pair of accounts, identify which account would be reported on the balance sheet and which would be reported on the income statement. For each balance sheet account, identify its classification. For each income statement account, identify which subtotal(s) of income would be affected by the account.

18. Multi-Step Income Statement   LO4

The following are all independent cases:

	The Bike Shop	The Rental Center	The Uniform Center
Sales	$ _____	$ 78,000	$ 35,000
Cost of sales	45,000	_____	_____
Gross profit	18,000	_____	7,000
Selling expenses	_____	9,000	3,000
Administrative expenses	2,800	_____	_____
Total operating expenses	8,800	13,600	_____
Operating profit	9,200	25,400	_____
Income tax expense	_____	11,000	1,000
Net income	7,700	_____	1,500

Required

Fill in each blank with the appropriate dollar amount.

19. Multi-Step Income Statement   LO4

These items were taken from the financial records of Brown's Used Cars:

Utilities expense	$ 17,650
Interest expense	50
Selling expense	14,600
Administrative expense	15,230
Interest revenue	500
Cost of sales	75,620
Net sales	154,900

Required

Prepare a multi-step income statement assuming Brown's falls into the 30% tax bracket and has a December 31 year end.

20. Multi-Step Income Statement   LO4

The following income statement items are taken from the records of Matthews Music Group for the year ending December 31:

Advertising expense	$ 6,210
Cost of sales	83,910
Income tax expense	2,250
Insurance expense	3,960
Interest expense	4,115
Interest revenue	6,055
Rent expense	11,410
Salaries expense	28,525
Sales	153,010
Supplies expense	5,600

Required

Prepare a multi-step income statement for the year ending December 31.

21. Completing a Multi-Step Income Statement LO4

The following multi-step income statement was provided by Reece Corp.:

Reece Corp. Income Statement For the Year Ending December 31	
Net sales	$ (a)
(b)	96,000
(c)	$92,000
Insurance expense	(d)
Salaries expense	11,500
(e)	$52,500
Interest revenue	9,200
Interest expense	(f)
(g)	$ (h)
(i)	14,990
Net income	$28,310

Required

Identify the missing amounts and descriptions.

22. Financial Statement Accounts LO3, 4, 6

The following is a list of accounts:

Treasury stock	Interest payable
Interest revenue	Common stock
Buildings	Cost of sales
Dividends	Administrative expense
Accounts payable	Additional paid-in capital
Retained earnings	Cash

Required

Identify if each account would appear on the balance sheet, income statement, and/or statement of stockholders' equity.

23. Horizontal and Vertical Analyses LO4, 5

Comparative income statements are available for Johanna's Fine Furs:

	2012	2011
Sales	$850,000	$800,000
Cost of sales	325,000	275,000
Gross profit	525,000	525,000
Operating expenses	175,000	120,000
Operating profit	350,000	405,000
Income tax expense	105,000	121,500
Net income	$245,000	$283,500

Required

Perform horizontal and vertical analyses on each of the items in the above comparative income statements. Round percentages to one decimal point (i.e., 10.1%).

24. Horizontal and Vertical Analyses LO4, 5

The following condensed balance sheets are available for Delta Electronics:

	2012	2011
Cash	$ 142	$ 160
Accounts receivable	35	30
Inventory	428	382
Current assets	605	572
Equipment, net	880	790
Total assets	$1,485	$1,362
Accounts payable	$ 201	$ 220
Salaries payable	169	162
Current liabilities	370	382
Bonds payable	350	300
Total liabilities	720	682
Retained Earnings	382	300
Common Stock	383	380
Total equity	765	680
Total liabilities and equity	$1,485	$1,362

Required

Perform horizontal and vertical analyses on each of the items in the above comparative balance sheets. Round percentages to one decimal point (i.e., 10.1%).

25. Horizontal and Vertical Analyses LO3, 5

Comparative balance sheet data is available for Ellis Enterprises:

	2012	2011
Total assets	$850,000	$700,000
Total liabilities	$240,000	$280,000
Total equity	$610,000	$420,000

Required

Perform horizontal and vertical analyses on each of the items above. Round percentages to one decimal point (i.e., 10.1%). If generating assets through debt is considered more risky than generating assets through equity, is Ellis more or less risky in 2012?

26. Horizontal and Vertical Analyses LO5

A company provides the following information:

	Current Year	Prior Year
Net sales	$121,345	$119,872
Accounts receivable	$ 30,192	$ 12,676
Total assets	$246,933	$250,361

Required

Should the company be concerned about its performance? Use horizontal and vertical analyses to "prove" why or why not. Round percentages to one decimal point (i.e., 10.1%).

27. Financial Accounting Terms   LO5, 7

The following are various terms and definitions from financial accounting:

a. Common-size financial statement
b. Notes to the financial statements
c. Management's Discussion and Analysis
d. Auditor's Report
e. Vertical analysis
f. Horizontal analysis

1. A technique that compares account balances within one year by stating each account balance as a percentage of a base amount.
2. Textual and numerical information immediately following the financial statement's disclosing information such as accounting methods used, detail and explanation of account balances, and information not recognized in the financial statements.
3. A statement in which all accounts have been standardized by the overall size of the company.
4. A discussion and analysis of the financial activities of the company by the company's management.
5. A report, prepared by a certified public accountant for the public shareholder, stating an opinion on whether the financial statements present fairly in conformity with GAAP the company's financial condition and results of operations and cash flows.
6. A technique that calculates the change in an account balance from one period to the next and expresses that change in both dollar and percentage terms.

Required

Match each term with the appropriate definition.

28. Prepare a Classified Balance Sheet   LO3

Bay Company thinks there may be a problem with its balance sheet:

Bay Company Classified Balance Sheet For the Year Ending December 31	
Assets	
Current assets	
Buildings	$ 70,000
Interest revenue	11,000
Equipment	41,000
Cash	8,000
Other current assets	4,000
Total current assets	134,000
Accounts receivable	12,000
Land	20,000
Interest payable	14,000
Total noncurrent assets	46,000
Total assets	$180,000
Liabilities and Stockholders' Equity	
Current liabilities	
Accounts payable	$ 16,000
Interest expense	39,000
Total current liabilities	55,000
Stockholders' equity	
Retained earnings	50,000
Common stock	35,000
Bonds payable	40,000
Total stockholders' equity	125,000
Total liabilities and stockholders' equity	$180,000

Required

Prepare a corrected classified balance sheet.

29. Prepare a Multi-Step Income Statement LO4

The auditor for Foshee Corporation noticed that its income statement was incorrect:

Foshee Corporation
Income Statement
December 31

Sales		$130,000
Cost of sales		80,000
Accounts receivable		19,500
Gross profit		30,500
Interest expense	$15,000	
Selling expense	13,000	
Total operating expenses		28,000
Operating profit		2,500
Interest revenue	16,500	
Interest payable	4,000	8,500
Income before taxes		11,000
Income tax expense		12,850
Net income (loss)		$ (1,850)

Required
Prepare a corrected multi-step income statement.

30. Multi-Step Income Statement and Classified Balance Sheet LO3, 4

The following items were taken from the financial statements of Wilson Inc. for 2012:

Accounts payable	$15,780
Accounts receivable	8,470
Advertising expense	4,200
Cash	16,080
Common stock	15,400
Cost of sales	41,250
Dividends	2,310
Equipment, net	45,420
Income tax expense	3,260
Insurance expense	4,680
Long-term liabilities	9,920
Prepaid insurance	5,970
Retained earnings, Jan. 1	28,450
Salaries expense	17,420
Salaries payable	5,210
Sales	78,420
Utilities expense	4,180

Required
Prepare a multi-step income statement for the year ending December 31, 2012, and a classified balance sheet at December 31, 2012. Hint: You must calculate ending retained earnings.

31. Prepare and Analyze the Classified Balance Sheet LO3, 5

The following balance sheet items are available from Carnell Inc. as of December 31, 2012:

	2012	2011
Accounts payable	$ 75,500	$ 35,035
Accounts receivable	50,000	85,065
Bonds payable, due 12/31/2016	125,000	25,000
Buildings, net	240,000	300,000
Capital stock, $5 par	100,000	80,000
Cash	15,000	25,635
Equipment, net	24,000	24,000
Income taxes payable	12,250	16,465
Interest payable	13,755	7,550
Inventory	25,650	27,270
Land	300,000	200,000
Long-term investments	125,000	100,000
Notes payable, due 6/30/2013	100,000	100,000
Supplies	12,500	13,500
Additional paid-in capital	200,000	190,000
Patents	6,000	6,000
Prepaid rent	10,150	12,275
Retained earnings	146,295	306,135
Salaries payable	35,500	33,560

Required
a. Prepare a comparative, classified balance sheet for Carnell Inc.
b. Perform horizontal and vertical analyses and interpret the results. Round percentages to one decimal point (i.e., 10.1%).
c. Assume the same information above except that in 2012, Bonds payable is $0 while Retained earnings is $271,295. Does this new information change any interpretations previously made?

32. Prepare and Analyze the Multi-Step Income Statement LO4, 5

The following income statement items are available from Dansby Inc. for the years ending December 31:

	2012	2011
Advertising expense	$ 7,765	$ 9,789
Commissions expense	4,879	6,010
Cost of sales	48,596	58,896
Income tax expense	2,217	2,684
Insurance expense	4,897	5,236
Interest expense	2,584	2,695
Interest revenue	4,287	4,189
Sales	95,950	106,569
Supplies expense	1,654	2,106
Salaries expense	19,320	21,012
Rent expense	7,634	7,856

Required

a. Prepare a comparative, multi-step income statement for Dansby Inc.

b. Perform horizontal and vertical analyses and interpret the results. Round percentages to one decimal point (i.e., 10.1%).

c. Assume the following change in information: Cost of sales in 2012, $62,470 and in 2011, $45,670. Does this new information change any interpretations previously made?

33. Horizontal Analysis of the Income Statement LO5

The following items were taken from a recent income statement of PepsiCo:

	Current Year	Prior Year
Net sales	$43,251	$39,474
Cost of sales	20,351	18,038
Selling and administrative expenses	15,965	14,266
Operating income	6,935	7,170
Other income	86	461
Income before taxes	7,021	7,631
Provision for income taxes	1,879	1,973
Net income	5,142	5,658

Required

Perform a horizontal analysis on each account. Round percentages to one decimal point (i.e., 10.1%). What conclusions can you make about PepsiCo?

34. Using Horizontal and Vertical Analyses LO5

The president of ABC Inc. is disappointed that the company was less profitable this year than last year. Comparative income statements for ABC Inc. are as follows:

	Current Year	Prior Year
Sales	$800,000	$500,000
Cost of sales	300,000	200,000
Gross profit	$500,000	$300,000
Operating expenses	167,000	130,000
Operating income	$333,000	$170,000
One-time gain		180,000
Net income	$333,000	$350,000

Required

Why was ABC's net income lower in the current year? Use horizontal and vertical analyses to show the ways in which ABC was more profitable in the current year. Round percentages to one decimal point (i.e., 10.1%).

CASES

35. Reading and Analyzing Financial Statements LO3, 4, 5

Refer to **Home Depot's** Annual Report contained in Appendix C of the textbook.

Required

a. Identify the company's current-year and prior-year balances in total current assets, net property and equipment, total assets, total current liabilities, total liabilities, and total stockholders' equity.

b. Conduct horizontal analysis on each account balance in part a. What broad trend is indicated by the calculations? Round percentages to one decimal point (i.e., 10.1%).

c. Identify the company's current-year and prior-year gross profit, operating income, earnings before income taxes, and net earnings.

d. Conduct horizontal analysis on each account balance in part c. What broad trend is indicated by the calculations? Round percentages to one decimal point (i.e., 10.1%).

36. Understanding Financial Statements LO3

Refer to Home Depot's classified balance sheet contained in Appendix C of the textbook.

Required

a. The current liability section contains an account entitled "Current Installments of Long-Term Debt." Explain what this account represents and why it is included in current liabilities if it relates to long-term debt.

b. The liability section contains an account entitled "Long-Term Debt, excluding current installments." Examine the fifth note to the financial statements and identify how many different "Senior Notes" are included in the account balance.

c. The current liability section contains an account entitled "Deferred Revenue." Read the "Revenues" and "Services Revenue" paragraphs in the first note to the financial statements. What two general activities are captured in the "Deferred Revenue" account?

37. Understanding Financial Statements LO4

Refer to Home Depot's income statement contained in Appendix C of the textbook.

Required

a. Identify the line item just above Net Earnings. Explain in your own words what you think this line item represents.

b. Look at the fourth note to the financial statements. What was the item that gave rise to the line on the income statement?

c. Do you think that this item should be reported separately on the income statement? Why or why not?

38. Research and Analysis LO4, 5

Access the 2010 annual report for **AnnTaylor Stores** by clicking on the *Investors* and *Annual Reports* links at www.anninc.com.

Required

Conduct horizontal analysis of the company's net sales, cost of sales, and gross profit for the current year and vertical analysis for the same accounts for both the current and prior year. Round percentages to one decimal point (i.e., 10.1%). What conclusions can you draw about the company's ability to earn a profit from its sales?

39. Communication in Accounting LO4, 5

You and some friends have decided to start an investment club. Several of the new members of the club, however, have no knowledge of financial statements, particularly the income statement. They understand that a company must "make money," but they get confused when they read a multi-step income statement.

Required

Prepare a short memo for current and future members that describes the subtotals of income on a multi-step income statement.

IT'S ALL ABOUT
THE HOMEWORK!

CengageNOW™ is an **easy-to-use online resource** that helps you **study in less time** to **get the grade you want** – NOW.

CengageNOW™ is your online resource for ACCT2 and features:
- All end-of-chapter homework from the textbook written by the authors
- Additional hints and guidance during homework via enhanced feedback
- Interactive eBook
- Personalized Study Plan, including pre- and post-test assessments, videos, games, E-lectures, and more!

How to Register Your Access Code:
1. Launch a Web browser. Go to login.cengagebrain.com and click on "Create a New Account." Already have an account? Enter your email/password under "Log In."
2. Enter your access code in the field provided, exactly how it appears on your card.
3. New users: Enter your account information and click "Continue."
4. Record your email address and password below and store it in a secure location for future visits.

   [Email Address: _____]
   [Password: _____]

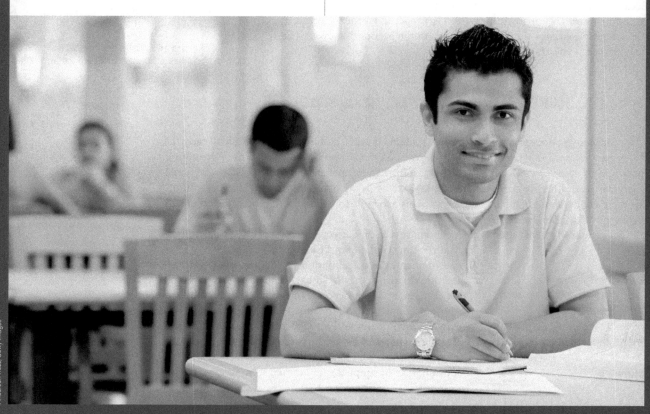

Recording
Accounting Transactions

Introduction

The first two chapters of this book focused on how economic information is communicated to users through financial statements: the balance sheet, the income statement, the statement of stockholders' equity, and the statement of cash flows. This chapter and Chapter 4 focus on how the activities of a business are captured by the accounting system so that these financial statements can be prepared. More specifically, Chapters 3 and 4 describe the accounting cycle. Because financial statements must be prepared periodically, the process of capturing and reporting information is a repetitive process, or cycle. This chapter explores the first three steps in the accounting cycle. The next chapter explores the remaining steps.

Learning Objectives

After studying the material in this chapter, you should be able to:

LO1 Describe the purpose of an accounting information system.

LO2 Analyze the effect of accounting transactions on the accounting equation.

LO3 Understand how T-accounts and debits and credits are used in a double-entry accounting system.

LO4 Describe the purpose of the journal, ledger, and trial balance.

LO5 Record and post accounting transactions and prepare a trial balance and financial statements.

LO1 The Accounting Information System

A company's **accounting information system** is the system that identifies, records, summarizes, and communicates the various transactions of a company. Accounting information systems vary widely, ranging from manual, pencil-and-paper systems in some organizations to highly complex electronic systems in other organizations. However different their forms, though, all accounting systems are built to capture and report the effects of a company's *accounting transactions*.

An **accounting transaction** is any economic event that affects a company's assets, liabilities, or equity at the time of the event. Examples include the purchase of equipment, the consumption of supplies in operations, and the issuance of debt or stock. In each of these examples, the event increases or decreases a specific asset, liability, or equity account of the company. Accounting transactions between a company and an external party (for example, an equipment purchase or the issuance of stock) are *external* transactions, while transactions within a company (the consumption of supplies) are *internal* transactions.

Accounting information system The system that identifies, records, summarizes, and communicates the various transactions of a company.

Accounting transaction Any economic event that affects a company's assets, liabilities, or equity at the time of the event.

Much like a video camera, an accounting information system captures business activity so that others can view it.

Jeff Greenberg/Alamy

ACCT

To record accounting transactions and summarize the resulting information, companies use accounts. An **account** is an accounting record that accumulates the activity of a specific item and yields the item's balance. For example, a company's cash account is increased and decreased as cash is received and paid, and it shows the amount of cash held at any point in time. The various accounts that a company uses to capture its business activities are often listed in a **chart of accounts**. An example chart of accounts, complete with numerical references for each account, is found in Exhibit 3-1.

Charts of accounts will vary across companies. For example, a bank will have accounts relating to customer deposits while a biotech company will have accounts relating to research and development. Of course, there certainly will be many

Account An accounting record that accumulates the activity of a specific item and yields the item's balance.

Chart of accounts The list of accounts that a company uses to capture its business activities.

You can tell a lot about what a company does if you have its chart of accounts.

Exhibit 3-1 Chart of Accounts

100–199	ASSETS
100	Cash
101	Accounts Receivable
110	Supplies
120	Equipment
200–299	LIABILITIES
210	Accounts Payable
211	Unearned Revenues
230	Notes Payable
300–399	EQUITY
300	Common Stock
350	Retained Earnings
400–499	REVENUES
400	Service Revenue
500–599	EXPENSES
501	Administrative Expense
502	Advertising Expense
600–699	DIVIDENDS

commonalities across charts of accounts—for example, practically every company will have an account for cash—but there will be differences depending on the company's activities. As a result, you can tell a lot about what a company does if you have its chart of accounts.

Dual nature of accounting Every accounting transaction must affect at least two accounts.

LO₂ Accounting Transactions and the Accounting Equation

All accounting transactions must be recorded in the accounting information system. To understand the nature of recording transactions, it is best to start with the fundamental accounting equation:

$$\text{Assets} = \text{Liabilities} + \text{Equity}$$

The equation states that a company's assets must always equal the sum of its liabilities and equity. This means that any change to one part of the equation must be accompanied by a second change to another part. For example, suppose that a transaction increases an asset account. For the equation to stay in balance, the transaction must also either decrease another asset account or increase a liability or equity account. This means that every accounting transaction must affect at least two accounts. This is known as the **dual nature of accounting**.

Transaction Analysis

To illustrate how accounting transactions affect the accounting equation, consider the following ten transactions in the first month of operations of Circle Films, a company that documents weddings, birthdays, and other significant life events. Although the example is a small hypothetical company, the transactions would be treated in the same way by all companies, large or small.

HOME DEPOT ANALYSIS

Look at Home Depot's balance sheet in Appendix C and determine how many accounts it uses to report its assets, liabilities, and equity. Also, consider the scenario when one stockholder of Home Depot sells his or her stock to another stockholder. Is this an economic event relating to Home Depot? Is it an accounting transaction?

Home Depot's balance sheet reports 29 different accounts: 14 asset accounts, 10 liability accounts, and 5 equity accounts.

When Home Depot's stock is sold on the New York Stock Exchange, the sale is an economic event of interest to Home Depot. However, because Home Depot is not involved in the transaction, it is not an accounting transaction.

TRANSACTION #1: Circle Films incorporates in the state of Texas and issues 3,000 shares of common stock to investors for $15,000 cash. Because Circle Films receives cash of $15,000, assets increase. Its equity also increases because investors have contributed cash for an ownership interest in the company. More specifically, Circle Films' common stock increases.

	Assets	=	Liabilities	+	Equity
	Cash	=		+	Common Stock
Prior Bal.	$ 0				$ 0
#1	+$15,000				+$15,000
New Bal.	$15,000				$15,000
	$15,000	=	$0	+	$15,000

TRANSACTION #2: Circle Films purchases a video camera for $9,000 and memory cards for $1,000. In this transaction, the company is exchanging one asset (cash) for other assets (equipment and supplies). Therefore, assets both increase and decrease by $10,000. The net effect is no change in total assets.

	Assets			=	Liabilities	+	Equity
	Cash	Supplies	Equipment	=		+	Common Stock
Prior Bal.	$15,000	$ 0	$ 0				$15,000
#2	−$10,000	+$1,000	+$9,000				
New Bal.	$ 5,000	$1,000	$9,000				$15,000
	$15,000			=	$0	+	$15,000

TRANSACTION #3: Circle Films receives a $1,500 payment immediately after filming a customer's wedding. Because Circle Films is receiving cash, assets increase. But unlike the previous transaction in which assets were exchanged, the increase in assets in this transaction results from filming the wedding. Recall from Chapter 1 that an inflow of assets from providing a service is a revenue. Revenues increase net income and therefore retained earnings. As a result, Circle Films' equity increases.

	Assets			=	Liabilities	+	Equity	
	Cash	Supplies	Equipment	=		+	Common Stock	Retained Earnings
Prior Bal.	$5,000	$1,000	$9,000				$15,000	$ 0
#3	+$1,500							+$1,500
New Bal.	$6,500	$1,000	$9,000				$15,000	$1,500
	$16,500			=	$0	+	$16,500	

TRANSACTION #4: Circle Films receives a $2,000 deposit from a customer to film her parents' fiftieth wedding anniversary. In this transaction, Circle Films again receives cash from a customer, so assets increase. However, it has not yet provided the service, so it has an obligation to the customer. As a result, Circle Films' liabilities increase for the amount of cash received.

	Assets			=	Liabilities	+	Equity	
	Cash	Supplies	Equipment	=	Unearned Revenue	+	Common Stock	Retained Earnings
Prior Bal.	$6,500	$1,000	$9,000		$ 0		$15,000	$1,500
#4	+$2,000				+$2,000			
New Bal.	$8,500	$1,000	$9,000		$2,000		$15,000	$1,500
		$18,500		=	$2,000	+	$16,500	

TRANSACTION #5: Circle Films paid $250 cash to run an ad in the local paper. Because Circle Films paid cash, assets decrease. The decrease in assets results from advertising its business. Recall from Chapter 1 that a decrease in assets from operating a business is an expense. Expenses decrease net income and therefore retained earnings. As a result, Circle Films' equity decreases.

	Assets			=	Liabilities	+	Equity	
	Cash	Supplies	Equipment	=	Unearned Revenue	+	Common Stock	Retained Earnings
Prior Bal.	$8,500	$1,000	$9,000		$2,000		$15,000	$1,500
#5	−$ 250							−$ 250
New Bal.	$8,250	$1,000	$9,000		$2,000		$15,000	$1,250
		$18,250		=	$2,000	+	$16,250	

TRANSACTION #6: Circle Films films a dance competition, leaving a $3,500 invoice with the customer. Because Circle Films receives no cash at the time of the competition, it is tempting to conclude that there is no accounting transaction and therefore no effect on the accounting equation. However, not all accounting transactions affect cash. By completing the job and leaving an invoice with the customer, Circle Films now has a receivable from the customer. Therefore, assets increase. And because the receivable is generated by providing a service, the firm has additional revenues and therefore more equity. So, equity increases as well. Note that this transaction is very similar to transaction #3, with the only difference being the type of asset that increases.

	Assets				=	Liabilities	+	Equity	
	Cash	Accounts Receivable	Supplies	Equipment	=	Unearned Revenue	+	Common Stock	Retained Earnings
Prior Bal.	$8,250	$ 0	$1,000	$9,000		$2,000		$15,000	$1,250
#6		+$3,500							+$3,500
New Bal.	$8,250	$3,500	$1,000	$9,000		$2,000		$15,000	$4,750
		$21,750			=	$2,000	+	$19,750	

TRANSACTION #7: Circle Films purchases another $9,000 video camera by signing a two-year promissory note requiring the payment of principal and interest at maturity. Interest is charged at a 6% annual rate. Like transaction #2, Circle Films receives equipment, so assets increase. Unlike transaction #2, though, Circle Films promises to pay in two years rather than today. Therefore, its liabilities increase.

	Assets				=	Liabilities		+	Equity	
	Cash	Accounts Receivable	Supplies	Equipment	=	Unearned Revenue	Notes Payable	+	Common Stock	Retained Earnings
Prior Bal.	$8,250	$3,500	$1,000	$ 9,000		$2,000	$ 0		$15,000	$4,750
#7				+$ 9,000			+$9,000			
New Bal.	$8,250	$3,500	$1,000	$18,000		$2,000	$9,000		$15,000	$4,750
		$30,750			=		$11,000	+		$19,750

TRANSACTION #8: Circle Films receives $3,500 from the customer in payment of the open invoice from transaction #6. In this transaction, Circle Films exchanges one asset for another. It receives cash in satisfaction of the receivable that was created when the service was performed. As a result, cash increases while receivables decrease. There is no change in total assets.

	Assets				=	Liabilities		+	Equity	
	Cash	Accounts Receivable	Supplies	Equipment	=	Unearned Revenue	Notes Payable	+	Common Stock	Retained Earnings
Prior Bal.	$ 8,250	$3,500	$1,000	$18,000		$2,000	$9,000		$15,000	$4,750
#8	+$ 3,500	−$3,500								
New Bal.	$11,750	$ 0	$1,000	$18,000		$2,000	$9,000		$15,000	$4,750
		$30,750			=		$11,000	+		$19,750

TRANSACTION #9: Circle Films pays salaries of $2,000 to its employees. In this case, its cash decreases by $2,000, so its assets decrease. Since the payments are an outflow of assets from operating the business, the payments are an expense, which is a reduction to equity. Therefore, equity decreases.

	Assets				=	Liabilities		+	Equity	
	Cash	Accounts Receivable	Supplies	Equipment	=	Unearned Revenue	Notes Payable	+	Common Stock	Retained Earnings
Prior Bal.	$11,750	$0	$1,000	$18,000		$2,000	$9,000		$15,000	$4,750
#9	−$ 2,000									−$2,000
New Bal.	$ 9,750	$0	$1,000	$18,000		$2,000	$9,000		$15,000	$2,750
		$28,750			=		$11,000	+		$17,750

TRANSACTION #10: At the end of the month, Circle Films pays its owners a $1,500 cash dividend. In this transaction, cash and therefore assets decrease. Payments to a company's owners are dividends. Recall from Chapter 1 that dividends decrease retained earnings, so equity decreases as well.

	Assets				=	Liabilities		+	Equity	
	Cash	Accounts Receivable	Supplies	Equipment	=	Unearned Revenue	Notes Payable	+	Common Stock	Retained Earnings
Prior Bal.	$9,750	$0	$1,000	$18,000		$2,000	$9,000		$15,000	$2,750
#10	−$1,500	—	____	____		____	____		____	−$1,500
New Bal.	$8,250	$0	$1,000	$18,000		$2,000	$9,000		$15,000	$1,250
		$27,250			=	$11,000		+	$16,250	

Summary of Transactions

The ten transactions of Circle Films are summarized in Exhibit 3-2. Circle Films started the month with nothing but an idea and ended the month with $27,250 in assets, $11,000 in liabilities, and $16,250 in equity. As you review the exhibit, note that changes to the left side of the equation equaled changes to the right side of the equation for all transactions. As a result, the accounting equation was always in balance. Note also that every transaction affected at least two specific accounts. Sometimes the transaction affected two asset accounts (#2 and #8), sometimes an asset and a liability account (#4 and #7), and sometimes an asset and an equity account (#1, #3, #5, #6, #9, and #10). Any combination affecting assets, liabilities, and equity can occur, as long as the equation stays in balance.

Exhibit 3-2 Transaction Summary for Circle Films

	Assets				=	Liabilities		+	Equity	
	Cash	Accounts Receivable	Supplies	Equipment	=	Unearned Revenue	Notes Payable	+	Common Stock	Retained Earnings
#1	+15,000				=			+	+15,000	
#2	−10,000		+1,000	+9,000	=			+		
#3	+1,500				=			+		+1,500
#4	+2,000				=	+2,000		+		
#5	−250				=			+		−250
#6		+3,500			=			+		+3,500
#7				+9,000	=		+9,000	+		
#8	+3,500	−3,500			=			+		
#9	−2,000				=			+		−2,000
#10	−1,500				=			+		−1,500
	$8,250	$0	$1,000	$18,000	=	$2,000	$9,000	+	$15,000	$1,250
		$27,250			=	$11,000		+	$16,250	

LO3 The Double-Entry Accounting System

While the preceding analysis is an excellent way to understand and visualize the effect of accounting transactions, accounting information systems do not record transactions using plusses and minuses in a tabular format since such an approach, while accurate, would be very cumbersome. Rather, they use a *double-entry system* that traces its origins back to a mathematical treatise written in the fifteenth century by a Franciscan monk, Luca Pacioli. The double-entry system is based on the dual nature of accounting demonstrated in the preceding transaction analyses. That is, every accounting transaction affects at least two accounts, so accounting systems record those transactions with a "double" or "two-fold" entry. The following sections explain the mechanics of this double-entry system, starting with the T-account.

The T-Account

All accounts can be characterized or represented in the following form known as a T-account due to its resemblance to a capital T.

Account Name	
Debit Side	Credit Side

The name of the account is listed at the top with two columns appearing below. The left column is the *debit* side while the right column is the *credit* side. The term **debit** simply means left side of an account while the term **credit** simply means right side of an account.

T-accounts work as follows. When a transaction affects an account balance, the amount of the transaction is entered on the account's debit side or credit side, depending on the transaction. You will see how transactions are recorded shortly. An entry on the debit side is called a "debit," while an entry on the credit side is called a "credit." Once all entries are made, the balance in an account is determined by separately adding up all debits and all credits and subtracting the smaller total from the larger, leaving the difference as the account balance. The following three examples illustrate this process.

Examples of T-Account Mechanics

Asset		Liability		Equity	
1,000	5,000	2,000	6,000	7,000	2,000
4,000	3,000	1,000	4,000		3,000
8,000		3,000			3,000
5,000			4,000		1,000

The areas between the horizontal lines contain the activity in each account, with the account balance below. The asset account has three debit entries totaling $13,000 and two credit entries totaling $8,000, leaving a debit balance of $5,000. The liability account has debit entries totaling $6,000 and credit entries totaling $10,000, resulting in a $4,000 credit balance. The equity account has a $1,000 credit balance after having $7,000 of debit entries and $8,000 of credit entries.

It is no coincidence that in this example the asset account has a debit balance while the liability and equity accounts have credit balances. In a double-entry system, asset accounts should normally have debit balances while liability and equity accounts should normally have credit balances. Such "normal" balances mirror the accounting equation, where assets are on the left side of the equal sign and liabilities and equity are on the right side.

Normal Account Balances

Asset Accounts		Liability Accounts		Equity Accounts	
Normal Balance			Normal Balance		Normal Balance

Accounting Equation

Assets	=	Liabilities	+	Equity

This arrangement of normal balances is the key to how a double-entry system works. To keep the accounting equation balanced, a double-entry system must keep debit balances equal to credit balances. This means that every accounting transaction must be recorded with equal changes to debit and credit balances. That, again, is why the system is "double-entry." How debits and credits are used to change account balances is discussed next.

Debit The left side of an account.

Credit The right side of an account.

> ## Any change to the accounting equation must be accompanied by a second change.

Debit and Credit Rules

In a double-entry system, changes in account balances are recorded according to the following basic rules.

To *increase* an account balance	Record transaction on the same side as the normal balance.
To *decrease* an account balance	Record transaction on the opposite side as the normal balance.

These two rules seem simple enough, but their application can be confusing at first because different accounts have different normal balances. The following sections demonstrate how these rules are applied to asset, liability, and equity accounts. Also demonstrated is how these rules are applied to the three types of accounts that affect equity: revenues, expenses, and dividends. Once you have mastered the mechanics of these six types of accounts, you should be able to record most any accounting transaction correctly.

Asset Accounts Asset accounts have normal debit balances. Therefore, increases to assets are recorded on the debit side while decreases are recorded on the credit side.

Asset Accounts	
Record increases on debit side	Record decreases on credit side
Balance	

To illustrate, suppose that a company starts the day with $5,000 in cash, receives $300 from a customer, and pays $250 to a vendor. The beginning balance of $5,000 is recorded on the debit side of the cash T-account. The increase of $300 is also recorded on the debit side, but the $250 decrease in cash is recorded on the side opposite of the normal balance—the credit side. Netting the debit and credit sides yields a debit balance of $5,050.

Cash	
5,000	250
300	
5,050	

Liability and Equity Accounts Liability and equity accounts have normal credit balances. Therefore, increases are recorded on the credit side, while decreases are recorded on the debit side.

Liability and Equity Accounts	
Record decreases on debit side	Record increases on credit side
	Balance

To illustrate a liability account, suppose that a company owing $2,500 to a vendor buys an additional $150 of product on account and then pays $850 of its obligation. The beginning balance of $2,500 is recorded on the credit side of the Accounts Payable T-account. The additional payable of $150 is also recorded on the credit side. In contrast, the $850 payment, which is a reduction to the payable, is recorded on the debit side. Netting the debit and credit sides yields a credit balance of $1,800.

Accounts Payable	
850	2,500
	150
	1,800

To illustrate an equity account, suppose that a company has $34,000 of common stock outstanding. The company then issues additional common stock for $10,000 and later buys back and retires $6,000 of stock. The original $34,000 balance appears on the credit side of the Common Stock T-account. Since the Common Stock account has a normal credit balance, the $10,000 increase is recorded on the credit side while the $6,000 decrease is recorded on the opposite or debit side of the account. Netting the debit and credit sides yields a credit balance of $38,000.

Common Stock	
6,000	34,000
	10,000
	38,000

Revenue Accounts When a company generates a revenue, it is increasing its equity. As demonstrated previously, increasing an equity account requires a credit entry. Therefore, revenue accounts are set up so that they also are increased with a credit entry. That is, revenue accounts have normal credit balances and are increased with credit entries and decreased with debit entries.

Revenue Accounts

Record decreases on debit side	Record increases on credit side
	Balance

To illustrate, suppose that a company has $115,000 in existing service revenue. The company then earns an additional $13,000 in revenue. Since the Service Revenue account has a normal credit balance, both the existing $115,000 balance and the $13,000 increase are shown on the credit side, resulting in a balance of $128,000.

Service Revenue

	115,000
	13,000
	128,000

Expense and Dividend Accounts When a company incurs expenses or pays dividends, it is decreasing its equity. As demonstrated previously, decreasing equity requires a debit entry. Therefore, for expense and dividend accounts to effectively reduce equity, they have normal debit balances. Expense and dividend accounts are therefore increased with debit entries and decreased with credit entries.

Expense and Dividend Accounts

Record increases on debit side	Record decreases on credit side
Balance	

To illustrate an expense, suppose that a company has $66,000 in salaries expense when it incurs an additional $6,000 in salaries expense. Since the Salaries Expense account has a normal debit balance, both the $66,000 in existing expense and the $6,000 increase should be recorded on the debit side of the account, yielding a balance of $72,000.

Salaries Expense

66,000	
6,000	
72,000	

Summary of Debit and Credit Rules

You have now seen each major type of account and how the debit and credit columns are used to increase or decrease those accounts. For asset, expense, and dividend accounts, increases are recorded in the debit column and decreases are recorded in the credit column. For liability, equity, and revenue accounts, increases are recorded in the credit column and decreases are recorded in the debit column. A summary of these rules is presented in Exhibit 3-3.

Exhibit 3-3 Summary of Debit and Credit Rules

Type of Account	Normal Balance	Increase with a	Decrease with a
Asset	Debit	Debit	Credit
Liability	Credit	Credit	Debit
Equity	Credit	Credit	Debit
Revenue	Credit	Credit	Debit
Expense	Debit	Debit	Credit
Dividend	Debit	Debit	Credit

HOME DEPOT ANALYSIS

Look at **Home Depot's** income statement in Appendix C. Which of the accounts would be increased with a credit entry? Would the remaining accounts be increased with a debit entry?

Home Depot's income statement lists eight different accounts. Of those accounts, Net Sales and Interest and Investment Income would be increased with a credit entry. Both of these accounts are revenue accounts. The other six accounts are expense accounts and are increased with a debit entry.

In a double-entry system, asset accounts have debit balances while liability and equity accounts have credit balances.

LO4 Recording Transactions in the Accounting System

This section examines the actual process of recording accounting transactions in a double-entry system. Accounting transactions are not recorded directly in T-accounts. Instead, accounting transactions are first recorded in a journal. Once recorded, the information is transferred or posted to a ledger. Information in the ledger is then summarized in a worksheet known as a trial balance. Financial statements are then prepared from the information in the trial balance.

The Journal

A **journal** is a chronological record of transactions. Because the journal is where transactions are first recorded into the accounting system, it is often called the book of original entry. Entries recorded in the journal are called *journal entries*. Companies can have various types of journals in which they record transactions, but since the mechanics of all journals are the same, we will focus on the most basic of journals, the general journal. The general journal and an example journal entry take the form shown in Exhibit 3-4.

Exhibit 3-4 General Journal Form

Date	Accounts and Explanation	Debit	Credit
Date of transaction	Account(s) Debited	Amount	
	Account(s) Credited		Amount
	(Explanation of transaction)		

Journal A chronological record of transactions.

Ledger A collection of accounts and their balances.

At the far left of the journal is a column for the transaction date. To the right of the date is a column to record the names of the accounts affected by the transaction and an explanation. The account(s) receiving debit entries are listed first followed by the account(s) receiving credit entries, which are slightly indented. To the right of the account names are debit and credit columns to record the monetary amounts of the transaction. As explained previously, the totals in the debit and credit columns should be the same for each transaction. When an accounting transaction is recorded in the general journal, we often say that the transaction has been *journalized*.

The general journal is useful in that it contains in one place a chronological record of all the accounting transactions of a company. Thus, a company can examine its journal if it has a question about whether a transaction was recorded or whether it was recorded correctly. However, the general journal is not very useful if a company is trying to determine the balance in a particular account. To get an account balance, one would have to find all journal entries affecting that account and then compute a balance. To avoid such a time-consuming task, the information recorded in the general journal is transferred to a *ledger*.

The Ledger

A **ledger** is a collection of accounts and their balances. While most companies have various types of ledgers containing different accounts, we will focus on the most basic type of ledger, the general ledger. The general ledger is nothing more than a collection of T-accounts for a company, which means that the general ledger contains both the activity and balances of all company accounts.

Account balances in the general ledger are updated as follows. When an accounting transaction is recorded in the general journal, the amounts recorded in the debit and credit columns are transferred to the debit and credit columns of the respective T-accounts in the ledger. This process of copying or transferring the information from the journal to the ledger is called *posting* and results in up-to-date account balances. Thus, companies look to the ledger for balances in their accounts.

When an accounting transaction is recorded in the general journal, we often say that the transaction has been *journalized*.

The Trial Balance

After accounting transactions are recorded in the journal and posted to the ledger, companies prepare a trial balance. A **trial balance** is a listing of accounts and their balances at a specific point in time. In a trial balance, all accounts in a company's ledger are listed in a column on the left. Asset accounts are listed first, followed by liability accounts, equity accounts, and then revenue, expense, and dividend accounts. Each account's balance from the ledger is listed in the appropriate debit or credit column. At the bottom of each column, a total is calculated. The form of the trial balance is shown in Exhibit 3-5.

Exhibit 3-5 Trial Balance Form

	Debit	Credit
Asset Account(s)	Amount	
Liability Account(s)		Amount
Equity Account(s)		Amount
Revenue Account(s)		Amount
Expense Account(s)	Amount	
Dividends	Amount	
Totals	Total Debits	Total Credits

Trial balance A listing of accounts and their balances at a specific point in time.

MAKING IT REAL

Although the text primarily discusses a manual accounting system, there are several popular computerized accounting information systems utilized by small businesses. Two of the most popular are QuickBooks® and Peachtree®.

QuickBooks is favored largely for its simplicity and ease of use for individuals with little to no accounting experience. Peachtree is a more sophisticated accounting system designed for a user with more accounting knowledge than the average person.

Both systems provide banking, general ledger, accounts payable, accounts receivable, payroll, and

inventory features and can keep track of income and expenses by customer, job, and department. Many reports can be created by both systems to analyze business performance. Both systems also provide security features to ensure only authorized users are accessing the businesses' accounting information.

Overall, such computerized systems are a great tool for businesses because they help ensure that a company's accounting information is captured and communicated effectively and efficiently.

A trial balance serves several functions. First and foremost, a trial balance proves that total debit balances equal total credit balances. If they are unequal, then the accounting equation is out of balance and a correction is warranted. Second, a trial balance summarizes in one place all accounts of an entity and their respective balances. Financial statements are then prepared from those balances. Finally, a trial balance is helpful in making any necessary adjustments to account balances at the end of an accounting period. We will see this function in Chapter 4.

LO5 Comprehensive Example: Journal Entries to Financial Statements

The following section uses the Circle Films transactions to demonstrate the recording of transactions in the journal, the posting of information to the ledger, the preparation of a trial balance, and the preparation of financial statements.

Recording Transactions in the Journal and Posting to the Ledger

Circle Films entered into ten transactions. A four-step process will be used to demonstrate how to properly record each transaction and post it to the ledger. First, the accounts affected by the transaction will be identified. Second, the relevant debit/credit rules for those accounts will be identified. Third, the transaction will be recorded in the journal. Fourth, the transaction will be posted to the ledger. This four-step process can be followed when recording and posting any accounting transaction.

Transaction #1   Circle Films issued 3,000 shares of common stock for $15,000.

Step 1—What accounts are affected and how?
Circle Films receives cash, so cash increases. Circle Films issues common stock, so common stock increases.

Step 2—What debit and credit entries are required?
Cash is an asset, so debit the Cash account to increase it. Common Stock is an equity account, so credit the Common Stock account to increase it.

Step 3—Record the journal entry.

#1	Cash	15,000	
	Common Stock		15,000
	(Owners invest cash in business)		

| Assets | = | Liabilities | + | Equity |
| +15,000 | | | | +15,000 |

Step 4—Post the information to the ledger.

Cash		Common Stock	
15,000			15,000
15,000			15,000

Transaction #2   Circle Films buys a $9,000 video camera and $1,000 of memory cards for $10,000 cash.

Step 1—What accounts are affected and how?
Circle Films receives a camera and some tapes, so both equipment and supplies increase. Circle Films pays with cash, so cash decreases.

Step 2—What debit and credit entries are required?
Equipment and supplies are assets, so debit the Equipment and Supplies accounts to increase them. Cash is also an asset, so credit the Cash account to decrease it.

Step 3—Record the journal entry.

#2	Equipment	9,000	
	Supplies	1,000	
	Cash		10,000
	(Purchase video camera and tapes)		

Assets	=	Liabilities	+	Equity
+9,000				
+1,000				
−10,000				

Step 4—Post the information to the ledger.

Cash		Supplies		Equipment	
15,000	10,000	1,000		9,000	
5,000		1,000		9,000	

Transaction #3   Circle Films films a wedding for $1,500 cash.

Step 1—What accounts are affected and how?
Circle Films receives cash, so cash increases. The increase in cash results from Circle Films providing its service, so service revenue increases.

Step 2—What debit and credit entries are required?
Cash is an asset, so debit the Cash account to increase it. Revenues increase equity, so credit the Service Revenue account to increase it.

Step 3—Record the journal entry.

#3	Cash	1,500	
	Service Revenue		1,500
	(Provide service to customer)		

Assets	=	Liabilities	+	Equity
+1,500				+1,500

Step 4—Post the information to the ledger.

Cash		Service Revenue	
15,000	10,000		1,500
1,500			
6,500			1,500

Transaction #4   Circle Films receives $2,000 to film a future reception.

Step 1—What accounts are affected and how?
Circle Films receives cash, so cash increases. Because Circle Films has not yet performed the required service, it has a new liability to the customer called unearned revenue.

Step 2—What debit and credit entries are required?
Cash is an asset, so debit the Cash account to increase it. Unearned Revenue is a liability, so credit the Unearned Revenue account to increase it.

Step 3—Record the journal entry.

#4	Cash	2,000	
	Unearned Revenue		2,000
	(Cash received in advance of		
	providing service to customer)		

Assets	=	Liabilities	+	Equity
+2,000		+2,000		

Step 4—Post the information to the ledger.

Cash		Unearned Revenue	
15,000	10,000		2,000
1,500			
2,000			2,000
8,500			

Transaction #5   Circle Films pays $250 cash for advertising.

Step 1—What accounts are affected and how?
Circle Films pays cash, so cash decreases. The decrease in cash results from Circle Films' advertising its service, so advertising expense increases.

Step 2—What debit and credit entries are required?
Cash is an asset, so credit the Cash account to decrease it. Expenses decrease equity, so debit the Advertising Expense account to increase it.

Step 3—Record the journal entry.

#5	Advertising Expense	250	
	Cash		250
	(Pay for advertising)		

Assets	=	Liabilities	+	Equity
−250				−250

Step 4—Post the information to the ledger.

Cash		Advertising Expense	
15,000	10,000	250	
1,500	250		
2,000		250	
8,250			

Transaction #6   Circle Films films an event for $3,500 and leaves an invoice with the customer.

Step 1—What accounts are affected and how?
Circle Films performed a service for a customer, so its service revenue increases. Circle Films has not yet received any payment from the customer, so its accounts receivable also increases.

Step 2—What debit and credit entries are required?
Accounts Receivable is an asset, so debit the Accounts Receivable account to increase it. Revenues increase equity, so credit the Service Revenue account to increase it.

Step 3—Record the journal entry.

#6	Accounts Receivable	3,500	
	Service Revenue		3,500
	(Provide service to customer		
	on account)		

Assets	=	Liabilities	+	Equity
+3,500				+3,500

Step 4—Post the information to the ledger.

Accounts Receivable		Service Revenue	
3,500			1,500
			3,500
3,500			5,000

Transaction #7 Circle Films buys another camera by signing a $9,000 promissory note.

Step 1—What accounts are affected and how?
Circle Films receives a camera, so equipment increases. It signs a note for payment, so notes payable increases.

Step 2—What debit and credit entries are required?
Equipment is an asset, so debit the Equipment account to increase it. Notes Payable is a liability, so credit the Notes Payable account to increase it.

Step 3—Record the journal entry.

#7	Equipment	9,000	
	Notes Payable		9,000
	(Purchase of a video camera with a promissory note)		

Assets	=	Liabilities	+	Equity
+9,000		+9,000		

Step 4—Post the information to the ledger.

Equipment		Notes Payable	
9,000			9,000
9,000			9,000
18,000			

Transaction #8 Circle Films receives $3,500 from a customer in payment of services provided.

Step 1—What accounts are affected and how?
Circle Films receives cash, so cash increases. Circle Films collects a receivable from a customer, so its accounts receivable decreases.

Step 2—What debit and credit entries are required?
Cash is an asset, so debit the Cash account to increase it. Accounts Receivable is also an asset account, so credit the Accounts Receivable account to decrease it.

Step 3—Record the journal entry.

#8	Cash	3,500	
	Accounts Receivable		3,500
	(Receive payment from customer)		

Assets	=	Liabilities	+	Equity
+3,500				
−3,500				

Step 4—Post the information to the ledger.

Cash		Accounts Receivable	
15,000	10,000	3,500	3,500
1,500	250	0	
2,000			
3,500			
11,750			

Transaction #9 Circle Films pays $2,000 in salaries to employees.

Step 1—What accounts are affected and how?
Circle Films pays cash, so cash decreases. This reduction in cash results from salaries paid to employees, so salaries expense increases.

Step 2—What debit and credit entries are required?
Cash is an asset, so credit the Cash account to decrease it. Expenses decrease equity, so debit the Salaries Expense account to increase it.

Step 3—Record the journal entry.

#9	Salaries Expense	2,000	
	Cash		2,000
	(Pay salaries to employees)		

Assets	=	Liabilities	+	Equity
−2,000				−2,000

Step 4—Post the information to the ledger.

Cash		Salaries Expense	
15,000	10,000	2,000	
1,500	250	2,000	
2,000	2,000		
3,500			
9,750			

Transaction #10 Circle Films pays $1,500 in dividends to the owners.

Step 1—What accounts are affected and how?
Circle Films pays cash, so cash decreases. The cash payment is a distribution of company assets to the owners, so dividends increase.

Step 2—What debit and credit entries are required?
Cash is an asset, so credit the Cash account to decrease it. Dividends decrease equity, so debit the Dividends account to increase it.

Step 3—Record the journal entry.

#10	Dividends	1,500	
	Cash		1,500
	(Pay dividends to owners)		

Assets	=	Liabilities	+	Equity
−1,500				−1,500

Step 4—Post the information to the ledger.

Cash		Dividends	
15,000	10,000	1,500	
1,500	250	1,500	
2,000	2,000		
3,500	1,500		
8,250			

Summary After recording and posting the ten transactions, Circle Films' complete Journal and Ledger would appear as follows:

General Journal

Transaction	Accounts	Debit	Credit
#1	Cash	15,000	
	Common Stock		15,000
#2	Equipment	9,000	
	Supplies	1,000	
	Cash		10,000
#3	Cash	1,500	
	Service Revenue		1,500
#4	Cash	2,000	
	Unearned Revenue		2,000
#5	Advertising Expense	250	
	Cash		250
#6	Accounts Receivable	3,500	
	Service Revenue		3,500
#7	Equipment	9,000	
	Notes Payable		9,000
#8	Cash	3,500	
	Accounts Receivable		3,500
#9	Salaries Expense	2,000	
	Cash		2,000
#10	Dividends	1,500	
	Cash		1,500

General Ledger

Cash		Accounts Receivable		Supplies	
15,000	10,000	3,500	3,500	1,000	
1,500	250				
2,000	2,000	0		1,000	
3,500	1,500				
8,250					

Equipment		Unearned Revenue		Notes Payable	
9,000			2,000		9,000
9,000					
18,000			2,000		9,000

Common Stock		Service Revenue		Advertising Expense	
	15,000		1,500	250	
			3,500		
	15,000		5,000	250	

Salaries Expense		Dividends	
2,000		1,500	
2,000		1,500	

Preparing a Trial Balance

Once all transactions are recorded in the journal and posted to the ledger, a trial balance can be prepared. Recall that a trial balance is a listing of all accounts

Circle Films
Trial Balance
May 31

	Debit	Credit
Cash	$ 8,250	
Supplies	1,000	
Equipment	18,000	
Unearned Revenue		$ 2,000
Notes Payable		9,000
Common Stock		15,000
Service Revenue		5,000
Advertising Expense	250	
Salaries Expense	2,000	
Dividends	1,500	
Totals	$31,000	$31,000

and their balances at a specific point in time, starting with assets and followed by liabilities, equity, revenues, expenses, and dividends. Therefore, it is a summary of the balances in the ledger. You can confirm that the trial balance includes only the balances from the general ledger by reviewing again Circle Films' ledger on the previous page. As expected, total debit balances of $31,000 equal total credit balances of $31,000 in the trial balance.

Preparation of Financial Statements

Once the trial balance is finished, the final product of the accounting system can be prepared—the financial statements. As demonstrated in Chapter 1, the income statement must be prepared first, followed by the statement of retained earnings, and then the balance sheet.

The income statement shows a company's revenues and expenses. Circle Films' May 31 trial balance contains only one revenue account and two expense accounts. Therefore, its income statement for the month of May would appear as follows:

Circle Films Income Statement For the Month Ending May 31		
Service revenue		$5,000
Expenses		
Advertising expense	$ 250	
Salaries expense	2,000	
Total expenses		2,250
Net income		$2,750

With net income calculated, Circle Films' statement of retained earnings can be prepared. Recall from Chapter 1 that the statement of retained earnings takes the beginning balance in retained earnings, adds net income, and subtracts dividends to yield the current balance in retained earnings. Its May 31 trial balance shows no balance in beginning retained earnings because it just started its business. It also shows a $1,500 balance in dividends. Combining these two balances with net income yields the following statement of retained earnings for the month of May:

Circle Films Statement of Retained Earnings For the Month Ending May 31	
Retained earnings, May 1	$ 0
+ Net income	2,750
− Dividends	1,500
Retained earnings, May 31	$1,250

With retained earnings calculated, the company's balance sheet can be prepared. A balance sheet shows a company's assets, liabilities, and equity at a point in time. Circle Films' May 31 trial balance shows three asset accounts, two liability accounts, and one equity account (Common Stock). These six accounts, along with the amount of retained earnings from the May statement of retained earnings, should be included on the balance sheet. Therefore, its May 31 balance sheet would appear as follows:

Circle Films Balance Sheet May 31		
Cash		$ 8,250
Supplies		1,000
Equipment		18,000
Total assets		$27,250
Unearned revenue	$ 2,000	
Notes payable	9,000	
Total liabilities		$11,000
Common stock	15,000	
Retained earnings	1,250	
Total stockholders' equity		16,250
Total liabilities and stockholders' equity		$27,250

Chapter review card

- ➲ Learning Objective and Key Concept Reviews
- ➲ Key Definitions and Formulas

Online (Located at www.cengagebrain.com)

- ➲ Flash Cards and Crossword Puzzles
- ➲ Games and Quizzes
- ➲ E-Lectures
- ➲ Homework Assignments (as directed by your instructor)

CONCEPT QUESTIONS

1. (LO1) What is an accounting information system?
2. (LO1) What is an accounting transaction?
3. (LO1) What is the main function of an account?
4. (LO1) What does a chart of accounts contain?
5. (LO2) What is the fundamental accounting equation?
6. (LO2) Do accounting transactions have to affect both sides of the fundamental accounting equation? Explain.
7. (LO3) Does the double entry system mean that each transaction is recorded twice? Explain.
8. (LO3) True or false: debit means "increase" and credit means "decrease." Why?
9. (LO3) What are the normal account balances for the following accounts: a) Equipment; b) Unearned Revenue; c) Supplies Expense; d) Accounts Payable; e) Retained Earnings?
10. (LO3) What is used to decrease an asset account, a liability account, a revenue account, and an expense account?
11. (LO4) Where are transactions first recorded?
12. (LO4) What is a ledger, and from where does the input for a ledger come?
13. (LO4) In what order are accounts listed in a trial balance?
14. (LO4) To what does the term "posting" refer?
15. (LO4) What are the three main purposes of a trial balance?

MULTIPLE CHOICE

1. (LO1) When considering accounting information systems, which of the following is false?
   a. Accounting information systems vary in size across companies
   b. An accounting information system records and summarizes economic events
   c. All accounting information systems use the same basic procedures to identify, record, and communicate the effects of economic events
   d. Accounting information systems record all economic events

2. (LO1) Which of the following would be considered an accounting transaction?
   a. Hiring a new CEO
   b. Selling an in-house developed patent
   c. Establishing a new company dress code
   d. Posting journal entries to the general ledger

3. (LO1) Which of the following would not be an account found in the financial statements?
   a. Equipment
   b. Salaries Payable
   c. Employees' Personal Data
   d. Dividends

4. (LO1) Which of the following is false regarding a chart of accounts?
   a. The total number of asset accounts must equal the total number of liability accounts
   b. A chart of accounts is a listing of all the accounts that a company uses to record accounting information

c. Each account listing contains an account name and a numerical reference

d. Charts of accounts will vary across companies

5. (LO2) Which of the following is false?
   a. A company can have a transaction that affects only the left side of the fundamental accounting equation
   b. In each accounting transaction, total debits to assets must equal total credits to liabilities
   c. The fundamental accounting equation will always balance after each correctly recorded accounting transaction
   d. All of the above are true

6. (LO3) Which of the following is true?
   i. In the double-entry system, each accounting transaction is recorded twice
   ii. Each journal entry will at least affect two accounts.
   a. i. only
   b. ii. only
   c. Both i. and ii.
   d. Neither i. nor ii.

7. (LO3) Which of the following groups of accounts shows only accounts that are increased with a debit?
   a. Assets, Liabilities, Dividends
   b. Assets, Equity, Dividends
   c. Assets, Expenses, Dividends
   d. Assets, Equity, Expenses

8. (LO3) Which of the following is true?
   i. Paying out a dividend of $1,000 would result in a debit to the Dividends account.
   ii. In the general ledger, this $1,000 would be entered on the right side of the Dividends T-account.
   a. i. only
   b. ii. only
   c. Both i. and ii.
   b. Neither i. nor ii.

9. (LO3) What would be the result of a credit to these accounts?

	Cash	Service Revenue	Common Stock
a.	Increase	Increase	Decrease
b.	Decrease	Increase	Increase
c.	Decrease	Increase	Decrease
d.	Increase	Decrease	Increase

10. (LO4) The general journal:
    a. pulls all information from the general ledger.
    b. only contains revenue and expense accounts.
    c. is where transactions are recorded.
    d. is a collection of all of the accounts maintained by a company.

11. (LO4) The general ledger:
    a. is the first place a transaction is recorded.
    b. records economic events as well as accounting transactions.
    c. shows the activity in, and balances for, all of the company's accounts.
    d. requires adjusting entries in order for total debit balances to equal total credit balances.

12. (LO4) Which of the following is false?
    a. A trial balance is considered to be a financial statement
    b. In a trial balance, total debit balances must equal total credit balances
    c. A trial balance summarizes in one place all accounts of an entity and their respective balances
    d. Preparation of a trial balance is part of the accounting cycle

13. (LO4) Which of the following would cause a trial balance not to balance?
    a. Recording a $350 purchase of supplies on account as a debit to Supplies and a credit to Cash
    b. A $425 payment on account is unrecorded
    c. A $400 purchase on account is debited to Supplies for $400 and credited to Accounts Payable for $4,000
    d. A $500 purchase of supplies on account is credited to Supplies and debited to Accounts Payable

14. (LO4) Which of the following is not a purpose of the trial balance?
    a. To summarize in one place all accounts of an entity and their respective balances
    b. To provide a chronological order of a company's transactions
    c. To serve as a helpful tool in preparing financial statements
    d. To prove that total debit balances equal total credit balances

15. (LO4) A journal entry does not contain:
    a. the date of the transaction.
    b. the balance of the accounts involved.
    c. an explanation of the transaction.
    d. at least two accounts.

16. (LO2, 5) Incurring $500 in salaries while earning $1,500 of revenue would result in a:
    a. $1,500 net increase in net income.
    b. $1,000 net increase in net income.
    c. $2,000 net increase in net income.
    d. none of the above.

17. (LO5) Which of the following properly demonstrates the flow of information through the accounting system?
    a. Journal ⇒ Ledger ⇒ Trial Balance ⇒ Financial Statements
    b. Ledger ⇒ Journal ⇒ Trial Balance ⇒ Financial Statements
    c. Journal ⇒ Trial Balance ⇒ Ledger ⇒ Financial Statements
    d. Trial Balance ⇒ Ledger ⇒ Journal ⇒ Financial Statements

BRIEF EXERCISES

1. Chart of Accounts   LO1

The following accounts were taken from the charts of accounts of a retailer, a bank, and/or a chemical company:

Cash	Property and Equipment
Research and Development Expense	Dividends Payable
Retained Earnings	Salaries Expense
Mortgage Receivable	Sales Returns

Required

Indicate whether each account would likely appear in the chart of accounts of the retailer (R), the bank (B), the chemical company (C), or all three (A).

2. Accounting Transactions   LO1

A company enters into the following economic events:
1. Hired a new receptionist.
2. Billed customers for services performed.
3. Announced the signing of a contract that should produce $100,000 of new revenue.
4. Paid for insurance that will not be used until next year.

Required

Indicate whether each economic event would be considered an accounting transaction.

3. Analyze Transactions   LO2

EA Systems entered into the following transactions during the month of August:
1. Received $6,350 for services performed during August.
2. Purchased $1,200 of supplies on account.
3. Paid employee salaries of $3,280 for the first week of August.
4. Paid $900 towards the previous purchase of supplies.

Required

Indicate whether each transaction increases, decreases, or has no effect on assets, liabilities, and equity. If a transaction affects equity, indicate whether the transaction affects revenues or expenses.

4. Journalize Transactions   LO3

Review the EA Systems information in the preceding Brief Exercise.

Required

Prepare journal entries for each transaction (omitting explanations).

5. T-Accounts   LO3

A company reports the following asset and liability T-accounts:

Account #1		Account #2		Account #3	
1,000	6,000	8,400	3,250	4,280	3,600
4,000	3,000		2,120	1,660	1,120

Required

Determine the balance in each account and identify whether each account would most likely be an asset account or a liability account.

6. Normal Balances   LO3

The following is a list of possible accounts found in a trial balance:
1. Equipment
2. Notes Payable
3. Dividends
4. Supplies
5. Rent Expense
6. Service Revenue
7. Unearned Revenue

Required

Indicate each account's normal balance and the effect of a debit and credit to the account.

7. Posting Transactions   LO3

A company records the following transactions during November:

Date	Account Title	Debit	Credit
Nov. 1	Accounts Receivable	3,200	
	Service Revenue		3,200
Nov. 6	Cash	1,000	
	Accounts Receivable		1,000
Nov. 15	Utilities Expense	250	
	Cash		250
Nov. 26	Inventory	2,360	
	Accounts Payable		2,360

Required

Post the transactions to appropriate T-accounts and prepare a Trial Balance.

8. Recording Transactions   LO2, 3, 5

Barrett Fisher, a clerk for Naval Supplies, received a payment from a customer and recorded the following journal entry:

Date	Account Title	Debit	Credit
Mar. 1	Cash	1,000	
	Accounts Payable		1,000

Required

Is this entry correct or not? Explain why it is or is not correct.

9. Trial Balance LO4

Harris Consulting provides the following incomplete trial balance:

Harris Consulting Trial Balance September 30		
	Debit	Credit
(a)	$ 8,850	
Accounts Receivable	(b)	
Supplies	1,625	
Notes Payable		$ 3,000
Common Stock		10,000
Retained Earnings		(c)
Service Revenue		15,630
Salaries Expense	10,560	
Utilities Expense	2,350	
Totals	$33,765	$ (d)

Required

Determine the missing values.

10. Prepare Financial Statements LO4

Review the Harris Consulting information in the preceding Brief Exercise.

Required

Using the given information and your answers for a-d, prepare Harris' income statement and statement of retained earnings for September and its balance sheet at September 30.

EXERCISES

11. Transaction Analysis LO2

The following is a list of independent economic events:

1. Purchased inventory on account.
2. Paid dividends at the end of the year.
3. Received cash in payment for services.
4. Issued common stock for cash.
5. Paid rent in cash.
6. Received a bill for utilities incurred.
7. Bought equipment for cash.
8. Billed customers for services.

Required

Indicate a) the accounts that would be affected by each transaction and b) whether each transaction increases, decreases, or has no effect on assets, liabilities, and stockholders' equity.

12. Transaction Analysis LO2

The following are a few possible ways in which the accounting equation can be affected by a transaction:

Assets	= Liabilities	+	Stockholders' Equity
1. Increase	Increase		
2. Decrease			Decrease
3. Increase			Increase
4. Increase/Decrease			
5. Decrease	Decrease		

Required

Describe at least two situations that could result in each of the five scenarios listed.

13. Transaction Analysis LO2

Handyman Services was founded on January 1 and entered into the following transactions during January:

1. Issued common stock of $30,000 in exchange for cash.
2. Purchased an old warehouse for $50,000 by issuing notes payable.
3. Purchased a truck for $15,000 cash.
4. Purchased shop supplies for $5,000 on account.
5. Provided services of $15,325, receiving $12,200 in cash.
6. Paid $1,000 for local advertising for January.
7. Received payment of $3,125 from customers in #5.
8. Paid $4,000 on open account from #4.
9. Paid dividends of $1,000 to stockholders.
10. Paid employee salaries of $4,000 for January.
11. Billed customers $3,500 for services provided during January.
12. Paid $100 interest on notes payable.

Required

a. Show the effects of each transaction on the accounting equation by preparing a tabular analysis using the following column headings: Cash, Accounts Receivable, Supplies, Property and Equipment, Accounts Payable, Notes Payable, Common Stock, Retained Earnings.
b. Calculate Handyman's net income for the month of January.

14. Normal Balances LO3

The following is a list of possible accounts found in a trial balance:

1. Accounts Receivable
2. Common Stock
3. Cash
4. Retained Earnings
5. Accounts Payable
6. Salaries Expense
7. Long-term Investments
8. Service Revenue
9. Dividends

Required

Indicate each account's normal balance and the effect of a debit and a credit to the account.

15. T-account Mechanics LO3

The general ledger for TPC Company contains the following accounts:

Cash		Notes Payable	
2,000	3,000	10,000	5,500
8,000	(a)		18,100
4,000			(b)

Salaries Expense		Accounts Payable	
13,500		23,850	45,300
(c)		(d)	12,775
15,900			17,300

Service Revenue		Accounts Receivable	
	(e)	(f)	3,500
	33,210	2,500	9,570
	88,690	7,660	

Required
Determine the missing values.

16. Transaction Analysis LO2, 3

Tsunami, Inc., entered into the following transactions during one month of operations:
1. Purchased $3,000 of computer equipment on account.
2. Issued $7,500 of common stock to investors in exchange for cash.
3. Purchased supplies for $300 in cash.
4. Billed customers $25,000 for services rendered.
5. Paid salaries of $3,500 to employees.
6. Paid dividends to stockholders in the amount of $1,000.
7. Received $5,000 cash in payment of services earned and billed in the previous month.
8. Paid cash for the purchase in #1.
9. Borrowed $50,000 from the bank.

Required
a. Indicate the specific accounts affected by each transaction.
b. Indicate whether those accounts were increased or decreased.
c. Designate the normal balances for each of the specific accounts.

17. Recording Transactions LO3, 4, 5

Prepare journal entries for the transactions listed in the preceding exercise (omitting explanations).

18. Recording Transactions LO3, 4, 5

The following information pertains to York Rafting Company:
Jan. 2 Issued common stock to investors for $25,000.
   3 Bought $3,500 of supplies on account.
   4 Paid rent for January in the amount of $1,200.
   9 Billed a customer $7,000 for services provided.
   16 Paid $1,500 cash to vendor for the January 3 purchase.

24 Borrowed $10,000 from local bank.
26 Received payment for billing made on January 9.

Required
Prepare journal entries for each transaction (omitting explanations).

19. Posting Transactions LO4, 5

Post the journal entries prepared in the preceding exercise to their appropriate T-accounts and prepare a trial balance at January 31.

20. Recording Transactions LO3, 4, 5

In the month of March, C. D. Goose, Inc. entered into the following transactions:
Mar. 2 Bought a new building for $135,000.
   3 Paid February utility bill of $860.
   11 Issued common stock to investors in return for $5,000.
   13 Hired a new administrative assistant for a $35,000 salary.
   19 Received payment in the amount of $750 for service billed in February.
   31 Paid dividends of $1,000.

Required
Prepare all necessary journal entries for March (omitting the explanations).

21. Recreate Journal Entries LO3, 4

The general ledger for King Consulting contains the following accounts:

Cash		Accounts Receivable	
23,500	7,200	14,200	13,000
13,000	10,500	19,300	15,000
15,000	1,000	5,500	
32,800			

Salaries Expense		Accounts Payable	
10,500		7,200	8,100
10,500			900

Service Revenue		Supplies	
	14,200	8,100	
	19,300		
	33,500	8,100	

Dividends		Common Stock	
1,000			23,500
1,000			23,500

Required
Recreate the nine journal entries that resulted in King's ledger balances.

22. Transaction Analysis LO2, 4, 5

The following is a tabular analysis of transactions in the month of September for the Fresh Company:

	Cash	+	Accounts Receivable	+	Supplies	+	Equipment	=	Accounts Payable	+	Stockholders' Equity	Additional Information
1.	+2,000		+7,000								+9,000	Service Revenue
2.					+1,000				+1,000			
3.	−500								−500			
4.	−1,500										−1,500	Dividends
5.	−750										−750	Advertising
6.	+10,000										+10,000	Common Stock
7.	+5,000		−5,000									
8.	−2,000										−2,000	Rent
9.									+2,500		−2,500	Utilities
10.							+5,000		+5,000			

Required
a. Provide a probable explanation for each individual event.
b. Recreate the appropriate journal entries.
c. Prepare an income statement for the month of September.
d. Prepare a statement of retained earnings for the month of September. Assume beginning Retained Earnings is $1,000.

23. Accounting Terms   LO1, 2, 3, 4

The following is a list of various terms and definitions associated with accounting information systems:

a. Accounting information system
b. Accounting transaction
c. Account
d. Double-entry accounting
e. Chart of accounts
f. Debit
g. Credit
h. Journal
i. Ledger
j. Trial balance

1. A listing containing a name and a numerical reference for all the accounts that a company uses to record accounting information.
2. A recording system in which at least two accounts will be affected when recording every accounting transaction.
3. The system that identifies economic events to be recorded, measures and records those events, and then processes the resulting information so that financial statements can be prepared.
4. An accumulation of the activity and balance for a specific item.
5. Any economic event that affects specific asset, liability, or equity accounts at the time of the event.
6. The right side of an account.
7. The left side of an account.
8. A collection of accounts and their balances.
9. A listing of all accounts and their balances at a specific point in time.
10. A chronological record in which transactions are first recorded.

Required
Match terms a–j with their appropriate definitions.

24. Errors in Recording Transactions   LO4, 5

Chappy's Chapstick, Inc. recently hired a new accountant, who made the following errors:
1. Recorded a $200 cash purchase of inventory as a debit to inventory and a credit to accounts payable.
2. Failed to record the payment of $300 for advertising for the period.
3. Debited supplies for $150 and credited cash for invoice amount of $510.
4. Recorded $100 cash received for services but forgot to record the service revenue.

Required
a. Recreate each entry that was made and prepare each entry that should have been made.
b. Which of the four errors would result in the trial balance being out of balance?

25. Posting Information   LO4, 5

The following is the general journal of Dee's Fur Company for the month of November:

Date	Account Titles	Debit	Credit
Nov. 1	Cash	15,000	
	Common Stock		15,000
8	Equipment	5,000	
	Accounts Payable		3,000
	Cash		2,000
11	Accounts Receivable	7,500	
	Service Revenue		7,500
18	Accounts Payable	1,700	
	Cash		1,700
21	Cash	5,000	
	Notes Payable		5,000
24	Dividends	1,500	
	Cash		1,500
25	Cash	3,500	
	Accounts Receivable		3,500

Required
a. Post the journal entries to the appropriate T-accounts assuming Dee's Fur starts its business in November.
b. Prepare a trial balance for the month ending November 30.

26. Trial Balance   LO4, 5
Saxon Company provides the following account balances as of July 31:

Accounts Payable	$12,445
Accounts Receivable	12,300
Buildings	99,840
Cash	33,200
Common Stock	15,000
Dividends	4,000
Notes Payable	33,000
Salaries Expense	45,205
Retained Earnings	45,700
Service Revenue	49,700
Supplies	6,980

Required
Prepare a trial balance as of July 31.

27. Trial Balance   LO4, 5
During the audit of Hines Brewery, the auditor discovered the following errors:
1. A purchase of equipment in the amount of $3,500 was recorded as a debit to Equipment for $350 and a credit to Accounts Payable for $350.
2. A credit of $5,600 to Service Revenue in the general journal was posted to the general ledger at $6,500.
3. $1,000 cash paid for salaries incurred in previous months was recorded as a debit to Salaries Expense and a credit to Cash.
4. A journal entry recording a purchase of $1,200 of supplies on account was posted twice to the general ledger.
5. A credit posting to Service Revenue of $4,000 was omitted.

Required
For each error, indicate whether or not the trial balance will still balance after the error is made. Also, indicate the manner in which the trial balance will be incorrect (for example, Service Revenue will be overstated by $500).

28. Transaction Analysis   LO2
Gels and Shells, Inc., was established on January 1 and entered into the following transactions during its first month of business:
1. Issued common stock of $50,000 in exchange for cash.
2. Purchased equipment for $24,000 cash.
3. Purchased supplies of $6,000 on account.
4. Received $235 bill for January advertising in the newspaper.
5. Billed customers $14,680 for services.
6. Paid salaries of $2,015.
7. Received payment of $6,023 from customers for bills in #5.
8. Received $5,000 cash for services to be performed in March.
9. Paid $4,500 to suppliers for purchase in #3.
10. Received bill for January utilities in the amount of $175.
11. Paid dividends of $300 to stockholders.
12. Borrowed $10,000 from bank on a long-term basis.
13. Paid $100 interest on the bank loan.

Required
a. Show the effects of each transaction on the accounting equation by preparing a tabular analysis using the following column headings: Cash, Accounts Receivable, Supplies, Property and Equipment, Accounts Payable, Unearned Revenue, Notes Payable, Common Stock, Retained Earnings.
b. Prepare an income statement for the month of January.
c. Prepare a statement of retained earnings for the month of January.
d. Prepare a balance sheet at January 31.

29. Recording Transactions   LO3, 4, 5
Darby Consulting, Inc., was established on March 1, and during March, Darby entered into the following transactions:

Mar. 1 Issued $10,000 common stock in exchange for cash.
   3 Purchased $300 of supplies on account.
   7 Prepaid $1,500 total for April, May, and June rent.
   8 Paid $175 towards the March 3 purchase of supplies.
   11 Billed customers $5,780 for services rendered.
   12 Paid $700 for March advertising.
   25 Received $4,500 from customers billed on March 11.
   28 Paid $200 in dividends to stockholders.
   29 Paid $1,200 for March salaries.
   29 Paid $760 for March utilities.

Required

a. Prepare journal entries for each transaction (omitting explanations).
b. Post journal entries to appropriate T-accounts.
c. Prepare a trial balance at March 31.
d. Prepare an income statement and a statement of retained earnings for the month of March. Prepare a balance sheet at the end of March.

30. Recording Transactions   LO3, 4, 5

The trial balance for ShirtCraft, Inc., at January 31 is shown as follows:

ShirtCraft, Inc. Trial Balance January 31		
	Debit	Credit
Cash	$ 5,600	
Accounts Receivable	12,890	
Supplies	9,235	
Prepaid Rent	1,500	
Equipment	30,500	
Accounts Payable		$ 7,625
Unearned Revenue		6,400
Notes Payable		15,000
Common Stock		25,000
Service Revenue		9,650
Salaries Expense	2,300	
Utilities Expense	650	
Dividends	1,000	
Totals	$63,675	$63,675

During February the following transactions occurred:

Feb. 1 Billed customers $2,500 for services rendered.
1 Paid $150 interest on note from bank.
4 Received $4,500 from customers billed in January.
8 Bought $560 of office supplies on account.
12 Completed a $3,500 service for which payment was received in January.
18 Paid $1,895 towards a January purchase of supplies on account.
26 Paid $1,000 in dividends to stockholders.
27 Paid $2,100 for February salaries and $775 for February utilities.

Required

a. Prepare opening T-accounts for the month of February.
b. Prepare journal entries for transactions in the month of February.

c. Post journal entries to appropriate T-accounts.
d. Prepare a trial balance at February 28.

31. Recording Transactions   LO3, 4, 5

On November 1, Josh White started an amusement park. The park experienced the following transactions during the first month of operations:

Nov. 1 Stockholders contributed $50,000 in exchange for common stock.
2 Hired six employees to staff the park.
3 Purchased go-carts for $12,500 on account.
3 Borrowed $10,000 from bank.
3 Purchased arcade games for $4,000.
4 Paid $1,000 to advertise the park's opening.
7 Purchased bumper boats for $11,750 on account.
10 Billed Mr. Jones $1,100 for his son's birthday party.
11 Received cash of $2,200 for entry fees into the park.
15 Paid $5,000 cash towards go-cart bill.
20 Received $3,400 for entry fees into the park.
25 Received full payment from Mr. Jones.
28 Paid utilities in the amount of $560.
30 Paid $100 interest on loan.

Required

Prepare journal entries for each transaction, including explanations.

32. Recording and Posting Journal Entries   LO3, 4, 5

Carbon Company entered into the following transactions during November:

Nov. 1 Issued common stock in exchange for $15,000 cash.
4 Purchased $6,500 of equipment, paying $4,000 in cash and the remainder on account.
8 Paid $5,000 for investments, which will mature in six months.
12 Billed customers $12,550 for services rendered.
16 Hired office assistant at a salary equal to being paid $1,000 every two weeks.
21 Received $8,950 from customers billed on Nov. 12.
22 Purchased $1,500 of supplies on account.
24 Paid $1,000 towards the remaining balance on the equipment purchase.
29 Paid $500 in dividends to stockholders.
30 Paid $3,400 for November salaries.

After journalizing these transactions, Carbon Company's general ledger appeared as follows:

Cash			
1st	15,000	4th	4,000
21st	8,950	8th	5,000
		24th	1,000
		30th	3,400

Accounts Payable			
24th	1,000	4th	2,500
		16th	1,000
		22th	1,500

Accounts Receivable	
12th 12,550	

Common Stock			
29th	500	1st	15,000

Supplies	
22th 1,500	

Service Revenue		
	12th	12,550
	21th	8,950

Short-Term Investments	
8th 5,000	

Salaries Expense	
16th 1,000	
30th 4,300	

Equipment	
4th 6,500	

Dividends	
29th 500	

Required

a. Reproduce Carbon Company's journal entries for November.
b. Post the journal entries to the appropriate T-accounts.
c. Compare your postings to those of Carbon Company and identify Carbon's recording errors.
d. Prepare a trial balance at November 30.

CASES

33. Read and Interpret Financial Statements LO3, 4, 5

Access **Walgreens'** balance sheet in its 2010 annual report by clicking on the *Investor Relations* and *Annual Report/Proxies* links at www.walgreens.com.

Required

a. Identify the dollar change in the following subtotals: total current assets; total non-current assets; total current liabilities; total non-current liabilities; and total shareholders' equity. (For example, total current assets increased $1,616.)
b. Identify whether the accounting system would

debit or credit each subtotal to achieve the change. Treat each subtotal description as if it were an account. (For example, an increase of $1,616 in total current assets would be accomplished with a debit to that account.)
c. Prepare one journal entry that records the changes in all subtotals. Again, use the subtotal descriptions as if they were actual accounts.
d. Does the entry in part c balance? Should it? Explain why or why not.

34. Ethics in Accounting LO3, 4, 5

You are a staff accountant at a large service provider. Your company is under tremendous pressure to meet earnings targets so that the company stock price can continue to grow and the company can continue to acquire other companies. For the current year, it appears that the company will miss its earnings targets. Your boss, who has been a mentor to you, asks you to prepare a journal entry to record $100,000 of revenue for a fictitious job. He provides a fabricated invoice as documentation. He states that as soon as the new year begins, he will make a reversing entry that removes the receivable from the books. He asks you to do this as a personal favor to him.

Required

a. Identify the ethical issues associated with this scenario.
b. What factors other than accounting are at play here?
c. What are your alternatives?

35. Written Communication LO3, 4

Since you are enrolled in an introductory accounting class, a friend asks you the following: "I've never understood debits and credits. All I know is that debit means bad and credit means good."

Required

Write a brief explanation of the terms *debit* and *credit* and how they are used in an accounting information system. Explain why debit and credit cannot mean good and/or bad.

Accrual Accounting
and Adjusting Entries

Introduction

Chapter 3 introduced the first three steps in the accounting cycle—recording transactions, posting information to the ledger, and preparing a trial balance from which financial statements are prepared. This chapter explores the remaining steps in the cycle. This includes the adjusting process that leads to accrual-based financial statements and the closing process that prepares the accounting system for the next period. Both the adjusting and closing processes occur at the end of each accounting period.

LO1 Accrual and Cash Bases of Accounting

One of the main functions of the accounting information system is to record the revenues and expenses that a business generates. In accounting, there are two possible bases for recording revenues and expenses—the cash basis and the accrual basis. The main difference between the two is the timing of when revenues and expenses are recorded.

The **cash basis of accounting** records revenues when cash is received and records expenses when cash is paid. The best example of a cash basis accounting system is your personal checking account. Revenues such as job wages are recorded only when you are paid. Expenses such as utilities are recorded only when you write the check.

In contrast, the **accrual basis of accounting** records revenues when they are earned and records expenses when they are incurred. This is an application of the revenue recognition and matching principles, respectively, discussed in Chapter 1. In an accrual accounting system, revenues such as job wages are recorded when earned, regardless of when payment is received. Likewise, expenses such as utilities are recorded when used, regardless of when payment is made. A summary of each basis is as follows.

> **Cash basis of accounting** Records revenues when cash is received and records expenses when cash is paid.
>
> **Accrual basis of accounting** Records revenues when they are earned and records expenses when they are incurred.

Learning Objectives

After studying the material in this chapter, you should be able to:

LO1 Describe how income is measured and reported under the accrual and cash bases of accounting.

LO2 Identify the four major circumstances in which adjusting journal entries are necessary.

LO3 Record and post adjusting journal entries, and prepare an adjusted trial balance and financial statements.

LO4 Describe the purpose of the closing process and prepare closing entries.

LO5 Describe the steps of the accounting cycle.

When a retailer like American Eagle Outfitters sells a gift card, it records a liability. It records a revenue when the customer redeems the card.

AP Photo/Gene J. Puskar

	Cash Basis	Accrual Basis
Record revenues when:	Cash is received	Revenue is earned
Record expenses when:	Cash is paid	Expense is incurred

To illustrate the difference between the cash and accrual bases, suppose that a neighbor leaves town for the months of June and July and asks you to collect his mail and newspapers. Before he leaves, he pays you $100. Suppose further that you agree to pay a friend $40 to do the work, but you pay him at the end of July after the work is completed. Income for June and July under each basis would be calculated as follows.

The best example of a cash basis accounting system is your personal checking account.

Under the cash basis, June revenues are $100 because you received $100 during the month. Likewise, June expenses are $0 because you paid nothing during the month. As a result, June income is $100. For July, you received no money but paid your friend $40, so revenues are $0 and expenses are $40. Therefore, July income is a loss of $40.

	Cash Basis			Accrual Basis		
	June	July	Total	June	July	Total
Revenues	$100	$ 0	$100	$50	$50	$100
− Expenses	0	40	40	20	20	40
Net Income	$100	$(40)	$ 60	$30	$30	$ 60

Under the accrual basis, revenues for June are $50 because you earned half of the $100 during June. And, even though you don't pay your friend until July, he provided half of the agreed labor in June, so June expenses are $20. As a result, June income is $30. Because the exact same circumstances occur in July, income for July is also $30.

The comparative income statements show that although each basis results in the same $60 of cumulative income, monthly income varies considerably. The cash-based statement reports that you generated a $100 profit one month and a $40 loss the next, while the accrual-based statement reports that you generated $30 in profits each month. Given that your activities were exactly the same each month, accrual-based income of

$30 each month makes more sense than a $100 profit and a $40 loss. Even though both bases result in the same $60 income over the long term, the accrual basis provides a better representation of income over the two shorter periods of time. As a result, the accrual basis is required by Generally Accepted Accounting Principles.

Reporting Accrual- and Cash-Based Income

Because Generally Accepted Accounting Principles require the accrual basis, income statements report accrual-based income. However, cash basis information is also useful in understanding the financial condition of a company. A company that generates accrual income but never generates cash is a company that will soon fail. As a result, cash-based income is reported on the statement of cash flows. Recall from Chapter 1 that the operating activities section of a company's statement of cash flows calculates and reports the cash generated from operating the business. Cash generated from operations is the same as cash-based income.

To illustrate, consider the following condensed version of the operating activities section of **American Eagle Outfitters'** statement of cash flows shown in Exhibit 4-1.

American Eagle Outfitters uses the indirect method of reporting operating cash flows, which means that it calculates cash-based income by adjusting accrual-based income. The top line shows income on an accrual basis. For the current year, American Eagle Outfitters generated over $140 million of income under the accrual basis. This number would also be found on American Eagle Outfitters' income statement. After $220 million of adjustments, cash basis income is determined to be over $402 million. As you can see, American Eagle Outfitters' cash-based income is greater than its accrual-based income in all three years reported. The nature of these differences will be explored further in Chapter 11.

Exhibit 4-1 American Eagle Outfitters' Condensed Statement of Cash Flows—Operating Activities

(in thousands) For the Years Ended	01/29/11	01/30/10	01/31/09
Operating activities:			
Net income	$140,647	$169,022	$179,061
Adjustments to reconcile net income to cash provided:			
Depreciation and amortization	145,548	139,832	126,362
⋮	⋮	⋮	⋮
Accrued liabilities	(12,457)	(1,993)	(1,930)
Total adjustments	220,660	186,928	115,128
Net cash provided by operating activities	$402,594	$400,326	$345,112

LO2 Adjusting Journal Entries

To ensure that revenues and expenses are properly recorded under an accrual basis, accounting information systems use adjusting journal entries. **Adjusting journal entries** are entries made in the general journal to record revenues that have been earned but not recorded and expenses that have been incurred but not recorded. The process of recording and posting adjusting entries is the fourth step in the accounting cycle and occurs at the end of each accounting period after the trial balance is prepared. After adjusting entries are journalized and posted, an "adjusted" trial balance is then prepared, from which financial statements are generated.

While adjusting entries can vary significantly across companies, they all arise because the exchange of cash does not always coincide with the earning of a revenue or incurrence of an expense. For example, sometimes cash is received *before* a revenue is earned while at other times cash is received *after* a revenue is earned. Likewise, sometimes cash is paid *before* an expense is incurred while at other times cash is paid *after* an expense is incurred. These four basic scenarios are the reasons that adjusting journal entries are necessary. Each scenario is listed in the following table and is discussed in the following sections.

The process of recording and posting adjusting entries is the fourth step in the accounting cycle and occurs at the end of each accounting period after the trial balance is prepared.

Scenario	Classification of Adjusting Entry
1. Cash is received before revenue is earned	Deferred Revenue
2. Cash is received after revenue is earned	Accrued Revenue
3. Cash is paid before expense is incurred	Deferred Expense
4. Cash is paid after expense is incurred	Accrued Expense

Adjusting journal entries Entries made in the general journal to record revenues that have been earned but not recorded and expenses that have been incurred but not recorded.

HOME DEPOT ANALYSIS

In Appendix C, look at the Revenues paragraph in Home Depot's Note 1: Summary of Significant Accounting Policies. How can you tell from that paragraph that Home Depot uses the accrual basis of accounting?

Also, look at Home Depot's statement of cash flows in Appendix C. Over the three years presented, what was the total net income on a cash basis and how does that compare to total net income on an accrual basis?

The Revenues paragraph states that the company recognizes revenues when the customer takes possession of the merchandise or receives the service (that is, when the revenue is earned). It further states that when

a customer pays in advance, the company records a "Deferred Revenue" because it has not yet earned the revenue, even though cash has been received.

The company's statement of cash flows shows that cash basis income was greater than accrual basis income in all years presented.

	2011	2010	2009	Total
Net income (cash basis):	$4,585	$5,125	$5,528	$15,238
Net income (accrual basis):	$3,338	$2,661	$2,260	$ 8,259

ook at the Revenues, Prepaid Advertising, and Self-Insurance paragraphs in Home Depot's Note 1: Summary of Significant Accounting Policies, found in Appendix C. Do these paragraphs represent examples of deferred revenues, accrued revenues, deferred expenses, or accrued expenses?

The Revenues paragraph explains the example of receiving payment before providing the good or service (deferred revenue). The Prepaid Advertising paragraph explains the example of making payment before consuming the advertising (deferred expense). The Self-Insurance paragraph explains the recording of a liability before payment of claims against the company (accrued expense).

Scenario 1: Deferred Revenue

Companies sometimes receive cash before they earn the revenue. For example, airlines get your money before you fly. When a company receives cash before it provides the service, it has a *deferred revenue*. The term *deferred* is used because at the time of cash receipt, the company has not yet provided the promised service and therefore cannot record a revenue in its accounting system. Instead, it must record a liability. Recording of the revenue must be *deferred* until the revenue is earned.

Subscription Revenue To illustrate a deferred revenue adjustment, suppose that a company sells 12-month subscriptions to its monthly magazine. On October 1, the company receives a total of $1,200 for 20 subscriptions. To record this transaction, the company would record the following entry in its general journal:

Oct. 1	Cash	1,200	
	Unearned Revenue		1,200
	(To record cash received for future magazines)		

$$\begin{array}{ccccc} \text{Assets} & = & \text{Liabilities} & + & \text{Equity} \\ +1,200 & & +1,200 & & \end{array}$$

This entry first increases the Cash account by the amount received. And, because the company now has an obligation to its customers to deliver the magazines, the entry also increases a liability account called Unearned Revenue. As a result, both assets and liabilities

are increasing. The entry would then be posted to the relevant T-accounts as follows:

Cash		Unearned Revenue		Service Revenue	
1,200			1,200		0
1,200			1,200		0

Suppose further that the company prepares financial statements at the end of each month. As of October 31, the company has provided one month of magazines and has therefore earned one month of revenue, or $100 ($1,200 ÷ 12 months). Because the accounting system does not yet reflect this earned revenue, the following adjusting journal entry should be made on October 31:

Oct. 31	Unearned Revenue	100	
	Service Revenue		100
	(To record revenue earned during October)		

$$\begin{array}{ccccc} \text{Assets} & = & \text{Liabilities} & + & \text{Equity} \\ & & -100 & & +100 \end{array}$$

This entry increases the Service Revenue account by the amount earned during the month and decreases the liability account Unearned Revenue by the same amount. As a result, liabilities are decreasing and equity is increasing. The entry would be posted to the relevant T-accounts as follows:

Cash		Unearned Revenue		Service Revenue	
1,200			1,200		0
		100			100
1,200			1,100		100

After posting, the Service Revenue T-account reflects the $100 earned in the current period while the Unearned Revenue T-account reflects the remaining $1,100 to be earned over the next 11 months. These two accounts have been *adjusted* so that they properly reflect revenues earned during October and liabilities owed on October 31. The Cash account is not affected by the adjusting journal entry. Cash was exchanged and recorded on October 1.

General Rule When a company receives cash before it provides a service, the company should always increase a liability account for the amount received. As the company provides the service, the liability account is adjusted down (decreased) and the related revenue account is adjusted up (increased). So, the adjusting journal entry for this scenario will always be a reduction to a liability account and an increase to a revenue account, as shown in Exhibit 4-2.

Scenario 2: Accrued Revenue

Companies often provide a service and then collect the cash. When a company earns a revenue before it receives cash, it has an *accrued revenue*. The term *accrue* means to accumulate or increase. An accrued revenue is another name for a receivable.

Exhibit 4-2 Entries in a Deferred Revenue Scenario

Cash Exchange   **Adjusting Entry**

1 Receive cash and record liability   **2** Provide service   **3** Record revenue and reduce liability

MAKING IT REAL

Although gift cards have existed for many years, their ever-growing popularity in recent times is causing some accounting issues for retailers.

Many people would assume that retailers record revenue with each gift card purchased. However, the transfer of merchandise is required for revenue to be recognized. Therefore, gift card sales represent a deferred revenue, which is a liability. Revenue is not generated until the gift card is redeemed. For companies like American Eagle Outfitters, this liability is significant and, as a result, is a separate line item on the balance sheet. American Eagle Outfitters reports over $41 million in unredeemed gift cards at January 29, 2011.

© Mark erickson/Getty Images

Gift cards create another accounting challenge because of "breakage"—gift cards that are never redeemed. When a retailer determines that a card will not be redeemed, it can reduce its liability and increase its revenue for the breakage estimate. American Eagle Outfitters follows this practice. In the notes to its financial statements, the company states that it "determines an estimated gift card breakage rate by continuously evaluating historical redemption data and the time when there is a remote likelihood that a gift card will be redeemed. The Company recorded gift card breakage of $5.5 million, $6.8 million, and $12.2 million during Fiscal 2010, Fiscal 2009, and Fiscal 2008, respectively."

Service Revenue   To illustrate an accrued revenue adjustment, suppose that an accounting firm agrees to provide a service to a client for a $1,000 fee. The firm completes its work on September 23, bills the client on October 10, and receives payment on October 21. Suppose further that the accounting firm prepares its own financial statements at the end of each month, which in this case is September 30.

Because the accrual basis requires that revenues be recorded in the period in which they are earned, the accounting firm must record the $1,000 of revenue on September 30 with the following adjusting journal entry:

Sept. 30	Accounts Receivable	1,000	
	Service Revenue		1,000
	(To record revenue earned during September)		

Assets	=	Liabilities	+	Equity
+1,000				+1,000

The entry increases the Accounts Receivable account for the amount that the client owes the firm and increases the Service Revenue account for the amount that the firm has earned. As a result, both assets and equity are increasing. The preceding entry would be posted to the relevant T-accounts as follows:

Cash		Accounts Receivable		Service Revenue	
0		1,000			1,000
0		1,000			1,000

After posting, the Service Revenue T-account reflects the $1,000 earned in the current period while the Accounts Receivable T-account reflects the $1,000 of expected cash receipts from the client. These two accounts have been *adjusted* so that they properly reflect revenues earned during September and receivables held on September 30.

When the customer pays cash on October 21, the following entry is made:

Oct. 21	Cash	1,000	
	Accounts Receivable		1,000
	(To record receipt of cash)		

Assets	=	Liabilities	+	Equity
+1,000				
−1,000				

This entry increases the Cash account and decreases the Accounts Receivable account for the amount collected. As a result, although specific asset accounts are changing, total assets remain unchanged. No revenue is recorded because it was recorded in the prior period when it was earned. The entry would be posted to the relevant T-accounts as follows:

Cash		Accounts Receivable	
0		1,000	
1,000			1,000
1,000		0	

General Rule   When a company earns a revenue before it receives cash, the company should always increase a receivable account and a revenue account for the amount earned. In other words, the receivable account should be adjusted up (increased) and the revenue account should also be adjusted up (increased). When the company collects the receivable, the receivable account is decreased and the cash account is increased. So, the adjusting journal entry for this scenario will always be an increase to an asset account and an increase to a revenue account, as shown in Exhibit 4-3.

Exhibit 4-3 Entries in an Accrued Revenue Scenario

	Adjusting Entry	Cash Exchange
1 Provide service	**2** Record revenue and resulting receivable	**3** Receive cash and reduce receivable

Scenario 3: Deferred Expense

Companies often pay cash before they incur an expense. You need look no further than your own personal expenses to find numerous examples of payments made before you use the service. One example is insurance. You pay for insurance for several months in advance and are then covered.

When a company pays for a resource before it uses or consumes it, the company has a *deferred expense*. We use the term *deferred* because at the time of cash payment for the resource, the company has yet to use or consume the resource it is acquiring and therefore cannot record an expense in the accounting system. Instead, it records an asset. Recording of the expense must be *deferred* until the expense is incurred. You should note that a *deferred expense* is nothing more than an asset—a resource to be used.

Insurance Expense To illustrate a deferred expense adjustment, suppose that on March 1, a company purchases a 12-month general liability insurance policy for $36,000. To record this transaction, the company would record the following entry in its general journal:

Mar. 1	Prepaid Insurance	36,000	
	Cash		36,000
	(To record purchase of insurance)		

Assets	=	Liabilities	+	Equity
−36,000				
+36,000				

This entry increases the asset account Prepaid Insurance to reflect the amount of insurance bought and decreases the Cash account for the same. Since both of these accounts are assets, this entry does not change total assets. The entry would then be posted to the relevant T-accounts as follows. For illustration purposes, assume that the Cash account has a $100,000 balance prior to the entry.

Cash		Prepaid Insurance		Insurance Expense	
100,000	36,000	36,000		0	
64,000		36,000		0	

Suppose further that the company prepares financial statements at the end of March. As of March 31, the company has been covered for one month and has therefore consumed one month of insurance, or $3,000 ($36,000 ÷ 12 months). Because the accounting system does not yet reflect this expense, the following adjusting journal entry should be made on March 31:

Mar. 31	Insurance Expense	3,000	
	Prepaid Insurance		3,000
	(To record expense incurred during March)		

Assets	=	Liabilities	+	Equity
−3,000				−3,000

This entry increases the Insurance Expense account by the amount consumed during the month and decreases the asset account Prepaid Insurance by the same amount. As a result, both assets and equity are decreasing. The entry would be posted to the relevant T-accounts as follows:

Cash		Prepaid Insurance		Insurance Expense	
100,000	36,000	36,000		0	
			3,000	3,000	
64,000		33,000		3,000	

After posting, the Insurance Expense T-account reflects the $3,000 of insurance that was consumed in the current period while the Prepaid Insurance T-account reflects the remaining $33,000 of insurance to be consumed over the next eleven months. These two accounts have been *adjusted* so that they properly reflect expenses incurred during March and unexpired assets on March 31. The Cash account is not affected by the adjusting journal entry. Cash was exchanged and recorded on March 1.

Depreciation Expense Another example of an expense where cash is paid before the expense is incurred is depreciation. Depreciation is the process of spreading out over their useful lives the cost of non-current assets such as equipment and buildings. For example, suppose that on August 1, a company purchases a delivery truck for $40,000. This transaction would be recorded into the accounting system as follows:

Aug. 1	Equipment	40,000	
	Cash		40,000
	(To record purchase of truck)		

Assets	=	Liabilities	+	Equity
−40,000				
+40,000				

This entry increases the asset account Equipment to reflect the cost of the truck and decreases the Cash account for the same. Since both of these accounts are assets, this entry does not change total assets. The entry would then be posted to the relevant T-accounts as follows. We will assume that the Cash account has a $70,000 balance prior to the entry.

Cash		Equipment		Depreciation Expense	
70,000	40,000	40,000		0	
30,000		40,000		0	

Suppose further that the company prepares financial statements at the end of August. As of August 30, the company has used the truck for one month and should therefore record some amount of expense associated with the use of the truck. If we assume for simplicity that the amount of expense to be recognized in the current month is $1,000, the following adjusting journal entry should be made on August 31:

Aug. 31	Depreciation Expense	1,000	
	Accumulated Depreciation		1,000
	(To record expense incurred		
	during August)		

Assets	=	Liabilities	+	Equity
−1,000				−1,000

This entry increases the Depreciation Expense account by the amount of expense allocated to the current month. However, instead of decreasing the Equipment account directly, the entry increases Accumulated Depreciation. We discuss accumulated depreciation in detail in Chapter 8, but for now you should know that the account is a contra-asset account that accumulates depreciation expense to date and is subtracted from the Equipment account to yield the net balance of the asset. As a result of the entry, both assets and equity are decreasing. Equity is decreasing because the company recorded an expense. Assets are decreasing because the net balance of Equipment and Accumulated Depreciation at the end of August is now $39,000 ($40,000 – $1,000). The entry would be posted to the relevant T-accounts as follows:

Equipment		Accumulated Depreciation		Depreciation Expense	
40,000			0	0	
			1,000	1,000	
40,000			1,000	1,000	

The Depreciation Expense and Accumulated Depreciation accounts have been *adjusted* so that they properly reflect the $1,000 of expenses incurred during August and the $39,000 of net unexpired balance of Equipment on August 31.

General Rule   When a company pays cash before it incurs an expense, the company should always increase an asset account for the amount paid. As the company consumes the asset, the asset account is adjusted down (decreased) and the related expense account is adjusted up (increased). Depending on the type of asset, either the actual asset account will be decreased or a related contra-asset account will be increased. So, the adjusting journal entry for this scenario will always be a reduction to an asset account and an increase to an expense account, as shown in Exhibit 4-4.

Exhibit 4-4 Entries for a Deferred Expense Scenario

Scenario 4: Accrued Expense

Companies often incur expenses and pay for them later. A good example is employee salaries. Practically all companies pay their employees after the employees have provided labor for the company. When this occurs, the company has an *accrued expense*. An accrued expense is another name for a liability.

Salaries Expense To illustrate an accrued expense adjustment, suppose that a company's daily payroll is $1,000. The company pays its employees via direct deposit every Saturday for the work the employees have provided Monday through Friday. Suppose further that the company prepares its financial statements on April 30, which is a Friday.

Because the accrual basis requires that expenses be recorded in the period in which they are incurred, the company must record $5,000 of expense on April 30 with the following adjusting journal entry:

Apr. 30	Salaries Expense	5,000	
	Salaries Payable		5,000
	(To record salaries incurred during April)		

Assets	=	Liabilities	+	Equity
		+5,000		−5,000

The preceding entry increases the Salaries Expense account for the $5,000 of salaries incurred for the week and increases the Salaries Payable account for the same since it owes the employees those salaries. As a result, liabilities are increasing and equity is decreasing. The preceding entry would be posted to the relevant T-accounts as follows:

Cash		Salaries Payable		Salaries Expense	
8,000			5,000	5,000	
8,000			5,000	5,000	

After posting, the Salaries Expense T-account reflects the $5,000 incurred in the current period while the Salaries Payable T-account reflects the $5,000 owed to employees on April 30. These two accounts have been *adjusted* so that they properly reflect expenses incurred during April and the payable owed on April 30.

The Cash account is not affected by the adjusting journal entry. Cash, which has an $8,000 balance for illustrative purposes, will be paid on Saturday, May 1.

When the company pays its employees, the following entry would be made:

May 1	Salaries Payable	5,000	
	Cash		5,000
	(To record payment of cash)		

Assets	=	Liabilities	+	Equity
−5,000		−5,000		

The entry decreases the Cash account for the $5,000 paid to employees and decreases the Salaries Payable account by the same $5,000. No expense is recorded because it was recorded in the prior period when the expense was incurred. As a result, both assets and liabilities are decreasing. The entry would be posted to the relevant T-accounts as follows:

Cash		Salaries Payable	
8,000			5,000
	5,000	5,000	
3,000			0

Interest Expense Interest is another example of incurring an expense before cash is paid. For example, suppose that a company borrows $10,000 on November 1. The annual interest rate on the loan is 6%, and interest is payable on the first day of each month. Suppose further that the company prepares its financial statements on November 30.

As of November 30, the company has used the borrowed money for one month, so it has incurred one month's worth of interest. To calculate the amount of interest, we simply multiply the principal amount ($10,000) by the annual interest rate (6%) and by the relevant number of periods (1 month out of 12, or 1/12). So, interest for the month of November is:

$$\text{Principal} \times \text{annual rate} \times \text{time} = \$10,000 \times 0.06 \times 1/12$$
$$= \$50$$

Therefore, the following adjusting journal entry should be made on November 30:

Nov. 30	Interest Expense	50	
	Interest Payable		50
	(To record interest incurred during November)		

Assets	=	Liabilities	+	Equity
		+50		−50

The preceding entry increases the Interest Expense account for the $50 of interest for November and increases the Interest Payable account for the same. As a result, liabilities are increasing and equity is decreasing. The preceding entry would be posted to the relevant T-accounts as follows:

Cash		Interest Payable		Interest Expense	
1,000			50	50	
1,000			50	50	

After posting, the Interest Expense T-account reflects the $50 incurred in the current period and the Interest Payable T-account reflects the $50 owed to the bank on November 30. These two accounts have been *adjusted* so that they properly reflect expenses incurred during November and the payable owed on November 30.

The Cash account is not affected by the adjusting journal entry. Cash, which has a $1,000 balance for illustrative purposes, will be paid on December 1. On that date, the following entry would be made:

Dec. 1	Interest Payable	50	
	Cash		50
	(To record payment of cash)		

Assets	=	Liabilities	+	Equity
−50		−50		

The preceding entry decreases the Cash account for the $50 paid to the bank and decreases the Interest Payable account by the same $50. As a result, both assets and liabilities are decreasing. The entry would be posted to the relevant T-accounts as follows:

Cash		Interest Payable	
1,000			50
	50	50	
950			0

General Rule   When a company incurs an expense before it pays cash, the company should always increase a payable account and an expense account for the amount incurred. In other words, the payable account should be adjusted up (increased) and the expense account should also be adjusted up (increased). When the company pays the liability, the liability account is reduced and the cash account is decreased. So, the adjusting journal entry for this scenario will always be an increase to a liability account and an increase to an expense account, as shown in Exhibit 4-5.

Summary of Adjusting Journal Entries

Exhibit 4-6 summarizes the four scenarios that give rise to adjusting journal entries and the characteristics of the relevant entries.

As you review this exhibit, consider the following generalizations of all adjusting entries:

1. The purpose of adjusting entries is to record revenues that have been earned but not recorded and expenses that have been incurred but not recorded.

Exhibit 4-5 Entries in an Accrued Expense Scenario

Exhibit 4-6 Summary of Adjusting Journal Entry Scenarios

Scenario	Classification	Entry Before End of Period		Adjusting Entry at End of Period		Entry After End of Period	

Cash is received *before* revenue is earned	Deferred Revenue	Cash
		  Liability
			$$
			  $$
				Liability
				  Revenue
					$$
					  $$		

Cash is received *after* revenue is earned	Accrued Revenue			Receivable
				  Revenue
					$$
					  $$
						Cash
						  Receivable
							$$
							  $$

Cash is paid *before* expense is incurred	Deferred Expense	Asset
		  Cash
			$$
			  $$
				Expense
				  Asset
					$$
					  $$		

Cash is paid *after* expense is incurred	Accrued Expense			Expense
				  Payable
					$$
					  $$
						Payable
						  Cash
							$$
							  $$

2. Every adjusting journal entry will affect at least one revenue or one expense account. In addition, every adjusting journal entry will affect at least one asset or liability account. This means that every adjusting entry will affect at least one account from the income statement and one account from the balance sheet.

3. Adjusting journal entries arise because the timing of revenue and expense recognition differs from the exchange of cash. Therefore, cash will never be increased or decreased in an adjusting entry.

LO3 Comprehensive Example: Adjusting Journal Entries

To illustrate the process of making adjusting journal entries from a trial balance and then preparing an adjusted trial balance, the Circle Films example from Chapter 3 will be continued. As a result of the transactions entered into by Circle Films during its first month of operations, the following unadjusted trial balance was prepared at May 31. Notice that it is an *unadjusted* trial balance because adjusting entries have not yet been made.

Circle Films
Unadjusted Trial Balance
May 31

	Debit	Credit
Cash	$ 8,250	
Supplies	1,000	
Equipment	18,000	
Unearned Revenue		$ 2,000
Notes Payable		9,000
Common Stock		15,000
Service Revenue		5,000
Advertising Expense	250	
Salaries Expense	2,000	
Dividends	1,500	
Totals	$31,000	$31,000

In addition to these accounts and balances, the following information was available on May 31:

1. On May 31, Circle Films filmed the retirement reception for the customer who paid $2,000 on May 10 (see transaction #4 in Chapter 3 on page 58).

2. On May 31, Circle Films filmed the first night of a two-night local play. The second night will be filmed on June 1, at which time Circle Films will bill the customer. The customer has agreed to pay Circle Films $1,500 for each night.

3. After a physical count, Circle Films determined that it had $650 of supplies remaining.

4. The interest rate for the promissory note is 6%.

5. Circle Films estimates that depreciation for May on its two cameras totals $600.

Given this information, the following adjusting entries can be prepared.

Journalizing and Posting Adjusting Entries

Adjustment #1 (Deferred Revenue) Circle Films has now filmed the retirement reception, so it no longer has a liability to the customer. It has a revenue instead. However, the trial balance still shows the $2,000 liability. Thus, the adjusting entry to adjust the liability down and the revenue up is as follows:

May 31	Unearned Revenue	2,000	
	Service Revenue		2,000
	(To record revenue earned)		

Assets	=	Liabilities	+	Equity
		−2,000		+2,000

The entry would be posted to the relevant T-accounts as follows:

Unearned Revenue			Service Revenue	
	2,000			5,000
2,000				2,000
	0			7,000

Adjustment #2 (Accrued Revenue) Circle Films filmed one night of a local play. Therefore, it has earned revenue for one night, or $1,500. The trial balance does not reflect this because Circle Films has not issued a bill, so the adjusting journal entry to adjust receivables and revenues up is as follows:

May 31	Accounts Receivable	1,500	
	Service Revenue		1,500
	(To record revenue earned)		

Assets	=	Liabilities	+	Equity
+1,500				+1,500

The entry would be posted to the relevant T-accounts as follows:

Accounts Receivable			Service Revenue	
0				5,000
1,500				2,000
				1,500
1,500				8,500

Adjustment #3 (Deferred Expense) Circle Films has $650 in supplies on hand. However, the trial balance shows $1,000 in the Supplies account, which is the amount that Circle Films originally purchased. Therefore, Circle Films must have used $350 of supplies ($1,000 − $650). To adjust the Supplies account down from $1,000 to $650 and to record the $350 in expense, the following adjusting journal is required.

May 31	Supplies Expense	350	
	Supplies		350
	(To record expense incurred)		

Assets	=	Liabilities	+	Equity
−350				−350

The entry would be posted to the relevant T-accounts as follows:

Supplies			Supplies Expense	
1,000			0	
	350		350	
650			350	

Adjustment #4 (Accrued Expense) Circle Films must pay interest on the promissory note at a 6% annual rate. Therefore, after one month, Circle Films has incurred $45 of interest expense ($9,000 × 6% × 1/12). This expense and the related obligation are not reflected in the trial balance because they have not yet been recorded. To record them, the following adjusting entry is required:

May 31	Interest Expense	45	
	Interest Payable		45
	(To record expense incurred)		

Assets	=	Liabilities	+	Equity
		+45		−45

Once an adjusted trial balance is prepared, financial statements can be generated.

The entry would be posted to the relevant T-accounts as follows:

Interest Payable			Interest Expense	
	0		0	
	45		45	
	45		45	

Adjustment #5 (Deferred Expense) Circle determines that depreciation on its cameras should be $600 for the month of May. To record this depreciation, the following adjusting entry is required:

May 31	Depreciation Expense	600	
	Accumulated Depreciation		600
	(To record expense incurred)		

Assets	=	Liabilities	+	Equity
−600				−600

The entry would be posted to the relevant T-accounts as follows:

Equipment		Depreciation Expense		Accumulated Depreciation	
18,000		0			0
		600			600
18,000		600			600

Preparing an Adjusted Trial Balance

Once all of the preceding adjusting entries are journalized and posted to the ledger, an adjusted trial balance can be prepared. Like the previous trial balance, the adjusted trial balance simply lists all balances from the ledger. Since the ledger now reflects several adjustments, so does the adjusted trial balance.

The following is Circle Films' May 31 adjusted trial balance. The accounts that were either created or adjusted by the adjusting entries are highlighted.

Zeffss1/iStockphoto.com

Circle Films Adjusted Trial Balance May 31		
	Debit	**Credit**
Cash	$ 8,250	
Accounts Receivable	1,500	
Supplies	650	
Equipment	18,000	
Accumulated Depreciation		$ 600
Interest Payable		45
Unearned Revenue		0
Notes Payable		9,000
Common Stock		15,000
Service Revenue		8,500
Advertising Expense	250	
Depreciation Expense	600	
Interest Expense	45	
Salaries Expense	2,000	
Supplies Expense	350	
Dividends	1,500	
Totals	$33,145	$33,145

Preparing Financial Statements

Once all revenues and expenses are recorded and an adjusted trial balance is prepared, financial statements can be generated. Recall from Chapter 1 that the income statement should be prepared first. Using the adjusted revenue and expense account balances from the adjusted trial balance, Circle Films' income statement for the month of May would appear as follows:

Circle Films Income Statement For the Month Ending May 31		
Service revenue		$ 8,500
Expenses		
Advertising expense	$ 250	
Depreciation expense	600	
Interest expense	45	
Salaries expense	2,000	
Supplies expense	350	
Total expenses		3,245
Net income		$ 5,255

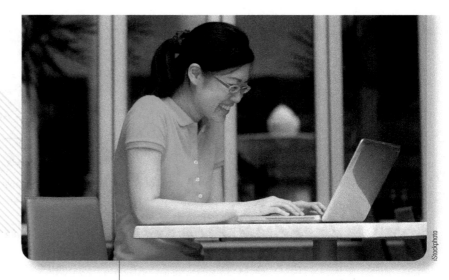

After a period ends and financial statements are prepared, all temporary accounts must be reset to zero for the start of the next period.

With net income calculated, Circle Films' statement of retained earnings can be prepared. Recall that the statement of retained earnings takes the beginning balance in Retained Earnings, adds net income, and subtracts dividends to yield the current balance in Retained Earnings. Circle Films' May 31 adjusted trial balance shows no balance in beginning Retained Earnings and a $1,500 balance in dividends. Therefore, Circle Films' statement of retained earnings for the month of May would appear as follows:

Circle Films Statement of Retained Earnings For the Month Ending May 31	
Retained earnings, May 1	$ 0
+ Net income	5,255
− Dividends	1,500
Retained earnings, May 31	$ 3,755

With Retained Earnings calculated, Circle Films' balance sheet can be prepared. Circle Films' May 31 adjusted trial balance shows several balance sheet accounts, starting with Cash and continuing through Common Stock. These accounts, along with the amount of Retained Earnings from the May statement of retained earnings, should be included on the balance sheet. Therefore, Circle Films' May 31 balance sheet would appear as follows.

Closing process The process of transferring all revenue, expense, and dividend account balances to the Retained Earnings account.

Temporary accounts Accounts that accumulate balances only for the current period.

Circle Films Balance Sheet May 31		
Cash		$ 8,250
Accounts receivable		1,500
Supplies		650
Equipment	$18,000	
Less: Accumulated depreciation	600	17,400
Total assets		$27,800
Interest payable	$ 45	
Notes payable	9,000	
Total liabilities		$ 9,045
Common stock	$15,000	
Retained earnings	3,755	
Total stockholders' equity		18,755
Total liabilities and stockholders' equity		$27,800

LO4 Closing Process

After financial statements are prepared, companies conduct the closing process. The **closing process** is the process of transferring all revenue, expense, and dividend account balances to the Retained Earnings account. This transfer is necessary for two reasons.

First, revenue, expense, and dividend accounts are **temporary accounts**, meaning that they accumulate balances only for the current period. After the period ends and financial statements are prepared, all temporary accounts must be reset to zero for the start of the next period.

Second, the transfer updates the Retained Earnings account to its proper end-of-period balance. In the preceding example, the balance in Retained Earnings is generated from the statement of retained earnings, not the adjusted trial balance. The closing process is the mechanism that updates the actual Retained Earnings account balance in the ledger.

The closing process is accomplished with several entries. **Closing entries**, which are made in the journal and posted to the ledger, eliminate the balances in all temporary accounts and transfer those balances to the Retained Earnings account. Usually, one entry is made for revenues, one for expenses, and a final entry for dividends. To illustrate, the temporary accounts from Circle Films' adjusted trial balance are shown in the following partial adjusted trial balance:

Circle Films
Partial Adjusted Trial Balance
May 31

	Debit	Credit
Service Revenue		$8,500
Advertising Expense	$ 250	
Depreciation Expense	600	
Interest Expense	45	
Salaries Expense	2,000	
Supplies Expense	350	
Dividends	1,500	

Circle Films has one revenue account with an $8,500 credit balance. To eliminate that balance and transfer it to the Retained Earnings account, the following closing entry is required:

May 31	Service Revenue	8,500	
	Retained Earnings		8,500
	(To close revenue account)		

In this entry, the revenue balance is eliminated while the Retained Earnings account is increased.

Expense and dividend accounts are closed in a similar fashion. To eliminate those balances and transfer them to Retained Earnings, the following closing entries are required:

May 31	Retained Earnings	3,245	
	Advertising Expense		250
	Depreciation Expense		600
	Interest Expense		45
	Salaries Expense		2,000
	Supplies Expense		350
	(To close expense accounts)		

May 31	Retained Earnings	1,500	
	Dividends		1,500
	(To close dividend account)		

In the first entry, all expense accounts are eliminated, and the Retained Earnings account is decreased for the same. In the second entry, the dividend account is eliminated, and the Retained Earnings account is decreased for the same.

All three closing entries would be posted to the appropriate T-accounts as follows:

Retained Earnings		Service Revenue		Advertising Expense	
	8,500		8,500	250	
3,245		8,500			250
1,500					
	3,755		0	0	

Depreciation Exp.		Interest Expense		Salaries Expense	
600		45		2,000	
	600		45		2,000
0		0		0	

Supplies Expense		Dividends	
350		1,500	
	350		1,500
0		0	

Notice that after the closing entries are posted, all revenue, expense, and dividend accounts have zero balances as desired. They are now ready to begin the next reporting period. Also, Retained Earnings has a $3,755 credit balance. This is the balance reported on Circle Films' statement of retained earnings and balance sheet. In other words, the Retained Earnings account now has the proper balance at the end of the period.

As a final check that all accounts have been properly closed, a new trial balance is prepared. Appropriately called a post-closing trial balance, it contains all account balances for the beginning of the next accounting period. Circle Films' post-closing trial balance is as follows:

Closing entries Entries made in the journal and posted to the ledger that eliminate the balances in all temporary accounts and transfer those balances to the Retained Earnings account.

Circle Films Post-Closing Trial Balance May 31		
	Debit	**Credit**
Cash	$ 8,250	
Accounts Receivable	1,500	
Supplies	650	
Equipment	18,000	
Accumulated Depreciation		$ 600
Interest Payable		45
Notes Payable		9,000
Common Stock		15,000
Retained Earnings		3,755
Totals	$28,400	$28,400

LO5 The Accounting Cycle— A Summary

This and the previous chapter covered the accounting cycle. The **accounting cycle** is the sequence of steps in which an accounting information

Accounting cycle The sequence of steps in which an accounting information system captures, processes, and reports a company's accounting transactions during a period.

system captures, processes, and reports a company's accounting transactions during a period. Chapter 3 demonstrated the first three steps—how to record journal entries in the journal, post the information to the ledger, and prepare a trial balance. This chapter demonstrated the two major processes that occur at the end of the period—adjusting and closing. The adjusting process includes the recording and posting of adjusting entries and the preparation of an adjusted trial balance, from which financial statements are prepared. The closing process includes the recording and posting of closing entries and the preparation of a post-closing trial balance. Once closing is completed, the accounting information system is prepared to begin the next period. Exhibit 4-7 summarizes these steps.

Exhibit 4-7 The Accounting Cycle

1. Journalize and post accounting transactions.
2. Prepare a trial balance.
3. Journalize and post adjusting entries.
4. Prepare an adjusted trial balance.
5. Prepare financial statements.
6. Journalize and post closing entries.
7. Prepare a post-closing trial balance.

STUDY TOOLS 4

Chapter review card

- ● Learning Objective and Key Concept Reviews
- ● Key Definitions and Formulas

Online (Located at www.cengagebrain.com)

- ● Flash Cards and Crossword Puzzles
- ● Games and Quizzes
- ● E-Lectures
- ● Homework Assignments (as directed by your instructor)

1. (LO1) When are revenues and expenses recognized under the cash basis of accounting?
2. (LO1) When are revenues and expenses recognized under the accrual basis of accounting?
3. (LO1) Which basic accounting principle(s) does the cash basis of accounting violate?
4. (LO1) Income under the cash basis of accounting is not reported at all under Generally Accepted Accounting Principles. Do you agree or disagree? Explain.
5. (LO1) Why will income under the cash basis and the accrual basis be the same in the long run?
6. (LO2) What is the purpose of adjusting journal entries, and when are they made?
7. (LO2) What circumstances give rise to a deferred revenue? a deferred expense?
8. (LO2) What circumstances give rise to an accrued revenue? an accrued expense?
9. (LO2) List the four basic classifications of adjusting entries and describe the nature of each adjusting entry.
10. (LO2) Deferred expense and accrued expense are interchangeable terms. Explain why this statement is false.
11. (LO3) Is it possible for adjusting entries to affect only the balance sheet? Why or why not?
12. (LO3) How is the adjusted trial balance used to prepare financial statements?
13. (LO4) What does the term "temporary accounts" mean? List the general types of accounts that fall under this classification.
14. (LO4) At the beginning of an accounting period, a company's revenue, expense, and dividend accounts will always have zero balances. Do you agree or disagree? Explain.
15. (LO4) Describe the three possible closing entries.

MULTIPLE CHOICE

1. (LO1) The cash basis of accounting:
   a. is a basis for when to record revenues and expenses.
   b. is required by Generally Accepted Accounting Principles.
   c. records expenses when they are incurred.
   d. records revenues only when they have been earned.
2. (LO1) On December 31, a company receives a $5,000 payment for services not yet rendered and a $500 electric bill for the month of December. Under the cash basis of accounting, this company would recognize:
   a. $4,500 of revenue and $500 of expense.
   b. $5,000 of revenue and $0 of expense.
   c. $5,000 of revenue and $500 of expense.
   d. $0 of revenue and $500 of expense.

3. (LO1) On December 31, a company receives a $5,000 payment for services not yet rendered and a $500 electric bill for the month of December. Under the accrual basis of accounting, this company would recognize:
   a. $4,500 of revenue and $500 of expense.
   b. $5,000 of revenue and $0 of expense.
   c. $5,000 of revenue and $500 of expense.
   d. $0 of revenue and $500 of expense.
4. (LO2) Which of the following situations would likely not require an adjusting entry?
   a. Revenue is earned before cash is received
   b. Expense is incurred before cash is paid
   c. Cash is received before revenue is earned
   d. Cash is paid before equipment is received
5. (LO2) Which of the following accounts is most likely associated with a deferred revenue?
   a. Depreciation Expense
   b. Salaries Payable
   c. Unearned Revenue
   d. Accounts Receivable
6. (LO2) Which of the following accounts is most likely associated with an accrued expense?
   a. Depreciation Expense
   b. Salaries Payable
   c. Unearned Revenue
   d. Accounts Receivable
7. (LO2) Which of the following is false?
   a. Adjusting entries are made at the end of an accounting period
   b. Adjusting entries are not necessary under the cash basis of accounting
   c. The cash account will always be affected by adjusting journal entries
   d. Adjusting journal entries always affect at least one revenue or expense account and at least one asset or liability account
8. (LO1, 2) A company prepays rent of $500 and receives a $3,000 payment for services not yet rendered. Under the accrual basis of accounting, these two transactions will:
   a. increase net income $2,500.
   b. increase net income $3,000.
   c. decrease net income $500.
   d. have no effect on net income.
9. (LO2) A company has $3,000 of supplies on hand at the beginning of the year. During the year, the company buys $7,500 of supplies. At the end of the year, supplies on hand total $4,000. What is the amount of Supplies Expense reported on the company's income statement?
   a. $4,000
   b. $7,500
   c. $6,500
   d. $10,500
10. (LO2) On December 1, Smiles, Inc. prepays $2,400 for three months of rent. On December 31, Smiles prepares financial statements. After the appropriate

adjusting entry for rent, Smiles' balance sheet would show:
a. prepaid Rent of $2,400.
b. rent Expense of $800.
c. prepaid Rent of $1,600.
d. prepaid Rent of $800.

11. (LO2) A company has a $4,000 balance in Unearned Revenue on its unadjusted trial balance. At the end of the year, the company has earned all but one-fourth of the revenue. The adjusting journal entry necessary at year-end would include:
a. a debit to Service Revenue of $4,000.
b. a credit to Unearned Revenue for $3,000.
c. a debit to Unearned Revenue for $3,000.
d. a credit to Service Revenue of $1,000.

12. (LO2) A company fails to record the expiration of insurance that it purchased previously. Because of this error, the company's assets and equity are:
a. overstated.
b. understated.
c. unaffected.
d. cannot tell from the given information.

13. (LO2, 3) A company's unadjusted trial balance shows a $12,000 balance in Salaries Expense while the adjusted trial balance shows a balance of $13,000. Which of the following best describes the reason for the difference?
a. An adjusting entry to reduce Salaries Expense by $1,000 was prepared
b. An adjusting entry to reduce Salaries Payable by $1,000 was prepared
c. An adjusting entry to record the payment of $1,000 of salaries was prepared
d. An adjusting entry to increase Salaries Expense by $1,000 was prepared

14. (LO2, 3) Tom and Judy's Bed and Breakfast received the following bills for December utilities:
 i. Electricity - $500 on December 31, 2011
 ii. Water - $750 on December 29, 2011
 iii. Telephone - $375 on January 1, 2012
On the December 31, 2011, financial statements, Tom and Judy's should show accrued expenses of:
a. $1,625.
b. $1,250.
c. $500.
d. None of the above.

15. (LO4) The closing process:
a. updates the retained earnings account.
b. prepares all revenue and expense accounts for the next period.
c. puts any dividend account to zero.
d. all of the above.

16. (LO4) Claw's Irrigation, Inc. paid $2,000 of dividends in the prior year and $4,500 of dividends in the current year. The closing entry for the current year would include:
a. a debit to Retained Earnings for $6,500.
b. a credit to Dividends for $6,500.
c. a credit to Dividends for $4,500.
d. a credit to Retained Earnings for $4,500.

17. (LO4) Collins Construction Co. uses the accrual basis of accounting. During the year, Collins reported $45,000 of revenue, $12,500 of expenses, and $1,200 of dividends. On December 31, Collins prepares all closing entries. The net effect on Retained Earnings is a:
a. decrease of $1,200.
b. increase of $42,500.
c. increase of $31,300.
d. decrease of $13,700.

18. (LO4) Which of the following is not a possible closing entry?
a. A debit to Retained Earnings and a credit to Dividends
b. A debit to Revenue and a credit to Retained Earnings
c. A debit to Retained Earnings and a credit to Expense
d. A debit to Expense and a credit to Retained Earnings

19. (LO5) Which of the following is not a step in the accounting cycle?
a. Prepare an adjusted trial balance
b. Prepare and post closing entries
c. Prepare financial statements
d. Each of the above is a step in the accounting cycle

20. (LO5) Which of the following best summarizes the order of the accounting cycle?
a. Journalize, post, adjust, close
b. Journalize, adjust, post, close
c. Journalize, close, adjust, post
d. Journalize, post, close, adjust

BRIEF EXERCISES

1. Cash and Accrual Basis   LO1
During the year, Black Diamond Company earned $86,500 in revenue. At year-end, only $65,000 of that revenue had been collected. Also, Black Diamond incurred $44,000 of expenses of which only $35,000 had been paid.

Required
Determine net income for the year under (a) the cash basis of accounting and (b) the accrual basis of accounting.

2. Adjusting Journal Entries   LO2, 3
Consider the following incomplete adjusting journal entries:

1.	Utilities Expense	2,900	
	(a)		2,900
2.	(b)	19,500	
	Service Revenue		19,500
3.	(c)	7,000	
	Prepaid Insurance		7,000
4.	Unearned Revenue	4,650	
	(d)		4,650

Required

Identify the likely account(s) that would complete each adjusting journal entry.

3. Adjusting Journal Entries LO2

Consider the four entries in the preceding brief exercise.

Required

Identify each entry as an accrued expense, an accrued revenue, a deferred expense, or a deferred revenue.

4. Adjusting Journal Entry—Revenue LO2, 3

On March 1, Global Airlines received $3,500 cash from customers who bought tickets. Only half of the tickets were used by the end of March, and the remaining tickets were expected to be used in April. Global prepares adjusting entries monthly.

Required

a. Determine whether the revenue is a deferred or accrued revenue and explain why.
b. Prepare the journal entries that Global would make on March 1 and March 31.

5. Adjusting Journal Entry—Expense LO2, 3

White Star Enterprises records salaries expense each Friday when employees are paid. The company is preparing its financial statements on June 30, which is a Wednesday. Salaries are $5,000 a week.

Required

a. Prepare any adjusting journal entry necessary on June 30.
b. Explain if this situation is a deferred or accrued expense.
c. Show the T-accounts with the adjusting journal entry posted to them.

6. Adjusting Journal Entry—Expense LO2, 3

On January 1, PGD Corporation bought equipment for $20,000 cash. For the year, PGD calculates a total of $1,250 of depreciation on the equipment. PGD records depreciation annually on December 31.

Required

a. Prepare all journal entries relating to the purchase and depreciation of the equipment.
b. Post the December 31 journal entry to the relevant T-accounts.

7. Adjusting Journal Entry Errors LO2, 3

Suppose that a company fails to make the proper adjusting journal entries associated with the following expenses and revenues:
1. Prepaid insurance that has expired
2. Interest that has accrued on notes payable
3. Unearned revenue that has now been earned

Required

Determine the likely accounts that are affected by each error and whether those accounts are understated or overstated as a result of the error.

8. Calculate Expenses and Revenues LO2, 3

The current- and prior-year balance sheets of Banter Company show the following account balances:

	Current Year	Prior Year
Supplies	$3,000	$4,500
Unearned Revenue	7,200	7,000

During the current year, Banter purchased $11,300 of supplies and received $9,200 of cash for services to be performed later.

Required

Using T-accounts, determine Banter Company's supplies expense and service revenue for the current year.

9. Adjusting Journal Entries LO2, 3

Big E Services provides the following selected information from its trial balance and adjusted trial balance at August 31:

Big E Services Trial Balance August 31				
	Unadjusted		**Adjusted**	
	Debit	**Credit**	**Debit**	**Credit**
Accounts Receivable	$8,910		$9,240	
Supplies	3,400		2,200	
Service Revenue		$17,480		$17,810
Supplies Expense	5,320		6,520	

Required

Prepare the adjusting journal entries that Big E must have made at August 31.

10. Prepare Financial Statements from Trial Balance LO3

The adjusted trial balance for Handle Coffee is as follows:

Handle Coffee Adjusted Trial Balance November 30		
	Debit	**Credit**
Cash	$2,500	
Accounts Receivable	350	
Supplies	1,800	
Accounts Payable		$ 750
Salaries Payable		2,000
Retained Earnings		1,000
Service Revenue		4,400
Salaries Expense	2,900	
Supplies Expense	600	
Total	$8,150	$8,150

Required

Prepare Handle's income statement and statement of retained earnings for the month of November and its balance sheet at November 30.

11. Closing Entries LO4

Ivey Publishing generates and records $15,000 of revenues and $12,000 of expenses during the month. It also pays and records $500 in dividends for the month.

Required

Prepare Ivey's closing entries for the month and determine the net change in Retained Earnings as a result of those entries.

12. Adjusting and Closing Process LO3, 4, 5

Consider the following accounts:

Cash
Accounts Receivable
Interest Payable
Common Stock
Service Revenue
Salaries Expense

Required

Determine which accounts fall into the following categories: A) Accounts that can be adjusted and closed; B) Accounts that can be adjusted but not closed; C) Accounts that are not normally adjusted nor closed.

EXERCISES

13. Cash and Accrual Income LO1

During 2012, Stacker Enterprises earned $55,000 from services provided and incurred $15,500 of expenses. At the end of the year, Stacker had received cash for $35,750 of the revenues and had paid $11,600 of the expenses. Also during 2012, Stacker received $3,500 cash for services to be performed in 2013 and paid $4,500 for rent for the first six months of 2013.

Required

Determine 2012 net income under (a) the cash basis and (b) the accrual basis of accounting.

14. Adjusting Journal Entries LO2, 3

Following are several independent accounting situations:

1. Interest of $1,500 on a loan outstanding during 2012 is due on January 1, 2013.
2. Received $100,000 in 2012 for a service project that is 45% complete at year-end.

3. Received a $450 utility bill for the month of December on January 3, 2013.
4. $750 of prepaid rent for the month of December has expired.
5. $5,000 of revenue for services performed on December 14, 2012, is uncollected.
6. Prepay $6,500 of insurance on December 31, 2012, for the entire year of 2013.
7. Intend to buy a warehouse on January 1, 2013, for $125,000.
8. Equipment depreciation is $5,000 for the year.

Required

For each independent situation, determine the basic type of adjustment, if any, that is needed on December 31, 2012 (deferred revenue, deferred expense, accrued revenue, accrued expense). What would be the cumulative effect on 2012 net income of all adjustments made in situations 1–8?

15. Adjusting Journal Entries LO2, 3

The following selected accounts were taken from the general ledger of the Cone Corporation on September 30 before adjusting entries have been made. Cone makes adjusting entries *quarterly*.

	Debit	Credit
Supplies	4,000	
Prepaid Rent	5,400	
Building	100,000	
Notes Receivable	25,000	
Accumulated Depreciation		20,000
Unearned Revenue		8,500

Additional Information:

1. Rent expires at a rate of $900 per month.
2. Supplies on hand total $2,000.
3. Utilities incurred in September but not yet recorded or paid are $500.
4. The building depreciates at a rate of $2,700 per quarter.
5. $5,000 of the $8,500 unearned revenue has been earned during the quarter.
6. Interest of $250 on the notes receivable has been earned but not yet recorded.

Required

Prepare the necessary adjusting journal entries at September 30.

16. Adjusting Journal Entries LO2, 3

For each of the transactions for Cone Corporation in Exercise 15, indicate the amount of the increase or decrease on the appropriate element of the balance sheet or income statement. The first transaction has been completed as an example.

Transaction	Balance Sheet			Income Statement		
	Assets	Liability	Equity	Revenues	Expenses	Net Income
1.	−2,700	NE	−2,700	NE	+2,700	−2,700
2.						
3.						
4.						
5.						
6.						

17. Adjusting Journal Entries LO2, 3

In its first year of operations, Lien Corporation entered into the following transactions, among others:

1. January 1: Bought equipment, $105,000.
2. March 31: Prepaid one year's rent, $24,000.
3. July 1: Took out a one year loan from the bank at an annual interest rate of 8%, $20,000.
4. August 1: Received payment for services not yet rendered, $12,000.

On December 31, Lien has earned $8,000 of the $12,000 in transaction 4 and has incurred but not recorded $450 of utilities. Lien prepares adjusting entries on an annual basis.

Required

Prepare journal entries for transactions 1–4. Prepare any adjusting journal entries needed at December 31. Assume that the equipment depreciates $15,000 annually.

18. Adjusting Journal Entries LO 2,3

Mikato Company's annual accounting period ends on June 30, 2012. Mikato makes adjusting journal entries semiannually, and the following information applies to all necessary adjusting journal entries at June 30, 2012:

1. Mikato carries the following two insurance policies:

Policy	Purchase Date	Policy Length	Cost at Purchase Date
A	July 1, 2010	5 years	$48,000
B	July 1, 2011	2 years	16,000

2. At January 1, 2012, office supplies totaled $1,800. In the past six months, additional supplies of $2,700 were purchased, and a count revealed $2,150 available supplies at June 30, 2012.
3. Mikato owns one building:

Cost	Useful Life	Annual Depreciation
$150,000	25	$6,000

4. Mikato decides to rent out a portion of its building. On June 1, 2012, Mikato received a prepayment of $5,700 for rent for the months of June, July, and August.

5. The Mikato staff consists of seven employees. Each employee earns a total of $1,200 a week and is paid each Monday for the previous week's work. June 30, 2012, falls on Thursday.

Required

Prepare all necessary adjusting entries at June 30, 2012, and indicate whether each entry relates to a deferred revenue, deferred expense, accrued revenue, or accrued expense.

19. Errors in Adjusting Journal Entries LO2, 3

Consider the following independent situations.

1. A company provides a service but has not yet received payment. Therefore, the company does not record any revenue for the service.
2. A company receives cash in advance of providing a service and properly records a liability to the customer. At year-end, the company has not provided any of the service. The company does not adjust the liability at year-end.
3. Half of a company's prepaid insurance expires during the year, but the company does not adjust the prepaid insurance account to reflect the expiration.
4. A company incurs legal expenses associated with defending a lawsuit. No bill has been received at year-end, so the company does not record any expenses associated with the lawsuit.

Required

For each independent scenario, determine whether the company's accounting was correct or incorrect. If it was incorrect, determine whether the error resulted in the company's assets, liabilities, equity, revenues, and expenses being correct, understated, or overstated.

20. Adjusting Journal Entries LO2, 3

Coy Williams, a first-year accountant at Protein Plus, has asked you to review the following items for potential errors. Protein Plus has a December 31 year-end.

1. Did not adjust the Prepaid Insurance account for the $6,600 of insurance that expired during the year.
2. Recorded a full year of accrued interest on a $20,000, 10% note payable that was entered into on July 1. Interest is payable each July 1.

3. Did not record $8,500 of depreciation on an office building.
4. Recorded revenues of $12,000 when payment was received for a job that will be completed next year.
5. Recorded $600 of utilities expense for December utilities even though Protein Plus will not pay the bill until January of next year.

Required
Determine if Coy made any errors in the five items. For those in which an error was made, prepare the entry that Coy should have made. What was the net effect of Coy's errors on the net income of Protein Plus?

21. Closing Entries LO4
Ivey Publishing provides the following trial balance at March 31:

Ivey Publishing Trial Balance March 31		
	Debit	Credit
Cash	$ 4,280	
Prepaid Insurance	3,500	
Unearned Revenue		$ 3,000
Retained Earnings		2,380
Service Revenue		14,820
Insurance Expense	2,300	
Salaries Expense	8,920	
Dividends	1,200	
Totals	$20,200	$20,200

Required
Prepare Ivey's closing entries at March 31 and its Post-Closing Trial Balance.

22. Closing Process LO4
A partial adjusted trial balance is shown as follows for Sparks Electricity:

Sparks Electricity Partial Adjusted Trial Balance June 30		
	Debit	Credit
Retained Earnings		$17,150
Service Revenue		30,500
Advertising Expense	$ 1,200	
Depreciation Expense	10,750	
Interest Expense	560	
Salaries Expense	5,000	
Supplies Expense	2,500	
Utilities Expense	2,080	
Dividends	1,000	

Required
a. Prepare Sparks' income statement and statement of retained earnings for the month of June.
b. Prepare the appropriate closing entries at June 30.
c. What is the purpose of "closing the books" at the end of an accounting period?

23. Closing Process LO4
The following T-accounts contain the December postings to the general ledger of Swoops, Inc. The December 1 postings are beginning balances, while the December 31 postings are closing entries.

Service Revenue

12/31	75,000	12/1	64,000
		12/8	4,000
		12/24	3,000
		12/30	4,000

Salaries Expense

12/1	15,000	12/31	17,000
12/15	1,000		
12/30	1,000		

Supplies Expense

12/1	1,800	12/31	2,500
12/30	700		

Depreciation Expense

12/1	4,400	12/31	4,800
12/30	400		

Interest Expense

12/1	1,500	12/31	1,800
12/24	300		

Retained Earnings

12/31	2,500	12/1	51,550
12/31	26,100	12/31	75,000

Dividends

12/1	2,000	12/31	2,500
12/15	500		

Required
Recreate the closing journal entries made by Swoops on December 31.

24. Errors in Closing Entries LO4

Landers Manufacturing prepares the following three closing entries at the end of the year:

#1 Retained Earnings	45,550	
Service Revenue		45,550
#2 Retained Earnings	39,200	
Advertising Expense		10,400
Rent Expense		4,500
Salaries Expense		18,800
Supplies Expense		4,500
#3 Retained Earnings	2,000	
Dividends Payable		2,000

Required

Identify the potential error(s) in Landers' closing entries.

25. Match Terms and Definitions LO1, 2, 3, 4

The following is a list of various accounting terms and definitions:

1. Accrual basis of accounting
2. Cash basis of accounting
3. Adjusting journal entries
4. Deferred revenue
5. Accrued revenue
6. Deferred expense
7. Accrued expense
8. Closing process

a. The final step in the accounting cycle whereby all revenue, expense, and dividend account balances are transferred to the Retained Earnings account.

b. Cash is received before revenue is earned.

c. Entries made into the general journal at the end of an accounting period that record previously unrecorded revenues or expenses.

d. Expense is incurred before cash is paid.

e. Revenues are recorded only when cash is received, and expenses are recorded only when cash is paid.

f. Cash is paid before expense is incurred.

g. Revenues are recorded only when they are earned, and expenses are recorded only when they are incurred.

h. Revenue is earned before cash is received.

Required

Match each accounting term with the appropriate definition.

PROBLEMS

26. Cash and Accrual Income LO1, 2

Olga Industries keeps records under the cash basis of accounting rather than the accrual basis. Olga's 2012 income statement and additional data from 2011 and 2012 are as follows:

Olga Industries Cash-Basis Income Statement For the Year Ending December 31, 2012	
Revenues	$54,000
Expenses	35,000
Net income	$19,000

Additional Information:

	12/31/11	12/31/12
Accrued Revenues	6,000	8,000
Deferred Revenues	13,000	4,500
Accrued Expenses	5,000	4,000
Deferred Expenses	10,000	9,500

All accrued revenues and expenses as of 12/31/11 were collected and paid, respectively, in 2012. All deferred revenues and expenses as of 12/31/11 were earned and used, respectively, in 2012.

Required

Convert revenues and expenses from the cash basis to the accrual basis and recalculate income. Briefly explain why each adjustment is made.

27. Adjusting Entries and Trial Balance LO2, 3

The unadjusted trial balance of Sweet Cheeks Facial Spa is shown as follows:

Sweet Cheeks Facial Spa Unadjusted Trial Balance September 30		
	Debit	**Credit**
Cash	$ 4,300	
Supplies	2,250	
Equipment	18,000	
Accumulated Depreciation		$ 2,400
Unearned Revenue		1,500
Notes Payable		10,000
Common Stock		10,000
Service Revenue		4,000
Advertising Expense	650	
Depreciation Expense	1,200	
Interest Expense	400	
Salaries Expense	600	
Dividends	500	
Totals	$27,900	$27,900

Additional Information:
1. On September 30, Sweet Cheeks completed a service for which it had received payment in August, $1,500.
2. On September 30, Sweet Cheeks determined that it had earned but not yet billed revenues of $500.
3. Monthly depreciation on Sweet Cheeks' equipment is $150.
4. The interest rate on the promissory note is 6%.
5. A count of the supplies revealed $500 of supplies remaining on September 30.
6. Assume the trial balance was last adjusted on August 31.

Required
Prepare all necessary adjusting entries for the month of September and prepare an adjusted trial balance as of September 30.

28. Adjusting Entries and Closing Entries
LO2, 3, 4
The unadjusted and adjusted trial balances of HD Rizzle, Inc. are as follows:

HD Rizzle, Inc.
Trial Balance
December 31

	Unadjusted Debit	Unadjusted Credit	Adjusted Debit	Adjusted Credit
Cash	$ 3,500		$ 3,500	
Accounts Receivable	8,250		10,750	
Prepaid Insurance	4,600		3,400	
Supplies	600		200	
Buildings	165,000		165,000	
Land	75,000		75,000	
Accumulated Depreciation		$ 15,000		$ 31,500
Accounts Payable		9,950		11,000
Salaries Payable		0		1,800
Unearned Revenue		12,050		10,050
Notes Payable		50,000		50,000
Common Stock		100,000		100,000
Retained Earnings		34,600		34,600
Service Revenue		48,550		53,050
Advertising Expense	5,600		5,600	
Depreciation Expense			16,500	
Insurance Expense			1,200	
Salaries Expense	7,600		9,400	
Supplies Expense			400	
Utilities Expense			1,050	
Totals	$270,150	$270,150	$292,000	$292,000

Required
a. Compare the two trial balances and recreate all adjusting journal entries that were made at December 31.
b. What is the net effect of the adjusting journal entries on net income?

29. Adjusting Entries and Financial Statements   LO2, 3
The June 30 unadjusted trial balance of Prime Realty appears as follows:

Prime Realty
Unadjusted Trial Balance
June 30

	Debit	Credit
Cash	$ 6,900	
Accounts Receivable	4,500	
Prepaid Rent	6,300	
Supplies	2,250	
Equipment	18,000	
Accumulated Depreciation		$ 900
Unearned Revenue		1,500
Notes Payable		10,000
Common Stock		8,000
Retained Earnings, Jan. 1		12,200
Service Revenue		11,200
Advertising Expense	650	
Depreciation Expense	900	
Interest Expense	150	
Rent Expense	2,100	
Salaries Expense	1,700	
Dividends	350	
Totals	$43,800	$43,800

Additional Information:
1. Rent expires at a rate of $700 per month.
2. Monthly depreciation on equipment is $300.
3. Interest on the 6% promissory note is paid quarterly on April 1, July 1, October 1, and January 1.
4. Performed services for which payment was received in April, $800.
5. Received utility bill to be paid next month, $500.
6. Services to customers earned during June but unrecorded at June 30, $2,500.
7. Supplies on hand totaled $1,500 at June 30.
8. Owed employees for salaries for the last week of June to be paid in July, $800.
9. Prime Realty prepares adjusting entries each quarter. Adjustments were last made on March 31.

Required
a. Prepare all adjusting journal entries for the quarter ending June 30.
b. Post journal entries to T-accounts using totals on the unadjusted trial balance as the opening balances.
c. Prepare an adjusted trial balance as of June 30.
d. Prepare an income statement and a statement of retained earnings for the six months ending June 30.
e. Prepare a classified balance sheet as of June 30.

30. Adjusting Entries and Closing Entries
LO2, 3, 4

The unadjusted and adjusted trial balances of Wang, Inc. are shown as follows:

	Wang, Inc. **Trial Balance** **December 31**			
	Unadjusted Trial Balance		**Adjusted Trial Balance**	
	Debit	**Credit**	**Debit**	**Credit**
Cash	$ 8,000		$ 8,000	
Accounts Receivable	12,250		16,250	
Prepaid Insurance	6,400		5,600	
Supplies	2,400		1,200	
Buildings	250,000		250,000	
Land	75,000		75,000	
Accumulated Depreciation		$ 25,000		$ 50,000
Salaries Payable				2,000
Unearned Revenue		9,500		7,000
Utilities Payable		15,450		20,950
Notes Payable		75,000		75,000
Common Stock		150,000		150,000
Retained Earnings		22,100		22,100
Service Revenue		75,500		82,000
Advertising Expense	8,500		8,500	
Depreciation Expense			25,000	
Insurance Expense			800	
Salaries Expense	8,000		10,000	
Supplies Expense			1,200	
Utilities Expense			5,500	
Dividends	2,000		2,000	
Totals	$372,550	$372,550	$409,050	$409,050

Required
a. Compare the unadjusted trial balance and the adjusted trial balance and recreate all adjusting journal entries that were made at December 31.
b. Prepare the income statement and a statement of retained earnings for the year. Also prepare a classified balance sheet at December 31.
c. Prepare necessary closing entries.

31. The Accounting Cycle LO2, 3, 4, 5

Ruberstein, Inc. was founded on April 1 and entered into the following transactions:

Apr. 1 Issued common stock to shareholders in exchange for cash, $20,000.
1 Purchased a delivery van (equipment), $13,000.
1 Purchased a one-year insurance policy to be consumed evenly over the next 12 months, $4,800.
1 Took out a loan from First Bank, $20,000.
6 Hired two new employees on salary of $1,000 a month each.
6 Received prepayment for a contracted job to be performed in May, $4,500.
7 Purchased office supplies on credit, $1,200.
8 Billed customers for services provided, $7,500.
12 Paid to have an ad placed on a billboard during April, $1,300.
18 Billed customers for services provided, $8,600.
24 Paid dividends to stockholders, $1,000.
30 Received utility bills for the month of April to be paid next month, $740.
30 Prepaid the next six months of rent starting with May, $3,600.

Additional Information:
1. April depreciation for the delivery van is $217.
2. Interest on the loan from the bank is paid annually at a rate of 6%.
3. An inventory count of office supplies at April 30 showed $500 of supplies on hand.
4. Prepaid insurance has expired.
5. Employees' salaries earned during April but to be paid in May, $2,000.

Required
a. Journalize the transactions for the month of April.
b. Post the journal entries to the general ledger using T-accounts.
c. Prepare a trial balance as of April 30.
d. Prepare all necessary adjusting journal entries and post the entries to the appropriate T-accounts.
e. Prepare an adjusted trial balance as of April 30.
f. Prepare an income statement and a statement of retained earnings for the month of April. Also prepare a classified balance sheet as of April 30.
g. Prepare all closing entries for the temporary accounts and post the entries to the appropriate T-accounts.
h. Prepare a post-closing trial balance as of April 30.

32. Locate and Understand Accounting Information

Access the latest annual report for Starbucks Corporation by clicking on the *Investor Relations* and *Annual Reports* links at www.starbucks.com.

Required

Review the first note to the financial statements and answer the following questions.

a. When does Starbucks recognize revenue from stored value cards? Where does it report outstanding customer balances? Is this an example of a deferred or accrued revenue?

b. When does Starbucks recognize retail revenues?

c. When does Starbucks recognize revenues from product sales such as coffee, tea, and related products?

d. Does Starbucks recognize all advertising costs as they are incurred? If not, does it treat those advertising costs as a deferred or accrued expense?

33. Communication Activity

You are the chief financial officer of a small corporation, and the date is December 31. You recently asked the new accountant to prepare the initial draft of the financial statements for your review. However, when you receive the draft, you quickly notice that no adjusting journal entries were made.

Required

Write a short memo explaining the importance of adjusting entries and the potential misstatements that can result from their exclusion.

34. Ethics and Adjusting Entries

Traction Tires is a large producer of automobile tires. During the current year, Traction was on pace to have record revenues and profits. However, towards the end of the current year, a string of accidents linked to Traction's tires resulted in numerous lawsuits and a product recall of Traction's Premiere line. Traction's President, Hal Marker, recently approached chief accountant Ronnie Williams about the inevitable losses next year and asked Ronnie to defer all possible revenue until next year and to accrue all possible expenses to the current year. "We have so much revenue to spare this year," Hal said, "but next year, we will need all the help we can get."

Required

a. What ethical issues are involved in this scenario?

b. If Hal gets his way, what accounting principles would be violated?

c. Some may say that Hal is simply managing his earnings like he manages all other aspects of his business. What is your opinion of "earnings management"?

35. Ethics and Adjusting Entries

You are a service associate with a major company. When you sell a service, the customer pays cash and you provide the service. At the end of each year, you are required to estimate how much of each outstanding service contract has been earned. At year-end, you have $100,000 of outstanding contracts. You estimate that you have earned somewhere between 40% and 60% of those contracts.

Required

Under the following independent conditions, identify the amount of outstanding contracts that you would report earned. Explain why you would report those amounts.

a. Your compensation is based on performance, and you are $80,000 short of your quota before your estimate.

b. Your compensation is based on performance, and you are $50,000 short of your quota before your estimate.

c. Your compensation is based on your group's performance, and while you have met your quota before your estimate, the group needs $60,000 to meet the group quota.

REVIEW!

ACCT2 puts a multitude of study aids at your fingertips. After reading the chapters, check out these resources for further help:

- **Review Cards,** found in the back of your book, include all learning objectives, key terms and definitions, and visual summaries for each chapter.

- **Online Printable Flash Cards** give you additional ways to check your comprehension of key accounting concepts.

- **Animations**, found in the **CengageNOW™** Personalized Study Plan, offer dynamic, visual examples based around key concepts. One example is the "Make-or-Buy Decision" based on Birdie Maker Golf Company in Chapter 7.

- **Interactive games** include Beat the Clock, a timed quiz for each chapter, and Quiz Bowl—a Jeopardy-style game that helps test your knowledge and understanding of the critical concepts within the chapter.

Find these and other great resources online as part of **CengageNOW™** for **ACCT2**. Sign on at www.cengagebrain.com.

reviewcard

Learning Objectives

LO1 Describe the four assumptions made when communicating accounting information.

LO2 Describe the purpose and structure of an income statement and the terms and principles used to create it.

LO3 Describe the purpose and structure of a balance sheet and the terms and principles used to create it.

LO4 Describe the purpose and structure of a statement of retained earnings and how it links the income statement and the balance sheet.

LO5 Describe the purpose and structure of a statement of cash flows and the terms and principles used to create it.

LO6 Describe the qualitative characteristics that make accounting information useful.

LO7 Describe the conceptual framework of accounting.

Key Concepts

When communicating accounting information, accountants assume that the activities of a company can be separated from those of the owners, that economic information can be effectively communicated in dollars over short periods of time, and that the business will continue into the foreseeable future.

An income statement reports a company's revenues and expenses over a period of time. A revenue is an inflow of resources from providing services, while an expense is an outflow of resources from providing services. Revenues are recorded when they are earned (revenue recognition principle), and expenses are recorded when they are incurred (matching principle). When revenues exceed expenses, a company generates net income.

A balance sheet reports a company's assets, liabilities, and equity accounts at a point in time. An asset is a resource of a business. A liability is an obligation of a business. Equity is the difference between assets and liabilities. Assets are recorded at their costs (cost principle). Assets are always equal to liabilities plus equity.

A statement of retained earnings reports the change in a company's retained earnings balance over a period of time. The statement links the income statement and the balance sheet. Net income reported on the income statement is used to calculate the retained earnings balance reported on the balance sheet.

A statement of cash flows reports a company's sources and uses of cash over a period of time. Cash inflows and outflows are categorized into operating, investing, or financing activities.

Accounting information is useful only if it possesses several qualitative characteristics. It should be understandable, relevant, reliable, easily comparable, and consistent across time.

The conceptual framework is the collection of concepts that guide the practice of accounting. It includes the principles followed, the assumptions made, and the terms and statements used to communicate accounting information. It also includes the qualitative characteristics that make the information useful.

Key Definitions

Accounting The process of identifying, measuring, and communicating economic information to permit informed judgments and decisions. (p. 2)

Asset An economic resource that is objectively measurable, results from a prior transaction, and will provide future economic benefit. (p. 7)

Balance sheet A financial statement that reports a company's assets, liabilities, and equity at a specific point in time. (p. 8)

Comparability The ability to use accounting information to compare or contrast the financial activities of different companies. (p. 12)

Conceptual framework of accounting The collection of concepts that guide the manner in which accounting is practiced. (p. 14)

Conservatism The manner in which accountants deal with uncertainty regarding economic situations. (p. 14)

Consistency The ability to use accounting information to compare or contrast the financial activities of the same entity over time. (p. 13)

Contributed capital The resources that investors contribute to a business in exchange for ownership interest. (p. 7)

Cost principle The principle that assets should be recorded and reported at the cost paid to acquire them. (p. 7)

Dividends Profits that are distributed to owners. (p. 7)

Economic entity assumption Accountants assume that the financial activities of a business can be separated from the financial activities of the business's owner(s). (p. 3)

Equity The difference between a company's assets and liabilities, representing the share of assets that is claimed by the company's owners. (p. 7)

Expense A decrease in resources resulting from the sale of goods or provision of services. (p. 5)

Going concern assumption Accountants assume that a company will continue to operate into the foreseeable future. (p. 4)

Income statement A financial statement that reports a company's revenues and expenses over a specific period of time. (p. 6)

Liability An obligation of a business that results from a past transaction and will require the sacrifice of economic resources at some future date. (p. 7)

Matching principle The principle that expenses should be recorded in the period resources are used to generate revenues. (p. 5)

Materiality The threshold at which a financial item begins to affect decision making. (p. 13)

Monetary unit assumption Accountants assume that the dollar is the most effective means to communicate economic activity. (p. 4)

Relevance The capacity of accounting information to make a difference in decisions. (p. 12)

Reliability The extent to which accounting information can be depended upon to represent what it purports to represent, both in description and in number. (p. 12)

Retained earnings Profits that are retained in the business. (p. 7)

Revenue An increase in resources resulting from the sale of goods or the provision of services. (p. 5)

Revenue recognition principle The principle that a revenue should be recorded when a resource has been earned. (p. 5)

Statement of cash flows A financial statement that reports a company's sources and uses of cash over a specific period of time. (p. 10)

Statement of retained earnings A financial statement that reports the change in a company's retained earnings over a specific period of time. (p. 8)

Time period assumption Accountants assume that economic information can be meaningfully captured and communicated over short periods of time. (p. 4)

Understandability The ability of accounting information to "be comprehensible to those who have a reasonable understanding of business...and are willing to study the information with reasonable diligence." (p. 11)

Demonstration Problem

On August 1, Sarah begins a tutoring service that she will operate for four months. With $40 borrowed from a friend and $20 of her own money, she rents an accounting textbook for $40 a month and buys $8 of school supplies. Sarah promises to pay her friend $1 at the end of each month and to pay back the full $40 at the end of December.

Sarah charges $20 per tutoring session. During August, she conducted ten sessions and bought $10 of additional school supplies. At the end of the month, Sarah has not collected on four of the ten sessions, and she has $5 of school supplies left over. Prepare Sarah's income statement and statement of retained earnings for the month ending August 31 and her balance sheet on August 31.

Key Formulas

Income Statement	Revenues − Expenses = Net Income or Net Loss
Balance Sheet	Assets = Liabilities + Equity
Statement of Retained Earnings	Retained Earnings, Beginning Balance +/− Net Income/Loss − Dividends = Retained Earnings, Ending Balance
Statement of Cash Flows	Cash Flows Provided (Used) by Operating Activities +/− Cash Flows Provided (Used) by Investing Activities +/− Cash Flows Provided (Used) by Financing Activities = Net Increase (Decrease) in Cash

Demonstration Problem Solution

Sarah's Tutoring Service
Income Statement
For the Month Ending August 31

Revenues:		$200
Expenses:		
Rent	$ 40	
Supplies	13	
Interest	1	
Total expenses		54
Net income		$146

Sarah's Tutoring Service
Statement of Retained Earnings
For the Month Ending August 31

Retained earnings, August 1	$ 0
Add: Net income	146
Less: Dividends	0
Retained earnings, August 31	$146

Sarah's Tutoring Service
Balance Sheet
August 31

Cash	$121	
Accounts receivable	80	
Supplies	5	
Total assets		$206
Note payable	$ 40	
Total liabilities		$ 40
Contributed capital	$20	
Retained earnings	146	
Total equity		166
Total liabilities and equity		$206

reviewcard

Learning Objectives	Key Concepts	Key Definitions
LO1 Describe the three major forms of business.	The three major forms of business are sole proprietorship, partnership, and corporation. A sole proprietorship is owned by one person. A partnership is owned by multiple partners. A corporation is established in a state and is owned by investors who purchase the corporation's stock. Corporations whose stock is available to the public at large are called public corporations.	**American Institute of Certified Public Accountants** The professional organization of certified public accountants whose board establishes rules that are often more technical and more specific to certain industries. (p. 27)
		Classified balance sheet A type of balance sheet that groups together accounts of similar nature and reports them in a few major classifications. (p. 28)
LO2 Define generally accepted accounting principles and their origins.	Generally accepted accounting principles are the accounting standards, rules, principles, and procedures that comprise authoritative practice for financial accounting. They have been developed over time by several regulatory bodies, including the Securities and Exchange Commission, the Financial Accounting Standards Board, and the American Institute of Certified Public Accountants.	**Common-size financial statement** A statement in which all accounts have been standardized by the overall size of the company. (p. 35)
		Contributed capital The amount of equity a company generates through the sale of stock to investors. (p. 30)
		Corporation A separate legal entity that is established by filing articles of incorporation in a state. (p. 26)
		Cost of sales The cost of the inventory sold during a period. (p. 31)
LO3 Describe the main classifications of assets, liabilities, and equity in a classified balance sheet.	A classified balance sheet summarizes an entity's financial position at a point in time by grouping similar asset, liability, and equity accounts together and reporting them in several major classifications. Assets are classified into current assets, long-term investments, fixed assets, intangible assets, and other assets. Liabilities are classified into current liabilities and long-term liabilities. Equity is classified into contributed capital and retained earnings.	**Current asset** Any asset that is reasonably expected to be converted to cash or consumed within one year of the balance sheet date. (p. 28)
		Current liability An obligation that is reasonably expected to be satisfied within one year. (p. 30)
		Financial Accounting Standards Board The standard-setting body whose mission is "to establish and improve standards of financial accounting and reporting for the guidance and education of the public, including issuers, auditors, and users of financial information." (p. 27)
LO4 Describe the main subtotals of income on a multi-step income statement.	A multi-step income statement calculates income in multiple steps by grouping certain revenues and expenses together and calculating several subtotals of income. These subtotals include gross profit, operating profit, income before taxes, and net income.	**Fixed assets** The tangible resources that are used in a company's operations for more than one year and are not intended for resale. (p. 28)
		Generally accepted accounting principles The accounting standards, rules, principles, and procedures that comprise authoritative practice for financial accounting. (p. 26)

Learning Objectives		Key Concepts	Key Definitions (continued)
LO5	Analyze the balance sheet and the income statement using horizontal and vertical analyses.	Horizontal analysis calculates the change in an account balance from one period to the next and expresses that change in both absolute and percentage terms. Because a horizontal analysis shows the growth or decline in each account, it is useful for identifying trends. Vertical analysis states each account balance as a percentage of some base account—sales on the income statement and total assets on the balance sheet. Because a vertical analysis standardizes each account by a measure of company size, it is useful in comparing different companies. The product of a vertical analysis is called a common-size statement.	**Gross profit** The profit that a company generates when considering only the sales price and the cost of the product sold. (p. 31) **Horizontal analysis** A method of analyzing a company's account balances over time by calculating absolute and percentage changes in each account. (p. 33) **Income before taxes** The profit that a company generates when considering all revenues and expenses except for income taxes. (p. 32) **Independent auditor's report** A report, prepared by a certified public accountant for the public shareholder, stating an opinion on whether the financial statements present fairly, in conformity with GAAP, the company's financial condition and results of operations and cash flows. (p. 40)
LO6	Describe the purpose of a statement of stockholders' equity.	The statement of stockholders' equity shows the changes in all equity accounts, including retained earnings and contributed capital, over a period of time.	**Intangible asset** A resource that is used in operation for more than one year, is not intended for resale, and has no physical substance. (p. 29) **International Accounting Standards Board** A board, similar to the FASB, whose mission is to develop a single set of high-quality standards requiring transparent and comparable information. (p. 27)
LO7	Describe the types of information usually disclosed along with financial statements.	In addition to its financial statements, a company will include the following in its annual report distributed to stockholders: notes to the financial statements, the auditor's report, and management's discussion and analysis.	**International Financial Reporting Standards** Standards issued by the International Accounting Standards Board. (p. 27) **Long-term investments** The investments in the common stock or debt of another entity that will not be sold within a year. (p. 28) **Long-term liability** An obligation that is not expected to be satisfied within one year. (p. 30) **Management's Discussion and Analysis** A discussion and analysis of the financial activities of the company by the company's management. (p. 41) **Multi-step income statement** Calculates income by grouping certain revenues and expenses together and calculating several subtotals of income. (p. 30) **Net income** The final income measure after the provision for income taxes is subtracted from income before taxes. (p. 33) **Notes to the financial statements** The additional textual and numerical information immediately following the financial statements. (p. 40)

Operating expenses Recurring expenses that a company incurs during normal operations. (p. 31)

Operating profit The profit that a company generates when considering both the cost of the inventory and the normal expenses incurred to operate the business. (p. 32)

Other assets Resources that do not fit well into one of the other asset classifications or are small enough that they do not warrant separate reporting. (p. 29)

Other revenue and expenses Revenues and expenses generated outside of normal operations. (p. 32)

Partnership A business that is formed when two or more proprietors join together to own a business. (p. 25)

Provision for income taxes The amount of income tax expense for a given period. (p. 32)

Public corporation A separate legal entity in which ownership is available to the public at large. (p. 26)

Retained earnings The amount of equity a company generates by being profitable and retaining those profits in the business. (p. 30)

Sales The resources that a company generates during a period from selling its inventory. (p. 31)

Securities and Exchange Commission The federal agency charged to protect investors and maintain the integrity of securities markets. (p. 26)

Single-step income statement Calculates total revenues and total expenses and then determines net income in one step by subtracting total expenses from total revenues. (p. 30)

Sole proprietorship A business owned by one person. (p. 24)

Statement of stockholders' equity A financial statement that shows how and why each equity account in the company's balance sheet changed from one year to the next. (p. 38)

Vertical analysis A method of comparing a company's account balances within one year by dividing each account balance by a base amount to yield a percentage. (p. 35)

Key Formulas

Classified Balance Sheet

Assets
   Current assets
   Long-term investments
   Fixed assets
   Intangible assets
   Other assets
      Total assets

Liabilities and Equity
   Current liabilities
   Long-term liabilities
      Total liabilities
   Contributed capital
   Retained earnings
      Total equity
      Total liabilities and equity

Multi-Step Income Statement

Net sales or revenues
$-$ Cost of goods sold
Gross profit
$-$ Operating expenses
Operating profit
$+/-$ Other revenues and expenses
Income before taxes
$-$ Income tax expense
Net income

Horizontal Analysis

Dollar change in account balance $=$ Current-year balance $-$ Prior-year balance

$$\text{Percentage change in account balance} = \frac{\text{Dollar change}}{\text{Prior-year balance}}$$

Vertical Analysis

	For the Balance Sheet	For the Income Statement
Percentage	$\dfrac{\text{Account balance}}{\text{Total Assets}}$	$\dfrac{\text{Account balance}}{\text{Net Sales or Revenue}}$

Demonstration Problem

The following items were taken from the financial statements of Columbia Sportswear Company. Use the items to prepare a multi-step income statement for the year ending December 31 and a classified balance sheet at December 31. For each statement, prepare a vertical analysis. All dollar amounts are in thousands of dollars.

Accounts payable	$ 62,432
Accounts receivable	206,024
Accrued liabilities	43,789
Cash and cash equivalents	264,585
Common stock	205,465
Cost of sales	511,101
Current portion of long-term debt	4,596
Deferred tax asset, current	17,442
Deferred tax liability, long-term	7,716
Goodwill	12,157
Income tax expense	70,548
Income taxes payable	8,069
Intangibles and other assets	24,475
Interest expense	1,627
Interest revenue	2,107
Inventories	126,808
Long-term debt	16,335
Net sales	951,786
Prepaid expenses and other current assets	6,028
Property, plant, and equipment, net	126,247
Retained earnings	435,364
Selling, general and administrative expenses	250,496

Demonstration Problem Solution

Columbia Sportswear Company
Income Statement
For the Year Ending December 31

Net sales	$951,786	100.0%
Cost of sales	511,101	53.7%
Gross profit	$440,685	46.3%
Selling, general, and administrative expenses	250,496	26.3%
Operating profit	$190,189	20.0%
Other revenues and expenses:		
Interest revenue	2,107	0.2%
Interest expense	(1,627)	0.2%
Income before income tax	$190,669	20.0%
Income tax expense	70,548	7.4%
Net income	$120,121	12.6%

Columbia Sportswear Company
Balance Sheet
December 31

Assets

Current assets:		
Cash and cash equivalents	$264,585	33.8%
Accounts receivable, net	206,024	26.3%
Inventories, net	126,808	16.2%
Deferred tax asset	17,442	2.2%
Prepaid expenses and other current assets	6,028	0.8%
Total current assets	$620,887	79.2%
Property, plant, and equipment, net	126,247	16.1%
Intangibles and other assets	24,475	3.1%
Goodwill	12,157	1.6%
Total assets	$783,766	100.0%

Liabilities and Shareholders' Equity

Current liabilities:		
Accounts payable	$ 62,432	8.0%
Accrued liabilities	43,789	5.6%
Income taxes payable	8,069	1.0%
Current portion of long-term debt	4,596	0.6%
Total current liabilities	$118,886	15.2%
Long-term debt	16,335	2.1%
Deferred tax liability	7,716	1.0%
Total liabilities	$142,937	18.2%
Shareholders' equity:		
Common stock	$205,465	26.2%
Retained earnings	435,364	55.6%
Total shareholders' equity	$640,829	81.8%
Total liabilities and shareholders' equity	$783,766	100.0%

review card CHAPTER 3
Recording Accounting Transactions

Learning Objectives	Key Concepts
LO1 Describe the purpose of an accounting information system.	The purpose of an accounting information system is to identify economic events to be recorded, to measure and record those events, and to process the resulting information so that financial statements can be prepared.
LO2 Analyze the effect of accounting transactions on the accounting equation.	All accounting transactions must affect at least two accounts so that the fundamental accounting equation remains in balance. This is known as the dual nature of accounting.
LO3 Understand how T-accounts and debits and credits are used in a double-entry accounting system.	The double entry accounting system uses debits and credits to record accounting transactions. For every transaction, total debit entries must equal total credit entries. Asset, expense, and dividend accounts have debit balances, so they are increased with debit entries and decreased with credit entries. Liability, equity, and revenue accounts have credit balances, so they are increased with credit entries and decreased with debit entries.
LO4 Describe the purpose of the journal, ledger, and trial balance.	Accounting transactions are recorded in the general journal, which captures information chronologically. Information in the general journal is posted to the general ledger, which summarizes information by account. Balances from the general ledger are listed on a trial balance, which contains all account balances and proves that debit balances equal credit balances.
LO5 Record and post accounting transactions and prepare a trial balance and financial statements.	After determining which accounts are affected by an accounting transaction, the transaction is recorded and posted. Once all transactions are posted, a trial balance is prepared, from which financial statements are prepared.

Key Definitions

Account An accounting record that accumulates the activity of a specific item and yields the item's balance. (p. 55)

Accounting information system The system that identifies, records, summarizes, and communicates the various transactions of a company. (p. 54)

Accounting transaction Any economic event that affects a company's assets, liabilities, or equity at the time of the event. (p. 54)

Chart of accounts The list of accounts that a company uses to capture its business activities. (p. 55)

Credit The right side of an account. (p. 61)

Debit The left side of an account. (p. 61)

Dual nature of accounting Every accounting transaction affects at least two accounts. (p. 56)

Journal A chronological record of transactions. (p. 63)

Ledger A collection of accounts and their balances. (p. 64)

Trial balance A listing of accounts and their balances at a specific point in time. (p. 65)

Key Exhibit

Debit and Credit Rules	Type of Account	Normal Balance	Increase with a	Decrease with a
	Asset	Debit	Debit	Credit
	Liability	Credit	Credit	Debit
	Equity	Credit	Credit	Debit
	Revenue	Credit	Credit	Debit
	Expense	Debit	Debit	Credit
	Dividend	Debit	Debit	Credit

Demonstration Problem

The following transactions occurred during the first month of operations for Auburn Windows, Inc. Prepare all necessary journal entries, post the information to the ledger, and prepare a trial balance at March 31.

Mar. 1 Issued 15,000 shares of common stock for $20,000 cash.	Mar. 20 Paid $2,300 cash for employee salaries.
1 Purchase equipment for $7,200 cash.	21 Collected $4,000 cash from customers billed on March 12.
3 Purchased cleaning supplies for $5,000 cash.	25 Billed customers $5,200 for cleaning services.
5 Paid $2,400 cash on a one-year insurance policy effective March 1.	31 For the month, paid for and used $600 of fuel.
12 Billed customers $4,800 for cleaning services.	31 Declared and paid $200 cash dividend.

Demonstration Problem Solution

Mar. 1	Cash	20,000	
	Common Stock		20,000
	(Initial investment by owner)		
Mar. 1	Equipment	7,200	
	Cash		7,200
	(Purchase of equipment)		
Mar. 3	Supplies	5,000	
	Cash		5,000
	(Purchase of supplies)		
Mar. 5	Prepaid Insurance	2,400	
	Cash		2,400
	(Purchase of insurance policy)		
Mar. 12	Accounts Receivable	4,800	
	Service Revenue		4,800
	(Provide services on account)		
Mar. 20	Salaries Expense	2,300	
	Cash		2,300
	(Pay employees)		
Mar. 21	Cash	4,000	
	Accounts Receivable		4,000
	(Collect receivables from customers)		
Mar. 25	Accounts Receivable	5,200	
	Service Revenue		5,200
	(Provide services on account)		
Mar. 31	Fuel Expense	600	
	Cash		600
	(Pay for fuel consumed)		
Mar. 31	Dividends	200	
	Cash		200
	(Pay for dividends)		

Cash

20,000	7,200
4,000	5,000
	2,400
	2,300
	600
	200
6,300	

Accounts Receivable

4,800	4,000
5,200	
6,000	

Equipment

7,200	
7,200	

Prepaid Insurance

2,400	
2,400	

Supplies

5,000	
5,000	

Common Stock

	20,000
	20,000

Service Revenue

	4,800
	5,200
	10,000

Salaries Expense

2,300	
2,300	

Fuel Expense

600	
600	

Dividends

200	
200	

Trial Balance
March 31

Cash	$ 6,300	
Accounts Receivable	6,000	
Prepaid Insurance	2,400	
Supplies	5,000	
Equipment	7,200	
Common Stock		$20,000
Service Revenue		10,000
Fuel Expense	600	
Salaries Expense	2,300	
Dividends	200	
Totals	$30,000	$30,000

review card

Learning Objectives	Key Concepts	Key Definitions
LO1 Describe how income is measured and reported under the accrual and cash bases of accounting.	The cash basis records revenues when cash is received and expenses when cash is paid. The accrual basis records revenues when they are earned and expenses when they are incurred. Although both bases result in the same income over the long term, the accrual basis best reflects income over short periods of time, so it is required by GAAP.	**Accounting cycle** The sequence of steps in which an accounting information system captures, processes, and reports a company's accounting transactions during a period. (p. 96)
LO2 Identify the four major circumstances in which adjusting journal entries are necessary.	Adjusting journal entries are necessary to record revenues that have been earned and expenses that have been incurred. The four scenarios in which adjusting entries arise are (1) a deferred revenue—revenue is earned after cash is received, (2) an accrued revenue—revenue is earned before cash is received, (3) a deferred expense—an expense is incurred after cash is paid, and (4) an accrued expense—an expense is incurred before cash is paid.	**Accrual basis of accounting** Records revenues when they are earned and records expenses when they are incurred. (p. 80) **Adjusting journal entries** Entries made in the general journal to record revenues that have been earned but not recorded and expenses that have been incurred but not recorded. (p. 83) **Cash basis of accounting** Records revenues when cash is received and records expenses when cash is paid. (p. 80)
LO3 Record and post adjusting journal entries, and prepare an adjusted trial balance and financial statements.	At the end of an accounting period, adjusting journal entries are prepared to properly record revenues and expenses. Once these entries are posted to the ledger, an adjusted trial balance is prepared, from which financial statements are created.	**Closing entries** Entries made in the journal and posted to the ledger that eliminate the balances in all temporary accounts and transfer those balances to the Retained Earnings account. (p. 95) **Closing process** The process of transferring all revenue, expense, and dividend account balances to the Retained Earnings account. (p. 94)
LO4 Describe the purpose of the closing process and prepare closing entries.	The purpose of the closing process is to (1) update the Retained Earnings account to reflect all revenues, expenses, and dividends from the period and (2) prepare all revenue, expense, and dividend accounts for the next period by setting their balances to zero. The closing process is accomplished through "closing entries" recorded in the journal after financial statements are prepared.	**Temporary accounts** Accounts that accumulate balances only for the current period. (p. 94)
LO5 Describe the steps of the accounting cycle.	The steps in the accounting cycle are as follows: (1) journalize and post transactions, (2) prepare a trial balance, (3) journalize and post adjusting entries, (4) prepare an adjusted trial balance, (5) prepare financial statements, (6) journalize and post closing entries, (7) prepare a post-closing trial balance.	

Demonstration Problem

Given the following March 31 Unadjusted Trial Balance and the additional information at the end of the month, prepare all necessary adjusting journal entries and prepare an Adjusted Trial Balance as of March 31.

Unadjusted Trial Balance
March 31

	Debit	Credit
Cash	$ 6,300	
Accounts Receivable	6,000	
Equipment	7,200	
Prepaid Insurance	2,400	
Supplies	5,000	
Common Stock		$20,000
Service Revenue		10,000
Fuel Expense	600	
Salaries Expense	2,300	
Dividends	200	
Totals	$30,000	$30,000

Additional Information:

1. Depreciation on equipment is $150 monthly.

2. One-twelfth of the insurance expired during the month.

3. An inventory count shows $1,000 of cleaning supplies on hand at March 31.

4. Earned but unpaid employee salaries were $250 on March 31.

Demonstration Problem Solution

Adjusting Journal Entries on March 31

1	Depreciation Expense	150	
	Accumulated Depreciation		150
	(To record depreciation on the equipment: $150 is given)		
2	Insurance Expense	200	
	Prepaid Insurance		200
	(To record expired insurance: $2,400 × 1/12)		
3	Supplies Expense	4,000	
	Supplies		4,000
	(To record supplies used: $5,000 − $1,000)		
4	Salaries Expense	250	
	Salaries Payable		250
	(To record salaries earned but not paid: $250 is given)		

Adjusted Trial Balance
March 31

	Debit	Credit
Cash	$ 6,300	
Accounts Receivable	6,000	
Prepaid Insurance	2,200	
Supplies	1,000	
Equipment	7,200	
Accumulated Depreciation		$ 150
Salaries Payable		250
Common Stock		20,000
Service Revenue		10,000
Depreciation Expense	150	
Fuel Expense	600	
Insurance Expense	200	
Salaries Expense	2,550	
Supplies Expense	4,000	
Dividends	200	
Totals	$30,400	$30,400

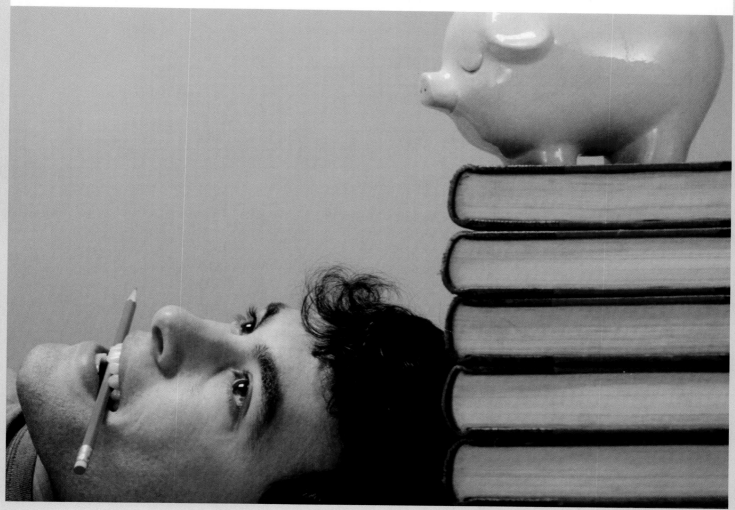

Introduction to
Managerial Accounting

Introduction

Learning Objectives

After studying the material in this chapter, you should be able to:

LO1 Describe the contemporary view of accounting information systems and describe and give examples of financial and nonfinancial accounting information.

LO2 Compare and contrast managerial accounting with financial accounting and distinguish between the information needs of external and internal users.

LO3 Recognize the role of relevant factors in decision making.

LO4 Understand sources of ethical issues in business and the importance of maintaining an ethical business environment.

Business environments have changed dramatically in the past few decades. Companies of all sizes can now compete in a dynamic global marketplace through electronic commerce (e-business) and other emerging technologies. Downsizing, combined with a more mobile workforce, has placed a premium on retaining talented, knowledge-able employees. Customers demand specialized products and services and real-time information concerning product availability, order status, and delivery times. Suppliers need information on their buyers' sales and inventory levels in order to tailor their production schedules and delivery times to meet the buyers' demands. Shareholders demand greater value from their investments. Although these changes have provided opportunities for those companies which are able to adapt and take advantage of them, they have also resulted in challenges. Above all else, such changes require more effective management of knowledge within an organization. In today's business environment, knowledge is power and must be managed for a company to remain competitive.

Although the terms are sometimes used interchangeably, *knowledge* should not be confused with *data* or *information*. Companies generate literally tons of **data**—financial statements, customer lists, inventory records, and the number and type of products and services sold. However, translating those data into an accessible and usable form is another matter. When data are organized, processed, and summarized, they become **information**. When that information is shared and exploited so that it adds value to an organization, it becomes **knowledge**.

All types of organizations, from large multinational manufacturing companies like **Ford Motor Company** to small manufacturers of items like custom furniture, have a need for accounting information. Retailers, such as **Wal-Mart** and locally owned hardware stores; large service companies, such as **FedEx** and local certified public accounting (CPA) and law firms; and even nonprofit organizations, such as the **American Red Cross** and small local museums and homeless shelters, need accounting

Data Reports such as financial statements, customer lists, and inventory records.

Information Data that have been organized, processed, and summarized.

Knowledge Information that is shared and exploited so that it adds value to an organization.

Turning data into knowledge is a key to business success.

information. Accounting information is used by internal managers in their day-to-day decision making and also by external users, such as investors, creditors, donors, and even the Internal Revenue Service.

LO₁ **Accounting Information**

Accounting information is provided by a company's **accounting information system (AIS)**. Traditionally, the AIS was simply a transaction-processing system that captured financial data resulting from accounting

> **Accounting information system (AIS)** A transaction-processing system that captures financial data resulting from accounting transactions within a company.

Accounting information includes both financial and nonfinancial information used by decision makers.

transactions. For example, the AIS would document a transaction to purchase materials by recording a journal entry showing the date of purchase, an increase to raw materials inventory, and a corresponding increase to accounts payable or decrease in cash.

Under this view of AIS, accounting information was simply financial information (sales, net income, total assets, costs of products, and so on) expressed in terms of dollars or other monetary units (e.g., yen, euros, pesos). Other, nonfinancial information—such as the number of units of materials or inventory on hand, the number of budgeted labor hours to produce a product, the number of units necessary to break even, and the time it takes to manufacture a product—were likely collected and processed outside the traditional AIS. The use of multiple information systems within a company causes a number of problems. It is costly to support multiple systems. Perhaps more important, it is difficult to integrate information coming from various systems and to make decisions for a company with multiple sources of information. In addition, other useful transaction information—such as the quality of the material purchased, the timeliness of its delivery, or customer satisfaction with an order—may not be captured at all and therefore not evaluated by management.

Over the past few years, enterprise resource planning (ERP) systems have been developed in an attempt to address these shortcomings. ERP systems integrate the traditional AIS with other information systems to

capture both quantitative and qualitative data, to collect and organize those data into useful information, and to transform that information into knowledge that can be communicated throughout an organization.

Throughout our study of accounting information and its use in decision making, we emphasize the importance of considering both quantitative and qualitative information. In order to provide managers with the information they need to make effective business decisions, financial data must be linked to nonfinancial data, transformed into useful information and knowledge, and communicated throughout an organization (see Exhibit 1-1).

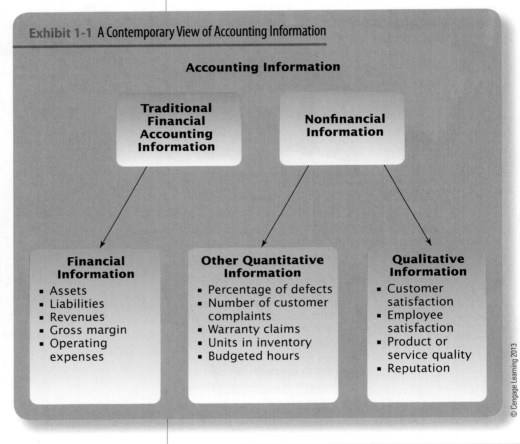

Exhibit 1-1 A Contemporary View of Accounting Information

Accounting Information

Traditional Financial Accounting Information

Nonfinancial Information

Financial Information
- Assets
- Liabilities
- Revenues
- Gross margin
- Operating expenses

Other Quantitative Information
- Percentage of defects
- Number of customer complaints
- Warranty claims
- Units in inventory
- Budgeted hours

Qualitative Information
- Customer satisfaction
- Employee satisfaction
- Product or service quality
- Reputation

© Cengage Learning 2013

LO2 A Comparison of Financial and Managerial Accounting

Financial accounting is the area of accounting concerned primarily with the preparation of general-use financial statements for creditors, investors, and other users outside the company (external users). By contrast, **managerial accounting** is concerned primarily with generating financial and nonfinancial information for use

© Dmitriy Shironosov/Shutterstock.com

Financial accounting information is focused on the information needs of external users, whereas managerial accounting information is focused on the information needs of internal users.

by managers in their decision-making roles within a company (internal users). This information typically is not shared with those outside the company. Although both financial accounting information and managerial accounting information are generated from the same AIS, the information is used in different ways by the various stakeholders of the company. A stakeholder is any person or group that either affects or is affected by the company's actions and decisions. As such, stakeholders include both external and internal users of information.

External Users

Stockholders, potential investors, creditors, government taxing agencies and regulators, suppliers, and customers are all **external users**. What type of information do external users need? Stockholders and potential investors want information to help them analyze the current and future profitability of an organization. Companies that have issued stock to the public (or those which plan to) provide this information in the form of annual reports, registration statements, prospectuses, and other reports issued to shareholders, potential investors, and the Securities and Exchange Commission (SEC). The information required in these reports and the accounting methods used to prepare them are governed by the Financial Accounting Standards Board (FASB) and the SEC. Although this information is primarily financial (e.g., sales and net income), it also may include nonfinancial information, such as units shipped and market share. In addition, it may include qualitative

information typically described in the "Management's Discussion and Analysis" section of annual reports.

What about smaller companies that are owned by just a few members of a family (called closely held companies) or nonprofit organizations, such as the Red Cross? External users of financial information, such as banks or potential donors to nonprofit organizations, still need accounting information to make the proper decision about lending or donating money. However, their needs may differ from those of stockholders and potential investors.

Creditors generally want to assess a company's overall financial health and may be particularly interested in a company's cash flow and ability to repay its loans. Potential contributors to nonprofit organizations may have a need for both financial information, such as how much of the Red Cross's budget is spent for charitable purposes, and nonfinancial information, such as how many women with children are served by the local homeless shelter.

Financial accounting The area of accounting concerned primarily with the preparation and use of financial statements by creditors, investors, and other users outside the company.

Managerial accounting The area of accounting concerned primarily with generating financial and nonfinancial information for use by managers in their decision-making roles within a company.

External users Stockholders, potential investors, creditors, government taxing agencies, regulators, suppliers, customers, and others outside the company.

Government agencies (federal, state, and local) have very specific information needs, including the measurement of income, payroll, and assets for purposes of assessing taxes. This accounting information is typically provided on income tax returns, payroll reports, and other forms designed specifically to meet the requirements of each agency.

Generally, accounting information provided to shareholders, creditors, and government agencies is characterized by a lack of flexibility (its content is often dictated by the user), the reporting of past events by using historical costs (financial statements for the previous three years), and an emphasis on the organization as a whole.

Suppliers and customers are also external users. However, their accounting information needs are likely to be very different from those of other external users and may be more clearly aligned with the needs of internal users. For example, suppliers of car parts to **General Motors** need detailed information on inventory levels of specific parts in order to know when to manufacture and ship parts. Bank customers may want to check on their account or loan balances before making a major purchase. Someone buying a new computer may want to check on the expected delivery date or whether a product is back ordered before placing an order. This type of information needs to be much more detailed and timely than that provided to most other external users.

Internal Users

Internal users of accounting information include individual employees as well as teams, departments, regions, and top management of an organization. For convenience,

---

Internal users Individual employees, teams, departments, regions, top management, and others inside the company—often referred to as managers.

Planning The development of both the short-term (operational) and long-term (strategic) objectives and goals of an organization and the identification of the resources needed to achieve them.

Operational planning The development of short-term objectives and goals (typically, those to be achieved in less than one year).

Strategic planning Addresses long-term questions of how an organization positions and distinguishes itself from competitors.

Operating activities The day-to-day operations of a business.

Controlling activities The motivation and monitoring of employees and the evaluation of people and other resources used in the operation of the organization.

---

these internal users are often referred to as managers. Managers are involved in three primary activities, commonly referred to as planning, operating, and controlling.

Planning Activities **Planning** involves the development of both the short-term (operational) and long-term (strategic) objectives and goals of an organization and the identification of the resources needed to achieve them. **Operational planning** involves the development of short-term objectives and goals (typically, those to be achieved in less than one year). Examples of operational planning for **Ben & Jerry's** include planning the raw material and production needs for each type of ice cream for the next four quarters and determining the company's short-term cash needs. Operational planning for a hospital would include budgeting for the number of physicians, nurses, and other staff needed for the upcoming month or determining the appropriate level of medical supplies to have in inventory. Operational planning also involves determining short-term performance goals and objectives, including meeting customer service expectations, sales quotas, and time budgets.

Strategic planning addresses long-term questions of how an organization positions and distinguishes itself with respect to competitors. For example, **Ben & Jerry's** strategy for producing high-quality ice cream is very different from that used by a company producing a store brand of lower priced ice cream. Long-term decisions about where to locate plants and other facilities, whether to invest in new, state-of-the-art production equipment, and whether to introduce new products or services and enter new markets are strategic planning decisions. Strategic planning also involves the determination of long-term performance and profitability measures, such as market share, sales growth, and stock price.

Operating Activities **Operating activities** encompass what managers must do to run the business on a day-to-day basis. Operating decisions for manufacturing companies include whether to accept special orders, how many parts or other raw materials to buy (or whether to make the parts internally), whether to sell a product or to process it further, whether to schedule overtime, which products to produce, and what prices to charge. Other operating decisions affecting all organizations include assigning tasks to individual employees, choosing whether to advertise (and predicting the corresponding impact of advertising on sales and profits), and choosing whether to hire full-time employees or to outsource.

Controlling Activities **Controlling activities** involve the motivation and monitoring of employees and the evaluation of people and other resources used in the organization's operations. The purpose of control is to make sure that the goals of the organization are being attained. It includes using incentives and other rewards to motivate employees to accomplish an organization's goals and using mechanisms to detect and correct deviations from those goals. Control often involves the comparison of actual outcomes (cost of products, sales, and so on) with desired outcomes (as stated in the organization's operating and strategic plans). Control decisions include questions of how to evaluate performance, what measures to use, and what types of incentives to implement. For example, a company that emphasizes high-quality products and excellent customer service may evaluate and reward production workers who have exceeded goals that are based on these virtues. (Such goals may involve specifying the percentage of allowable defective units or scrap, monitoring customer complaints, or myriad other factors.)

The Functional Areas of Management

Managers are found in all functional areas of an organization, including operations and production, marketing, finance, and human resources. Although managers rely on the same information provided to external users, they have other needs as well.

The Operations and Production Function The **operations and production function** produces the products or services that an organization sells to its customers. Operations and production managers are concerned with providing quality products and services that can compete in a global marketplace. They need accounting information to make planning decisions affecting how and when products are produced and services are provided. They need to know the costs of producing and storing products in order to decide how much inventory to keep on hand. They need to know the costs of labor when making decisions on whether to schedule overtime to complete a production run or when deciding how many physicians are needed in an emergency room. These decisions are also influenced by information provided by the marketing managers, including the expected customer reaction if products are not available when orders are placed or if doctors are not available when patients need them.

The Marketing Function The **marketing function** is involved with the process of developing, pricing, promoting, and distributing goods and services sold to customers. Marketing managers need to know how much a product costs in order to help establish a reasonable selling price. They need to know how a given advertising campaign and its resulting impact on the number of units sold is expected to affect income. They need to know how enhancing a product's features or changing its packaging will influence its cost. Commissions paid to sales representatives may be based on a company's profits. All these marketing decisions require accounting information.

The Finance Function The **finance function** is responsible for managing the financial resources of the organization. Finance managers make decisions about how to raise capital as well as where and how to invest it. Finance managers need accounting information to answer such questions as whether money should be raised through borrowing (issuing bonds) or selling stock. Finance managers also make decisions concerning whether a new piece of manufacturing equipment should be purchased or leased and whether a plant expansion should be paid for in cash or by borrowing money from the bank.

The Human Resource Function Although all managers who supervise, motivate, and evaluate other employees are human resource managers, the **human resource function** is concerned with the utilization of human resources to help an organization reach its goals. More specifically, human resource managers support other functions and managers by recruiting and staffing, designing compensation and benefit packages, ensuring the safety and overall health of personnel, and providing training and development opportunities for employees. These decisions require input from all other functional areas. What kind of accounting information do human resource managers need? Human resource decisions, such as hiring new employees, are often made under budget constraints. Ensuring safe workplaces for employees may involve the redesign of manufacturing processes. Accountants can provide information regarding the cost of the redesign. The decision to train employees to use new equipment may require an analysis of the costs and benefits of the new program.

> **Operations and production function** Produces the products or services that an organization sells to its customers.
>
> **Marketing function** Involved with the process of developing, pricing, promoting, and distributing goods and services sold to customers.
>
> **Finance function** Responsible for managing the financial resources of the organization.
>
> **Human resource function** Concerned with the utilization of human resources to help an organization reach its goals.

The Information Needs of Internal and External Users

As you can see, the information needs of internal users and external users differ in significant ways. Because of the varying needs of internal users, managerial accounting is more flexible than financial accounting. Although financial accounting is geared toward the preparation of financial statements and other reports according to generally accepted accounting principles

part of the manager's job, and in order to plan effectively, managers need up-to-date information. Although the timeliness of information is paramount, managerial accounting information frequently is less precise than financial accounting information and often includes the use of estimates.

Exhibit 1-2 summarizes the external and internal users of accounting information, the type of information typically needed by these users, and the source of the information.

Exhibit 1-2 External and Internal Users of Accounting Information

	Users	Type of Accounting Information Needed	Source
External	Shareholders and creditors	Sales, gross profit, net income, cash flow, assets and liabilities, earnings per share, etc. Although such information is primarily financial, it may also include nonfinancial information (units in inventory). This information is often provided in summary form (for the company as a whole) and typically is historical in nature.	Annual reports, financial statements, and other available documents
External	Government agencies	Varies by agency but includes taxable income, sales, assets, comparisons of actual expenditures with budgets, etc. This information is usually provided for the company as a whole and is historical in nature. It can include both financial and nonfinancial information.	Tax returns and other reports
External	Customers and suppliers	Order status, shipping dates, inventory levels, etc. This information must be very detailed and timely to be useful.	Limited-access databases available to specific customers and suppliers
Internal	Marketing, operations and production, finance, and human resource managers	Timely and detailed information on sales and expenses, product costs, budgetary considerations, and measures of performance. Often includes nonfinancial data (direct labor hours, units to break even, etc.). Accounting information is frequently needed for segments of an organization and is more likely future oriented than historical.	Cost reports, budgets, and other internal documents

© Cengage Learning 2013

(GAAP) and other rules, managerial accounting can be customized to a specific company or segment of a company. Although financial accounting is concerned primarily with reporting on the company as a whole, managerial accounting emphasizes the various segments of a company, such as divisions, departments, sales regions, and product lines.

Because of the decision focus of internal managers, managerial accounting information must focus on the future rather than the past. Planning is an integral

The Role of the Managerial Accountant

What is the role of the managerial accountant in providing information to this diverse group of internal users? Managerial accountants have traditionally been thought of as the bean counters or number crunchers in an organization. However, advances in AIS and other changes in the past decade have resulted in the automation of traditional accounting functions involving data collection, data entry, and data reporting and a corresponding

Managerial accountants facilitate management decision making.

shift of those functions from management accounting to clerical staff.

As a result, managerial accountants in many companies now focus on analyzing information and creating knowledge from it rather than collecting data. Managerial accountants have become decision-support specialists who see their role as interpreting information, putting it into a useful format for other managers, and facilitating management decision making.[1]

LO3 Relevant Factors and Decision Making

Although the problems and questions facing marketing, production, finance, and human resource managers of organizations differ, the decision-making process that they follow is remarkably uniform. In fact, it is the same decision-making model that you are likely to use when making nonbusiness decisions. Do you remember the decision-making process you went through the last time you made a major decision? It could have been a decision to purchase or sell a car, a computer, or a stereo system. It could have been a decision to attend a particular college, accept a summer job, or perhaps even get married.

Decisions have many variables or factors that must be considered. If you were making a decision to purchase a car, you would consider such variables as its cost, features, color, and financing options. If you were making a decision about what college to attend, factors might include the cost, proximity to your home, and academic

reputation. Different decision makers might even consider different factors for the same decision situation. For example, the color of a car may be unimportant to one buyer but critical to another. The number and type of variables considered might differ for each individual and for each decision that individual makes.

Decisions may have to be made under time, budget, or other constraints. Your choice of a car may be limited to those which cost under $10,000. Your decision to accept a summer job may be limited to those which are within 30 miles of your home. Your decision to attend a college may have to be made by a certain date. In addition, many decisions are made with missing information or at least with imperfect information. In deciding which car to buy, you would probably want to consider the cost of future repairs for various models. Although you might estimate these costs by using such sources as *Consumer Reports*, you will not know the costs with certainty. Decisions may not be perfect, but they should be the best you can make given the information that is available to you at the time. The process you go through is to gather all the information you can to reduce the risk of an incorrect or less-than-optimal decision.

Decisions often lead to other decisions. Once you have decided to buy a car or a stereo, you need to make other decisions, such as whether to pay cash or to finance the purchase or whether to buy an extended warranty. Life does seem like a never-ending string of decisions.

Decision making is the process of identifying different courses of action and selecting one appropriate to a given situation. All decisions require using judgment, and the quality of a decision often depends on how good that judgment is. Judgment refers to the cognitive aspects of the decision-making process. By cognitive, we mean taking a logical, rational approach to making decisions rather than making decisions impulsively, on the spur of the moment.

Decision making The process of identifying alternative courses of action and selecting an appropriate alternative in a given decision-making situation.

[1]Institute of Management Accountants, *Counting More, Counting Less: The 1999 Practice Analysis of Management Accounting* (Montvale, New Jersey: Institute of Management Accountants, 1999).

Relevant Costs

What should you consider in making a decision? An effective approach is to focus on factors that affect a particular decision. That is, relevant factors are those which differ among alternatives. For example, if you were deciding which automobile to purchase and each automobile you were considering had the same options at the same cost (air-conditioning, CD player, and so on), you would conclude that those options are not relevant to the decision because they do not differ among the various automobiles. Very often, cost is a key factor that must be considered in decisions. **Relevant costs** are those which differ among alternatives. Another way to view relevant costs is to identify those which are avoidable, or those which can be eliminated by choosing one alternative over another. In choosing among automobiles, if one car has air-conditioning and another does not, the cost of air-conditioning is relevant because choosing one of the other automobiles could eliminate that cost.

Sunk Costs

Sunk costs are costs that have already been incurred. Because sunk costs cannot be avoided, they are not relevant in a decision. In your decision to trade in your old vehicle, the amount that you paid for it may appear to be important. However, because that cost is sunk, it cannot be avoided, is not relevant, and should not be considered in your decision.

As another example, assume you are the production manager of a company and that you have the opportunity to purchase a new piece of equipment that can reduce the cost of making a product by 30 percent. However, your boss says that you can't buy the new equipment until the old equipment is fully depreciated, in two more years. Is the depreciation on the old machine a relevant cost? As was the case in the previous scenario, the cost of the old equipment (and the corresponding depreciation) is

Sunk costs and future costs that do not differ among alternatives are not relevant. Opportunity costs, however, are relevant.

a sunk cost, cannot be avoided, is not relevant, and should not be considered in the decision.

If sunk costs are not relevant, what about costs that will be incurred in the future? Are all costs that are not sunk relevant? Again, the key is that relevant costs are avoidable costs. If future costs do not differ among alternatives, they are not avoidable (they will be incurred regardless of the alternative chosen) and therefore not relevant. In your choice among automobiles, if the cost of an option is the same, that cost is not relevant in your decision.

Opportunity Costs

Opportunity costs are the benefits forgone by choosing one alternative over another and are relevant costs for decision-making purposes. For example, in choosing to go to college, you are forgoing the salary you could receive by working full time. Almost all alternatives have opportunity costs. In choosing to work instead of going to school, the opportunity cost is the higher salary that you might later earn if you choose to go to school. Opportunity costs are sometimes difficult to quantify but nevertheless should be considered in making decisions (see Exhibit 1-3).

Relevant costs
Costs which differ among alternatives.

Sunk costs Costs that have already been incurred.

Opportunity costs The benefits forgone by choosing one alternative over another.

Exhibit 1-3 Relevant and Irrelevant Costs

Relevant Costs		Irrelevant Costs	
Future costs that differ among alternatives	Opportunity costs—benefits that are forgone by choosing one alternative over another	Future costs that do not differ among alternatives	Sunk costs—costs that have already been incurred

© Cengage Learning 2013

LO4 Ethics and Decision Making

Business managers make ethical decisions every day. Although some might argue that business decisions are simply a matter of economics, there are also ethical dimensions to most of these decisions. In today's business environment, companies have to be aware not only of the economic impact of their decisions but also of their ethical impact.

Ethical problems arise in organizations for a variety of reasons. For example, undue pressure to achieve short-term productivity and profitability goals may lead to unethical behavior, such as requiring employees to work long hours that exceed limits set by state and federal agencies, intentionally ignoring product safety concerns, or falsifying accounting records or other documentation. Such unethical behavior often occurs in corporate environments in which employees feel that they have no choice but to follow their superiors' orders and directives. Strictly adhering to an organizational hierarchy can be problematic if employees blindly follow orders.

Famed economist Milton Friedman once argued that the only social responsibility of corporations was to increase their profits. Further, he stated that business managers should not be expected to make socially responsible decisions because they are not trained to

> Establishing an ethical business environment encourages employees to act with integrity and conduct business in a fair and just manner.

do so.[2] Given the world in which we now live, this perspective may no longer be valid. Managers simply cannot make business decisions without carefully considering their ethical dimensions. As you continue this study of managerial accounting, thoughtfully consider how managers can use information for both good and bad ends. Doing so will increase the likelihood that you will be prepared to make informed and ethical choices as a business manager.

Business ethics results from the interaction of personal morals and the processes and objectives of business. That is to say, business ethics is nothing more than our personal views of right and wrong applied in a business setting. For example, business practices

[2]Milton Friedman, "The Social Responsibility of Business Is to Increase Its Profits," *New York Times Magazine,* September 30, 1970.

MAKING IT REAL

The World's Most Ethical Companies

Each year, the Ethisphere Institute identifies the world's most ethical companies by ranking the companies on seven key dimensions: corporate citizenship and responsibility; corporate governance; innovation that contributes to public well-being; industry leadership; executive leadership and tone from the top; legal, regulatory, and reputation track record; and internal systems and ethics/compliance programs. Among the 100 winners in 2010 were the following U.S. based companies: **Patagonia**, **Ford Motor Company**, **Ecolab**, **Trader Joe's**, **Caterpillar**, **Google**, **Zappos**, **Waste Management**, **Starbucks**, **UPS**, **T-Mobile**, and **Cisco Systems**.

© 119/ZUMA Press/Newscom

Source: http://ethisphere.com/wme2010/.

Don't Be Evil

"**G**ooglers generally apply those words to how we serve our users. But "Don't be evil" is much more than that. Yes, it's about providing our users unbiased access to information, focusing on their needs and giving them the best products and services that we can. But it's also about doing the right thing more generally—following the law, acting honorably, and treating each other with respect.

The Google Code of Conduct is one of the ways we put "Don't be evil" into practice. It's built around the recognition that everything we do in connection with our work at Google will be, and should be, measured against the highest possible standards of ethical business conduct.

© Alex Segre/Alamy

We set the bar that high for practical as well as aspirational reasons: We hire great people who work hard to build great products, and it's essential that we build an environment of trust—among ourselves and with our users. That trust and mutual respect underlie our success, and we need to earn it every day.

So, please do read the Code, and follow it, always bearing in mind that each of us has a personal responsibility to incorporate, and to encourage other Googlers to incorporate, the principles of the Code into our work. And if you have a question or ever think that one of your fellow Googlers or the company as a whole may be falling short of our commitment, don't be silent. We want—and need—to hear from you."

Source: http://investor.google.com/conduct.html.

---

that are viewed as unethical include managers lying to employees, stealing from a company, divulging confidential information, and taking credit for the work of others. Consider how these unethical business practices could occur in your personal life. For example, a child may lie to her mother, a roommate may steal money from you while you are in class, a friend may tell another person about a "private" conversation that you and he had, and a group member may contribute nothing to a group project yet accept full credit for the project. Business ethics is, in many ways, an extension of our personal ethics. Of course, the stakes are often much higher, or at least very different. Consider the many billions of dollars that the tobacco industry paid in damages because its members lied to consumers and the government about the harmful effects of nicotine.

In addition, managers must consider various stakeholders when evaluating ethical dilemmas. A chief executive officer cannot simply make the decision that is best for her without considering the interests of other employees, stockholders, customers, suppliers, creditors, and so forth.

Integrity is the cornerstone of ethical business practices. Failure to build a business on integrity carries costs. For example, deceptive business practices may harm a company's standing in the community, decrease employee productivity, reduce customer loyalty, build resentment among employees, increase the likelihood of further unethical behavior by employees, and cause scrutiny by government agencies. Although the costs of some of these consequences are difficult to quantify, there is no doubt that they can be substantial.

Ethics Programs

Ethics programs Company programs or policies created for the express purpose of establishing and maintaining an ethical business environment.

Companies frequently create **ethics programs** to establish and help maintain an ethical business environment. Some of the most common elements of ethics programs are written codes of conduct, employee hot lines and ethics call centers, ethics training, processes to register anonymous complaints about wrongdoing, and ethics offices.

Corporate Wrongdoing

Although companies establish ethics programs to encourage employees to act with integrity, some individuals engage in behaviors that are not only unethical but also fraudulent. The case of **Enron** is one example where an ethics program was not effective. In late 2001, the once high-flying company filed for bankruptcy protection. Investigations into the company's failure revealed a series of questionable transactions designed by the company's top officials to enrich themselves. The company's former chief financial officer and two former chief executive officers were found guilty of fraud. Though the actual cost of **Enron**'s collapse will never be known, estimates are that shareholders and creditors lost more than $60 billion.

Sarbanes–Oxley Act of 2002

As a response to the rash of corporate scandals and frauds that began in the early 2000s with the implosion of **Enron** in late 2001, the U.S. Congress passed the Sarbanes–Oxley Act. Sarbanes–Oxley includes a number of significant provisions. For example, the law requires management to assess whether internal controls over financial reporting (ICFR) are effective. In addition, the company's external financial statement auditor is required to audit ICFR and assess whether those controls are effective in preventing and detecting financial misstatements. These assessments are part of the so-called Section 404 report called for under the law. Because Congress wanted to include a significant deterrent, Sarbanes–Oxley also increases the criminal penalties associated with financial statement fraud to a maximum fine of $5 million and imprisonment for 20 years. Another provision of the law requires companies to establish procedures to allow employees to lodge complaints about accounting and auditing matters directly with members of the audit committee. Furthermore, companies must ensure that employees who make such complaints are not harassed or otherwise discriminated against by others within the organization. In sum, the Sarbanes–Oxley Act has increased the level of scrutiny of public companies' financial statements. Many observers believe that the law has improved the quality of financial reporting in the United States and helped to rebuild the public's trust in the nation's financial markets.

STUDY TOOLS 1

Chapter review card

- ➲ Learning Objective and Key Concept Reviews
- ➲ Key Definitions and Formulas

Online (Located at www.cengagebrain.com)

- ➲ Flash Cards and Crossword Puzzles
- ➲ Games and Quizzes
- ➲ Buycostumes.com Video and E-Lectures
- ➲ Homework Assignments (as directed by your instructor)

BRIEF EXERCISES

1. Data, Information, and Knowledge LO1

The following statements relate to various types of data, information, and knowledge in a business setting.

a. The sales price for a particular inventory item
b. Dimensions of a company's manufacturing facility
c. Customer purchasing patterns used to launch a new advertising campaign
d. Summary of cash disbursements by vendor
e. Summary of product sales by product and region
f. Statistical analysis of production defects, resulting in changes to production and inspection processes

Required
Classify each of the following as *data, information,* or *knowledge.*

2. Managerial vs. Financial Accounting LO2

Financial and managerial accounting information serve different purposes. The following phrases are commonly used to describe either financial or managerial accounting.
—Must follow GAAP
—Focused on past performance
—Timeliness is critical
—Emphasizes reporting on the whole company
—Information is often less precise
—Future orientation
—Information is often "old"
—Reports results by segments
—Highly customizable

Required
Indicate whether each of the preceding phrases describes financial accounting or managerial accounting.

3. Factors in Decision Making LO3

Decision making requires the consideration of various factors and matters, some quantitative and others qualitative. The following statements describe various aspects of decision making.

a. Cost is rarely a factor in decisions and should be considered only when financial resources are plentiful.
b. Relevant costs are those costs which can be avoided by choosing one alternative over another.
c. Future costs that do not differ across alternatives are always relevant.
d. Only historical costs are sunk costs.
e. Opportunity costs that are not quantifiable need not be considered in decision making.

Required
Indicate whether each of the preceding statements is true or false.

4. Ethics and Decision Making LO4

Many decisions have ethical implications. Therefore, understanding the ethical dimensions of business decisions is important.

a. The famed economist, _____, once argued that the only social responsibility of a corporation is to increase profits.
b. Common elements of ethics programs include _____, _____, and _____.
c. Corporate scandals such as that at Enron led to the passage of the _____.
d. _____ is the cornerstone of ethical business practices.
e. Managers should always consider the views of various _____ when evaluating ethical dilemmas.

Required
Use the following terms to complete the preceding sentences about ethics and decision making: *stakeholders, employee hot lines, Milton Friedman, integrity, written codes of conduct, Sarbanes–Oxley Act,* and *ethics training.*

EXERCISES

5. Users of Accounting Information LO2

Accounting information is used by a variety of individuals and organizations for numerous purposes. Following is a small set of potential users of accounting information.

a. Bank loan officer
b. Employee labor union
c. Production manager
d. Current stockholder
e. Sales manager
f. Company president

Required
Identify the types of accounting information that may be of interest to each of these potential users. Be specific if possible.

6. Types of Business Managers LO2

Business managers do not all have the same information needs. Some require detailed production data, whereas others require detailed data about sales and marketing performance. Read the following statements that describe business managers.

a. These managers make decisions about how to raise capital as well as where and how it is invested.
b. These managers need to know how much a product costs in order to help establish a reasonable selling price.
c. These managers support other managers by recruiting and staffing, designing compensation and benefit packages, and providing training and development opportunities for employees.

d. These managers make decisions about how and when products and services are produced or provided.

Required

Identify the type of business manager described in each of the preceding statements.

7. Decision Making and Ethics LO4

Henry Powell, Inc., produces batteries for riding lawn mowers. The company provides the batteries to some of the largest manufacturers of riding lawn mowers in the United States. In the last few months, the company has received reports of batteries exploding as a result of high heat. The incidents have all been in southern states and have occurred with only one particular brand and model of lawn mower. In these models, the batteries are installed beneath the seats of the mower. In more than one case, the exploding batteries have resulted in serious injuries. Powell officials are aware of the potential danger, but have been unable to determine the cause of the problem. Some company officials think that the problem may be with the lawn mower and not with the batteries, and internal testing has been inconclusive.

Required

A. In your opinion, what responsibility does the company bear for the potential dangers of the battery?
B. Should company officials try to shift blame to the manufacturer of the lawn mower, as the problems are with only one particular brand of mower?
C. Identify the stakeholders who are affected by the issue, and discuss ethical considerations faced by company officials in this situation.

PROBLEMS

8. Financial vs. Managerial Accounting LO2

Imagine that you are home during a break from school and are talking to a friend about classes. You tell your friend, who is not a college student, that you are taking managerial accounting this term. Your friend says that she remembers that you took accounting last term and wonders why you have to take another accounting course. You look a little perplexed and decide to give that question some thought.

Required

As you think about your friend's question, you decide to answer the following questions:

A. What are the differences between financial and managerial accounting? (Explain concisely.)
B. Why do the two types of accounting exist?
C. Who are the users of financial accounting information? Who are the users of managerial accounting information?

9. Decision Making and Relevant Factors LO3

You have an opportunity to choose a flight for your upcoming spring break trip to Mexico. After a lot of thought and research, you have narrowed your options to four different flights. If there are no delays, each should get you to your destination on time. (It is important to arrive on time, as you have to meet a bus at a particular time to take you and other students to your final destination.) If any of the flights are late, arranging for alternative transportation will be difficult. Basic information about each flight is presented in the following table:

	Flight 1	Flight 2	Flight 3	Flight 4
Base Price	$300	$400	$500	$600
Flight Time and Connections	12 hours/3	6 hours/2	5 hours/1	3 hours/ direct flight
First-Class Upgrade	Not available	$250	$200	$300
Meals (Airport and Plane)	$30	$15	$10	Included in airfare
Wireless Internet Access	Not available	$20	$25	Included in airfare
Beverages	$10	$10	$10	Included in airfare
Total Price (all options)	$340	$695	$745	$900

Required

What are the relevant factors affecting your choice of flight?

10. Decision Making and Ethics LO3, 4

Ken Martin is an engineer with a multinational aerospace firm that produces a jet engine that is widely used by airplane manufacturers. Ken recently became aware of a potential defect in an engine part. As the lead engineer responsible for the part, Ken directed that tests be performed to ascertain the conditions under which the part might fail. The results of the tests indicate that at low temperatures a critical seal may crack, possibly allowing fluids to leak into other portions of the engine. Although the risks of such a leak are very low, the consequences are potentially disastrous.

Required

A. What are some of the objectives that Ken might identify when dealing with this dilemma?
B. What options are available to Ken?
C. Does the company have an ethical responsibility to fix the part?
D. Should the company consider the estimated cost of fixing the part in its decision-making process? Why or why not?

Product Costing:
Manufacturing Processes, Cost Terminology, and Cost Flows

Introduction

Every company provides a product or a service to customers and clients. **Manufacturing companies** (such as **Toyota** and **Dell Computer**) take raw materials and produce new products from them. **Merchandising companies** sell products that someone else has manufactured. Examples are large department stores, such as **Wal-Mart** and **Target**, as well as the independent music shop or clothing store on the corner. In contrast to manufacturing and merchandising companies, **service companies** do not sell a tangible product as their primary business. Service providers include such diverse companies and industries as airlines, hospitals, automobile repair shops, brokerage firms, law firms, and CPA firms. Service providers are the fastest-growing segment of the U.S. economy, employing roughly 75 percent of the workforce.

Regardless of the type of company involved, costs are associated with the products and services produced and sold. Although it might appear simple to determine the cost of a product or service, the process can be quite complicated, as you will see in the next few chapters. How should companies determine the costs of producing products and providing services? What costs should be included? Before we can answer these questions, we should also ask why companies want to determine their product costs. For example, a company might be preparing financial statements for a bank to use in determining whether to make a loan to the company or may be filing its income tax return for the year. Generally accepted accounting principles (GAAP) and tax laws govern costing for financial statement purposes and for tax purposes, respectively. In contrast, a company might want to determine the cost of a particular product in order to determine its sales price or to estimate a product's profitability.[1] Cost information is also helpful for budgeting and evaluation purposes.

Learning Objectives

After studying the material in this chapter, you should be able to:

LO1 Describe basic production processes used by manufacturing companies.

LO2 Identify the key characteristics and benefits of lean production and JIT manufacturing.

LO3 Distinguish manufacturing costs from nonmanufacturing costs and classify manufacturing costs as direct materials, direct labor, or overhead.

LO4 Diagram the flow of costs in manufacturing, merchandising, and service companies and calculate the cost of manufacturing or selling goods and services.

LO5 Evaluate the impact of product costs and period costs on a company's income statement and balance sheet.

Manufacturing companies Companies that purchase raw materials from other companies and transform those raw materials into a finished product.

Merchandising companies Companies that sell products that someone else has manufactured.

Service companies Companies that do not sell a tangible product as their primary business.

[1]Note that companies might want to cost other objects in addition to products. For example, a company might want to know the costs of a particular department or division or even the costs of servicing a particular customer.

Businesses use sophisticated information systems to manage inventories so that they can be responsive to consumer demands.

© Kayte Deioma/PhotoEdit

LO₁ **The Production Process**

Manufacturing companies purchase raw materials from other companies and transform them into a finished product. This transformation typically requires labor and the incurring of other costs, such as the cost of utilities, the depreciation of factory equipment, and the cost of supplies. Manufacturing companies may produce a single product or many products. Likewise, companies may have only a few customers or many thousands. The process used to manufacture these products depends on the specific product or products made, the customers who buy the product(s), and the company itself. Some companies are very labor intensive, whereas others rely heavily on automation. Some companies choose to

> Production processes require the combination of raw materials, labor, and other items, such as electricity and supplies, to create finished goods.

make very high quality products, whereas other companies emphasize low cost. Some companies choose to carry large amounts of inventory, whereas others manufacture their products in small batches and make them just in time to meet customer demand.

Manufacturing in a Traditional Environment

Traditionally, the factory of a manufacturing company was organized with similar machines grouped together. For example, a furniture manufacturer still using traditional processes might have areas devoted to cutting and rough sanding, shaping the cut lumber into furniture pieces (such as chair legs), using lathes and routers, drilling holes and dovetailing joints, assembling the furniture pieces, and finishing. As raw material (in this case, lumber) is processed in each area, it is "pushed" to the next area for further processing. Lumber is brought into the factory from the warehouse and is cut and rough sanded according to specifications for specific products. It is then moved to another area in the factory for shaping the rough lumber into chair legs, bedposts, and tabletops. Next, the lumber might

move to an area containing drill presses and machines to make dovetail joints. After drilling and jointing, it would be moved to still another area for assembly. In this area, workers glue or screw the various parts together and attach necessary hardware and glass. After assembly, the furniture is moved to an area where it is sanded again and varnish or paint finishes are applied. It would not be unusual for one or more of these areas to be in different buildings or sometimes in entirely different plants. After leaving the finishing department, the furniture is ready for packing and selling to customers.

In this traditional system, it was normal (and perhaps even desirable) to accumulate **raw materials inventory** and **finished-goods inventory** to serve as buffers in case of unexpected demand for products or unexpected problems in production. It was also normal to accumulate inventories of partially completed products (called **work in process inventory, or WIP**). WIP might result, for example, when furniture pieces that have been drilled and jointed are pushed to the assembly area before the workers in that area are ready for them.

LO2 Lean Production and Manufacturing in a JIT Environment

One of the big changes affecting companies in the past 20 to 25 years has been the adoption of **lean production** systems and **just-in-time (JIT) manufacturing**. In an effort to reduce costs and increase efficiency, companies began to focus on the costs and problems associated with the traditional manufacturing facility and the practice of carrying large amounts of inventory.

Lean production is focused on eliminating waste associated with holding more inventory than is required, making more product than is needed, overprocessing a product (doing more than a customer values), moving products (and people) farther than is required, and experiencing downtime caused by people waiting for work to do and products waiting in mid-assembly.

One of the key aspects of lean production is managing inventory. Carrying large amounts of inventory results in storage and insurance costs. Traditional manufacturing systems may result in other, not-so-obvious problems, including the production of lower quality products with more defects. The buffers that seem so

---

Raw materials inventory Inventory of materials needed in the production process but not yet moved to the production area.

Finished-goods inventory Inventory of finished product waiting for sale and shipment to customers.

Work in process (WIP) inventory Inventory of unfinished product (in other words, what is left in the factory at the end of the period).

Lean production A system focused on eliminating waste associated with holding more inventory than is required, making more product than is needed, overprocessing a product, moving products (and people) farther than is required, and waiting.

Just-in-time (JIT) manufacturing The philosophy of having raw materials arrive just in time to be used in production and for finished-goods inventory to be completed just in time to be shipped to customers.

© Dmitriy Shironosov/Shutterstock.com

Lean production and JIT provide many benefits, including improved production quality and reduced processing time.

desirable may in fact lead workers to pay less attention to detail and work less efficiently. In addition, the organization of factories in which similar machines are grouped together greatly increases the time necessary to manufacture products and makes it more difficult to meet special orders or unexpected increases in demand without having large amounts of inventory on hand.

In a just-in-time system, materials are purchased and products are made "just in time" to meet customer demand. Unlike traditional production, the process begins with a customer order, and products are "pulled" through the manufacturing process. Under ideal conditions, companies operating in a JIT environment would reduce inventories of raw materials, work in process, and finished goods to very low levels or even zero.

With only a small buffer of extra finished goods and raw materials, it is imperative that companies employing JIT be able to procure supplies and raw materials on a timely basis. This requires that companies work with suppliers that can deliver goods on time and free of defects. Typically, JIT companies rely on only a few suppliers that have proven to be highly reliable.

In order to successfully implement lean production and JIT manufacturing systems, companies must be able to manufacture products very quickly. This often entails restructuring the factory itself. In the traditional factory,

MAKING IT REAL

Embracing "Lean" at Starbucks

The recession, together with increased competition from mom-and-pop coffee shops, has forced Starbucks to seek ways to become more efficient and reduce waste. Using lean techniques, the company studied ways to reduce the time its employees (called partners by Starbucks) spend setting up the store each day and the time baristas spend making a drink. Simple changes

© Frances M. Roberts/Newscom

such as (1) color-coding and moving bins of coffee beans to the top of the counter so that baristas don't have to bend over every time they scoop coffee and (2) moving items closer to where drinks are handed to customers shaved seconds off the time it took to make and serve drinks to customers. In a business where annual labor costs are about $2.5 billion, time is money.

Source: Julie Jargon, "Latest Starbucks Buzzword: 'Lean' Japanese Techniques," *The Wall Street Journal*, August 4, 2009.

How Much Is Enough When Disaster Strikes?

As hospitals focus on cutting costs, inventory management has gained importance. As a result, most hospitals carry no more than a 30-day supply of drugs. Although this is adequate in normal situations, hospitals and other health care organizations may not have enough medical supplies on hand to deal with a pandemic flu outbreak or other emergencies.

For example, as the world faced an outbreak of swine flu in the spring of 2009, reports found that while affluent countries like Japan, Britain, and the United States had enough Tamiflu and other antiviral medicines to treat up to half of their citizens, poorer countries, including Guatemala, India, and Mexico (where the outbreak began), had enough supplies for less than 2 percent of their populations.

Source: Bernard Wysocki, Jr., and Sarah Lueck, "Just-in-Time Inventories Make U.S. Vulnerable in a Pandemic," *The Wall Street Journal*, January 12, 2006, A1; and Gregory Katz, "Tamiflu Stockpiles Vary Widely Throughout World," Associated Press, May 1, 2009.

---

similar machines were often grouped together, resulting in raw materials and unfinished products being handled and moved a great deal from area to area. In the traditional factory, it also was difficult and time consuming to switch production from one product to another (from tables to chairs, for example) because the same machines were used for both. In contrast, factories in a JIT environment are typically organized so that all the machinery and equipment needed to make a product is available in one area. These groupings of machines are called manufacturing cells. The use of cells minimizes the handling and moving of products. It also reduces or eliminates setup time (the time needed to switch production from one product to another). Sometimes, workers are trained to operate all the machinery in a manufacturing cell, increasing speed and efficiency even more.

Although it is easy to think of lean production and JIT as inventory management tools only, successful implementation provides an array of benefits, including the following:

1. reduced waste and scrap

2. improved product quality

3. lower overall production costs (although the costs of raw materials may increase in some cases)

4. lower labor costs

5. reduced inventory

6. reduced processing time

7. increased manufacturing flexibility

These benefits often lead to increased customer satisfaction, increased motivation within the workforce, and increased profits.

However, disruptions in supply can wreak havoc on companies that rely on just-in-time purchasing of parts and supplies. These disruptions may result from strikes by factory workers of the supplier, natural disasters, or the unexpected closing of national borders (when suppliers are located in other countries).

For example, in the days following the terrorist attacks on the World Trade Center on September 11, 2001, delayed shipments of air freight and heightened security at border crossings slowed the delivery of parts, forcing several automakers to temporarily shut down assembly lines. More recently, Hurricane Katrina caused disruptions in the supply of gasoline when oil refineries and ports along the Gulf Coast were damaged and shipping routes along the Mississippi River, railways, and highways were made inaccessible. In a similar fashion, the devastating earthquake and tsunami that struck Japan in March 2011 disrupted deliveries of auto parts from suppliers located in Japan, shutting down vehicle assembly operations not only in Japan but around the globe.[2]

LO3 Product Costs in a Manufacturing Company

Regardless of the size of the company involved, the number of products made, or the type of manufacturing system used, manufacturing companies must know how much their products cost. It is useful to distinguish between direct and indirect costs. **Direct costs** are costs that are directly attached to the finished product and can be conveniently traced to that product. **Indirect costs** are costs that are attached to the product but cannot be conveniently traced to each separate product. It is also convenient to distinguish **manufacturing costs** (those costs incurred in the manufacture of a product) from nonmanufacturing costs (those costs incurred elsewhere in the company). Manufacturing costs typically consist of three components: *direct materials, direct labor,* and *manufacturing overhead* (see Exhibit 2-1).

Direct Materials

Direct materials are defined as materials that can be directly and conveniently traced to a particular product or other cost object *and* that become an integral part of the finished product. At **Ford Motor Company**, sheet metal and tires are direct materials. At **Dell Computer**, the computer chips made by **Intel** and used in **Dell** computers are direct materials.

Direct materials typically cause few problems in the costing of products. The amount of direct materials used in making products can usually be accurately

[2]Yoshio Takahashi, "Car Plants to Restart Operations in Japan," *The Wall Street Journal*, March 21, 2011, p. B1.

measured by engineering studies, and the accounting systems of most companies are capable of tracing the materials used and the costs of those materials to specific products. However, questions do arise, and judgment is often needed to correctly classify materials as direct or indirect.

Direct Labor

Direct labor is the labor cost (including fringe benefits) of all production employees who work directly on the product being made or service being provided. Sometimes, direct labor is called *touch labor* to reflect the hands-on relationship between the employee and the product or service. Assembly-line workers are the clearest example of direct labor. As with direct materials, the identification of direct labor cost is usually straightforward and accurate. Time sheets may be used to keep track of the work employees perform on different products and the wages they are paid.

Manufacturing Overhead

All costs incurred in the factory that are not properly classified as direct materials or direct labor are

> **Direct costs** Costs that are directly attached to the finished product and can be conveniently traced to that product.
>
> **Indirect costs** Costs that are attached to the product but cannot be conveniently traced to each separate product.
>
> **Manufacturing costs** Costs incurred in the factory or plant to produce a product; typically consist of three elements: direct materials, direct labor, and manufacturing overhead.
>
> **Direct materials** Materials that can easily and conveniently be traced to the final product.
>
> **Direct labor** Labor that can easily and conveniently be traced to particular products.

Exhibit 2-1 Manufacturing Costs

Direct Materials	Direct Labor	Manufacturing Overhead
Various materials that can be directly and conveniently traced to a product	Labor costs of assembly-line workers	Indirect materials such as welding material, glue, and screws
		Indirect labor such as factory maintenance workers and factory janitors
		Other factory costs

© Cengage Learning 2013

called **manufacturing overhead**. Manufacturing overhead includes both **indirect materials** and **indirect labor**. Materials that we know are used in the manufacture of products but cannot be measured with reasonable accuracy and easily and conveniently traced to a particular product are called indirect materials. For example, the rivets and welding materials used by an automobile manufacturer and the screws and glue used by a furniture manufacturer would probably be classified as indirect materials. Likewise, certain labor costs that are not directly associated with production are classified as indirect labor and included in manufacturing overhead. Examples include labor costs of janitorial staff and maintenance workers in a factory and supervisors who do not directly work on a product.

Manufacturing overhead also includes utilities, depreciation of factory equipment and buildings, rent, repairs and maintenance, insurance, and other factory costs. In a traditional manufacturing environment, the costs included in manufacturing overhead are most often indirect in nature and cannot be conveniently and accurately traced and assigned to a specific product. Remember, the machinery and equipment are typically used to make multiple products, making it difficult to trace the cost of a machine to a specific product. Although many overhead costs in a JIT environment will also be indirect in nature (rent and utilities, for example), more of the costs are likely to be direct in nature. For instance, in a JIT environment, the cost of machinery in a manufacturing cell can be traced to a specific product (such as tables) if it is used only to make that product.

Because of the indirect nature of most overhead costs and the inability of companies to directly measure the amount of overhead included in products or to trace

> *Manufacturing costs are incurred in the production facility, whereas nonmanufacturing costs are incurred elsewhere in the company, such as in the marketing department.*

manufacturing overhead to products, accountants have come up with various methods of allocating manufacturing overhead to products. Traditional methods of allocating overhead using job, process, and operations costing are discussed in Chapter 3. A more modern method, called activity-based costing, is discussed in Chapter 4.

Manufacturing costs are also called **product costs** or inventoriable costs because they attach to products as they go through the manufacturing process. Direct material, direct labor, and overhead costs remain with the product until it is sold. Only when the product is sold are these costs expensed on the income statement as cost of goods sold.

Nonmanufacturing Costs

Nonmanufacturing costs consist of those costs which are incurred outside the plant or factory and typically are categorized as selling and administrative costs. Although nonmanufacturing costs are necessarily incurred in running a business, they are not directly incurred in the production of products. A general rule of thumb is to imagine the product not being produced. If a particular cost would still occur, it is generally a nonmanufacturing cost. Common examples of nonmanufacturing costs include advertising costs, commissions paid to salespersons, administrative and accounting salaries, and the cost of office supplies. Nonmanufacturing costs also include rent, insurance, taxes, the cost of utilities, and depreciation of equipment when used in selling and administrative activities. Nonmanufacturing costs are called **period costs**. In contrast to manufacturing costs, nonmanufacturing costs are expensed on the income statement in the period incurred. Exhibit 2-2 lists several examples of manufacturing and nonmanufacturing costs.

Manufacturing overhead The cost of indirect materials and labor and any other expenses related to the production of products but not directly traceable to the specific product.

Indirect materials Materials used in the production of products but not directly traceable to the specific product.

Indirect labor Labor used in the production of products but not directly traceable to the specific product.

Product costs Costs that attach to the products as they go through the manufacturing process; also called inventoriable costs.

Nonmanufacturing costs Costs that include selling and administrative costs.

Period costs Costs that are expensed in the period incurred; attached to the period as opposed to the product.

Exhibit 2-2 Manufacturing and Nonmanufacturing Costs

Description	Manufacturing Cost	Nonmanufacturing Cost
Depreciation of factory machinery	Yes	No
Depreciation of vehicles used by sales staff	No	Yes
Lease expense on factory equipment	Yes	No
Lease expense on office computer	No	Yes
Lubricants used for maintenance of factory machinery (indirect materials)	Yes	No
Supplies used in the human resources office	No	Yes
Utilities used in the factory building	Yes	No
Utilities used in the administrative headquarters	No	Yes
Salary of a supervisor in the factory (indirect labor)	Yes	No
Salary of a supervisor in the marketing department	No	Yes

LO4 Cost Flows in a Manufacturing Company—Traditional Environment with Inventory

If companies simply used all the materials they purchased to make one product, finished making all the units of that product that they started, and sold everything they finished, then calculating the income or loss from selling the product would be relatively easy. However, when multiple products are made or when materials are not all used, goods are not all finished, or products are not all sold, the process becomes more difficult.

To accurately determine the cost of manufactured products, a company must trace or allocate manufacturing costs to each individual product as it is being produced and then follow those costs through various inventory accounts as the product progresses toward eventual completion and sale. At the point of sale, the cost of producing the product (the cost of goods sold) must be matched with the sales price to compute a profit or loss on the sale (called

gross margin, or gross profit). Subtracting nonmanufacturing costs from the gross margin provides a measure of profitability for the company as a whole. When materials are not all used in production, goods are not finished, or finished goods are not all sold, costs must be accounted for in the appropriate raw materials, work in process, or finished-goods inventory accounts.

Manufacturing costs include the costs of direct materials, direct labor, and manufacturing overhead. These costs are also called product costs because they attach to the product as it goes through the production process. Picture a product moving down an assembly line. As labor, material, and overhead costs are incurred, they attach to the product being produced and remain with that product (in an inventory account) until it is sold. Costs flow in the same way that products flow through a production facility (see Exhibit 2-3).

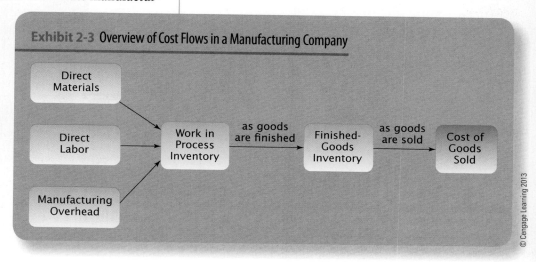

Exhibit 2-3 Overview of Cost Flows in a Manufacturing Company

© Cengage Learning 2013

This basic cost flow model is appropriate (with slight variations) for companies using either job-costing, operations-costing, or process-costing systems. The differences between the costing systems are discussed more fully in Chapter 3.

The Cost-of-Goods-Sold Model for a Traditional Manufacturing Company with Inventory

To illustrate the production process and some of the associated problems with costing products, we will use a fictional company called Northern Lights Custom Cabinets. Northern Lights Custom Cabinets manufactures and sells custom-ordered kitchen and bathroom cabinets. The company sells primarily to building contractors but occasionally deals directly with homeowners. Northern Lights is located in Anchorage, Alaska, and has been in business only a few years, so management is still learning the business and how to properly determine the cost of each cabinet.

Northern Lights has an engineering and design division, which is involved in all custom-cabinet jobs. Quality control dictates that the engineering and design division must design all cabinets. Northern Lights strives to minimize the costs of production without sacrificing quality. Once the design phase of each cabinet job is complete, the material must be ordered. The material is stored in the raw materials warehouse until needed for the job and is then moved to the production area.

The production factory is separated into three distinct areas (see Exhibit 2-4): cutting, assembly, and finishing. In the cutting area, all wood is cut into the required pieces, based on the plans from the engineering and design division. The pieces are all numbered and bundled for each particular section of the cabinet job. After cutting is completed, the bundles are moved to the assembly area, where the cabinets are constructed with the use of glue and wood dowels. The assembled cabinets are then moved to the finish area, where they are finished and stored for delivery to the home. This process can take up to one month to complete and is very labor intensive. Because each cabinet is custom made, Northern Lights also provides installation services for an extra charge.

Northern Lights purchases raw materials and stores the materials in a warehouse that is separate from the production facility, or factory. While these materials are in the warehouse, the costs of the raw materials are included in a raw materials inventory account. Northern Lights began 2011 with raw materials costing $10,000 on hand and purchased an additional $40,000 of raw materials during the year. Therefore, the company had $50,000 of raw materials available for use during the year.

The Purchase of Raw Materials		
Description	**Item**	**Amount**
Raw materials on hand to start the period	Beginning inventory of raw materials	$10,000
Purchases of raw materials during the period	+ Cost of raw materials purchased	+ 40,000
The pool of raw materials available for use during the period	= Raw materials available for use	= $50,000

Exhibit 2-4 The Northern Lights Production Process

Cutting
All wood is cut into required pieces.

Assembly
The cabinets are constructed by using glue and wood dowels.

Finishing
The cabinets are finished and stored for delivery.

© Cengage Learning 2013

The journal entry to record the purchase of raw materials is as follows:

Raw Materials Inventory	40,000	
Accounts Payable (or Cash)		40,000

When the raw materials are moved to the factory, the raw material costs move with the material to a work in process (WIP) inventory account. Any raw materials not used during the year remain in the raw materials inventory account. As shown next, if Northern Lights has $5,000 of raw materials in ending inventory at the end of the year, the raw materials used in production equal $45,000.

Transferring Raw Materials to Work in Process

scription	Item	Amount
w materials on hand to start the period	Beginning inventory of raw materials	$10,000
rchases of raw materials during the riod	+ Cost of raw materials purchased	+ 40,000
e pool of raw materials available for use ring the period	= Raw materials available for use	=$50,000
w materials on hand at the end of the riod	− Ending inventory of raw materials	− 5,000
e amount of raw materials used in oduction (and moved to work in process)	= Raw materials used in production	=$45,000

Raw Materials		Work in Process	
$10,000	= $45,000		
+ 40,000		$45,000	
− $ 5,000			

The journal entry to record the transfer of raw materials from raw materials inventory to WIP inventory is as follows:

Work in Process Inventory	45,000	
Raw Materials Inventory		45,000

As direct labor costs of $65,000 are incurred (factory workers work on the cabinets), the cost of the workers is added to the raw material cost in the WIP inventory account. Likewise, as manufacturing overhead costs ($85,000 of machine costs, rent, depreciation, the cost of utilities, the cost of indirect materials, and so forth) are incurred, they are added to the WIP account. As long as each set of cabinets remains in the factory, the costs associated with them are recorded in the WIP account.

The journal entry to record the incurrence of direct labor costs is as follows:

Work in Process Inventory	65,000	
Salaries and Wages Payable (or Cash)		65,000

The journal entry to record the incurrence of manufacturing overhead costs is as follows:

Work in Process Inventory	85,000	
Accounts Payable (or Cash)		85,000

Note that as the actual manufacturing overhead costs are incurred, they are entered directly into the WIP account, with corresponding credits to accounts payable or cash. This system of product costing using the actual overhead costs incurred is called **actual costing**. For a number of reasons discussed in Chapter 3, most companies utilize a system of product costing called **normal costing**, in which a manufacturing overhead clearing account is used and predetermined overhead rates are employed to apply overhead to the WIP account.

If there is no beginning inventory of work in process and everything that is started in 2011 is finished (there is no ending inventory of WIP), the cost of goods manufactured is simply the sum of raw materials used, direct labor, and manufacturing overhead. When beginning or ending inventories exist, the cost of goods manufactured must be adjusted accordingly. At the beginning of 2011, Northern Lights had $15,000 of unfinished cabinets (started in 2010) in the factory. These cabinets were completed in early 2011. However, the company got even further behind in 2011, resulting in $20,000 of cabinets being partially finished at the end of the year. Therefore, the cost of goods (cabinets) manufactured in 2011 and transferred to finished goods was $190,000.

The Calculation of Cost of Goods Manufactured

Description	Item	Amount
Work in process on hand at the beginning of the period	Beginning inventory of WIP	$ 15,000
The amount of raw materials used in production	+ Raw materials used	+ 45,000
The amount of direct labor cost incurred	+ Direct labor	+ 65,000
The amount of manufacturing overhead incurred	+ Manufacturing overhead	+ 85,000
Work in process at the end of the period	− Ending inventory of WIP	− 20,000
The cost of goods manufactured during the period	= Cost of goods manufactured	=$190,000

Actual costing A product costing system in which actual overhead costs are entered directly into work in process.

Normal costing A product costing system in which estimated or predetermined overhead rates are used to apply overhead to work in process.

The Calculation of Cost of Goods Manufactured (cont.)

Work in Process		Finished Goods
$15,000	= $190,000	
+ 45,000		
+ 65,000		
+ 85,000		$190,000
− $20,000		

The journal entry to record the transfer of finished goods from WIP to finished goods inventory is as follows:

Finished-Goods Inventory	190,000	
Work in Process Inventory		190,000

When a cabinet is sold, the accumulated costs in the finished-goods inventory account are moved to the cost-of-goods-sold account. If there is no beginning inventory of finished goods, and all the goods finished in the current year are sold (there is no ending inventory), the cost of goods sold is equal to the cost of goods manufactured. However, when beginning and ending inventories exist, the cost of goods sold must be adjusted accordingly. Northern Lights had one order (costing $30,000) that was not delivered to customers by the end of 2010. Likewise, at the end of 2011, the company had $5,000 of cabinets that were finished but not sold. Therefore, the cost of goods (cabinets) sold during 2011 was $215,000.

The Calculation of Cost of Goods Sold

Description	Item	Amount
Finished goods on hand at the beginning of the period	Beginning inventory of finished goods	$ 30,000
The cost of goods manufactured during the period	+ Cost of goods manufactured	+ 190,000
Finished goods on hand at the end of the period	− Ending inventory of finished goods	− $ 5,000
The cost of goods sold during the period	= Cost of goods sold	= $215,000

Finished Goods		Cost of Goods Sold
$ 30,000	= $215,000	
+ 190,000		$215,000
− $ 5,000		

The journal entry to record the cost of goods sold and the transfer of goods out of finished-goods inventory as the product is sold is as follows:

Cost of Goods Sold	215,000	
Finished-Goods Inventory		215,000

In sum, the flow of costs from the raw materials storeroom to WIP inventory, from WIP inventory to finished-goods inventory, and from finished-goods inventory to cost of goods sold is accounted for as shown in Exhibit 2-5.

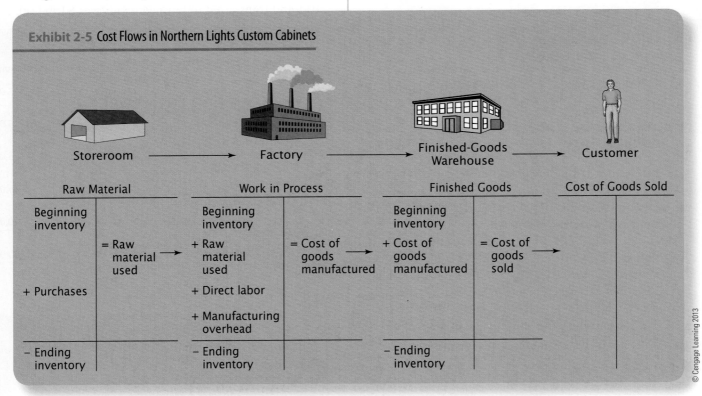

Exhibit 2-5 Cost Flows in Northern Lights Custom Cabinets

© Cengage Learning 2013

A schedule of cost of goods manufactured and a schedule of cost of goods sold for Northern Lights Custom Cabinets are presented in Exhibit 2-6.

Given that Northern Lights had sales of $500,000 and selling and administrative expenses of $175,000, the company's 2011 income statement is presented in Exhibit 2-7.

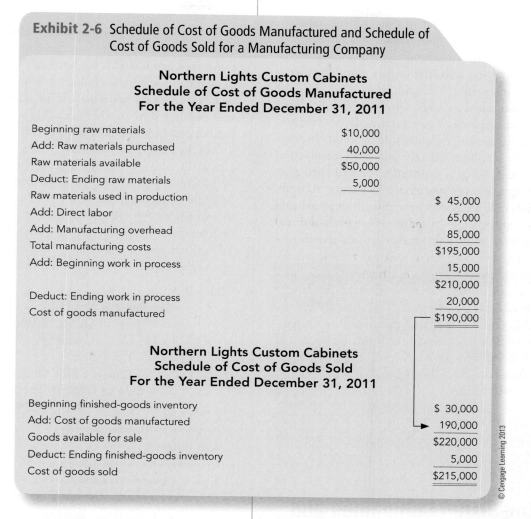

Exhibit 2-6 Schedule of Cost of Goods Manufactured and Schedule of Cost of Goods Sold for a Manufacturing Company

Northern Lights Custom Cabinets
Schedule of Cost of Goods Manufactured
For the Year Ended December 31, 2011

Beginning raw materials	$10,000	
Add: Raw materials purchased	40,000	
Raw materials available	$50,000	
Deduct: Ending raw materials	5,000	
Raw materials used in production		$ 45,000
Add: Direct labor		65,000
Add: Manufacturing overhead		85,000
Total manufacturing costs		$195,000
Add: Beginning work in process		15,000
		$210,000
Deduct: Ending work in process		20,000
Cost of goods manufactured		$190,000

Northern Lights Custom Cabinets
Schedule of Cost of Goods Sold
For the Year Ended December 31, 2011

Beginning finished-goods inventory	$ 30,000
Add: Cost of goods manufactured	190,000
Goods available for sale	$220,000
Deduct: Ending finished-goods inventory	5,000
Cost of goods sold	$215,000

© Cengage Learning 2013

Exhibit 2-7 Income Statement for a Manufacturing Company

Northern Lights Custom Cabinets
Income Statement
For the Year Ended December 31, 2011

Sales		$500,000
Cost of goods sold:		
Beginning finished-goods inventory	$ 30,000	
Add: Cost of goods manufactured	190,000	
Goods available for sale	$220,000	
Deduct: Ending finished-goods inventory	5,000	215,000
Gross margin		$285,000
Less: Selling and administrative expense		175,000
Net operating income		$110,000

© Cengage Learning 2013

Cost Flows in a Manufacturing Company—JIT Environment

How do cost flows differ in a manufacturing company utilizing JIT? Remember, in a JIT environment, the physical flow of goods is streamlined by the use of manufacturing cells that largely eliminate inventories of raw materials, WIP, and finished goods. Cost flows are streamlined as well. Direct materials, direct labor, and overhead costs can essentially be accumulated directly in a cost-of-goods-sold account. Because raw materials are immediately put into production when purchased, there is no need to record their purchase in a separate raw materials inventory account. Likewise, because all goods are typically finished and shipped out immediately to customers, there is no reason to keep track of WIP or finished-goods inventories.

The Calculation of Cost of Goods Sold—JIT Environment

Description	Item	Amount
The amount of raw materials purchased and used in production	Raw materials purchased and used	$ 50,000
The amount of direct labor costs incurred	+ Direct labor	+ 65,000
The amount of overhead cost incurred	+ Manufacturing overhead	+ 85,000
The cost of goods sold during the period	= Cost of goods sold	= $200,000

Merchandising Companies and the Cost of Products

Wholesalers and retailers purchase merchandise in finished form from other companies. With the exception of packaging and other minor changes, they simply offer the products for resale to other companies (wholesalers) or to the ultimate consumers (retailers). Therefore, the product cost of a wholesaler or retailer is simply the purchase price of the merchandise the wholesaler or retailer sells.

Because merchandising companies simply purchase goods for resale, the flow of costs in a retail or wholesale establishment is fairly simple. On the balance sheet, merchandising companies use a single account for inventory, called merchandise inventory. The costs incurred in inventory are simply the costs to purchase the inventory.

How are the costs incurred in purchasing inventory for resale expensed? You may recall from financial accounting that the principle of matching revenue from sales with the costs associated with that revenue means that the cost of purchasing merchandise is expensed as cost of goods sold as the merchandise is sold. However, the cost of goods sold is not necessarily equal to the cost of merchandise purchased during the period. If merchandise is purchased and not sold or if merchandise that was purchased in another period is sold in the current period, cost of goods sold must be adjusted accordingly.

In the example that follows, Cheryl's Bike Shop begins 2011 with a beginning inventory of bikes and parts of $15,000. During the year, the company purchases $63,000 of merchandise and has $78,000 of merchandise available for sale. At the end of 2011, $18,000 of merchandise inventory remains on hand, resulting in $60,000 of cost of goods sold. The company's Schedule of Cost of Goods Sold is shown in Exhibit 2-8.

Exhibit 2-8 Schedule of Cost of Goods Sold for a Merchandising Company

Cheryl's Bike Shop
Schedule of Cost of Goods Sold
For the Year Ended December 31, 2011

Beginning merchandise inventory	$15,000
Add: Purchases	63,000
Goods available for sale	$78,000
Deduct: Ending merchandise inventory	18,000
Cost of goods sold	$60,000

© Cengage Learning 2013

© steamroller_blues/Shutterstock.com

The Calculation of Cost of Goods Sold for a Merchandising Company

Description	Item	Amount
Merchandise on hand to start the period	Beginning inventory	$15,000
Acquisitions of merchandise during the period	+ Cost of goods purchased	+ 63,000
The pool of merchandise available for sale during the period	= Cost of goods available for sale	= 78,000
Merchandise on hand at the end of the period	− Ending inventory	− 18,000
The expense recognized on the income statement	= Cost of goods sold	= $60,000

With sales of $175,000 and selling and administrative expenses totaling $40,000, the income statement is shown in Exhibit 2-9.

Exhibit 2-9 Income Statement for a Merchandising Company

Cheryl's Bike Shop
Income Statement
For the Year Ended December 31, 2011

Sales		$175,000
Cost of goods sold:		
Beginning merchandise inventory	$15,000	
Add: Purchases	63,000	
Goods available for sale	$78,000	
Deduct: Ending merchandise inventory	18,000	60,000
Gross margin		$115,000
Less: Selling and administrative expense		40,000
Net operating income		$ 75,000

© Cengage Learning 2013

Service Companies and the Cost of Services

Many similarities exist between the costing of products in a manufacturing company and the costing of services. Rather than costing products that are manufactured and sold, service providers must calculate the costs associated with the revenue earned by the company from selling its services. Income statements of service providers typically refer to the "cost of services" as the "cost of revenue." Like product costs, the cost of services includes three components: direct materials, direct labor, and overhead. However, the proportions of each may vary dramatically. Service companies typically have a small amount of material costs and large amounts of labor and overhead.

Although service companies have both direct and indirect costs, they generally have larger proportions of indirect costs. For example,

- In a movie studio, costumes and props are direct materials and the salaries of actors and directors are direct labor. Overhead would include the costs of the studio itself and all the recording and production equipment. Camera operators and other support people would more than likely be classified as indirect labor because they would probably work on more than one film at a time.
- In a CPA firm, material costs would probably be very small. Although paper and other materials are used in the preparation of tax returns, the materials would probably be considered an indirect cost and classified as overhead. In contrast, direct labor costs for a CPA firm would be very large.
- In a hospital, although the costs of specific drugs and special tests or X-rays can be traced to a specific patient, the costs of operating rooms and equipment and the salaries of administrators, discharge personnel, orderlies, and maintenance workers would all be indirect.

Although service companies typically have little need for raw materials accounts and finished-goods inventory accounts, work in process (WIP) accounts are commonly used on projects that were incomplete at month's end, such as audits by CPA firms, lengthy legal cases by law firms, and consulting engagements that are long term.

LO5 Product Costs and Period Costs

As previously discussed, manufacturing costs, or product costs, attach to products as they go through the manufacturing process. Until the sale of the product, the costs of manufacturing are included in one of three inventory accounts: raw materials, work in process, and finished goods. These inventory accounts appear on the balance sheet along with other assets and liabilities. Only when a product is sold are manufacturing costs expensed as cost of goods sold on the income statement. By contrast, nonmanufacturing costs, or period costs, are expensed immediately on the income statement in the period in which they are incurred (see Exhibit 2-10).

> *Product costs attach to the product and are expensed only when the product is sold, whereas period costs are expensed in the period in which they are incurred.*

Exhibit 2-10 The Path to the Income Statement—Product and Period Costs

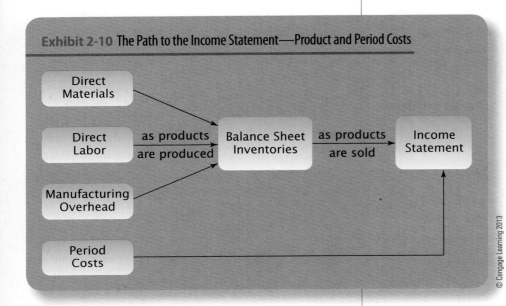

© Cengage Learning 2013

For external financial reporting purposes, information on the cost of goods sold (frequently called the cost of sales) and the amount of inventory owned by a company is provided in financial statements and included in the company's annual report.

STUDY TOOLS 2

Chapter review card

➔ Learning Objective and Key Concept Reviews

➔ Key Definitions and Formulas

Online (Located at www.cengagebrain.com)

➔ Flash Cards and Crossword Puzzles

➔ Games and Quizzes

➔ Washburn Guitars Video and E-Lectures

➔ Homework Assignments (as directed by your instructor)

1. Understanding the Production Process LO_1

An understanding of production processes is important to accurate costing of products. The following statements describe different aspects of production processes.

a. Manufacturing companies must produce their own raw materials to manufacture other products for customers.

b. There are only two inputs into the production process: raw materials and labor.

c. In the traditional manufacturing environment, similar machines are grouped together.

d. Products that have been partially manufactured are often called "work in process inventory."

e. The three types of inventory in a traditional manufacturing environment are direct materials, raw materials and finished goods.

Required

Indicate whether each of the above statements is true or false.

2. JIT and Lean Production LO_2

Just-in-time and lean production systems are widely viewed as improving the competitive position of companies. Complete the following sentences describing the effects of JIT and lean production using the words *increase(s)* or *decrease(s)*.

a. Storage and other inventory carrying costs _____.

b. The time required to make products typically _____.

c. Customer satisfaction _____.

d. The cost of raw materials may _____.

e. Product quality improves because the number of defective units _____.

f. Production flexibility _____ because employees are highly trained.

g. The number of suppliers often _____ because companies must have highly reliable suppliers that can deliver raw materials whenever needed.

3. Manufacturing vs. Nonmanufacturing Costs LO_3

The following costs were incurred by a manufacturer of breakfast cereals.

a. Heat, water, and power used in the factory

b. Cost of repairing mixing machines and ovens

c. Wheat, sweetener, and coloring used in production

d. Lease payments for salespersons' company cars

e. Wax paper used to package cereals

f. Overtime paid to office employees

Required

Indicate whether each of the preceding costs is a manufacturing cost or a nonmanufacturing cost.

4. Features of Lean Production LO_2

The sentences that follow describe key features of a lean production system. Indicate whether the statements are true or false.

a. Lean production is focused on eliminating waste associated with holding more inventory than is required.

b. Lean production is focused on having extra inventory on hand in case customer demand rises unexpectedly.

c. Lean production is focused on exceeding a customer's needs.

d. Lean production is focused on minimizing the amount of movement of products and people.

e. Lean production is focused on reducing waiting time.

5. Types of Manufacturing Costs LO_3

The following costs are manufacturing costs for a producer of personal computers.

a. Wages of employees who conduct quality testing

b. Purchase cost of processor chips included in the manufactured computers

c. Wages paid to maintenance workers

d. Property taxes paid for the manufacturing facility

e. Salaries paid to a staff nurse who provides care for manufacturing employees

f. Wages paid to assembly-line employees

g. Small screws and fasteners

Required

Indicate whether each of the preceding costs is direct material (DM), direct labor (DL), indirect material (IM), indirect labor (IL), or another manufacturing overhead cost (MOH).

6. Product Costs LO3

The Perfect Smile manufactures extra-whitening toothpaste. During the year the company had the following costs:

Direct materials used	$41,000
Direct labor	28,000
Factory rent	12,000
Factory depreciation	9,000
Office depreciation	4,050
Selling expenses	3,500
Administrative expenses	50,000

The company had no beginning or ending work in process inventory, no beginning finished goods inventory, and started and completed 45,000 units of toothpaste during the year.

Required
A. Calculate the total manufacturing costs for the year.
B. Calculate the product cost on a per-unit basis.

EXERCISES

7. Product Costs LO3

Berry Brothers is a new company that manufactures desks. In its first month of operation, it began and completed 500 desks. The following production information has been provided:

Direct material cost per unit	$ 18
Indirect labor costs	400
Indirect material costs	220
Marketing expenses	750
Cost per direct labor hour	15
Factory rent	2,000
Administrative expenses	1,600
Direct labor per unit	4 hours

Required
A. Calculate the cost of direct labor for one desk.
B. Calculate the total overhead costs for the first month of production.
C. Calculate the total manufacturing costs for the first month of production.

8. Direct and Indirect Labor LO3

Comfort Quilts manufactures decorative quilts and incurred the following wage and salary expenses for the most recent year:

Machine operators	$100,000
Quality control supervisors	50,000
Fabric cutters	25,000
Factory janitor	8,000
Company president	100,000

Required
Determine the amount of direct labor incurred during the year.

9. Raw Material Used LO3

Fun Central produces a variety of popular board games. The company has decided to strategically position itself in the industry with unique handcrafted game boards and game pieces. The company's controller has accumulated the following data regarding raw materials used in production:

Pounds of laminated corrugated material purchased	15,000
Board games produced	10,000
Average pounds of laminated corrugated material per board	0.80
Average cost per pound of laminated corrugated material	$ 1.24
Board games sold during the period	7,850

Required
Given that the company did not have any laminated corrugated board at the beginning of the period, calculate the amount of raw material cost that is included in the product cost for the period.

10. Cost Flows: Raw Materials Used LO4

At the beginning of the month, AGN Manufacturing had the following information available for the month of September:

	Beginning	Ending
Raw materials inventory	$25,000	$32,000
Work in process inventory	60,000	85,000
Finished-goods inventory	10,000	2,000

During the month of September, the company purchased $120,000 of raw materials. How much raw material was used in September?

11. Cost of Goods Manufactured LO4

Candy's Chocolate Shoppe had the following information available for the month of September:

	Beginning	Ending
Raw materials inventory	$40,000	$20,000
Work in process inventory	25,000	15,000
Finished-goods inventory	10,000	20,000
Raw materials purchased		75,000
Direct labor (3,000 hrs @ $10)		30,000
Overhead		50,000

Required
Calculate the cost of goods manufactured for the month.

12. Cost of Goods Manufactured LO4

Shelly's Bakery had the following information available for the month of January:

	Beginning	Ending
Raw materials inventory	$30,000	$20,000
Work in process inventory	20,000	15,000
Finished-goods inventory	15,000	20,000
Raw materials purchased		80,000
Direct labor (2,500 hrs @ $12)		30,000
Overhead		60,000

Required
Calculate the cost of goods manufactured for the month.

13. Cost of Goods Sold LO4

Memories, Inc., which produces specialty picture frames, had the following summary cost information:

Direct materials used	$24,000
Direct labor	22,000
Factory rent	6,000
Equipment depreciation	7,500
Marketing expense	15,000
Administrative expense	18,000
Number of units produced	25,000

The company had no beginning or ending work in process inventory and no beginning finished-goods inventory. The company sold 24,000 units.

Required
Calculate the cost of goods sold.

14. Basic Cost Flows: Raw Materials Used LO4

At the beginning of the month, Chateo, Inc., had raw materials of $54,000. During the month, the company purchased an additional $38,000 of raw materials. If the company used $63,000 of the raw materials for the month's production needs, what is the company's ending raw materials inventory balance?

15. Calculation of Net Income LO5

Classic Coolers manufactures portable coolers adorned with college logos. During the first quarter of the year, the company had the following costs:

Direct materials used	$56,000
Direct labor	38,000
Factory rent	24,000
Factory equipment depreciation	10,000
Office equipment depreciation	1,400
Marketing expenses	5,500
Administrative expenses	12,000

The company had no beginning or ending work in process inventory and no beginning finished-goods inventory. Although 8,000 units were started and finished during the quarter, just 5,300 were sold, for an average price of $25 each.

Required
Calculate Classic Coolers' net income for the first quarter.

16. Basic Cost Flows: Raw Materials Used LO4

BMV Automotive Manufacturers had the following information available for the month of January related to their current production of sports cars:

	Beginning	Ending
Raw materials inventory	$20,000	$37,000
Work in process inventory	55,000	80,000
Finished-goods inventory	10,000	3,000

During the month of January, BMV purchased $140,000 of raw materials. How much raw material was used in January?

17. Cost of Goods Sold LO4

Bell Computers, which produces made-to-order laptops, had the following summary cost information:

Direct materials used	$18,000
Direct labor	21,000
Factory rent	5,000
Equipment depreciation	7,500
Marketing expense	12,000
Administrative expense	16,000
Shipping charges	4,500
Number of units produced	20,000

The company had no beginning or ending work in process inventory and no beginning finished-goods inventory.

Required
Calculate the cost of goods sold if 18,000 units are sold.

18. Cost of Goods Sold and Merchandise Available for Sale in a Merchandising Company LO4

Dash Department Store features women's fashions. At the beginning of the year, the store had $514,000 in merchandise. Total purchases for the year were $463,000.

Required
A. Calculate the cost of goods sold for the year, assuming that the year-end inventory was $488,000.
B. What was the total amount of merchandise available for sale during the year?

19. Cost of Goods Sold and Sales for a Merchandising Company LO4

Roy's Selection is a local men's clothing store. Roy's buys clothing and accessories from manufacturers and marks them up by 55 percent. Roy's began the year with $155,000 of inventory ($240,250 retail value) and bought $350,000 of inventory (retail value $542,500) during the year. Ending inventory is $95,000 (retail value $147,250).

Required
A. Calculate Roy's cost of goods sold for the year.
B. Calculate Roy's sales for the year.

20. Calculation of Net Income LO5

You are the president of Our Bakery. Your new accountant, who recently graduated from a local university, presented you with the following income statement for the month of January:

Sales revenues	$660,000
Less: Total January expenses	595,000
Net income	$ 65,000

By talking to the production departments, you learn that 60,000 units were produced in January at a total cost of $420,000. The sales department notes that 55,000 units were sold for $11 each. Monthly administrative and marketing expenses totaled $75,000.

Required
Based on the preceding information, calculate the correct amount of net income for January.

21. Product vs. Period Cost LO5

Columbia Brick, a manufacturing company, prepays its insurance coverage for a three-year period. The premium for the three years is $21,000 and is paid at the beginning of the first year. Three-fourths of the premium relates to factory operations, and one-fourth relates to selling and administrative activities.

Required
A. Calculate the amount of the premium that should be recorded as a product cost each year.
B. Calculate the amount of the premium that should be recorded as a period cost each year.

PROBLEMS

22. Cost of Goods Manufactured, Cost of Goods Sold, and Impact on Financial Statements LO3, 4, 5

The accounting information system of Bosch, Inc., reported the following cost and inventory data for the year:

Costs Incurred		
Raw materials purchased		$125,000
Direct labor		75,000
Indirect labor		40,000
Equipment maintenance		10,000
Insurance on factory		12,000
Rent on factory		30,000
Equipment depreciation		20,000
Factory supplies		11,000
Advertising expenses		15,000
Selling and administrative expenses		21,000

Inventories	Beginning Balance	Ending Balance
Raw materials	$10,000	$17,000
Work in process	20,000	31,000
Finished goods	30,000	25,000

Required

A. Calculate the cost of goods manufactured.
B. Calculate the cost of goods sold.
C. List the costs not included in the calculations of cost of goods manufactured and cost of goods sold, and discuss why you excluded them from those calculations.
D. If raw materials and work in process inventories had decreased during the year, would the financial statements be different? How?

23. Cost of Goods Manufactured and Cost of Goods Sold LO3, 4, 5

The accounting information system of Textbook Co. reported the following cost and inventory data for the year:

Costs Incurred	
Raw materials purchased	$100,000
Direct labor	50,000
Indirect labor	35,000
Equipment maintenance	9,000
Insurance on factory	11,000
Rent on factory	40,000
Equipment depreciation	20,000
Factory supplies	12,000
Advertising expenses	18,000
Selling and administrative expenses	25,000
Net revenue	350,000

Inventories	Beginning Balance	Ending Balance
Raw materials	$15,000	$18,000
Work in process	20,000	29,000
Finished goods	35,000	30,000

Required

A. Calculate the cost of goods manufactured.
B. Calculate the cost of goods sold.
C. Calculate the gross margin and operating income.

24. Decision Focus: Impact on Financial Statements LO3, 4, 5

B&B Manufacturing Co. was organized on January 1 of the current year. Outside investors who financed the business stipulated that the company must show a profit by the sixth month or the financing will be stopped. B&B reported losses for the first four months, but expected to show a profit in the fifth (the current) month. After reviewing the income statement for the fifth month (May), the president,

Craig, was disappointed with the performance and called an employee meeting. At the meeting, Craig informed the employees that, on the basis of the performance for the first five months and, in particular, the month of May, he saw very little hope of a profit by the sixth month. He also informed the employees that they should prepare to close the business. After the meeting, the controller quit, leaving you in charge of the accounting function. The latest financial information is as follows:

B&B Manufacturing Co. Income Statement For the Month Ended May 31		
Sales		$325,000
Less: Raw materials purchased	$140,000	
Direct labor	75,000	
Indirect labor	10,000	
Utilities	25,000	
Depreciation	30,000	
Insurance	15,000	
Rent	12,000	
Selling & administrative	30,000	
Advertising	25,000	
		362,000
Net loss		$ (37,000)

Other Information

Inventory	May 1 Balance	May 31 Balance
Raw materials	$10,000	$30,000
Work in process	15,000	22,000
Finished goods	50,000	70,000

Seventy-five percent of utilities, depreciation, insurance, and rent are related to production operations, whereas 25 percent of those costs are related to selling and administrative activities.

Required

A. Prepare the income statement for May on the basis of the information provided previously. (Include a statement of cost of goods manufactured and a statement of cost of goods sold.)
B. Do you agree with the president's assessment of the situation? Why or why not?
C. How will you explain to the investors why your income statement is different from the one prepared by the controller?

25. Decision Focus: Service Company LO3, 5

Mead & Lawson, LLP, is a local CPA firm that prepares approximately 1,000 tax returns each year for its clients. The managing partner of the firm has asked for information concerning the costs of preparing tax returns. He has been provided with the following data:

Average wage per hour of tax preparation staff	$35
Average wage per hour of clerical staff	$12
Average number of hours per return (preparation)	10
Average number of hours per return (clerical)	2

Required

A. What is Mead & Lawson's average direct labor cost of preparing a tax return?
B. Think creatively about options that might be used to reduce the cost of preparing tax returns. What are the implications of the options you envision?
C. Mead & Lawson has an opportunity to purchase tax preparation software for $5,000 per year. If the software is used, the hours needed to prepare the return would decrease to three hours per return and the clerical time would increase to four hours because of additional computer operator time. How would the purchase affect the cost of labor on a per–tax return basis?
D. Does it appear to be a good business decision to purchase the software? What other costs must be considered?
E. What are the qualitative aspects of the preceding decision?

26. Basic Cost Flows, Income Statement LO4, 5

Business managers frequently operate in a world where data are not readily available. Imagine a situation in which a company experiences a catastrophic event (for example, a hurricane, flood, or fire) and must reconstruct its accounting data. Consider the following independent situations in which selected data are missing:

	Company 1	Company 2
Direct materials used	$ 9,000	$19,000
Direct labor	4,000	14,000
Manufacturing overhead	11,000	?
Total manufacturing costs	$?	$35,000
Beginning work in process	?	11,000
Ending work in process	6,000	13,500
Cost of goods manufactured	$21,000	$?
Sales	$35,000	$50,000
Beginning finished-goods inventory	$ 7,000	$?
Cost of goods manufactured	?	?
Goods available for sale	$?	$?
Ending finished-goods inventory	10,000	14,000
Cost of goods sold	$?	$25,500
Gross margin	$?	$?
Selling and administrative expenses	7,000	?
Net operating income	$?	$15,500

Required

A. Supply the missing data for each independent situation.
B. Prepare an income statement for each independent situation.

27. Basic Cost Flows LO4, 5

Home Cabinets manufactures and sells custom-ordered kitchen and bathroom cabinets. The company sells primarily to building contractors but occasionally deals directly with homeowners. Following is a summary of inventory and cost information for the year:

	Beginning Balance	Ending Balance
Raw materials inventory	$10,000	$15,000
Work in process inventory	15,000	12,000
Finished-goods inventory	30,000	32,000

During the year, raw material purchases totaled $350,000. Home Cabinets incurred $200,000 in labor costs in the factory and $175,000 in manufacturing overhead for the year.

Required

A. Calculate the amount of direct materials transferred to work in process during the year.
B. Calculate total manufacturing costs for the year.
C. Calculate the total cost of goods manufactured for the year.
D. Calculate the cost of goods sold for the year.

28. Basic Cost Flows, Income Statement LO4, 5

Business managers frequently operate in a world where data are not readily available. Two independent situations follow:

	Company 1	Company 2
Direct materials used	$10,000	$20,000
Direct labor	5,000	13,000
Manufacturing overhead	12,000	?
Total manufacturing costs	?	35,000
Beginning work in process	?	15,000
Ending work in process	6,000	17,500
Cost of goods manufactured	$23,000	?
Sales	$35,000	$50,000
Beginning finished-goods inventory	10,000	?
Cost of goods manufactured	?	?
Goods available for sale	?	?
Ending finished-goods inventory	12,000	15,000
Cost of goods sold	?	26,000
Gross margin	?	?
Selling and administrative expenses	9,500	?
Net operating income	$?	$17,000

Required

A. On the basis of the preceding information, reconstruct the accounting data for each company.

B. Prepare an income statement for each company.

29. Basic Cost Flows, Income Statement LO4, 5

Venus Corporation's accounting manager recently left the company without completing the company's schedule of cost of goods manufactured. The company's president is unsure what to do. He is unable to complete the schedule and has turned to you for help.

Venus Corporation Schedule of Cost of Goods Manufactured For the Month Ended December 31, 2011		
Direct Materials:		
Beginning raw materials	$ 16,000	
Raw material purchases	?	
Raw materials available	164,000	
Ending raw materials	?	
Raw materials used in production		$154,500
Direct Labor		?
Manufacturing Overhead:		
Indirect labor	$?	
Glue and fasteners	1,080	
Equipment depreciation	11,210	
Factory depreciation	4,300	
Factory insurance	2,420	
Property taxes	3,600	
Utilities	2,100	
Total manufacturing overhead		52,010
Total manufacturing costs		$269,760
Add: Beginning work in process		?
		$288,590
Deduct: Ending work in process		12,940
Cost of goods manufactured		$?

Inventories	Beginning Balance	Ending Balance
Raw materials	$ 16,000	$?
Work in process		12,940
Finished goods	23,000	17,830

Required

A. Supply the missing data.

B. Prepare an income statement for the month. Sales totaled $415,000 for December, and selling and administrative expenses were $31,900.

30. Cost Flows and Financial Statements LO4, 5

New River Computer Company began manufacturing personal computers for small businesses at the beginning of 2011. During the year, New River purchased 30,000 mouse pads with the company's name and logo at a cost of $2.50 each. The marketing manager used 2,500 of the pads as an advertising gimmick at a local trade show, and 25,000 of the pads were packaged with computers that were manufactured during 2011. Eighty percent of the computers were sold in 2011.

Required

A. Determine the cost of the mouse pads that would be included in the following accounts as of December 31, 2011:
   a. Raw materials
   b. Finished goods
   c. Cost of goods sold
   d. Advertising expense
B. On which basic financial statement do the accounts in question A appear? Why does it matter on which basic financial statement the amounts associated with purchasing the computer mouse pads appear?

CASES

31. JIT Implementation, Financial Statements LO2, 5

You recently began work at Colt Kitchen, Ltd. The company is a well-known distributor of gourmet foods. Like many similar companies, Colt Kitchen currently maintains a relatively large warehouse in which a wide variety of products are stored. Most other food wholesalers also maintain large warehouses; however, Sharon Oblinger, the company's president, is very concerned about the company's ability to maintain and sell the freshest products. She has also grown increasingly concerned about the company's cash management practices. She has accumulated the following inventory data:

Spices	$ 28,000
Coffee and tea	61,060
Pasta	32,140
Vegetables	108,460
Health supplements	84,700
Dairy	46,975
Meats	185,610
Personal products	71,440
Household	88,200
Pet care	15,920

Ken Martin, cofounder and chief strategist, is equally concerned about the company, but he believes that specialty food shops that sell the company's products expect to be able to order items from Colt Kitchen and have them shipped immediately. In short, Ken thinks that maintaining an adequate inventory is crucial to the company's future. Sharon and Ken have set a meeting for late next week to decide on the company's adoption

of a just-in-time inventory management system. Sharon is proposing that inventory be reduced by 80 percent and that warehouse employment be decreased by 30 percent. Currently, the 10 warehouse employees earn an average gross pay of $350 per week.

Required

A. What impact will reducing inventory by 80 percent have on Colt Kitchen's ability to meet its customer demand?
B. If Sharon and Ken agree to reduce inventory, how should the company accomplish the reduction?
C. Assume that Colt Kitchen can invest cash that would otherwise be "tied up" in inventory. Calculate the potential interest income if the company were to receive an annual interest rate of 3.5 percent on the cash that would otherwise be invested in the inventory (represented by the 80 percent reduction).
D. Although annual sales are currently $3.8 million, Ken believes that adopting a just-in-time system will ultimately cause problems such that customers will turn to other wholesalers for their needs. Ken is estimating lost revenues of 20 percent. If the company's gross profit is 30 percent of sales, what impact will the lost revenues have on the company's income statement?
E. Should Colt Kitchen adopt the just-in-time inventory management system? Why or why not?

32. Manufacturing Costs versus Nonmanufacturing Costs, Income Statements LO3, 5

Fancy Glassware is a producer of heirloom-quality glassware. The company has a solid reputation and is widely regarded as a model corporate citizen. Your friend began working for the company last year as a financial analyst and has recently begun to question the company's squeaky-clean image. Because you graduated with an accounting degree from a well-regarded university, your friend has asked you to look over Fancy Glassware's income statement and answer a few questions. The income statement appears as follows:

Fancy Glassware, Inc. Statement of Income For the Year Ended October 31, 2011	
Sales revenue	$12,008,450
Cost of goods sold	8,475,361
Gross profit	3,533,089
Selling & administrative expenses	1,845,902
Net operating income	$ 1,687,187

Your friend also asked that you look over the following supplementary schedule:

Fancy Glassware, Inc. Manufacturing Overhead Schedule For the Year Ended October 31, 2011	
Indirect labor	$ 743,012
Supplies	41,950
Advertising	210,375
Equipment depreciation	96,210
Factory depreciation	32,900
Factory insurance	22,420
Property taxes	18,600
Utilities	27,100
Management salary allocation	194,800
Total manufacturing overhead	$1,387,367

You are a little surprised to see the inclusion of advertising expense in the manufacturing overhead schedule, and you really have no idea why the "management salary allocation" would be considered overhead.

Required

A. Where would you expect to see advertising expense included on an income statement? Does the inclusion of advertising in the overhead amount seem reasonable to you? Why might Fancy Glassware want to include advertising expense in manufacturing overhead?

B. Your friend explains to you that the "management salary allocation" is the result of a corporate strategy of requiring that each part of the business bear some of the costs associated with management's functions. You learn that none of the salary allocation relates to management members who are associated with production operations. Is the inclusion of the salary allocation legitimate?

C. What is the impact on the financial statement of including advertising expenses and an allocation for management's salaries in manufacturing overhead?

Job Costing, Process
Costing, and Operations Costing

Introduction

One of the most important roles of managerial accountants is to help determine the cost of the products or services being produced and sold by a company. Cost information is equally important for manufacturing and service businesses and is used by managers across the organization. Pricing decisions made by marketing managers, manufacturing decisions made by production managers, and finance decisions made by finance managers are all influenced by the cost of products.

For example, marketing managers need to set a competitive price that will capture the needed market share and provide a fair profit. On the one hand, if the price of the product is set too low, a larger market share may be captured but the business may not earn a satisfactory profit. On the other hand, if the price of the product is too high, the business may not capture sufficient market share to remain competitive. These pricing decisions require product cost information in order for an optimal price to be set.

LO1 Product Costing Systems

Just as companies use different techniques to manufacture products or to provide services, companies also use various product costing systems to accumulate, track, and assign the costs of production to the goods produced and services provided.

Job Costing

Companies that manufacture customized products or provide customized services to clients use a costing system called **job costing,** which accumulates, tracks, and assigns costs for each job. Jobs are simply the individual units of a product. For a builder of custom homes, each house is a job. For a CPA firm, a job might be an individual tax return, an audit engagement,

Job costing A costing system that accumulates, tracks, and assigns costs for each job produced by a company.

Learning Objectives

After studying the material in this chapter, you should be able to:

LO1 Contrast job costing, process costing, and operations costing and explain how they are used to accumulate, track, and assign product costs.

LO2 Recognize issues related to the measurement of direct material and direct labor costs in job costing.

LO3 Recognize issues related to the allocation of manufacturing overhead cost to products.

LO4 Explain the need for using predetermined overhead rates and calculate overhead applied to production.

LO5 Determine whether overhead has been over- or underapplied and demonstrate the alternative treatments of the over- or underapplied amount.

LO6 Describe basic process costing and the calculation of equivalent units of production.

LO7 Compare and contrast the weighted-average and first-in, first-out (FIFO) methods of process costing and apply each step of the four-step process costing system under both methods.

LO8 Allocate service department costs using the direct and step-down methods.

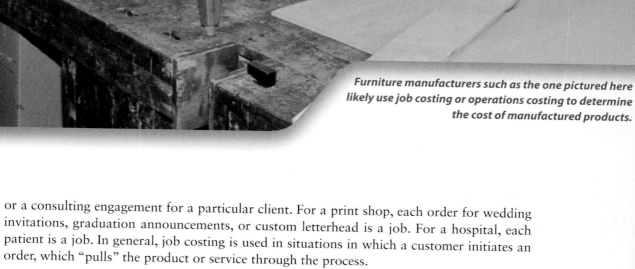

Furniture manufacturers such as the one pictured here likely use job costing or operations costing to determine the cost of manufactured products.

or a consulting engagement for a particular client. For a print shop, each order for wedding invitations, graduation announcements, or custom letterhead is a job. For a hospital, each patient is a job. In general, job costing is used in situations in which a customer initiates an order, which "pulls" the product or service through the process.

Process Costing

Companies that produce a homogeneous product on a continuous basis (oil refineries, breweries, paint and paper manufacturers, for example) use **process costing** to accumulate, track, and assign costs to products. In general, process costing is used by companies that

> **Process costing** A costing system that accumulates and tracks costs for each process performed and then assigns those costs equally to each unit produced.

© Marka/Alamy

The type of costing system used depends upon the manufacturing process and the nature and availability of cost data.

forecast demand and consequently "push" a product through the manufacturing process. Rather than accumulating the costs for each unit produced and directly tracking and assigning costs to each unique unit, process costing accumulates and tracks costs for each process as products pass through the process and then assigns costs equally to the units that come out of each process. A process is simply the work that is performed on a product. For a paint manufacturer, blending and pouring are processes. For a bread baker, mixing, baking, and slicing are processes.

Operations Costing

Operations costing is a hybrid of job and process costing and is used by companies, such as clothing or automobile manufacturers, that make products in batches—large numbers of products that are standardized within a batch. For example, a clothing manufacturer might make 5,000 identical shirts in one batch. Each batch is costed like a job in job costing, but each shirt in the batch is costed like a homogeneous product in process costing. Exhibit 3-1 summarizes the types of products that would most likely be costed by using job, operations, and process costing.

LO2 Basic Job Costing for Manufacturing and Service Companies

Charles' Custom Furniture (CCF) uses job costing to accumulate, track, and assign costs to the cabinets it produces. CCF builds furniture based on customer orders, so each piece is unique. The direct material, direct labor, and overhead costs for a specific job are accumulated on a job cost report. This report may be prepared manually or be totally automated. Regardless, its role is to keep track of the material, labor, and overhead costs that are incurred for a particular job. A job cost report for CCF is shown in Exhibit 3-2.

Measuring and Tracking Direct Materials

© iStockphoto.com/Olga Utlyakova

Direct material costs include the costs of the primary materials used in production. In addition to the cost of the materials themselves, direct material costs include shipping costs (if paid by the purchaser), sales tax paid on the purchase (if any), and other costs incurred in delivering the materials to the factory.

Measuring direct material costs should be a relatively easy task for CCF. The company has to identify only the amount of material actually used in each job and attach the proper cost to it. CCF uses a variety of materials, including wood, fabric, glue, screws, dowels, and stain, in constructing a finished piece of furniture. Although some of the more common materials are stored in inventory, exotic and more expensive wood, fabric, and hardware such as handles are typically purchased just in time for their use in a particular job. Raw materials are recorded on the job cost report as they are needed for a particular job.

In Exhibit 3-2, you can see that CCF used oak, maple, particleboard, and glass in the manufacture

Exhibit 3-1 Product Costing Systems

	Costing System		
	Job Costing	**Operations Costing**	**Process Costing**
Type of Product	Custom	Standardized within batches	Homogeneous
Examples	Construction, movie studios, hospitals, print shops, CPA and law firms	Automobile and clothing manufacturers	Beverages, oil refineries, paint, paper, rolled steel

© Cengage Learning 2013

Operations costing A hybrid of job and process costing; used by companies that make products in batches.

Exhibit 3-2 Job Cost Report

Charles' Custom Furniture

Job Number: 101
Date Started: March 6
Description: TV Cabinet

Customer: Robyn Gray
Date Finished: March 19

Direct Materials		Direct Labor			Manufacturing Overhead		
Type	Cost	Employee	Hours	Amount	Hours	Rate	Amount
Oak	$ 875.00	Staley	12.6	$255.15	22.4	$12.50	$280.00
Maple	600.00	Chen	4.5	91.13			
Particle-board	78.00	Kent	5.3	107.33			
Glass	330.00						
	$1,883.00		22.4	$453.61	22.4		$280.00

Cost Summary		
	Direct Materials	$1,883.00
	Direct Labor	453.61
	Manufacturing Overhead	280.00
	Total	$2,616.61

© Cengage Learning 2013

> *Direct material costs include the cost of the primary materials used in production, along with shipping costs and sales taxes.*

the hospital. Doctors need to know exactly what medications have been given and when. So, although it may also provide a way to charge patients for the cost of medications they consume during a hospital stay, the costing of the medications is probably not as important as the tracking itself.

of Job 101. These materials can all be traced directly to Job 101 and are treated as direct materials.

CCF also uses a variety of wooden dowels, screws, glues, and finishing nails in the construction of Job 101. However, you should note that these items are not listed as direct materials on the job cost report in Exhibit 3-2. Although it may be physically possible to track the specific screws, glue, and nails to a particular job, the cost of doing so is great and the benefits are few. CCF has chosen to treat these materials as indirect materials that will be allocated to the job as part of overhead.

Companies that primarily provide services to clients or have minimal material costs may not treat any materials as direct. For example, a law firm that primarily prepares wills and other paper documents may choose to treat the cost of paper as an indirect material cost (part of overhead). Likewise, although CPA firms may use a lot of paper and other materials in processing tax returns for clients, they may not track the paper to specific jobs on a job cost report.

In contrast, a hospital might choose to itemize every pill (even aspirin) and other medication given to a patient and every bandage used in an operation on a patient's job cost report (the patient's case file). Tracking the use of pills and other medications to a patient provides other valuable benefits to doctors and

Measuring and Tracking Direct Labor

The costs of direct labor are the wages earned by production workers for the actual time spent working on a product. The measurement of direct labor cost also should be a relatively easy task. Direct labor cost refers to labor that is directly related to manufacturing a product or providing a service. Assembly-line workers in a manufacturing setting and CPAs working on tax returns are examples of direct labor. By contrast, manufacturing supervisors, janitorial staff, and maintenance personnel in a manufacturing company and secretarial staff in a CPA firm are considered indirect labor and are included in overhead. The costs of direct labor for a specific job may be accumulated on a job cost report, but most companies keep track of each employee's time by requiring the completion of time sheets. Time sheets may be prepared by hand or be totally automated and integrated with the company's accounting information system (AIS). Regardless of the form used, employees must keep track of how much time they spend on specific jobs. For assembly-line workers, management needs to know how much time is spent manufacturing a specific product. For CPAs and attorneys, the managing partner needs to know how many hours are spent serving a particular client.

Charging for Shop Supplies

"Why did I get charged for shop supplies when I took my car to the dealer for repairs? Is this a legitimate expense?" That was the question asked of Tom and Ray Magliozzi (also known as Click and Clack, the Tappet Brothers) of *Car Talk* fame on their Web site (www.cartalk.com). Ray explains that shop supplies refer to things like solvents, cleaners, and small quantities

© iStockphoto.com/1001nights

of fluids that are used in servicing a vehicle. Although small shops may track the shop supplies that were used for a particular job and itemize them on your bill, larger shops often have difficulty keeping track of the supplies on a job-by-job basis. Accordingly, they may treat the supplies as overhead and either increase the labor rate charged to the job or charge customers a percentage of the repair cost.

Source: http://www.cartalk.com/content/columns/Archive/2008/January/06.html; accessed on January 31, 2008.

The cost of direct labor is calculated simply by multiplying a wage rate for each employee by the number of hours that each employee works on each product.

Fringe Benefits In addition to the hourly cost of labor, wage rates must include the cost of **fringe benefits**. These fringe benefits include the employer's cost for health, dental, and other insurance; retirement plans; and so on. The employer portion of social security tax and state and federal unemployment taxes would also be included. Studies have shown that fringe benefits typically cost a company 30 to 35 percent of the base wage of each full-time employee. The job cost report in Exhibit 3-2 shows that three employees of CCF worked 22.4 hours on Job 101 at a cost of $20.25 per hour. This cost includes a $15 hourly wage rate plus benefits of $5.25 per hour.

Idle Time As a result of a power outage, CCF incurred **idle time** while working on Job 101. Would CCF most likely treat this idle time as overhead or as an additional cost of direct labor assigned directly to Job 101? Not all the time that direct labor workers are paid for is spent productively. For example, if machinery and equipment break down or if materials are not available when needed, idle time results. Although idle time could be traced to a specific job (the job that is being worked on when the idle time occurs), most companies choose to treat idle time as an overhead cost rather than a cost of a specific job.

Overtime **Overtime premiums** paid to direct labor workers cause similar classification problems. Overtime is typically paid at 150 percent of the normal wage rate (sometimes called "time and a half") for hours worked in excess of 40 per week. For example, let's assume that the hourly pay for an assembly-line worker is $15. An overtime premium for this worker would be $7.50 per hour, increasing the total hourly wage to $22.50. With fringe benefits at 35 percent, the cost of labor rises to $30.38 per hour.

Overtime may be incurred for a number of reasons. Sometimes, production problems cause a company to get behind on a job. When this happens, the company may choose to incur overtime costs (work over the weekend) to finish up the job on time. In other situations, a company might accept an order, knowing that it will require the scheduling of overtime.

In practice, the treatment of overtime costs depends on the reason the overtime is incurred. For most companies, if overtime is incurred as a result of production

Fringe benefits Payroll costs in addition to the basic hourly wage.

Idle time Worker time that is not used in the production of the finished product.

Overtime premium An additional amount added to the basic hourly wage owing to overtime worked by the workers.

problems, it is treated as overhead. By contrast, if the overtime results from the acceptance of a rush order, most companies would treat the overtime as a direct labor cost that would be assigned to the specific job (and would most likely be included in determining its price).

For example, on a Friday morning, the customer who had ordered Job 101 called CCF and said she needed the TV cabinet next Monday instead of next Wednesday. CCF craftspeople worked eight hours on Saturday, and the company incurred overtime premiums, in order to finish the job by the new due date. CCF likely would treat the overtime premium as a direct labor cost in this situation.

In highly automated manufacturing environments, the cost of direct labor has been reduced significantly as automated machinery and robotics have replaced direct labor workers. This shift in product costs from labor to overhead has had important implications for product costing. Whereas the cost of direct labor is relatively easy to accumulate, track, and assign to products, overhead costs are a different matter.

LO3 Manufacturing Overhead

Overhead is the most difficult product cost to accumulate, track, and assign to products. Unlike direct materials and direct labor, overhead is made up of several seemingly unrelated costs: rent and lease payments for machinery and equipment used in the factory; depreciation on the factory equipment and building; factory supplies and other indirect materials; electricity, natural gas, and other utility costs for operating the manufacturing facilities and equipment; indirect labor costs for employees who perform maintenance on the equipment and clean the manufacturing area; repair and maintenance costs related to the manufacturing equipment and facilities; and insurance and property taxes on the manufacturing equipment and facilities. In addition, overhead is generally indirect in nature. As a result, overhead cannot be directly tracked to products and services but must instead be allocated in order for managers to determine the true cost of manufacturing a product or providing a service.[1]

Allocation involves finding a logical method of assigning overhead costs to the products or services a

[1]Generally accepted accounting principles (GAAP) require that manufacturing overhead be allocated to inventory and cost of goods sold for financial accounting purposes.

Overhead cannot be directly tracked to products and services but must instead be allocated with the use of cost drivers.

company produces or provides. If a company produced only one product, the allocation would be simple. We could simply divide the total overhead cost by the total number of units produced. If our total overhead costs incurred during the year were $100,000 and we produced 20,000 identical tables during the year, it would be logical to assign $5 of overhead to each table ($100,000 ÷ 20,000 tables). However, what if we make 10,000 tables and 10,000 chairs? Does it still make sense to allocate overhead on the basis of the number of units produced? Probably not. A more logical approach might be to allocate the overhead to the tables and chairs on the basis of the number of direct labor hours or machine hours consumed in the manufacture of each. If chairs take twice as long to manufacture as tables, twice as much overhead would be allocated to them. The choice of an allocation base requires a thorough understanding of what causes overhead costs to be incurred.

Cost Drivers and Overhead Rates

Understanding what causes overhead costs to be incurred is the key to allocating overhead. The choice of a logical base on which to allocate overhead depends on finding a cause-and-effect relationship between the base and the overhead. A good allocation base is a base that drives the incurrence of the overhead cost. Therefore, allocation bases are often referred to as **cost drivers**.

A cost driver for overhead is an activity that causes overhead to be incurred. If we wanted to allocate the cost of utilities incurred to run machines in the factory to products, we would want to find a cost driver that causes the utility costs to be incurred. In this case, the time the machines were in use (machine hours) might be an appropriate allocation base. If it takes twice as many machine hours to make chairs as it does to make tables, chairs would correspondingly be allocated twice

Allocation The process of finding a logical method of assigning overhead costs to the products or services a company produces or provides.

Cost drivers Factors that cause, or drive, the incurrence of costs.

© lightpoet/Shutterstock.com

Understanding what causes overhead costs to be incurred (what drives them) is the key to allocating overhead.

as much utility cost. In more labor-intensive companies, the cost of utilities might be allocated by using direct labor hours instead of machine hours as the cost driver. The choice of cost driver depends on the specific company and the processes it utilizes in manufacturing products and providing services to customers.

Overhead consists of a variety of costs with potentially different drivers for each. For example, the salaries of janitors and supervisors in the factory are overhead costs. The costs of rent and insurance for the factory building are overhead costs. The costs of indirect materials are overhead costs. Instead of identifying cost drivers for each component of overhead, companies have traditionally lumped overhead into similar **cost pools** to simplify the task. In the most extreme case, companies lump all overhead costs into one cost pool for the entire factory. Other companies have separate pools of overhead costs for each department. Still others use cost pools for each activity performed in making a product. Regardless of the number of cost pools and method of overhead allocation used, overhead rates are calculated with the same basic formula:

$$\text{Overhead rate} = \frac{\text{Manufacturing overhead}}{\text{Cost driver}}$$

CCF incurs utility costs of $1,000 during a month and starts and finishes 12 jobs. Each job requires machine time, but the time varies greatly, depending on the materials used and the difficulty of the job. Job 101 required 22.4 labor hours, whereas Job 104 required 60 hours. Labor hours during that month totaled 500. If CCF allocates utility cost with labor hours as the cost driver, how much of the utility cost should be allocated to Job 101? How much to Job 104? The overhead rate for utility costs is $2 per direct labor hour ($1,000 ÷ 500 direct labor hours). Therefore, $44.80 of utility costs (22.4 hours × $2 per hour) should be allocated to Job 101, whereas $120 of utility costs (60 hours × $2 per hour) should be allocated to Job 104.

Plantwide Overhead Rates

In labor-intensive manufacturing companies and service industries, direct labor hours or direct labor cost have often served as cost drivers. In automated manufacturing environments, machine hours historically have been used as the cost driver. Direct labor hours and machine hours are both volume-based cost drivers; that is, they are directly related to the volume or number of units produced. Allocating overhead based on the basis of direct labor hours or machine time works well when companies make only a few products, when they incur relatively small overhead costs compared with labor and material costs, and when that overhead is related to the volume of products produced.

For example, as demonstrated in Exhibit 3-3, a pizza restaurant might apply overhead by using a single predetermined overhead rate for the entire restaurant. The costs of pizza ovens, rent, and utilities, as well as other overhead costs, would be lumped into one cost pool and allocated to products (pizzas), based on the amount of labor time (direct labor hours, or DLHs) it takes to make each pizza. In this case, the cost of overhead is relatively small and is likely to be related to the number of pizzas made.

Cost pools Groups of overhead costs that are similar; used to simplify the task of assigning costs to products with ABC costing.

Exhibit 3-3 Applying Overhead by Using a Plantwide Rate

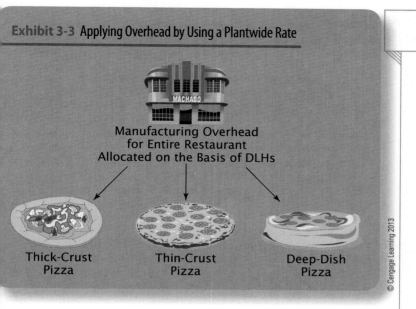

Manufacturing Overhead
for Entire Restaurant
Allocated on the Basis of DLHs

Thick-Crust Pizza   Thin-Crust Pizza   Deep-Dish Pizza

© Cengage Learning 2013

In Exhibit 3-4, overhead costs total $8,000 per month. If direct labor hours per month are 800, the overhead rate is equal to $10.00 per direct labor hour. If a thick-crust pizza takes 10 minutes of direct labor time to produce, a thin-crust pizza takes 6 minutes to produce, and a deep-dish pizza takes 15 minutes to produce, the amount of overhead allocated to each is $1.66, $1.00, and $2.50, respectively.

Exhibit 3-4 Overhead Allocation Using Direct Labor Hours as the Cost Driver

Overhead Costs Per Month:

Depreciation on pizza ovens	$1,500
Rent	2,000
Utilities	1,000
Other	3,500
Total	$8,000
Direct labor hours (DLHs) per month	800 direct labor hours
Overhead per direct labor hour	($8,000 ÷ 800 DLHs) = $10.00 per DLH

Direct labor hours per pizza:

Thick crust	10 minutes
Thin crust	6 minutes
Deep dish	15 minutes

Allocation of Overhead for Each Type of Pizza:

Thick crust	$10.00 × 1/6 hour of labor	= $1.66
Thin crust	$10.00 × 1/10 hour of labor	= $1.00
Deep dish	$10.00 × 1/4 hour of labor	= $2.50

LO4 The Use of Estimates

It is not unusual for managers to want to estimate the cost of a product before it is actually produced or before the actual costs are known with certainty. Having timely cost information is useful for pricing decisions as well as for production decisions. However, because the actual amount of many overhead items will not be known until the end of a period (perhaps when an invoice is received), companies often estimate the amount of overhead that will be incurred in the coming period. For example, a manufacturer of computers that are custom made to meet customer requirements needs to know the cost of producing each computer so that it can establish a sales price. Customers place orders 24 hours a day, and the company's policy is to ship computers to customers within 48 hours of the order. Although the company has records of each component and other materials used in the assembly of the computer and knows the exact amount of time workers spent putting the computer together (remember the job cost report discussed earlier), calculating the actual amount of overhead cost incurred is virtually impossible to do in a timely manner.

Why? Because the amount of most overhead items, such as utilities expense, maintenance expense, supplies expense, and so forth, will not be known until after the computer is assembled and shipped. The only alternative, short of requiring the customer to wait until the end of the period to know the actual price of the computer, is to estimate the amount of overhead on each computer and to set the sales price accordingly. Using estimates has another advantage as well. It is not unusual for overhead to fluctuate during the year. For example, the utilities costs incurred by **Ben & Jerry's** (whose factory is located in Vermont) during the winter are likely to be higher than those incurred in the summer. If **Ben & Jerry's** used actual overhead costs to cost products, the ice cream the company makes in February would cost more than the ice cream it makes in May. Using estimates smoothes out, or normalizes, seasonal and random fluctuations in overhead costs. Thus, this method of costing is often called **normal costing**.

Normal costing A method of costing using an estimate of overhead and predetermined overhead rates instead of the actual amount of overhead.

© Cengage Learning 2013

In order to provide relevant information for decision making, overhead must often be estimated.

Predetermined Overhead Rates

Companies that estimate the amount of overhead cost incurred in costing products allocate overhead by using predetermined overhead rates. **Predetermined overhead rates** are calculated by using a slight modification of the basic overhead rate formula:

$$\text{Predetermined overhead rate (for a cost pool)} = \frac{\text{Estimated overhead for the cost pool}}{\text{Estimated units of the cost driver}}$$

Predetermined overhead rates are typically calculated by using annual estimates of overhead and cost drivers, although some companies do more frequent calculations.

The Application of Overhead to Products The allocation of overhead using predetermined overhead rates is called an application of overhead. The amount of overhead applied to a product is calculated by multiplying the predetermined overhead rate by the actual units of the cost driver incurred in producing the product or service:

$$\text{Applied overhead} = \text{Predetermined overhead rate} \times \text{Actual units of cost driver}$$

The cost of a product or a service for a company utilizing normal costing therefore includes the costs of an actual amount of direct material, an actual amount of direct labor, and an applied amount of manufacturing overhead based on estimates.

Predetermined overhead rates Used to apply overhead to products; calculated by dividing the estimated overhead for a cost pool by the estimated units of the cost driver.

Overapplied overhead The amount of applied overhead in excess of actual overhead.

Underapplied overhead The amount of actual overhead in excess of applied overhead.

Calculating predetermined overhead rates is a three-step process. Step 1 involves the identification and estimation of the overhead costs included in the plantwide or departmental cost pool. Step 2 involves the identification and estimation of the appropriate allocation base (the cost driver). Step 3 is the actual computation of the predetermined overhead rate.

As an example, let's assume that CCF has chosen to lump all overhead into one cost pool for the entire factory (a plantwide cost pool). The company identifies overhead costs as the cost of utilities, insurance, and rent for the factory building; depreciation and repairs and maintenance of manufacturing equipment; the cost of supplies used in the factory; and the salaries of a production supervisor and janitor in the factory. The company further estimates that these costs should total about $100,000 in the next year. Because CCF is very labor intensive, it has chosen labor hours as the cost driver and estimates using 8,000 labor hours during the next year. Dividing the estimated overhead of $100,000 by the estimated allocation base of 8,000 labor hours results in a predetermined overhead rate of $12.50 per labor hour:

$$\frac{\$100,000}{8,000} = \$12.50 \text{ per labor hour}$$

In other words, for every labor hour worked on a product, the company should apply $12.50 in overhead cost. As shown in Exhibit 3-2 (page 43), since Job 101 required 22.4 labor hours, it was allocated $280.00 of overhead.

LO5 The Problem of Over- and Underapplied Overhead

Because overhead is applied to products by using predetermined overhead rates based on estimates, it is likely that actual overhead costs (when they become known) will differ from those applied. If applied overhead is greater than actual overhead, the company **overapplied overhead**. If applied overhead is less than actual overhead, the company **underapplied overhead** for the period. Over- and underapplied overhead can occur for a couple of reasons: estimating the overhead incorrectly or estimating the cost driver incorrectly. As shown in Exhibit 3-5, CCF had a predetermined overhead rate of $12.50 per direct labor hour, based on estimated overhead of $100,000 and estimated direct labor hours of 8,000. If, during the year, 8,100 direct labor

Under normal costing, the cost of a product includes the costs of the actual amount of direct materials, the actual amount of direct labor, and an applied amount of manufacturing overhead.

The manufacturing overhead account essentially serves as a clearing account. At this point (see Exhibit 3-6), the manufacturing overhead account has a debit balance of $102,000 and a credit balance of $101,250.

Exhibit 3-6 The Manufacturing Overhead Account

Manufacturing Overhead	
$102,000	$101,250
Actual overhead costs as incurred	Overhead applied to WIP by using the predetermined overhead rate

© Cengage Learning 2013

Exhibit 3-5 The Calculation of Applied Overhead

Estimated overhead	$100,000
Estimated units of cost driver	8,000 direct labor hours
Predetermined overhead rate	$12.50 ($100,000 ÷ 8,000 DLHs)
Applied overhead = Predetermined overhead rate × actual direct labor hours	
Applied overhead	$101,250 ($12.50 per DLH × 8,100 DLHs)

© Cengage Learning 2013

hours are actually incurred in making furniture, CCF's applied overhead will be $101,250.

Now, assume that the actual overhead costs for CCF total $102,000. Under a normal costing system, as actual overhead costs are incurred throughout the year, the manufacturing overhead account is increased (debited) for the amount of the actual costs. The journal entry to record the payment of overhead expenses and the transfer of those costs to manufacturing overhead is

Manufacturing Overhead	102,000	
Accounts Payable or Cash		102,000

Likewise, as individual jobs are completed throughout the year, overhead is applied to work in process by using the predetermined overhead rate.

As shown in Exhibit 3-5, CCF's applied overhead was $101,250. The journal entry to record the application of overhead to work in process requires a debit to work in process and a credit to manufacturing overhead:

Work in Process Inventory	101,250	
Manufacturing Overhead		101,250

CCF's actual overhead is greater than the applied overhead by $750. Consequently, CCF has underapplied overhead in the amount of $750. What impact does the underapplied overhead have on the cost of furniture produced by CCF?

Because applied overhead is accumulated in work in process (WIP), transferred to finished goods as units are completed, and then transferred to cost of goods sold as units are sold, if everything is sold, adjusting for over- or underapplied overhead involves adjusting the balance of the cost-of-goods-sold account. In practice (particularly in a just-in-time [JIT] manufacturing environment), this is likely to be the case. Jobs are typically completed and sold before any adjustment can be made to an inventory account. In our case, if CCF sells all the furniture it produces, its cost of goods sold will be understated by $750 and our adjustment will increase cost of goods sold by $750. But what if some of the furniture is not sold or perhaps not even finished? Then, the $750 might be allocated in some fashion to WIP, finished goods, and cost of goods sold to recognize that all three accounts are too low. This allocation is usually based on the amount of overhead in each account. As an alternative, if the amount of the adjustment is immaterial, companies may choose to adjust only the cost-of-goods-sold account. Assume that the amount of overhead in WIP, finished goods, and cost of goods sold is as follows:

Work in process	$ 20,250	(20% of total)
Finished goods	30,375	(30% of total)
Cost of goods sold	50,625	(50% of total)
Total	$101,250	

If the amount of underapplied overhead is considered immaterial, the cost of goods sold is adjusted by the entire $750. The balance after adjustment is $51,375:

	Original Balance		Underapplied Overhead		Adjusted Balance
Cost of goods sold	$50,625	+	$750	=	$51,375*

*Note that the underapplied overhead increases the cost-of-goods-sold amount. If overhead had been overapplied, the adjustment would have decreased the cost-of-goods-sold balance.

The journal entry to record the adjustment to cost of goods sold is

Cost of Goods Sold	750	
Manufacturing Overhead		750

If, however, the amount of underapplied overhead is considered material, the underapplied overhead might be allocated to WIP, finished goods, and cost of goods sold according to the percentages shown on the previous page. For example, 20 percent of the underapplied overhead, or $150, would be allocated to WIP ($750 × 20%), while 30 percent of the underapplied amount, or $225, would be allocated to finished goods and 50 percent ($375) would be allocated to cost of goods sold. After adjustment, the amount of overhead in each inventory account is as follows:

	Original Balance		Underapplied Overhead		Adjusted Balance
Work in process	$ 20,250	+	$150	=	$ 20,400
Finished goods	30,375	+	225	=	30,600
Cost of goods sold	50,625	+	375	=	51,000
Total	$101,250	+	$750	=	$102,000

The journal entry to allocate the underapplied overhead to the three accounts is

Work in Process	150	
Finished Goods	225	
Cost of Goods Sold	375	
Manufacturing Overhead		750

LO6 Basic Process Costing

Companies that produce beverages or other products (for example, paint, paper, oil, and textiles) in a continuous flow production process typically use process costing. As mentioned previously, instead of accumulating, tracking, and assigning direct material and direct labor costs to each job, process costing systems accumulate and track direct material and direct labor costs by department and then assign the costs evenly to the products that pass through each department. Likewise, instead of applying overhead to each specific job, overhead is applied to each department and then assigned evenly to each product that passes through. Although the application to job or department differs, the amount of overhead applied is calculated in exactly the same way. After predetermined overhead rates are developed, overhead is applied by multiplying the predetermined overhead rate by the actual units of cost driver incurred in each department. A comparison of the cost flows in job costing and process costing is shown in Exhibit 3-7.

In companies with no beginning or ending inventories (all units are finished), the mechanics of process costing are very simple. Because all the units produced are identical, costs accumulated and tracked in each department can simply be averaged across all the units that are produced. If $30,000 of direct material costs and $70,000 of direct labor and overhead costs are incurred in the blending department of a paint manufacturer, and 10,000 gallons of product are produced, the cost of blending each gallon is $10 per gallon and the 10,000 finished units cost $100,000 to produce.

However, problems quickly arise when companies have inventories. Let's assume that the blending department finishes blending only 8,000 gallons and that 2,000 gallons are left in ending WIP at the end of the year. These 2,000 gallons are 50 percent complete and will require additional materials, labor, and overhead during the next period before they are finished. Should each gallon (finished or unfinished) still cost $10 in this case? That would mean that our 8,000 finished units cost $80,000 and our 2,000 unfinished units cost $20,000. Of course, that would not make sense, because we would expect our finished units to cost more per gallon than those which are only half finished!

> Process costing assigns costs to products as they pass through departments, rather than to each individual product.

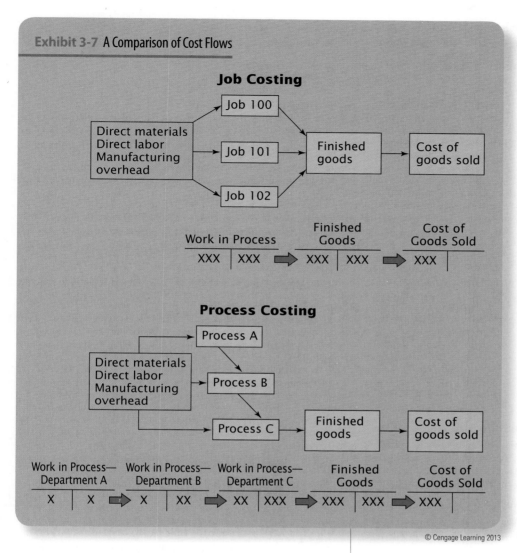

Exhibit 3-7 A Comparison of Cost Flows

Job Costing

Process Costing

© Cengage Learning 2013

To get around this problem, we need to calculate the number of **equivalent units** completed during the period. If two units are uniformly 50 percent finished at the end of a period, we have finished the equivalent of one complete unit. In the previous example, we partially finished 2,000 units, with each unit uniformly 50 percent complete. How many finished units could we have completed by using the same amount of direct materials, labor, and overhead? The 2,000 units, that are 50 percent finished are the equivalent of 1,000 finished units. Therefore, our total equivalent units finished during the period equals 9,000—the 8,000 units we actually finished plus another 1,000 equivalent finished units in ending WIP.

Our cost per equivalent unit is therefore $11.11 ($100,000 ÷ 9,000 equivalent units) and the 8,000 finished units cost $88,880, whereas the 2,000 units in ending inventory (1,000 equivalent units) cost $11,120 ($100,000 − $88,880). Process costing and

the calculation of equivalent units are substantially more complicated when companies have both beginning and ending inventories of WIP.

Another difference between job costing and process costing is that process cost systems often require multiple WIP accounts—one for every process. As products are moved from one process to another, the costs of the previous process are simply transferred to the next process. For example, a paint manufacturer accumulates and tracks direct material, direct labor, and overhead costs to a WIP account for each process (blending and pouring). The total costs for each process are then assigned to the paint by dividing by the number of gallons of paint that come out of each process. The total cost of each gallon is therefore the sum of the costs assigned from each process and an average of the costs incurred in each process.

Materials, Labor, and Overhead Cost Journal Entries

The use of multiple WIP accounts in process costing introduces some peculiarities in recording the flow of costs by means of journal entries. Although the journal entries to record the flow of costs through a process costing system are similar to those in job costing, there are a few key differences.

Material Costs As materials are drawn from the raw materials inventory storeroom, the costs are traced to processing departments rather than individual jobs.

> **Equivalent units** The number of finished units that can be made from the materials, labor, and overhead included in partially completed units.

The journal entry to record the materials used in processing department A is as follows:

Work in Process Inventory—Process A	xx	
Raw Materials Inventory		xx

Note that materials can be added in any processing department. For example, if materials are also used in process B, a similar journal entry would record the materials used in that processing department:

Work in Process Inventory—Process B	xx	
Raw Materials Inventory		xx

Labor Costs Likewise, labor costs are traced directly to a processing department rather than to individual jobs. As labor costs are incurred in processing department A, the journal entry to record the labor costs is as follows:

Work in Process Inventory—Process A	xx	
Salaries and Wages Payable		xx

If labor costs are incurred in process B or process C, similar journal entries would be used to record the labor costs in those departments.

Overhead Costs Predetermined overhead rates are typically used in process costing to apply overhead. However, instead of applying overhead to a particular job, overhead is applied as follows to units of product as they move through each processing department:

Work in Process Inventory—Process A	xx	
Manufacturing Overhead		xx

As with material and labor costs, as overhead costs are incurred in process B or C, similar journal entries would record the cost flows.

Transferring Costs from Process to Process As work is completed within a processing department, the accumulated costs of materials, labor, and overhead must be transferred to the next processing department. For example, once processing is complete in process A, the accumulated costs in the WIP account would be transferred to the WIP account in process B as follows:

Work in Process Inventory—Process B	xx	
Work in Process Inventory—Process A		xx

Likewise, as work is completed in process B, the accumulated costs would be transferred to process C:

Work in Process Inventory—Process C	xx	
Work in Process Inventory—Process B		xx

Transferring Costs to Finished Goods As work is completed in process C, the product is ready for transfer to finished goods. The journal entry to transfer the costs of the completed units to finished-goods inventory is as follows:

Finished-Goods Inventory	xx	
Work in Process Inventory—Process C		xx

Recording the Cost of Goods Sold As the finished goods are sold, the cost of the goods is transferred out of finished-goods inventory and recognized as the cost of goods sold:

Cost of Goods Sold	xx	
Finished-Goods Inventory		xx

LO7 Additional Topics in Process Costing

When a company has both beginning and ending inventories of WIP, process costing becomes more complicated. In this situation, it is useful to view process costing in four steps.

In Step 1, the physical flow of units and their associated costs are analyzed. In this step, it is essential to note the percentage of completion of both the beginning and ending inventories of WIP. For example, let's assume that the blending department of a paint manufacturer has 2,000 gallons of paint that is 80 percent complete in its beginning inventory of WIP. These units were started last period but not completed by the end of the period and will be finished this period. In addition, let's assume that $1,600 of direct material costs and $1,000 of conversion costs (the costs of direct labor and overhead incurred to convert the direct materials to a finished product) have already been incurred in blending these 2,000 gallons of partially completed paint.

During the current period, another 12,000 gallons of paint are started in the blending department, so 14,000 gallons are now in process. The company incurs another $20,000 of direct material costs (DM) and $7,370 of conversion costs (CC) working on these 14,000 gallons. The total costs incurred in the blending department now include $21,600 for direct material ($1,600 incurred last period and $20,000 incurred this period) and $8,370 for conversion costs ($1,000 incurred last period and $7,370 incurred this period).

Of the 14,000 gallons of paint now in process in the blending department, 13,000 gallons are finished by the end of the period. Consequently, 1,000 gallons remain in ending inventory. Let's assume that these 1,000 gallons are 50 percent complete (see Exhibit 3-8).

Exhibit 3-8 Step 1—The Physical Flow of Units and Their Associated Costs

© Cengage Learning 2013

The goal of a process costing system is to allocate the $29,970 of manufacturing costs that have been incurred in the blending department ($21,600 of DM and $8,370 of CC) to the 13,000 gallons of paint that are finished and transferred out (in this case, to the next processing department) and to the 1,000 gallons of paint that remain in the blending department's ending inventory.

Equivalent units of production can be calculated in two different ways: the first-in, first-out (FIFO) method or the weighted-average method. In the FIFO method, the equivalent units and unit costs for the current period relate only to the work done and the costs incurred in the current period. In contrast, in the weighted-average method, the units and costs from the current period are combined with the units and costs from last period in the calculation of equivalent units and unit costs.

First-In, First-Out (FIFO)

With the FIFO method, the 2,000 gallons in beginning WIP are assumed to be the first units finished. Consequently, of the 12,000 gallons started this period, 11,000 are finished whereas 1,000 gallons are partially completed and remain in ending WIP (Exhibit 3-9).

In Step 2, equivalent units of production (EU) are calculated. With the FIFO method, the equivalent units in beginning WIP (the units considered already complete at the beginning of the period) are correctly excluded from the calculation of equivalent units of production for the current period. Basically, we want to know the number of equivalent units completed in *this* period.

The formula for computing the equivalent units of production under the FIFO method consists of three separate calculations:

Equivalent units of production	=	Equivalent units required to complete beginning inventory*
		+ Units started and completed during the period
		+ Equivalent units in ending inventory at the end of the period

* Units in beginning inventory × (100% − percent completion of beginning inventory)

In our example, the 2,000 gallons are 80 percent complete at the beginning of the period. This is equivalent to 1,600 EUs (2,000 × 80 percent). If 80 percent of the work was completed last period, 20 percent will be completed this period. Therefore, we will complete 400 equivalent units (2,000 × 20 percent) out of the beginning inventory *this* period.

Exhibit 3-9 Step 1—The Physical Flow of Units with FIFO

© Cengage Learning 2013

What about the 12,000 gallons started new this period? According to Exhibit 3-10, 11,000 of the 12,000 gallons are completely finished (11,000 EUs) whereas another 1,000 are 50 percent finished (500 EUs). As shown in Exhibit 3-10, the total equivalent units are 11,900 (400 from beginning inventory, plus 11,000 units started and completely finished, plus 500 units in ending inventory).

Exhibit 3-10 Step 2—Calculation of Equivalent Units with FIFO

Equivalent units required to complete beginning inventory	2,000 units × 20%* =	400 units
Equivalent units started and completed this period		11,000 units
Equivalent units of ending WIP completed this period	1,000 units × 50% =	500 units
Total equivalent units		**11,900 units**

*The beginning inventory was 80 percent complete, so 20 percent is left to complete this period.

In Step 3, manufacturing costs per equivalent unit are calculated (see Exhibit 3-11). With the FIFO method, only the current-period costs ($20,000 of DM and $7,370 of CC) are included in the calculation. Last period's costs of $2,600 ($1,600 of DM and $1,000 of CC) are correctly segregated from the costs incurred this period. This allocation is consistent with including only the percentage of beginning inventory, completed this period in the calculation of equivalent units.

Exhibit 3-11 Step 3—Calculation of Cost per Equivalent Unit with FIFO

Current-period costs	$27,370
Equivalent units of production	÷ 11,900 EUs
Cost per equivalent unit	**$2.30 per EU**

In Step 4, the $29,970 of costs incurred ($2,600 from last period associated with the beginning inventory and $27,370 incurred this period) are allocated to the 13,000 gallons of completely finished paint and the 1,000 gallons of partially finished paint.

Because all 2,000 units in beginning inventory are assumed to be completed this period, the $2,600 of costs associated with those units will be allocated to the costs of the 13,000 finished units. Of course, we incur additional costs this period to finish the 2,000 units and to start and finish another 11,000 units. How much are these additional costs? According to our calculation in Exhibit 3-11, it cost $2.30 per equivalent unit to blend paint in this period. As calculated in Exhibit 3-12, the 13,000 gallons of completely finished paint cost $28,820.

Exhibit 3-12 Step 4—Allocating Costs to the Finished Units

Cost of the 2,000 units from beginning inventory:	
Cost incurred last period	$ 2,600
Cost to finish the units this period	
DM and CC ($2.30 per EU × 400 EUs*)	920
Cost of the 11,000 units started and finished this period	
DM and CC ($2.30 per EU × 11,000 EUs)	25,300
Total cost	**$28,820**

*The beginning inventory was 80 percent complete, so 20 percent is left to complete this period (2,000 units × 20 percent = 400 EUs).

The 1,000 units in ending work in process inventory are easier to cost. All are considered to come from the 12,000 units started this period and cost $2.30 per equivalent unit. As shown in Exhibit 3-13, the cost of the 1,000 units (500 equivalent units) in ending WIP is $1,150.

Exhibit 3-13 Step 4—Allocating Costs to the Ending WIP

Cost of the 1,000 units in ending WIP	
DM and CC ($2.30 per EU × 500 EUs)	$1,150

Note that the total cost allocated to the 13,000 units of finished paint and the 1,000 units of ending WIP must total $29,970. Consequently, if the finished units cost $28,820, the ending inventory must cost $1,150 ($29,970 − $28,820).

FIFO with Different Percent of Completion for DM and CC

Products may not be uniformly complete with respect to direct materials and conversion costs. In that case, equivalent units of production must be calculated separately for each component.

For example, let's assume that rather than being uniformly 80 percent complete, the beginning inventory of WIP is 90 percent complete as to direct materials and

70 percent complete as to conversion costs. Likewise, let's assume that the ending inventory of 1,000 units is 60 percent complete with respect to direct materials and 40 percent complete with respect to conversion costs. Exhibit 3-14 shows the physical flow of the units and their associated costs.

Exhibit 3-14 Step 1—The Physical Flow of Units and Their Associated Costs

90% complete DM   70% complete CC

WIP—Blending Department

Beginning Inventory	2,000 gallons $3,740 DM $1,440 CC	
Units Started	12,000 gallons $20,060 DM $ 6,600 CC	= 13,000 gallons completed
Ending Inventory	1,000 gallons	

60% complete DM   40% complete CC

As with our earlier example, the 2,000 units in beginning inventory are assumed to be the first units finished under FIFO. Accordingly, the 13,000 gallons completed during the period consist of 2,000 gallons from the beginning inventory and 11,000 gallons of the 12,000 gallons started during the period.

In Step 2 (see Exhibit 3-15), equivalent units of production are calculated.

Exhibit 3-15 Step 2—Calculation of Equivalent Units with FIFO

	Materials	Conversion Costs
Equivalent units required to complete beginning inventory:		
2,000 units × 10%	200	
2,000 units × 30%		600
Equivalent units started and completed this period	11,000	11,000
Equivalent units of ending WIP completed this period:		
1,000 units × 60%	600	
1,000 units × 40%		400
Total equivalent units	**11,800 units**	**12,000 units**

In Step 3, manufacturing costs per equivalent unit are calculated (see Exhibit 3-16). With the FIFO method, only the current-period costs ($20,060 of DM and $6,600 of CC) are included in the calculation. Last period's costs of $5,180 are correctly segregated from the costs incurred this period.

Exhibit 3-16 Step 3—Calculation of Cost per Equivalent Unit with FIFO

	Materials	Conversion Costs
Current-period costs	$20,060	$ 6,600
÷ Equivalent units of production	11,800	12,000
Cost per equivalent unit	$ 1.70	$ .55

In Step 4, the $31,840 of costs incurred ($5,180 from last period and $26,660 from the current period) are allocated to the 13,000 gallons of completely finished paint and the 1,000 gallons of paint remaining in ending work in process inventory. Because the 2,000 units in beginning inventory are the first units completed this period, the $5,180 of costs associated with those units will be allocated to the costs of the 13,000 finished units. The additional cost incurred to finish the 2,000 units is found by multiplying the respective cost per equivalent unit by the equivalent units in beginning inventory that are left to complete this period (2,000 × 10%, or 200 units, for DM, and 2,000 × 30%, or 600 units, for

CC). Costing the 11,000 units started and completed this period is more straightforward. As shown in Exhibit 3-17, each unit started and completed this period costs $2.25 per unit ($1.70 for DM and $.55 for CC). The total cost of the 13,000 finished units is $30,600.

WIP must total $31,840. Consequently, if the finished units cost $30,600, the ending inventory must cost $1,240 ($31,840 − $30,600).

Exhibit 3-19 shows a completed **production report**. The cost reconciliation section of the production report

Exhibit 3-17 Step 4—Allocating Costs to the Finished Units

		Equivalent Units	
	Cost	Materials	Conversion
Cost of the 2,000 units from beginning WIP:			
Cost incurred last period	$ 5,180.00		
Cost to finish the units this period			
Materials at $1.70	$ 340.00	200	
Conversion at $.55	$ 330.00		600
Cost of the 11,000 units started and finished this period at $2.25 per EU ($1.70 + $.55)	$ 24,750.00	11,000	11,000
Total cost of units transferred out	**$30,600.00**		

© Cengage Learning 2013

As in the previous example, the 1,000 units in ending work in process inventory are easier to cost. All are considered to come from the 12,000 units started this period and cost $1.70 per equivalent unit for direct material and $.55 per equivalent unit for conversion costs. As shown in Exhibit 3-18, the cost of the 1,000 units (600 EU for materials and 400 EU for conversion costs) in ending inventory is $1,240.

Note that the total cost allocated to the 13,000 units of finished paint and the 1,000 units of ending

shows the total costs charged to the department during the period as well as the allocation of those costs to finished units and ending work in process.

Weighted-Average Method

In contrast to the FIFO method, the weighted-average method treats the units in beginning inventory as if they were started in the current period. That is, we combine

Exhibit 3-18 Step 4—Allocating Costs to the Ending WIP

		Equivalent Units	
	Cost	Materials	Conversion
Cost of the 1,000 units in ending WIP:			
Material at $1.70	$ 1,020.00	600	
Conversion costs at $.55 per EU	$ 220.00		400
Total ending WIP	**$1,240.00**		

© Cengage Learning 2013

Production report Report that provides a summary of the units moving through a processing department during the period as well as a computation of equivalent units of production and the costs per equivalent unit.

the units we know were partially completed last period with the units started this period. Consequently, the 13,000 gallons of completed units and the 1,000 gallons of paint in ending WIP are both assumed to come from the 14,000 units we treat as having been started in the current period (Exhibit 3-20). The formula for

Exhibit 3-19 Production Report Using FIFO

Units to be accounted for:	Quantity		
Beginning WIP (DM, 90% complete; CC, 70% complete)	2,000		
Units started in production	12,000		
Units to be accounted for	14,000		

		Equivalent Units	
Units accounted for as follows:		**Materials**	**Conversion**
Transferred out from beginning WIP	2,000	200	600
Units started and completed	11,000	11,000	11,000
Ending WIP (DM, 60% complete; CC, 40% complete)	1,000	600	400
Total units accounted for	14,000	11,800	12,000

Cost per equivalent units			
Costs to be accounted for:			
Beginning WIP	$ 5,180		
Costs added during the period	$26,660	$20,060	$ 6,600
Total costs to be accounted for	$31,840		
Equivalent units		11,800	12,000
Cost per equivalent unit	$ 2.25	$ 1.70	$ .55

Cost reconciliation

		Equivalent Units	
	Total cost	**Materials**	**Conversion**
Cost accounted for as follows:			
From beginning inventory	$ 5,180		
Costs to complete these units:			
Materials at $1.70	$ 340	200	
Conversion costs at $.55	$ 330		600
Total costs from beginning inventory	$ 5,850		
Units started and completed at $2.25	$24,750	11,000	11,000
Total costs of units transferred out	$30,600		
Ending WIP			
Materials at $1.70	$ 1,020	600	
Conversion costs at $.55	$ 220		400
Total ending WIP	$ 1,240		
Total costs accounted for	$31,840		

© Cengage Learning 2013

Exhibit 3-20 Step 1—The Physical Flow of Units with Weighted Average

WIP—Blending Department (Weighted Average)

Beginning Inventory	0 gallons	
Units Started	14,000 gallons	13,000 gallons (Units completed) (all started this period)
Ending Inventory	1,000 gallons (all started this period)	

© Cengage Learning 2013

computing the equivalent units of production under the weighted-average method is simpler than the calculation of equivalent units under FIFO. Because the units in beginning inventory are considered to be started in the current period, the calculation simplifies to the following:

Equivalent units of production = Units completely finished during the period and transferred to finished goods + Equivalent units in WIP inventory at the end of the period

The calculation of equivalent units under the weighted-average method is shown in Exhibit 3-21.

Exhibit 3-21 Step 2—Calculation of Equivalent Units with Weighted Average

Equivalent units started and completed this period:		
Units completely finished		13,000 units
Equivalent units of ending WIP completed this period	1,000 units × 50% =	500 units
Total equivalent units		**13,500 units**

With the weighted-average method, last period's costs are combined with the current period's costs in the calculation of cost per equivalent unit in Step 3 (see Exhibit 3-22). This approach is consistent with treating the units in beginning inventory as if they were started this period in the calculation of equivalent units.

Exhibit 3-22 Step 3—Calculation of Cost per Equivalent Unit with Weighted Average

Total costs	$29,970
Equivalent units of production	÷ 13,500 EUs
Cost per equivalent unit	**$2.22 per EU**

As with the FIFO method, in Step 4 the $29,970 of costs incurred are allocated to the 13,000 gallons of completely finished paint and the 1,000 gallons of partially finished paint. As calculated in Exhibit 3-23, the 13,000 gallons of completely finished paint cost $28,860.

Exhibit 3-23 Step 4—Allocating Costs to the Finished Units

Cost of the 13,000 units started and completely finished DM and CC ($2.22 per EU × 13,000 EUs)	$28,860

The 1,000 units in ending inventory must also have come from the 14,000 units assumed to have been started this period. Consequently, the cost of the 1,000 units (500 equivalent units) in ending inventory is $1,110 (see Exhibit 3-24).

Exhibit 3-24 Step 4—Allocating Costs to the Ending WIP

Cost of the 1,000 units in ending WIP DM and CC ($2.22 per EU × 500 EUs)	$1,110

Once again, note that regardless of whether FIFO or the weighted-average method is used, the costs allocated to the finished units and ending WIP total $29,970.

Weighted Average with Different Percentages of Completion for DM and CC

As with the FIFO example, when products are not uniformly complete, equivalent units must be calculated separately for direct materials and conversion costs. Exhibit 3-25 shows the physical flow of the units and their associated costs under the weighted-average method. Remember, under that method, the beginning inventory and related costs are treated as if they were started in the current period.

Exhibit 3-25 Step 1—The Physical Flow of Units with Weighted Average

WIP—Blending Department

Beginning Inventory	0 gallons		
			= 13,000 gallons completed
Units Started	14,000 gallons $23,800 DM $ 8,040 CC		
Ending Inventory	1,000 gallons		

60% complete DM   40% complete CC

In Exhibit 3-26, we show the calculation of equivalent units using the weighted-average method when the

Exhibit 3-26 Step 2—Calculation of Equivalent Units with Weighted Average

	Materials	Conversion Costs
Equivalent units started and completed this period:		
Units completely finished and transferred to finished goods	13,000 units	13,000 units
Equivalent units of WIP inventory at the end of the period	600 units	400 units
Total equivalent units	**13,600 units**	**13,400 units**

percentage of completion is different with regard to materials and conversion costs.

When using the weighted-average method, last period's costs are combined with the current period's costs in the calculation of cost per equivalent unit. In Step 3 (see Exhibit 3-27), the $31,840 of total costs incurred ($23,800 for DM and $8,040 for CC) are divided by the equivalent units for DM and CC to arrive at the cost per equivalent unit.

Exhibit 3-27 Step 3—Calculation of Cost per Equivalent Unit with Weighted Average

	Materials	**Conversion Costs**
Total costs	$23,800	$ 8,040
÷Equivalent units of production	13,600	13,400
Cost per equivalent unit	$ 1.75	$ .60

In Step 4, the total costs of $31,840 are allocated to the 13,000 gallons of completely finished paint and the 1,000 gallons of partially finished paint. As shown in Exhibit 3-28, the 13,000 gallons of completely finished paint cost $30,550 (13,000 × $2.35 per EU).

The 1,000 units in ending inventory must also have come from the 14,000 units assumed to be started this period. The cost of the 1,000 units is calculated in Exhibit 3-29.

Exhibit 3-30 shows a completed production report for the period.

Which method is preferable? Although the FIFO method is conceptually superior, the weighted-average method will provide similar cost calculations when inventory levels are small (as in a JIT environment) or when costs are relatively stable from period to period. Also, note that the total costs of $31,840 allocated to finished units and ending inventory remain the same.

Exhibit 3-28 Step 4—Allocating Costs to the Finished Units

Cost of the 13,000 units started and completely finished this period	**Cost**
Materials at $1.75 per EU	$22,750
Conversion costs at $.60 per EU	7,800
Total cost of finished units	**$30,550**

Exhibit 3-29 Step 4—Allocating Costs to the Ending WIP

		Equivalent Units	
	Cost	**Materials**	**Conversion**
Cost of the 1,000 units in ending WIP:			
Materials at $1.75	$1,050.00	600	
Conversion costs at $.60 per EU	$ 240.00		400
Total ending WIP	**$1,290.00**		

Exhibit 3-30 Production Report Using Weighted-Average Costing

Units to be accounted for:	**Quantity**		
Beginning WIP (DM, 90% complete; CC, 70% complete)	2,000		
Units started in production	12,000		
Units to be accounted for	14,000		

		Equivalent Units	
Units accounted for as follows:		**Materials**	**Conversion**
Units transferred out to finished goods	13,000	13,000	13,000
Ending WIP (DM, 60% complete; CC, 40% complete)	1,000	600	400
Total units accounted for	14,000	13,600	13,400
Costs per equivalent unit			
Costs to be accounted for:			
Beginning WIP	$ 5,180	$ 3,740	$ 1,440
Costs added during the period	$26,660	$20,060	$ 6,600
Total costs to be accounted for	$31,840	$23,800	$ 8,040
Equivalent units		13,600	13,400
Cost per equivalent units	$ 2.35	$ 1.75	$ .60

		Equivalent Units	
Cost reconciliation	**Total cost**	**Materials**	**Conversion**
Costs accounted for as follows:			
Transferred out to finished goods	$30,550	13,000	13,000
Ending WIP			
Materials at $1.75	$ 1,050	600	
Conversion Costs at $.60	$ 240		400
Total ending WIP	$ 1,290		
Total cost accounted for	$31,840		

LO8 Allocation of Service Department Costs to Production Departments

Many large organizations have both production departments and service departments. The production departments are involved in the direct manufacturing of the company's product or the provision of a service to external customers. In contrast, service departments provide various services to other departments within the organization. As shown in Exhibit 3-31, examples include cafeterias, accounting departments, custodial services, and so on.

Exhibit 3-31 Service Departments with Common Cost Drivers

Service Department	Common Cost Drivers
Cafeteria	Meals served
Accounting	Staff hours worked
Custodial services	Staff hours worked or square footage of space cleaned
Maintenance	Staff hours worked or service calls made
Materials handling	Work orders handled or volume of materials handled
Human resources	Number of employees served
Data processing	Computer time or operator hours

© Cengage Learning 2013

The allocation of service department costs to production departments that consume the services is one of the first steps in the overall product-costing process. Costs must be allocated on the basis of an allocation or cost driver that is related to the particular costs incurred. For example, a cafeteria's costs would typically be allocated on the basis of the number of meals served to a production department. Other common cost drivers for various service departments are listed in the second column of Exhibit 3-31.

Direct method A method of allocating service department costs that allocates costs directly to production departments.

Step-down or **sequential method** Recognizes that service departments consume resources of other service departments and allocates those costs to other service departments and then to production departments in a sequential fashion.

Companies allocate service department costs to production for various reasons, such as the following:

- To provide more accurate product cost information
- To improve decisions concerning scarce resources
- To hold service departments accountable for the costs they incur
- To hold production departments accountable for the services they consume

Service department costs can be allocated on the basis of actual or budgeted costs. In general, budgeted costs should be allocated to production departments because allocating actual costs would allow the service department to pass cost inefficiencies in their departments to the production departments that consume their services.

There are three methods of allocating service department costs. The **direct method** is the most widely used. It allocates each service department's costs directly to the production departments and ignores the fact that service departments often provide services to other service departments. The **step-down** or **sequential method** recognizes that service departments consume resources of other service departments and allocates those costs to other service departments, and then to production departments, in a sequential fashion. The reciprocal method is similar to the step-down method in that it recognizes that service departments consume resources of other service departments. However, this method allocates costs back and forth among the service departments in a reciprocal fashion. In practice, it is rarely used and is not discussed in this text.

The Direct Method

As an example, let's consider Camelback Mountain Community Bank, which has two service departments (a cafeteria and a custodial department) and two production departments (a commercial loan department and a consumer loan department). As shown in the table that follows, the cafeteria has $60,000 of total costs and the custodial department has $50,000 of total costs. Prior to any allocation of service department costs, the commercial loan department has costs of $300,000 and the consumer loan department has costs of $200,000. The cafeteria's costs are allocated on the basis of the number of meals served, whereas the custodial department allocates costs on the basis of the square footage of the space cleaned.

	Service Departments		Production Departments	
	Cafeteria	Custodial Services	Commercial Lending	Consumer Lending
Departmental costs before allocation	$60,000	$50,000	$300,000	$200,000
Meals consumed	10	10	30	20
Square footage	3,000	2,000	40,000	20,000

Exhibit 3-32 illustrates the direct method of allocating the costs in the two service departments to the bank's loan departments. Note that there is no attempt in the direct method to allocate cafeteria costs to the custodial department or custodial costs to the cafeteria, even though the cafeteria consumes resources of the custodial department and the custodial department consumes resources of the cafeteria. Once the allocation is complete, all of the service department costs will have been allocated to the production departments. The total costs of the production departments will now include the direct costs of the production departments in addition to a portion of the costs of each service department. The total costs of the production departments can now be allocated to products and services with the

The direct method allocates the costs of service departments directly to production departments, whereas the step-down method allocates service department costs to other service departments and production departments in a sequential fashion.

use of traditional overhead allocation techniques or ABC. Although the direct method is simple, it ignores the consumption of services among service departments and thus is not as accurate as other methods.

The Step-Down or Sequential Method

The step-down method differs from the direct method in that the costs of a service department are allocated to other service departments and production departments in a sequential fashion. The allocation typically begins with the service department that provides the greatest percentage of service to other service departments or the service department with the highest costs. In this case, let's assume that the cafeteria's costs are allocated first. As illustrated in

Exhibit 3-32 The Direct Method of Service Department Cost Allocation

	Service Departments		Production Departments	
	Cafeteria	Custodial Services	Commercial Lending	Consumer Lending
Departmental costs before allocation	$60,000	$50,000	$300,000	$200,000
Allocation: Cafeteria costs	(60,000)		36,000*	24,000*
Allocation: Custodial costs		(50,000)	33,333**	16,667**
Departmental costs after allocation	$ 0	$ 0	$369,333	$240,667

*The allocation of cafeteria costs is based on the number of meals consumed in the two producing departments. Accordingly, 30/50, or 60%, of the costs are allocated to the commercial loan department and 20/50, or 40%, of the costs are allocated to the consumer loan department.

**The allocation of custodial costs is based on the square footage in the two producing departments. Accordingly, 40,000/60,000, or two-thirds, of the costs are allocated to the commercial loan department and 20,000/60,000, or one-third, of the costs are allocated to the consumer loan department.

© Cengage Learning 2013

Exhibit 3-33, the cafeteria's costs will be allocated to the custodial department as well as the commercial loan and consumer loan departments. Following that allocation, the custodial department's costs (which now include a portion of the cafeteria's costs) will be allocated only to the commercial loan and consumer loan departments in a step-down fashion. Note that after the cafeteria's costs have been allocated, costs of other service departments will not be allocated back to it.

Exhibit 3-33 The Step-Down Method of Service Department Cost Allocation

	Service Departments		Production Departments	
	Cafeteria	Custodial Services	Commercial Lending	Consumer Lending
Departmental costs before allocation	$60,000	$50,000	$300,000	$200,000
Allocation: Cafeteria costs	(60,000)	10,000*	30,000*	20,000*
Allocation: Custodial costs		(60,000)	40,000**	20,000**
Departmental costs after allocation	$ 0	$ 0	$370,000	$240,000

*The allocation of cafeteria costs is based on the number of meals consumed in the custodial department as well as the two producing departments. Accordingly, 10/60, or 16.67%, of the costs are allocated to the custodial department, 30/60, or 50%, of the costs are allocated to the commercial loan department, and 20/60, or 33.33%, of the costs are allocated to the consumer loan department.
**The allocation of custodial costs is based on the square footage in the two producing departments. None of the custodial department's costs are allocated back to the cafeteria. Accordingly, 40,000/60,000, or two-thirds, of the costs are allocated to the commercial loan department and 20,000/60,000, or one-third, of the costs are allocated to the consumer loan department.

© Cengage Learning 2013

STUDY TOOLS 3

Chapter review card

➲ Learning Objective and Key Concept Reviews

➲ Key Definitions and Formulas

Online (Located at www.cengagebrain.com)

➲ Flash Cards and Crossword Puzzles

➲ Games and Quizzes

➲ BP Video and E-Lectures

➲ Homework Assignments (as directed by your instructor)

BRIEF EXERCISES

1. Product Costing Systems LO1

Product costing systems are quite varied. The three fundamental costing systems are job costing, process costing, and operations costing. The following statements describe different aspects of these costing systems.

a. This costing technique is generally used by companies that forecast demand and "push" a product through the manufacturing process.

b. This costing technique is used by companies that produce goods in large batches with products that are standardized within a batch.

c. A large automobile manufacturer that produces cars that are mostly built with standard features, but that allows customers to select some custom features, likely uses this costing system.

d. Companies that need to track production costs for individual projects because of their custom nature most likely use this costing system.

e. This costing technique is often used when customers initiate orders, which "pull" the product or service through the manufacturing process.

f. This costing technique does not attempt to assign costs to specific individual units, but assigns costs equally to units as they pass through the production processes.

Required

Indicate which type of costing system (i.e., job costing, process costing, or operations costing) is described by each statement.

2. Basics of Job Costing LO2

Job costing is commonly used by small companies that specialize in custom products and services. The following statements describe job costing and its application to business.

a. The costs of direct labor include production workers and supervisors.

b. Shipping costs related to direct materials should be treated as manufacturing overhead.

c. A job cost report provides data regarding direct labor, direct materials, and manufacturing overhead.

d. The cost of fringe benefits is not included in direct labor, but is included in manufacturing overhead.

e. Most companies treat the cost of idle time of production employees as manufacturing overhead.

f. The use of job cost reports eliminates the need for tracking direct labor costs on a job-by-job basis.

Required

Indicate whether each of the preceding statements is true or false.

3. Overhead Rates LO3

Companies calculate overhead rates so that they can have a more accurate estimate of the cost of production. Manufacturing overhead is often a significant component of production cost. The following are calculations of overhead by a hypothetical company:

Rent on factory building	$15,000
Wages paid to supervisors	3,500
Utilities paid for factory	1,500
Wages paid to production workers	8,000
Depreciation expense for production equipment	10,000
Estimated number of hours of direct labor	1,200

Required

Calculate the overhead rate on the basis of the preceding information. Use direct labor hours as the cost driver.

4. Predetermined Overhead Rate and Applied Overhead LO4

Bostock's Building Blocks uses number of minutes in its firing oven to allocate overhead costs to products. In a typical month, 5,000 firing minutes are expected, and average monthly overhead costs are $3,500. During January, 4,800 firing minutes were used and total overhead costs were $2,750.

Required

Compute Bostock's predetermined overhead rate and the amount of applied overhead for January.

5. Overapplied Overhead LO5

Because manufacturing overhead is applied to production based on estimates of overhead costs and levels of cost driver activity, applied manufacturing overhead is rarely equal to actual manufacturing overhead. At the end of the year, Jenkins Manufacturing has the following amounts of actual and applied overhead:

Actual manufacturing overhead	$1,050,000
Applied manufacturing overhead	$1,240,000

	Amount of Overhead (%)
Work in process	30
Finished goods	10
Cost of goods sold	60

Required

Prepare the journal entry to adjust the accounts for the overapplied overhead, assuming that the amount is considered material by the company.

6. Process Costing: Equivalent Units with FIFO LO6, 7

The calculation of equivalent units is a necessary step when using process costing to assign costs to production. A dairy producer has the following production data for the first quarter of the year:

	Number of Gallons
Beginning work in process (70% complete)	50,000
Production started this period	65,000
Ending work in process (40% complete)	30,000

Required

If the company uses FIFO for costing purposes, how many equivalent units of production (gallons), in total, did the dairy produce in the first quarter of the year?

7. Process Costing: Equivalent Units with Weighted Average LO6, 7

Refer to the information provided in Brief Exercise 6.

Required

If the company uses weighted average for costing purposes, how many equivalent units of production (gallons), in total, did the dairy produce in the first quarter of the year?

8. Service Department Allocation Using the Direct Method LO8

Costs of operating service departments can be allocated across a company in a variety of ways, including the most widely used approach: the direct method. The following table includes costs for two service departments and the two production departments they support:

	Service A	Service B	Production A	Production B
Department costs	$48,000	$75,000	$210,000	$180,000
Number of calls	750	240	2,400	1,600
Number of employees	20	25	35	15

Service A allocates costs on the basis of the number of calls, and Service B allocates costs on the basis of the number of employees.

Required

Use the direct method to allocate the costs of the two service departments to the two production departments. What is the total cost for Production A and Production B after the allocation?

9. Job vs. Process Costing LO1

Product (service) costing systems are customized to provide accurate and timely cost data. A company should select a costing system that is appropriate for its production process. The following is a list of different organizations and selected products or services they provide.
a. Physical therapy clinic (mobility therapy)
b. Graphic design studio (logo design)
c. Auto repair shop (miscellaneous auto repairs)
d. Local bakery (wheat bread)
e. Dairy (whole milk)
f. Oil refinery (motor oil)
g. Construction contractor (custom-built homes)

Required

Indicate whether each of the preceding organizations would most likely choose *job costing* or *process costing*.

10. Job Costing LO2

Love's Pottery Barn had the following costs for June:

Direct labor	$ 400
Manufacturing overhead	375
Beginning work in process	0
Ending work in process	0
Costs of goods manufactured	1,050
Beginning finished goods	2,450
Ending finished goods	3,400

Required

What was the cost of direct material used during June?

11. Direct Labor vs. Indirect Labor LO2, 3

Jim Wilson is a typical manufacturing employee who commonly works 40 hours per week and is paid $14 per hour. During the last pay period, Jim performed the following activities:

Assembling products	29.5 hours
Cleaning his work area	5.0
Attending a workplace safety meeting	2.5
Talking with a supervisor about football	1.0
Giving a tour of the plant to schoolchildren	2.0

Required

Jim's employer uses job costing to measure and track production costs. The company is very concerned with maintaining accurate cost data. Determine the amount of labor costs that should be allocated to direct labor and indirect labor as manufacturing overhead.

12. Job Costing LO3

Walter Meyer Productions had the following costs for March:

Purchases of direct materials	$ 30,000
Indirect labor	20,000
Ending direct materials inventory	10,000
Beginning direct materials inventory	0
Total manufacturing costs	115,000
Direct labor	25,000

Required

How much manufacturing overhead was incurred during March?

13. Identification of Cost Drivers LO3

Overhead costs are rarely directly linked to the production of a specific product or group of products. Generally, overhead costs are only indirectly linked to production, so they must be allocated. Understanding the relationship between overhead costs and production activities is challenging for most businesses. Consider the following:

a. Architectural design firm: designer hours, _____

b. Caterer and party consultancy firm: number of party guests, _____

c. Furniture manufacturer: direct labor hours, _____

d. Printer and copy shop: size of print or copy job, _____

e. Textbook binder: machine hours, _____

f. Automobile repair shop: technician labor hours, _____

g. Winemaker: pounds of grapes used, _____

Required

Identify one additional potential cost driver that each of the organizations in "a" through "g" could use to allocate overhead to its products or services.

14. Overhead Costs, Cost Pools, Cost Drivers LO3, 4

The following statements describe various aspects of overhead costs and the roles of cost pools and cost drivers in the allocation of overhead.

a. Overhead costs cause cost drivers.

b. In traditional manufacturing environments, most overhead costs are directly related to production activities.

c. Overhead rates are calculated by multiplying manufacturing overhead costs by the volume of cost pool activity.

d. Companies that are labor intensive are likely to allocate overhead costs such as utilities expense on the basis of direct labor hours.

e. More overhead costs in a just-in-time environment are direct in nature as opposed to indirect.

f. A "good" allocation base is one that drives the incurrence of overhead costs.

g. Companies generally allocate overhead equally to all products produced during a given period.

Required

Indicate whether each of the preceding statements is true or false.

15. Predetermined Overhead Rate and Applied Overhead LO4

Rabbit Enterprises calculates predetermined overhead rates for each department. In the feeding department, total overhead costs were $19,240 in 2011 and they are expected to be $21,700 in 2012. The company maintained 515 rabbit pens in 2011 and plans to have 520 pens in 2012.

Required

A. If the number of rabbit pens is used as the cost driver, what is the company's 2012 predetermined overhead rate?

B. What amount of overhead was applied in 2012 if there were actually 530 pens?

16. Predetermined Overhead Rate and Applied Overhead LO4, 5

Ben Whitney manufactures holiday decorations. Overhead is applied to products on the basis of direct labor hours. Last year, total overhead costs were expected to be $85,000. Actual overhead costs totaled $88,750 for 8,400 actual hours. At the end of the year, overhead was underapplied by $4,750.

Required

A. Calculate the predetermined overhead rate.

B. How much overhead should be applied to a job that was completed in three direct labor hours?

17. Predetermined Overhead Rate and Applied Overhead LO4, 5

Speedy Shoe Factory manufactures running shoes. Overhead is applied to the shoes on the basis of direct labor hours. Last year, total overhead costs were expected to be $72,000. Actual overhead costs totaled $80,000 for 8,000 actual hours. At the end of the year, overhead was underapplied by $5,000.

Required

A. Calculate the predetermined overhead rate.

B. How much overhead should be applied to a job that was completed in three direct labor hours?

18. Applied Overhead and Predetermined Overhead Rate LO4, 5

Enrique Mares Enterprises uses direct labor hours to apply overhead. The following data are available for the year:

Expected direct labor hours	600,000
Actual direct labor hours	545,000
Overhead applied	$2,937,550
Actual overhead	$2,800,000

Required

What predetermined overhead rate did Enrique Mares use?

19. Process Costing: FIFO Method LO6, 7

O'Callahan Snack Company produces gourmet chips and other snack foods. One of the company's most popular snacks is a combination of several varieties of organic potatoes. The snack food goes through several processes, including a potato-peeling operation. Costs for operations during April are as follows (note: production costs include the costs of direct materials and conversion costs for the department):

	Number of Bags	Production Costs
Beginning work in process (10% complete)	3,000	$10,000
Current-period production	20,000	70,240
Ending work in process (85% complete)	5,000	

O'Callahan Snack Company uses the first-in, first-out method of computing equivalent units and assigning product costs.

Required

A. How many bags of the popular snack were completed during April?
B. Of the bags completed during April, how many bags were started and completed during the month?

20. Process Costing: Weighted-Average Method LO6, 7

For this exercise, use the information provided in Exercise 19.

Required

If O'Callahan Snack Company uses the weighted-average method of process costing, how would your answers to requirements A and B change?

21. Process Costing: Equivalent Units Using FIFO Method LO6, 7

O'Callahan Snack Company produces gourmet chips and other snack foods. One of the company's most popular snacks is a combination of several varieties of organic potatoes. The snack food goes through several processes, including a potato-peeling operation. Costs for operations during April are as follows (note: production costs include the cost of direct materials and conversion costs for the department):

	Number of Bags	Production Costs
Beginning work in process (10% complete)	3,000	$10,000
Current-period production	20,000	70,240
Ending work in process (85% complete)	5,000	

O'Callahan Snack Company uses the first-in, first-out method of computing equivalent units and assigning product costs.

Required

A. How many equivalent units did O'Callahan complete during April?
B. Calculate the cost of the ending work in process inventory.

22. Process Costing: Equivalent Units Using Weighted-Average Method LO6, 7

Use the information provided in Exercise 21. If O'Callahan Snack Company used the weighted-average method of process costing, how would your answers to the following two questions change?

Required

A. How many equivalent units did O'Callahan complete during April?
B. Calculate the cost of the ending work in process inventory.

23. Process Costing: Equivalent Units Using Weighted-Average Method LO6, 7

Mike Aliscad is widely known as an exceptional winemaker. He has developed a production process that has several distinct processes, including "speed crushing," which involves the breaking down of the grape skin and pulverizing of the grape fruit to produce a juice-like product. The following data relate to Aliscad's crushing process for October (note: production costs include the cost of direct materials and conversion costs for the department):

	Pounds of Grapes	Production Costs
Beginning work in process (15% complete)	2,000	$ 8,040
Current-period production	11,000	22,960
Ending work in process (60% complete)	3,000	

Aliscad uses the weighted-average method of computing equivalent units and assigning product costs.

Required
How many equivalent units were produced during October?

24. Process Costing: Cost per Equivalent Unit Using Weighted Average LO6, 7

Arnsparger Outdoors produces climbing gear specially designed to weather the toughest conditions. Arnsparger has developed and patented a process that leads to a substantially stronger rope than its competitors sell. The strengthening process is complicated and has increased the time required to produce rope, but Arnsparger believes the additional time is worth the effort. The following data relate to the process for the month of June (note: production costs include the cost of direct materials and conversion costs for the department):

	Feet of Rope	Production Costs
Beginning work in process (10% complete)	4,000	$ 4,000
Current-period production	13,000	26,000
Ending work in process (50% complete)	4,000	

Arnsparger Outdoors uses the weighted-average method of computing equivalent units and assigning product costs.

Required
A. Calculate the number of equivalent units produced during June.
B. What is the production cost per equivalent unit?

25. Service Department Cost Allocation LO8

The Sawyer Company has two service departments and two production departments. The following data are available from last year:

	Service 1	Service 2	Production 1	Production 2
Department costs	$63,000	$42,000	$200,000	$100,000
Number of transactions	10,000	12,000	14,000	16,000
Square feet occupied	2,000	1,000	3,000	2,000

The costs of Service Departments 1 and 2 are allocated on the basis of number of transactions and square feet occupied, respectively.

Required
A. Assuming that the Sawyer Company allocated service department costs by the direct method, how much overhead would be allocated from each service department to each producing department?
B. Assuming that the Sawyer Company allocated service department costs by the step-down method, starting with Service Department 1, how much overhead would be allocated from each service department to each producing department?

26. Service Department Cost Allocation LO8

Kenan Mortgage Company has two service departments (human resources and accounting) and two production departments (commercial lending and consumer lending) that relate to its mortgage writing and servicing business. The following data are available from last year:

	Service Departments		Production Departments	
	HR	Accounting	Commercial	Consumer
Department costs	$300,000	$240,000	$800,000	$600,000
Number of employees	5	3	19	11
Number of transactions	800	200	1,200	2,000

The costs of the HR department are allocated on the basis of the number of employees in each department, whereas the costs of the accounting department are allocated on the basis of the number of financial transactions processed in each department.

Required
A. Assuming that Kenan Mortgage Company allocates service department costs by the direct method, how much overhead would be allocated from each service department to each producing department?
B. Assuming that Kenan Mortgage Company allocates service department costs by the step-down method, starting with the HR Department, how much overhead would be allocated from each service department to each producing department?

27. Job Costing LO1, 2, 3

The Orville Smith Company, a small manufacturer, uses a job-costing system to measure and track product costs for its line of specialty outdoor clothing and uses normal costing to allocate overhead costs to its products. For the coming year, Kristin George, the company's controller, estimates total overhead costs to be $100,000. Production manager Portia Kabler told Kristin that her best estimate for total production time for the year is 20,000 hours. Production data for the first quarter of the year is as follows:

	Parkas	Shirts	Pants	Shoes
Direct materials used	$16,000	$12,000	$9,500	$11,500
Direct labor cost	13,000	10,000	7,000	9,500
Direct labor hours	1,500	1,250	850	950

Required
A. Calculate the company's predetermined overhead rate on the basis of direct labor hours.
B. Calculate the overhead costs to be assigned to parkas, shirts, pants, and shoes.
C. Calculate the total manufacturing cost of parkas, shirts, pants, and shoes.
D. On the basis of your knowledge of costing systems described in the chapter, which other method(s) might the company consider to measure and track the cost of its products? Why would the company choose to continue using job costing as it currently does?

28. Job Costing: Supply the Missing Data LO2, 3, 4

Grandma Whitney knits made-to-order blankets. The following is an incomplete job cost report for a Flower Petal blanket ordered by Anna Schotten.

	Direct Materials			Direct Labor		Overhead
Type of Yarn	Total Cost	Date	Knitting Hours	Total Cost	Total Applied
Blue—4 skeins	$14.00	January 23	5	$40.00	$4.50
Brown—2 skeins	11.00	January 24	7	?	?
Green—2 skeins	13.00	January 25	3	24.00	2.70

Required
A. What is the direct labor cost per hour?
B. What is the direct labor cost for January 24?
C. On the basis of this job cost report, how is overhead being assigned to each blanket? Do you believe that the chosen cost driver is appropriate in this instance? Why or why not?
D. How much overhead should be applied on January 24?
E. What is the total manufacturing cost for this blanket?

29. Comprehensive Job Costing LO2, 3, 4, 5

Kurtis Kabinets produces custom cabinetry for homes, which is sold nationwide. The company adds overhead costs to cabinetry projects at the rate of $7.75 per direct labor hour. The company accumulates overhead costs in a separate manufacturing overhead account and uses normal costing to assign overhead. The following data provide details of the company's activity and balances during the last half of the year:

	July 1	December 31
Direct materials inventory	$ 60,250	$61,750
Work in process inventory	44,000	43,500
Finished-goods inventory	24,150	23,000
Monthly production data:		
Direct materials purchased	$155,000	
Direct labor costs ($15/hr.)	270,000	

Required
A. Calculate the cost of direct materials used during the period.
B. Calculate the cost of goods manufactured during the period.
C. At the end of December, Kurtis found that it had actually incurred overhead costs of $145,000. If the company adjusts over- or underapplied overhead to cost of goods sold at the end of the year, what is the company's cost of goods sold after adjustment?

30. Comprehensive Job Costing LO2, 3, 4, 5

Geoff's Golf Clubs produces custom golf clubs, which are sold nationwide. The company adds overhead costs to jobs at the rate of $8.00 per direct labor hour. It accumulates overhead costs in a separate manufacturing overhead account and uses normal costing to assign overhead. The following data provide details of the company's activity and balances during the last half of the year:

	July 1	December 1
Direct materials inventory	$62,250	$63,750
Work in process inventory	46,000	45,500
Finished-goods inventory	26,150	25,000
Monthly production data:		
Direct materials purchased	$157,000	
Direct labor costs ($17/hr.)	272,000	

Required
A. Calculate the cost of direct materials used during the period.
B. Calculate the cost of goods manufactured during the period.
C. At the end of December, Geoff's found that it had actually incurred overhead costs of $123,000. If Geoff's adjusts over- or underapplied overhead to cost of goods sold at the end of the year, what is Geoff's cost of goods sold after adjustment?

31. Comprehensive Job Costing LO2, 4, 5

Moody Blues Chocolate Factory uses job costing to cost its products. In its first quarter of operations, the company incurred the following material and labor costs in manufacturing a batch of its chocolate candies (the company uses normal costing to apply overhead to products and uses machine hours as the cost driver):

Materials data:	
Direct material purchases	$100,000
Direct materials used in production (cost)	85,000
Labor data:	
Direct labor costs	60,000
Manufacturing overhead data:	
Overhead application rate per machine hour	9.00
Machine hours used	10,000
Inventory data:	
Transferred to finished goods	210,000
Cost of goods sold during quarter	190,000

Required
A. Calculate the direct materials ending inventory.
B. Calculate the work in process ending inventory.
C. Calculate the finished-goods ending inventory.
D. At the end of the quarter, Moody Blues' actual manufacturing overhead costs totaled $80,000. Calculate the over- or underapplied overhead for the period.

32. Comprehensive Job Costing LO2, 4, 5

Gordon Hammock Company produces a variety of hammocks and other outdoor products. The company uses job costing and applies overhead to work in process using a predetermined overhead rate, with direct labor hours as the cost driver. At the beginning of the year, the company estimated its overhead for the next year to be $66,000 and estimated that it would incur 4,800 direct labor hours. The company had no beginning inventories of raw materials, WIP, or finished goods, and it experienced the following events during the year:

Purchased $100,000 of raw materials
Direct materials used in production amounted to $70,000
Production employees worked 4,500 labor hours
Production employees' pay averaged $11 per hour
$180,000 of completed products were transferred to finished goods
Products costing $160,000 were sold

Required
A. Calculate the ending balance of direct materials inventory.
B. Calculate the ending balance of work in process inventory.
C. Calculate the ending balance of finished-goods inventory.

D. At the end of the year, the Gordon Hammock Company had incurred actual overhead costs of $65,000. Did the company over- or underapply overhead for the year? Is the cost of goods sold too high or too low?

33. Plantwide vs. Departmental Overhead Rates LO3, 4

Mollie Schlue started Mollie's Magnets seven years ago. This small company creates special-order magnets with varying logos and designs, and for different purposes. Mollie estimates her overhead costs to be $12,000 per month. In addition, she expects employees to work 2,000 hours, and there are usually 1,500 machine hours in a given month. Mollie's Magnets has two departments. The assembly department gives rise to 1,800 of the labor hours, and the finishing department requires 1,200 of the machine hours. The $12,000 in overhead is allocated as follows: $9,000 is traced to the assembly department and $3,000 is traced to the finishing department. During January, the following jobs were completed:

	Job 101	Job 102
Direct materials used	$1,100	$1,450
Direct labor cost	2,300	1,250
Direct labor hours	150	25
Machine hours	25	230

Required
A. What is the company's plantwide predetermined overhead rate? Use direct labor hours as the base.
B. What is the company's plantwide predetermined overhead rate? Use machine hours as the base.
C. How much overhead would be applied to each job if direct labor hours were used as the cost driver for overhead?
D. How much overhead would be applied to each job if machine hours were used as the cost driver for overhead?
E. If Mollie's Magnets decided to use department overhead rates, what would the overhead rates be for each department? The assembly department allocates overhead on the basis of direct labor hours, and the finishing department allocates overhead on the basis of machine hours.
F. Explain why it is important for Mollie's company to use departmental rates, as opposed to a single plantwide rate, to allocate overhead costs.

34. Comprehensive Process Costing: FIFO Method LO6, 7

The Maxma Beverage Corporation manufactures flavored bottled water and uses process costing to account for the cost of the products manufactured.

Raw material and conversion costs are incurred at the same rate during the production process. Data for the company's mixing department for March are as follows:

	Units	Production Costs
Work in process, March 1 (80% complete)	5,000	$ 60,000
Started during March	100,000	1,187,500
Work in process, March 31 (40% complete)	10,000	

Maxma uses the first-in, first-out method to calculate equivalent units.

Required
A. How many units were completed in March?
B. How many equivalent units were completed in March?
C. What is the cost per equivalent unit?
D. What is the cost of the ending WIP?
E. What is the cost of the units transferred out of the mixing department? That is, what is the cost of goods manufactured during March?

35. Process Costing Using the FIFO Method LO6, 7

Timmy's T-Shirts manufactures tie-dyed t-shirts for college sporting events. Each batch of shirts is identical, and the costs of a batch are determined by process costing. The following information is related to the production process for the month of February:

	Number of Shirts	Production Costs
Beginning work in process (25% complete)	20,000	$ 42,776
Current-period production	85,000	160,024
Ending work in process (70% complete)	12,000	

Timmy's T-Shirts uses the FIFO method of computing equivalent units and assigning product costs. Production costs include both the cost of raw materials and conversion costs, which are incurred uniformly in the production process.

Required
A. How many t-shirts were completed during February?
B. Of the t-shirts completed, how many were started and completed during the month?
C. How many equivalent finished units did the company complete in February?
D. What is the cost per equivalent unit?
E. Calculate the cost of the ending work in process inventory and the cost of goods manufactured in February.

36. Process Costing Using the Weighted-Average Method LO6, 7

How would your answers in Problem 35 change if Timmy's used the weighted-average method of process costing?

37. Process Costing Using the FIFO Method LO6, 7

Riley's Paper Company manufactures computer paper for laser printers. The following information is related to production costs incurred in the manufacturing process during the month of March:

	Reams of Paper	Production Costs
Beginning work in process (40% complete)	35,000	$ 89,170
Current-period production	93,000	394,830
Ending work in process (65% complete)	20,000	

The company uses the FIFO method of computing equivalent units and assigning product costs. Production costs include both the cost of raw materials and conversion costs that are incurred uniformly in the production process.

Required
A. How many reams of paper were completed in March?
B. Of the reams of paper completed in March, how many were started and completed during the month?
C. How many equivalent finished units did the company complete in March?
D. What is the cost per equivalent unit?
E. Calculate the cost of the ending work in process inventory and the cost of goods manufactured in March.

38. Process Costing Using the Weighted-Average Method LO7

How would your answers in Problem 37 change if Riley's used the weighted-average method of process costing?

39. Comprehensive Process Costing: Weighted-Average Method LO6, 7

The Gibson & Zorich Bakery bakes breads and muffins for wholesale to restaurants. The company uses process costing to account for the cost of the breads and muffins that it produces. Raw material (for example, flour, sugar, flavoring, fruits) and conversion costs are incurred at the same rate during the production process. Data for Gibson & Zorich's blending department for December are as follows:

	Units	Production Costs
Work in process, December 1 (80% complete)	5,000	$ 140,000
Started during December	100,000	1,060,000
Work in process, December 31 (50% complete)	10,000	

Gibson & Zorich Bakery uses the weighted-average method to compute equivalent units.

Required

A. How many units were completed in December?
B. How many equivalent units were completed in December?
C. What is the cost per equivalent unit?
D. What is the cost of the ending WIP?
E. What is the cost of the units transferred out of the blending department? That is, what is the cost of goods manufactured during December?

40. Comprehensive Process Costing: FIFO Method LO6, 7

AJ's Bakery bakes apple fritters for sale to area grocery stores. The company uses the FIFO method of process costing to account for the cost of the apple fritters it produces. Raw materials (flour, sugar, flavoring, apples) and conversion costs are incurred at the same rate during the production process. Data for AJ's Bakery are as follows:

	Units	Production Costs
Work in process, December 1:	4,000	
Raw materials (90% complete)		$ 2,132
Conversion costs (60% complete)		$ 976
Started during December	50,000	
Raw materials		$40,188
Conversion costs		$ 9,744
Work in process, December 31:	11,000	
Raw materials (90% complete)		
Conversion costs (60% complete)		

Required

A. How many units were completed in December?
B. How many equivalent units were completed in December for raw materials and conversion costs?
C. What is the cost per equivalent unit for raw materials and conversion costs?
D. What is the cost of ending WIP?
E. What is the cost of the units transferred out of work in process inventory to finished-goods inventory? That is, what is the cost of goods manufactured during December?

41. Comprehensive Process Costing: Weighted-Average Method LO6, 7

AJ's Bakery bakes apple fritters for sale to area grocery stores. The company uses the weighted-average method of process costing to account for the cost of the apple fritters it produces. Raw materials (flour, sugar, flavoring, apples) and conversion costs are incurred at the same rate during the production process. Data for AJ's Bakery are as follows:

	Units	Production Costs
Work in process, December 1:	4,000	
Raw materials (90% complete)		$ 2,132
Conversion costs (60% complete)		$ 976
Started during December	50,000	
Raw materials		$40,188
Conversion costs		$ 9,744
Work in process, December 31:	11,000	
Raw materials (90% complete)		
Conversion costs (60% complete)		

Required

A. How many units were completed in December?
B. How many equivalent units were completed in December for raw materials and conversion costs?
C. What is the cost per equivalent unit for raw materials and conversion costs?
D. What is the cost of ending WIP?
E. What is the cost of the units transferred out of work in process inventory to finished-goods inventory? That is, what is the cost of goods manufactured during December?

42. Comprehensive Process Costing: FIFO Method LO6, 7

Lulu's makes women's shoes for sale to boutique shoe stores. Lulu's uses the FIFO method of process costing to account for the cost of its shoes. Raw materials consist of leather and other processed materials. The shoes are handmade, so labor is a major part of the conversion costs. Data for Lulu's for the month of January are as follows:

	Units	Production Costs
Work in process, January 1:	12,000	
Raw materials (80% complete)		$ 331,140
Conversion costs (50% complete)		$ 24,000
Started during January	150,000	
Raw materials		$2,998,860
Conversion costs		$4,080,000
Work in process, January 31:	20,000	
Raw materials (90% complete)		
Conversion costs (70% complete)		

Required:
A. How many units were completed in January?
B. How many equivalent units were completed in January for raw materials and conversion costs?
C. What is the cost per equivalent unit for raw materials and conversion costs?
D. What is the cost of ending WIP?
E. What is the cost of the units transferred out of work in process inventory to finished-goods inventory? That is, what is the cost of goods manufactured during January?

43. Comprehensive Process Costing: Weighted-Average Method LO6, 7

Lulu's makes women's shoes for sale to boutique shoe stores. Lulu's uses the weighted-average method of process costing to account for the cost of its shoes. Raw materials consist of leather and other processed materials. The shoes are hand-made, so labor is a major part of the conversion costs. Data for Lulu's for the month of January are as follows:

	Units	Production Costs
Work in process, January 1:	12,000	
Raw materials (80% complete)		$ 331,140
Conversion costs (50% complete)		$ 24,000
Started during January	150,000	
Raw materials		$2,998,860
Conversion costs		$4,080,000
Work in process, January 31:	20,000	
Raw materials (90% complete)		
Conversion costs (70% complete)		

Required
A. How many units were completed in January?
B. How many equivalent units were completed in January for raw materials and conversion costs?
C. What is the cost per equivalent unit for raw materials and conversion costs?
D. What is the cost of ending WIP?
E. What is the cost of the units transferred out of work in process inventory to finished-goods inventory? That is, what is the cost of goods manufactured during January?

CASES

44. Problems with Overhead Application: Decision Focus LO3, 4

Bergan Brewery uses the latest in modern brewing technology to produce a prizewinning beer. In both 2011 and 2012, Bergan produced and sold 100,000 cases of beer and had no raw materials, work in process, or finished goods inventory at the beginning or end of either year. At the end of 2011, the company installed machines to perform some of the repetitive tasks previously performed with direct labor. At the beginning of 2012, Bergan's bookkeeper estimated that net income would increase from $530,000 in 2011 to $706,000 in 2012:

	2011 (Actual)	2012 (Estimated)
Beer sales (100,000 cases)	$1,000,000	$1,000,000
Less: Cost of goods sold		
Direct material	150,000	150,000
Direct labor	125,000	25,000
Applied overhead*	95,000	19,000
Gross profit	$ 630,000	$ 806,000
Less: Selling and administrative costs	100,000	100,000
Net income	$ 530,000	$ 706,000

*For 2012, overhead was applied at the 2011 rate of $9.50 per direct labor hour for an estimated 2,000 hours of direct labor. A total of 10,000 direct labor hours were worked in 2011. Bergan's bookkeeper estimates that 5,000 machine hours will be worked in 2012.

However, when actual overhead was used to calculate net income at the end of the year, net income decreased from $530,000 in 2011 to $435,000 in 2012:

	2011 (Actual)	2012 (Actual)
Beer sales (100,000 cases)	$1,000,000	$1,000,000
Less: Cost of goods sold		
Direct material	150,000	150,000
Direct labor	125,000	25,000
Actual overhead:		
Lease expense	25,000	25,000
Utilities expense	15,000	30,000
Depreciation (equipment)	50,000	200,000
Equipment maintenance	5,000	35,000
Gross profit	$ 630,000	$ 535,000
Less: Selling and administrative costs	100,000	100,000
Net income	$ 530,000	$ 435,000

Required

A. What potential problems do you see in the book-keeper's income estimate for 2012?

B. On the basis of the information given, would you change the cost driver or predetermined overhead rate for 2012? What cost driver would you suggest? What would be the new predetermined overhead rate?

C. Using the cost driver and predetermined overhead rate you suggested in B, and assuming that 5,000 machine hours will be incurred, recalculate Bergan's estimated net income for 2012.

D. Bergan has set a goal of increasing net income to $550,000 in 2013. However, sales are expected to be flat. How might the company reach its goal of increasing income to $550,000? What qualitative factors should be considered in its decision?

45. Decision Focus: The Choice of Cost Driver   LO3, 4, 5

Thiel Boots manufactures hunting boots. The company's president, Dick Thiel, has become increasingly doubtful about the firm's current overhead allocation. As a consequence, Dick has asked the company's controller to prepare some basic data so that other allocation methods can be investigated. The estimated income statement that follows was prepared under the following basic assumptions: The company expects to sell 10,000 pairs of boots in the coming year, estimates that production employees will work 10,000 hours, and expects that production equipment will operate 8,000 hours in total.

Thiel Boots Estimated Income Statement For the Year Ending November 30, 2012		
Sales		$1,000,000
Cost of goods sold:		
Direct materials	300,000	
Direct labor	160,000	
Estimated overhead	240,000	700,000
Gross profit		300,000
Selling and administrative expenses		175,000
Net income		$ 125,000

Required

A. Compute the predetermined overhead rate for Thiel, using the following three cost drivers: direct labor hours, direct labor dollars, and machine hours.

B. If actual labor costs were $170,000 for 10,500 direct labor hours and actual machine hours used were 7,800, what would be the applied overhead, according to the three predetermined overhead rates computed in part A?

C. Compute the amount of the over- or underapplied overhead, assuming that actual overhead is $229,000. You should assume that overhead was applied as computed by you in requirement B.

D. Take a moment to compare the overapplied or underapplied overhead amounts calculated in part C. Why do the different cost drivers result in such different applied overhead amounts? Is there one "best" cost driver? What basis should Dick Thiel use to select a cost driver?

E. What options are available to Thiel Boots to dispose of the over- or underapplied overhead amounts? Which option do you recommend? Why?

Activity-Based
Costing

Introduction

The previous chapter examined a number of problems associated with the application of overhead to products and services. Owing to the indirect nature of overhead and the fact that overhead consists of a variety of seemingly unrelated costs, it is often difficult to determine how much overhead should be included when costing specific products and services. To complicate matters further, overhead costs must often be estimated in order to provide timely cost information to managers.

In the past, overhead typically made up a smaller portion of the total cost of a product or service. The environment was one of "labor-intensive" manufacturing. With labor as the dominant activity and therefore the cost driver, direct labor hours worked was a logical activity base to use to allocate overhead to products. As the manufacturing environment has matured and the use of machines or robotics in production has increased, overhead cost has become a larger percentage of the total manufacturing cost. In heavily automated manufacturing environments, direct labor costs have shrunk to as little as 5 percent of total production costs, whereas overhead costs have soared to 60 percent or more of total product costs (see Exhibit 4-1). It's not difficult to see why.

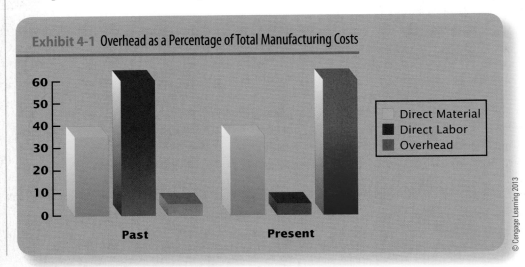

Exhibit 4-1 Overhead as a Percentage of Total Manufacturing Costs

Legend: Direct Material, Direct Labor, Overhead

Past — Present

© Cengage Learning 2013

Activity-based costing highlights the effects that common business activities have on costs.

Consider a modern automobile-manufacturing plant. High-tech computers control robots that weld, paint, and perform other jobs that used to be done by human labor. High-tech computer-operated equipment such as robots is very expensive and is treated as part of overhead cost. As overhead costs increase and make up a larger portion of the total costs of products, accuracy in overhead application has become much more important. At the same time, advances in information technology have allowed even the smallest businesses to take advantage of computers. These advances have provided more and more timely information to managers than ever before.

LOı Unit-, Batch-, Product-, and Facility-Level Costs

Traditional overhead allocation methods, which use volume-based cost drivers to assign overhead costs to products, can provide misleading product-cost information in heavily automated manufacturing environments in which companies make a variety of diverse products. Traditional, volume-based allocation methods work best if the manufacturing environment includes mostly **unit-level costs** (costs that vary with every unit produced or with the volume of production). Activity-based costing provides an alternative to traditional methods by allocating overhead costs on the basis of activities that lead to the overhead costs.

Costs incurred in setting up machinery to make different products, costs incurred in designing a new model, and costs incurred in providing manufacturing facilities are not incurred every time an individual unit (e.g., a table) is produced. Rather, **batch-level costs,** such as machine setups, are incurred only when a batch of products (say, 100 tables) is produced. Likewise, **product-level costs** (designing a new model) are incurred only when a new product is introduced. Finally, **facility-level costs,** such as the rent on the factory building, are incurred to sustain the overall manufacturing processes and do not vary with the number or type of products produced.[1]

Examples of unit-, batch-, product-, and facility-level overhead costs are provided in Exhibit 4-2.

Exhibit 4-2 Overhead Costs and Cooper's Hierarchy

Unit-Level Costs

Supplies for factory

Depreciation of factory machinery

Energy costs for factory machinery

Repairs and maintenance of factory machinery

Batch-Level Costs

Salaries related to purchasing and receiving

Salaries related to moving material

Quality control costs

Depreciation of setup equipment

Product-Level Costs

Salaries of engineers

Depreciation of engineering equipment

Product development costs (testing)

Quality control costs

Facility-Level Costs

Depreciation of factory building or rent

Salary of plant manager

Insurance and taxes on factory building

Employee training

© Cengage Learning 2013

When costing is concentrated at the unit level, it makes sense that the number of units produced should be correlated with the amount of overhead costs allocated to each unit. However, as companies incur more and more batch-, product-, and facility-level costs, the correlation between the number of products produced and the allocation of overhead becomes very fuzzy.

LO2 Activity-Based Costing

Activity-based costing (ABC) provides an alternative to traditional costing methods by allocating overhead costs on the basis of activities that drive costs. **Activities** are procedures or processes that cause work to be accomplished. Activities consume resources, and products consume activities.

Overhead costs are assigned to products in an ABC system in two stages.

Stage 1—Identification of Activities

In Stage 1, activities are identified. Examples of typical activities of a company are shown in the first column of Exhibit 4-3. Note that overhead costs can be traced to more than one activity. For example, utilities may be

Unit-level costs Costs that are incurred each time a unit is produced.

Batch-level costs Costs that are incurred each time a batch of goods is produced.

Product-level costs Costs that are incurred as needed to support the production of each type of product.

Facility-level costs Costs that are incurred to sustain the overall manufacturing process.

Activity-based costing (ABC) A system of allocating overhead costs that assumes that activities, not volume of production, cause overhead costs to be incurred.

Activities Procedures or processes that cause work to be accomplished.

[1]This classification of unit-level, batch-level, product-level, and facility-level costs is commonly referred to as *Cooper's hierarchy.*

Activity-based costing allocates costs on the basis of activities that drive overhead rather than on the basis of simple volume- or unit-based measures.

Exhibit 4-3 Activities and Cost Drivers

Activity	Level	Typical Cost Drivers
Repair and maintenance of factory equipment	Unit	Machine hours, labor hours, or number of units
Machining of products	Unit	Machine hours
Purchasing	Batch	Number of purchase orders or number of parts
Receiving	Batch	Amount of material or number of receipts
Setting up equipment	Batch	Number of setups
Product testing	Product	Number of change orders, number of tests, or hours of testing time
Engineering	Product	Number of engineering hours or number of products
Product design	Product	Number of new or revised products
Quality control	Unit, batch, product	Number of inspections, hours of inspection, or number of defective units

© Cengage Learning 2013

allocated to products or are allocated to products in an arbitrary manner. For example, plant occupancy is a facility-level activity that would include such costs as plant managers' salaries, depreciation of the factory building, rent, taxes, and insurance. Allocation of these costs would depend on the use of arbitrary cost drivers such as square footage, number of employees, labor hours, or machine hours.

It should be recognized that because of different types of production processes and products, every business will have a different set of activities and cost drivers. In addition, the more complex the business or the production process, the more complex the ABC system is likely to be.

ABC Systems in Nonmanufacturing Environments

Service providers currently make up the fastest-growing segment of the U.S. economy, employing almost 75 percent of the workforce. As service companies expand the scope and quality of services they offer, the need for fast, accurate costing information becomes more important. Can ABC be used to cost services as well as products? Do the same principles that we learned for manufacturing companies apply to service businesses? The answer is yes! In fact, ABC is every bit as important for service providers as it is for manufacturing companies. Although ABC was developed for use primarily by manufacturing companies, it has gained widespread acceptance in the service sector. For example, the U.S. Postal Service used activity-based costing to help determine the costs and benefits of allowing customers to pay with debit and credit cards. In this effort aimed at continuous improvement, the post office focused on the impact of payment flexibility on customer satisfaction even though cost savings were also likely to be realized.

However, implementing ABC in service companies is not without its problems. One common problem is that the type of work done by service companies tends to be nonrepetitive. Unlike highly automated manufacturing companies, analyzing the activities of a service provider can be difficult when the activities

related to purchasing, engineering, and machining activities. Thus, an employee who provides maintenance services and runs machines in the factory might have his or her salary split between machining and maintenance activities. Likewise, whereas depreciation of factory equipment is related to machining, depreciation of other equipment might be related to maintenance or quality control activities.

Stage 2—Identification of Cost Drivers

In Stage 2, cost drivers for activities are chosen. As discussed in Chapter 3, cost drivers should cause, or drive, the incurrence of costs. For example, costs of purchasing might be driven by the number of purchase orders processed, whereas engineering costs might be driven by the number of parts in a product. Typical cost drivers for the activities identified in Exhibit 4-3 are provided in the third column of that exhibit.

Unit-, batch-, and product-level activities are assigned to products by using cost drivers that capture the underlying behavior of the costs that are being assigned. Facility-level costs, however, are usually not

> Although there are common activities that drive overhead costs, every company should evaluate its activities carefully.

differ greatly for each customer or service. In addition, service-oriented companies are likely to have proportionately more facility-level costs than manufacturing companies have. Remember from our earlier discussion that facility-level costs are allocated arbitrarily to goods and services (if they are allocated at all).

Service providers will also have different activities and cost drivers, compared with traditional manufacturing companies. For example, CPA firms and law firms might want to measure costs for activities, such as professional development and client development, along with basic activities, such as planning, data collection, and review time. In addition to obvious activities, such as drink and food preparation, employees at coffee shops like **Starbucks** are engaged in activities related to setting up and closing the store each day, cleaning the food and drink preparation areas, processing customer orders (and payments), and so on.

In applying the principles of ABC to nonmanufacturing activities, instead of computing the manufacturing cost of a product or a service, the goal is to determine the total cost of a product or service. ABC can also be used to determine the cost of providing a particular nonmanufacturing activity. For example, a company might use ABC to determine the cost of providing payroll services. This information can then be used to help management determine whether to continue processing payroll in-house or to outsource.

LO3 Traditional Overhead Allocation and ABC—An Example

As an example, let's consider TopSail Construction, a modular home builder based in North Carolina. The company has been asked to construct a new modular home. These homes will be used in areas of the country affected by hurricanes and other natural disasters to provide safe, temporary housing for families whose houses were destroyed or severely damaged by storms. TopSail Construction usually builds about 300 units each year. On average, it takes about two weeks to assemble the components for each model and then one to two days to assemble the units on-site. As with all manufactured products, the cost of a house consists of three main components: direct materials, direct labor, and overhead.

Many types of materials are used in the construction of a modular home. Raw materials needed in home construction include lumber, roofing, insulation, wallboard, and siding. The costs for these types of raw materials can usually be accumulated, tracked, and assigned to specific homes with relative ease, so such materials are classified as direct materials. Indirect materials include such items as nails, screws, fasteners, basic hardware, glue, and other materials that are difficult to trace to a particular unit.

Direct labor is also fairly straightforward in the construction business. Like many home-building companies, TopSail does not employ carpenters or brick masons; rather, the company uses subcontractors to perform this work. Because subcontractor labor can be traced directly to each house, these costs are classified as direct labor. TopSail has 140 full-time employees working in the factory. Most of these employees are carpenters who work in the assembly of modular homes, so their wages are classified as direct labor. The company also employs electricians and plumbers whose wages are also classified as direct labor. Some employees are construction supervisors whose primary job is to supervise and inspect the work done on each unit. TopSail consequently classifies their salaries as indirect labor.

TopSail also has a purchasing department that handles the ordering of raw materials and processing of purchase orders for the manufacturing operations of the company, as well as purchases of supplies and equipment for nonmanufacturing operations. The company also has an administrative department that handles payroll, billing, accounts payable, and other accounting and administrative tasks related to the business. A portion of the costs of both service departments is allocated to the manufacturing operations of TopSail.

In addition to overhead costs associated with the service departments just described, TopSail incurs other manufacturing overhead costs, including the cost of tools (saws and drills) and of trucks used for delivery of the completed modular homes. TopSail estimates that its manufacturing overhead costs will total $3,830,000 in 2012. Exhibit 4-4 provides a breakdown of this estimate.

Exhibit 4-4 Estimated Manufacturing Overhead Costs for 2012

Overhead Item	Estimated Cost
Indirect materials	$1,800,000
Indirect labor:	
Construction supervisors	500,000
Part-time workers	200,000
Other overhead:	
Allocated service department costs	780,000
Tools	150,000
Trucks and other equipment	400,000
Total	$3,830,000

© Cengage Learning 2013

If TopSail produced only one type of modular home, the overhead allocation process would be very simple. As discussed in Chapter 3, all the company would have to do is divide the total overhead of $3,830,000 by the number of modular homes constructed. For example, if TopSail constructed 300 identical modular homes in 2012, $12,767 of overhead costs would be allocated to each unit.

However, to meet the specific needs of its customers, TopSail builds two basic models: a 1,200-square-foot two-bedroom unit and a 1,600-square-foot three-bedroom unit. These units are similar, except for size. Consequently, TopSail applies overhead on the basis of the square footage of each model. On the basis of an expected production of 150 two-bedroom units and 150 three-bedroom units in 2012, TopSail estimates that it will manufacture units with total floor space of 420,000 square feet [(150 two-bedroom units × 1,200 square feet) + (150 three-bedroom units × 1,600 square feet) = 420,000]. The company's predetermined overhead rate for 2012 is $9.12 per square foot ($3,830,000 ÷ 420,000 square feet = $9.12). A two-bedroom model with 1,200 square feet of floor space would thus be allocated $10,944 of overhead (1,200 square feet × $9.12), whereas a three-bedroom unit with 1,600 square feet of floor space would be allocated $14,592 of manufacturing overhead (1,600 square feet × $9.12).

The Federal Emergency Management Agency (FEMA) and other emergency organizations' expressed interest in emergency housing has caused TopSail to design the new 500-square-foot "Katrina cottage," which can be constructed and shipped to a site within one week of receiving the order. The cottages are set on a concrete slab or a cement block foundation and can be used later as a guest cottage or storage building. The company expects to manufacture 1,000 of these units in 2012.

According to FEMA, a cottage's total price may not exceed $37,500. In order to earn a sufficient profit, TopSail estimates that its costs must not exceed $30,000. TopSail will also offer these cottages for sale to others, just as it does with its regular models. The addition of the cottage to the company's product line will lead

© iStockphoto.com/james steidl

to more overhead and will require TopSail to give more attention to the proper allocation of overhead costs to each house. The estimated manufacturing overhead is expected to increase to $6,720,000.

If TopSail uses its traditional method of applying overhead based on square footage, the predetermined overhead rate would be $7.30 per square foot ($6,720,000 ÷ 920,000 total square feet [420,000 square feet from two- and three-bedroom units + 500,000 square feet from the Katrina cottages]). Accordingly, TopSail would allocate $8,760 of overhead to a two-bedroom unit (1,200 square feet × $7.30), $11,680 of overhead to a three-bedroom unit (1,600 square feet × $7.30), and $3,650 of overhead to a cottage (500 square feet × $7.30).

As shown in Exhibit 4-5, when the company uses its traditional method of applying overhead based on the square footage of the unit, the $30,650 cost of the cottage exceeds the target cost by $650 per unit.

Exhibit 4-5 Costs per Unit Using Volume-Based Overhead Allocation

	Two-Bedroom Unit	Three-Bedroom Unit	Cottage
Number of units	150	150	1,000
Direct material	$30,000	$40,000	$16,500
Direct labor	18,000	24,000	10,500
Overhead	8,760	11,680	3,650
Total cost per unit	$56,760	$75,680	$30,650

© Cengage Learning 2013

The company's chief financial officer (CFO) has some reservations about costing the new cottage by the traditional method of allocating overhead based on square footage. The cottage is expected to be simpler to build and does not need to be assembled on-site, thus requiring fewer resources than the current two-bedroom and three-bedroom modular units. Accordingly, she has recommended investigating the use of activity-based costing (ABC) because she has heard that this method will likely provide more accurate allocations of overhead.

TopSail's Stage 1: Identification of Activities

The first step in TopSail's implementation of an ABC system is the identification of activities and the tracing of overhead costs to each activity. Remember that activities are processes or procedures that cause work

to be accomplished. TopSail Construction has identified four primary activities that consume company resources:

1. Inspections
2. Purchasing
3. Supervision
4. Delivery and setup

Exhibit 4-6 shows the overhead costs associated with each activity. Note that the total overhead is $6,720,000, regardless of whether it is allocated by means of volume-based cost drivers or ABC.

Exhibit 4-6 Estimated Overhead Costs for 2012 (with addition of cottage)

Activity	Estimated Cost
Inspections	$ 900,000
Purchasing	500,000
Supervision	1,400,000
Delivery and setup	3,920,000
Total overhead	$6,720,000

© Cengage Learning 2013

TopSail's Stage 2: Identification of Cost Drivers and Allocation of Costs

Once the activities have been identified and overhead costs traced to each activity, cost drivers must be identified for each activity. The cost drivers are as follows:

Activity	Cost Driver
Inspections	Number of inspections
Purchasing	Number of purchase orders
Supervision	Hours of supervisory time
Delivery and setup	Setup time (days)

Each of these cost drivers is directly associated with the related activity. Accordingly, the cost of inspections is driven by the number of inspections, the cost of purchasing is driven by the number of purchase orders processed, and so on. It simply makes more sense to allocate the cost of supervision on the basis of the hours of supervisor time rather than on the amount of floor space in a unit.

The 1,200-square-foot two-bedroom unit is estimated to require 25 inspections, whereas the larger 1,600-square-foot three-bedroom unit is estimated to require 35 inspections. The cottage will require only 10 inspections. The cottage will also require the processing of fewer purchase orders (10) and less supervision (10 hours) than the other units. The two-bedroom unit requires the processing of 30 purchase orders and 72 hours of supervision, and the three-bedroom unit requires the processing of 40 purchase orders and 96 hours of supervision. Finally, whereas the two-bedroom unit requires four days to deliver and set up and the three-bedroom unit requires six days to deliver and set up, the cottage can generally be delivered and set up in only one day. Exhibit 4-7 summarizes the total number of cost driver units for each activity.

In Exhibit 4-8, predetermined activity rates are calculated for each activity and cost driver, just as they were in Chapter 3, using a plantwide overhead rate with volume-based cost drivers.

Exhibit 4-9 illustrates the total cost of each unit built by TopSail Construction, using an activity-based costing system.

If we compare the two methods of allocating overhead cost to the three modular homes produced by TopSail Construction, we can see why volume-based allocation and ABC result in different amounts of applied overhead. Under the traditional overhead allocation method based on square footage, the three-bedroom unit was allocated 320 percent more overhead than the cottage ($11,680, compared with $3,650) because it was 3.2 times larger (1,600 square feet, compared with 500 square feet).

Exhibit 4-7 Estimated Cost Driver Activity

Cost Driver	Two-Bedroom Unit	Three-Bedroom Unit	Cottage	Total
Number of inspections	(25 × 150) = 3,750	(35 × 150) = 5,250	(10 × 1,000) = 10,000	19,000
Number of purchase orders processed	(30 × 150) = 4,500	(40 × 150) = 6,000	(10 × 1,000) = 10,000	20,500
Hours of supervisory time	(72 × 150) = 10,800	(96 × 150) = 14,400	(10 × 1,000) = 10,000	35,200
Days of delivery and setup time	(4 × 150) = 600	(6 × 150) = 900	(1 × 1,000) = 1,000	2,500

© Cengage Learning 2013

Exhibit 4-8 The Calculation of Predetermined Activity Rates

Activity	Total Estimated Cost	Cost Driver and Estimated Amount	Predetermined Overhead Rate
Inspections	$ 900,000	Number of inspections (19,000)	$47.37 per inspection
Purchasing	500,000	Number of purchase orders (20,500)	$24.39 per purchase order
Supervision	1,400,000	Hours of supervisory time (35,200)	$39.77 per supervisory hour
Delivery and setup	3,920,000	Setup time (days) (2,500)	$1,568.00 per day

© Cengage Learning 2013

Exhibit 4-9 Cost of Units Based on Activity-Based Costing

Cost	Two-Bedroom Unit	Three-Bedroom Unit	Cottage
Direct materials	$ 30,000	$ 40,000	$ 16,500
Direct labor	18,000	24,000	10,500
Inspections	1,184	1,658	474
Purchases	732	976	244
Supervision	2,864	3,818	398
Delivery and setup	6,272	9,408	1,568
Total cost per unit	$59,052	$79,860	$29,684

© Cengage Learning 2013

Volume-based costing methods and ABC result in different allocations of overhead if products consume activities in different proportions. Allocating overhead costs with an ABC system results in greater allocations of overhead to the two- and three-bedroom units than under the traditional method of allocating overhead based on square footage. This is because the two- and three-bedroom units consume more of the inspection, purchasing, supervision, and delivery and setup activities (relative to the square footage of the units) than the cottage does. For example, whereas the three-bedroom unit is just over three times as large as the cottage, it requires 350 percent more inspections, 400 percent more purchase orders, 960 percent more supervision time, and 600 percent more delivery and setup time than the cottage.

In Exhibit 4-10, notice that, compared with costing under ABC, using traditional costing methods resulted in overcosting the cottage and undercosting the

> *Volume-based costing systems often result in overcosting high-volume products and undercosting low-volume products. This cross subsidy is eliminated by the use of ABC.*

are allocated too little overhead. This cross subsidy may make high-volume products appear unprofitable when they may not be, or it may make them appear to show less profit than they actually do. Activity-based costing systems eliminate the cross subsidy between high- and low-volume products.

Although the differences in cost may seem small, consider the impact on TopSail's pricing policy (see

Exhibit 4-10 Cost Comparison between Traditional and Activity-Based Costing

	Two-Bedroom Unit	Three-Bedroom Unit	Cottage
Traditional costing	$56,760	$75,680	$30,650
Activity-based costing	$59,052	$79,860	$29,684
Difference in cost	$2,292 higher with ABC	$4,180 higher with ABC	$966 lower with ABC

© Cengage Learning 2013

two- and three-bedroom units. In general, when there are batch- and product-level costs, ABC will typically shift costs from high-volume products produced in large batches to low-volume products produced in small batches. On a per-unit basis, this shift usually results in a greater impact on the low-volume products than on the high-volume products.

One important aspect of ABC systems is the elimination of cross subsidies between products. Cross subsidies occur when high-volume products, such as the cottage, are assigned more than their fair share of overhead costs. At the same time, more complicated low-volume products, such as the two- and three-bedroom units,

Exhibit 4-11). On the one hand, TopSail typically establishes a sales price equal to 125 percent of total manufacturing costs. Under ABC, TopSail would price the two-bedroom unit $2,865 higher, and the three-bedroom model $5,225 higher, than when using traditional costing. If these price increases can be made without affecting sales, total revenue for the two- and three-bedroom units will increase by $1,213,500 [(150 × $2,865) + (150 × 5,225)].

On the other hand, TopSail's goal was to produce the new cottage for less than $30,000, which would allow the company to sell it to FEMA at a price of $37,500.

Exhibit 4-11 Price Comparison between Traditional and Activity-Based Costing

	Two-Bedroom Unit	Three-Bedroom Unit	Cottage
Sales price based on traditional costing	$70,950	$94,600	$38,313
Sales price based on activity-based costing	$73,815	$99,825	$37,104
Difference in price	$2,865 higher with ABC	$5,225 higher with ABC	$1,209 lower with ABC

© Cengage Learning 2013

© Kristian Sekulic/Shutterstock.com

ABC systems generally improve the accuracy of cost data, but are often time consuming and expensive to develop.

Whereas traditional costing and overhead allocation based on square footage would have resulted in the company not being able to earn its desired profit, the revised ABC cost estimates indicate that the cottage can be manufactured for $29,684 and sold to FEMA for $37,104.

As this example illustrates, the allocation of costs by means of activity-based costing is more accurate and reflects the consumption of costs on the basis of the activities that drive them rather than on one volume-based cost driver. In addition to providing management with more accurate cost information for pricing decisions, it also affects a variety of other decisions discussed in the remainder of this book.

LO4 **Benefits and Limitations of ABC**

Because of the increase in global competition, companies must strive to achieve and sustain a competitive advantage. This requires organizations to continually improve performance in all aspects of their business operations. By focusing on continuous improvement, organizations can minimize scrap in the manufacturing process, reduce lead times for customer deliveries or vendor shipments, increase the quality of their products and services, control manufacturing and nonmanufacturing costs, and increase customer satisfaction.

Activity-based costing systems provide more, and more accurate, cost information that focuses managers on opportunities for continuous improvement. Throughout their planning, operating, and control activities, managers use the information provided by ABC systems. In Chapter 1, planning was defined as

the development of short- and long-term objectives and goals of an organization and the identification of the resources needed to achieve them. Using ABC in the budgeting process provides more accurate estimates of these resources.

One of the biggest advantages of ABC is the increased accuracy of cost information it provides for day-to-day decision making by managers (operating decisions). Managers use ABC information to make better decisions related to adding or dropping products, making or buying components used in the manufacturing process, marketing and pricing strategies, and so forth.

ABC also provides benefits related to the control function of managers. Costs that appear to be indirect under volume-based costing systems now are traced to specific activities by using cost drivers. This method allows managers to better see what causes costs to be incurred, leading to better control.

However, ABC is not for everyone, and the benefits of increased accuracy do not come without costs. Accumulating, tracking, and assigning costs to products and services with ABC requires the use of multiple activity pools and cost drivers. High measurement costs associated with ABC systems are a significant limitation. Companies may decide that the measurement costs associated with implementing ABC systems are greater than the expected benefit from having more accurate cost information. For example, if the market dictates prices, as it does with commodity products, and companies have little control over pricing their products, then highly reliable product costs may not be necessary for pricing. However, ABC may still prove valuable for planning and cost-reduction efforts.

In general, companies that have a high potential for cost distortions are more likely to benefit from ABC. Cost distortions are likely when companies make diverse products that consume resources differently. Products that vary a great deal in complexity are typically diverse, but differences in color or other seemingly minor differences in products can lead to product diversity when these differences materially change the products and affect the resources they consume.

Companies that have a large proportion of non-unit-level costs are also likely to benefit from ABC. Remember, unit-level costs vary with the number of units produced and can be allocated with reasonable accuracy by using volume-based cost systems and drivers. However, volume-based costing systems can result in distortions when a company allocates batch-, product-, and facility-level costs.

Companies that have relatively high proportions of overhead compared with direct materials and direct labor are likely to benefit from ABC as well. This situation is often the case with highly automated manufacturing companies or with companies that have adopted JIT techniques. Note that service companies, such as law or CPA firms, may also have high overhead costs compared with direct materials and direct labor costs and likewise may benefit from the implementation of ABC.

Diverse products Products that consume resources in different proportions.

STUDY TOOLS 4

Chapter review card

- Learning Objective and Key Concept Reviews
- Key Definitions and Formulas

Online (Located at www.cengagebrain.com)

- Flash Cards and Crossword Puzzles
- Games and Quizzes
- Cold Stone Creamery Video and E-Lectures
- Homework Assignments (as directed by your instructor)

BRIEF EXERCISES

1. **Cost Classifications** LO1

Hendee Cable Systems manufactures a variety of products for the fiber-optic industry in its facility in San Bernardino, California. The following are examples of the activities performed by various personnel at Hendee.

a. Purchase orders are generated for raw materials purchases from suppliers. Hendee orders raw materials as needed to fill customer orders and maintains a very small amount of raw materials inventory.

b. Engineers conduct research and development activities aimed at identifying new technologies for data transmission.

c. Hendee conducts continuous quality inspections during the production process. All cable is 100 percent guaranteed to be free of defects.

d. Machine operators must calibrate production equipment whenever production is started on a new order.

e. Maintenance personnel regularly inspect the manufacturing facility's heating and cooling systems to ensure adequate conditions within the manufacturing environment.

f. Hendee recently hired several new engineers to begin work on the development of a new product line.

g. Accounting personnel were billed for, and paid, property taxes on the manufacturing facility.

h. Hendee launched a Web site to auction excess cable to interested parties.

i. A new facility was built to house all design engineers in one central location. This new facility will be depreciated over 20 years.

Required

Classify each of the activities as a unit-level, batch-level, product-level, or facility-level activity.

2. ABC Activities and Cost Drivers LO2

Jakubielski and Martin, CPAs, is a full-service CPA firm that provides accounting, tax, and consulting services to its clients. The firm is considering changing to an activity-based costing system and has asked for your input regarding the design of the system. The firm has identified certain activities that are integral to the practice, and it would like your suggestions regarding potential cost drivers.

Activity	Cost Driver
a. Client interview	1. Professional staff hours
b. Tax return preparation	2. Transactions
c. Tax return review	3. Number of pages
d. Data input	4. Number of employees
e. Report assembly	5. Machine hours
f. Research	6. Clerical staff hours
g. Report writing	
h. Site visits	

Required

Match each of the activities with a potential cost driver. Note that you may not use all drivers and some may be used more than once.

3. ABC Overhead Calculation LO3

Timeless Timepieces produces and sells watches. The following data are available for various activities within the company:

Activity	Allocation Base	Number of Activities	Overhead Cost
Unpacking	Number of boxes unpacked	10,000	$40,000
Inspecting	Number of batches inspected	1,800	36,000
Packing	Number of watches packed	56,000	28,000

Required

Calculate the overhead rates for each of the three activities.

4. Benefits and Limitations of ABC LO4

Activity-based costing can aid companies in understanding their overhead costs. The following statements describe some of the benefits and limitations of ABC:

a. ABC is useful for understanding overhead costs, but it is not very useful for identifying opportunities for continuous improvement.

b. One significant advantage of ABC is the increased accuracy of cost information that it provides.

c. Traditional costing methods allow managers to better see what causes costs to be incurred than does ABC.

d. One of the biggest disadvantages of implementing an ABC system is the cost.

e. Companies that produce a limited number of products, most of which have similar features, would likely benefit more from implementing an ABC system than would companies that produce a large number of products with many different features.

Required

Indicate whether each of the preceding statements is true or false.

EXERCISES

5. ABC Activities and Cost Drivers LO2

The University of Tennessee has asked for your help with implementing an activity-based costing system for the admissions office. The following activities and cost drivers were identified by the chief admissions officer for the university:

Activity	Cost Driver
a. Receiving applications	1. Number of students
b. Processing applications	2. Number of acceptances
c. Receiving student inquiries	3. Number of applications
d. Responding to student inquiries	4. Labor hours
e. Accepting students	5. Number of inquiries
f. Enrolling students	

Required

Match each of the activities with a potential cost driver. Note that you may not use all drivers and some may be used more than once.

6. ABC Overhead Calculation LO3

Tip Top Company sells umbrellas suited for small and large picnic tables. In accordance with the advice of its accountant, Tip Top is considering whether to adopt an activity-based costing system. To evaluate the possible impact on cost, the company has accumulated the following data from last year:

Activity	Allocation Base	Overhead Cost
Purchasing	Number of purchase orders	$300,000
Receiving	Number of shipments received	150,000
Sales	Number of sales orders	150,000

The numbers of activities relating to small and large umbrellas were as follows:

	Small	Large
Purchase orders	10,000	5,000
Shipments received	12,500	7,500
Sales orders	8,500	6,500

Required

A. Calculate the overhead rates for the following activities: purchasing, receiving, and sales.

B. Calculate the dollar amount of overhead that should be assigned to small and large umbrellas for each of the three activities.

7. ABC Overhead Calculation LO3

The Bouncy Baby Crib Mattress Company sells firm and extra-firm mattresses. The company's president, Anna Greer, has become interested in the possibility of improving company performance by more closely monitoring overhead costs. She has decided to adopt an activity-based costing system for the current year. Last year, the company incurred $2,000,000 in overhead costs related to the following activities:

Activity	Allocation Base	Overhead Cost
Materials processing	Number of parts	$1,400,000
Firmness testing	Number of tests	400,000
Customer calls	Number of customer calls	200,000

During the year, 100,000 parts were handled (75,000 for firm mattresses and 25,000 for extra-firm mattresses), 20,000 firmness tests were conducted (12,500 for firm and 7,500 for extra-firm), and 10,000 customer calls were answered (7,500 for firm and 2,500 for extra-firm).

Required

A. On the basis of an activity-based approach, determine the total amount of overhead that should be assigned to firm and extra-firm mattresses.

B. If a firm mattress requires five parts, two tests, and one customer call, then what amount of overhead should be assigned to that mattress?

8. ABC Overhead Calculation: Traditional vs. ABC LO3

The following overhead cost information is available for the Christopher Corporation for the previous year:

Activity	Allocation Base	Overhead Cost
Purchasing	Number of purchase orders	$400,000
Receiving	Number of shipments received	100,000
Machine setups	Number of setups	400,000
Quality control	Number of inspections	150,000

During the year, 8,000 purchase orders were issued; 25,000 shipments were received; 4,000 machine setups occurred; and 7,500 inspections were conducted. Employees worked a total of 10,000 hours on production. The corporate managers are trying to decide whether they should use a traditional overhead allocation method based on direct labor hours or switch to an activity-based costing system.

Required

A. Determine the overhead rate, using the traditional overhead allocation method based on direct labor hours.

B. Determine the overhead rate for each of the activities, assuming that activity-based costing is used.

9. ABC Overhead Calculation: Traditional vs. ABC LO3

The following overhead cost information is available for the Bright LCD Corporation, a manufacturer of computer monitors:

Activity	Allocation Base	Overhead Cost
Purchasing	Number of purchase orders	$400,000
Receiving	Number of shipments of material	100,000
Machine setups	Number of setups	300,000
Assembly	Direct labor hours	125,000
Quality control	Number of inspections	75,000

During the year, 1,000 purchase orders were issued; 300 shipments of material were received; 600 machine setups occurred; and 750 inspections were conducted. Employees worked a total of 10,000 direct labor hours on assembly of the monitors. The corporate managers are trying to decide whether they should use a traditional overhead allocation method based on direct labor (assembly) hours or switch to an activity-based costing system. Assume that a batch of 200 monitors has resulted in the following cost activity:

Purchase orders	7
Shipments of material received	12
Machine setups	2
Direct labor assembly hours	50
Inspections	3

A. Determine the overhead allocation for the batch of 200 monitors under the traditional overhead allocation based on direct labor hours.

B. Determine the overhead allocation for the batch under activity-based costing.

10. ABC Overhead Calculation: Traditional vs. ABC LO3

The following overhead cost information is available for the Herbert Love Corporation for the previous year:

Activity	Allocation Base	Overhead Cost
Purchasing	Number of purchase orders	$400,000
Receiving	Number of shipments received	100,000
Machine setups	Number of setups	400,000
Quality control	Number of inspections	150,000

During the year, 8,000 purchase orders were issued; 25,000 shipments were received; 4,000 machine setups occurred; and 7,500 inspections were conducted. Employees worked a total of 10,000 hours on production. The corporate managers are trying to decide whether they should use a traditional overhead allocation method based on direct labor hours or switch to an activity-based costing system. Assume that a batch of products has the following specifications:

Direct labor hours	7
Purchase orders	7
Shipments received	10
Machine setups	3
Inspections	3

Required

A. Determine the overhead allocation for the batch under the traditional overhead allocation based on direct labor hours.
B. Determine the overhead allocation for the batch under activity-based costing.

11. ABC Overhead Calculation LO2, 3, 4

Elise Entertainment is a progressive company that is considering the implementation of activity-based costing techniques to better understand and control costs associated with its human resources (HR) department. Currently, the department incurs annual costs of $750,000. Claire Elise, the company's president, believes that there are four primary activities within the department: recruiting new employees, responding to employee questions about benefits, general employee administration, and employee termination/separation. She asked the HR manager to identify possible drivers and costs associated with each of these activities. The manager provided the following data:

Activity	Allocation Base	Overhead Cost
Recruitment	Number of applicants	$250,000
Query response	Number of questions	156,000
Administration	Number of employees	294,000
Separation	Number of terminations/separations	50,000

The HR manager determined that in the most recent year there were 2,000 applications received; 2,400 benefits-related questions from employees; an average monthly employment of 600 individuals; and 100 employees who either were terminated or otherwise left the company.

Required

A. Estimate the overhead cost for each activity.
B. Which activity is the most expensive and which is the least expensive?

12. ABC: Comparison with Traditional Costing LO2, 3, 4

Surfs Up manufactures surfboards. The company produces two models: the small board and the big board. Data regarding the two boards are as follows:

Product	Direct Labor Hours per Unit	Annual Production	Total Direct Labor Hours
Big	1.5	10,000 boards	15,000
Small	1.0	35,000 boards	35,000

The big board requires $75 in direct materials per unit, whereas the small board requires $40. The company pays an average direct labor rate of $13 per hour. The company has historically used direct labor hours as the activity base for applying overhead to the boards. Manufacturing overhead is estimated to be $1,664,000 per year. The big board is more complex to manufacture than the small board because it requires more machine time.

Blake Moore, the company's controller, is considering the use of activity-based costing to apply overhead because the surfboards require such different amounts of machining. Blake has identified the following four separate activity centers:

Activity Center	Cost Driver	Traceable Costs	Volume of Annual Activity	
			Big Board	Small Board
Machine setup	Number of setups	$100,000	100	100
Special design	Design hours	364,000	900	100
Production	Direct labor hours	900,000	15,000	35,000
Machining	Machine hours	300,000	9,000	1,000

Required

A. Calculate the overhead rate on the basis of traditional overhead allocation with direct labor hours as the base.
B. Determine the total cost required to produce one unit of each product. (Use the overhead rate calculated in question A.)
C. Calculate the overhead rate for each activity center on the basis of activity-based costing techniques.
D. Determine the total cost required to produce one unit of each product. Use the overhead rates calculated in question C.
E. Explain why overhead cost shifted from the high-volume product to the low-volume product under activity-based costing.

13. Traditional Costing vs. ABC LO2, 3, 4

Fairchild, Inc., manufactures televisions that are designed for use in sports bars. The company has budgeted manufacturing overhead costs for the year as follows:

Type of Cost	Cost Pools
Electric power	$2,500,000
Inspection	1,500,000

Under a traditional cost system, the company estimated the budgeted capacity for machine hours to be 40,000 hours. The company is considering changing to an activity-based cost system. As part of its consideration of the new costing system, the company developed the following estimates:

Type of Cost	Activity-Based Cost Drivers
Electric power	50,000 kilowatt hours (KWH)
Inspection	10,000 inspections (INSP)

The following information related to the production of 2,000 units of Model #1003 was accumulated:

Direct materials cost	$50,000
Direct labor costs	$75,000
Machine hours	10,000
Direct labor hours	5,000
Electric power—kilowatt hours	20,000
Number of inspections	1,000

On the basis of the data, Fairchild's accounting department provided management with the following report:

Traditional Costing System Estimate:		
Overhead rate per machine hour	$100.00	
Manufacturing costs for 2,000 units:		
Direct materials	$ 50,000	
Direct labor	75,000	
Applied overhead	1,000,000	
Total cost	$1,125,000	
Cost per unit		$562.50
Activity-Based Costing System Estimate:		
Electric power overhead rate (per KWH)	$ 50.00	
Inspection cost overhead rate (per INSP)	$150.00	
Manufacturing costs for 2,000 units:		
Direct materials	$ 50,000	
Direct labor	75,000	
Applied overhead	1,150,000	
Total cost	$1,275,000	
Cost per unit		$637.50

Required

A. Explain the difference between activity-based costing and traditional costing, and describe how ABC might enhance the financial reporting of Fairchild.
B. If Fairchild were setting a sales price based on a 20 percent markup, how would profit be affected if the company did not change to an ABC system?

14. Traditional vs. ABC LO2, 3, 4

The following cost information is available for Senkowski, Ltd.:

Activity	Allocation Base	Volume of Activity	Overhead Cost
Purchasing	Purchase orders	30,000	$150,000
Receiving	Shipments received	15,000	60,000
Machine setups	Setups	2,500	200,000
Quality control	Inspections	18,000	90,000

Direct materials are $15 per unit for luxury handbags and $11 per unit for deluxe handbags. There were 12,500 direct labor hours, each of which was charged to inventory at $18 per hour.

Required

A. Management is trying to decide between using the traditional allocation method based on direct labor hours and using activity-based costing. Calculate the overhead rates for each method.
B. One particular batch of 40 luxury handbags had the following specifications:

Direct labor hours	8
Purchase orders	4
Shipments received	3
Setups	2
Inspections	12

Calculate the overhead to be allocated to the bags under the traditional and activity-based costing techniques.
C. Which costing method do you think is better for the company? Why?

15. Traditional vs. ABC: Advantages of ABC LO2, 3, 4

David Mayes, Inc., manufactures plastic and ceramic outdoor dinnerware. The company's western plant has changed from a manual-labor operation to a robotics-intensive environment. As a result, management is considering moving from a direct-labor-based overhead rate to an activity-based costing system. The controller has chosen the following activity cost pools and cost drivers for factory overhead:

Overhead	Cost Information	Cost Driver	Driver Activity
Purchase orders	$200,000	Number of orders	25,000
Setup costs	300,000	Number of setups	15,000
Testing costs	420,000	Number of tests	16,000
Machine maintenance	800,000	Machine hours	50,000

Required

A. Calculate the overhead rate for each cost driver.
B. An order for 50 ceramic dish sets had the following requirements:

Number of purchase orders	3
Number of setups	20
Number of product tests	7
Machine hours	150

How much overhead should be assigned to this order?
C. Would you expect the new activity-based system to allocate a different amount of overhead?
D. Discuss why using an activity-based system could provide better information to decision makers regarding the setting of sales prices. What other advantages might David Mayes, Inc., realize from the new costing system?

16. Decision Focus: Traditional vs. ABC LO2, 3, 4

Gramercy, Inc., manufactures sailboats and has two major categories of overhead: materials handling and quality inspection. The costs expected for these categories for the coming year are as follows:

Materials handling (based on 500 material moves)	$100,000
Quality inspection (based on 200 inspections)	$300,000

The plant currently applies overhead based on direct labor hours. The estimated amount of direct labor hours is 50,000. Polly Richardson, the plant manager, has been asked to submit a bid and has assembled the following data on the proposed job:

Direct materials	$3,700
Direct labor (1,000 hours)	$17,000
Overhead	?
Number of material moves	10
Number of inspections	5

Polly has been told that many similar companies use an activity-based approach to assign overhead to jobs. Before submitting a bid, Polly wants to assess the effects of this alternative approach.

Required

A. Use the traditional overhead application to calculate the total cost of the potential job.
B. Use activity-based costing with the new cost drivers to calculate the total cost of the job.
C. Discuss the difference in the costs calculated under the two overhead allocation methods and what impact the change to activity-based costing might have on the pricing decision.

17. Decision Focus: ABC LO2, 3, 4

The HITEC Company manufactures multimedia equipment designed to be sold to universities. The company's southeastern plant has undergone production changes that have resulted in decreased usage of direct labor and increased usage of automated processes. As a result, management no longer believes that its overhead allocation method is accurate and is considering changing from a traditional overhead allocation to an activity-based method. The controller has chosen the following activity centers and cost drivers for overhead:

Overhead	Cost Information	Cost Driver	Driver Activity
Purchase orders	$200,000	Number of orders	25,000
Setup costs	300,000	Number of setups	15,000
Testing costs	420,000	Number of tests	16,000
Machine maintenance	800,000	Machine hours	50,000

Required

A. Calculate the overhead rate for each cost driver.
B. An order for 1,000 video projectors had the following requirements:

Number of purchase orders	3
Number of setups	5
Number of product tests	20
Machine hours	1,500

How much total overhead should be assigned to this order?
C. What could management do to reduce the overhead costs assigned to these video projectors? What would be the impact on company net income of reducing overhead assigned to the video projectors?

18. The Impact of ABC and JIT LO2, 4

Pritchett Enterprises manufactures hiking and outdoor equipment. The company's plant in western Colorado has recently seen dramatic changes in manufacturing processes. Management is concerned that the current cost system no longer captures the impact of the diversity of activities involved in its production processes. As a result, management is evaluating whether activity-based costing may provide more accurate and meaningful cost data. The production environment includes the following primary activities and cost drivers:

Overhead	Cost Information	Cost Driver	Driver Activity
Purchase orders	$200,000	Number of orders	10,000
Receiving orders	25,000	Number of orders	10,000
Setup costs	25,000	Number of setups	5,000
Testing costs	48,000	Number of tests	6,000
Machine maintenance	350,000	Machine hours	10,000

The company has decided to implement just-in-time inventory management techniques. Using JIT will reduce the amount of inventory on hand at any point in time and save approximately $50,000 annually on inventory carrying costs. In addition, there will be 70 percent fewer purchase orders for inventory issued, but twice as many setups for production runs. The company will also be able to receive a 2 percent discount on raw materials purchases because of the long-term nature of the orders.

Required

A. If raw materials purchases are $1,000,000 per year (that is, the cost before the aforementioned changes are implemented), what quantitative impact will the change to JIT have on the overall costs for the company?

B. What qualitative factors will be affected by the change to JIT?

C. Does it appear that the move to JIT will be positive or negative for the company? Why or why not?

19. ABC LO3

The following cost information is available for the Stuart and Hahn Corporation:

Direct material	$14 per unit for deluxe pillows
	$10 per unit for regular pillows
Direct labor	$20 per hour (including benefits)

Activity	Allocation Base	Overhead Cost
Purchasing	Number of purchase orders	$150,000
Receiving	Number of shipments received	50,000
Machine setups	Number of setups	250,000
Quality control	Number of inspections	125,000

During the year, 30,000 purchase orders were issued; 20,000 shipments were received; machine set-ups numbered 2,500; and 25,000 inspections were conducted.

A customer has contacted the company requesting comparative bids for an order of 100 deluxe pillows and 100 regular pillows. The company adds a 20 percent markup on deluxe pillows and 15 percent on regular pillows for its profits. The company's records indicate that the following activities would be required to complete an order of 100 deluxe and regular pillows:

	Regular	Deluxe
Direct labor hours	7	10
Purchase orders	7	7
Shipments received	10	10
Setups	3	4
Inspections	3	4

Required

Compute the bids for deluxe and regular pillows on a total-order basis.

20. Traditional vs. ABC LO3, 4

Grandma's Rocking Chair Company produces 1,000 units each of the Kennedy Rocker and the Bentwood Rocker. Currently, the company uses a traditional cost system, but is considering an activity-based cost system. The company is committed to producing only the highest-quality chairs. Consequently, the management group wants to know what the cost of inspection would be for both products, given the following data:

Number of inspections per unit:	
Kennedy	3
Bentwood	1
Inspection cost (in total)	$50,000
Direct labor hours:	
Kennedy	3,000
Bentwood	2,000

Required

A. Under traditional costing, how much of the inspection cost would be allocated to Kennedy Rockers and Bentwood Rockers, respectively?

B. Using activity-based costing, how much of the inspection cost would be allocated to Kennedy Rockers and Bentwood Rockers, respectively?

C. Discuss what caused the difference. Would this difference affect management decisions? How? Which method is more accurate? Why?

CASES

21. Traditional versus ABC LO1, 2, 3, 4

Duffy and Rowe is a full-service legal firm. During the year, corporate clients required 5,000 hours of legal services whereas individuals required 3,000 hours. In the past, the firm has assigned overhead to client engagements on the basis of direct labor hours. However, Duffy suspects that legal services to corporate clients drive firm overhead more than legal services to individuals and believes that adopting activity-based costing will allow a more accurate allocation of costs to various clients. The firm's revenues and costs for the year are as follows:

	Corporate	Individual	Total
Revenue	$150,000	$150,000	$300,000
Expenses			
Lawyers' salaries	100,000	50,000	150,000
Overhead			
Filing			$ 10,000
Quality control			5,000
Data entry			25,000
Total overhead			$ 40,000

Duffy and Rowe has kept records of the following data for use in the new activity-based costing system:

Overhead Cost	Cost Driver	Activity Level	
		Corporate	Individual
Filing	Number of clients	5	5
Quality control	Number of hours spent	75	25
Data entry	Number of pages entered	1,000	1,500

The accounting manager has prepared the following pro forma income statements:

Income Statement Using Traditional Costing			
	Corporate	Individual	Total
Revenue	$150,000	$150,000	$300,000
Expenses			
Salaries	100,000	50,000	150,000
Overhead	25,000	15,000	40,000
Total expenses	$125,000	$ 65,000	$190,000
Operating profit	$ 25,000	$ 85,000	$110,000

Income Statement Using Activity-Based Costing			
	Corporate	Individual	Total
Revenue	$150,000	$150,000	$300,000
Expenses			
Salaries	100,000	50,000	150,000
Overhead			
Filing			
($1,000 × 5)	5,000	5,000	10,000
Quality costs			
($50 × 75)	3,750		3,750
($50 × 25)		1,250	1,250
Data entry			
($10 × 1,000)	10,000		10,000
($10 × 1,500)		15,000	15,000
Total overhead	$ 18,750	$ 21,250	$ 40,000
Total expenses	$118,750	$ 71,250	$190,000
Operating profit	$ 31,250	$ 78,750	$110,000

Required

Calculate the overhead rate for individual and corporate clients for the traditional income statement. Compare those rates with the rates for the activity-based costing income statement. Discuss the best way to allocate costs in this example, and include the approximate difference in profits between corporate and individual clients. Why would activity-based costing be preferred as a cost allocation method?

22. Decision Focus: ABC LOI, 2, 3, 4

Worth Hawes Manufacturing has just completed a major change in its quality control (QC) process. Previously, QC inspectors had reviewed products at the end of each major process and the company's 10 QC inspectors were charged as direct labor to the operation or job. In an effort to improve efficiency and quality, Worth Hawes purchased a computer video QC system for $250,000. The system consists of a minicomputer, 15 video cameras, other peripheral hardware, and software.

The new system uses cameras stationed by QC engineers at key points in the production process. Each time an operation changes or a new operation begins, the cameras are moved and a QC engineer loads a new master picture into the computer. The camera takes pictures of the unit in process, and the computer compares them with the picture of a "good" unit. Any differences are sent to a QC engineer, who removes the bad units and immediately discusses the flaws with the production supervisors. The new system has replaced the 10 QC inspectors with two QC engineers.

The operating costs of the new QC system, including the salaries of the QC engineers, have been included as overhead in calculating the company's plantwide factory overhead rate, which is based on direct labor dollars.

In short, the company's president is confused. The vice president of production has been commenting on how efficient the new system is, yet the president has observed that there has been a significant increase in the factory overhead rate. The computation of the rate before and after implementation of the new QC system is as follows:

	Before	After
Budgeted overhead	$1,900,000	$2,100,000
Budgeted direct labor	$1,000,000	$ 700,000
Budgeted overhead rate	190%	300%

"Three hundred percent," lamented the president. "How can we compete with such a high factory overhead rate?"

Required

A. Discuss the development of factory overhead rates. Why do we need factory overhead rates, and how are they computed? Discuss the accuracy of the computation of a factory overhead rate.

B. Explain why the increase in the overhead rate should not have a negative impact on Worth Hawes Manufacturing.

C. Explain, in the greatest detail possible, how the company could change its overhead accounting system to eliminate confusion over product costs.

D. Discuss how an activity-based costing system might benefit Worth Hawes Manufacturing.

Cost Behavior

Introduction

I n Chapter 5, we focus our attention on the behavior of costs. As production volume changes, some costs may increase or decrease and other costs may remain stable, but specific costs behave in predictable ways as volume changes. This concept of predictable **cost behavior** based on volume is very important to the effective use of accounting information for managerial decision making.

LO1 **Fixed and Variable Costs**

Fixed costs are costs that remain the same in total, but vary per unit, when production volume changes. Facility-level costs, such as rent, depreciation of a factory building, the salary of a plant manager, insurance, and property taxes, are likely to be fixed costs. Summarizing this cost behavior, fixed costs stay the same in total but vary when expressed on a per-unit basis.

Learning Objectives

After studying the material in this chapter, you should be able to:

LO1 Describe the nature and behavior of fixed and variable costs.

LO2 Use regression analysis and the high/low method to define and analyze mixed costs.

LO3 Illustrate the impact of income taxes on costs and decision making.

LO4 Identify the difference between variable costing and absorption costing.

LO5 Identify the impact on the income statement of variable costing and absorption costing.

LO6 Recognize the benefits of using variable costing for decision making.

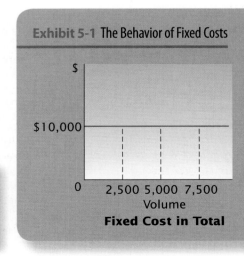

Exhibit 5-1 The Behavior of Fixed Costs

Fixed Cost in Total

Fixed Cost per Unit

© Cengage Learning 2013

Cost behavior How costs react to changes in production volume or other levels of activity.

Fixed costs Costs that remain the same in total when production volume increases or decreases but that vary per unit.

Understanding how costs behave with changes in production is crucial for managers of an organization.

© Henner Frankenfeld/Bloomberg via Getty Images

Rent is a good example. If the cost to rent a factory building is $10,000 per year and 5,000 units of product are produced, the rent per unit is $2.00 ($10,000 ÷ 5,000). If production volume decreases to 2,500 units per year, the cost per unit will increase to $4.00 ($10,000 ÷ 2,500). If production volume increases to 7,500 units, the cost per unit decreases to $1.33 ($10,000 ÷ 7,500). However, the total rent remains $10,000 per year (see Exhibit 5-1).

On the other hand, **variable costs** vary in direct proportion to changes in production volume but are constant when expressed as per-unit amounts. As production increases, variable costs increase in direct proportion to the change in volume; as production decreases, variable costs decrease in direct proportion to the change in volume. Examples include direct material, direct labor (if paid per unit of output), and other unit-level costs, such as factory supplies, energy costs to run factory machinery, and so on.

> **Variable costs** Costs that stay the same per unit, but change in total, as production volume increases or decreases.

Consider the behavior of direct material costs as production increases and decreases. If the production of a standard classroom desk requires $20 of direct materials (wood, hardware, and so on), the total direct material costs incurred will increase or decrease proportionately with increases and decreases in production volume. If 5,000 desks are produced, the total direct material cost will be $100,000 (5,000 × $20). If production volume is increased to 7,500 units (a 50 percent increase), direct material costs will also increase 50 percent, to $150,000 (7,500 × $20). However, the cost per unit is still $20. Likewise, if production volume is decreased to 2,500 desks, direct material costs will decrease by 50 percent, to $50,000. But once again, the cost per unit remains $20 (see Exhibit 5-2).

> *Within the relevant range, fixed costs are constant in total and vary per unit, and variable costs vary in total and are constant per unit.*

Exhibit 5-2 The Behavior of Variable Costs

Variable Cost in Total

Variable Cost per Unit

© Cengage Learning 2013

A current trend in manufacturing is to automate—to replace direct factory labor with robotics and other automated machinery and equipment. This trend has the effect of increasing fixed costs (depreciation) and decreasing variable costs (direct labor). Although there are many advantages to automation, the impact of automation on the employee work force and on day-to-day decisions made by managers must not be ignored.

Strictly speaking, a cost that varies in direct proportion to changes in volume requires a linear (straight-line) relationship between the cost and volume. However, in reality, costs may behave in a curvilinear fashion. Average costs or cost per unit may increase or decrease

as production increases. For example, utility costs per kilowatt-hour may decrease at higher levels of electricity use (and production). Managerial accountants typically get around this problem by assuming that the relationship between cost and volume is linear within the relevant range of production. In other words, the cost per unit is assumed to remain constant over the relevant range. The **relevant range** is the normal range of production that can be expected for a particular product and company. The relevant range can also be viewed as the volume of production for which the fixed and variable cost relationships hold true. As you can see in Exhibit 5-3, within this narrower range of production, a curvilinear cost can be approximated by a linear relationship between the cost and volume.

Relevant range The normal range of production that can be expected for a particular product and company.

Exhibit 5-3 Curvilinear Costs and the Relevant Range

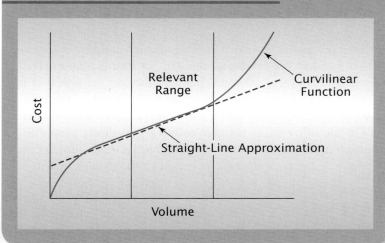

© Cengage Learning 2013

Direct Labor as a Fixed Cost

For years, U.S. car manufacturers have had contracts with their workers' unions that require the companies to pay their assembly-line workers even when they are not on the assembly line. These contracts essentially transform direct labor costs into fixed costs. More recently, as the recession has resulted in idle assembly lines, Toyota has done likewise. However, unlike the U.S. companies, which often send their workers home, at Toyota the workers might attend training classes, repair and maintain equipment, or brainstorm in an effort to identify new cost-savings or quality-improvement initiatives.

© Jessica Rinaldi/Reuters/Landov

Source: "Toyota Keeps Idled Workers Busy Honing Their Skills," by Kate Linebaugh, *The Wall Street Journal*, October 13, 2008.

Step Costs

The classification of costs is not always a simple process. Some costs vary but only with relatively large changes in production volume. Batch-level costs related to moving materials may vary with the number of batches of product produced but not with every unit of product. Product-level costs associated with quality control inspections may vary when new products are introduced. Costs like these are sometimes referred to as **step costs**. In practice, step costs may look like and be treated as either variable costs or fixed costs. Although step costs are technically not fixed costs, they may be treated as such if they remain constant within a relatively wide range of production. Consider the costs of janitorial services within a company. As long as production is below 7,500 desks, the company will hire one janitor with salary and fringe benefits totaling $25,000. The cost is fixed as long as production remains below 7,500 units. But if desk production exceeds 7,500, increasing the amount of waste and cleanup needed, it may be necessary to hire a second janitor at a cost of another $25,000. However, within a relevant range of production between 7,501 and 15,000 units, the cost is essentially fixed ($50,000).

Relevant Costs and Cost Behavior

As mentioned in Chapter 1, relevant costs are those which are avoidable or can be eliminated by choosing one alternative over another. Relevant costs are also known as differential, or incremental, costs. In general, variable costs are relevant in production decisions because they vary with the level of production. Likewise, fixed costs are generally not relevant, because they typically do not change as production changes. However, variable costs can remain the same between two alternatives, and fixed costs can vary between alternatives. For example, if the direct material cost of a product is the same for two competing designs, the material cost is not a relevant factor in choosing a design. However, other qualitative factors relating to the material, such as durability, may still be relevant. Likewise, fixed costs can be relevant if they vary between alternatives. Consider rent paid for a facility to store inventory. Although the rent is a fixed cost, it is relevant to a decision to reduce inventory storage costs through just-in-time production techniques if the cost of the rent can be avoided (by subleasing the space, for example) by choosing one alternative over another.

The Cost Equation

Expressing the link between costs and production volume as an algebraic equation is useful. The equation for a straight line is

$$y = a + bx$$

Step costs Costs that vary with activity in steps and may look like and be treated as either variable costs or fixed costs; step costs are technically not fixed costs but may be treated as such if they remain constant within a relevant range of production.

The *a* in the equation is the point where the line intersects the vertical (*y*) axis (the *y*-intercept), and *b* is the slope of the line. In Exhibit 5-4, if *y* = total direct material costs and *x* = units produced, then *y* = $0 + $20*x*. The *y*-intercept is zero and the slope of the line is 20. For

It can be misleading to always view variable costs as relevant and fixed costs as irrelevant.

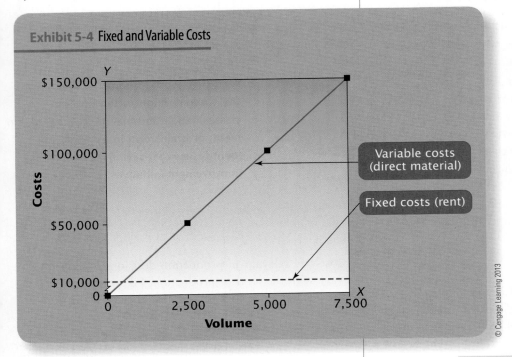

Exhibit 5-4 Fixed and Variable Costs

Variable costs (direct material)

Fixed costs (rent)

© Cengage Learning 2013

every one-unit increase (decrease) in production (*x*), direct material costs increase (decrease) by $20. You can see that direct material costs are variable because they stay the same on a per-unit basis but increase in total as production increases. Likewise, we can express the fixed-cost line as an equation. If *y* = cost of rent and *x* = units produced, then *y* = $10,000 + $0*x*. In this case, the *y*-intercept is $10,000 and the slope is zero. In other words, fixed costs are $10,000 at any level of production within the relevant range.

LO2 Mixed Costs

The presence of **mixed costs** presents a unique challenge because they include both a fixed and a variable component. Consequently, it is difficult to predict

> **Mixed costs** Costs that include both a fixed and a variable component, making it difficult to predict the behavior of a mixed cost as production changes, unless the cost is first separated into its fixed and variable components.

the behavior of a mixed cost as production changes, unless the cost is first separated into its fixed and variable components. A good example of a mixed cost is the overhead costs of KenCor Pizza Emporium. Overhead typically has both a fixed and a variable component. For example, rent and insurance paid by KenCor would be fixed components of overhead, whereas utilities and supplies would likely be variable costs.

In the first seven weeks of operations, KenCor incurred the following overhead costs:

Week	Pizzas	Total Overhead Costs	Cost per Unit
1 (Start-up)	0	$ 679	N/A
2	423	1,842	$4.35
3	601	2,350	3.91
4	347	1,546	4.46
5	559	2,250	4.03
6	398	1,769	4.44
7	251	1,288	5.13

Is the overhead cost a fixed, variable, or mixed cost? Clearly, the cost is not fixed, because it changes each week. However, is it a variable cost? Although the cost changes each week, it does not vary in direct proportion to changes in production. In addition, remember that variable costs remain constant when expressed per unit. In this case, the amount of overhead cost per pizza changes from week to week. A cost that changes in total and also changes per unit is a mixed cost. As you can see in Exhibit 5-5, a mixed cost looks somewhat like a variable cost. However, the cost does not vary in direct proportion to changes in the level of production (you can't draw a straight line through all the data points), and if

Exhibit 5-5 Mixed Costs

Graph showing Overhead Costs ($) on the y-axis ranging from $0 to $2,500, and Pizzas on the x-axis ranging from 0 to 700, with data points for Overhead plotted along an upward trend line.

© Cengage Learning 2013

a line were drawn through the data points back to the y-axis, we would still incur overhead cost at a production volume of zero. Like a fixed cost, a mixed cost has a component that is constant regardless of production volume.

Once we know that a cost is mixed, we are left with the task of separating the mixed cost into its fixed and variable components. However, it is not clear how much of the overhead cost is fixed and how much is variable. In the next section, we will demonstrate the use of a statistical tool called regression analysis to estimate the fixed and variable components of a mixed cost.

A variety of tools can be used to estimate the fixed and variable components of a mixed cost. When we separate a mixed cost into its variable and fixed components, what we are really doing is generating the equation for a straight line, with the y-intercept estimating the fixed cost and the slope estimating the variable cost per unit.

Continuing our example of KenCor Pizza Emporium, we see that after the initial seven-week start-up period, the company's accountant compiles data regarding the total overhead cost

and the number of pizzas produced in the next 12 months (see Exhibit 5-6). As you can see, because the overhead cost varies in total and on a per-unit basis, it must be a mixed cost. A graph of the data is shown in Exhibit 5-7.

Exhibit 5-6 Overhead Costs per Pizza

Month	Pizzas	Overhead	Per Pizza
1	2,100	$ 8,400	$4.00
2	2,600	10,100	3.88
3	2,300	8,800	3.83
4	2,450	9,250	3.78
5	2,100	8,050	3.83
6	2,175	8,200	3.77
7	1,450	6,950	4.79
8	1,200	6,750	5.63
9	1,350	7,250	5.37
10	1,750	7,300	4.17
11	1,550	7,250	4.68
12	2,050	7,950	3.88

© Cengage Learning 2013

Regression Analysis

A statistical technique used to estimate the fixed and variable components of a mixed cost is called least squares regression. **Regression analysis** uses statistical

> **Regression analysis** The procedure that uses statistical methods (least squares regression) to fit a cost line (called a regression line) through a number of data points.

© iStockphoto.com/Todd Smith

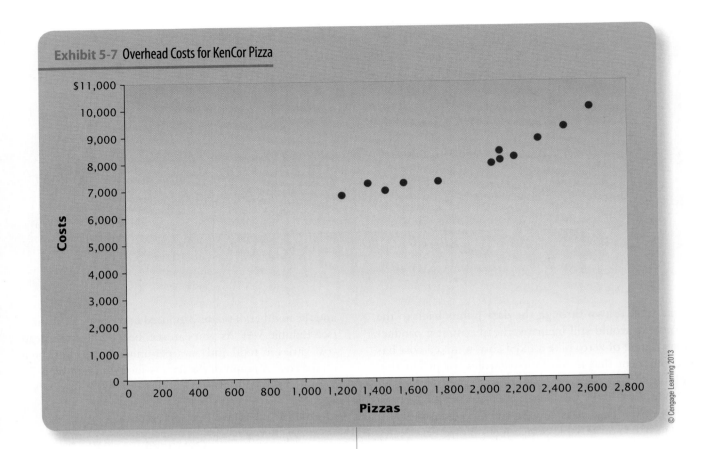

Exhibit 5-7 Overhead Costs for KenCor Pizza

© Cengage Learning 2013

methods to fit a cost line (called a regression line) through a number of data points. Note that although the data points in our example do not lie along a straight line, regression analysis statistically finds the line that minimizes the sum of the squared distances from each data point to the line (hence the name *least squares regression*).

Using a Spreadsheet Program to Perform Regression Analysis Using a spreadsheet program to produce regression results is a relatively simple process. We are going to use Microsoft Excel in this example, but all spreadsheet programs are similar. The first step is to enter the actual values for our mixed cost (called the **dependent variable** in regression analysis because the amount of cost is dependent on production) and the related volume of production (called the **independent variable** because it drives the cost of the dependent

Dependent variable The variable in regression analysis that is dependent on changes in the independent variable.

Independent variable The variable in regression analysis that drives changes in the dependent variable.

variable) into a spreadsheet, using one column for each variable. Employing data from KenCor Pizza Emporium for overhead costs incurred and pizzas produced for the first 12 months of operations, we see the data shown in the Excel spreadsheet in Exhibit 5-8.

The next step in Excel (see Exhibit 5-9) is to click on the Data tab and choose *data analysis* from the Analysis ribbon. From the data analysis screen, scroll down, highlight *regression*, and either double-click or choose OK.

The regression screen will prompt you to choose a number of options. The first step is to input the *y* range. The *y* range will be used to identify the dependent variable (overhead costs), found in column C of your spreadsheet. You can either type in the range of cells or simply highlight the cells in the spreadsheet (be sure not to include the column heading), and click on the icon in the *y*-range box. The next step is to select the *x* range for the independent variable (volume of pizzas). Once again, you can enter the cells directly or highlight the cells in the second column of your spreadsheet.

After inputting the appropriate *y* and *x* ranges, your Excel spreadsheet should look like the example shown in Exhibit 5-10. Click OK, and the regression model summary output appears as shown in Exhibit 5-11.

Exhibit 5-8 Regression Analysis—Step 1

	A	B	C
1	Month	Pizzas	Overhead
2	1	2,100	$8,400.00
3	2	2,600	$10,100.00
4	3	2,300	$8,800.00
5	4	2,450	$9,250.00
6	5	2,100	$8,050.00
7	6	2,175	$8,200.00
8	7	1,450	$6,950.00
9	8	1,200	$6,750.00
10	9	1,350	$7,250.00
11	10	1,750	$7,300.00
12	11	1,550	$7,250.00
13	12	2,050	$7,950.00
14			
15			

Exhibit 5-9 Regression Analysis—Step 2

Exhibit 5-10 Regression Analysis—Step 2 (continued)

Exhibit 5-11 Regression Analysis—Summary Output

How is the summary output interpreted? First, note toward the bottom of Exhibit 5-11 that the estimated coefficient (value) of the intercept (the y-intercept) is 3,998.25 and the estimated coefficient (value) of the x variable (the slope) is 2.09. This means that the fixed-cost component of our mixed overhead cost is estimated to be $3,998.25 and the variable-cost component is estimated to be $2.09 per pizza.

Using the least squares regression results, we can compute the regression line for overhead costs at KenCor Pizza Emporium:

Total overhead cost = Fixed cost + (Variable cost/unit × Volume)
Total overhead cost = $3,998.25 + ($2.09 × Volume)

Graphically, the line for the total overhead costs can be expressed as shown in the following illustration:

We can use the preceding equation to help predict the total amount of overhead costs that will be incurred for any number of pizzas within the relevant range. The relevant range is that range of activity within which management expects to operate, or the range in which the equation in question is useful or meaningful. Our predictions should be limited to those activity levels within the relevant range. On the basis of last year's data, KenCor expects to produce between 1,200 and 2,600 pizzas each month. Next month, KenCor expects to produce 1,750 pizzas. Using the regression equation, KenCor estimates total overhead costs to be $7,655.75 ($3,998.25 + [$2.09 × 1,750 pizzas]).

Regression Statistics The regression statistics section at the top of Exhibit 5-11 provides useful diagnostic tools. The multiple R (called the *correlation coefficient*) is a measure of the proximity of the data points to the regression line. In addition, the sign of the statistic

(+ or −) tells us the direction of the correlation between the independent and dependent variables. In this case, there is a positive correlation between the number of pizzas produced and the total overhead costs. *R square* (often represented as R^2 and called the *coefficient of determination*) is a measure of goodness of fit (how well the regression line "fits" the data). An R^2 of 1.0 indicates a perfect correlation between the independent and dependent variables in the regression equation; in other words, 100 percent of the data points are on the regression line. R^2 can be interpreted as the proportion of dependent-variable variation that is explained by changes in the independent variable. In this case, the R^2 of 0.8933 indicates that over 89 percent of the variation in overhead costs is explained by increasing or decreasing pizza production.

A low value of R^2 may indicate that the chosen independent variable is not a very reliable predictor of the dependent variable or that other independent variables may have an impact on the dependent variable. For example, the outside temperature and other environmental factors might affect overhead costs incurred by KenCor.

The presence of outliers in the data may also result in low R^2 values. Outliers are simply extreme observations—that is, observations so far from the normal activity that they may not be representative of normal business levels (they are outside of the relevant range). Under the least squares method, a regression line may be pulled disproportionately toward the outlier and result in misleading estimates of fixed and variable costs and measures of goodness of fit.

Estimating Regression Results with the High/Low Method

If we did not have access to a computer regression program or for some reason did not want to use this tool, we could estimate the regression equation by using a simpler technique called the high/low method. The

R square (R²) A measure of goodness of fit (how well the regression line "fits" the data).

high/low method uses only two data points (related to the high and low levels of activity) and mathematically derives an equation for a straight line intersecting those two data points. Though technically inferior to regression analysis (which uses all the data points), from a practical perspective the high/low method can often provide a reasonable estimate of the regression equation.

In Exhibit 5-6, the high level of activity occurred in month 2, when 2,600 pizzas were produced and $10,100 of overhead cost was incurred. The low level of activity occurred in month 8, when only 1,200 pizzas were produced and overhead costs totaled $6,750. The slope of the line connecting those two points can be calculated by dividing the difference between the costs incurred at the high and low levels of activity by the difference in volume (number of pizzas) at those levels. Remember, the slope of a line is calculated as the change in cost over the change in volume, in this case the difference in cost to produce pizzas over the difference in volume of pizzas made. As with the regression equation, the slope of the line is interpreted as the variable-cost component of the mixed cost:

$$\frac{\text{Change in cost}}{\text{Change in volume}} = \text{Variable cost per unit}$$

Inserting the data for KenCor Pizza Emporium, we find that the variable cost is $2.39 per unit ($10,100 − $6,750) ÷ (2,600 − 1,200). This result compares with our regression estimate of $2.09. We then solve for the fixed-cost component by calculating the total variable cost incurred at either the high or the low level of activity and subtracting the variable costs from the total overhead cost incurred at that level. Mathematically, if

$$\text{Total overhead costs} = \text{Fixed costs} + \\ (\text{Variable cost per unit} \times \text{number of pizzas})$$

then

$$\text{Total overhead costs} - \text{Variable costs} = \text{Fixed costs}$$

At the high level of activity, total overhead costs are $10,100 and variable costs equal $6,214 (2,600 pizzas × $2.39 per pizza). Therefore, the fixed-cost component of overhead costs is estimated to be $3,886 (total overhead costs of $10,100, less variable costs of $6,214), and the total overhead cost is estimated to be $3,886 + ($2.39 × number of pizzas produced).

Why is this equation different from the least squares regression equation? Regression is a statistical tool that fits the "best" line through all 12 data points, whereas the high/low method mathematically derives a straight line between just two of the data points. By using the two points at the highest and lowest levels of activity, we are forcing a line between those points without regard to the remaining data points. If one or both of the points we selected is unusual (an outlier), the result will be a cost line that is skewed and therefore may not be a good measure of the fixed and variable components of the mixed cost.

In the case of KenCor Pizza Emporium, let's see how the high/low estimate would affect our prediction of total overhead costs next month, when 1,750 pizzas will be produced. Using the high/low estimate of the cost equation, we would predict total overhead costs of $8,068.50 ($3,886 + [$2.39 × 1,750 pizzas]). This result compares with our estimate of $7,655.75 using the cost equation generated from the regression analysis.

Given the simplicity of generating regression equations with spreadsheet packages and handheld calculators, the need for using the high/low method for computing cost equations in practice is questionable. However, it remains an easy-to-use tool for estimating cost behavior.

LO3 The Impact of Income Taxes on Costs and Decision Making

We always need to consider tax laws and the impact income and other taxes have on costs, revenues, and decision making. Just as an individual should consider the impact of income taxes on a decision whether to hold or sell a stock, managers must consider the impact of taxes for a variety of decisions. The first key to understanding the impact of taxes on costs and revenues is the recognition that many costs of operating businesses are deductible for income tax purposes and that most business revenues are taxable.

After-Tax Costs and Revenues

Consider an example in which your current taxable cash revenue is $100 and tax-deductible cash expenses equal $60. As shown in Exhibit 5-12, taxable income therefore equals $40. If the income tax rate is 40 percent, $16 of income taxes will be paid, leaving you with

© Yuri Arcurs/ShutterStock.com

Managers must consider the impact of taxes when making decisions.

the "real" cost of a tax-deductible expense to the business and to increase cash flow.

Income taxes also have an impact on cash revenues received by a business. Continuing our original example in Exhibit 5-12, if taxable cash revenue increases by $20, taxable income will increase to $60 ($120 − $60). After payment of $24 of income taxes, you will be left with $36 of cash. An increase in revenue of $20 increases your cash flow by only $12 ($36 − $24). Why? Because the $20 is taxable and results in the payment of an additional $8 of income tax ($20 × 0.40). Mathematically, the formula to find the after-tax benefit associated with a taxable cash revenue is analogous to the formula for after-tax cost. The after-tax benefit of a taxable cash receipt can be found by subtracting the additional income tax to be paid from the before-tax receipt or by simply multiplying the pretax receipt by (1 − tax rate):

Exhibit 5-12 The Impact of Income Taxes on Cash Flow

	Current	Increase Spending by $20	Increase Revenue by $20
Revenue	$100	$100	$120
Expense	− 60	− 80	− 60
Taxable income	$ 40	$ 20	$ 60
Tax (rate = 40%)	− 16	− 8	− 24
After-tax cash flow	$ 24	$ 12	$ 36

© Cengage Learning 2013

$24 cash after tax. Now consider the impact of spending an additional $20 on tax-deductible expenditures. This reduces your taxable income to $20. With a 40 percent income tax rate, $8 of income taxes will be paid instead of $16 (you saved $8 of income tax) and you will be left with $12 after tax. Even though you spent an additional $20, your cash flow decreased by only $12 ($24 less $12). Mathematically, the after-tax cost of a tax-deductible cash expenditure can be found by subtracting the income tax savings from the before-tax cost or by simply multiplying the before-tax amount by (1 − tax rate):

> After-tax cost = Pretax cost × (1 − tax rate)

So, if the before-tax cost is $20 and the income tax rate is 40 percent, the after-tax cost is $12 ($12 = $20 × [1 − 0.40]). In this case, the impact of income taxes is to reduce

> After-tax benefit = Pretax receipts × (1 − tax rate)

So, if the before-tax receipt is $20 and the tax rate is 40 percent, the after-tax benefit is $12 ($12 = $20 × [1 − 0.40]). In this case, the impact of income taxes is to decrease cash flow to the business.

Before- and After-Tax Income

In a similar fashion, managers can calculate the impact of income taxes on income. If we have an income tax rate of 40 percent and operating income of $1,000,000, we will have a tax liability of $400,000 (40 percent of the $1,000,000) and be left with $600,000 of after-tax income. This is exactly the same thing that happens

Chapter 5: Cost Behavior 103

to our paychecks as individuals. If an individual earns $1,000 per week and faces a 30 percent income tax rate, the individual's take-home pay (after considering income tax withholding) is only $700. Mathematically,

$$\text{After-tax income} = \text{Pretax income} \times (1 - \text{tax rate})$$

Although tax laws are highly complex and computing tax due is rarely as simple as applying one rate to income, estimating the impact of income tax and other taxes on cash receipts and disbursements is important in managerial decision making.

LO4 A Comparison of Absorption Costing and Variable Costing

Earlier in this chapter, we introduced the concept of cost behavior—that is, how costs behave in relation to production volume—and described the behavior of fixed and variable costs.

Absorption Costing

In Chapter 2, a system of product costing was introduced in which all manufacturing costs, fixed and variable, were treated as product costs. Product costs include the costs of direct materials, direct labor, and all manufacturing overhead (both fixed and variable). You will recall that product costs attach to the product and are expensed only when the product is sold. Commonly called **absorption costing**, or **full costing**, this method is required both for external financial statements prepared under generally accepted accounting principles (GAAP)

and for income tax reporting. Selling, general, and administrative costs, also called period costs, are expensed immediately in the period in which they are incurred.

In contrast, **variable costing**, or **direct costing**, treats only variable product costs (the costs of direct materials, direct labor, and variable manufacturing overhead) as product costs and treats fixed manufacturing overhead as a period cost (along with selling, general, and administrative costs). Variable costing is more consistent with the focus of cost–volume–profit analysis (discussed in Chapter 6) on differentiating fixed from variable costs, and it provides useful information for internal decision making that is often not apparent when using absorption costing.

Variable Costing

Exhibit 5-13 provides a summary of the two costing methods. As you can see, *the only difference between absorption and variable costing is the treatment of fixed overhead*. Under absorption costing, fixed overhead is treated as a product cost, added to the cost of the product and expensed only when the product is sold. Under variable costing, fixed overhead is treated as a period cost and is expensed when incurred. The impact of this difference on reported income becomes evident when a company's production and sales are different (that is, when the number of units produced is greater than or less than the number of units sold).

Because absorption costing treats fixed overhead as a product cost, if units of production remain unsold at year's end, fixed overhead remains attached to those units and is included on the balance sheet as an asset as part of the cost of inventory. With variable costing, all fixed overhead is expensed each period, regardless of the level of production or sales. Consequently, when production is greater than sales and inventories increase, absorption costing will result in higher net income than variable costing.

Absorption (full) costing A method of costing in which product costs include the costs of direct materials, direct labor, and fixed and variable overhead; required for external financial statements and for income tax reporting.

Variable (direct) costing A method of costing in which product costs include the costs of direct materials, direct labor, and variable overhead; fixed overhead is treated as a period cost; variable costing is consistent with CVP's focus on cost behavior.

Exhibit 5-13 Absorption and Variable Costing

Absorption Costing		Variable Costing	
Product Costs	**Period Costs**	**Product Costs**	**Period Costs**
Direct materials		Direct materials	
Direct labor	Selling, general, and administrative costs	Direct labor	Selling, general, and administrative costs
Variable overhead		Variable overhead	
Fixed overhead			***Fixed overhead***

© Cengage Learning 2013

LO5 The Impact of Absorption Costing and Variable Costing on the Income Statement

> The only difference between absorption and variable costing is the treatment of fixed overhead.

LuLu's Lockets is a custom jeweler manufacturing unique lockets. LuLu's CFO, Elise, is concerned about choosing the best costing method (variable vs. absorption) to allow her to make the best decision regarding management compensation and to more easily understand the impact of production volume on the income statement. LuLu's Lockets produces 100,000 units each year, with the following per-unit costs: direct material of $0.30, direct labor of $0.35, and variable overhead of $0.10 per unit. Fixed manufacturing overhead costs are $30,000. The company also has variable selling and administrative costs of $0.05 per unit sold and fixed selling and administrative costs of $10,000.

The selling price of each locket is $2. The cost of one unit of product under absorption costing and variable costing is calculated as follows:

Product Costs			
Absorption Costing		**Variable Costing**	
Direct material	$0.30	Direct material	$0.30
Direct labor	0.35	Direct labor	0.35
Variable overhead	0.10	Variable overhead	0.10
Fixed overhead	0.30		
Total per unit	$1.05	Total per unit	$0.75

The only difference between the two methods is $0.30 of fixed overhead ($30,000 ÷ 100,000 units), which is treated as a product cost under absorption costing and a period cost under variable costing.

Year 1 Income Comparison

Let's assume that in year 1 all 100,000 units that are produced are sold. Then how much income would be reported under each method? To answer this question, remember that, under absorption costing, fixed manufacturing overhead costs are expensed as part of cost of goods sold. Under variable costing, fixed manufacturing overhead costs are deducted as a fixed period cost. Regardless, when all units produced are sold, the net operating income reported under each method would be the same.

Year 1 Comparison of Absorption and Variable Costing			
(100,000 Units Produced and Sold)			
Absorption Costing		**Variable Costing**	
Sales	$200,000	Sales	$200,000
Less: Cost of goods sold	105,000	Less: Variable costs	80,000
Gross profit	$ 95,000	Contribution margin	$120,000
Less: S&A costs	15,000	Less: Fixed costs	40,000
Net operating income	$ 80,000	Net operating income	$ 80,000

Year 2 Income Comparison

Let's suppose that in the next year LuLu's Lockets produces 100,000 units (for the same costs) but, because of a very slow Christmas season, sells only 80,000 units. In this case, the variable-costing method would expense the entire $30,000 of fixed manufacturing overhead as a period cost, whereas the absorption-costing method would expense only $24,000 (80,000 units sold × $0.30 per unit). When production exceeds sales, absorption costing will report higher net operating income than variable costing will. Part of the $30,000 of fixed overhead (20,000 unsold units × $0.30 per unit, or $6,000) remains in inventory until those units are sold. The question for Elise is which method more closely represents what actually happened in the second year, when production exceeded sales. Fixed overhead does not change with changes in sales volume, so variable costing seems to report a more accurate picture of the company's actual costs. Variable costing allows Elise to look at the contribution of each item sold to the

© Scott Rothstein/Shutterstock.com

Year 2 Comparison of Absorption and Variable Costing

(100,000 Units Produced and 80,000 Units Sold)

Absorption Costing		Variable Costing	
Sales	$160,000	Sales	$160,000
Less: Cost of goods sold*	84,000	Less: Variable costs	64,000
Gross profit	$ 76,000	Contribution margin	$ 96,000
Less: S&A costs	14,000	Less: Fixed costs†	40,000
Net operating income	$ 62,000	Net operating income	$ 56,000

* Cost of goods sold includes $24,000 (80,000 × $0.30) of fixed manufacturing overhead.
† Fixed costs include $30,000 of fixed manufacturing overhead.

company's overall profit, whereas absorption costing distorts that analysis by including fixed manufacturing overhead in the sales data when, in fact, that cost is incurred regardless of the sales volume.

Year 3 Income Comparison

In Year 3, LuLu's Lockets holds production constant at 100,000 units, but increases sales to 120,000 units (the 20,000 units left over from Year 2 were sold, in addition to all of the production for the third year). In this case, under variable costing, $30,000 of fixed manufacturing overhead would be expensed as a period cost. Under absorption costing, the $30,000 would be expensed along with an additional $6,000 related to the 20,000 units produced in Year 2 and sold in Year 3 (20,000 units × $0.30 per unit = $6,000). When units sold exceed units produced, variable costing will report higher net operating income than will absorption costing. Remember from our previous discussion of cost behavior that fixed costs

Year 3 Comparison of Absorption and Variable Costing

(100,000 Units Produced and 120,000 Units Sold)

Absorption Costing		Variable Costing	
Sales	$240,000	Sales	$240,000
Less: Cost of goods sold *	126,000	Less: Variable costs	96,000
Gross profit	$114,000	Contribution margin	$144,000
Less: S&A costs	16,000	Less: Fixed costs†	40,000
Net operating income	$ 98,000	Net operating income	$104,000

* Cost of goods sold includes $36,000 (120,000 × $0.30) of fixed manufacturing overhead.
† Fixed costs include $30,000 of fixed manufacturing overhead.

remain constant from year to year regardless of sales volume. Absorption costing delays the expensing of a portion of the fixed cost incurred in Year 2 until all units are sold in Year 3. By contrast, variable costing results in the expensing of fixed costs in the year in which they are incurred.

Note that, over the three-year period, the total income is the same under each method. Why? Because when units produced are equal to units sold, the net operating income reported under each method is the same. Although production was greater than sales in Year 2 and sales were greater than production in Year 3, over the three-year period the company produced and sold 300,000 units.

	Year 1	Year 2	Year 3	Total
Production	100,000	100,000	100,000	300,000
Sales	100,000	80,000	120,000	300,000
Absorption Costing				
Sales	$200,000	$160,000	$240,000	$600,000
Less: Cost of goods sold	105,000	84,000	126,000	315,000
Gross margin	$ 95,000	$ 76,000	$114,000	$285,000
Less: S&A costs	15,000	14,000	16,000	45,000
Net operating income	$ 80,000	$ 62,000	$ 98,000	$240,000
Variable Costing				
Sales	$200,000	$160,000	$240,000	$600,000
Less: Variable costs	80,000	64,000	96,000	240,000
Contribution margin	$120,000	$ 96,000	$144,000	$360,000
Less: Fixed costs	40,000	40,000	40,000	120,000
Net operating income	$ 80,000	$ 56,000	$104,000	$240,000

To summarize (see Exhibit 5-14), in Year 1, when *units sold equaled units produced,* net operating income was the same under both costing methods. In Year 2, when *units produced exceeded units sold,* absorption costing reported higher net operating income than variable costing did. In Year 3, when *units sold exceeded units produced,* variable costing reported higher net operating income than absorption costing did.

Exhibit 5-14 Production, Sales, and Income Under Absorption Costing and Variable Costing

When Production = Sales	Absorption Income = Variable Income
When Production > Sales	Absorption Income > Variable Income
When Production < Sales	Absorption Income < Variable Income

© Cengage Learning 2013

LO6 Variable Costing and Decision Making

> *Variable costing is consistent with CVP's focus on differentiating fixed and variable costs and provides useful decision-making information that is often not apparent when using absorption costing.*

The use of absorption costing for internal decision making can result in less-than-optimal decisions. For example, consider the case of the unemployed executive who offered his services to a manufacturing company for only $1 per year in salary and a bonus equal to 50 percent of any increase in net income generated for the year. Reviewing the absorption-costing income statement for the previous year, he learned that although 10,000 units of product were produced and sold, the company had the capacity to produce 20,000 units. In addition, variable production costs were $40 per unit, variable selling and administrative (S&A) costs were $10 per unit sold, fixed manufacturing overhead costs were equal to $300,000 ($30 per unit produced), and fixed selling and administrative costs were equal to $100,000. As shown here, the previous year's net operating income was $100,000:

Absorption Costing Income (10,000 Units Produced)	
Sales (10,000 units)	$1,000,000
Less: Cost of goods sold*	700,000
Gross profit	$ 300,000
Less: S&A costs	200,000
Net operating income	$ 100,000

*Includes $300,000 (10,000 units × $30) of fixed manufacturing overhead.

By increasing production to 20,000 units, the allocation of fixed manufacturing overhead is reduced to $15 per unit ($300,000 ÷ 20,000 units = $15). Remember that, under absorption costing, fixed overhead is a product cost and is expensed only when the product is sold. Therefore, only $150,000 of fixed overhead costs will be expensed. The remaining $150,000 of fixed manufacturing overhead costs is included in inventory and is reported as an asset on the balance sheet. The cost of goods sold is reduced to $550,000, and net income is increased by $150,000, to $250,000. The manager is entitled to a bonus of $75,000, whereas the company is saddled with 10,000 units of unsold inventory and the attendant costs of storing and insuring it!

Absorption Costing Income (20,000 Units Produced)	
Sales (10,000 units)	$1,000,000
Less: Cost of goods sold*	550,000
Gross profit	$ 450,000
Less: S&A costs	200,000
Net operating income	$ 250,000

*Includes $150,000 (10,000 units × $15) of fixed costs.

If income had been measured with a variable costing approach, net operating income would be the same each year and the manager would not have been able to pull off his scheme.

Variable Costing Income			
(10,000 units produced)		(20,000 units produced)	
Sales (10,000 units)	$1,000,000	Sales (10,000 units)	$1,000,000
Variable costs	500,000	Variable costs	500,000
Contribution margin	$ 500,000	Contribution margin	$ 500,000
Fixed costs	400,000	Fixed costs	400,000
Net operating income	$ 100,000	Net operating income	$ 100,000

So, where are the costs that resulted from the increased production? Under variable costing, those production costs are attached to the inventory and are on the balance sheet as inventory. The fixed costs, under variable costing, are expensed each period in total, regardless of the level of production.

Problems like these are less common in a just-in-time (JIT) environment, in which inventory levels are minimized and companies strive to produce only enough products to meet demand.

Choosing the Best Method for Performance Evaluation

For external reporting purposes, managers have no choice but to use absorption costing, as it is required by GAAP. Managers are also required to use absorption costing for filing annual income tax returns. However, for internal decision making, variable costing is often the best choice. If income is used to evaluate the performance of a manager of a division or segment of a company, it seems logical that the measure of income should reflect managerial effort and skill. If sales decrease from one period to another with no changes in production or other factors, it seems logical that income should decrease as it does under variable costing. In contrast, increasing income by increasing production with no corresponding increase in sales (as is possible with absorption costing) is counterintuitive. All other things being equal, increases in sales should result in increases in income and decreases in sales should result in decreases in income.

So, using variable costing for internal decision making removes the impact of changing production levels on income. Accordingly, calculations of income are more likely to reflect managerial skill rather than simply an increase in production. If a manager's compensation package is based on net income, using absorption costing may motivate that manager to increase production simply to increase income. Under variable costing, managers are more likely to make optimal production volume decisions.

Variable costing offers many benefits that focus on managerial performance and cost behavior.

Advantages of Variable Costing

Absorption costing is required by GAAP and must be used whenever a company provides financial statements to individuals outside the company. However, for internal management purposes, variable costing would seem to be a better choice. Variable costing has the following advantages:

- Changes in production and inventory levels do not affect the calculation of profits.
- Variable costing focuses attention on relevant product costs. That is, attention is focused on variable product costs, which can be avoided, rather than on fixed product costs, which are often unavoidable.
- Under variable costing, cost behavior is emphasized and fixed costs are separated from variable costs on the income statement.
- Variable costing is consistent with variance analysis, an important tool used to manage a business.
- Variable costing income is more closely aligned with a company's cash flows.

STUDY TOOLS 5

Chapter review card

- Learning Objective and Key Concept Reviews
- Key Definitions and Formulas

Online (Located at www.cengagebrain.com)

- Flash Cards and Crossword Puzzles
- Games and Quizzes
- Zingerman's Deli Video and E-Lectures
- Homework Assignments (as directed by your instructor)

BRIEF EXERCISES

1. Understanding Fixed Costs and Variable Costs LO1

Cost behavior is fundamentally important concept to managerial accounting. The following statements describe various aspects of cost behavior:

a. Facility-level costs include production labor, raw materials, and utilities.

b. Fixed costs vary in direct proportion to changes in production volume, but are constant when expressed on a per-unit basis.

c. The normal range of production expected for a particular product and company is called the relevant range.

d. Assumptions about the behavior of fixed and variable costs are expected to hold inside and outside the relevant range.

e. Costs that vary, but only with relatively large changes in production volume, are often called step costs.

f. The cost equation $y = a + bx$ can be used to describe fixed costs, but not variable costs.

Required
Indicate whether each of the preceding statements is true or false.

2. Mixed Costs Using High/Low Method LO2

PG Phones accumulated the following production and overhead cost data for the past five months related to its production of cell phones:

	Production (cell phones)	Overhead Cost
January	13,600	$34,500
February	11,500	29,500
March	12,750	30,100
April	14,300	35,940
May	13,250	32,650

Required
A. Use the high/low method to calculate the variable cost per unit and fixed costs for PG Phones.
B. What are estimated total costs for production of 13,000 cell phones?

3. The Impact of Income Taxes LO3

Decisions frequently have income tax implications for a business. The following table includes data about mutually exclusive income tax scenarios:

Before-Tax Revenue	Tax Rate	After-Tax Revenue
?	30%	$63,000
$78,000	?	58,500
125,000	20%	?

Before-Tax Cost	Tax Rate	After-Tax Cost
$60,000	15%	?
?	25%	$60,000
96,000	?	62,400

Required
Calculate the missing values for each of the preceding transactions.

4. Absorption Costing vs. Variable Costing LO4

The difference between absorption costing and variable costing is relatively straightforward, but students often have difficulty mastering the material.

Item	Absorption Costing	Variable Costing
Direct materials		
Variable manufacturing overhead		
Fixed selling and administrative costs		
Direct labor		
Fixed manufacturing overhead		
Variable selling and administrative costs		

Required
Label each of the preceding items as to whether it is treated as a *product cost* or a *period cost* for absorption costing and variable costing.

5. Calculating Unit Cost under Absorption Costing and Variable Costing LO5

Companies use absorption costing and variable costing for different purposes. Understanding the difference in unit cost that results from these methods is necessary for sound decision making. The following production, cost, and pricing data are available:

Units in beginning inventory	0
Units produced	12,000
Units sold	10,500
Sales price per unit	$22
Variable costs per unit:	
Direct materials	$7
Direct labor	4
Manufacturing overhead	2
Selling and administrative	1
Fixed costs in total:	
Manufacturing overhead	$36,000
Selling and administrative	50,000

Required
Calculate the cost per unit, using absorption costing and variable costing.

6. Comparing Income under Absorption and Variable Costing LO6

Refer to the data in Brief Exercise 5.

Required
Calculate the net operating income for the company, using absorption costing and variable costing.

EXERCISES

7. Cost Behavior LO1

Baby Toys Co. produces fine porcelain dolls that are sold in exclusive gift shops. The controller and sales manager are discussing possible price increases and have started looking at various costs to consider their potential impact on price. The following are several of the costs they are discussing:

a. Advertising
b. Packaging (each doll is carefully packaged in a nicely designed collectible carton)
c. Supervisors' salaries
d. Fabric used in production (each doll is adorned in unique fabrics)
e. Assembly labor
f. Mortgage payment on the production facility
g. Production facility utilities
h. Quality assurance (each doll is carefully inspected)

Required
Assist the controller and sales manager by indicating whether each of the preceding costs is most likely a fixed cost (FC) or a variable cost (VC).

8. Calculation of Total Costs LO1

Doors and Keys, Inc., provides custom creation of door locks for expensive homes. The company has recently become concerned about its ability to plan and control costs. Howard Lockwood, the company's founder, believes that he can summarize the company's monthly cost with a simple formula that appears as "Cost = $12,800 + $25.00 per labor hour."

Required
If Doors and Keys's employees work 850 hours in a single month, calculate an estimate of the company's total costs.

9. Cost Behavior Analysis LO1

Sisters Erin Joyner and Teresa Hayes have started separate companies in the same city. Each company provides party-planning services for weddings, birthday parties, holiday parties, and other occasions. Erin and Teresa graduated from Upper State University and completed a managerial accounting course, so they both understand the importance of managing their company's costs. On the one hand, Erin has estimated her cost equation to be "Total cost = $4,000 + $40 per planning hour." On the other hand, Teresa has estimated her cost equation to be "Total cost = $250 + $60 per planning hour."

Required
A. What could explain such a difference in the cost equations?
B. If each sister works a total of 135 planning hours, what total costs would each report?

10. Mixed Costs and the Cost Equation LO1

Carla Janes and Associates incurred total costs of $10,000 to produce 500 custom mirrors. A total of 550 direct labor hours was required for the production of the mirrors. Direct labor is variable and costs $10 per hour.

Required
How much fixed cost did Carla Janes and Associates incur?

11. Cost Behavior: Step Costs LO1

Sara Ouellette has leased a new automobile under a special lease plan. If she drives the car 1,000 miles or less during a one-month period, the lease payment is $250. If the mileage ranges between 1,001 and 1,500 miles, the lease payment becomes $300. If the mileage ranges between 1,501 and 2,000 miles, the lease payment rises to $350.

Required
A. What type of cost is the lease?
B. If Sara drives the car only between 1,200 and 1,400 miles per month, then what type of cost does the lease effectively become?

12. Fixed and Variable Cost Behavior LO1

Killy's Baskets has the following current-year costs:

Variable costs	$6 per unit
Fixed costs	$7,000

Killy and a key supplier have entered into an arrangement that will result in a per-unit decrease in Killy's variable cost of $0.50 next year. Rental space will also be reduced, thereby decreasing fixed costs by 10 percent.

Required
A. If the company makes these changes, what is the new cost equation?
B. Given the new cost equation, determine estimated total costs if production remains at 12,000 units.

13. Regression Analysis: Calculation of Total Cost LO2

Valentine is a manufacturer of fine chocolates. Recently, the owner, Melinda Gross, asked her controller to perform a regression analysis on production costs. Melinda believes that pounds of chocolate produced drive all of the company's production costs. The controller generated the following regression output:

R Square	0.50688	
Standard Error	1.43764	

Analysis of Variance

	DF	Sum of Squares	Mean Square
Regression	1	418.52992	481.52992
Residual	197	407.16375	2.06682
$F = 202.49935$	Signif. $F = 0.0000$		

Variables in the Equation

Variable	Coefficients	Standard Error	t Stat	P-Value
Pounds	7.940	0.055794	14.230	0.0000
Intercept	204.070	0.261513	20.780	0.4361

Required

Calculate an estimated total cost, assuming that Valentine manufactures 5,000 pounds of chocolate.

14. Mixed Costs Using High/Low Method LO2

Gregory's Gems accumulated the following production and overhead cost data for the past five months:

	Production (units)	Overhead Cost
January	10,600	$40,250
February	10,500	40,000
March	11,500	44,250
April	12,500	45,500
May	11,000	43,750

Required

A. Use the high/low method to calculate the variable cost per unit and fixed costs for Gregory's Gems.
B. What are estimated total costs for production of 12,000 units?

15. Mixed Costs Using High/Low Method LO2

Captain Co. used the high/low method to derive the cost formula for electrical power cost. According to the cost formula, the variable cost per unit of activity is $3 per machine hour. Total electrical power cost at the high level of activity was $7,600 and was $7,300 at the low level of activity. The high level of activity was 1,200 machine hours.

Required

Calculate the low level of activity.

16. Calculate Variable Cost Using High/Low Method LO2

Delia, Inc., is preparing a budget for next year and requires a breakdown of the cost of steam used in its factory into fixed and variable components. The following data on the cost of steam used and direct labor hours worked are available for the last six months:

	Cost of Steam	Direct Labor Hours
July	$ 15,850	3,000
August	13,400	2,050
September	16,370	2,900
October	19,800	3,650
November	17,600	2,670
December	18,500	2,650
	$101,520	16,920

Required

A. Use the high/low method to calculate the estimated variable cost of steam per direct labor hour.
B. Prepare a graph of the cost of steam and the direct labor hours. Show labor hours on the x-axis and cost on the y-axis. What can you observe from the graph you prepared? (Hint: Set the minimum y-axis value to $11,000.)

17. Impact of Income Taxes LO3

Ben Rakusin is contemplating an expansion of his business. He believes he can increase revenues by $9,000 each month if he leases 1,500 additional square feet of showroom space. Rakusin has found the perfect showroom. It leases for $4,000 per month. Ben's tax rate is 30 percent.

Required

What estimated after-tax income will Rakusin earn from his expansion?

18. Impact of Income Taxes LO3

Most business transactions have tax consequences. Understanding the after-tax effects of transactions is fundamentally important. Consider the following:

Before-Tax Revenue	Tax Rate	After-Tax Revenue
$100,000	40%	?
200,000	20%	?
135,000	35%	?
Before-Tax Cost	**Tax Rate**	**After-Tax Cost**
$25,000	40%	?
50,000	20%	?
35,000	35%	?

Required

Calculate the after-tax revenue or after-tax cost for each of the preceding transactions.

19. Impact of Income Taxes LO3

Barnett Corporation anticipates net operating income (before tax) of $1,200,000 this year. The company is considering signing an equipment lease that would result in a $175,000 deductible expense this year. The company's tax rate is 35 percent.

Required

A. What are the tax expense and net income after taxes for the anticipated net income without the lease of the equipment?
B. What are the tax expense and net income after taxes if the equipment is leased?

20. Variable Costing: Calculation of Unit Variable Cost LO4, 5

Yankee Doodle Dandy Candy Company manufactures a single product, an awesome chocolate bar. Last year, the company produced 4,000 bars and sold 3,500 of them. Yankee Doodle Dandy had no candy bars at the beginning of the year. The company has the following costs:

Variable costs per unit:	
Production	$ 4.00
Selling and administrative	$ 1.00
Fixed costs in total:	
Production	$12,000
Selling and administrative	$ 8,000

Required

Calculate the unit product cost, assuming that the company uses variable costing.

21. Absorption Costing vs. Variable Costing LO4, 5, 6

Munn Bicycle Company manufactures bicycles specifically for college campuses. The bicycles sell for $100 and are very sturdy, with built-in saddlebags on the rear designed to carry backpacks. Selected data for last year's operations are as follows:

Units in beginning inventory	0
Units produced	20,000
Units sold	18,000
Units in ending inventory	2,000
Variable costs per unit:	
Direct materials	$40
Direct labor	20
Variable manufacturing overhead	5
Variable selling and administrative	2
Fixed costs:	
Fixed manufacturing overhead	$250,000
Fixed S&A	$100,000

Required

A. What is the product cost per bicycle if the company uses absorption costing?
B. What is the product cost per bicycle if the company uses variable costing?

22. Absorption Costing: Calculation of Unit Variable Cost LO5

Lisa's Lockets manufactures a single product, a diamond locket. Last year, the company produced 4,000 lockets and sold 3,500 of them. They had no lockets at the beginning of the year. The company has the following costs:

Variable costs per unit:	
Production	$ 4.00
Selling and administrative	$ 1.00
Fixed costs in total:	
Production	$12,000
Selling and administrative	$ 8,000

Required

Calculate the unit product cost, assuming that the company uses absorption costing.

23. Absorption Costing vs. Variable Costing: Calculation of Net Operating Income LO4, 5, 6

Refer to the data in Exercise 21.

Required

A. Prepare income statements for each costing method.
B. Explain the difference between the two income statements.
C. If, in the next year of operation, 20,000 units are produced and 21,000 units are sold, what would the net operating income be under each costing method? Explain the difference. (Assume that there is no change in the variable cost per unit or the fixed costs.)

24. Absorption Costing vs. Variable Costing: Calculation of Net Operating Income LO4, 5, 6

Posey Manufacturing has the following cost information available for the most current year.

Direct materials	$6.00 per unit
Direct labor	$4.00 per unit
Variable manufacturing overhead	$2.00 per unit
Variable S&A costs	$1.00 per unit
Fixed manufacturing overhead	$80,000
Fixed S&A costs	$25,000

During the year, Posey produced 12,500 units, out of which 11,000 were sold for $60 each.

Required

A. Produce an income statement using variable costing.
B. Produce an income statement using absorption costing.
C. If Posey needs to take one of these income statements to the bank to apply for a loan, which one should he use? Why?
D. For internal decision making, which income statement would be more useful? Why?

25. Absorption Costing vs. Variable Costing LO4, 5

McIntyre Manufacturing produces a single product. Last year, the company produced 20,000 units, out of which 18,000 were sold. There were no units in beginning inventory. The company had the following costs:

Variable costs per unit:	
Production	$ 10.00
S&A	$ 4.00
Fixed costs (total):	
Production	$40,000
S&A	$20,000

Required

A. Calculate McIntyre's product cost per unit, assuming that the company uses variable costing.
B. Calculate McIntyre's product cost per unit, assuming that the company uses absorption costing.
C. Calculate McIntyre's total period cost, assuming that the company uses variable costing.
D. Calculate McIntyre's total period cost, assuming that the company uses absorption costing.
E. Explain the differences in product cost and period cost between the two costing methods.

26. Variable Costing: Calculation of Net Operating Income LO5

Kristi Bostock started Bostock Boutique three years ago. Her business has grown handsomely, and she now produces and sells thousands of items each year. Selected operational and financial data are as follows:

Units in beginning inventory	0
Units produced	20,000
Units sold	19,000
Selling price per unit	$ 100
Variable costs per unit:	
Direct materials	$ 12.00
Direct labor	25.00
Manufacturing overhead	3.00
Selling and administrative	2.00
Fixed costs in total:	
Manufacturing overhead	$500,000
Selling and administrative	$600,000

Required

Calculate Bostock Boutique's net operating income, assuming that the company uses variable costing.

27. Absorption Costing: Calculation of Net Operating Income LO5

Refer to the data in Exercise 26.

Required

Calculate Bostock Boutique's net operating income, assuming that the company uses absorption costing.

28. Absorption Costing vs. Variable Costing: Calculation of Net Operating Income LO5, 6

Simmons Products has the following cost information available for the most recent year.

Direct materials	$4.00 per unit
Direct labor	$3.00 per unit
Variable manufacturing overhead	$2.00 per unit
Variable S&A costs	$1.00 per unit
Fixed manufacturing overhead	$25,000
Fixed S&A costs	$10,000

During the year, Simmons produced 5,000 units, out of which 4,600 units were sold for $30 each.

Required

A. Calculate Simmons's net operating income, assuming that the company uses variable costing.
B. Calculate Simmons's net operating income, assuming that the company uses absorption costing.

29. Variable Costing and Absorption Costing: Calculation of Net Operating Income LO5, 6

Graham Warner started Warner's Watches four years ago. His business has grown handsomely, and he now produces and sells thousands of watches each year. Selected operational and financial data are as follows:

Units in beginning inventory	0
Units produced	25,000
Units sold	20,000
Selling price per unit	$ 100
Variable costs per unit:	
Direct materials	$ 10.00
Direct labor	30.00
Manufacturing overhead	4.00
Selling and administrative	1.00
Fixed costs in total:	
Manufacturing overhead	$400,000
Selling and administrative	$300,000

Required

A. Calculate Warner's Watches's net operating income, using variable costing.
B. Calculate Warner's Watches's net operating income, using absorption costing.

30. Variable Costing and Absorption Costing: Calculation of Net Operating Income LO5, 6

Gumby's Gum produces large amounts of gum each year. This year, Gumby's produced 45,000 packs of gum but sold only 42,000 of the packs. Each pack sells for $1.50. Selected operational and financial data are as follows:

Variable costs per unit:	
Production	$ 0.50
S&A	0.10
Fixed costs in total:	
Production	$6,000
S&A	$3,000

Required

A. Calculate Gumby's net operating income, using variable costing.
B. Will operating income be higher or lower if calculated with absorption costing?
C. By how much?

31. Variable Costing and Absorption Costing: Calculation of Net Operating Income LO5, 6

Entel Corporation creates an accounting computer program. This year, Entel Corporation produced 20,000 units of its program and sold 22,000 units. Each unit sells for $250. Selected operational and financial data are as follows:

Variable costs per unit:	
Direct materials	$ 15.00
Direct labor	40.00
Manufacturing overhead	5.00
Selling and administrative	2.00
Fixed costs per unit:	
Manufacturing overhead	$200,000
Selling and administrative	$150,000

Required

A. Calculate Entel's net operating income, using absorption costing.
B. Will operating income be higher or lower if calculated with variable costing?
C. By how much?

32. Absorption Costing vs. Variable Costing: Benefits and Calculation of Net Operating Income LO5, 6

Tammond Tire Manufacturing produces truck tires. Current market conditions indicate a significant increase in demand in 2013 for their tires. In anticipation of that increase, the CEO has ordered the production plants to increase production by 25 percent in 2012. Because sales are projected to remain stable in 2012, that will result in a 25 percent increase in inventory levels by the end of 2012.

Required

Discuss the impact on operating income in 2012, using variable and absorption costing. What causes the difference? Tammond Tire is required to provide the bank with financial statements at the end of each year. What do you think the bank will think of the 2012 income statement? If the market projections prevail and sales increase by 25 percent in 2013, what will be the impact on the 2013 income statement, using both costing methods?

PROBLEMS

33. Regression vs. High/Low Method LO1, 2

Tools Are Us Corporation produces toolboxes used by construction professionals and homeowners. The company is concerned that it does not have an understanding of its utility consumption. The company's president, George, has asked the plant manager and cost accountant to work together to get information about utilities cost. The two of them accumulated the following data for the past 14 months (production volume is presented in units):

	Production	Utility Cost
January	113,000	$1,712
February	114,000	1,716
March	90,000	1,469
April	110,000	1,600
May	112,000	1,698
June	101,000	1,691
July	104,000	1,700
August	105,000	1,721
September	115,000	1,619
October	97,000	1,452
November	98,000	1,399
December	98,000	1,403
January	112,000	1,543
February	107,000	1,608

Required

A. Use the high/low method to determine the company's utility cost equation.
B. What would be the expected utility cost of producing 120,000 units? (The relevant range is 85,000 to 125,000 units of production.)
C. Using the data shown and a spreadsheet program, perform a regression analysis. Discuss any differences in the results and the potential impact on decision making.

34. Regression Analysis Interpretation LO1, 2

Global Office Services & Supplies sells various products and services in the greater Wentworth area. Duplicating is one of its most popular services for corporate customers and individuals alike. Selected data from the Duplicating Department for the previous six months are as follows:

	Number of Copies Made	Duplicating Department's Costs
January	20,000	$1,700
February	25,000	1,950
March	27,000	2,100
April	22,000	1,800
May	24,000	1,900
June	30,000	2,400

Regression output based on the previous data is as follows:

Coefficient of intercept	280.79
R square	0.967696
Number of observations	6
X coefficient (independent variable)	0.0687

Required

A. What is the variable cost per copy for Global Office Services & Supplies?
B. What is the fixed cost for the Duplicating Department?
C. Given the limited regression output shown, what cost formula should be used to compute an estimate of future total costs in the Duplicating Department?
D. If 26,000 copies are made next month, what total cost would be predicted?
E. On the basis of the information given, how accurate will the cost formula developed in response to question C be at predicting total Duplicating Department costs each month?

35. Basic Cost Behavior, High/Low Method LO1, 2

Simon and Garfunkel operate separate, but related, businesses in the same town. The two have been debating which of them has the least amount of fixed costs. Simon, because he has always come first, believes his business has lower fixed costs than Garfunkel's business. Of course, Garfunkel disagrees, saying that his business has lower fixed costs. The two have accumulated the following activity and cost data and have asked that you help them resolve their debate:

Simon's Business Data

Units Produced	Utilities	Rent	Indirect Labor
1,000	$10,000	$15,000	$13,000
1,500	12,500	15,000	15,600

Garfunkel's Business Data

Units Produced	Utilities Expense	Rent	Indirect Labor
2,000	$24,250	$21,000	$22,000
8,000	66,250	21,000	88,000

Required

A. Classify each of Simon's and Garfunkel's expenses as a fixed, variable, or mixed cost.
B. Calculate the total-cost formula for each business. Which business has lower fixed costs?
C. If Simon produces 1,300 units, what would his total costs be?
D. If Garfunkel produces 1,300 units, what would his total costs be?

36. Regression Analysis LO1, 2

Same Day Delivery wants to determine the cost behavior pattern of maintenance costs for its delivery vehicles. The company has decided to use linear regression to examine the costs. The previous year's data regarding maintenance hours and costs are as follows:

	Hours of Activity	Maintenance Costs
January	480	$4,200
February	320	3,000
March	400	3,600
April	300	2,820
May	500	4,350
June	310	2,960
July	320	3,030
August	520	4,470
September	490	4,260
October	470	4,050
November	350	3,300
December	340	3,160

Required

A. Perform a regression analysis on the given data. What maintenance costs should be budgeted for a month in which 420 maintenance hours will be worked?
B. What is the percentage of the total variance that can be explained by your analysis?
C. Use the high/low method to estimate a cost formula for Same Day. How similar is your high/low solution to the regression solution?

37. Regression Analysis LO1, 2

Pine Side Hospital wants to determine the cost behavior pattern of maintenance costs for its X-ray machines. The hospital has decided to use linear regression to examine the costs. The previous year's data regarding maintenance hours and costs are as follows:

	Hours of Activity	Maintenance Costs
January	500	$3,950
February	450	3,800
March	300	3,220
April	375	3,380
May	425	3,700
June	520	4,000
July	410	3,650
August	380	3,400
September	440	3,780
October	390	3,470
November	400	3,590
December	330	3,310

Required

A. Perform a regression analysis on the given data. What maintenance costs should be budgeted for a month in which 430 maintenance hours will be worked?

B. What is the percentage of the total variance that can be explained by your analysis?

C. Use the high/low method to estimate a cost formula for Pine Side. How similar is your high/low solution to the regression solution?

38. Regression Analysis: Impact of Outliers
LO1, 2

Chris Gill founded Gill's Grill over 20 years ago. The business has grown so much and been so successful that Chris is now considering selling franchises. Chris knows that potential franchisees will want access to certain operational data. Gill's Grill is probably best known for its incredible "potato flats," a french fry–like item served with a special secret sauce. Chris is concerned that some of the potato flats data are unusual and out of the ordinary. The following production data related to "potato flats" have been compiled:

	Pounds of Potatoes	Food Preparation Costs
January	20,000	$17,000
February	25,000	11,000
March	27,000	27,000
April	22,000	18,000
May	24,000	30,000
June	30,000	24,000
July	22,000	18,000
August	23,000	18,500
September	34,000	26,000
Regression Output		
Coefficient of intercept	4,104.372	
R square	0.244367	
X coefficient	0.672073	

Required

A. Should Chris remove some of the data? In other words, are any of the months unusual relative to the others? If so, identify likely outliers from the data and state reasons that you would remove them.

B. Do you think removing the data points would change the regression output? Perform a regression analysis to find out the correct answer.

39. Cost Behavior, High/Low Method LO1, 2

Ullrich Framing is well known for the quality of its picture framing. Lucinda Ullrich, the company's president, believes that the number of linear feet of framing used is the best predictor of framing costs for her company. She asked her assistant to look into the matter, and he accumulated the following data:

	Linear Feet of Framing	Number of Mats	Framing Costs
January	20,000	7,100	$17,000
February	25,000	8,120	19,500
March	27,000	8,500	21,000
April	22,000	8,400	18,000
May	24,000	8,300	19,000
June	30,000	10,600	24,000

Required

A. Use the high/low method to develop a total cost formula for Ullrich Framing. You will need to perform two separate calculations, one for number of feet of framing and one for number of mats.

B. Compare the cost formulas developed in question A. Why are there differences?

C. On what basis should Ullrich select a formula to predict framing costs? Would you recommend that Ullrich rely on the results of the high/low method?

40. Absorption Costing vs. Variable Costing: Benefits and Calculation of Net Operating Income LO4, 5, 6

HD Inc. produces a variety of products for the computing industry. CD burners are among its most popular products. The company's controller, Katie Jergens, spoke to the company's president at a meeting last week and told her that the company was doing well, but that the financial picture depended on how product costs and net operating income were calculated. The president did not realize that the company had options in regard to calculating these numbers, so she asked Katie to prepare some information and be ready to meet with her to talk more about this issue. In preparing for the meeting, Katie accumulated the following data:

Units produced	100,000
Units sold	95,000
Fixed manufacturing overhead	$300,000
Direct materials per unit	$55.00
Direct labor per unit	$25.00
Variable manufacturing overhead per unit	$15.00

Required

A. Compute the cost per unit, using absorption costing.

B. Compute the cost per unit, using variable costing.

C. Compute the difference in net operating income between the two methods. Which costing method results in the higher net operating income?

D. Assume that production was 100,000 units and sales were 100,000 units. What would be the difference in net operating income between the two methods?

E. Which method is required by generally accepted accounting principles?

41. Absorption Costing vs. Variable Costing: Benefits and Calculation of Net Operating Income LO4, 5, 6

Boots R Us produces a variety of products for the fashion industry. Cowboy-type boots are among its most popular products. The company's controller spoke to the company's president at a meeting last week and told her that the company was doing well, but that the financial picture depended on how product costs and net operating income were calculated. The president did not realize that the company had options with regard to calculating these numbers, so she asked the controller to prepare some information and be ready to meet with her to talk more about this issue. In preparing for the meeting, the controller accumulated the following data:

Beginning inventory	25,000
Units produced	100,000
Units sold	105,000
Fixed manufacturing overhead	$400,000
Direct materials per unit	$25.00
Direct labor per unit	$35.00
Variable manufacturing overhead per unit	$15.00

Required

A. Compute the cost per unit, using absorption costing.
B. Compute the cost per unit, using variable costing.
C. Compute the difference in net operating income between the two methods. Which costing method results in the higher net operating income?
D. Assume that production was 100,000 units and sales were 70,000 units. What would be the difference in net operating income between the two methods? Which costing method shows the greater net operating income?
E. Assume that production was 100,000 units and sales were 100,000 units. What would be the difference in net operating income between the two methods?
F. Which method is required by generally accepted accounting principles?

42. Absorption vs. Variable Costing: Benefits and Calculation of Net Operating Income LO4, 5, 6

Oliver, Inc., produces an oak rocking chair that is designed to ease back problems. The chairs sell for $200 each. Results from last year's operations are as follows:

Inventory and production data:	
Units in beginning inventory	0
Units produced during the year	20,000
Units sold during the year	18,000
Variable costs (unit):	
Direct materials	$ 70.00
Direct labor	20.00
Variable manufacturing overhead	15.00
Variable selling and administrative	10.00
Fixed costs:	
Fixed manufacturing overhead	$500,000
Fixed selling and administrative	$530,000

Required

A. Compute the unit product cost for one rocking chair, assuming that the company uses variable costing.
B. Prepare an income statement based on variable costing.
C. Compute the unit product cost for one rocking chair, assuming that the company uses absorption costing.
D. Prepare an income statement based on absorption costing.
E. Compare the two income statements. What causes the net operating income to differ?
F. If the company produced 18,000 chairs and sold 20,000 chairs (assume that the additional 2,000 chairs were in the beginning inventory), what would be the impact on the two income statements? In other words, which method provides the higher net operating income?

CASES

43. Decision Focus: Comprehensive Regression Analysis LO1, 2

Last Minute Cruise Co. has been operating for more than 20 years. The company has recently undergone several major management changes and needs accurate information to plan new cruises. You have been retained as a consultant to provide a cruise-planning model. The company's accounting department provided you with the data that follow regarding last year's average costs for 12 cruises on the MS *Robyn*, a cruise ship that has a maximum capacity of 525 passengers and a crew of 250. All cruises on the MS *Robyn* are for either 7 or 10 days. The total cost shown includes all costs of operating the ship (fuel, maintenance, depreciation, etc.) as well as meals, entertainment, and crew costs.

Cruise	Days	Passengers	Total Cost
1	7	455	$315,010
2	7	420	297,525
3	7	473	317,595
4	7	510	326,615
5	7	447	314,510
6	7	435	310,015
7	10	445	365,015
8	10	495	370,015
9	10	480	367,035
10	10	505	375,000
11	10	471	367,500
12	10	439	365,090

Required

A. Using the number of passengers as the independent variable, perform a regression analysis to develop the total-cost formula for a cruise.

B. How accurate is the model calculated in question A? (Hint: Look at how much variance in total cost is explained by the number of passengers.)

C. What are the total fixed costs per cruise? (Round your answer to the nearest cent.)

D. What are the variable costs per passenger? (Round your answer to the nearest cent.)

E. What other independent variable might Last Minute Cruise Co. use to predict total cruise costs? Using regression analysis, develop another total-cost formula based on the new independent variable.

F. Using the best planning model you can develop from the data provided, what is the estimated cost of a 10-day cruise at full capacity of 525 passengers? (Round your answer to the nearest cent.)

44. Decision Focus: Comprehensive Regression Analysis LO1, 2, 3

Perlman-Douglas, a major retailing and mail-order operation, has been in business for the past 10 years. During that time, the mail-order operations have grown from a sideline to more than 80 percent of the company's annual sales. Of course, the company has suffered growing pains. There were times when overloaded or faulty computer programs resulted in lost sales. And, hiring and scheduling temporary employees to augment the permanent staff during peak periods has always been a problem.

Gail Lobanoff, manager of mail-order operations, has developed procedures for handling most problems. However, she is still trying to improve the scheduling of temporary employees to take telephone orders from customers. Under the current

system, Lobanoff keeps a permanent staff of 60 employees who handle the basic workload. On the basis of her estimate of the upcoming week's telephone volume, she determines the number of temporary employees needed. The permanent employees are paid an average of $10 per hour plus 30 percent fringe benefits. The temporary employees are paid $7 per hour with no fringe benefits. The full-time employees are seldom sent home when volume is light, and they are not paid for hours missed. Temporary employees are paid only for their hours worked. Perlman-Douglas normally has three supervisors who earn $1,000 per month, but one additional supervisor is hired when temporary employees are used.

Lobanoff has decided to try regression analysis as a way to improve the prediction of total costs of processing telephone orders. By summarizing the daily labor hours into monthly totals for the past year, she was able to determine the number of labor hours incurred each month. In addition, she summarized the number of orders that had been processed each month. After entering the data into a spreadsheet, Lobanoff ran two regressions. Regression 1 related the total hours worked (permanent and temporary employees) to the total cost of operating the phone center. Regression 2 related the number of orders taken to the total cost. The data used and regression output are as follows:

Month	Total Cost	Total Hours	Number of Orders
January	$134,000	9,600	10,560
February	133,350	9,550	10,450
March	132,700	9,500	10,200
April	134,000	9,600	10,700
May	133,675	9,575	10,400
June	139,900	10,100	10,700
July	143,820	10,500	11,100
August	140,880	10,200	10,450
September	137,940	9,900	10,200
October	153,620	11,500	12,200
November	163,420	12,500	12,900
December	150,680	11,200	11,490

Regression equation: TC = FC + VC (hours) or TC = FC + VC (orders), where TC = total cost, FC = fixed cost, and VC = variable cost per hour or order.

	Regression 1	Regression 2
Intercept (FC)	36,180.42	21,595.15
X Variable (VC)	10.21475	10.95427
R square	0.997958	0.890802

Required

A. What is the total-cost formula for each of the preceding regressions? State each formula, using costs that are rounded to the nearest cent.

B. Gail Lobanoff estimates that 12,470 orders will be received and 12,000 hours will be worked during January. Use each cost formula you developed in question A to predict the total cost of operating the phone center. Round your answers to the nearest dollar.

C. Gail needs to select one of the models for use in predicting total phone center costs for next year's monthly budget.
   (1) What are the objectives in selecting a prediction model?
   (2) What options are available to Gail? That is, what other independent variables might be used to predict the costs of the phone center?

45. Absorption Costing versus Variable Costing: Benefits and Calculation of Net Operating Income LO4, 5, 6

Crystal Glass is a producer of heirloom-quality glassware. The company has a solid reputation and is widely regarded as a model corporate citizen. You have recently been hired as a staff accountant at a time when the company is experiencing rapid growth and is looking for a substantial increase in its line of credit at the local bank. Crystal Glass also is planning on trying to take the company public in the next three to five years. At the present time, the company is a closely held family-owned business. One of your first jobs is to review the current month's income statement for accuracy. The income statement appears as follows:

Crystal Glass, Inc. Statement of Income For the Year Ended October 31, 2011	
Sales revenue	$12,008,450
Variable costs	8,475,361
Contribution margin	3,533,089
Fixed costs	1,845,902
Net operating income	$ 1,687,187

You are given the following additional information:

Variable costs:	
Manufacturing	$6,356,521
S&A	$2,118,840
Fixed costs:	
Manufacturing	$1,476,722
S&A	$369,180
Beginning inventory	250,000 units
Production	500,000 units
Sales	600,000 units

Required

A. What type of costing method is used by Crystal Glass?

B. Does the method comply with GAAP? If not, what costing method should be used? What would net operating income be?

C. Could the statements be misleading to the bank? Why or why not?

D. What are your options as the new staff accountant? Who are the stakeholders affected?

Cost–Volume–Profit
Analysis

Introduction

Some of the more important decisions managers make involve analyzing the relationships among the cost, volume, and profitability of products produced and services provided by a company. **Cost–volume–profit (CVP) analysis** focuses on the relationships among the following five factors and the overall profitability of a company:

1. The prices of products or services

2. The volume of products or services produced and sold

3. The per-unit variable costs

4. The total fixed costs

5. The mix of products or services produced

As in any form of analysis involving projections of the future, certain assumptions must be considered. The major assumptions are as follows:

1. The selling price is constant throughout the entire relevant range. In other words, we assume that the sales price of the product will not change as the volume changes.

2. Costs are linear throughout the relevant range. As discussed in Chapter 5, although costs may behave in a curvilinear fashion, they can often be approximated by a linear relationship between cost and volume within the relevant range.

3. The sales mix used to calculate the weighted-average contribution margin is constant.

4. The amount of inventory is constant. In other words, the number of units produced is equal to the number of units sold.

Although some of these assumptions are often violated in real business settings, the violations are usually minor and have little or no impact on management decisions. CVP analysis can still be considered valid and very useful in decision making.

> **Cost–volume–profit (CVP) analysis** A tool that focuses on the relationships among a company's profits and (1) the prices of products or services, (2) the volume of products or services, (3) the per-unit variable costs, (4) the total fixed costs, and (5) the mix of products or services produced.

Learning Objectives

After studying the material in this chapter, you should be able to:

LO1 Use the contribution margin in its various forms to determine the impact of changes in sales on income.

LO2 Analyze what-if decisions by using CVP analysis.

LO3 Compute a company's break-even point in single- and multiproduct environments.

LO4 Analyze target profit before and after the impact of income tax.

LO5 Compute a company's operating leverage and understand the relationship of leverage to cost structure.

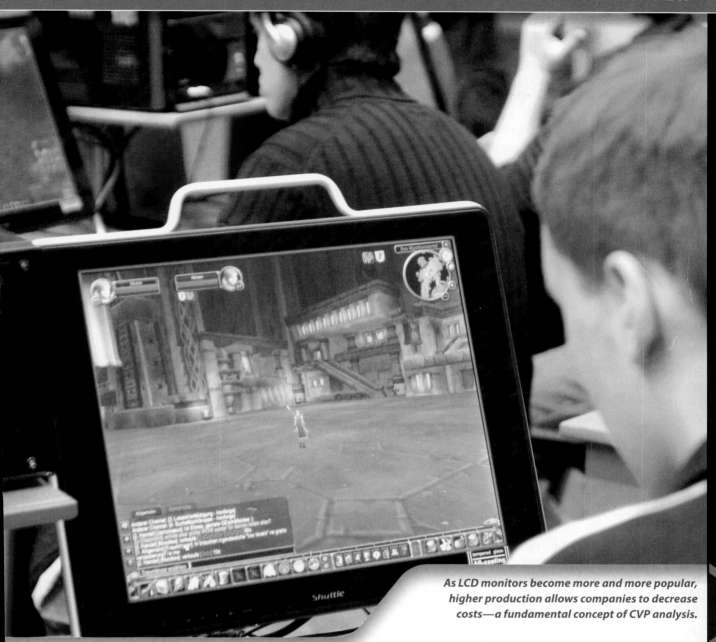

As LCD monitors become more and more popular, higher production allows companies to decrease costs—a fundamental concept of CVP analysis.

© kolvenbach/Alamy

LO1 The Contribution Margin and Its Uses

As mentioned in Chapter 5, the traditional income statement required for external financial reporting focuses on function (product costs versus period costs) in calculating the cost of goods sold and a company's gross profit. **Gross profit** is the difference between sales and cost of goods sold. However, because cost of goods sold includes both fixed costs (facility-level costs, such as rent) and variable costs (unit-level costs, such as direct materials), the behavior of cost of goods sold and gross profit is difficult to predict when production increases or decreases.

> **Gross profit** The difference between sales and cost of goods sold.

ACCT

In contrast, the contribution margin income statement is structured by behavior rather than by function. In Exhibit 6-1, a traditional income statement and a contribution margin income statement are shown side by side so that you can see the difference.

As you can see, although the net income is the same for both statements, the traditional statement focuses on the function of the costs, whereas the contribution margin income statement focuses on the behavior of the costs. In the traditional income statement, the cost of goods sold and selling, general, and administrative

> The contribution margin income statement is structured to emphasize cost behavior as opposed to cost function.

Exhibit 6-1 Comparison of Income Statements

Traditional

Sales		$1,000
Less: Cost of goods sold:		
Variable costs	$350	
Fixed costs	150	
Total cost of goods sold		500
Gross profit		$ 500
Less: S, G, & A costs:		
Variable costs	$ 50	
Fixed costs	250	
Total S, G, & A costs		300
Net operating income		$ 200

Contribution Margin

Sales		$1,000
Less: Variable costs:		
Manufacturing costs	$350	
S, G, & A costs	50	
Total variable costs		400
Contribution margin		$ 600
Less: Fixed costs:		
Manufacturing costs	$150	
S, G, & A costs	250	
Total fixed costs		400
Net operating income		$ 200

© Cengage Learning 2013

(S, G, & A) costs include both variable and fixed costs. In the contribution margin income statement, costs are separated by behavior (variable versus fixed) rather than by function. Note, however, that the contribution margin income statement combines product and period costs. Variable costs include both variable product costs (direct materials) and variable selling, general, and administrative costs (commissions on sales), whereas fixed costs likewise include both product and period costs.

Contribution Margin per Unit

To illustrate the many uses of the contribution margin income statement in managerial decision making, let's look at the income statement of Happy Daze Games. Happy Daze, unlike large established firms such as

Blizzard Entertainment and Bioware Corp., is a start-up company and produces just one game but plans to increase its product line to include more games in the near future.

A contribution margin income statement for Happy Daze Game Company follows.

	Total	Per Unit
Sales (8,000 units)	$100,000	$12.50
Less: Variable costs	72,000	9.00
Contribution margin	$ 28,000	$ 3.50
Less: Fixed costs	35,000	
Net operating income (loss)	$ (7,000)	

Note that, in addition to the total sales, variable costs, and contribution margin, per-unit cost information is also shown in the statement. Happy Daze sells each game for $12.50, and the variable cost of manufacturing each game is $9.00. As you can see, the **contribution margin per unit** is $3.50 and can be found by subtracting the per-unit variable costs of $9.00 from the per-unit

Contribution margin per unit The sales price per unit of product, less all variable costs to produce and sell the unit of product; used to calculate the change in contribution margin resulting from a change in unit sales.

sales price of $12.50. The contribution margin per unit can also be calculated by dividing the contribution margin (in dollars) by the number of units sold:

$$\text{Contribution margin (per unit)} = \frac{\text{Contribution margin (in \$)}}{\text{Units sold}}$$
$$= \frac{28{,}000}{8{,}000} = \$3.50$$

What exactly does this tell us? It tells us that every game that is sold adds $3.50 to the contribution margin. Assuming that fixed costs don't change, net operating income increases by the same $3.50.

What happens if sales increase by 100 games? Because we know that the contribution margin is $3.50 per game, if sales increase by 100 games, net operating income will increase by $350 ($3.50 × 100). In a similar fashion, if sales were to decrease by 200 games, then net operating income would decrease by $700 ($3.50 × −200).

As summarized in Exhibit 6-2, the use of contribution margin per unit makes it very easy to predict how both increases and decreases in sales volume affect contribution margin and net income.

> *The contribution margin per unit and the contribution margin ratio will remain constant as long as sales vary in direct proportion to volume.*

The **contribution margin ratio** is calculated by dividing the contribution margin in dollars by sales in dollars:

$$\text{Contribution margin ratio} = \frac{\text{Contribution margin (in \$)}}{\text{Sales (in \$)}}$$

Exhibit 6-2 The Impact of Changes in Sales on Contribution Margin and Net Income

	Decreased by 200 units	Original Total	Increased by 100 units
	7,800 units	8,000 units	8,100 units
Sales (sales price, $12.50/unit)	$97,500	$100,000	$101,250
Less: Variable costs ($9/unit)	70,200	72,000	72,900
Contribution margin ($3.50/unit)	$27,300	$ 28,000	$ 28,350
Less: Fixed costs	35,000	35,000	35,000
Net operating income (loss)	$ (7,700)	$ (7,000)	$ (6,650)
Change in income	Decreased by $700		Increased by $350
	(200-unit decrease × $3.50)		(100-unit increase × $3.50)

© Cengage Learning 2013

Contribution Margin Ratio

The contribution margin income statement can also be presented in terms of percentages, as shown in the following income statement:

	Total	Percentage
Sales (8,000 units)	$100,000	100
Less: Variable costs	72,000	72
Contribution margin	$ 28,000	28 ($28,000/$100,000)
Less: Fixed costs	35,000	
Net operating income (loss)	$ (7,000)	

The contribution margin ratio can be viewed as the amount of each sales dollar contributing to the payment of fixed costs and increasing net operating profit; that is, 28 cents of each sales dollar contributes to the payment of fixed costs or increases net income.

Contribution margin ratio The contribution margin divided by sales; used to calculate the change in contribution margin resulting from a dollar change in sales.

Like the contribution margin per unit, the contribution margin ratio will remain constant as long as sales vary in direct proportion to volume.

Like contribution margin per unit, the contribution margin ratio allows us to very quickly see the impact of a change in sales on contribution margin and net operating income. As you saw in Exhibit 6-2, a $1,250 increase in sales (100 units) will increase contribution margin by $350 ($1,250 × 28%). Assuming that fixed costs don't change, this $350 increase in contribution margin increases net operating income by the same amount. Likewise, in Exhibit 6-2, we decreased sales by 200 units ($2,500), resulting in a decrease in contribution margin and net operating income of $700 ($2,500 × 28%).

LO2 What-If Decisions Using CVP

Continuing with our example, we note that Happy Daze had a net loss of $7,000 when 8,000 units were sold. At that level of sales, the total contribution margin of $28,000 is not sufficient to cover fixed costs of $35,000. The CEO of the company would like to consider options to increase net income while maintaining the high quality of the company's products. After consultation with marketing, operations, and accounting managers, the CEO identifies three options that she would like to consider in more depth:

1. Reducing the variable costs of manufacturing the product

2. Increasing sales through a change in the sales incentive structure or commissions (which would also increase variable costs)

3. Increasing sales through improved features and increased advertising

Option 1—Reduce Variable Costs

When variable costs are reduced, the contribution margin will increase. So the question becomes, What can be done to reduce the variable costs of manufacturing? Happy Daze could find a less expensive supplier of raw materials. The company could also investigate the possibility of reducing the amount of labor used in the production process or of using lower wage employees in the production process.

In either case, qualitative factors must be considered. If Happy Daze finds a less expensive supplier of raw materials, the reliability of the supplier (shipments may be late, causing downtime) and the quality of the material (paper products are not as good, adhesive is not bonding) must be considered. Reducing labor costs also has both quantitative and qualitative implications. If less labor is involved in the production process, more machine time may be needed. Although this option certainly lowers variable costs, it may also raise fixed costs. Using lower skilled workers to save money could result in more defective products, owing to mistakes made by inexperienced workers. Another possible result of using fewer workers is that it can adversely affect employee morale. Being short staffed can cause stress on workers, owing to the likelihood that they will be overworked.

Happy Daze decides to decrease variable costs by reducing the costs of direct labor. The operations manager assures the CEO that the change can be made by outsourcing some of the current production activities. This change reduces variable costs by 10 percent and, as shown in the following analysis, results in an overall increase in net operating income of $7,200:

Impact of Reducing Variable Costs By 10 Percent		
	Current	Option 1
Sales	$100,000	$100,000
Less: Variable costs	72,000	64,800
Contribution margin	$ 28,000	$ 35,200
Less: Fixed costs	35,000	35,000
Net operating income (loss)	$ (7,000)	$ 200

Option 2—Increase Sales Incentives (Commissions)

The CEO of Happy Daze would also like to consider providing additional sales incentives to motivate the sales staff in an effort to increase sales volume. The marketing manager estimates that if Happy Daze raises the sales commission by 10 percent on all sales above the present level, sales will increase by $40,000, or 3,200 games. (The additional sales commission will be $4,000.)

Happy Daze can increase net operating income by $7,200 by increasing the sales commission by 10 percent on all sales of more than $100,000. The new variable costs are calculated by using a variable-cost percentage of 72 percent on sales up to $100,000 and 82 percent on all sales of more than $100,000. As you can see in the following income statement, if sales increase by $40,000, operating income will increase by $7,200, and Happy Daze will report net operating income of $200:

Impact of Increasing Sales Incentives (Sales Increase to $140,000)		
	Current	Option 2
Sales	$100,000	$140,000
Less: Variable costs	72,000	104,800
Contribution margin	$ 28,000	$ 35,200
Less: Fixed costs	35,000	35,000
Net operating income (loss)	$ (7,000)	$ 200

In Option 1 and Option 2, the ultimate change in net income can be determined by focusing solely on the change in contribution margin. Fixed costs are not relevant in either analysis because they do not vary. However, as you will see in Option 3, that is not always the case.

Option 3—Change Game Features and Increase Advertising

Changes can be made to more than one variable at a time. In fact, changes in cost, price, and volume are never made in a vacuum and almost always affect one or both of the other variables. Happy Daze has decided to change some key features of its game. Although this change will add $0.25 to the variable cost per game, the marketing manager estimates that with additional advertising of $5,000, sales volume will increase by 40 percent, or 3,200 units. In order to offset some of these costs, the accounting manager proposes an increase of $0.75 per unit in the sales price. As shown next, this option increases the contribution margin per unit to $4.00 per unit. The new sales price per unit is $13.25, and variable costs increase from $9.00 to $9.25 per unit. The increase in contribution margin of $16,800 is more than enough to offset the $5,000 increase in fixed costs and results in an overall increase of $11,800 in net operating income.

MAKING IT REAL

As consumer spending slowed during the recent recession, managers and owners of both large and small companies employed CVP analysis in an effort to bolster income. For example, Drue Sanders, founder of Drue Sanders Custom Jewelers, created a new line of jewelry using silver rather than more costly gold and platinum as the main component. This approach allowed the company to sell items for $150 to $200 rather than the normal $500 and up prices she normally charged. The result was increased volume as consumers reacted to the lower pricing.

In a similar fashion, in order to lure cost-conscious customers, PC makers such as Hewlett-Packard Co. and Dell shifted their product lines toward cheaper laptops and notebooks that sold for as little as $399. With consumers balking at spending thousands of dollars on a new computer, offering lower priced computers with fewer (and less expensive) features allowed the companies to continue making sales in a difficult economy.

© Jana Birchum/Getty Images

Source: "Smart Ways to Cut Prices," by Diana Ransom, and "Leaner Laptops, Lower Prices," by Justin Scheck and Loretta Chao, The Wall Street Journal, April 22, 2009.

Impact of Changes to Cost, Price, and Volume

	Current (8,000 units)	Option 3 (11,200 units)
Sales	$100,000 ($8,000 × $12.50)	$148,400 (11,200 × $13.25)
Less: Variable costs	72,000 (8,000 × $9.00)	103,600 (11,200 × $9.25)
Contribution margin	$ 28,000 (8,000 × $3.50)	$ 44,800 (11,200 × $4.00)
Less: Fixed costs	35,000	40,000
Net operating income (loss)	$ (7,000)	$ 4,800

How well does each option meet the stated objectives of increasing net operating income while maintaining a high-quality product? The CEO of Happy Daze should analyze each alternative solution in the same manner and choose the best course of action on the basis of both quantitative and qualitative factors.

From a quantitative perspective, Option 1 results in an increase in net operating income of $7,200, Option 2 increases net operating income by the same $7,200, and Option 3 increases net operating income by $11,800. The CEO must also assess the risk inherent in each option, including the sensitivity of a decision to make changes in key assumptions. For example, although Option 1 appears to have little quantitative risk because the decrease in costs is known with certainty and no increase in sales is projected, Happy Daze should consider whether reducing labor costs in Option 1 will have a negative impact on the quality of its product. If the reduction in labor costs results from using lower paid but inadequately skilled workers, quality may be adversely affected.

LO3 Break-Even Analysis

In addition to considering what-if analysis, it is useful for managers to know the number of units sold or the dollar amount of sales that is necessary for a company to break even. The **break-even point** is the level of sales at which the contribution margin just covers fixed costs and, consequently, income is equal to zero. Break-even analysis is really just a variation of CVP analysis in

Break-even point The level of sales at which the contribution margin just covers fixed costs and income is equal to zero.

which volume is increased or decreased in an effort to find the point at which income is equal to zero.

Break-even analysis is facilitated through the use of a mathematical equation derived directly from the contribution margin income statement. Another way to look at these relationships is to put the income statement into equation form:

$$\text{Sales} - \text{Variable Costs} - \text{Fixed Costs} = \text{Income}$$
$$SP(x) - VC(x) - FC = I$$

where

$$SP = \text{Sales price per unit}$$
$$VC = \text{Variable costs per unit}$$
$$FC = \text{Total fixed costs}$$
$$I = \text{Income}$$
$$x = \text{Number of units sold}$$

At the break-even point, income is equal to zero, so

$$SP(x) - VC(x) - FC = 0$$

Rearranging and dividing each side by $SP - VC$, we find that the number of units (x) that must be sold to reach the break-even point is

$$(SP - VC)(x) = FC$$
$$\text{and } x = \frac{FC}{CM}$$

Because the selling price per unit (SP) less variable costs per unit (VC) is equal to the contribution margin per unit, by dividing the contribution margin of each product into the fixed cost, we are calculating the number of units that must be sold to cover the fixed costs—the break-even point:

$$\text{Break-even (units)} = \frac{\text{Fixed costs}}{\text{Contribution margin per unit}}$$

At that point, the total contribution margin will be equal to the fixed cost and net income will be zero.

For example, if Happy Daze has fixed costs of $35,000 and the contribution margin per unit is $3.50, the break-even point is computed as follows:

$$\text{Break-even (units)} = \frac{\text{Fixed costs}}{\text{Contribution margin per unit}}$$
$$= \$35,000 \div \$3.50$$
$$= 10,000 \text{ units}$$

We can use a similar formula to compute the amount of sales dollars needed to break even:

$$\text{Break-even (\$)} = \frac{\text{Fixed costs}}{\text{Contribution margin ratio}}$$

Using the amounts from the previous example gives

$$\text{Break-even (\$)} = \frac{\$35,000}{28\% \ (\text{see page } 123)}$$
$$= \$125,000$$

Graphically, the break-even point can be found by comparing a company's total revenue with its total costs (both fixed and variable). As shown in Exhibit 6-3, the break-even point is the volume at which total revenue is equal to total cost.

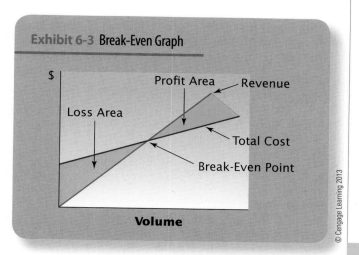

Exhibit 6-3 Break-Even Graph

© Cengage Learning 2013

Break-Even Calculations with Multiple Products

Break-even calculations become more difficult when more than one product is produced and sold. In a multiproduct environment, a manager calculating the break-even point is concerned not so much with the unit sales or the dollar sales of a single product but with the amount of total sales necessary to break even. This requires the calculation of an "average" contribution margin for all the products produced and sold. This calculation in turn requires an estimate of the sales mix: the relative percentage of total units or total sales dollars expected from each product.[1] However, customers (and sales volume) will not always behave in the manner that we predict. For example, although the expected sales product mix may be 600 units of Product A and 400 units of Product B, we can estimate our customers' buying habits only from past experience. If the sales product mix ends up being 700 units of A and 300 units of B, the break-even analysis will change accordingly.

[1]Calculating the optimum mix of products to produce given limited resources and demand constraints is addressed in Chapter 7. The optimum mix will result in the highest overall contribution margin and also the highest overall profit for a company.

> A thorough understanding of fixed and variable costs is necessary before a manager can calculate and understand a break-even analysis.

Now, assume that Happy Daze adds another game to its product line. The company estimates that the new game will achieve sales of approximately 4,500 units. The expected sales product mix (in units) is therefore 64 percent (8,000 ÷ 12,500) old game and 36 percent (4,500 ÷ 12,500) new game. The new game will be priced at $15 per unit and requires $11 of variable production, selling, and administrative costs, so the contribution margin per unit is $4. The game will also require an investment of $15,000 in additional fixed costs. A summary of the price and cost of the old and new games follows:

Happy Daze Game Company				
	Old Game (8,000 units)	Per Unit	New Game (4,500 units)	Per Unit
Sales	$100,000	$12.50	$67,500	$15.00
Less: Variable costs	72,000	9.00	49,500	11.00
Contribution margin	$ 28,000	$ 3.50	$18,000	$ 4.00
Less: Fixed costs	35,000		15,000	
Net operating income (loss)	$ (7,000)		$ 3,000	

The average contribution margin can be found by weighting the contribution margins per unit for the old game and the new game by the relative sales mix and then summing the products. The weighting is as follows:

Old game = 0.64 × $3.50 = $2.24
New game = 0.36 × $4.00 = $1.44

The weighted-average contribution margin for Happy Daze Game Company is therefore $3.68 per game ($2.24 + $1.44). The amount can also be calculated by dividing the total contribution margin earned by selling both games ($46,000) by the total number of units sold (12,500 games) ($46,000 ÷ 12,500 games = $3.68

per game). The break-even formula for a company with multiple products is as follows:

$$\text{Break-even (units)} = \frac{\text{Fixed costs}}{\text{Weighted-average contribution margin per unit}}$$

Happy Daze's break-even point is therefore 13,587 units ($50,000 ÷ $3.68). How is this number interpreted? Remember that the weighted-average contribution margin is dependent on the sales mix. Likewise, the break-even point is dependent on the sales mix. Assuming a sales mix of 64 percent old games and 36 percent new games, Happy Daze must sell 8,696 old games and 4,891 new games to break even:

$$\text{Old game} = 13,587 \times 0.64 = 8,696$$
$$\text{New game} = 13,587 \times 0.36 = 4,891$$

If the sales mix changes to 50 percent old games and 50 percent new games, what will be the impact on the break-even point? What if the sales mix changes to 40 percent old games and 60 percent new games? With the sales mix at 50 percent old and 50 percent new, the weighted-average contribution margin becomes $3.75 [(0.50 × $3.50) + (0.50 × $4.00)]. When the mix changes to 40 percent old and 60 percent new, the weighted-average contribution margin changes to $3.80 [(0.40 × $3.50) + (0.60 × $4.00)]. Notice that when the volume shifts toward selling more of the product with the highest contribution margin, the weighted-average contribution margin increases. As the weighted-average contribution margin increases, the break-even point will decrease.

The break-even point calculated with a weighted-average contribution margin for multiple products is valid only for the sales mix used in the calculation. If the sales mix changes, the break-even point will also change. The more products involved in the sales mix, the more sensitive the calculation becomes to changes in sales mix.

LO4 Target Profit Analysis (Before and After Tax)

The goal of most businesses is not to break even but to earn a profit. Luckily, we can easily modify the break-even formula to compute the amount of sales needed to earn a target profit (before tax). Instead of solving for the sales necessary to earn a net income of zero, we simply solve for the sales necessary to reach a target profit:

Sales − Variable costs − Fixed costs = Target profit (before tax)
$$SP(x) − VC(x) − FC = TP,$$

where

$$SP = \text{Sales price per unit}$$
$$VC = \text{Variable costs per unit}$$
$$FC = \text{Total fixed costs}$$
$$TP = \text{Target profit (before tax)}$$
$$x = \text{Number of units sold}$$

Rearranging and dividing each side by SP − VC, we find the number of units (x) that must be sold to earn a before-tax target profit by dividing the sum of the fixed costs and the target profit by the contribution margin (CM) per unit:

$$(SP − VC)(x) = (FC + TP)$$

$$x = \frac{[FC + TP \text{ (before tax)}]}{CM}$$

Consequently,

$$\text{Sales volume (to reach a target profit before tax)} = \frac{[FC + TP \text{ (before tax)}]}{CM}$$

Happy Daze has decided that it must earn a target profit of $100,000 on sales of the old game or the owners will not want to continue their investment in the business. The question is how many old games does the company have to sell to earn that amount of profit?

$$\text{Sales volume (to reach a target profit before tax)} = \frac{(\$35,000 + \$100,000)}{\$3.50}$$

$$= 38,571 \text{ units (rounded)}$$

Although Happy Daze must sell only 10,000 old games to break even, the company must sell 38,571 old games to reach a before-tax target profit of $100,000. In fact, once we know that Happy Daze's break-even point is 10,000 units, we can directly calculate the sales necessary to reach a target profit of $100,000 by using the CM per unit. Because each additional unit sold (above the break-even point) will contribute $3.50 toward net income, Happy Daze must sell an additional 28,572 units ($100,000 ÷ $3.50) to earn a profit of $100,000.

The multiple-product break-even formula can be modified in a similar fashion to solve for the sales necessary to reach a target profit. In a multiple-product environment,

$$\text{Sales volume (to reach target profit)} = \frac{\text{(Fixed costs + Target profit)}}{\text{Weighted-average contribution margin per unit}}$$

The Impact of Taxes

The payment of income taxes also needs to be considered in the target profit formula. If Happy Daze sells 38,572 games and earns the projected $100,000 in target profit, the company still won't have $100,000 in cash flow to distribute to the owners as dividends, because it must pay income tax on the profit. If we assume that the income tax rate for Happy Daze is 35 percent, the company will have to pay $35,000 in income tax ($100,000 × 35%) and will be left with after-tax profit of $65,000. The after-tax profit can be found by multiplying the before-tax profit by (1 − tax rate). Correspondingly, the before-tax profit equals the after-tax profit divided by (1 − tax rate):

$$\text{Before-tax profit} = \frac{\text{After-tax profit}}{\text{(1 − tax rate)}}$$

If Happy Daze desires to earn an after-tax profit of $100,000, the company must earn a before-tax profit of $153,846 (rounded):

$$\text{Before-tax profit} = \frac{\$100,000}{\text{(1 − 0.35)}} = \$153,846$$

Consequently, Happy Daze must sell 53,956 units of the old game in order to reach a before-tax profit of $153,846 and an after-tax profit of $100,000:

$$\text{Sales volume (to reach an after-tax target profit)} = \frac{\text{(\$35,000 + \$153,846)}}{\$3.50}$$

$$= 53,956 \text{ units}$$

This is confirmed in the following income statement for Happy Daze:

Sales (53,956 units)	$674,450
Less: Variable costs	485,604
Contribution margin	$188,846
Less: Fixed costs	35,000
Income before taxes	$153,846
Less: Income tax @35%	53,846
Net income after tax	$100,000

> The payment of income taxes is an important variable in target profit and other CVP decisions if managers are to understand the bottom-line effect of their decisions.

LO5 Cost Structure and Operating Leverage

As mentioned in Chapter 5, *cost structure* refers to the relative proportion of fixed and variable costs in a company. On the one hand, highly automated manufacturing companies with large investments in property, plant, and equipment are likely to have cost structures dominated by fixed costs. On the other hand, labor-intensive companies such as home builders are likely to have cost structures dominated by variable costs. Even companies in the same industry can have very different cost structures. A company's cost structure is important because it directly affects the sensitivity of that company's profits to changes in sales volume. Consider, for example, two companies that make the same product (furniture), with the same sales and same net income. Company A is highly automated and uses state-of-the-art machinery to design, cut, and assemble its products. Company B is highly labor intensive and uses skilled craftspeople to cut and assemble its products. Contribution margin income statements for both companies are provided in Exhibit 6-4.

Which company would you prefer to run? Although you might opt for Company A, with its high level of

Exhibit 6-4 Contribution Margin Ratio and Operating Leverage

	Company A	Company B
Sales	$200,000	$200,000
Less: Variable costs	40,000	80,000
Contribution margin	$160,000	$120,000
Less: Fixed costs	80,000	40,000
Net operating income	$ 80,000	$ 80,000
Contribution margin ratio	80%	60%
Operating leverage	2.0	1.5

© Cengage Learning 2013

automation and correspondingly higher contribution margin ratio relative to Company B, consider the impact of changes in sales volume on the net income of each company. Although *increasing* sales will benefit Company A more than Company B, what happens when sales *decline*? If sales decline by 10 percent ($20,000), the income of Company A will decline by $16,000 ($20,000 × 80%), whereas the income of Company B will decline by $12,000 ($20,000 × 60%).

A company with a cost structure characterized by a large proportion of fixed costs relative to variable costs will experience wider fluctuations in net income as sales increase and decrease than a company with more variable costs in its cost structure.

Operating Leverage

Operating leverage is a measure of the proportion of fixed costs in a company's cost structure and is used as an indicator of how sensitive profit is to changes in sales volume. A company with high fixed costs in relation to variable costs will have a high level of operating leverage. In this case, net income will be very sensitive to changes in sales volume. In other words, a small percentage increase in sales dollars will result in a large percentage increase in net income. In contrast, a company with high variable costs in relation to fixed costs will have a low level of operating leverage and income will not be as sensitive to changes in sales volume. Operating leverage is computed with the following formula:

$$\text{Operating leverage} = \frac{\text{Contribution margin}}{\text{Net operating income}}$$

In Exhibit 6-4, Company A has an operating leverage of 2.0 ($160,000 ÷ $80,000) whereas Company B has an operating leverage of 1.5 ($120,000 ÷ $80,000). What does this mean? When sales increase (decrease) by a given percentage, the operating income of Company A will increase (decrease) by 2 times that percentage

Operating leverage The contribution margin divided by net income; used as an indicator of how sensitive net income is to a change in sales.

increase (decrease), whereas the operating income of Company B will increase (decrease) by 1.5 times the percentage change in sales. When sales increase by 10 percent, the operating income of Company A will increase by 20 percent, or $16,000 ($80,000 × 20%). In other words, when sales of Company A increase to $220,000, operating income will increase to $96,000. The operating income of Company B will increase by 15 percent, or $12,000 ($80,000 × 15%), to a new operating income of $92,000. Likewise, when sales decrease by 10 percent, the operating income of Company A will decrease by 20 percent whereas the operating income of Company B will decrease by 15 percent.

As summarized in Exhibit 6-5, when operating leverage is high, a change in sales results in large changes in profit. By contrast, when operating leverage is low, a change in sales results in small changes in profits.

Exhibit 6-5 Operating Leverage and the Impact on Profit

	Operating Leverage	
	High	Low
Percent increase in profit with increase in sales	Large	Small
Percent increase in loss with decrease in sales	Large	Small

© Cengage Learning 2013

Unlike measures of contribution margin, operating leverage changes as sales change (see Exhibit 6-6). At a sales level of 1,000 units ($200,000), Company B's operating leverage is 1.5. A 10 percent increase in sales increases net income by 15 percent. At a sales level of 500 units, operating leverage increases to 3.0 and a 10 percent increase in sales will increase net income by 30 percent (3 × 10%). At a sales level of 2,000 units, operating leverage is reduced to 1.2 and a 10 percent increase in sales will increase income by 12 percent.

As a company gets closer and closer to the break-even point, operating leverage will continue to increase and income will be very sensitive to changes in sales.

Exhibit 6-6 Company B—Operating Leverage at Various Levels of Sales

	500 Units	1,000 Units	2,000 Units
Sales	$100,000	$200,000	$400,000
Less: Variable costs	40,000	80,000	160,000
Contribution margin	$ 60,000	$120,000	$240,000
Less: Fixed costs	40,000	40,000	40,000
Net operating income	$ 20,000	$ 80,000	$200,000
Operating leverage	$\frac{\$60,000}{\$20,000} = 3.0$	$\frac{\$120,000}{\$80,000} = 1.5$	$\frac{\$240,000}{\$200,000} = 1.2$

© Cengage Learning 2013

© Yuri Arcurs/Shutterstock.com

> A company operating near the break-even point will have a high level of operating leverage, and income will be very sensitive to changes in sales volume.

For example, when Company B sells 334 units (see Exhibit 6-7), the contribution margin is equal to $40,080, operating income is equal to $80, and operating leverage is equal to 501 ($40,080 ÷ $80). A 10 percent increase in sales at this point will increase net operating income by a whopping 5,010 percent.

Understanding the concepts of contribution margin and operating leverage and how they are used in CVP analysis is very important in managerial decision making. Using these tools, managers can quickly estimate the impact on net income of changes in cost, sales volume, and price.

Exhibit 6-7 Company B—Operating Near the Break-Even Point

Sales (334 units)	$66,800
Less: Variable costs	26,720
Contribution margin	$40,080
Less: Fixed costs	40,000
Net operating income	$ 80
Operating leverage	$\dfrac{\$40,080}{\$80} = 501$

© Cengage Learning 2013

STUDY TOOLS 6

Chapter review card

- ➔ Learning Objective and Key Concept Reviews
- ➔ Key Definitions and Formulas

Online (Located at www.cengagebrain.com)

- ➔ Flash Cards and Crossword Puzzles
- ➔ Games and Quizzes
- ➔ Boyne Resorts Video and E-Lectures
- ➔ Homework Assignments (as directed by your instructor)

1. Contribution Margin LO1

Companies that wish to distribute their income statements to outside parties such as banks must prepare those statements by using the traditional income statement format. These same companies may also prepare contribution margin income statements to more fully understand their costs. The following terms are commonly used in describing contribution margin income statements and related topics:

Gross profit	Decrease
Contribution margin	Fixed costs
Net income	Contribution margin ratio
Variable costs	Increase

Required

Choose the term from the preceding list that most appropriately completes the following statements.

a. Once a company has paid all of its fixed costs, net income increases in an amount equal to _____ for each unit sold to customers.

b. When production and sales are equal, whether a company prepares a traditional income statement or a contribution margin income statement, two numbers do not change. One of these is sales, and the other is _____.

c. _____, the difference between sales and cost of goods sold, is not reported on the contribution margin income statement.

d. For every unit sold, contribution margin will _____ in total.

e. The _____ is computed by dividing the contribution margin by sales dollars.

f. Of these two cost categories, only _____ increases and decreases contribution margin.

g. If a company is unable to increase sales or _____ variable costs, the company can increase net income by reducing _____.

2. What-If Analysis LO2

Mike's Motorcycles has enjoyed several years of business success, but recently the company has seen some indications of a slowdown in sales. The company's owner has decided to increase the advertising budget by 10% and reduce sales prices by 4%. The following partial income statement shows the company's results for the most recent quarter:

Mike's Motorcycles	
Partial Income Statement	
Sales	$800,000
Less: Variable costs	560,000
Contribution margin	240,000
Less: Fixed costs	175,000
Net operating income	$ 65,000

Required

Assuming that the advertising budget was $30,000 for the quarter and was included in the fixed costs, calculate Mike's Motorcycles' new net income or loss if the changes are made. You should assume that the variable costs will not change if Mike implements the preceding changes.

3. Break-Even Analysis LO3

Katie and Holly founded Hokies Plumbing Company after graduating from college. They wanted to be competitive, so they set their rate for house calls at a modest $100. After paying the company's gas and other variable costs of $60, the women thought there would be enough profit. Because they were ready to live life a bit, they set their salaries at $100,000 each. There were no other fixed costs at all.

Required

Calculate the number of house calls that Hokies Plumbing must make to break even.

4. Target Profit Analysis LO4

Nellie's Nursery has the following information related to sales of one popular type of spring flower that is widely sold to landscapers in a multistate region of the country:

Sales price per flower	$ 0.70
Variable costs per flower	0.20
Total fixed costs for the type of flower	$20,000

Required

If Nellie's Nursery wishes to earn a before-tax profit of $30,000 on this type of flower, how many flowers must be sold to landscapers?

5. Operating Leverage LO5

Naru's has the following information for the most recent year:

Naru's	
Partial Income Statement	
Sales	$1,200,000
Less: Variable costs	700,000
Contribution margin	500,000
Less: Fixed costs	250,000
Net operating income	$ 250,000

Required

What is Naru's operating leverage?

6. CVP: The Impact on Income LO2

Eric Ziegler started a lawn-mowing service in high school. He currently prices his lawn-mowing service at $35 per yard. He estimates that variable expenses related to gasoline, supplies, and depreciation on his equipment total $21 per yard.

Required

If Eric wants to increase his price by 40 percent, how many fewer yards can he mow before his net income decreases?

7. CVP: What-If Analysis LO2

Last year, Mayes Company had a contribution margin of 30 percent. This year, fixed expenses are expected to remain at $120,000 and sales are expected to be $550,000, which is 10 percent higher than last year.

Required

What must the contribution margin ratio be if the company wants to increase net income by $15,000 this year?

8. What-If Decisions with Changing Fixed Costs LO2

Walker Company has current sales of $600,000 and variable costs of $360,000. The company's fixed costs are equal to $200,000. The marketing manager is considering a new advertising campaign, which will increase fixed costs by $10,000. She anticipates that the campaign will cause sales to increase by 5 percent as a result.

Required

Should the company implement the new advertising campaign? What will be the impact on Walker's net operating income?

9. Operating Leverage LO2, 5

Burger Queen Restaurant had the following information available related to its operations from last year:

Sales (150,000 units)	$500,000
Variable costs	200,000
Contribution margin	$300,000
Fixed costs	150,000
Net operating income	$150,000

Required

A. What is Burger Queen's operating leverage?

B. If sales increased by 30 percent, what would Burger Queen's net operating income be?

10. Break-Even Analysis LO3

Jimmy's Seafood Restaurant is a family-owned business on the North Carolina coast. In the last several months, the owner has seen a drop-off in business. Last month, the restaurant broke even. The owner looked over the records and saw that the restaurant served 1,000 meals last month (variable cost is $10 per meal) and incurred fixed costs totaling $25,000.

Required

Calculate Callahan's average selling price for a meal.

11. Break-Even Analysis LO3

Lincoln Company sells logs for an average of $18 per log. The company's president, Abraham, estimates that the variable manufacturing and selling costs total $6 per log. Logging operations require substantial investments in equipment, so fixed costs are quite high and total $108,000 per month. Abraham is considering making an investment in a new piece of logging equipment that will increase monthly fixed costs by $12,000.

Required

Assist Abraham by calculating the number of additional logs that must be sold to break even after investing in the new equipment.

12. Break-Even Analysis: Multiproduct Environment LO3

Kim Johnson's company produces two well-known products: Glide Magic and Slide Magic. Glide Magic accounts for 60 percent of her sales, and Slide Magic accounts for the rest. Glide currently sells for $16 per tube and has variable manufacturing and selling costs of $8. Slide sells for just $12 and has variable costs of $9 per tube. Kim's company has total fixed costs of $36,000.

Required

Calculate the total number of tubes that must be sold for Kim's company to break even.

13. Break-Even Analysis: Multiproduct Environment LO3

Donald Tweedt started a company to produce and distribute natural fertilizers. Donald's company sells two fertilizers that are wildly popular: green fertilizer and compost fertilizer. Green fertilizer, the most popular among environmentally minded consumers, commands the highest price and sells for $16 per 30-pound bag. Green fertilizer also requires additional processing and includes environmentally friendly ingredients that increase its variable costs to $10 per bag. Compost fertilizer sells for $12 and has easily acquired ingredients that require no special processing. It has variable costs of $8 per bag. Tweedt's total fixed costs are $35,000. After some aggressive marketing efforts, Tweedt has been able to drive consumer demand to be equal for each fertilizer.

Required

Calculate the number of bags of green fertilizer that will be sold at break-even.

14. Sales to Reach After-Tax Profit LO4

Lockwood Company currently sells its deadbolt locks for $30 each. The locks have a variable cost of $10, and the company's annual fixed costs are $150,000. The company's tax rate is 40 percent.

Required

Calculate the number of locks that must be sold to earn an after-tax profit of $24,000.

15. Target Profit Analysis LO4

Kingman Corp. has been concerned with maintaining a solid annual profit. The company sells a line of fire extinguishers that are perfect for homeowners, for an average of $10 each. The company has perfected its production process and now produces extinguishers with a variable cost of $4 per extinguisher. Kingman's annual fixed costs are $92,000. Kingman's tax rate is 40 percent.

Required

Calculate the number of extinguishers Kingman must sell to earn an after-tax profit of $60,000.

PROBLEMS

16. Multiproduct Break-Even Analysis LO1, 3

Don Waller and Company sells canisters of three mosquito-repellant products: Citronella, DEET, and Mean Green. The company has annual fixed costs of $260,000. Last year, the company sold 5,000 canisters of its mosquito repellant in the ratio of 2:4:4. Waller's accounting department has compiled the following data related to the three mosquito repellants:

	Citronella	DEET	Mean Green
Price per canister	$11.00	$15.00	$17.00
Variable costs per canister	6.00	12.00	16.00

Required

A. Calculate the total number of canisters that must be sold for the company to break even.
B. Calculate the number of canisters of Citronella, DEET, and Mean Green that must be sold to break even.
C. How might Don Waller and Company reduce its break-even point?

17. CVP: What-If Analysis LO1, 2, 3

Hacker Aggregates mines and distributes various types of rocks. Most of the company's rock is sold to contractors who use the product in highway construction projects. Treva Hacker, company president, believes that the company needs to advertise to increase sales. She has proposed a plan to the other managers that Hacker Aggregates spend $100,000 on a targeted advertising campaign. The company currently sells 25,000 tons of aggregate for total revenue of $5,000,000. Other data related to the company's production and operational costs follow:

Direct labor	$1,500,000
Variable production overhead	200,000
Fixed production overhead	350,000
Selling and administrative expenses:	
Variable	50,000
Fixed	300,000

Required

A. Compute the break-even point in units (i.e., tons) for Hacker Aggregates.
B. Compute the contribution margin ratio for Hacker Aggregates.
C. If Treva decides to spend $100,000 on advertising and the company expects the advertising to increase sales by $200,000, should the company increase the advertising? Why or why not?

18. CVP and Break-Even Analysis LO1, 2, 3

Lauren Tarson and Michele Progransky opened Top Drawer Optical seven years ago with the goal of producing fashionable and affordable eyewear. Tarson and Progransky have been very pleased with their revenue growth. One particular design, available in plastic and metal, has become one of the company's best sellers. The following data relate to this design:

	Plastic Frames	Metal Frames
Sales price	$ 60.00	$ 80.00
Direct materials	20.00	18.00
Direct labor	13.50	13.50
Variable overhead	6.50	8.50
Budgeted unit sales	10,000	30,000

Currently, the company produces exactly as many frames as it can sell. Therefore, it has no opportunity to substitute a more expensive frame for a less expensive one. Top Drawer Optical's annual fixed costs are $1.225 million.

Required

Each of the following is an independent situation.
A. Calculate the total number of frames that Top Drawer Optical needs to produce and sell to break even.
B. Calculate the total number of frames that Top Drawer Optical needs to produce and sell to break even if budgeted direct material costs for plastic frames decrease by $10 and annual fixed costs increase by $12,500 for depreciation of a new production machine.

C. Tarson and Progransky have been able to reduce the company's fixed costs by eliminating certain unnecessary expenditures and downsizing supervisory personnel. Now, the company's fixed costs are $1,122,000. Calculate the number of frames that Top Drawer Optical needs to produce and sell to break even if the company sales mix changes to 35 percent plastic frames and 65 percent metal frames.

19. Decision Focus: Basic CVP and Break-Even Analysis LO1, 2, 3

Gigi LeBlanc founded a company to produce a special bicycle suspension system several years ago after her son, who worked for a bicycle delivery service, was hurt in a riding accident. The market's response has been overwhelmingly favorable to the company's new suspension system. Riders report feeling that they experience fewer "unpredictable" bumps than with traditional suspension systems. Gigi made an initial investment of $100,000 and has set a target of earning a 30 percent return on her investment. Gigi expects her company to sell approximately 10,000 suspension systems in the coming year. Based on this level of activity, variable manufacturing costs will be $5 for each suspension system. Fixed selling and administrative expenses will be $2 per system, and other fixed costs will be $1 per system.

Required
A. Calculate the sales price that Gigi LeBlanc's company must charge for a suspension system if she is to earn a 30 percent return on her investment.
B. Calculate the company's break-even point.
C. Assuming that Gigi's company maintains the current activity level, how can she increase her return on investment to 35 percent?

20. Break-Even and Target Profit LO1, 2, 3, 4

Matthew Hagen started his company, The Sign of Things to Come, three years ago after graduating from Upper State University. While earning his engineering degree, Matthew became intrigued by all of the neon signs he saw at bars and taverns around the university. Few of his friends were surprised to see him start a neon sign company after leaving school. Matthew is currently considering the introduction of a new custom neon sign that he believes will sell like hot cakes. In fact, he is estimating that the company will sell 700 of the signs. The new signs are expected to sell for $75 and require variable costs of $25. The new signs will require a $30,000 investment in new equipment.

Required
A. How many new signs must be sold to break even?
B. How many new signs must be sold to earn a profit of $15,000?
C. If 700 new signs are sold, how much profit will they generate?

D. What would be the break-even point if the sales price decreased by 20 percent? Round your answer to the next-highest number.
E. What would be the break-even point if variable costs per sign decreased by 40 percent?
F. What would be the break-even point if the additional fixed costs were $50,000 rather than $30,000?

21. Decision Focus: Break-Even and Target Profit LO1, 2, 3, 4

ZIA Motors is a small automobile manufacturer. Chris Rickard, the company's president, is currently evaluating the company's performance and is considering options that might be effective at increasing ZIA's profitability. The company's controller, Holly Smith, has prepared the following cost and expense estimates for next year, on the basis of a sales forecast of $3,000,000:

Direct materials	$ 800,000
Direct labor	700,000
Factory overhead	750,000
Selling expenses	300,000
Other administrative expenses	100,000
	$2,650,000

After Chris received and reviewed the cost and expense estimates, he realized that Holly had given him all the data without breaking it out into fixed and variable components. He called her, and she told him the following: "Factory overhead and selling expenses are 40 percent variable, but other administrative expenses are 30 percent variable."

Required
A. How much revenue must ZIA generate to break even?
B. Chris Rickard has set a target profit of $700,000 for next year. How much revenue must ZIA generate to achieve Chris's goal?

22. Decision Focus: Multiproduct Break-Even Analysis LO4

Clean Skin Company sells bottles of three face-wash products: Daily Wash, Mud Mask, and Face Cleanser. The company has annual fixed costs of $300,000. Last year, the company sold 7,500 bottles of its face-wash products in the ratio of 4:2:4. Clean Skin's accounting department has compiled the following data related to the three face-wash products:

	Daily Wash	Mud Mask	Face Cleanser
Price per bottle	$12.00	$20.00	$14.00
Variable costs per bottle	2.00	8.00	6.00

A. Calculate the total number of bottles that must be sold for the company to break even.
B. Calculate the number of bottles of Daily Wash, Mud Mask, and Face Cleanser that must be sold to break even.
C. How might Clean Skin Company reduce its break-even point?

CASES

23. CVP Analysis: Target Profit with Constraints
LO1, 2, 4

Moore, Inc., invented a secret process to double the growth rate of hatchery trout. The company manufactures a variety of products related to this process. Each product is independent of the others and is treated as a separate division. Product managers have a great deal of freedom to manage their divisions as they think best. Failure to produce target division income is dealt with severely; however, rewards for exceeding one's profit objective are, as one division manager described them, lavish.

The Morey Division sells an additive that is added to pond water. Morey has had a new manager in each of the three previous years because each manager failed to reach Moore's target profit. Bryan Endreson has just been promoted to manager and is studying ways to meet the current target profit for Morey.

The target profit for Morey for the coming year is $800,000 (20 percent return on the investment in the annual fixed costs of the division). Other constraints on division operations are as follows:

- Production cannot exceed sales, because Moore's corporate advertising stresses completely new additives each year, even though the "newness" of the models may be only cosmetic.
- The Morey selling price may not vary above the current selling price of $200 per gallon, but it may vary as much as 10 percent below $200 (i.e., $180).

Endreson is now examining data gathered by his staff to determine whether Morey can achieve its target profit of $800,000. The data are as follows:

- Last year's sales were 30,000 units at $200 per gallon.
- The present capacity of Morey's manufacturing facility is 40,000 gallons per year, but capacity can be increased to 80,000 gallons per year with an additional investment of $1 million per year in fixed costs.
- Present variable costs amount to $80 per unit, but if commitments are made for more than 60,000 gallons, Morey's vendors are willing to offer raw material discounts amounting to $20 per gallon, beginning with gallon 60,001.

Endreson believes that these projections are reliable, and he is now trying to determine what Morey must do to meet the profit objectives assigned by Moore's board of directors.

Required
A. Calculate the dollar value of Morey's current annual fixed costs.
B. Determine the number of gallons that Morey must sell at $200 per gallon to achieve the profit objective. Be sure to consider any relevant constraints. What if the selling price is $180?
C. Without prejudice to your previous answers, assume that Bryan Endreson decides to sell 40,000 gallons at $200 per gallon and 24,000 gallons at $180 per gallon. Prepare a pro forma income statement for Morey, showing whether Endreson's decision will achieve Morey's profit objectives.

24. Break-Even and Target Profit Analysis
LO1, 2, 3, 4

Boeing Corporation (formerly McDonnell Douglas Corporation) manufactures the C-17, the most flexible jet transport used by the U.S. Air Force. The company originally sold the C-17 for a "flyaway cost" of $175 million per jet. The variable production cost of each C-17 was estimated to be approximately $165 million. When the C-17 was first proposed in 1981, the Air Force expected to eventually purchase 400 jets. However, as of June 2011, only 232 C-17s have been produced and sold.

Production began, and at one point the company was faced with the following situation: With 20 jets finished, a block of 20 more in production, and funding approved for the purchase of a third block of 20 jets, the U.S. Congress began indicating that it would approve funding for the order and purchase of only 20 more jets (for a total of 80). This was a problem for the company because company officials had indicated previously that the break-even point for the C-17 project was around 100 aircraft.

Required
A. Given the previous facts concerning the sales price, variable cost, and break-even point, what were McDonnell Douglas's fixed costs associated with the development of the C-17?
B. What would the income or loss be if the company sold only 80 C-17s?
C. Assume that McDonnell Douglas had been told up front that the Air Force would buy only 80 jets. Calculate the selling price per jet that the company would have to charge to achieve a target profit (before tax) of $10 million per jet.
D. Assuming that the costs and sales price of the jet have remained the same over the years, how much income have McDonnell Douglas and Boeing made from the sale of the C-17?

IT'S ALL ABOUT
THE HOMEWORK!

CengageNOW™ is an **easy-to-use online resource** that helps you **study in less time** to **get the grade you want** – NOW.

CengageNOW™ is your online resource for ACCT2 and features:

- All end-of-chapter homework from the textbook written by the authors
- Additional hints and guidance during homework via enhanced feedback
- Interactive eBook
- Personalized Study Plan, including pre- and post-test assessments, videos, games, E-lectures, and more!

How to Register Your Access Code:

1. Launch a Web browser. Go to login.cengagebrain.com and click on "Create a New Account." Already have an account? Enter your email/password under "Log In."
2. Enter your access code in the field provided, exactly how it appears on your card.
3. New users: Enter your account information and click "Continue."
4. Record your email address and password below, and store it in a secure location for future visits.

[Email Address: _____]
[Password: _____]

ACCT

Relevant Costs and
Product-Planning Decisions

Introduction

As we discussed in Chapter 1, operating activities include a wide range of decisions that managers make on a day-to-day basis. The manager of a company that makes t-shirts must determine the price for a special onetime order. The manager of a restaurant must continually assess the status of its menu items, just as managers of a large manufacturer of stereo components must consider whether to add new products or drop unprofitable ones. Managers of a company that makes bicycles must decide whether to buy tires from another manufacturer or make them internally. Colleges and universities must decide whether to use their own employees to provide janitorial services in dorms and provide food service (cafeterias and so on) to students or to outsource those services to someone else. The manager of a hardware store must determine which products to put on the shelves, and a book publisher must determine which books to publish. All these decisions require relevant, timely accounting information to aid in the decision-making process. As discussed earlier in the book, relevant costs are costs that differ among alternatives—that is, costs that are avoidable or that can be eliminated by choosing one alternative over another. Because sunk costs have already been incurred and cannot be avoided, they are not relevant in decisions. Likewise, future costs that do not differ among alternatives are not relevant, because they cannot be eliminated by choosing one alternative over another. By contrast, opportunity costs are relevant in decision making. In this chapter, we discuss the tools that managers use to make these short-term tactical decisions.

Learning Objectives

After studying the material in this chapter, you should be able to:

LO1 Analyze the pricing of a special order.

LO2 Analyze a decision involving outsourcing labor or making or buying a component.

LO3 Analyze a decision dealing with adding or dropping a product, product line, or service.

LO4 Analyze a decision dealing with scarce or limited resources.

LO5 Describe the theory of constraints and explain the importance of identifying bottlenecks in the production process.

LO6 Analyze a decision dealing with selling a product or processing it further.

LO1 Special Orders

Special-order decisions Short-run pricing decisions in which management must decide which sales price is appropriate when customers place orders that are different from those placed in the regular course of business (onetime sale to a foreign customer, etc.).

Deciding whether to accept a special order is really just a pricing decision. However, **special-order decisions** are short-run decisions. Management must decide what sales price is appropriate when customers place orders that are different

Many of the costs of flying an airliner are fixed and don't vary with the number of passengers on the plane. Understanding cost behavior is critical for companies making everyday decisions such as those discussed in this chapter.

from those placed in the regular course of business (onetime sale to a foreign customer, etc.).[1] These decisions are affected by whether the company has excess production capacity and can produce additional units with existing machinery, labor, and facilities. A special order would almost never be accepted if a company does not have excess capacity. If a company does not have excess capacity, it will have to turn away current customers in order to fill a special order. These current customers may then turn to other companies to fill their needs. Filling a special order under such circumstances may permanently damage the relationship with those customers. Even if a special order is profitable from a quantitative perspective, the impact on customer relations should be considered before deciding whether to accept or reject the order.

[1]Although rush orders and orders requiring special handling, packaging, or different manufacturing specifications might be considered "special orders," these types of decisions are not discussed here.

If customers find other suppliers due to delivery delays, the overall profit of the company might decrease.

Even when a company has excess capacity, qualitative factors must be considered before deciding to accept a special order, particularly if the special-order price is below the price offered to regular customers. In these situations, care must be taken so that regular customers do not feel they have been treated unfairly.

Consider Sunset Airlines, a major regional airline. A large corporation has asked the company to provide 150 seats to San Diego for corporate executives attending a convention. The corporation offers the airline $125 per ticket, although the normal fare for this route is $275. The tickets can be used on only one day, and the executives need to be able to fly on one of five flights offered that day. The aircraft that Sunset Airlines flies on this route carries 180 passengers, so the five scheduled flights provide a capacity of 900 seats. The normal passenger load on the day requested is between 77 percent and 78 percent of available capacity (700 passengers), so Sunset should have plenty of excess capacity (40 seats per plane, or 200 seats total). However, should Sunset accept the special order at the discounted price of $125 per ticket? That depends on the company's objective.

The objective of Sunset Airlines is to maximize income in the short run without reducing income in the long run. The options in this case include selling the tickets for $125 (accepting the special order), letting the marketplace determine the level of sales at a predetermined price of $275, or selling the tickets at another price. An analysis of the options requires that the relevant costs and other factors be identified. The accounting department of Sunset Airlines has provided the following information:

	Per Passenger	Per Round Trip
Cost of meals and drinks	$ 6.50	$ 1,170
Cost of fuel	88.89	16,000
Cost of cabin crew (four flight attendants)	6.11	1,100
Cost of flight crew	11.11	2,000
Depreciation of aircraft	16.67	3,000
Aircraft maintenance	8.33	1,500
Total	$137.61	$24,770

This decision appears to be an easy one, as the special-order price of $125 is less than the total cost per passenger of $137.61. On the basis of the full cost reported by the accounting department, Sunset Airlines would be losing $12.61 on each passenger purchasing a ticket for $125. But would it? To analyze the options in this decision problem correctly, only the *relevant* costs should be considered. In this decision, the only costs that are relevant are those which will differ depending on whether the special order is accepted. Another way to look at the problem is by determining which costs can be avoided by choosing one alternative over the other.

In this case, almost all the costs are fixed with respect to the number of passengers on the plane. In fact, owing to the unique nature of the airline business, most operating costs are fixed. For example, the aircraft will require the same maintenance and flight crew costs regardless of how many passengers are on board. Although the costs of the cabin crew may vary, let us assume that in this situation regulations require four flight attendants for any flight with more than 125 passengers. In this case, four flight attendants are required regardless of whether the plane carries 125 passengers or 180 passengers, so acceptance of the special order will not change the cost of the cabin crew. In essence, the costs of the maintenance, flight crew, and cabin crew are fixed. Likewise, depreciation is a fixed cost. Even fuel costs would not be expected to vary much with the addition of 30 to 40 passengers. In fact, the only cost that would likely vary with the number of passengers on the plane is the small additional cost of meals and drinks. Because Sunset Airlines appears to have plenty of excess capacity (empty seats), any sales price above the variable costs of providing the seats will increase the income of the company. If the cost of meals and drinks is the only variable cost, Sunset should be willing to accept the special order at any price over $6.50. In situations in which excess capacity exists, the general rule is that in order to maximize income, the special-order price must simply be higher than the additional variable costs incurred in accepting the special order.

What if Sunset does not have any excess capacity? If the airline expects to sell all its tickets at the regular price of $275, accepting the special order involves an opportunity cost. The risk in this situation is that the airline will have to turn away full-fare passengers if it accepts the special order. Remember from Chapter 2 that an opportunity cost is the benefit forgone by choosing one alternative over another. If Sunset Airlines accepts the special order, it will forgo the receipt of $268.50 of contribution margin on each ticket (the $275 selling price, less the $6.50 variable cost of meals and drinks). Therefore, it would not be willing to accept a special order for any price below the $275 market price. The relevant costs in this case are the variable cost of $6.50 and the opportunity cost of $268.50.

> *The price of a special order must be higher than the additional variable costs plus any opportunity costs incurred in accepting the special order.*

As demonstrated in Exhibit 7-1, when Sunset Airlines has excess capacity, accepting the special order will result in a profit of $118.50 for each ticket sold. However, when there is insufficient capacity, Sunset Airlines can meet the special order only by turning away full-paying customers and incurring an opportunity cost. As a result, the company would lose $150.00 for each ticket sold.

Exhibit 7-1 The Special-Order Decision

	Excess Capacity	No Excess Capacity
Relevant costs:		
Meals	$ 6.50	$ 6.50
Opportunity costs from lost ticket revenue (Contribution margin lost)	0	$ 268.50
Total relevant costs	$ 6.50	$ 275.00
Special-order ticket price	125.00	125.00
Profit (loss) from accepting special order	$118.50	$(150.00)

© Cengage Learning 2013

Fixed costs can be relevant to a special-order decision when they change depending on the option chosen. For example, let's consider the case of flight attendants again. Instead of requiring four flight attendants for any flight with more than 125 passengers, let's assume that regulations require one flight attendant for every 35 passengers. Then, whereas four attendants are sufficient for a flight of 140 passengers, adding 30 additional passengers will require the addition of an extra flight attendant at a cost of $275, or $9.17 per additional passenger. Assuming that excess capacity exists, the special-order price would need to exceed $15.67 to be acceptable to Sunset Airlines.

Instead of 150 extra passengers flying on the five regularly scheduled flights, assume that Sunset Airlines has an additional airplane that is currently idle but can be chartered for the flight. In this case, fuel costs, salaries of the flight and cabin crews, and maintenance costs are

likely to be relevant, but depreciation is still not relevant. It is important to note that determining what is relevant and what is not depends on the specific situation.

A number of qualitative factors must also be considered in special-order decisions. First, if it accepts the special order on the basis of expected excess capacity but its passenger-load predictions are wrong, Sunset Airlines may have to turn away passengers who would otherwise pay full fare. If that happens and these passengers turn to competing airlines, Sunset Airlines faces the potential of losing long-term customers. Second, the impact of selling seats at a discount on those customers paying regular fares must be considered.

LO2 Outsourcing and Other Make-or-Buy Decisions

The decision to outsource labor or to purchase components used in manufacturing from another company rather than to provide the services or to produce the components internally affects a wide range of manufacturing, merchandising, and service organizations. For example, a university can contract with an outside company to provide janitorial and repair services for on-campus dormitories, or it can provide those services by using university employees. A local florist can provide payroll processing internally, or it can hire a CPA to provide those services. Hewlett-Packard can make carrying cases for its calculators internally, or it can buy them from an outside supplier.

Strategic Aspects of Outsourcing and Make-or-Buy Decisions

An analysis of outsourcing and **make-or-buy decisions** requires an in-depth analysis of relevant quantitative and qualitative factors and a consideration of the costs and benefits of outsourcing and vertical integration. For example, Sunset Airlines might consider outsourcing the

> **Make-or-buy decisions** Short-term decisions to outsource labor or to purchase components used in manufacturing from another company rather than to provide services or produce components internally.

maintenance function on its airplanes to an outside organization. Suppose that Sunset Airlines now pays all maintenance personnel $20 per hour plus 30 percent for fringe benefits. Total labor costs are $26 per hour. An outside agency offers to perform the maintenance for $22 per hour plus the cost of parts and supplies. From a quantitative perspective, this is a money-saving move. Let's assume that Sunset Airlines has 100 maintenance personnel who all work 40 hours per week. The savings from outsourcing would be $16,000 per week, or $832,000 per year. However, Sunset Airlines needs to consider a number of qualitative factors before making this decision. Is the quality of work the same? What are the risks associated with outsourcing maintenance if poor-quality work results in an airplane accident? How will outsourcing maintenance affect other employees of the airline, including ticket agents and ground service personnel? Other employees may become demoralized and worry about losing their own jobs. They may be less motivated to do the best job possible, leading to quality problems, operational slowdowns, and even employee strikes. They may very well leave the company if and when a better opportunity presents itself.

Vertical integration is accomplished when a company is involved in multiple steps of the value chain. In an extreme example, the same company might own a gold mine, a manufacturing facility to produce gold jewelry, and a retail jewelry store. Most companies operate with some form of vertical integration (they market the products they produce, or they develop the products they manufacture), but the extent of integration varies greatly from company to company and, indeed, from product to product within a company. All elements of the value chain—from initial research and development through design, manufacture, marketing, distribution, and customer service—must be considered in decisions about making or buying components needed for production of the final product.

There are advantages to making components internally instead of buying them from an outside supplier. Vertically integrated companies are not dependent on suppliers for the timely delivery of services or components needed in the production process or for the quality of those services and components. However, vertically integrated companies have disadvantages as well.

There are disadvantages to making parts internally. The supplier may be able to provide a higher quality part for less cost. For this reason, computer manufacturers do not produce their own computer chips. The producers of those chips produce in such large quantities that they can provide the chips more cheaply than the companies could produce them internally. Chip manufacturers also spend billions of dollars on research and development to ensure high-quality and high-performance chips.

The Make-or-Buy Decision

Birdie Maker Golf Company produces custom sets of golf clubs that are advertised to be far superior to other golf clubs on the market. Birdie Maker's golf clubs sell for $1,000 per set, and the company currently sells about 1,000 sets each year. Birdie Maker currently manufactures all the golf clubs in the set but is considering acquiring the putter from Ace Putters, Inc., a manufacturer of custom putters. The purchased putter would be customized for Birdie and matched to the other clubs, so customers should not be able to distinguish it from the rest of the clubs in the set. The costs incurred in the manufacture of the putter are as follows:

	Total (1,000 putters)	Per Unit
Direct materials	$ 5,000	$ 5.00
Direct labor	9,000	9.00
Variable manufacturing overhead	3,000	3.00
Fixed manufacturing overhead	9,500	9.50
Total cost	$26,500	$26.50

The expected production for the year is 1,000 putters, so the full cost of each putter is $26.50 ($26,500 ÷ 1,000). Ace Putters is offering to sell the putters to Birdie Maker for $25 per putter. Although this decision seems to be a very easy one ($25 is less than $26.50), the decision is more complex than it appears.

Although Birdie Maker would like to maximize income by producing or buying the putter at the lowest possible cost, the company is also very concerned about the quality of the putter and the potential impact of the putter on sales of other clubs.

As we discussed in Chapter 1, relevant costs are those which can be avoided by choosing one alternative over another. The key, then, is to analyze the costs of manufacturing the putter with an eye toward identifying those costs which can be *avoided* or eliminated if the putter is purchased from Ace Putters. If Birdie

Vertical integration Accomplished when a company is involved in multiple steps of the value chain.

A product should continue to be made internally if the avoidable costs are less than the additional costs that will be incurred by buying or outsourcing.

making this decision, the company must be convinced that it can manufacture a putter of acceptable quality and that it will be able to keep up with any technological changes affecting the manufacture of the putter in the future.

Sometimes, fixed costs are relevant to the analysis. For example, assume that $5,500 of the fixed manufacturing cost is for specialized machinery that is currently being leased under a month-to-month contract. If the putters are purchased from Ace Putters, the equipment will be returned to the lessor. That means that $5.50 of the fixed manufacturing costs ($5,500 ÷ 1,000 putters) is avoidable if the putter is bought from Ace Putters and that only $4.00 of fixed overhead will be incurred if the putter is purchased. The resulting analysis is shown in Exhibit 7-3.

Maker continues to manufacture the putter internally, the company will incur costs of $26,500. If Birdie Maker decides to purchase the putters from Ace Putters, Birdie Maker will incur costs of $25,000 ($25 × 1,000 putters) *plus* any manufacturing costs that are not avoidable. Although the costs related to direct materials, direct labor, and variable manufacturing overhead are variable (and thus avoidable), fixed manufacturing overhead is not.

So, although it appears on the surface that Birdie Maker can save $1,500 ($26,500 − $25,000) by buying the putters from Ace Putters, it will in reality cost Birdie an additional $8 per club, or $8,000, as you can see in Exhibit 7-2. Note that the fixed overhead of $9.50 per unit is incurred regardless of the decision to make or buy. We could

Exhibit 7-3 The Make-or-Buy Decision with Relevant Fixed Costs

	Cost to Make (Per Unit)	Cost to Buy (Per Unit)
Direct materials	$ 5.00	
Direct labor	9.00	
Variable manufacturing overhead	3.00	
Fixed manufacturing overhead	9.50	$ 4.00
Purchase price from Ace Putters		25.00
	$26.50	$29.00

© Cengage Learning 2013

Exhibit 7-2 The Make-or-Buy Decision

	Cost to Make (Per Unit)	Cost to Buy (Per Unit)
Direct materials	$ 5.00	
Direct labor	9.00	
Variable manufacturing overhead	3.00	
Fixed manufacturing overhead	9.50	$ 9.50
Purchase price from Ace Putters		25.00
	$26.50	$34.50

© Cengage Learning 2013

have come to the same conclusion by comparing the $17 variable costs of making putters ($5.00 of direct materials + $9.00 of direct labor + $3.00 of variable overhead) with the outside purchase price of $25. What is the best solution? From a purely quantitative perspective, Birdie Maker would maximize its income by choosing to continue making putters. However, before

Although it remains preferable to make the putters internally, the cost difference shrinks to $2.50 per putter instead of $8.00. In this situation, Birdie Maker must carefully consider the qualitative factors relevant to the decision, including the quality of the putters, the importance of keeping up with changing technology, and the dependability of the supplier.

Another way to look at the analysis is to compare the total avoidable costs with the purchase price. In this case, if the putter is purchased, the avoidable costs include the costs of direct materials ($5.00), direct labor ($9.00), variable manufacturing overhead ($3.00), and $5.50 per putter for fixed manufacturing overhead. The $22.50 of total avoidable costs should then be compared with the $25.00 purchase price. Regardless of how you choose to look at the problem, Birdie Maker is better off by $2.50 per putter if it continues making the putter.

Onshoring and Outsourcing

After decades of increased globalization accompanied by moving U.S. manufacturing offshore, **Caterpillar** and other U.S. companies are moving jobs back to the United States. Some of the "onshoring" is a result of problems overseas including political unrest, high shipping costs, complicated logistics, and problems with production quality. In addition, a weak U.S. dollar has made it costlier to import products from overseas. At the same time, in the face of a stronger yen, which makes Japanese goods more costly, Japanese manufacturers are moving more of their production abroad. For example, in 2010, 71 percent of **Nissan's** production was conducted abroad. **Toyota's** foreign production amounted to 57 percent and **Sony's** 55 percent.

Source: "Caterpillar Joins 'Onshoring' Trend," by Kris Maher and Bob Tita, *The Wall Street Journal*, March 12, 2010, and "Japanese Firms Send Work Overseas," by Mariko Sanchanta, *The Wall Street Journal*, October 24, 2010.

Opportunity costs should also be considered in make-or-buy decisions. Using the same facts as in Exhibit 7-2, consider the impact of renting out for $10,000 the factory space that is now used to manufacture putters.

Exhibit 7-4 shows that, by effectively reducing the cost to purchase the putters by $10,000, or $10 per putter, the effective cost to purchase the putter is reduced to $24.50, so Birdie Maker would be better off by $2.00 per putter by purchasing the putters.

Once again, as an alternative, we could treat the $10 opportunity cost as a relevant cost of making the putter internally. In that case, the total relevant cost of making the putter increases to $36.50, compared with the purchase price of $34.50. In addition to quality and reliability considerations, other factors to consider in this case include the long-term potential for renting out the unused space, potential other uses of the space, and so on.

LO3 The Decision to Drop a Product or a Service

The decision to drop a product or a service is among the most difficult that a manager can make. Like other decisions discussed in this chapter, the decision whether to drop an old product or product line hinges on an analysis of the relevant costs and qualitative factors affecting the decision. Qualitative factors are sometimes more important than a focus that is solely on income.

Clayton Herring Tire Company is considering dropping one of the 10 models of tires that it manufactures and sells. Sales of a special mud-and-snow tire have been disappointing, and on the basis of the latest

Exhibit 7-4 The Make-or-Buy Decision with Relevant Opportunity Costs

	Cost to Make (Per Unit)	Cost to Buy (Per Unit)
Direct materials	$ 5.00	
Direct labor	9.00	
Variable manufacturing overhead	3.00	
Fixed manufacturing overhead	9.50	$ 9.50
Purchase price from Ace Putters		25.00
Rental of unused factory space		(10.00)
	$26.50	$24.50

© Cengage Learning 2013

© iStockphoto.com/quavondo

A product should be dropped when the fixed costs that are avoided exceed the contribution margin that is lost.

financial information (shown in the following table), the tires appear to be losing money:

	Mud and Snow	All Other Tires	Total
Sales	$25,500	$150,000	$175,500
Less: Direct materials	12,000	50,600	62,600
Direct labor	5,000	30,000	35,000
Variable overhead	2,000	12,000	14,000
Contribution margin	$ 6,500	$ 57,400	$ 63,900
Less: Fixed overhead	7,000	21,000	28,000
Net operating income	$ (500)	$ 36,400	$ 35,900

Chris (the CEO of Clayton Herring Tire) asked Karen (the controller) why the mud-and-snow tires were losing money. Karen explained that the tires required more machine time than other tires required. Consequently, they were allocated a greater portion of fixed overhead. Chris then asked Karen whether she would recommend that production of the mud-and-snow tires be discontinued. Karen explained that, although it appears that net operating income for the company would increase to $36,400 if the mud-and-snow tires were dropped from the product line, further analysis had revealed that a large portion of the fixed overhead allocated to

the tires resulted from the rental of machines used to make the tires. On further inspection, Karen determined that these machines were used to make several models of tires and could not be disposed of if the mud-and-snow tires were dropped. Consequently, $5,000 of the fixed costs allocated to mud-and-snow tires would have to be reallocated to other product lines. These costs would remain even if the mud-and-snow tires were discontinued. On the basis of this new information, Karen prepared another report for Chris, showing the effect of dropping the mud-and-snow tires (see Exhibit 7-5).

Exhibit 7-5 The Decision to Drop a Product

	With Mud-and-Snow Tires	Without Mud-and-Snow Tires	Difference
Tire sales	$175,500	$150,000	
Less: Direct materials	62,600	50,600	
Direct labor	35,000	30,000	
Variable overhead	14,000	12,000	
Contribution margin	$ 63,900	$ 57,400	$(6,500)
Less: Fixed overhead	28,000	26,000	2,000
Net operating income	$ 35,900	$ 31,400	$(4,500)

© Cengage Learning 2013

Why would the income for the company decrease by $4,500 (from $35,900 to $31,400) if the mud-and-snow tires were dropped, even though they appear to be losing money? The answer is that the contribution margin decreases by $6,500, whereas fixed costs decrease by only $2,000 if the tires are dropped. Only

$2,000 of the fixed costs are avoidable and relevant to this decision. The other $5,000 of fixed costs originally allocated to the mud-and-snow tires would simply be reallocated to one or more of the other models of tires. A simple way to analyze this problem is to compare the contribution margin lost if the product line is dropped with the fixed costs that are avoided. In this case, Clayton Herring Tire Company loses $6,500 of contribution margin while saving (avoiding) only $2,000 of fixed overhead (see Exhibit 7-5).

If the machine used to produce the tires were used only for making these tires and could be disposed of, resulting in a savings of $5,000, how much would income increase (decrease) if the mud-and-snow tires were discontinued? (Assume that the other $2,000 of fixed overhead could still be avoided.) Although the contribution margin would still be reduced by $6,500, the entire $7,000 of fixed costs would be avoided, resulting in an overall increase in income of $500.

But what about qualitative factors in this decision? As we discussed earlier, qualitative factors are sometimes more important than quantitative factors in these decisions. For example, what impact will discontinuing the sale of mud-and-snow tires have on sales of the remaining product lines? Tire retailers are likely to prefer purchasing tires from a company offering a full line of tires. Retailers that cannot offer mud-and-snow tires may have difficulty selling tires to individuals in the winter.

LO4 Resource Utilization Decisions

A company faces a **constraint** when its capacity to manufacture a product or to provide a service is limited in some manner. A **resource utilization decision** requires an analysis of how best to use a resource that is available in limited supply. The limited resource may be a rare material or component used in manufacturing a product, but more likely is related to the time required to make a product or provide a service or to the space required to store a product. For example, building custom furniture requires skilled craftspeople, who may be

Constraint A restriction that occurs when the capacity to manufacture a product or to provide a service is limited in some manner.

Resource utilization decision A decision requiring an analysis of how best to use a resource that is available in limited supply.

in short supply. Deciding how best to utilize the limited labor time available is a resource utilization decision. The manufacture of golf clubs requires special machinery. If a company has only one machine that can be used to manufacture shafts for putters and other clubs, machine time may be a limited resource.

What is likely to be a limited resource in a grocery store? Grocery stores and other retail stores have limited shelf space. The resource utilization decision involves an analysis of how best to use this limited resource. Which products should be carried? How many? Although it may seem easy to conclude that stores should carry those products which are most profitable, decisions like this are complicated by the fact that the multitudes of products carried in large stores require different amounts of shelf space. Multipacks of paper towels take up several times the shelf space required for a box of macaroni and cheese. Although the multipack of paper towels may be more profitable per unit, this information has to be balanced with the requirement of more shelf space. A decision concerning how much of each product to have on hand must also consider the impact of qualitative factors, such as customer reaction if a product is not carried and the impact on sales of other products.

Resource utilization decisions are typically short-term decisions. In the short run, such resources as machine time, labor hours, and shelf space are fixed and cannot be increased. However, in the long run, new machines can be purchased, additional skilled laborers can be hired, and stores can be expanded. When faced with short-run constraints, managers must focus on the contribution margin provided by each product per unit of limited resource rather than on the profitability of each product.[2]

Birdie Maker produces two types of golf balls: the pro model and the tour model. The balls are sold to retailers in cartons containing 360 balls (30 boxes containing 4 sleeves per box, with each sleeve holding 3 balls). Both models are made with the same machines. The constraint, or limited resource, is the number of hours that the machines can run. The pro model golf ball takes 30 minutes of machine time to produce 360 balls, whereas the tour ball takes 45 minutes to produce the same number. The difference in production time results mainly from the different materials used in construction. Although weekend golfers purchase both models, professionals on the PGA Tour use the tour

[2]Decisions involving limited resources, or constraints, often include multiple constraints, such as storage space, machine time, labor hours, and even dollars available to invest. When we have more than one constraining factor, the decision-making process becomes more complicated and is facilitated by the use of computerized linear programming models. A discussion of linear programming is beyond the scope of this text.

model. The relevant data concerning the two models follows:

	Pro Model	Tour Model
Sales price (per carton)	$450	$540
Less: Direct materials	200	265
Direct labor	50	50
Variable overhead	50	75
Contribution margin	$150	$150

In this case, the contribution margin per carton is the same for both the pro model and the tour model. Other things being equal, each model is equally profitable. However, if we compute the contribution margin per unit of the constraint, or limited resource, we see that each carton of pro model balls has a contribution margin of $300 per hour of machine time whereas each carton of tour model balls has a contribution margin of $200 per hour of machine time (see Exhibit 7-6).

Exhibit 7-6 The Resource Utilization Decision

Sales price (per carton)	$450	$540
Less: Direct materials	200	265
Direct labor	50	50
Variable overhead	50	75
Contribution margin	$150	$150
Required machine time (in hours)	÷ 0.50	÷ 0.75
Contribution margin per machine hour	$300	$200

If demand is not a factor and qualitative considerations are not important, Birdie Maker will maximize profit by producing and selling only pro model golf balls. However, if demand for either product is limited, the company must decide on the optimal product mix. For example, if machine time is limited to 300 hours per month, the demand for the pro model is 400 cartons per month, and the demand for the tour model is 150 cartons, how much of each product should Birdie Maker produce? Although Birdie Maker has the capacity to produce 600 cartons (300 hours ÷ 0.5 hour) of pro model balls, it can sell only 400 cartons. Producing 400 cartons requires 200 machine hours, leaving 100 additional machine hours per month for the production of

© iStockphoto.com/Duncan Babbage

tour balls. Thus, Birdie Maker can maximize income by producing 400 cartons of pro balls and 133 cartons of tour balls each month.

Qualitative factors, including the impact of discontinuing the sale of the tour ball, must also be considered. Visibility of the tour ball on the professional tour may be a valuable source of advertising, contributing to sales of the pro model.

Other options include adding machines to increase the amount of available machine hours or reducing the machine time needed to produce a carton of balls. Maximizing profits by focusing on the constraint itself in order to loosen it is the focus of the theory of constraints.

LO5 The Theory of Constraints

The **theory of constraints** is a management tool for dealing with constraints. The theory of constraints identifies **bottlenecks** in the production process. Bottlenecks limit throughput, which can be thought of as the amount of finished goods that result from the production process. In the previous example, machine time is a bottleneck that limits the amount of throughput. In the airline industry, certain tasks performed while the aircraft is on the ground may delay departure and increase the turnaround time for the plane.

The key to the theory of constraints is identifying and managing bottlenecks. Once a bottleneck is identified, management must focus its time and resources on relieving the bottleneck. Utilizing resources to increase the efficiency of an operation that is not a bottleneck

Theory of constraints A management tool for dealing with constraints; identifies and focuses on bottlenecks in the production process.

Bottlenecks Production-process steps that limit throughput or the number of finished products that go through the production process.

> When faced with a limited resource, a company will maximize profit by making the product with the highest contribution margin per unit of the limited resource.

Bottlenecks must be identified and managed if a business is to be successful in overcoming constraints.

from Ace Putters. Options for relieving this bottleneck include requiring Ace Putters to reduce its delivery time. If Ace cannot speed up delivery, Birdie Maker might consider using another supplier or perhaps making the putters in-house instead of outsourcing them. Reducing the time spent manufacturing irons or woods will not reduce overall delivery time until the bottleneck with the putters is relieved.

will rarely increase throughput. For example, increasing the efficiency of machines with excess capacity in a factory or reducing the flight time for an airline will result in very limited increases in throughput (if any) until bottlenecks are relieved.

In Exhibit 7-7, Birdie Maker has discovered that delays in the delivery of golf clubs to customers result from the extra time it takes to order and receive putters

LO6 Decisions to Sell or Process Further

The decision whether to sell a product as is or to process it further to generate additional revenue is another common management decision. For

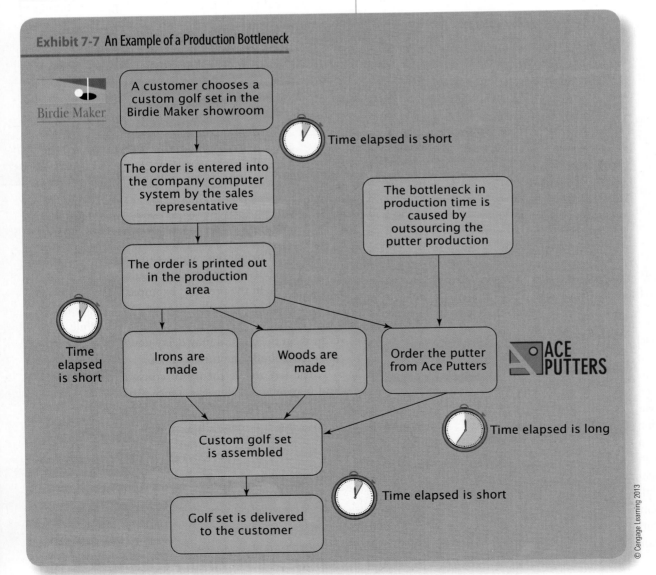

Exhibit 7-7 An Example of a Production Bottleneck

© Cengage Learning 2013

> *A product should be processed further if the additional (incremental) revenue exceeds the additional (incremental) cost of processing.*

example, furniture manufacturers may sell furniture unassembled and unfinished, assembled and unfinished, or assembled and finished (see Exhibit 7-8). The key in deciding whether to sell or process further is that all costs which are incurred up to the point where the decision is made are sunk costs and therefore not relevant.

The relevant costs are the incremental or additional processing costs. Managers should compare the additional sales revenue that can be earned from processing the product further with the additional processing costs. If the additional revenue is greater than the additional costs, the product should be processed further. If the additional costs exceed the revenues, the product should be sold as is.

For example, assume that unassembled and unfinished tables cost $100 to produce and can be sold for $150. The company is considering selling assembled and finished tables for $225 each. Additional assembly and finishing costs of $45 per table would be required. The following table sums up the situation:

	Unassembled and Unfinished Tables	Assembled and Finished Tables	Incremental Revenue and Cost
Sales price	$150	$225	$75
Cost to produce	100	145	45
Increase in income from further processing			$30

As shown in the table, the additional (incremental) revenue from selling assembled and finished furniture is $75 per unit. As long as the additional (incremental) costs of assembly and finishing are less than $75, the company will maximize profits by further processing of the tables. Assuming that it has sufficient demand for the assembled and finished tables, the company will make an additional $30 per table ($75 incremental revenue less $45 incremental costs) by selling assembled, finished tables. Note that the $100 cost of producing the unassembled and unfinished table is not relevant in the analysis, because it is a sunk cost. It is incurred regardless of the decision whether to sell unassembled and unfinished tables or to process further.

Exhibit 7-8 The Decision to Sell or Process Further

Unassembled and unfinished furniture → Assembled but unfinished furniture → Assembled and finished furniture

Compare costs to assemble with additional revenue from selling assembled furniture

Compare costs to finish with additional revenue from selling assembled and finished furniture

© Cengage Learning 2013

Chapter review card

- ➔ Learning Objective and Key Concept Reviews
- ➔ Key Definitions and Formulas

Online (Located at www.cengagebrain.com)

- ➔ Flash Cards and Crossword Puzzles
- ➔ Games and Quizzes
- ➔ Navistar International Video and E-Lectures
- ➔ Homework Assignments (as directed by your instructor)

BRIEF EXERCISES

1. Special-Order Pricing Decision LO1

Rick Nicotera sells special terra-cotta trays that are perfect for planting in dry climates. The trays have per-unit variable production costs of $15 and fixed costs of $4 (based on 8,000 units). Rick's company has excess capacity to accept a special order of up to 500 units.

Required
What is the minimum price that could be charged for this special order?

2. Make-or-Buy Decision LO2

Switzer Corporation makes motorcycle engines. The company's records show the following unit costs to manufacture part #61645:

Direct materials	$12
Direct labor	15
Variable overhead	20
Fixed overhead	10

Another manufacturer has offered to supply Switzer Corporation with part #61645 for a cost of $50 per unit. Switzer uses 1,000 units annually.

Required
If Switzer accepts the offer, what will be the short-run impact on income?

3. Basic Drop-a-Segment Decision LO3

Finlay Grace Sullivan & Company has two sales offices: one located in Portland, Maine, and one in Portsmouth, New Hampshire. Management is considering dropping the Portland office. The company's records report the following information:

	Portland	Portsmouth
Sales	$40,000	$50,000
Direct costs:		
Variable	15,000	25,000
Fixed	10,000	10,000

Required
What will be the effect on income if the Portland office is eliminated and half of its fixed costs are avoided?

4. Resource Utilization Decisions and Constraints LO4, 5

Companies regularly face limited resources. Maximizing the utilization of a scarce resource is a key to business success. The following statements relate to resource utilization decisions and the theory of constraints.

a. The goal of a resource utilization decision is to minimize the contribution margin per unit of the limited resource.

b. Limited resources likely include money and raw materials, but do not likely include machine capacity or direct labor time available.

c. Decision makers should consider qualitative factors when making resource utilization decisions.

d. One of the most effective ways of increasing throughput is to increase the efficiency of a nonbottleneck operation.

e. Bottlenecks are always a result of poor management decisions.

Required

Indicate whether each of the preceding statements is true or false.

5. Decision to Sell or Process Further   LO6

Swine Enterprises produces hams from locally raised pigs. The cost of getting the meat ready for market is $1 per pound. Hams weigh an average of 12 pounds and sell for $1.50 per pound. The company can smoke the hams for an additional $0.50 per pound. The smoked hams would sell for $2.25 per pound.

Required

Should the company smoke the hams? What if the selling price were $1.75 per pound?

EXERCISES

6. Special-Order Pricing Decision   LO1

Bob Johnson, Inc., sells a lounging chair for $25 per unit. It incurs the following costs for the product: direct materials, $11; direct labor, $7; variable overhead, $2; and fixed overhead, $1. The company has received a special order for 50 chairs. The order would require rental of a special tool for $300. Bob Johnson, Inc., has sufficient idle capacity to produce the chairs for this order.

Required

Calculate the minimum price per chair that the company could charge for this special order if management requires a $500 minimum profit on any special order.

7. Special-Order Decision: Relevant Costs   LO1

Husky Sports manufactures footballs. The forecasted income statement, not including any special orders, is as follows:

	Total	Per Unit
Sales	$4,000,000	$10.00
Manufacturing cost of goods sold	3,200,000	8.00
Gross profit	$ 800,000	$ 2.00
Selling expenses	300,000	0.75
Net income	$ 500,000	$ 1.25

Fixed costs included in the preceding forecasted income statement are $1,200,000 in manufacturing cost of goods sold and $100,000 in selling expenses. Husky Sports received a special order for 50,000 footballs at $7.50 each and has sufficient capacity to manufacture 50,000 more footballs.

Required

Calculate the relevant unit cost that Husky Sports should consider in evaluating this special order.

8. Special-Order Pricing Decision   LO1

Great Falls Brewery's regular selling price for a case of beer is $15. Variable costs are $8 per case, and fixed costs total $2 per case, based on production of 250,000 cases. The fixed costs remain unchanged within a relevant range of 50,000 to 300,000 cases. After sales of 180,000 cases were projected for the year, a special order was received for an additional 30,000 cases.

Required

Calculate Great Falls Brewery's minimum acceptable selling price for the special order of 30,000 cases.

9. Special Order: Effect on Income   LO1

Suckert Company manufactures lacrosse sticks. The company's capacity is 4,500 sticks per month; however, it currently sells only 3,000 sticks per month. Long Meadow Sports has offered to buy 700 lacrosse sticks for $50 each from Suckert. Normally, the company sells its sticks for $65. Suckert's accounting records report the cost of each stick to be $40, including fixed costs of $20 each.

Required

If Suckert were to accept Long Meadow's offer, what would be the impact on Suckert's income?

10. Make or Buy: Effect on Income   LO2

Engstrom, Inc., uses 10,000 pounds of a specific component in the production of life preservers each year. Presently, the component is purchased from an outside supplier for $11 per pound. For some time now, the factory has had idle capacity that could be utilized to make the component. Engstrom's costs associated with manufacturing the component are as follows:

Direct materials per lb	$3
Direct labor per lb	3
Variable overhead per lb	2
Fixed overhead per unit (based on annual production of 10,000 lb)	2

In addition, if the component is manufactured by Engstrom, the company will hire a new factory supervisor at an annual cost of $32,000.

Required

If Engstrom chooses to make the component instead of buying it from the outside supplier, what would be the change, if any, in the company's income?

11. Basic Make-or-Buy Decision LO2

Ice Cold Corporation makes dorm-size refrigerators. The company's records show the following unit costs to manufacture part #15498:

Direct materials	$15
Direct labor	18
Variable overhead	23
Fixed overhead	13

Another manufacturer has offered to supply Ice Cold Corporation with part #15498 for a cost of $60 per unit. Ice Cold uses 1,000 units annually.

Required

If Ice Cold Corporation accepts the offer, what will be the short-run impact on income?

12. Outsourcing Decision LO2

Humphrey Sports is considering outsourcing its maintenance work. The total labor cost for the maintenance department is $150,000, and the company has an offer from Robyn Maintenance to provide the service for $125,000. The maintenance equipment currently used by Humphrey cannot be sold and has annual depreciation of $10,000. The overhead allocated to the maintenance department is $20,000 per year and would not be avoidable. If the maintenance work is outsourced, all of Humphrey's maintenance workers will be terminated.

Required

On the basis of the information given, what should Humphrey Sports do with respect to outsourcing its maintenance work?

13. Outsourcing Decision LO2

State Hospital is considering outsourcing its maintenance work. The total labor cost for the maintenance department is $200,000, and the hospital has an offer from Jenny Maintenance to provide the service for $150,000. The maintenance equipment currently used cannot be sold and has annual depreciation of $10,000. The overhead allocated to the maintenance department is $20,000 per year and would not be avoidable.

Required

On the basis of the information given, what should State Hospital do with respect to outsourcing its maintenance work?

14. Impact of Dropping a Product Line LO3

Langer Company has three products (A, B, and C) that use common facilities. The relevant data concerning these three products follow:

	A	B	C	Total
Sales	$10,000	$30,000	$ 40,000	$ 80,000
Variable costs	5,000	20,000	25,000	50,000
Contribution margin	$ 5,000	$10,000	$ 15,000	$ 30,000
Fixed costs	5,000	15,000	30,000	50,000
Operating loss	$ 0	$ (5,000)	$(15,000)	$(20,000)

Required

If fixed costs allocated to product line C are not avoidable and if product line C is dropped, what will be the impact on income?

15. Impact of Dropping a Product Line LO3

Woodruff, Ltd., sells three rockers (Unfinished, Stained, and Painted) that use common facilities. The relevant data concerning these three products follow:

	Unfinished	Stained	Painted	Total
Sales	$10,000	$30,000	$ 40,000	$ 80,000
Variable costs	5,000	20,000	25,000	50,000
Contribution margin	$ 5,000	$10,000	$ 15,000	$ 30,000
Fixed costs	5,000	15,000	30,000	50,000
Operating loss	$ 0	$ (5,000)	$(15,000)	$(20,000)

Required

If $15,000 of the fixed costs allocated to the Painted rockers are avoidable and the company drops Painted rockers from its product line, what will be the impact on income?

16. Limited-Resource Decision LO4

Kerrie Velinsky Productions produces music videos in two lengths on separate compact discs. The company can sell its entire production of either product. The relevant data for these two products follow:

	Compact Disc 1	Compact Disc 2
Machine time per CD (hours)	2	5
Selling price per CD	$10	$20
Variable costs per CD	$2	$4

Total fixed overhead is $240,000. The company has only 100,000 machine hours available for production. Because of the constraint on the maximum number of machine hours, Kerrie must decide which CD to produce to maximize the company's income.

Required

Which product should the company select to maximize operating profits?

17. Maximizing Contribution Margin Given a Limited Resource LO4

Soft Mattress, Inc., produces both a queen- and a king-size soft mattress. Selected data related to each product follow:

	Queen	King
Sales price	$525.00	$635.00
Direct materials	$350.00	$365.00
Direct labor	$75.00	$85.00
Variable overhead	$25.00	$35.00
Stuffing hours per mattress	1	3

Only two employees are trained to stuff the secret soft ingredient into the mattresses. They have a maximum of 4,000 total stuffing hours per year.

Required

A. What is the contribution margin per limited resource for each type of bed?
B. Assuming that demand is not a constraint, how many queen- and king-size mattresses should be produced by Soft Mattress, Inc.?

18. Maximizing the Contribution Margin Given a Limited Resource LO4

Footballs Galore produces both pigskin and artificial leather footballs that are stitched by one of two machines. Selected data related to producing a batch of 10 footballs for each product follow:

	Pigskin	Artificial Leather
Sales price	$500.00	$250.00
Direct materials	$150.00	$50.00
Direct labor	$45.00	$40.00
Variable overhead	$30.00	$20.00
Stitching hours	2	1

Only two machines are capable of stitching the footballs. They have a maximum capacity of 3,000 total stitching hours per year.

Required

A. What is the contribution margin per limited resource for each type of football?
B. Assuming that demand is not a constraint, how many pigskin and artificial leather footballs should be produced by Footballs Galore?

19. Sell-or-Process Further Decision LO6

Ryan Miller Company manufactured 500 units of a defective product. The per-unit manufacturing costs of the products were as follows:

Direct materials	$30
Direct labor	24
Variable overhead	10
Fixed overhead	12

Each product normally sells for $100. The company can rework each unit of product at a cost of $20 for direct materials, $20 for direct labor, and $2 for variable overhead. In addition, fixed overhead will be applied at the rate of 75 percent of direct labor cost. Alternatively, the company could sell the defective products "as is" for a selling price of $70.

Required

What should management do to maximize profits?

20. Sell-or-Process Further Decision LO6

DePaulis Furniture Manufacturers makes unfinished furniture for sale to customers from its own stores. Recently, the company has been considering taking production one step further and finishing some of the furniture to sell as finished furniture. To analyze the problem, DePaulis is going to look at only one product, a very popular dining room chair. The chair can be produced now for $65 and sells for $85 unfinished. If DePaulis were to finish the chair, the cost would increase to $90, but the company could sell the finished chairs for $125.

Required

Should DePaulis finish the chairs or continue to sell them unfinished? Show computations to support your decision.

PROBLEMS

21. Special-Order Decision: Qualitative Factors LO1

Lindsey Smith, Inc., has the following cost structure for the upcoming year:

Sales (20,000 units @ $25)	$500,000
Manufacturing costs:	
Variable	$10 per unit
Fixed	$180,000
Marketing and administrative costs:	
Variable	$5 per unit
Fixed	$20,000

Required

A. What is the expected level of profit?
B. Should the company accept a special order for 1,000 units at a selling price of $20 if variable marketing expenses associated with the special order are $2 per unit? What will be the incremental profit if the order is accepted?
C. Suppose that the company received a special order for 3,000 units at a selling price of $19 with no variable marketing expenses. What would be the impact on profit?
D. Assume that if the special order were accepted, all the regular customers would be aware of the price paid for the special order. Would that influence your decision? Why?

22. Special-Order Decision: Qualitative Factors LO1

The Belik Company has the capacity to produce 5,000 units per year. Its predicted operations for the year are as follows:

Sales (4,000 units @ $20 each)	$80,000
Manufacturing costs:	
Variable	$5 per unit
Fixed	$10,000
Marketing and administrative costs:	
Variable	$1 per unit
Fixed	$8,000

The accounting department has prepared the following projected income statement for the coming year for your use in making decisions:

Sales		$80,000
Variable costs:		
Manufacturing ($5 × 4,000)	$20,000	
Marketing ($1 × 4,000)	4,000	24,000
Contribution margin		$56,000
Fixed costs:		
Manufacturing	$10,000	
Marketing	8,000	18,000
Operating profit		$38,000

Required

A. Should the company accept a special order for 500 units at a selling price of $8? Assuming that there are no variable marketing and administrative costs for this order and that regular sales will not be affected, what is the impact of this decision on company profits?

B. Suppose that the preceding order has a onetime setup fee of $1,000. Should the special order be accepted? Why or why not?

C. What other factors should be considered, and how would they affect your decision to accept the special order?

D. Disregarding questions A through C, suppose that regular sales would be reduced by 200 units if the special order were accepted. What impact would this have on the company's decision?

23. Make-or-Buy Decision: Relevant Costs and Qualitative Factors LO2

Jain Simmons Company needs 10,000 units of a certain part to be used in production. If Jain Simmons buys the part from Sullivan Company instead of making the part itself, Jain Simmons could not use its present facilities for another manufacturing activity. Sixty percent of the fixed overhead applied will continue regardless of what decision is made.

The following quantitative information is available regarding the situation presented:

Cost to make the part:	
Direct materials	$ 6
Direct labor	24
Variable overhead	12
Fixed overhead applied	15
	$57
Cost to buy the part:	$53

Required

A. In deciding whether to make or buy the part, what are Jain Simmons's total relevant costs to make the part?

B. Which alternative (make or buy) is more desirable for Jain Simmons and by what amount?

C. Suppose that Jain Simmons Company is in an area of the country with high unemployment and that it is unlikely that displaced employees will find other employment. How might that affect your decision?

24. Make-or-Buy Decision: Relevant Costs and Qualitative Factors LO2

Tony's Electronics Corporation needs 12,000 units of a certain part to be used in the production of its karaoke machines. If Tony's Electronics buys the part from Scott Company instead of making it, Tony's could not use the present facilities for another manufacturing activity. Sixty percent of the fixed overhead applied will continue regardless of what decision is made. The following quantitative information is available regarding the situation presented:

Cost to make the part:	
Direct materials	$ 5
Direct labor	25
Variable overhead	12
Fixed overhead applied	15
	$57
Cost to buy the part:	$45

Required

A. In deciding whether to make or buy the part, what are Tony's total relevant costs to make the part?

B. Which alternative (make or buy) is more desirable for Tony's and by what amount?

C. Suppose that Tony's Electronics Corporation is in an area of the country with high unemployment and that it is unlikely that displaced employees will find other employment. How might that affect your decision?

25. Make or Buy Decision: Qualitative Factors LO2

The Hemp Division of West Company produces rope. One-third (10,000 feet) of the Hemp Division's output is sold to the Hammock Products Division of West; the remainder (20,000 feet) is sold to outside customers. The Hemp Division's estimated sales and cost data for the fiscal year ending September 30 are as follows:

	Hammock Products	Outsiders Sales
Sales	$15,000	$40,000
Variable costs	10,000	20,000
Fixed costs	3,000	6,000
Gross margin	$ 2,000	$14,000
Unit sales	10,000	20,000

The Hemp Division has an opportunity to purchase 10,000 feet of identical-quality rope from an outside supplier at a cost of $1.25 per unit on a continuing basis. Assume that the Hemp Division cannot sell any additional product to outside customers.

Required

A. Should West allow its Hemp Division to purchase the rope from the outside supplier? Why or why not?
B. Assume that the Hemp Division is now at full capacity and that sufficient demand exists to sell all production to outsiders at present prices. What is the differential cost (benefit) of producing the rope internally?
C. Assume that the quality of the rope is found to be of a lesser, but still satisfactory, quality. What factors should be considered?
D. Assume that the quality of the rope is found to be of questionable quality but that the price is $1.00 per unit. What factors should be considered in the decision?

26. Temporary Suspension of Operations: Qualitative Factors LO3

Smoluk Mining Company currently is operating at less than 50 percent of capacity. The management of the company expects sales to drop below the present level of 10,000 tons of ore per month very soon. The sales price per ton is $3 and the variable cost per ton is $2. Fixed costs per month total $10,000.

Management is concerned that a further drop in sales volume will generate a loss and, accordingly, is considering the temporary suspension of operations until demand in the metals markets rebounds and prices once again rise. Over the past year, management has implemented a cost-reduction program that has been successful in reducing costs to the point that suspending operations appears to be the only viable alternative. Management estimates that suspending operations would reduce fixed costs by $6,000 per month.

Required

A. Why does management estimate that the fixed costs will persist at $4,000 even though the mine is temporarily closed?
B. At what sales volume will the loss be greater or less than the shutdown cost of $4,000 per month?
C. List any qualitative factors that you think management should consider in this decision, and discuss the potential impact of each factor on the decision.

27. Decision Focus: Eliminating Unprofitable Segments LO3

Casagrande Company is currently operating at 80 percent capacity. Worried about the company's performance, Mike, the general manager, reviewed the company's operating performance. Following are sales and related cost information about Casagrande, in millions of dollars:

	Segment			
	North	South	East	West
Sales	$30	$40	$20	$10
Less variable costs	12	8	21	8
Contribution margin	$18	$32	$ (1)	$ 2
Less fixed costs	9	12	6	3
Operating profit (loss)	$ 9	$20	$ (7)	$ (1)

Required

A. What is the current operating profit for the company as a whole?
B. Assume that all fixed costs are unavoidable. If Mike eliminated the unprofitable segments, what would be the new operating profit for the company as a whole?
C. What options does management have to maximize profits?
D. What qualitative factors do you think management should consider before making this decision? What impact could these qualitative factors have on the decision?

28. Decision Focus: Eliminating Unprofitable Segments LO3

Big Bucks Casino is currently operating at 80 percent capacity. Worried about the casino's performance, Grey, the general manager, reviewed the company's operating performance. Following are revenue and cost data relating to Big Bucks Casino, in millions of dollars:

	Segment			
	Card Tables	Slots	Craps	Roulette
Revenues	$25	$50	$15	$35
Less variable costs	12	20	9	15
Contribution margin	$13	$30	$ 6	$20
Less fixed costs	8	15	8	10
Operating profit (loss)	$ 5	$15	$ (2)	$10

Required

A. What is the current operating profit for the company as a whole?
B. Assume that all fixed costs are unavoidable. If Grey eliminated the unprofitable segments, what would be the new operating profit for the company as a whole?
C. What options does management have to maximize profits?
D. What qualitative factors do you think management should consider before making this decision? What impact could these qualitative factors have on the decision?

29. Limited-Resource Decision LO4, 5

Trailblazers produces two types of hiking boots: the men's boot and the women's boot. The two types of boots are similar, except that the women's boots are more stylish. Both types are made with the same machines. It takes 15 minutes of machine time to produce one pair of men's boots, whereas it takes 30 minutes of machine time to produce one pair of women's boots. The difference in production time results mainly from the different materials used in construction. The relevant data concerning the two types of boots are as follows:

	Men's	Women's
Sales price (per pair)	$35	$40
Less: Direct materials	10	13
Direct labor	4	4
Variable overhead	8	10
Contribution margin	$13	$13
Required machine time	¼ hour	½ hour

Required

A. If the amount of machine time available to Trailblazers is limited, which boot should be produced first?
B. If the total machine time available is 640 hours per month and the demand for each type of boot is 1,000 pairs per month, how many of each type should be produced to maximize profit? (Round your answer to the nearest pair.)
C. What other factors should be considered in this decision, and how would they affect the decision?

30. Limited-Resource Decision LO4, 5

Robinson's Grocery Store is a small corner grocery store in rural Montana, and shelf space is very limited. Management must decide how to allocate shelf space for salsa. Robinson's has been given an opportunity to sell a very popular brand of salsa produced by Bobby Tutor, a popular rock star. The unique bottle is taller and thinner than bottles from the other popular brands on the market, increasing its visibility on the shelf.

Following are sales and cost data on the new salsa and the three other brands presently sold by Robinson's:

	Salsa #1	Salsa #2	Salsa #3	New Salsa
Sales price per jar	$2.50	$2.75	$3.00	$4.00
Cost to purchase	1.25	1.35	1.50	3.20
Contribution margin	$1.25	$1.40	$1.50	$0.80
Bottles per foot of shelf space	10	9	7	12

Required

A. Rank the salsas on the basis of expected revenue if each is given 10 feet of shelf space and all bottles are expected to be sold.
B. On the basis of the information given, which salsa should get the most shelf space? Why?
C. What qualitative factors should be considered in this decision? How would these factors affect the decision?

31. Limited-Resource Decision LO4, 5

Sun Devil Golf Balls produces two types of golf balls: the pro model and the tour model. The balls are sold to retailers in cartons containing 360 balls (30 boxes containing 4 sleeves per box, with each sleeve holding 3 balls). Both models are made with the same machines. It takes 15 minutes of machine time to produce 360 pro model golf balls, whereas it takes 30 minutes to produce the same number of tour model balls. The difference in production time results mainly from the different materials used in construction. The relevant data concerning the two models are as follows:

	Pro Model	Tour Model
Sales price (per carton)	$500	$590
Less: Direct materials	200	265
Direct labor	50	50
Variable overhead	50	75
Contribution margin	$200	$200
Required machine time	1/4 hour	1/2 hour

Required

A. If the amount of machine time available to Sun Devil Golf Balls is limited, which golf ball should be produced in the larger quantity?
B. If the total machine time available is 110 hours per month and the demand for each model of golf ball is 108,000 balls per month, how many of each model should be produced to maximize profit? (Round your answer to the nearest carton.)
C. What other factors should be considered in this decision, and how would they affect the decision?

32. Sell-or-Process Further Decision LO6

DeBaca's Fish House buys fish from local fishermen and sells the fish to the public from its booth at the public market. Lately, the fish house has had a number of requests for smoked salmon and has decided to investigate whether that would be a profitable item. The salmon DeBaca's buys now costs the company $2 per pound. DeBaca's would have to take the new salmon to a smokehouse to have it smoked, which would increase the total cost to $3.25 for each pound of salmon. The salmon currently sells for $5.50 per pound but would sell for $6.50 per pound if it were smoked.

Required

A. On the basis of the facts given, would it be profitable to smoke the salmon? Why or why not?
B. If the cost of the smoking process could be reduced by $0.50 per pound, would it be profitable to smoke the salmon?
C. What qualitative factors should be considered before making a final decision?

CASES

33. Comprehensive Make-or-Buy Decision LO1

Foggy Mountain Company manufactures several styles of banjos. Management estimates that during the second quarter of the current year, the company will be operating at 80 percent of normal capacity. Because Foggy Mountain wants to increase utilization of the plant, the company has decided to consider special orders for its products.

Foggy Mountain has just received inquiries from a number of companies concerning the possibility of a special order and has narrowed the decision to two companies. The first inquiry is from CCR Company, which would like to market a banjo very similar to one of Foggy Mountain's. The CCR banjo would be marketed under CCR's own label. CCR has offered Foggy Mountain $57.50 per banjo for 20,000 banjos to be shipped by June 1. The cost data for the Foggy Mountain banjo are as follows:

Regular selling price per banjo	$90.00
Costs per unit:	
Raw material	$25.00
Direct labor (5 hours @ $6)	30.00
Overhead (2.5 machine hours @ $4)	10.00
Total costs	$65.00

According to the specifications provided by CCR, the banjo that the company wants requires less expensive raw material. Consequently, the raw material would cost only $22 per banjo. Foggy Mountain has estimated that all remaining costs would not change.

The second special order was submitted by Seager & Buffet Company for 7,500 banjos at $75 per banjo. These banjos would be marketed under the Seager & Buffet label and also would be shipped by June 1. However, the Seager & Buffet model is different from any banjo in the Foggy Mountain product line. The estimated per-unit costs are as follows:

Raw material	$32.50
Direct labor (5 hours @ $6)	30.00
Overhead (5 machine hours @ $4)	20.00
Total costs	$82.50

In addition, Foggy Mountain would incur $15,000 in additional setup costs and would have to purchase a $22,500 special machine to manufacture these banjos; this machine would be discarded once the special order has been completed.

The Foggy Mountain manufacturing capabilities are limited in the total machine hours available. The plant capacity under normal operations is 900,000 machine hours per year, or 75,000 machine hours per month. The budgeted fixed overhead for the year is $2,160,000. All manufacturing overhead costs are applied to production on the basis of machine hours at $4 per hour.

Foggy Mountain will have the entire second quarter to work on the special orders. Management does not expect any repeat sales to be generated from either special order. Company practice precludes Foggy Mountain from subcontracting any portion of an order when special orders are not expected to generate repeat sales.

Required

A. What is the excess capacity of machine hours available in the second quarter?
B. What is the variable overhead rate per machine hour?
C. On the basis of the preceding information and your analysis, would you accept CCR's offer?
D. What is the unit contribution margin per banjo for the Seager & Buffet order?
E. What is the actual gain (loss) incurred by accepting Seager & Buffet's offer?

34. Decision Focus: Comprehensive Make or Buy LO2, 4

Avery, Inc., is a wholesale distributor supplying a wide range of moderately priced sporting equipment to large chain stores. About 60 percent of Avery's products are purchased from other companies, and the remainder of the products are manufactured by Avery. The company has a plastics department that is currently manufacturing molded fishing tackle boxes. Avery is able to manufacture and sell 8,000 tackle boxes annually, making full use of its direct labor capacity at available workstations. The following table presents the selling price and costs associated with Avery's tackle boxes:

Selling price	$86.00
Costs per box:	
Molded plastic	$ 8.00
Hinges, latches, handle	9.00
Direct labor ($15/hour)	18.75
Manufacturing overhead	12.50
Selling and administrative cost	17.00* 65.25
Profit per box	$20.75

*Includes $6 per unit of fixed distribution costs.

Because Avery believes that it could sell 12,000 tackle boxes, the company has looked into the possibility of purchasing the tackle boxes from another manufacturer. Craig Products, a supplier of quality products, could provide up to 9,000 tackle boxes per year at a per unit price of $68. Variable selling and administrative costs of $4 per unit will be incurred if the tackle boxes are purchased from Craig Products.

Bart Johnson, Avery's product manager, has suggested that the company could make better use of its plastics department by purchasing the tackle boxes and manufacturing skateboards. To support his position, Johnson has a market study that indicates an expanding market for skateboards and a need for additional suppliers. Johnson believes that Avery could expect to sell 17,500 skateboards annually at a price of $45.00 per skateboard. Johnson's estimate of the costs to manufacture the skateboards is as follows:

Selling price per skateboard		$45.00
Costs per skateboard:		
Molded plastic	$5.50	
Wheels, plastic	7.00	
Direct labor ($15/hour)	7.50	
Manufacturing overhead	5.00	
Selling and administrative cost	9.00*	34.00
Profit per skateboard		$11.00

*Includes $6 per unit of fixed distribution costs.

In the plastics department, Avery uses direct labor hours as the base for applying manufacturing overhead. Included in the manufacturing overhead for the current year is $50,000 factorywide, fixed manufacturing overhead that has been allocated to the plastics department.

Required

A. Define the problem faced by Avery on the basis of the facts as presented.
B. What options are available to Avery in solving the problem?
C. Rank the options in order of preference on the basis of quantitative factors.
D. What qualitative factors should Avery consider in the decision?
E. Should Avery consider the potential liability that comes with selling skateboards? It has been shown that skateboards are responsible for 25 deaths per year and more than 500 serious accidents. Would that change your decision to make skateboards?

REVIEW!

ACCT2 puts a multitude of study aids at your fingertips. After reading the chapters, check out these resources for further help:

• **Review Cards,** found in the back of your book, include all learning objectives, key terms and definitions, and visual summaries for each chapter.

• **Online Printable Flash Cards** give you additional ways to check your comprehension of key accounting concepts.

• **Animations**, found in the CengageNOW™ Personalized Study Plan, offer dynamic, visual examples based around key concepts. One example is the "Make-or-Buy Decision" based on Birdie Maker Golf Company in Chapter 7.

• **Interactive games** include Beat the Clock, a timed quiz for each chapter, and Quiz Bowl—a Jeopardy-style game that helps test your knowledge and understanding of the critical concepts within the chapter.

Find these and other great resources online as part of **CengageNOW™** for **ACCT2.**

Long-Term
(Capital Investment) Decisions

Introduction

Capital investment decisions are made by all types and sizes of organizations and involve the purchase or lease of new machinery and equipment and the acquisition or expansion of facilities used in a business. A decision by a local florist to purchase or lease a new delivery van is a capital investment decision, as is the decision to upgrade the computer system at a law firm. A decision by **Wal-Mart** to build and open a new store and a decision by **Ford** to invest in new automated production equipment are capital investment decisions. Long-term purchasing decisions such as these often involve large sums of money and considerable risk because they commit companies to a chosen course of action for many years.

Two key factors to be considered in a long-term purchasing decision are the return of the investment and the return on the investment—in other words, whether the benefits of the investment exceed its cost. The costs and benefits include both qualitative and quantitative elements. Qualitative costs and benefits include the reactions of employees, customers, and the community to changes in location; the impact of automation on displaced employees; and quality improvements that result from new equipment. Quantitative costs and benefits include large initial outlays of cash, the need for future repairs and maintenance, the potential for increased sales, and reductions in production and other costs.

Because capital investments involve large sums of money and last for many years, a quantitative analysis of the costs and benefits of capital investment decisions must consider the **time value of money**. The focus of the time value of money is on cash flow, not accounting net income. Accounting net income and cash flow are often not the same. Accounting net income is calculated on the basis of the accrual of income and expenses rather than on the receipt and payment of cash. Whereas measurements of both income and cash flow are useful to managers, investors, and creditors, time-value-of-money calculations are based on the concept that a dollar received today is worth more than a dollar received in the future and thus focus on the cash flow of an organization.

Capital investment decisions Long-term decisions involving the purchase or lease of new machinery and equipment and the acquisition or expansion of facilities used in a business.

Time value of money The concept that a dollar received today is worth more than a dollar received in the future.

Learning Objectives

After studying the material in this chapter, you should be able to:

LO1 Use the NPV method to evaluate capital investment decisions.

LO2 Use the IRR method to evaluate capital investment decisions.

LO3 Distinguish between screening and preference decisions and use the profitability index to evaluate preference decisions.

LO4 Evaluate the impact of taxes on capital investment decisions.

LO5 Use the payback method to evaluate capital investment decisions, and discuss the limitations of the method.

> *Companies routinely use techniques that take into account the time value of money in order to evaluate the benefits and costs of investing in new equipment.*

Typical cash outflows include the original investment in the project, any additional working capital needed during the life of the investment, repairs and maintenance needed for machinery and equipment, and additional operating costs that may be incurred. Typical cash inflows include projected incremental revenues from the project, cost reductions in operating expenses, the salvage value (if any) of the investment at the end of its useful life, and the release of working capital at the end of a project's useful life.

With the exception of the initial cash outflow associated with the investment, other cash inflows and outflows are likely to be estimates. The extended time involved in long-term purchasing decisions makes the projection of these cash inflows and outflows difficult at best. The impact of uncertainty on capital investment decisions and the use of sensitivity analysis are discussed in more detail later in the chapter.

LO1 Net Present Value

The **net present value (NPV)** method requires the choice of a discount rate to be used in the analysis. Many companies choose to use the **cost of capital**. The cost of capital represents what the firm would have to pay to borrow (issue bonds) or to raise funds through equity (issue stock) in the financial marketplace. In NPV analysis, the **discount rate** serves as a minimum required rate of return, or a hurdle rate—the return that the company feels must be earned in order for any potential investment to be profitable. For purposes of this chapter, we will refer to this discount rate as the minimum required rate of return rather than the hurdle rate, although, in practice, it is commonplace to use both terms. The discount rate is often adjusted to reflect the risk and the uncertainty of cash flows that are expected to occur many years in the future.

Computing net present value requires comparing the present value of all cash inflows associated with a project with the present value of all cash outflows:

> NPV = Present value of cash inflows −
> present value of cash outflows

If the present value of the inflows is greater than or equal to the present value of the outflows (the NPV is greater than or equal to zero), then the investment provides a return at least equal to the discount rate (the minimum required rate of return) and the investment is acceptable. If the present value of the outflows is greater than the present value of the inflows, then the NPV will be negative and the investment will not be acceptable, because it provides a return less than the discount rate.

To illustrate NPV decisions, let's discuss Bud and Rose's Flower Shop, which is considering the purchase of a new refrigerated delivery van that will cost $50,000. Having the van will allow the

If the present value of cash inflows is greater than or equal to the present value of cash outflows (the NPV is greater than or equal to zero), then the investment provides a return at least equal to the discount rate (the minimum required rate of return) and the investment is acceptable.

company to accept large flower orders for weddings, receptions, and so on and is expected to increase cash income from sales (net of increased expenses) by $14,000 per year for six years. The van is not expected to have any salvage value at the end of the six years. Bud and Rose have a minimum required rate of return of 12 percent and use that as their discount rate.

The only cash outflow in this case is the initial purchase price of $50,000. The annual cash inflow of $14,000 can most easily be viewed as an ordinary annuity for purposes of calculating present value. NPV calculations using present-value factors are as follows:[1]

Transaction	Cash Flow	Year	Amount	12% Factor	Present Value
Purchase of refrigerated van	Initial investment	Now	$(50,000)	1.0000	$(50,000.00)
Sales of flowers	Annual cash income (net of increased expenses)	1–6	14,000	4.1114	57,559.60
	Net present value				$ 7,559.60

The built-in function =PV(12%,6,−14000) in Microsoft Excel returns a present value for the cash inflows that is equal to $57,559.70 (see Exhibit 8-1). The $0.10 difference results from rounding.

Because the NPV is positive, the delivery van should be purchased. Although the positive NPV tells us that the return on the investment is at least 12 percent, it does not tell us exactly what the return is. Is it 14 percent, 16 percent, or an even higher number? We could find the

Net present value (NPV) A technique for considering the time value of money whereby the present value of all cash inflows associated with a project is compared with the present value of all cash outflows.

Cost of capital What the firm would have to pay to borrow (issue bonds) or raise funds through equity (issue stock) in the financial marketplace.

Discount rate Used as a hurdle rate, or minimum rate of return, in calculations of the time value of money; adjusted to reflect risk and uncertainty.

[1]Extended present value tables can be found at the end of the Review Cards.

© iStockphoto.com/Sean Locke

© Cengage Learning 2013

Exhibit 8-1 Finding the Present Value by Using the PV Function in Excel

Function Arguments | ?| X|

PV

Rate	12%		= 0.12
Nper	6		= 6
Pmt	-14000		= -14000
Fv			= number
Type			= number

= 57559.70253

Returns the present value of an investment: the total amount that a series of future payments is worth now.

Pmt is the payment made each period and cannot change over the life of the investment.

Formula result = $57,559.70

Help on this function   OK   Cancel

actual return by trial and error. Remember, an NPV of zero means that an investment is earning exactly the discount rate used in the analysis. Increasing the discount rate to 14 percent reduces the NPV to $4,442. Going up to 16 percent reduces the NPV to $1,586, but going up to 18 percent results in a negative NPV of $1,034. The true yield of the investment must be somewhere between 16 percent and 18 percent and would be close to 17 percent. The present value of an annuity table can also be used to find the true rate of return for the delivery van.

As discussed in the appendix at the end of the text, the present value of an annuity (PVA) can be found with the formula

$$PVA = R(DFA_{n,r})$$

where R is the annual cash inflow, DFA is the discount factor for an ordinary annuity, and n is the number of periods. Then, knowing R, DFA, and n, we can solve indirectly for the interest rate r:

$$PVA_{6,??} = \$14{,}000(DFA_{6,??})$$

$$\$50{,}000 = \$14{,}000(DFA_{6,??})$$

$$DFA_{6,??} = 3.5714$$

Using the present value of annuity table in the back of your textbook and looking at the row for an n of 6, we see that a DFA of 3.5714 is about halfway between an r of 16 percent and an r of 18 percent.

LO2 Internal Rate of Return

The **internal rate of return (IRR)** is the actual yield, or return, earned by an investment. We can find the yield of an investment in a number of ways. One way of looking at IRR is that it is the discount rate that equates the present value of all cash inflows to the present value of all cash outflows. In other words, IRR is the discount rate that makes NPV = 0.

Although a present-value table *can* be used to calculate IRR, it is inconvenient in this case because the true yield lies between the rates provided in the table. However, IRR can easily be calculated with a financial calculator or Microsoft Excel (see appendix at the end of the text). In Excel, =RATE(6,−14000,50000,0,0) generates an annual yield of 17.191 percent (see Exhibit 8-2).

Internal rate of return (IRR) The actual yield, or return, earned by an investment.

The internal rate of return (IRR) is the actual yield, or return, earned by an investment.

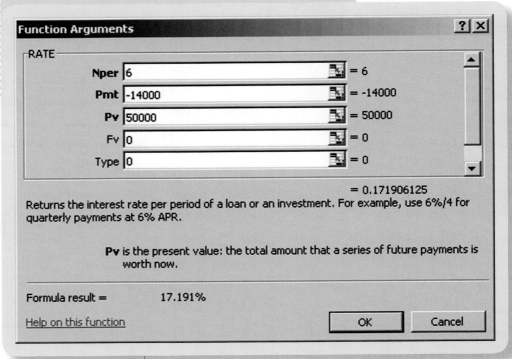

Exhibit 8-2 Finding the Internal Rate of Return by Using the Rate Function in Excel

Function Arguments ?×

RATE
Nper | 6 | = 6
Pmt | -14000 | = -14000
Pv | 50000 | = 50000
Fv | 0 | = 0
Type | 0 | = 0

= 0.171906125

Returns the interest rate per period of a loan or an investment. For example, use 6%/4 for quarterly payments at 6% APR.

Pv is the present value: the total amount that a series of future payments is worth now.

Formula result =   17.191%

Help on this function   OK   Cancel

© Cengage Learning 2013

The Problem of Uneven Cash Flows

Calculations of net present value and internal rate of return get significantly more difficult when cash inflows and outflows are more numerous and when cash flows are uneven. Consider an example in which Harbourside Hospital is contemplating the purchase of a new X-ray machine for cardiac care patients. Harbourside is a nonprofit hospital and has a minimum required rate of return of 10 percent. In addition, one of the hospital's objectives is to improve the quality of care provided to cardiac patients in the area. Currently, patients have to travel as far as 100 miles to a hospital equipped with this type of X-ray machine. The machine will cost $1,200,000 plus installation

costs of another $50,000 and will have a useful life of approximately six years. Owing to frequent changes in technology, the machine would have little salvage value at the end of its useful life; Harbourside expects that it can sell the machine to a hospital in a developing country for $20,000. The machine is expected to increase revenues by $400,000 per year but will require the hiring of two new technicians at $40,000 per year each, and it will require maintenance and repairs averaging $20,000 per year, resulting in a net annual cash flow of $300,000 ($400,000 − $80,000 − $20,000). In addition, the machine is expected to require the installation of a new X-ray tube at the end of years 3 and 5 at a cost of $50,000 for each tube. The detailed NPV analysis follows.

Transaction	Cash Flow	Year	Amount	10% Factor	Present Value
Purchase of new machine	Initial investment	Now	$(1,250,000)	1.0000	$(1,250,000)
Increased patient revenue less related expenses	Net annual cash inflows	1–6	300,000	4.3553	1,306,590
Repairs and maintenance	Cash outflow	3	(50,000)	0.7513	(37,565)
Repairs and maintenance	Cash outflow	5	(50,000)	0.6209	(31,045)
Sale of machine	Cash inflow	6	20,000	0.5645	11,290
	Net present value				$ (730)

In this case, NPV is negative, indicating that the investment would earn Harbourside less than its minimum required rate of return of 10 percent. Using Microsoft Excel's IRR function, we calculate the internal rate of return of the X-ray machine as 9.9796 percent (see Exhibit 8-3).

Key Assumptions of Discounted Cash Flow Analysis

In both the net present value and internal rate of return, two simplifying assumptions are made when discounting cash flows to their present value. The first is that all cash flows are assumed to occur at the end of each period (typically at the end of a year). Although most cost reductions and cash inflows resulting from increased sales actually occur uniformly throughout the year, this assumption greatly simplifies present-value calculations. The second assumption is that all cash inflows are immediately reinvested in another project or investment. This assumption is analogous to the immediate reinvesting of dividends in a stock investment. The rate of return assumed to be earned on the reinvested amounts depends on whether the NPV or the IRR method is used. Under the NPV method, cash inflows are assumed to be reinvested at the discount rate used in the analysis. Under the IRR method, cash inflows are assumed to be reinvested at the internal rate of return of the original investment.

Exhibit 8-3 Finding the Internal Rate of Return by Using the IRR Function in Excel

© Cengage Learning 2013

Although the quantitative analysis indicates that the investment is not acceptable, Harbourside should also consider qualitative factors in its decision. In this case, because improving the quality of patient care is very important to Harbourside, it may well approve the investment even though its IRR is slightly below the normal acceptable level. Harbourside must also consider the impact of uncertainty on the decision. In this case, the only cash flow known with certainty is likely to be the initial purchase price. Changes in assumptions about future revenue and costs are likely to affect the decision.

The time value of money is considered in capital investment decisions by using one of two techniques: net present value (NPV) or internal rate of return (IRR).[2]

The Importance of Qualitative Factors

Investments in automated and computerized design and manufacturing equipment and in robotics tend to be very large, although many of the benefits may be indirect and intangible or, at the very least, difficult to quantify (for example, increased quality resulting in fewer warranty expenses). These types of investments may be difficult to evaluate with the use of purely quantitative data. For this reason, it is critically important to consider the impact of qualitative factors in such decisions.

Automating a process in a manufacturing environment is much more extensive and expensive than just purchasing a piece of equipment. The total cost of automating a process can be as much as 30 or 40 times that of installing a single machine, owing to additional software needs, further training of personnel, and the

[2]The discussion that follows assumes that readers are already familiar with the basic concepts of discounting and the calculation of present value for single sums and annuities. If you are not familiar with this material, you should study the appendix at the end of the book.

development of new processes. The benefits of automating production processes include the following:

1. Decreased labor costs

2. An increase in the quality of the finished product or a reduction in defects, resulting in fewer inspections, less waste in the production process, less rework of defective goods, and less warranty work on defective goods

3. Increased speed of the production process

4. Increased reliability of the finished product

5. An overall reduction in the amount of inventory

These improvements not only will save costs but also may allow the company to increase its market share. When the competition has automated production systems, companies must often follow suit or risk loss of business. Although some of the preceding benefits are difficult to measure, they must nevertheless be considered in making capital investment decisions in the new manufacturing environment.

LO3 Screening Decisions and Preference Decisions

Capital investment decisions typically fall into one of two categories: screening decisions or preference decisions. **Screening decisions** involve deciding whether an investment meets a predetermined company standard (that is, whether the investment is acceptable), whereas **preference decisions** involve choosing among alternatives.

Typical problems addressed in capital investment decisions are as follows:

1. Should old equipment be replaced with new equipment that promises to be more cost efficient?

2. Should a new delivery vehicle be purchased or leased?

3. Should a manufacturing plant be expanded?

4. Should a new retail store be opened?

Screening decisions Decisions about whether an investment meets a predetermined company standard.

Preference decisions Decisions that involve choosing among alternatives.

Once the problem is defined, the next step is to identify objectives. Objectives include both quantitative factors (increase production, increase sales, reduce costs) and qualitative factors (make a higher quality product, provide better customer service). Analyzing the options involves both a quantitative analysis, using tools that recognize the time value of money, and a qualitative analysis. Once the potential investments are screened and analyzed, the best option is chosen.

Both NPV and IRR can be used as screening tools. They allow a manager to identify and eliminate undesirable projects. Although the two methods accomplish the same objective, it is important to remember that they are used in different ways. With net present value, the cost of capital is typically used as the discount rate to compute the net present value of each proposed investment. Any project that has a negative net present value should be rejected, unless qualitative reasons exist for considering the project further.

With the internal rate of return, the cost of capital or other measure of a company's minimum required rate of return is compared with the computed internal rate of return. If the internal rate of return is equal to or greater than the minimum required rate of return, the investment is acceptable, unless qualitative reasons exist for rejecting the project (see Exhibit 8-4).

The NPV method does have some advantages over the IRR method for making screening decisions. Adjusting the discount rate to take into account the increased risk and the uncertainty of cash flows expected to occur many years in the future is possible with NPV. By contrast, users of the IRR method have to modify cash flows directly to adjust for risk.

However, NPV (without adjustment) cannot be used to compare investments (make preference decisions) unless the competing investments are of similar magnitude. Consider, for example, two competing investments, each with a five-year useful life. The first is an investment of $10,000 and generates cash savings with a present value of $12,000 (cash inflows of $3,165.56 per year for five years, discounted at 10 percent). Its NPV is therefore $2,000. The second is an initial investment of $20,000 and generates cash inflows with a present value of $22,000 (cash inflows of $5,803.52 per year for five years). As you can see, both investments have the same NPV of $2,000:

	Investment 1	Investment 2
Initial investment	$(10,000)	$(20,000)
Present value of cash inflows	12,000	22,000
Net present value	$ 2,000	$ 2,000

Which is preferred? Intuitively, the $10,000 investment should be preferred to the $20,000 investment. Think of it this way. You could invest in two $10,000 projects and generate cash inflows of $6,331.12 ($3,165.56 × 2) per year instead of the $5,803.52 generated from one $20,000 investment.

Profitability Index

The NPV analysis can be modified slightly through the calculation of a profitability index to allow a better comparison of investments of different size. The **profitability index (PI)** is calculated by dividing the present value of the cash inflows (netted with the present value of any cash outflows occurring after the project starts) by the initial investment (netted with any other cash flows occurring on the project start date).

> Profitability Index = (Present value of cash inflows)/
> (Initial investment)

A PI greater than 1.0 means that the NPV is positive (the PV of the inflows is greater than the initial

> # The profitability index is a useful tool for making preference decisions because it can be used to compare projects that require investment of different amounts.

investment), and the project is acceptable. In comparing the PI of competing projects, the project with the highest PI is preferred. The PIs of investments 1 and 2 are calculated as follows:

	Investment 1	Investment 2
Present value of cash inflows	$12,000	$22,000
Initial investment	÷$10,000	÷$22,000
Profitability index	1.20	1.10

The $10,000 investment has a higher PI of 1.20 and is preferred over the $20,000 investment with a PI of 1.10. We can confirm this preference by calculating the IRR of both investments.

Using Microsoft Excel's RATE function, we see that the IRR of investment 1 is 17.55 percent (=RATE(5,3165.56,−10000,0,0) = 17.55%), whereas the IRR of investment 2 is only 13.84 percent (=RATE(5,5803.52,−20000,0,0) = 13.84%).

In cases like this, in which the investment lives are equal and the cash flows follow similar patterns (annual cash flows for five years), IRR can be used to make preference decisions. However, when asset lives

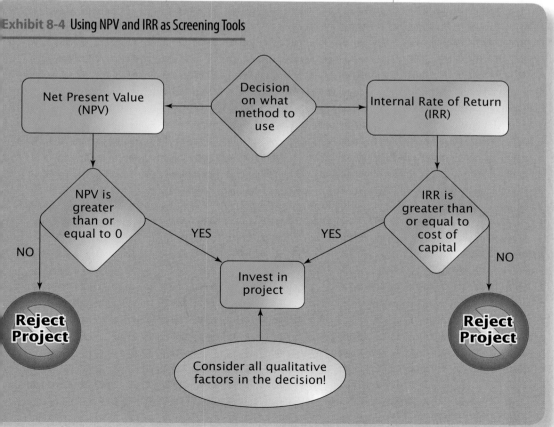

Exhibit 8-4 Using NPV and IRR as Screening Tools

Profitability index (PI)
Calculated by dividing the present value of cash inflows by the initial investment.

© Cengage Learning 2013

are unequal and cash flows follow different patterns, the use of IRR can result in incorrect decisions even when the initial investment is the same.

Consider the following example, in which two $20,000 projects are being contemplated: Project A reduces cash operating costs (increases cash flow) by $12,500 per year for the next two years, whereas project B reduces operating costs by $5,000 per year for six years. Assuming a discount rate of 10 percent, we calculate the NPV, PI, and IRR of each investment as follows:

	Project A	Project B
Initial investment	$(20,000.00)	$(20,000.00)
PV of cash inflows	21,693.75	21,776.50
NPV	$ 1,693.75	$ 1,776.50
PI	1.085	1.089
IRR	16.26%	12.98%

Although IRR would indicate that project A is preferable to project B, NPV and PI indicate that project B is better. Which is right? Well, it depends. As we discussed earlier in the chapter, the IRR method assumes that cash inflows are immediately reinvested at the IRR earned on the original investment—in this case, over 16 percent. In contrast, the NPV method assumes that cash inflows are reinvested at the cost of capital or other discount rate used in the analysis—10 percent in our analysis. If you can reinvest the large cash inflows received in project A at the end of years 1 and 2 at a high rate of return, project A would indeed be preferred. If not, project B, offering a return of almost 13 percent for six years, would be preferred. The use of IRR generally favors short-term investments with high yields, whereas NPV favors longer term investments even if the return is lower.

LO4 The Impact of Taxes on Capital Investment Decisions

Nonprofit organizations, such as Harbourside Hospital, do not pay income taxes and do not need to consider the impact of income taxes on capital investment decisions (or other decisions, for that matter).[3] However, profit-making companies must pay income taxes on any taxable income earned (just as individuals must) and must therefore consider the impact of income taxes on capital investment and other management decisions. With federal income tax rates on corporations ranging from 15 percent to 35 percent of taxable income (and state income taxes typically adding another 5 to 10 percent), taxes are a major source of cash outflows for many companies and must be taken into consideration in any long-term investment decision.

As demonstrated in Chapter 5, the after-tax benefit or cost of a taxable cash inflow or a tax-deductible cash outflow is found by multiplying the before-tax cash inflow or before-tax cash outflow by (1 − tax rate). For a company with a combined federal and state income tax rate of 40 percent, a taxable cash inflow of $100,000 results in a $60,000 after-tax cash inflow [$100,000 × (1 − 0.40)]. Likewise, a $20,000 tax-deductible cash outflow for repairs results in an after-tax outflow of only $12,000.

The disposal of assets may also have tax consequences. When an asset is sold or otherwise disposed of, the gain or loss is calculated on the difference between the sales price and the book value. Because current tax law rules do not consider salvage value in the computation of depreciation (assets are depreciated to zero even if they have a salvage value), the book value of an asset at the end of its useful life will be zero and any salvage value realized will be taxed as gain. The after-tax cash flow associated with the sale of an asset for its salvage value is therefore found by multiplying the salvage value by (1 − tax rate).[4] For simplicity, we will assume that a gain on the disposal of an asset is taxed at the same rate as the operating income of a company. In practice, the tax calculation on the sale of depreciable assets can be quite complicated.

The Depreciation Tax Shield

Not all tax-deductible expenses involve cash outflows. Depreciation is a tax-deductible expense that does not

[4]When assets are sold during their useful life, it is possible to generate tax-deductible losses as well as taxable gains. When assets are sold at a loss, their after-tax cash flow is more difficult to compute. It consists of the cash received from the sale *plus* the tax savings generated from the deductible loss.

[3]Hospitals, museums, churches, and a multitude of other organizations are often structured as organizations that are exempt from federal and state income taxes. In order to qualify, they must meet certain requirements specified by Congress and the Internal Revenue Service. These organizations may also be exempt from local property taxes.

Taxes are a major source of cash outflows for many companies and must be taken into consideration in calculations of the time value of money.

involve a direct payment of cash. Although depreciation does not result in a direct cash outflow, it does result in an indirect cash *inflow* owing to the impact of depreciation on income taxes paid. Depreciation expense reduces a company's taxable income and thus its income tax, resulting in an increase in cash flow.

For example, in Exhibit 8-5, the revenue and expenses of Company A and Company B are identical except for $10,000 of depreciation expense incurred by Company B. This depreciation reduces Company B's taxable income by $10,000 and reduces its income tax by $4,000. As a result, Company B's cash flow *increases* by $4,000. (Remember that the depreciation expense itself does not result in a cash outflow.)

Exhibit 8-5 Tax Savings from Depreciation

	Company A		Company B	
	Income	Cash Flow	Income	Cash Flow
Cash revenue	$100,000	$100,000	$100,000	$100,000
Cash expense	60,000	60,000	60,000	60,000
Depreciation	0	0	10,000	0
Income (before tax)	$ 40,000		$ 30,000	
Income tax (40% rate)	16,000	16,000	12,000	12,000
Net income	$ 24,000		$ 18,000	
Cash flow		$ 24,000		$ 28,000

© Cengage Learning 2013

The tax savings from depreciation (called the **depreciation tax shield**) can easily be found by multiplying the depreciation expense by the tax rate:

Tax Savings from Depreciation = Depreciation Expense × Tax Rate

In this case, Company B's $10,000 of depreciation expense multiplied by the 40 percent tax rate results in $4,000 of tax savings.

As an example, consider a company contemplating the purchase of a new piece of manufacturing equipment. The equipment will cost $50,000 and will generate cost savings of $13,000 per year for six years. The company has a cost of capital of 10 percent.

Let's assume that the equipment will be depreciated for federal income tax purposes over six years by the straight-line method.[5] Depreciation expense is equal

[5]Although the equipment would be depreciated over a useful life of five years, tax law generally requires the use of a convention whereby a half year of depreciation is deducted in the year of acquisition of the asset (regardless of when it is purchased) and a half year's depreciation is deducted in the sixth year. In addition, the tax law currently allows the use of an accelerated method of depreciation for machinery and equipment. The intricacies of tax depreciation rules are beyond the scope of this book.

to $5,000 for years 1 and 6 and $10,000 for years 2 through 5. Assuming an income tax rate of 40 percent, the depreciation deduction results in tax savings of $2,000 for years 1 and 6 ($5,000 × 40%) and $4,000 for years 2 through 5 ($10,000 × 40%), as shown in the following table.

The Impact of Depreciation on Cash Flow				
	Depreciation Expense Calculation		Tax Savings from Depreciation	
Year		Noncash Depreciation Expense	Depreciation Expense × Tax Rate	Cash Inflow
1	$50,000 ÷ 5 × 1/2	$ 5,000	$ 5,000 × 0.40	$2,000
2	$50,000 ÷ 5	10,000	10,000 × 0.40	4,000
3	$50,000 ÷ 5	10,000	10,000 × 0.40	4,000
4	$50,000 ÷ 5	10,000	10,000 × 0.40	4,000
5	$50,000 ÷ 5	10,000	10,000 × 0.40	4,000
6	$50,000 ÷ 5 × 1/2	5,000	5,000 × 0.40	2,000

Now let's calculate the after-tax NPV. In the following table, the annual cash inflow of $13,000 has been adjusted to the equivalent after-tax amount ($13,000 × 0.6 = $7,800) and the discount rate has been changed to its equivalent after-tax rate (10% × 0.6 = 6%):

Cash Flow	Year	After-Tax Amount	6% Factor	Present Value
Initial investment	Now	($50,000)	1.0000	($50,000.00)
Annual cash income	1–6	7,800	4.9173	38,354.94
Tax savings from depreciation	1	2,000	0.9434	1,866.80
	2	4,000	0.8900	3,560.00
	3	4,000	0.8396	3,358.40
	4	4,000	0.7921	3,168.40
	5	4,000	0.7473	2,989.20
	6	2,000	0.7050	1,410.00
Net present value				$ 4,707.74

Depreciation tax shield The tax savings from depreciation.

The NPV of the new equipment is positive, indicating that it will provide a return greater than the company's 6 percent after-tax cost of capital. Using Excel's IRR function, we find that the after-tax return of the investment is 8.938 percent (see Exhibit 8-6).

take for a project to pay for itself? Obviously, the quicker the payback, the more desirable is the investment. The formula used to compute the payback period is as follows:

$$\text{Payback period} = \frac{\text{Original investment}}{\text{Net annual cash inflows}}$$

Exhibit 8-6 The IRR Function in Excel

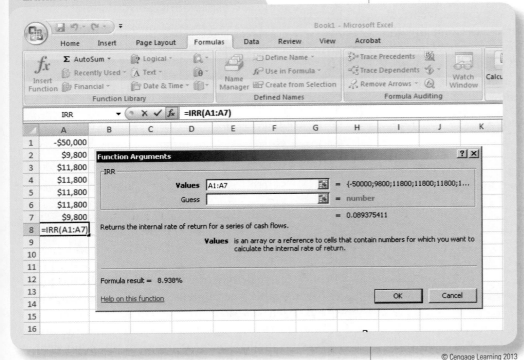

© Cengage Learning 2013

For example, using our earlier example of Bud and Rose's purchase of a delivery van (see pages 162 and 163), we find that the delivery van's payback period would be 3.57 years:

$$\frac{\$50,000 \text{ original investment}}{\$14,000 \text{ net annual cash inflow}} = 3.57 \text{ years}$$

Because the payback method ignores the time value of money, it must be used with caution. Consider our earlier example in which we were contemplating investing in either project A or project B, each requiring an initial investment of $20,000. Project A promises cash inflows of $12,500 per year for two years, whereas project B promises cash inflows of $5,000 per year for six years:

LO5 The Payback Method

Capital investment tools that recognize the time value of money and use discounted cash flow techniques are preferred by most decision makers when dealing with capital investment decisions. In practice, however, some managers still use nondiscounting methods. Although these methods are declining in popularity, the payback method can still be useful in some cases as a fast, easy approximation of the more complicated discounted cash flow methods.

The **payback period** is defined as the length of time needed for a long-term project to recapture, or pay back, the initial investment. In other words, how long does it

	Project A	Project B
Initial investment	$(20,000.00)	$(20,000.00)
Annual cash inflows	12,500.00	5,000.00
PV of cash inflows	21,693.75	21,776.50
NPV	$ 1,693.75	$ 1,776.50
PI	1.085	1.089
Payback	1.6 years ($20,000 ÷ $12,500)	4 years ($20,000 ÷ $5,000)

Although a manager using the payback method would prefer project A, the method ignores the time value of money and ignores any cash flow received after the initial investment is paid for. While NPV and PI signal that project B should be chosen, project A has the shorter payback period.

The payback method can be useful as a quick approximation of the discounted cash flow methods when

Payback period The length of time needed for a long-term project to recapture, or pay back, the initial investment.

© iStockphoto.com/alvarez

The payback method can be useful as a quick approximation of the discounted cash flow methods when the cash flows follow similar patterns.

the cash flows follow similar patterns. It can also be useful in screening decisions if cash flow is a serious concern and management wants to eliminate projects that would have adverse cash flow consequences. For example, smaller businesses, such as Bud and Rose's Flower Shop, may be concerned about cash flow in the short run even if the long-term profitability of a project is higher than that of alternative projects. In these situations, the amount of time needed to recover cash outlays may be a very important criterion when evaluating capital investment decisions.

What method is used in practice? According to one recent survey of chief financial officers (CFOs), most CFOs use the NPV or IRR techniques to evaluate long-term investment options. Only about half use the payback method. In addition, older CFOs and CFOs of smaller companies tend to use the payback method more frequently than younger CFOs or those working for larger companies.[6]

[6]John Graham and Campbell Harvey, "How Do CFOs Make Capital Budgeting and Capital Structure Decisions?" *The Journal of Applied Corporate Finance*, Vol. 15, No. 1, 8–22.

MAKING IT REAL

Capital Investment Decisions in the University

Discounted cash flow analysis and other quantitative methods may not be appropriate tools for making capital investment decisions in universities and other nonprofit organizations. Although a new university classroom building has definite costs, it may not generate cost savings or any additional revenue

© Pixland/Jupiterimages

in the traditional sense. However, projects such as these can still be analyzed and ranked according to qualitative factors. For example, when the University of Vermont needed a way to prioritize its many building projects, it created a model that evaluates the impact of the project on the university's mission, vision, and strategy.

Source: "What a University Can Teach You about Choosing Capital Projects," by Luke Dion, Geoffrey Robertson, and Susan B. Hughes, *Strategic Finance*, January 2009.

STUDY TOOLS 8

Chapter review card

○ Learning Objective and Key Concept Reviews

○ Key Definitions and Formulas

Online (Located at www.cengagebrain.com)

○ Flash Cards and Crossword Puzzles

○ Games and Quizzes

○ Hard Rock Cafe Video and E-Lectures

○ Homework Assignments (as directed by your instructor)

BRIEF EXERCISES

1. NPV: No Salvage Value or Taxes LO1

Kim Johnson purchased an asset for $80,000. Annual operating cash inflows are expected to be $30,000 each year for four years. At the end of the life of the asset, Kim will not be able to sell the asset because it will have no salvage value.

Required
What is the net present value if the cost of capital is 12 percent (ignore income taxes)?

2. IRR: Even Cash Flows LO2

Williams and Park Accounting Practice is considering investing in a new computer system that costs $9,000 and would reduce processing costs by $2,000 a year for the next six years.

Required
Calculate the internal rate of return, using the time-value-of-money charts located at the end of the Review Cards.

3. Screening and Preference Decisions LO3

Choosing among alternative capital investments requires an organization to consider various aspects of the alternative investments. The following statements relate to screening and preference decisions that may arise as an organization considers various investments.
a. A screening decision is the same as a preference decision.
b. NPV and IRR can be used as screening tools.

c. NPV should never be used to compare capital investments, unless the investments are of different magnitudes.
d. The profitability index is a modification of the NPV and can be used to compare investments of different magnitudes.
e. A preference decision involves deciding whether an investment exceeds an organization's minimum required return.

Required
Indicate whether each of the preceding statements is true or false.

4. Depreciation Tax Shield LO4

Harris Corp. recently purchased a manufacturing facility for $2.5 million. The company will depreciate the facility by recording $125,000 of depreciation expense each year for 20 years. Harris Corp. expects that its tax rate will be 35 percent in the coming year.

Required
What is the tax savings (that is, the depreciation tax shield) associated with the new facility in the coming year?

5. Payback Method with Uneven Cash Flows LO5

A particular project requires an initial investment of $10,000 and is expected to generate future cash flows of $4,000 for Year 1 and $3,000 for years 2 through 5.

Required
Calculate the project's payback period in years.

6. Basic NPV: No Salvage Value or Taxes LO1

Carrie Rushing is considering the purchase of a new production machine that costs $120,000. She has been told to expect decreased annual operating expenses of $40,000 for four years. At the end of the fourth year, the machine will have no salvage value and will be scrapped.

Required
What is the net present value of the machine if Carrie's cost of capital is 9 percent? (Ignore income taxes.)

7. Basic NPV with Salvage Value LO1

Schaefer Organic Farms purchased a new tractor at a cost of $80,000. Annual operating cash inflows are expected to be $30,000 each year for four years. At the end of the tractor's useful life, the salvage value of the tractor is expected to be $5,000.

Required
What is the net present value if the cost of capital is 12 percent? (Ignore income taxes.)

8. Basic NPV with Salvage Value LO1

Food Bear Grocery Store purchased a new U-Scan machine at a cost of $100,000. Annual operating cash inflows are expected to be $40,000 each year for four years. At the end of the U-Scan's useful life, the salvage value of the machine is expected to be $3,000.

Required
What is the net present value if the cost of capital is 12 percent? (Ignore income taxes.)

9. Understanding NPV LO1

Wilson, Inc., has a project with an expected cash inflow of $1 million at the end of Year 5. Wilson has a second project with an expected cash inflow of $200,000, to be received at the end of each year for the next five years.

Required
If both projects have the same total expected cash outflows, what can be said of the net present value of the first project compared with that of the second project?

10. NPV LO1

A planned factory expansion project has an estimated initial cost of $800,000. Based on a discount rate of 20 percent, the present value of the future cost savings from the expansion is $843,000.

Required
To yield exactly a 20 percent return on investment, the actual investment expenditure should not exceed the $800,000 estimated cost by more than what amount?

11. NPV and IRR Assumptions LO1, 2

Discounted cash flow analysis techniques are used by managers to understand the impact of investment decisions in terms of "today's dollars." Two common techniques that use discounted cash flows are net present value (NPV) and internal rate of return (IRR). Like most analysis techniques, each of these methods requires us to make certain assumptions.

Required
Describe the assumptions underlying NPV and IRR.

12. IRR: Even Cash Flows LO2

The Pearce Club, Inc., is considering investing in an exercise machine that costs $5,000 and would increase revenues by $1,500 a year for five years.

Required
Use Excel to calculate the equipment's internal rate of return. (Ignore income taxes.) Round your answer to two decimals.

13. IRR with Uneven Cash Flows LO2

Powers, Inc., has a project that requires an initial investment of $43,000 and has the following expected stream of cash flows:

Year 1	$20,000
Year 2	30,000

Required
Use Excel to calculate the project's internal rate of return.

14. IRR: Tax Effects LO2

The Golden Golf Club is considering an investment in golf carts that requires $21,000 and promises to return $29,000 in three years' time. The company will depreciate the golf carts via the straight-line method over three years. The carts will have no salvage value at the end of the three-year period. The company's income tax rate is 40 percent.

Required
Use Excel to calculate the equipment's internal rate of return. Round your answer to two decimals.

15. IRR: Tax Effects LO2, 4

The Pearce Club, Inc., is considering investing in an exercise machine that costs $5,000 and would increase revenues by $1,500 a year for five years. The machine would be depreciated over its five-year useful life via the straight-line method and would have no salvage value.

Required
Use Excel to calculate the equipment's internal rate of return. Assume that the tax rate is 30 percent. Round your answer to two decimals.

16. Profitability Index LO3

An investment manager is currently evaluating a project that requires an initial investment of $10,000 and will provide future cash flows that have a present value of $17,000.

Required
Calculate the project's profitability index and explain what the number means.

17. Profitability Index LO3

Kuntz Company has a project that requires an initial investment of $35,000 and has the following expected stream of cash flows:

Year 1	$25,000
Year 2	20,000
Year 3	10,000

Required
Assume that the company's cost of capital is 12 percent. What is the profitability index for the project?

18. After-Tax NPV LO4

Gemini, LLC, invested $1 million in a state-of-the-art information system that promises to reduce processing costs for its purchasing activities by $120,000 per year for the next 10 years. The company will scrap its old information system and will receive no money as a consequence. The new system will be depreciated over 10 years at a rate of $100,000 per year. Gemini's tax rate is 30 percent, and the company has a 7 percent after-tax cost of capital.

Required
What is the after-tax net present value of Gemini's new information system?

19. Depreciation Tax Shield LO4

Owens, Grubbs, and Riley, LLP, recently purchased a new facility to house the partnership's law practice. The facility cost $500,000. The partnership will depreciate the facility by recording $50,000 of depreciation expense each year for 10 years. Owens, Grubbs, and Riley, LLP, expects that its tax rate will be 35 percent in the coming year.

Required
What is the tax savings (that is, the depreciation tax shield) associated with the new facility in the coming year?

20. Payback Method LO5

The Happy Day Care Center is considering an investment that will require an initial cash outlay of $300,000 to purchase nondepreciable assets that have a 10-year life. The organization requires a minimum 4-year payback.

Required
Assume that the investment generates equivalent annual cash flow. What minimum amount of annual cash flows must be generated by the project for the company to make the investment?

PROBLEMS

21. Preference Decisions: NPV vs. IRR vs. Profitability Index LO1, 2, 3

Stephens Industries is contemplating four projects: Project P, Project Q, Project R, and Project S. The capital costs and estimated after-tax net cash flows of each project are shown in the table that follows. Stephens's after-tax cost of capital is 12 percent. Excess funds cannot be reinvested at greater than 12 percent.

	Project P	Project Q	Project R	Project S
Initial cost	$200,000	$235,000	$190,000	$210,000
Annual cash flows:				
Year 1	93,000	90,000	45,000	40,000
Year 2	93,000	85,000	55,000	50,000
Year 3	93,000	75,000	65,000	60,000
Year 4	0	55,000	70,000	65,000
Year 5	0	50,000	75,000	75,000
Net present value	$23,370	$29,827	$27,233	$(7,854)
Internal rate of return	18.7%	17.6%	17.2%	10.6%
Profitability index	1.12	1.13	1.14	0.95

Required
A. Which of the four projects are acceptable options? Why?
B. If only one project can be accepted, which one should the company choose?

22. NPV and Preference Decisions LO1, 3

Harriman Enterprises has three possible projects. Each project requires the same initial investment of $1,000,000. Harriman's chief financial officer has prepared the following cash flow projections for each project:

Year	Project X	Project Y	Project Z
1	$1,250,000	$ 0	$ 500,000
2	1,250,000	0	2,000,000
3	1,250,000	0	2,000,000
4	1,250,000	5,000,000	500,000

Jim Harriman, the company's president, is unsure of which project to pursue. Each holds promise for the company, but he is confused about what to do because each project generates the same amount of cash flow over the four-year period from beginning to end of the project.

Required

Ignoring taxes, compute the net present value of each project at a 15 percent cost of capital. Which project should be chosen? Why?

23. NPV vs. Payback Method: Impact of Varying Cash Flow Assumptions LO1, 2, 5

Winona Miller, president of CLJ Products, is considering the purchase of a computer-aided manufacturing system that requires an initial investment of $4,000,000 and is expected to provide cash benefits and savings for the next 10 years. CLJ Products's cost of capital is currently 12 percent. The annual cash benefits/savings associated with the system are as follows:

Decrease in defective products	$100,000
Revenue increase due to improved quality	150,000
Decrease in operating costs	300,000

Required

A. Calculate the payback period for the system. Assume that the company has a policy of accepting only projects with a payback of five years or less. Should the system be purchased?

B. Calculate the NPV and the IRR (use Excel to calculate the IRR) for the project. Should the system be purchased? What if the system does not meet the payback criterion?

C. The project manager reviewed the projected cash flows and pointed out that two items had been missed. First, the system would have a salvage value of $500,000 at the end of 10 years. Second, the increased quality of the company's products produced with the new system would allow the company to increase its market share by 30 percent, leading to additional annual cash inflows of $180,000. Given this new information, recalculate the payback period, NPV, and IRR. Would your recommendation change? Why or why not?

24. NPV vs. Payback Method vs. Profitability Index LO1, 3, 5

Alfred Stein is about to invest $1,000. Alfred is a very cautious man and would like to have some expert advice on which two projects is best for him. He has not told you his exact cost of capital because he likes to keep such information private, but he has told you to consider 8 percent, 10 percent, and 12 percent in your calculations. He has also told you that the salesperson from whom he expects to purchase his equipment has given him the following expected cost savings patterns:

Year	Project 1	Project 2
1	$600	$300
2	600	600
3	600	800
4	600	700

Required

A. Calculate the present value of each project at each of Alfred's potential costs of capital and indicate which project is acceptable at each.

B. Calculate the payback period for each project. Does your recommendation to Alfred change?

C. Calculate the profitability index for each project, using a cost of capital of 10 percent. Which project would you recommend Alfred pursue?

25. After-Tax NPV LO1, 4

Greer Law Associates is evaluating a capital investment proposal for new office equipment for the current year. The initial investment would require the firm to spend $50,000. The equipment would be depreciated on a straight-line basis over five years with no salvage value. The firm's accountant has estimated the before-tax annual cash inflow from the investment to be $15,000. The income tax rate is 40 percent, and all taxes are paid in the year that the related cash flows occur. The desired after-tax rate of return is 15 percent. All cash flows occur at year's end.

Required

What is the net present value of the capital investment proposal? Should the proposal be accepted? Why or why not?

26. NPV LO3

Tate Enterprises is a nonprofit organization that has a cost of capital of 10 percent. The organization is considering the replacement of its computer system. The old system has a net book value of $3,000 and a remaining useful life of five years, with no expected salvage value at the end of the five years. The company estimates the system's current salvage value to be $1,500. A new computer system will cost $10,000 and is expected to have a useful life of five years, with no salvage value. Annual cash operating costs are $4,000 for the old system and $2,000 for the new system.

Required

A. What is the present value of the operating cash outflows for the old system?

B. What is the present value of the operating cash outflows for the new system?

C. What is the present value of the salvage value of the old system if it is replaced now?

D. Would you advise the organization to replace the system? Show calculations to support your recommendation.

27. After-Tax NPV with Loss on Sale and Depreciation Tax Shield LO1, 4

Sullivan Company plans to acquire a new asset that costs $400,000 and is anticipated to have a salvage value of $30,000 at the end of four years. Sullivan's policy is to depreciate all assets with the use of straight-line depreciation with no half-year convention. The new asset will replace an old asset that currently has a tax basis of $80,000 and can be sold for $60,000 now. Sullivan will continue to earn the same revenues of $200,000 per year that it earned with the old asset. However, savings in operating costs will be $120,000 in each of the first three years and $90,000 in the fourth year. Sullivan is subject to a 40 percent tax rate and has an after-tax cost of capital of 10 percent.

Required

A. What is the present value of the depreciation tax shield for the new asset for Year 1?
B. What are the cash flows (net of tax) associated with the disposal of the old asset?
C. What is the investment's net present value (after tax)?

28. Decision Focus: Lease-or-Buy Decision by NPV Analysis LO1, 4

Bit and Byte is contemplating the acquisition of a computer system but is undecided whether it should be leased or purchased. Information regarding the system is as follows:

Equipment Purchase Information	
Cash purchase price	$275,000
Annual maintenance	25,000
Salvage value at the end of three years	120,000
Equipment Leasing Information	
Annual rental fee (includes maintenance)	$75,000 plus 10 percent of billings
Other Information	
Estimated billings:	
Year 1	$230,000
Year 2	250,000
Year 3	240,000
Income tax rate	40%
Depreciation method	Straight-line
Minimum desired after-tax rate of return	12%

Required

Prepare a net-present-value analysis that compares the purchase and leasing options. Which alternative is best for Bit and Byte?

29. Payback Method: After Tax LO4, 5

Stembridge Medical Associates is planning to acquire a $250,000 X-ray machine that promises to provide increased efficiencies and higher resolution X-rays. The medical group expects a reduction of $80,000 in annual operating costs. The machine will be depreciated by the straight-line method over five years (no half-year convention), with no salvage value at the end of the five years.

Required

Compute the X-ray machine's payback period, assuming a 40 percent income tax rate.

CASES

30. Decision Focus: Make-or-Buy Decision with NPV Analysis LO1, 4

Armstrong Company manufactures three models of paper shredders, including the waste container, which serves as the base. Whereas the shredder heads are different for all three models, the waste container is the same. The estimated numbers of waste containers that Armstrong will need during the next five years are as follows:

Year	Number of Containers
1	50,000
2	50,000
3	52,000
4	55,000
5	55,000

The equipment used to manufacture the waste container must be replaced because it is broken and cannot be repaired. The new equipment has a purchase price of $945,000 and is expected to have a salvage value of $12,000 at the end of its economic life in 5 years. The new equipment would be more efficient than the old equipment, resulting in a 25 percent reduction in direct materials.

The old equipment is fully depreciated and is not included in the fixed overhead. The old equipment can be sold for a salvage amount of $1,500. Armstrong has no alternative use for the manufacturing space at this time.

Rather than replace the equipment, one of Armstrong's production managers has suggested that the waste containers be purchased. One supplier has quoted a price of $27 per container. This price is $8 less than the current manufacturing cost, which is composed of the following costs:

Direct materials	$10.00	
Direct labor	8.00	
Variable overhead	6.00	$24.00
Fixed overhead:		
Supervision	$ 2.00	
Facilities	5.00	
General	4.00	11.00
Total manufacturing cost per unit		$35.00

Armstrong employs a plantwide fixed overhead rate in its operations. If the waste containers are purchased outside, the salary and benefits of one supervisor, included in the fixed overhead at $45,000, will be eliminated. There will be no other changes in the other cash and noncash items included in fixed overhead.

Armstrong is subject to a 40 percent income tax rate. Management assumes that all annual cash flows and tax payments occur at the end of the year and uses a 12 percent after-tax discount rate.

Required

A. Define the problem that Armstrong faces.
B. Calculate the net present value of the estimated after-tax cash flows for each option you identify.
C. What is your recommendation? Support your recommendation by explaining the logic behind it.

31. Comprehensive NPV LOI, 4

Rob Thorton is a member of the planning and analysis staff of Thurston, Inc., an established manufacturer of frozen foods. Rick Ungerman, chief financial officer of Thurston, Inc., has asked Thorton to prepare an analysis of net present value for a proposed capital equipment expenditure that should improve the profitability of the Southwestern plant. This analysis will be given to the board of directors for approval.

Several years ago, as director of planning and analysis, Ungerman was instrumental in convincing the board to open the Southwestern plant. However, recent competitive pressures have forced each of Thurston's manufacturing divisions to consider alternatives to improve their market position. To Ungerman's dismay, the Southwestern plant may be sold in the near future, unless significant improvements in cost control and production efficiency are achieved.

The Southwestern plant's production manager, an old friend of Ungerman's, has submitted a proposal for the acquisition of an automated materials-movement system. Ungerman is eager to have this proposal approved, as it will ensure the continuance of the Southwestern plant and preserve his friend's position. The plan calls for the replacement of a number of forklift trucks and operators with a computer-controlled conveyor belt system that feeds directly into the refrigeration units. This automation would eliminate the need for a number of materials handlers and increase the output capacity of the plant.

Ungerman has given this proposal to Thorton and instructed him to use the information in the subsequent table to prepare his analysis.

The forklift trucks have been fully depreciated and have a zero net book value. If the conveyor belt system is purchased now, these trucks will be sold for $100,000. Thurston has a 40 percent effective tax rate, has chosen the straight-line depreciation method, and uses a 12 percent after-tax discount rate. For the purpose of analysis, all tax effects and cash flows from the acquisition and disposal of equipment are considered to occur at the time of the transactions, whereas those from operations are considered to occur at the end of each year.

When Thorton completed his initial analysis, the proposed project appeared quite healthy. However, after investigating equipment similar to that proposed, he discovered that the estimated residual value of $850,000 was very optimistic; information that several vendors had previously provided estimates this value to be $100,000. Thornton also discovered that industry trade publications considered eight years to be the maximum life of similar conveyor belt systems. As a result, he prepared a second analysis, based on this new information. When Ungerman saw the second analysis, he told Thorton to discard this revised material, warned him not to discuss the new estimates with anyone, and ordered him not to present any of the new information, which follows, to the board of directors.

Projected useful life	10 years
Purchase/installation of equipment	$4,500,000
Increased working capital needed*	1,000,000
Increased annual operating costs (exclusive of depreciation)	200,000
Equipment repairs to maintain production efficiency (end of year 5)	800,000
Increase in annual sales revenue	700,000
Reduction in annual manufacturing costs	500,000
Reduction in annual maintenance costs	300,000
Estimated salvage value of conveyor belt system	850,000

*The working capital will be released at the end of the 10-year useful life of the conveyor belt system.

Required

A. Prepare an analysis of the net present value of the purchase and installation of the materials-movement system, using the revised estimates obtained by Thorton. Be sure to present supporting calculations.
B. Accurately describe the decision problem facing Thorton.
C. What alternatives does he have?
D. What is the best alternative from a quantitative analysis?
E. What other qualitative factors should be considered and why?

The Use of Budgets
in Planning and Decision Making

Introduction

Budgets are plans dealing with the acquisition and use of resources over a specified period. Everyone budgets, from the college student to the large multinational corporation. Although budgets are often thought of in terms of dollars (monetary or financial budgets), they are used for other purposes as well. For example, a college student carrying 15 credit hours, working 20 hours a week in a part-time job, and volunteering 10 hours per week at the local hospital might need to prepare a time budget to plan his or her use of time throughout the week.

Creating a monetary budget for a college student can be as simple as jotting down expected cash inflows from loans, parents, and maybe a part-time job and expected outflows for school and living expenses. At the other end of the budgeting spectrum, multinational companies may have very sophisticated budgets used to plan for the acquisition and use of thousands of different materials and the manufacture and sale of hundreds of products.

Managers use budgeting as they go about their **planning**, **operating**, and **control** activities (see Exhibit 9-1). Planning is the cornerstone of good management and requires the development of objectives and goals for the organization as well as the actual preparation of budgets. Operating activities entail day-to-day decision making by managers, which is facilitated by budgets. Control activities include ensuring that the objectives and goals developed by the organization are being attained. Control

Budgets Plans dealing with the acquisition and use of resources over a specified period.

Planning The cornerstone of good management; involves developing objectives and goals for the organization, as well as the actual preparation of budgets.

Operating Involves day-to-day decision making by managers, which is often facilitated by budgeting.

Control Involves ensuring that the objectives and goals developed by the organization are being attained; often involves a comparison of budgets with actual performance and the use of budgets for performance evaluation purposes.

Budgeting is a critical element in building and sustaining a successful business.

often involves a comparison of budgets with actual performance and the use of budgets for performance evaluation purposes. The use of budgets for cost control and performance evaluation is discussed in more depth in Chapter 10.

In this chapter, we emphasize the use of budgets in planning and operating activities, including decisions concerning how much of a product to produce, how much material to buy, how much labor to hire, and how much cash to borrow and invest. The concept of budgeting for cash is tied back to the operating cycle. The operating cycle focuses on cash flow, beginning with the investment of cash in inventory or the use of cash to manufacture products, continuing with the sale of those products to customers, and ending with the collection of cash from those customers (see Exhibit 9-2).

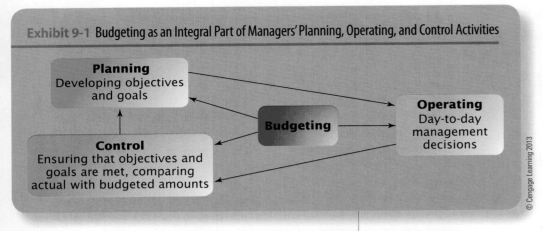

Exhibit 9-1 Budgeting as an Integral Part of Managers' Planning, Operating, and Control Activities

© Cengage Learning 2013

Exhibit 9-2 The Operating Cycle

© Cengage Learning 2013

One of the main reasons small businesses fail is the lack of adequate planning for cash needs. A small business that views budgeting for cash as too time consuming or expensive is destined for failure. With the availability and affordability of information systems in today's business environment, even the smallest business can easily perform the analysis necessary to successfully plan and budget for the future.

LO1 The Budget Development Process

One of the misconceptions about budgeting is that the budgeting process is just a mechanical

Zero-based budgeting Requires managers to build budgets from the ground up each year.

number-crunching task for bookkeepers. In reality, budgeting is a management task, not a bookkeeping task, and it requires a great deal of planning and thoughtful input from a broad range of managers in a company. Although budgeting is time consuming (it often takes as long as 60 to 90 days to prepare an annual budget), the use of spreadsheets, such as Microsoft Excel, makes the process simpler. A recent survey found that 81 percent of companies used spreadsheets either alone or in combination with a general ledger or enterprise resource planning (ERP) system to build their budgets. Although the survey found that large companies with annual revenues of $500 million and higher were more likely to use dedicated budgeting software, it also found that a majority still used spreadsheets alone or with other budgeting systems.

However, the widespread use of Excel spreadsheets is not without difficulty. Eighty percent of the survey respondents expressed frustration with Excel as a budgeting tool, complaining of difficulties in making changes, in "rolling up" numbers, and in creating "what-if" scenarios and lamenting the time-consuming nature of budgeting with spreadsheets.

The ability to conduct queries in ERP systems is a big advantage, as is the fact that ERP systems link data across all areas of a business, ensuring that the same assumptions are used throughout the different budgets.[1]

Some companies start their budget process on the basis of last year's numbers, whereas others employ **zero-based budgeting**. Zero-based budgets require managers to build budgets from the ground up each year, rather than just add a percentage increase to last year's numbers. Consequently, managers must justify all items in the budget, not just changes from last year's budget. Although zero-based budgeting is a good idea in theory,

[1]"Turning Budgeting Pain into Budgeting Gain," by John Orlando, *Strategic Finance*, March 2009, pp. 47–51.

> Budgets must start with a top-down strategic plan that guides and integrates the whole company and its individual budgets.

it can be very time consuming when done on an annual basis. In some cases, companies may require zero-based budgets only every few years or may rotate among departments the requirement that budgets be justified in full.

Although we typically think of budgets as being prepared annually, companies frequently use monthly budgets and rolling 12-month budgets to provide a mechanism for adjusting items in response to unforeseen circumstances. Many state governments prepare budgets biannually (every two years). This approach can cause major problems if unexpected costs are incurred because of a natural disaster or if tax revenue falls because of an unexpected downturn in the economy.

Participation in the Budget Development Process

Traditionally, budgeting is a bottom-up process dependent on departmental managers providing a detailed plan for the upcoming month, quarter, or year. Many companies use a system of **participatory budgeting**, which starts with departmental managers and then flows up through middle management and, ultimately, to top management. At each level, budget estimates are prepared and then submitted to the next level of management, which has responsibility for reviewing the budget and negotiating any changes that need to be made.

Regardless of the specific process used, budget development must be guided by a strategic plan that focuses attention on the company as a whole and integrates individual budgets. A budgeting process that is clearly guided and focused by a strategic plan makes managers more focused on important aspects of the budget and less worried about irrelevant details.[2] In addition, in order to motivate managers and other employees to meet the objectives and goals provided in budgets, companies should structure bonuses, merit pay, and other tangible and intangible rewards in ways that link these rewards to measurable goals outlined in the budgets.

[2] Tim Reason, "Budgeting in the Real World," *CFO Magazine*, http://www.cfo.com/magazine/, July 1, 2005.

Behavioral Implications of Budgeting

When budgets are used for both planning and control purposes, conflicts invariably arise. If managers are evaluated and compensated according to whether they "meet the budget," they may have incentives to pad the budget, thus making the targets easier to reach. For example, if a manager knows that she will receive a bonus if sales in her department exceed the budget, she may attempt to set the sales budget at an unrealistically low level. Likewise, if a manager is to receive a bonus if costs are held below budget, he may attempt to pad the budget by estimating that the costs will be higher than he really expects them to be.

Tying compensation to meeting targeted budgets also provides managers with an incentive to shift revenue and expenses from one period to another in order to make certain that the budget is met. For example, if a manager thinks that she is unlikely to meet a targeted cost budget, she may defer certain expenses, such as maintenance and repairs, until the following year. This type of behavior is unethical and clearly not beneficial for the company as a whole. Companies can reduce incentives for this type of behavior by holding managers accountable and punishing unethical behavior with strong sanctions. However, they can also reduce the likelihood of undesirable behavior by taking more positive steps, such as assuring managers that their performance evaluation will be done in a fair and equitable manner and will include other factors, such as customer satisfaction surveys, the quality of goods and services provided, and similar metrics.

Advantages of Budgeting

Budgeting has many advantages, including the following:

1. The budgeting process encourages communication throughout the organization.

2. The budgeting process encourages management to focus on the future and not be distracted by daily crises in the organization.

3. The budgeting process can help management identify and deal with potential bottlenecks or constraints before they become major problems.

Participatory budgeting A budgeting process that starts with departmental managers and flows up through middle management and then to top management. Each new level of management has responsibility for reviewing and negotiating any changes in the proposed budget.

4. The budgeting process can increase the coordination of organizational activities and help facilitate goal congruence. Implementing goal congruence means making sure that the personal goals of the managers are closely aligned with the goals of the organization.

5. The budgeting process can define specific goals and objectives that become benchmarks, or standards of performance, for evaluating future performance.

The Master Budget

The **master budget** consists of an interrelated set of budgets prepared by a business. A master budget for a

> **Master budget** Consists of an interrelated set of budgets prepared by a business.
>
> **Sales forecast** Combines with the sales budget to form the starting points in the preparation of production budgets for manufacturing companies, purchases budgets for merchandising companies, and labor budgets for service companies.
>
> **Sales budget** Used in planning the cash needs for manufacturing, merchandising, and service companies.

manufacturing company is shown in Exhibit 9-3, with a corresponding master budget for a merchandising company shown in Exhibit 9-4. The starting point in both is forecasting sales and preparing a sales budget.

LO2 The Sales Budget

All organizations require the forecasting of future sales volume and the preparation of a sales budget. A professional baseball team needs to forecast the number of fans who will attend home games each season. Airlines need to forecast the number of passengers who will fly on each route, and hotels need to forecast occupancy rates for various days and months. Retail stores, such as **Wal-Mart** and **JC Penney**, must forecast retail sales of many different products at many different locations. Manufacturing firms, such as **Ford**, **DaimlerChrysler**, and **General Motors**, must forecast consumer demand for each model of car or truck that they sell.

The **sales forecast** and **sales budget** are the starting points in the preparation of production budgets for manufacturing companies and purchases budgets for merchandising companies. The sales budget is a key component used in the overall strategic planning process

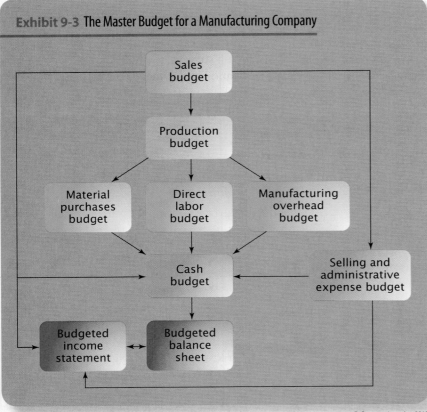

Exhibit 9-3 The Master Budget for a Manufacturing Company

© Cengage Learning 2013

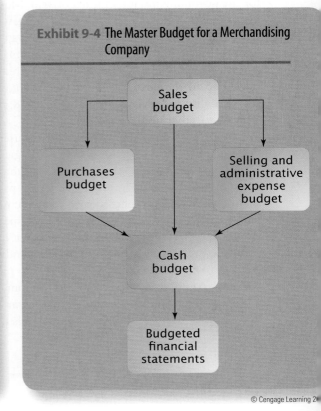

Exhibit 9-4 The Master Budget for a Merchandising Company

© Cengage Learning 2

Budgets are future oriented and make extensive use of estimates and forecasts.

and is also used in planning the cash needs of businesses.

There are numerous ways to forecast sales. Most forecasting will combine information from many different sources, either informally or through the use of computer programs. Regardless of the size of the company or the sophistication of the forecasting methods used, the usual starting point in sales forecasting is last year's level of sales. Other factors and information sources typically used in sales forecasting are as follows:

1. Historical data, such as sales trends for the company, competitors, and the industry (if available).

2. General economic trends or factors, such as inflation rates, interest rates, population growth, and personal spending.

3. Regional and local factors expected to affect sales.

4. Anticipated price changes in both purchasing costs and sales prices.

5. Anticipated marketing or advertising plans.

6. The impact of new products or changes in the product mix on the entire product line.

7. Other factors, such as political and legal events.

Every organization will have unique factors that it needs to consider, and each organization will also attach a different level of importance to each factor. For example, forecasting sales revenue (and the number of skiers) for a major ski resort requires not only the consideration of general economic conditions, the impact of new resorts, and the potential impact of advertising, but also a consideration of the weather. Although snowmaking equipment has reduced the dependence of resorts on natural snow, weather can sometimes affect these businesses in ways that cannot be easily predicted. In a recent winter, New England ski areas had plenty of snow, but the communities at lower elevations (from which most of their customers came) did not. Even though the ski resorts used extensive advertising to promote the good ski conditions, skiers stayed away from the slopes because of the warm weather and lack of snow at home.

The size and complexity of the organization will often determine the complexity of the sales forecasting system. In large companies, preparation of the sales forecast is usually accomplished by the marketing department and requires significant effort in the area of market research to arrive at an accurate forecast of expected sales. In smaller companies, the sales forecast may be made by an individual or a small group of managers. Some companies will use elaborate econometric planning models and regression analysis to forecast sales volume. Others may use informal models and rely heavily on the intuition and opinions of managers. Regardless of the level of sophistication, it is important to remember that sales forecasting is still just that—a forecast.

As you will see in the rest of this chapter, all the remaining budgets and the decisions that are made on the basis of their forecasts are dependent on this estimate of sales. For that reason, it is important to estimate sales with as much accuracy as possible. A small error in a sales forecast can cause larger errors in other budgets that depend on the sales forecast.

Operating budgets are used by companies to plan for the short term—usually one year or less. As an example of the budgeting process, let's consider the

Operating budgets Used to plan for the short term (typically one year or less).

The sales forecast (budget) is the starting point in the production budget.

case of Tina's Fine Juices, the orange juice bottler. Tina's produces bottled orange juice from fruit concentrate purchased from suppliers in Florida, Arizona, and California. The only ingredients in the juice are water and concentrate. The juice is blended, pasteurized, and bottled for sale in 12-ounce plastic bottles. The process is heavily automated and is centered on five machines that control the mixing and bottling of the juice. Each machine is run by one employee and can process 10 bottles of juice per minute, or 600 bottles per hour.

The juice is sold by a number of grocery stores under their store brand name and in smaller restaurants, delis, and bagel shops under the name of Tina's Fine Juices. Tina's has been in business for several years and uses a sophisticated sales forecasting model based on prior sales, expected changes in demand, and economic factors affecting the industry. Sales of juice are highly seasonal, peaking in the first quarter of the year. Forecasted sales for the first quarter of the year are as follows:

Sales Forecast	
January	250,000 bottles
February	325,000 bottles
March	450,000 bottles

Tina's sells the juice for $1.05 per 12-ounce bottle, in cartons of 50 bottles. A sales budget shows the projected volume of product to be sold times the expected sales price per unit (see Exhibit 9-5).

Production budget

Used to forecast how many units of product to produce in order to meet the sales projections.

LO3 Production Budget

For manufacturing companies, the next step in the budgeting process is to complete the **production budget**. Once the sales volume has been projected, companies must forecast how many units of product to produce in order to meet the sales projections. Although this might seem to be an easy task—just manufacture what you plan to sell—traditional manufacturing companies, as you will recall from Chapter 2, often choose to hold an established minimum level of finished-goods inventory (as well as direct materials inventory) to serve as buffers in case of unexpected demand for products or unexpected problems in production.

In this case, the sales forecast must be adjusted to account for any expected increase or decrease in finished-goods inventory. A basic production budget is shown in the following shaded box:

> Sales forecast (in units)
> + Desired ending inventory of finished goods
> = Total budgeted production needs
> − Beginning inventory of finished goods
> = Required production

Exhibit 9-5 Sales Budget

	January	February	March	1st Quarter
Tina's Fine Juices				
Sales Budget				
Budgeted sales in bottles	250,000	325,000	450,000	1,025,000
Selling price per bottle	$ 1.05	$ 1.05	$ 1.05	$ 1.05
Total budgeted sales	$262,500	$341,250	$472,500	$ 1,076,250

Tina's Fine Juices tries to maintain at least 10 percent of the next month's sales forecast in inventory at the end of each month. Because sales have been projected to increase very rapidly, the company does not want to run the risk of running out of juice to ship to customers, so Tina's Fine Juices keeps a minimum amount on hand at all times. Other problems, such as shipping delays or weather, could also affect the amount of desired ending inventory. On the basis of these requirements, Tina's would want to have 32,500 bottles of juice on hand at the end of January (10 percent of February's forecasted sales of 325,000). A production budget for Tina's Fine Juices is shown in Exhibit 9-6.

As shown in Exhibit 9-6, the arrows demonstrate that the projected ending inventory of finished goods for one month is the projected beginning inventory for the following month. The projected ending inventory for the quarter is the ending inventory on the last day of the quarter, in this case March 31, and the projected beginning inventory for the quarter is the beginning inventory on the first day of the quarter, or January 1.

Note that, to complete the production budget for the first quarter, we need to have some additional information. We need to know the forecasted sales for April in order to determine the projected ending inventory for the end of March. April sales are projected to be 500,000 units, so the projected ending inventory is 50,000 units.

The beginning inventory for January is 25,000 bottles. (This amount is also the ending inventory for December.) Closer examination of the production budget model will show that required production needs are just the budgeted sales plus or minus any projected change in finished-goods inventory during the month:

Required production = Budgeted sales $+(-)$ Increase (Decrease) in finished-goods inventory

In January, the budgeted sales are 250,000 units and inventories are projected to increase by 7,500 units (from 25,000 to 32,500). If we add the projected inventory increase to the sales projection, we have a required production level of 257,500 (250,000 + 7,500).

LO4 Material, Labor, Overhead, and Selling and Administrative Expense Budgets

Material Purchases Budget

Once the production budget is completed, the next budget to be prepared is the **material purchases budget**. Once again, because many traditional companies desire to keep materials on hand at all times in order to plan for unforeseen changes in demand, the desired ending inventory for materials must be added to the projected production needs for materials in order to arrive at the total expected needs for materials. Then an adjustment is made for any raw materials inventory on hand at the beginning

Exhibit 9-6 Production Budget

	January	February	March	1st Quarter
Tina's Fine Juices				
Production Budget				
Budgeted sales (Exhibit 9-5)	250,000	325,000	450,000	1,025,000
Add desired ending inventory of finished goods[1]	32,500	45,000	50,000	50,000
Total budgeted production needs	282,500	370,000	500,000	1,075,000
Less beginning inventory of finished goods[2]	25,000	32,500	45,000	25,000
Required production	257,500	337,500	455,000	1,050,000

[1] March ending inventory is calculated as follows: April sales are projected to be 500,000 units of finished goods. (500,000 x .10 = 50,000 units of finished goods.)

[2] January beginning inventory of 25,000 units of finished goods is given

Sales Budget   Production Budget   Purchases Budget - Concentrate   Purchases Budget - Bottles   Direct Lab

Material purchases budget Used to project the dollar amount of raw materials purchased for production.

© Cengage Learning 2013

Preparing budgets for material purchases, direct labor, overhead, and selling and administrative expenses is critical because these budgets often require companies to commit to expenditures months in advance.

of the month. A basic material purchases budget is shown in the following shaded box:

> Raw materials needed to meet the required production budget
> + Desired ending inventory of raw materials
> = Total raw materials needs
> − Beginning inventory of raw materials
> = Raw materials to be purchased

Tina's Fine Juices needs to prepare two purchases budgets: one for the concentrate used in its orange juice and one for the bottles that are purchased from an outside supplier. Tina's has determined that it takes one gallon of orange concentrate for every 32 bottles of finished product. Each gallon of concentrate costs $4.80. Tina's also requires 20 percent of next month's direct material needs to be on hand at the end of the budget period. Note that the starting point for this budget is the production budget. The next step in the preparation of the direct material purchases budget is to compute the raw materials needed on the basis of the projected production. In this case, we take the number of bottles to be produced and divide by 32, which is the number of bottles that can be produced with one gallon of concentrate. The ending inventory needs are then added to that figure to arrive at the projected direct materials needed to fulfill the production and ending inventory needs. Beginning inventory is then subtracted from the projected needs to arrive at

the projected purchases in gallons, and the last step is to convert that amount to dollars by multiplying the number of gallons by the price per gallon.

To calculate the projected ending inventory in March, Tina's must estimate sales for May. (April sales were already estimated to be 500,000 bottles.) If May sales are estimated at 400,000 bottles, April ending inventory will be estimated to be 40,000 bottles ($0.10 \times 400,000$) and April production will be 490,000 bottles (April sales of 500,000 bottles + ending inventory of 40,000 bottles − beginning inventory of 50,000 bottles). The production of 490,000 bottles in April requires 15,313 gallons of concentrate (490,000 bottles ÷ 32 bottles per gallon). Accordingly, Tina's will plan on holding 3,063 gallons of concentrate in inventory at the end of March (20 percent of the materials usage for April). The material purchases budget for orange concentrate is shown in Exhibit 9-7.

Tina's will prepare a similar budget for bottles. The bottles are purchased from an outside supplier for $0.10 per bottle. The supplier provides labels and

Exhibit 9-7 Material Purchases Budget—Orange Concentrate

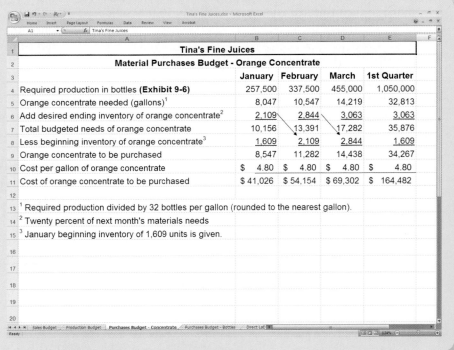

	January	February	March	1st Quarter
Tina's Fine Juices				
Material Purchases Budget - Orange Concentrate				
Required production in bottles **(Exhibit 9-6)**	257,500	337,500	455,000	1,050,000
Orange concentrate needed (gallons)[1]	8,047	10,547	14,219	32,813
Add desired ending inventory of orange concentrate[2]	2,109	2,844	3,063	3,063
Total budgeted needs of orange concentrate	10,156	13,391	17,282	35,876
Less beginning inventory of orange concentrate[3]	1,609	2,109	2,844	1,609
Orange concentrate to be purchased	8,547	11,282	14,438	34,267
Cost per gallon of orange concentrate	$ 4.80	$ 4.80	$ 4.80	$ 4.80
Cost of orange concentrate to be purchased	$ 41,026	$ 54,154	$ 69,302	$ 164,482

[1] Required production divided by 32 bottles per gallon (rounded to the nearest gallon).
[2] Twenty percent of next month's materials needs
[3] January beginning inventory of 1,609 units is given.

caps for the bottles as part of the purchase price. Tina's has the same inventory policy for bottles and orange concentrate. A material purchases budget for bottles is shown in Exhibit 9-8.

Exhibit 9-8 Material Purchases Budget—Bottles

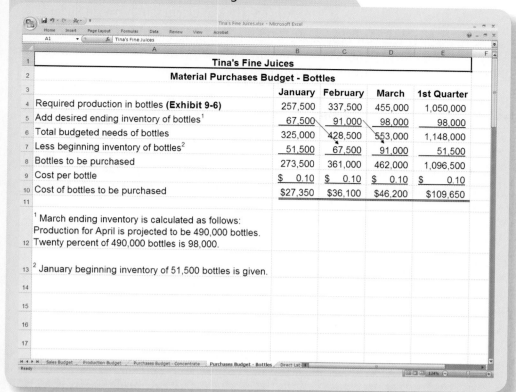

Tina's Fine Juices				
Material Purchases Budget - Bottles				
	January	February	March	1st Quarter
Required production in bottles **(Exhibit 9-6)**	257,500	337,500	455,000	1,050,000
Add desired ending inventory of bottles[1]	67,500	91,000	98,000	98,000
Total budgeted needs of bottles	325,000	428,500	553,000	1,148,000
Less beginning inventory of bottles[2]	51,500	67,500	91,000	51,500
Bottles to be purchased	273,500	361,000	462,000	1,096,500
Cost per bottle	$ 0.10	$ 0.10	$ 0.10	$ 0.10
Cost of bottles to be purchased	$27,350	$36,100	$46,200	$109,650

[1] March ending inventory is calculated as follows:
Production for April is projected to be 490,000 bottles.
Twenty percent of 490,000 bottles is 98,000.

[2] January beginning inventory of 51,500 bottles is given.

© Cengage Learning 2013

bottle shows that the amount of direct labor is $0.025 per bottle of juice ($15 ÷ 600 bottles). A direct labor budget for the first quarter is shown in Exhibit 9-9.

Manufacturing Overhead Budget

Preparation of the **manufacturing overhead budget** involves estimating overhead costs. As was discussed in detail earlier in this book, overhead can be estimated in a number of ways, by using plant-wide or departmental predetermined overhead rates or activity-based costing. At Tina's Fine Juices, most of the production process is automated, the juice is mixed by machine, and machines do the bottling

Direct Labor Budget

As with the material purchases budget, the **direct labor budget** starts with the production budget. However, because labor cannot be accumulated as raw materials can, no adjustments need to be made for beginning and ending inventory.

The direct labor budget is prepared by multiplying the number of units to be produced by the number of direct labor hours required to produce each unit. As was discussed earlier, the production process utilizes a worker assigned to each of the five mixing and bottling machines. Each machine (and thus each worker) can process 600 bottles of orange juice per hour. At Tina's Fine Juices, factory workers are paid an average of $15 per hour, including fringe benefits and payroll taxes. If the production schedule doesn't allow for full utilization of the workers and machines, one or more workers are temporarily moved to another department. Dividing the labor rate of $15 by the time required per

Exhibit 9-9 Direct Labor Budget

Tina's Fine Juices				
Direct Labor Budget				
	January	February	March	1st Quarter
Required production in bottles **(Exhibit 9-6)**	257,500	337,500	455,000	1,050,000
Direct labor hours per bottle	1/600	1/600	1/600	1/600
Total direct labor hours needed for production	429.17	562.50	758.33	1,750.00
Direct labor cost per hour	$ 15.00	$ 15.00	$ 15.00	$ 15.00
Total direct labor cost	$ 6,438	$ 8,437	$ 11,375	$ 26,250

© Cengage Learning 2013

Direct labor budget Used to project the dollar amount of direct labor cost needed for production.

Manufacturing overhead budget Used to project the dollar amount of manufacturing overhead needed for production.

and packaging. Overhead costs are incurred almost entirely in the mixing-and-bottling process. Consequently, Tina's has chosen to use a plantwide cost driver (machine hours) to apply manufacturing overhead to products.

However, as you will recall from Chapter 5, not all overhead is expected to behave in the same fashion as production increases and decreases each month. Although variable overhead costs will vary in direct proportion to the number of bottles of juice produced, fixed overhead costs will remain constant regardless of production. For budgeting purposes, Tina's separates variable overhead from fixed overhead and calculates a predetermined overhead rate for variable manufacturing overhead costs.

Tina's Fine Juices has estimated that variable overhead will total $438,000 for the year and that the machines will run approximately 8,000 hours at the projected production volume for the year (4,775,000 bottles). The estimated machine hours are 80 percent of capacity for the five machines. Therefore, Tina's predetermined overhead rate for variable overhead is $54.75 per machine hour ($438,000 ÷ 8,000 machine hours). Tina's has also estimated fixed overhead to be $1,480,000 per year ($123,333 per month), of which $1,240,000 per year ($103,333 per month) is depreciation on existing property, plant, and equipment.

The manufacturing overhead budget is presented in Exhibit 9-10. Note that variable overhead is budgeted on the basis of the predetermined overhead rate and varies with production each month, whereas fixed manufacturing overhead is budgeted at a constant $123,333 per month.

The material purchases budget, the direct labor budget, and the manufacturing overhead budget are summarized in a total manufacturing cost budget (see Exhibit 9-11). This budget provides

Tina's Fine Juices with an estimate of the total manufacturing costs expected to be incurred in the first quarter of the year.

Exhibit 9-10 Manufacturing Overhead Budget

Tina's Fine Juices
Manufacturing Overhead Budget

	January	February	March	1st Quarter
Budgeted machine hours[1]	429.17	562.50	758.33	1,750.00
Variable overhead rate	$ 54.75	$ 54.75	$ 54.75	$ 54.75
Variable manufacturing overhead	$ 23,497	$ 30,797	$ 41,519	$ 95,813
Fixed manufacturing overhead	$123,333	$123,333	$123,333	$ 369,999
Total manufacturing overhead[2]	$146,830	$154,130	$164,852	$ 465,812

[1] Budgeted machine hours are the same as budgeted labor hours **(Exhibit 9-9)**. Each machine can process 600 bottles of orange juice per hour.
[2] Total overhead each month includes $103,333 of noncash depreciation expense.

© Cengage Learning 20

Exhibit 9-11 Total Manufacturing Cost Budget

Tina's Fine Juices
Total Manufacturing Cost Budget

		January	February	March	1st Quarter
Budgeted material cost - concentrate	Exhibit 9-7	$ 41,026	$ 54,154	$ 69,302	$ 164,482
Budgeted material cost - bottles	Exhibit 9-8	$ 27,350	$ 36,100	$ 46,200	$ 109,650
Budgeted direct labor cost	Exhibit 9-9	$ 6,438	$ 8,437	$ 11,375	$ 26,250
Budgeted manufacturing overhead cos	Exhibit 9-10	$ 146,830	$ 154,130	$ 164,852	$ 465,812
Total budgeted manufacturing costs		$ 221,644	$ 252,821	$ 291,729	$ 766,194

© Cengage Learning 20

Selling and Administrative Expense Budget

A selling and administrative expense budget for Tina's includes variable expenses, such as commissions, shipping costs, and supplies, as well as fixed costs, such as rent, insurance, salaries, and advertising. Tina's commissions are a function of projected sales and are calculated as 10 percent of projected sales. Tina's selling and administrative expense budget is shown in Exhibit 9-12.

Exhibit 9-12 Selling and Administrative Expense Budget

Tina's Fine Juices				
Selling and Administrative Expense Budget				
	January	February	March	1st Quarter
Variable selling and administrative expenses				
Commissions[1]	$26,250	$34,125	$ 47,250	$ 107,625
Shipping costs	$10,500	$13,650	$ 18,900	$ 43,050
Supplies	$ 2,100	$ 2,720	$ 3,780	$ 8,600
Fixed selling and adminstrative expenses				
Rent	$20,000	$20,000	$ 20,000	$ 60,000
Insurance	$ 5,000	$ 5,000	$ 5,000	$ 15,000
Salaries	$15,000	$15,000	$ 15,000	$ 45,000
Advertising	$ 8,000	$ 8,000	$ 8,000	$ 24,000
Total selling and administrative expenses	$86,850	$98,495	$117,930	$ 303,275

[1] Commissions are based on 10% of projected sales (**Exhibit 9-5**).

LO5 Cash Budgets

Why Focus on Cash?

Many managers consider managing cash flow to be the single most important consideration in running a successful business. After all, cash, *not* income, pays the bills. Whereas income (earnings per share) is often important to external investors, cash flow frequently takes center stage for managers.

The timing of cash inflows and outflows is critical to the overall planning process. When cash inflows are delayed because of the extension of credit to buyers, there may not be sufficient cash to pay suppliers, creditors, and employee wages. Timely payment is necessary to maintain good business relationships with suppliers (and to keep employees happy) and to take the maximum discounts that may be available on purchases. Cash budgeting forces managers to focus on cash flow and to plan for the purchase of materials, the payment of creditors, and the payment of salaries. Sufficient cash must be available to pay dividends to stockholders and to acquire new fixed assets. As can be seen in the example in the next section, cash budgets also point out the need for borrowing cash or when excess cash can be invested or used to repay debt.

The Cash Receipts Budget—Sales

The first cash budget that must be prepared is the **cash receipts budget** for sales. The cash receipts budget for sales shows cash receipts that are generated from cash sales of inventory or services and from customer payments on account.

All the sales of Tina's Fine Juices are on account. On the basis of the company's experience in previous years, Tina's estimates that 50 percent of the sales each month will be paid for in the month of sale. Tina's also estimates that 35 percent of each month's sales will be collected in the month following sale and that 15 percent of each month's sales will be collected in the second month following sale.[3] As you will recall from the sales budget (Exhibit 9-5), sales for January, February, and March were projected to be $262,500, $341,250, and $472,500, respectively. Because collections lag sales by up to two months (some of November's

[3]It would not be unusual for some of the sales never to be collected. If Tina's thinks that some of the accounts receivable are uncollectible, the cash receipts budget should be adjusted accordingly.

> **Cash receipts budget** Used to project the amount of cash expected to be received from sales to customers and cash collections from customers.

sales will not be collected until January, and some of December's sales will not be collected until February), completing the cash receipts budget also requires that we include sales for November and December. November's sales were $200,000, and December's sales were $250,000.

The preparation of the cash receipts budget is straightforward once the payment scheme is set. In each month, we collect 50 percent of that month's sales (50 percent of January's sales are collected in January), 35 percent of the previous month's sales (35 percent of December's sales are collected in January), and 15 percent of the second previous month's sales (15 percent of November's sales are collected in January). Then the payment scheme is repeated for the remainder of the months in the budget. A cash receipts budget for cash received from sales is presented in Exhibit 9-13.

A closer look at the cash receipts budget shows that budgeted cash re-

ceipts are significantly different from budgeted sales revenue. In February and March, cash receipts are expected to be less than sales revenue. When sales are increasing and there is a lag between sales and the collection of cash, this is usually the case. It seems ironic,

Exhibit 9-13 Cash Receipts Budget—Sales

Month	Sales		January		February		March		1st Quarter
November	$200,000		$ 30,000	15%	$ -		$ -		$ 30,000
December	$250,000		$ 87,500	35%	$ 37,500	15%	$ -		$ 125,000
January	$262,500	Exhibit 9- 5	$ 131,250	50%	$ 91,875	35%	$ 39,375	15%	$ 262,500
February	$341,250	Exhibit 9- 5	$ -		$ 170,625	50%	$ 119,438	35%	$ 290,063
March	$472,500	Exhibit 9- 5	$ -		$ -		$ 236,250	50%	$ 236,250
Total cash receipts from sales			$ 248,750		$ 300,000		$ 395,063		$ 943,813

but businesses that are growing rapidly will often be short of cash.

The Cash Disbursements Budget— Manufacturing Costs

The next component in the cash budgeting process is the **cash disbursements budget** for manufacturing costs. The cash disbursements budget for manufacturing costs includes cash outflows resulting from payments to suppliers for materials, cash outflows for salaries and other labor costs, and cash outflows for overhead expenditures.

Budgeting for the cash disbursements related to materials, labor, and overhead is not as easy as just looking at the materials, labor, and overhead budgets. Purchases of materials are often made on account, resulting in lags between the date items are purchased and the date cash actually changes hands. The manufacturing overhead budget often includes noncash items, such as depreciation, that must be adjusted as well.

A cash disbursements budget for Tina's Fine Juices is shown in Exhibit 9-14. Tina's has a policy of paying 50 percent of the direct material purchases in the month of purchase and the balance in the month after purchase. This policy offsets to a certain extent the lag in cash receipts from sales. Purchases of direct materials are taken directly from the material purchases budgets (Exhibits 9-7 and 9-8), and then cash payments are adjusted for the payment lag. For example, in January, Tina's budgeted purchases of orange concentrate total $41,026 (see Exhibit 9-7). As shown in row 6 of the cash disbursements budget (Exhibit 9-14), 50 percent of this amount, or $20,513, will be paid in January, with the other 50 percent paid in February. Similar calculations are made for purchases of orange concentrate in February and March.

> **Accurate cash flow projections are critical if a company is to pay its employees, suppliers, and creditors on a timely basis.**

Exhibit 9-14 Cash Disbursements Budget— Manufacturing Costs

		January	February	March	1st Quarter
Tina's Fine Juices					
Cash Disbursements Budget - Manufacturing Costs					
Purchases of concentrate	Exhibit 9- 7				
December (given)		$ 18,220			$ 18,220
January		$ 20,513	$ 20,513		$ 41,026
February			$ 27,077	$ 27,077	$ 54,154
March				$ 34,651	$ 34,651
Purchases of bottles	Exhibit 9- 8				
December (given)		$ 12,146			$ 12,146
January		$ 13,675	$ 13,675		$ 27,350
February			$ 18,050	$ 18,050	$ 36,100
March				$ 23,100	$ 23,100
Total disbursements for material		$ 64,554	$ 79,315	$ 102,878	$ 246,747
Disbursements for direct labor	Exhibit 9- 9	$ 6,438	$ 8,437	$ 11,375	$ 26,250
Manufacturing overhead	Exhibit 9- 10				
December (given)		$ 20,917			$ 20,917
January		$ 21,748	$ 21,749		$ 43,497
February			$ 25,398	$ 25,399	$ 50,797
March				$ 30,759	$ 30,759
Total disbursements for manufacturing overhead		$ 42,665	$ 47,147	$ 56,158	$ 145,971
Total cash disbursements for manufacturing costs		$ 113,656	$ 134,899	$ 170,411	$ 418,967

© Cengage Learning 2013

Likewise, in January, Tina's budgeted purchases of bottles total $27,350 (see Exhibit 9-8). As with purchases of orange concentrate, half of this amount, or $13,675, will be paid in January and the other half in February (see row 11 of Exhibit 9-14). Similar calculations are made for purchases of bottles in February and March.

All direct labor costs are paid in the month incurred and come directly from the direct labor budget (see Exhibit 9-9).

> **Cash disbursements budget** Used to project the amount of cash to be disbursed during the budget period.

Like the cost of materials, manufacturing overhead costs are paid on a lag, with 50 percent paid for in the month incurred and 50 percent in the following month. However, the manufacturing overhead budget (Exhibit 9-10) must be adjusted for depreciation of property, plant, and equipment, which does not have a direct impact on cash flow.[4] Although total budgeted manufacturing overhead for January is estimated to be $146,830, $103,333 of this amount pertains to noncash depreciation and will not be included in the cash disbursements budget. Of the $43,497 of cash overhead expected in January ($146,830 − $103,333), 50 percent, or $21,748, will be paid in January, with the remaining $21,749 paid in February (see row 20 of Exhibit 9-14). Similar calculations are made for payments of manufacturing overhead expenses in February and March.

Summary Cash Budget

A basic summary cash budget is prepared in the following format:

    Beginning cash balance
  + Cash receipts
  ─────────────────────────────
  = Total cash available
  − Cash disbursements
  ─────────────────────────────
  = Cash balance before borrowing/repayment
  +/− Borrowing from/repayment of line of credit
  − Interest on line of credit
  ─────────────────────────────
  = Ending cash balance

Summary cash budgets can be fairly straightforward or very complex, depending on the size and complexity of the company. Tina's summary cash budget is shown in Exhibit 9-15.

[4]Recall from Chapter 8 that depreciation can have an indirect impact on cash flow through its impact on income taxes. The impact of income taxes is taken into account in the summary cash budget.

Summary cash budget Shows cash receipts and cash disbursements, along with any required borrowing or repayments made during the month.

Exhibit 9-15 Summary Cash Budget

© Cengage Learning 2013

Cash receipts from sales and cash disbursements related to manufacturing costs and to selling and administrative costs have already been summarized in Exhibits 9-12, 9-13, and 9-14. Tina's plans to buy some new machinery in February at a cost of $75,000 (see Exhibit 9-15, row 10). The company also plans on paying a dividend of $50,000 in January (see Exhibit 9-15, row 12). In addition, Tina's desires to keep a cash balance of at least $50,000 on hand at the end of any month. If the projected cash balance is less than that, a line of credit at Tina's local bank will be used to make up the shortage. If Tina's draws on the line of credit, the company is charged an interest rate of 10 percent annually. If the line of credit is used, money is borrowed at the beginning of the month. Repayments are made at the end of months in which there is sufficient excess cash (over $50,000) to pay back the entire line of credit. Last, but not least, Tina's pays estimated income taxes on a quarterly basis (in March, June, September, and December) on the income earned during the respective quarter. Tina's estimates that its federal tax liability is around 15 percent of taxable income.

LO6 Budgeted Financial Statements

Companies may also desire to prepare budgeted financial statements. These are used both for internal planning purposes and to provide information to external users. For example, a bank might want to examine a budgeted income statement and balance sheet before lending money to a company. The budgeted financial statements are often called **pro forma financial statements**.

Budgeted schedules of cost of goods manufactured and cost of goods sold are shown in Exhibits 9-16 and 9-17, respectively.

Note that the cost of goods manufactured and the cost of goods sold are calculated with absorption costing. Likewise, the budgeted income statement in Exhibit 9-18 is prepared in the traditional format with absorption costing. The budgeted balance sheet is shown in Exhibit 9-19.

As you can see, the set of operating budgets and budgeted financial statements form an interrelated set of planning tools that are vital for managers' decisions

Preparing budgeted, or pro forma, financial statements allows managers to determine the effects of their budgeting decisions on the company's financial statements.

affecting the number of units to produce, the amount of materials to purchase, how many employees to schedule for a particular period or shift (and when to schedule training, for example), the timing of major acquisitions and sales of equipment, and the overall management of cash.

Exhibit 9-16 Budgeted Cost of Goods Manufactured (Absorption)

	A	B	C	D
1	**Tina's Fine Juices**			
2	**Budgeted Cost of Goods Manufactured (Absorption)**			
3				
4	Beginning inventory of raw material[1]		$ 12,873	
5	Add purchases of raw material	Exhibit 9-7 and 9-8	$ 274,132	
6	Raw materials available for sale		$ 287,005	
7	Less ending inventory of raw material[2]		$ (24,502)	
8	Raw materials used in production			$ 262,503
9	Add direct labor	Exhibit 9-9		$ 26,250
10	Add manufacturing overhead	Exhibit 9-10		$ 465,812
11	Total manufacturing costs			$ 754,565
12	Add beginning inventory of WIP			$ -
13	Less ending inventory of WIP			$ -
14	Cost of goods manufactured			$ 754,565
15				
16	[1] The cost of the beginning inventory is given.			
17	[2] 3,063 gallons x $4.80 per gallon + 98,000 bottles x $.10 per bottle.			

Pro forma financial statements Budgeted financial statements that sometimes are used for internal planning purposes but more often are used by external users.

© Cengage Learning 2013

Exhibit 9-17 Budgeted Cost of Goods Sold (Absorption)

	A	B	C	D
1	**Tina's Fine Juices**			
2	**Budgeted Cost of Goods Sold (Absorption)**			
3	Beginning inventory of finished goods[1]		$ 17,966	
4	+ Cost of goods manufactured	**Exhibit 9-16**	$754,565	
5	= Cost of goods available for sale		$772,531	
6	- Ending inventory of finished goods[2]		$ (35,932)	
7	= Cost of goods sold		$736,599	
8				
9	[1] Beginning inventory of finished goods is given.			
10	[2] The cost of each of the 50,000 gallons is $.71863 per gallon ($754,565 cost of goods manufactured / 1,050,000 bottles produced).			
11				
12				
13				
14				

© Cengage Learning 2013

Exhibit 9-18 Budgeted Income Statement (Traditional)

	A	B	C	D
1	**Tina's Fine Juices**			
2	**Budgeted Income Statement (Traditional)**			
3				
4	Sales	**Exhibit 9-5**	$ 1,076,250	
5	Less cost of goods sold	**Exhibit 9-17**	$ 736,599	
6	Gross margin		$ 339,651	
7	Less selling and administrative expenses	**Exhibit 9-12**	$ (303,275)	
8	Net operating income		$ 36,376	
9	Less interest expense	**Exhibit 9-15**	$ (30,184)	
10	Income (before taxes)		$ 6,192	
11	Less income taxes (tax rate = 15%)		$ (929)	
12	Net income		$ 5,263	
13				

© Cengage Learning 2013

Exhibit 9-19 Budgeted Balance Sheet

	A	B	C
1		Tina's Fine Juices	
2		Budgeted Balance Sheet	
3	**Assets**		
4	Current assets:		
5	Cash	$ 115,458	Exhibit 9-15
6	Accounts receivable	$ 287,437	Exhibit 9- 5 ($341,250 x .15) + ($472,500 x .5)
7	Inventory: Direct materials	$ 24,502	Exhibit 9-16
8	Inventory: Finished goods	$ 35,932	Exhibit 9-17
9	Inventory: WIP	$ -	
10	Total current assets	$ 463,329	
11	Fixed assets (net of depreciation)	$ 5,075,000	$5,000,000 beginning balance (given) + $75,000 acquistions (Exhibit 9-15)
12	Total assets	$ 5,538,329	
13	**Liabilities and Equity**		
14	Current liabilities:		
15	Accounts payable	$ 88,511	Exhibits 9- 7, 9- 8 and 9- 10
16	Line of credit	$ -	
17	Income tax	$ 929	Exhibit 9-18
18	Total current liabilities	$ 89,440	
19	Long term liabilities	$ 1,500,000	
20	Total liabilities	$ 1,589,440	
21	Stockholders equity:		
22	Common stock	$ 3,500,000	Beginning balance (given)
23	Retained earnings	$ 448,889	Beginning balance of $493,626 (given) + income of $5,263 (Exhibit 9-18) - dividends paid of $50,000 (Exhibit 9-15)
24	Total liabilities and stockholders equity	$ 5,538,329	
25			
26			

© Cengage Learning 2013

LO7 Budgets for Merchandising Companies and Service Companies

The budgeting process for merchandising and service companies is similar to that for manufacturing companies, with a few important differences. It can also be every bit as complex. For example, consider the difficulty of budgeting for a professional baseball team like the Chicago White Sox. It can be a challenge to predict revenue from ticket sales because revenue is dependent on attendance and attendance is dependent on winning. Other revenue, such as that from parking, concessions, and souvenir sales, is also dependent on attendance. On the cost side, the number of security people hired depends on attendance. Accordingly, the budgeting process must be very adaptable. Sometimes budgets are even changed daily to take into account attendance fluctuations![5]

[5]Anita Dennis, "Budgeting for Curve Balls," *Journal of Accountancy,* Vol. 186, No. 3, 89–92.

Although service companies do not manufacture products, they may still prepare modified "production" budgets. For example, a CPA firm may budget not only for total revenues, but also for the amount of revenue expected to be generated by each type of engagement (tax, audit, and so forth), the number of those engagements expected (how many tax returns will be prepared), and the number of labor hours expected to be incurred in each. As a result, the main focus of budgeting for service companies will often be the labor budget. (The use of time budgets by service companies is discussed in more detail in the next section, on nonfinancial budgets.) Overhead is another important area of concern for service companies. A detailed budget of expected overhead expenditures (rent, utilities, insurance, and so on) is extremely useful in planning for cash outflows.

Merchandising companies are not involved in manufacturing the goods they sell. A merchandising company buys finished goods from manufacturing

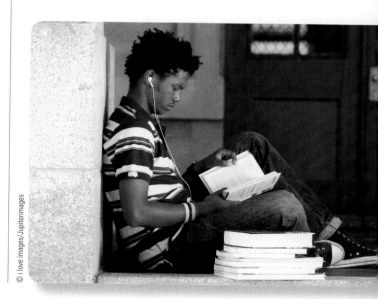

© i love images/Jupiterimages

companies and sells them to other companies for re-sale (wholesalers) or to final customers (retailers). Although merchandising companies will prepare a sales budget, they will not prepare budgets for production, direct material purchases, direct labor, or manufacturing overhead. However, merchandising companies will prepare a purchases budget (for goods to be sold to customers) based on the projections in the sales budget. In addition, many merchandising companies hold some level of merchandise inventory and will need to estimate desired inventory balances and adjust sales projections accordingly. The preparation of selling and administrative expense budgets, cash budgets, and budgeted financial statements in merchandising companies is similar to that in manufacturing companies.

LO8 Static versus Flexible Budgets

Static budgets are budgets that are established at the beginning of the period for one set level of activity and remain constant throughout the budget period. The budgets that are presented for Tina's Fine Juices are static budgets. Although static budgets are useful for planning and operating purposes, they can be problematic when used for control. As we discussed in Chapter 1, control involves motivating and monitoring employees and evaluating people and other resources used in the operations of an organization. The purpose of control is to make sure that the goals of the organization are being attained. Control requires the comparison of actual outcomes (cost of products, sales, and so on) with desired outcomes as stated in the organization's operating and strategic plans (including budgets). The idea is to compare budgeted amounts with actual results and then to analyze any differences for likely causes. However, when static budgets are used and actual sales are different from budgeted sales, such a comparison

Static budgets Budgets that are set at the beginning of the period and remain constant throughout the budget period.

Flexible budgets Budgets that take differences in spending owing to differences in volume out of the analysis by budgeting for labor (and other costs) on the basis of the *actual* number of units produced.

> *Flexible budgets are based on the actual number of units produced rather than on the budgeted units of production.*

is like comparing apples with oranges. If actual sales differ from projected sales, differences in production, material purchases, labor costs, and variable overhead should be expected. If actual sales are lower than budgeted sales, actual costs of materials, labor, and variable overhead *should* be lower than budgeted costs. The fact that a company's actual costs are lower than those budgeted under static conditions does not necessarily mean that the company (or its employees) was efficient.

For example, assume that Tina's Fine Juices produces 250,000 bottles of juice in January instead of the budgeted amount of 257,500 bottles. The projected direct labor cost (see Exhibit 9-9 on page 187) based on a static budget of 257,500 bottles was $6,438. At the end of January, Tina's had actual direct labor costs of $6,300. So Tina's spent $138 *less* than provided for in the static budget.

However, a comparison of actual labor costs to make 250,000 bottles with the budgeted labor costs to produce 257,500 bottles really does not make sense. Tina's ought to spend less for labor because fewer bottles were produced. The question then becomes, How much less? What we would really like to know is how much the labor costs should have been had we known that production was going to be 250,000 bottles instead of 257,500.

Flexible budgets do just that. Flexible budgets take differences in cost owing to differences in volume out of the analysis by budgeting for labor (and other costs) on the basis of the *actual number* of units produced.

A flexible direct labor budget for Tina's Fine Juices would budget labor costs on the basis of the actual January production of 250,000 bottles. Based on the labor time needed to produce 600 bottles and the direct labor rate per hour of $15, Tina's projected labor costs would then be $6,250 (250,000 bottles ÷ 600 bottles per hour = 416.666 hours; 416.666 × $15 per hour = $6,250), instead of $6,438. If we now compare the actual direct labor cost of $6,300 with the flexible budget amount of $6,250, we see that Tina's actually spent $50 *more* than expected instead of $138 *less* than expected:

	Flexible Budget	Actual	Difference
Production (bottles)	250,000	250,000	
Direct labor time per 600 bottles	1 hour		
Direct labor hours needed for production (250,000/600)	416.67		
Direct labor rate per hour	×$15		
Direct labor cost	$6,250	$6,300	$(50)

What explains the turnaround? By using flexible budgeting, Tina's removes any differences in cost caused by differences in volume of production and focuses only on differences arising from other factors.

What are those other factors? Perhaps Tina's paid more than $15 per hour for labor. However, another explanation is that Tina's used more than 417 labor hours or even some combination of the two. Without further analysis, we simply don't know. In Chapter 10, the use of flexible budgets is expanded to allow managers to break down these differences into variances resulting from either spending too much (or too little) or using too much (or too little). This process is called variance analysis.

STUDY TOOLS 9

Chapter review card

- ○ Learning Objective and Key Concept Reviews
- ○ Key Definitions and Formulas

Online (Located at www.cengagebrain.com)

- ○ Flash Cards and Crossword Puzzles
- ○ Games and Quizzes
- ○ High Sierra Video and E-Lectures
- ○ Homework Assignments (as directed by your instructor)

BRIEF EXERCISES

1. **Advantages of Budgeting** LO1

   Review the following incomplete statements regarding the advantages of budgeting.
   a. The budgeting process forces management to focus on the _____ and not be distracted by daily crises in the organization.
   b. The budgeting process can define specific _____ and objectives that can become _____, or standards of performance, for evaluating future performance.
   c. The budgeting process forces _____ throughout the organization.
   d. The budgeting process can increase the coordination of organizational activities and help facilitate goal _____.
   e. The budgeting process can help management identify and deal with potential _____ or constraints before they become major problems.

   Required
   Complete each of the preceding incomplete statements with the correct term or terms from the following list: *bottlenecks, communication, future, goals, congruence, benchmarks.*

2. Forecasting Sales LO2

Harriman Entertainment produced and sold 100,000 video games for $10 each last year. Demand is strong for the company's video games, and Harriman believes that volume will increase by 25 percent if the company increases the game price by 20 percent.

Required
What are Harriman's expected sales revenues for the coming year?

3. Purchases Budget LO4

Blanchard Company budgets on an annual basis for its fiscal year. The following beginning and ending inventory levels (in units) are planned for the fiscal year of July 1, 2011, through June 30, 2012:

	July 1, 2011	June 30, 2012
Raw materials*	40,000	50,000
Work in process	10,000	10,000
Finished goods	80,000	50,000

*Two units of raw material are needed to produce each unit of finished product.

Required
If Blanchard Company were to manufacture 500,000 finished units during the 2011–2012 fiscal year, how many units of raw material would it need to purchase?

4. Cash Receipts Budget LO5

Cookies and Cream begins business on January 1 of the current year and sells delicious chocolate chip cookies for $2.50 per box. The company's founder and lead marketing guru estimates first-quarter sales (in boxes) as follows:

January	1,500
February	1,200
March	1,600
Total	4,300

Cookies and Cream expects cash to be collected in the following manner:
55 percent of sales collected in month of sale
35 percent of sales collected in month following sale
10 percent of sales collected in second month following sale

Required
Prepare a cash receipts budget for the first quarter. How much will customers owe the company at the end of March if sales are exactly as estimated?

5. Budgeting Basics LO6, 7

Budgeting plays an important role in an organization's planning, operating, and control activities. The following statements relate to various aspects of budgeting.
a. Budgeted financial statements that are called pro forma financial statements should never be given to external parties such as banks.

b. Operating budgets and budgeted financial statements are combined to form an inter-related set of planning tools that managers use to make many decisions.
c. Although there are similarities between the budgeting process for a merchandising company and a manufacturing company, there are important differences, too.
d. A service company often spends a significant amount of time planning for and preparing a labor budget.
e. A merchandising company would likely prepare budgets for the following areas: sales, production, cash, and selling and administrative expenses.

Required
Indicate whether each of the preceding statements is true or false.

6. Flexible Budget LO8

Honolulu Hello produces pineapple candy. The company currently uses a static budget process. The company's controller prepared the following budget for April's production:

Estimated production	24,000 boxes
Direct labor per box	4 minutes
Direct labor required for estimated production	1,600 hours
Average direct labor rate per hour	$12.50
Estimated direct labor cost	$20,000

Actual production during April was 26,400 boxes and actual direct labor cost was $22,850.

Required
Prepare a flexible budget for Honolulu Hello that shows the projected direct labor cost and any difference between the budget and actual labor cost.

EXERCISES

7. Sales Budget LO2

Tim's Temple Tools sells small eyeglass repair tools for $1.25 each. Tim's marketing department prepared the following first-quarter sales forecast (in units):

January	125,000
February	135,000
March	170,000
Total	430,000

Required
Prepare Tim's sales budget for each month of the quarter.

8. Sales Budget LO2

Sarah's Salon performs manicures and pedicures for its clients. Sarah's also sells bottles of nail polish for $2.50 each. Sarah's marketing manager has prepared the following first-quarter sales forecast:

January	130 bottles
February	140 bottles
March	165 bottles
Total	435 bottles

Required

Prepare Sarah's sales budget for each month of the quarter.

9. Sales Forecast LO$_2$

Your friend Marcy Braeden has been working for the last two years with a small company that produces and sells a variety of small household items. Recently, she told you how amazed she is at how successful the company is in forecasting sales each year. She does not understand how the company does it.

Required

Help Marcy out by describing some of the factors that her employer may consider in forecasting sales.

10. Sales Budget LO$_{2,3}$

Lulu's Lockets sells small lockets for $1.50 each. The marketing department prepared the following first-quarter sales forecast:

January	135,000 units
February	125,000 units
March	155,000 units
Total	415,000 units

Required

Prepare the sales budget for Lulu's Lockets for each month of the quarter.

11. Production Budget LO$_3$

Mountain High makes and sells specialty mountain bikes. On June 30, the company had 50 bikes in finished-goods inventory. The company's policy is to maintain a bike inventory of 5 percent of the next month's sales. The company expects the following sales activity for the third quarter of the year:

July	1,200 bikes
August	1,000 bikes
September	900 bikes

Required

What is the projected production for August?

12. Purchases Budget LO$_4$

Lazy Day Donuts makes powdered donuts that are sold by the dozen. Each box of a dozen donuts requires ½ pound of flour. The company began the year with 20,000 pounds of flour on hand, but would like to have just 10,000 pounds of flour on hand at the end of the current year. Lazy Day expects to produce 200,000 boxes of donuts during the year.

Required

How many pounds of flour must be purchased during the year to have enough for production needs and the desired ending inventory?

13. Purchases Budget LO$_4$

Mandy's Modems estimates sales of 420,000 modems during the upcoming year. Each modem requires three internal memory chips. The company began the year with an inventory of 20,000 memory chips and no modems. The company's management wants to maintain an ending inventory of modems equal to 10 percent of the current year's sales and an ending inventory of chips equal to 10 percent of the current year's projected needs.

Required

How many memory chips must Mandy's Modems purchase during the year?

14. Purchases Budget LO$_4$

Crosser Company budgets on a quarterly basis. The following beginning and ending inventory levels (in units) are planned for the first and second quarters of 2012:

	Jan–March, 2012	April–June, 2012
Raw materials	40,000	50,000
Work in process	12,000	15,000
Finished goods	80,000	45,000
Two units of raw material are needed to produce each unit of finished product.		

Required

If Crosser Company were to manufacture 400,000 finished units (in total) during the first two quarters of 2012, how many units of raw material would it need to purchase? Prepare the purchases budget for the first six months of 2012.

15. Purchases Budget for a Merchandising Company LO$_4$

Loud Sounds sells specialty car stereo systems. On March 31, the company had 60 systems in inventory. The company's policy is to maintain inventory equal to 5 percent of next month's projected sales. The company expects the following sales activity for the second quarter of the year:

April	140 stereos
May	100 stereos
June	120 stereos

Required

Prepare a purchases budget for the month of May.

16. Direct Labor Budget LO4

Hammonds Hammocks produces and sells top-of-the-line Brazilian-style hammocks. The company prepared a production budget for the second quarter of the year which revealed that required production is 15,000 hammocks for April, 12,500 for May, and 12,500 for June. Each hammock requires 3 hours of direct labor at an average cost of $12 per hour (including all fringe benefits and taxes).

Required

Prepare Hammonds Hammocks's direct labor budget for the second quarter.

17. Selling and Administrative Budget LO4

Will's Wheel Shop sells high-end bicycles. Although business has been good, Will is concerned that some of the company's selling and administrative expenses are getting too high. He has asked you to help prepare a selling and administrative expense budget for him to review for the coming month. Another employee has accumulated information for you to use, but you should be careful because the employee does not know a lot about preparing this type of budget, so some items may not belong on the budget. Here is the other person's information:

Direct labor	$2,500
Store rental	1,200
Store supplies	450
Sales commission	925
Cost of bicycles	5,600
Advertising in the local paper	150
Insurance on bicycles in the store	100
Shipping costs for bicycle parts Will ordered	135

Required

Prepare a selling and administrative expense budget with separate sections for variable and fixed expenses.

18. Cash Receipts Budget LO5

Thirst Quencher sells plastic water bottles to outdoor enthusiasts for $1.25 each. The company's marketing manager prepared the following sales forecast (in units) for the first half of the year:

January	150,000
February	125,000
March	180,000
April	165,000
May	165,000
June	155,000
Total	940,000

Historically, the cash collection of sales has been as follows: 55 percent of sales collected in month of sale, 35 percent of sales collected in month following sale, and 9 percent of sales collected in second month following sale. The remaining 1 percent is never collected because customers do not pay.

Required

Prepare a cash receipts budget for each month of the second quarter (April, May, and June).

19. Cash Receipts Budget LO5

Art's Architecture Firm begins business on January 1 of the current year. The company charges $100 per hour for its services. Art estimates that first-quarter chargeable hours will be as follows:

January	100
February	500
March	400
Total	1,000

The firm expects cash to be collected in the following manner:

40 percent of revenues collected in the month of work

50 percent of revenues collected in the month following work

10 percent of revenues collected in second month following work

Required

Prepare a cash receipts budget for the first quarter. How much will clients owe the company at the end of March if revenues are exactly as estimated?

20. Cash Summary Budget LO5

The following records from Benson, Inc., are provided to assist you with the preparation of cash summary budgets. Benson requires a minimum cash balance of $7,000 to start each quarter. The following amounts are in thousands of dollars:

	Quarter			
	1	2	3	4
Beginning cash balance	$10	$?	$?	$?
Cash collections	?	?	126	80
Total cash available	$86	$?	$?	$?
Inventory purchases	41	59	?	33
Operating expenses	?	43	55	?
Equipment purchases	11	9	8	5
Dividends	3	3	3	3
Total disbursements	$?	$114	$?	$?
Excess (deficiency) of cash	(4)	?	30	?
Financing:				
Borrowings	?	21	—	—
Repayments*	—	—	(?)	(8)
Total	$?	$?	$?	$?
Ending cash balance	$?	$?	$?	$?

*Includes interest.

Required

Fill in the missing amounts in Benson's cash summary budget.

21. Cash Disbursements Budget LO5

Robyn's Rocket Shop sells various types of fireworks and firecrackers. The data that follow were taken from Robyn's detailed budgeted income statement for the month of June. Although the labor costs and rent will be paid during June, the advertising expense and inventory purchases will be paid for in July. Half of the selling expense is paid in June; the other half is not due until July. Here are the figures:

Labor expenses	$10,000
Advertising expenses	1,400
Rent on store	5,000
Inventory purchases	$3,800
Selling expenses	6,750

Required

Prepare a cash disbursements budget for Robyn's Rocket Shop for the month of June.

22. Budgeted Income Statement LO6

Robyn's Rocket Shop is in the midst of negotiating a loan from First National Bank. The bank has asked Robyn to prepare a budgeted income statement for the third quarter of the year (July through September). Robyn has accumulated the following data from various budgets for this purpose:

Sales forecast	$185,000
Interest expense	2,400
Selling and administrative expenses	74,450
Cost of goods sold	56,800

Required

Prepare a budgeted income statement for Robyn's Rocket Shop for the third quarter for presentation to First National Bank. Assume that the company's income tax rate is 30%.

23. Flexible Budget LO8

Ershey's Chocolates produces milk chocolate candy bars. The company currently uses a static budget process. The company's controller prepared the following budget for October's production:

Estimated production	50,000 bars
Direct labor per bar	3 minutes
Direct labor required for estimated production	2,500 hours
Average direct labor rate per hour	$15.00
Estimated direct labor cost	$37,500

Actual production during October was 53,000 bars and actual direct labor cost was $39,000.

Required

Prepare a flexible budget for Ershey's Chocolates that shows the projected direct labor cost and any difference between the flexible budget and actual labor costs. Were the company's labor costs over or under budget for the month?

PROBLEMS

24. The Sales Budget and CVP Analysis LO1, 2

CNX Motors is preparing a sales budget for the current year for the service department. The budget is based on last year's actual amounts. Management is interested in understanding what might happen if the service department has an increase in sales volume (i.e., the number of mechanic hours) or an increase in the average revenue per mechanic hour. They believe that, because of economic conditions in the local market, it is unlikely that both would increase. Last year's sales amounts were as follows:

	Mechanic Hours	Total Revenues
January	1,174	$11,681
February	1,057	10,538
March	1,125	11,261
April	1,516	15,008
May	1,724	16,981
June	2,515	25,014
July	2,746	27,185
August	3,107	30,604
September	2,421	23,823
October	2,211	22,154
November	1,709	17,090
December	1,524	15,125

Required

A. Compute the average revenue per mechanic hour for the current year on the basis of last year's actual data. Round the average hourly rate to the nearest penny.

B. Prepare a monthly sales budget for the current year, assuming that monthly sales volume (i.e., mechanic hours) will be 10 percent greater than it was in the same month last year. Assume that the average revenue per mechanic hour is the same as you computed in question A. Round budgeted hours to one decimal and budgeted revenues to the nearest dollar.

C. Prepare a monthly sales budget for the current year, assuming that the average revenue per mechanic hour computed in question A increased by 5 percent. Assume also that the number of mechanic hours stays the same as in the previous year. That is, there is no increase or decrease in the monthly sales volume. Round the rate per mechanic hour to two decimals and budgeted revenues to the nearest dollar.

D. For the current year in total, is it more advantageous to increase sales volume by 10 percent or average revenue per hour by 5 percent? Remember the impact of variable and fixed costs on these projections.

25. Sales, Production, and Material Purchases Budgets LO2, 3, 4

Curiosity Corner sells books and various other reading-related products. One of the store's most popular reading-related products is a book pillow for hard-cover and soft-cover books. The pillows sell for $8.00 each. Originally, the pillows were hand-made by a local artisan. The store's owner has been impressed with the demand for the pillow and has recently begun a small manufacturing company to produce and distribute the pillows to other stores. Estimated sales for the fourth quarter (in units) are as follows:

October	6,500
November	7,200
December	9,600
Total	23,300

Each pillow requires ½ yard of fabric that costs, on average, $6 per yard.

Required
A. Prepare a sales budget for the fourth quarter on the basis of the preceding information.
B. Prepare a production budget for the pillow-manufacturing company. The company did not have any inventory of pillows at the end of September, but the company does want to maintain a 10 percent inventory at the end of each month, based on the next month's estimated sales. January's sales are expected to be low, given the postholiday trends, and are estimated to be 4,800 units.
C. Prepare a fabric purchases budget. The company did not have any inventory of fabric at the end of September, but the company does want to maintain a fabric inventory equal to 20 percent of the next month's material needs. January's projected production is expected to be 4,820 units.

26. Sales and Cash Collections Budgets LO2, 5

Mountain Mash produces ice cream for wholesale distribution to grocers, restaurants, and independent ice cream shops. March, April, May, June, and July are busy months for the company as its customers gear up for the spring and summer rush. Mountain Mash has projected the following level of sales (in gallons) for March through July:

Month	Units	Month	Units
March	70,000	June	90,000
April	80,000	July	92,000
May	85,000		

The company has a set wholesale selling price of $3.50 per gallon. Mountain Mash's customers purchase ice cream on credit, with the agreement that they must pay invoices within 30 days. Nonetheless, not all customers pay within that time frame. Mountain Mash's credit manager has developed the following table to show the typical cash collection pattern:

70 percent of sales are collected in the month of sale
25 percent of sales are collected in the month following the month of sale
5 percent of sales are collected in the second month following the month of sale

Required
A. Prepare a sales budget for March, April, May, June, and July.
B. Prepare a cash receipts budget for May, June, and July. Be sure to remember the cash collections from months prior to May.
C. If sales and cash collections are exactly as the company estimates, how much will customers owe Mountain Mash as of the end of July?

27. Production and Purchases Budget LO3, 4

Alvarez Company produces various parts used in the automotive industry. The sales budget for the first eight months of 2012 shows the following projections:

Month	Units	Month	Units
January	25,000	May	31,400
February	27,000	June	34,500
March	32,000	July	36,700
April	28,500	August	35,000

Inventory on December 31 of the previous year was budgeted at 6,250 units. The desired quantity of finished-goods inventory at the end of each month in 2012 is to be equal to 25 percent of the next month's budgeted unit sales. Each unit of finished product requires three pounds of raw material. The company wants to have 30 percent of next month's required raw materials on hand at the end of each month.

Required
A. Prepare a production budget for January through June of 2012.
B. Prepare a material purchases budget for the same period, assuming that each pound of raw material costs $22.

28. Production and Direct Material Purchases Budget LO3, 4

Anderson Company produces decorative windows for residential and commercial applications. The company's marketing department has prepared a sales forecast for the first eight months of 2012 based on past sales trends and expected marketing and pricing plans. The vice president of marketing believes that the sales forecast is reasonable and hopes to grow sales in the coming year based partly on the marketing and pricing changes put in place during the year. The sales forecast for 2012 is as follows:

Month	Units	Month	Units
January	10,000	May	22,100
February	17,000	June	24,300
March	13,000	July	26,200
April	18,500	August	27,000

Inventory on December 31, 2011, was budgeted at 1,500 units. The desired quantity of finished-goods inventory at the end of each month in 2012 is to be equal to 15 percent of the next month's budgeted unit sales. Each completed unit of finished product requires 1.5 gallons of a special resin. The company has determined that it needs 20 percent of next month's raw material needs on hand at the end of each month.

Required

A. Prepare a production budget for January through June of 2012.

B. Prepare a material purchases budget for the same period, assuming that each gallon of the special resin costs $10.

29. Direct Labor and Manufacturing Overhead Budgets LO4

KenCor Pizza Emporium produces frozen pizzas for sale to grocery stores. The company has built a strong reputation for high-quality pizzas and has been profitable for a number of years. Because of increasing costs, KenCor is trying to control costs in the future. The CEO has asked the accounting and marketing departments to provide data related to labor costs and manufacturing overhead. The production budget for the upcoming year is as follows:

Month	Pizzas	Month	Pizzas
January	2,100	July	1,450
February	2,600	August	1,200
March	2,300	September	1,350
April	2,450	October	1,750
May	2,100	November	1,550
June	2,175	December	2,050

Each pizza requires ½ hour of direct labor to produce. The company currently applies manufacturing overhead to production at the rate of $2.50 per direct labor hour.

Required

A. Prepare a direct labor budget for the year. Direct labor averages $12 per hour.

B. Prepare a manufacturing overhead budget for the same period.

30. Direct Labor and Overhead Budgets LO4

Ash Company manufactures telephone handsets under various brand names. The company has built a strong reputation based on quality telephones and has been profitable for a number of years. Harriman Lassiter, the company's president, has decided to make a significant push for labor and overhead cost controls in the coming months because of increased overseas competition. Harriman has asked the marketing and accounting departments to provide data related to labor costs and manufacturing overhead. Production budgets for the period ending June 30 are as follows:

Month	Units	Month	Units
January	25,000	April	28,500
February	27,000	May	31,400
March	32,000	June	34,500

Each telephone requires 2.5 hours of direct labor for assembly and testing. The company currently applies manufacturing overhead to production at the rate of $7 per direct labor hour.

Required

A. Prepare a direct labor budget for January through June. Direct labor averages $15 per hour.

B. Prepare a manufacturing overhead budget for the same period.

31. Direct Labor and Overhead Budgets LO4

Babcock Builders is a well-regarded construction company that serves as a general contractor for both residential and commercial construction projects. One of the company's signature features is its cabinetry. The company's founder and president, Bill Babcock, began manufacturing cabinets six years ago in an effort to capitalize on the company's reputation and the skills of its craftsmen. The company's production budget for the first seven months of the year is as follows:

Month	Units	Month	Units
January	10,000	May	22,100
February	17,000	June	24,300
March	13,000	July	26,200
April	18,500		

Babcock's most popular cabinet is a small cherrywood cabinet typically used in bathrooms. Each completed unit requires 3.5 hours of direct labor, and the skilled labor costs an average of $25 per hour. The company applies overhead at the rate of $3 per direct labor hour.

Required

A. Prepare a direct labor budget for January through June.

B. Prepare a manufacturing overhead budget for the same period.

32. Cash Receipts Budget LO5

Barrera's Outdoor Outfitters sells many items that sporting enthusiasts find useful. The company sells shoes, pants, shirts, jackets, fly-fishing equipment, hiking equipment, hunting equipment, and various other products. The following sales projections were prepared by the company's sales manager and include all items for each of the first seven months of 2012:

Month	Sales Volume	Month	Sales Volume
January	25,000	May	31,400
February	27,000	June	34,500
March	32,000	July	36,700
April	28,500		

The average sales price per item is $12. The company estimates that it collects 70 percent of each month's sales in the month of sale and 20 percent the following month. The remaining outstanding sales are collected in the next month. The balance of accounts receivable on December 31, 2011, was $141,600. Of the accounts receivable balance, $33,600 represents uncollected November sales.

Required

Prepare a cash receipts budget for January through June of 2012.

33. Cash Receipts Budget LO5

Baum Bookstore is a tradition at State University. The store has served students and faculty for more than 50 years and is still regarded as the premier bookstore in the area. Baum Bookstore's sales budget shows the following projections (i.e., the number of units in each category) for the period ending May 31, 2012:

Month	Books	School Supplies	Software	Miscellaneous
January	4,000	2,700	240	1,700
February	1,400	1,450	190	1,400
March	1,000	1,310	175	1,500
April	500	1,600	100	1,650
May	1,800	1,850	145	2,125

The average sales price of each of the various items is as follows: books, $70; school supplies, $20; software, $90; and miscellaneous, $15. Because the store sells primarily to students and faculty, there are no credit sales.

Required

Prepare a cash receipts budget by item category for each month.

34. Cash Receipts, Disbursements, and Summary Budgets LO5

Hailey's Hats manufactures and distributes hats for every imaginable occasion. Henrietta Hailey started the company in her house three years ago and has been surprised at her success. She is considering an expansion of her business and needs to prepare cash-budgeting information for presentation to Second National Bank to secure a loan. Henrietta is not an accountant, so she has asked you to help her with preparing the necessary reports.

Hailey's Hats began the month with a bank balance of $10,000. The budgeted sales for March through June are as follows:

	March	April	May	June
Cash sales	$14,000	$16,500	$15,500	$17,500
Sales on account	29,000	30,000	40,000	50,000
Total sales	$43,000	$46,500	$55,500	$67,500

Henrietta has found that she generally collects payment for credit sales over a two-month period. Typically, 70 percent is collected in the month of sale and the remainder is collected in the next month. Her policy is to purchase inventory each month equivalent to 60 percent of that month's budgeted sales. She thinks that this provides her sufficient inventory levels to manage unanticipated changes in demand. Hailey's Hats pays for inventory purchases in the month following purchase. Selling and administrative expenses are budgeted to be 30 percent of each month's sales. One-half of the selling and administrative expenses is accounted for by depreciation on Henrietta's manufacturing equipment. The company purchased additional manufacturing equipment in April at a cost of $24,000. Henrietta does not receive a salary, but she does pay herself dividends as company performance allows. The first quarter of the year was very profitable, so Henrietta paid herself a dividend of $12,500 in April. Henrietta wants to maintain a minimum cash balance of $10,000 and has established a line of credit so that she can borrow enough money to make up any shortfall. If the company has excess cash on hand at the end of a month (in excess of $10,000), the line of credit will be paid back. Interest on the line of credit will not be paid until the end of the year. (Ignore any interest payments that the company would make on its borrowings.)

Required

A. Prepare a cash receipts budget for April, May, and June.
B. Prepare a cash disbursements budget for April, May, and June.
C. Prepare a summary cash budget for April, May, and June.

35. Cash Receipts, Disbursements, and Summary Budget LO5

Barley Restaurant Supply sells various equipment and supplies to restaurants in the local and surrounding communities. The company's controller, Barry Barley, has requested your help in preparing a cash budget for the month of June. Barry accumulated the following information for you:

a. The cash balance on June 1 was estimated to be $10,000.

b. Actual sales for April and May, and budgeted sales for June, are as follows:

	April	May	June
Cash sales	$16,500	$15,500	$17,500
Sales on account	30,000	40,000	50,000
Total sales	$46,500	$55,500	$67,500

Sales on account are collected over a two-month period, with 70 percent being collected in the first month and the remainder being collected in the second month.

c. Inventory purchases are expected to be $35,000 in June. The company pays for inventory purchases in the month following the purchase. The balance of May's purchases is $22,000.

d. Selling and administrative expenses are budgeted to be $14,000 for June. Of that amount, 50 percent is depreciation.

e. Equipment costing $14,000 will be purchased in June for cash.

f. Dividends in the amount of $2,500 will be paid.

g. The company wants to maintain a minimum cash balance of $10,000 and has set up a line of credit at the local bank that can be used to cover any shortage. If the company must borrow, the loan will be made at the beginning of the month and any repayment will be made at the end of the month of repayment.

Required

A. Prepare a cash receipts budget for June.
B. Prepare a cash disbursements budget for June.
C. Prepare a schedule that shows whether any borrowing against the line of credit is needed.

36. Budgeted Income Statement and Balance Sheet LO6

The Cold Mountain Furnace Company is a retail store with locations across the eastern United States. The company's income statement for its first year of operations, ended December 31, 2011, and its balance sheet as of December 31, 2011, are shown here:

Income Statement

Sales	$4,000,000
Less cost of sales	2,300,000
Gross margin	$1,700,000
Less selling, general, and administrative costs	800,000
Income before taxes	$ 900,000
Less income taxes	360,000
Net income	$ 540,000

Balance Sheet

Cash	$ 300,000
Accounts receivable	150,000
Inventory	400,000
Property, plant, and equipment (net of accumulated depreciation)	200,000
Total assets	$1,050,000
Accounts payable	$ 110,000
Common stock	400,000
Retained earnings	540,000
Total liabilities and owner's equity	$1,050,000

Additional information for 2012 is as follows:

a. **Sales Budget (Budgeted Sales) For 2012**

First quarter	$1,050,000
Second quarter	1,100,000
Third quarter	1,150,000
Fourth quarter	1,100,000

b. Sales are collected in two portions, consisting of 85 percent in the quarter of the sale and 15 percent in the quarter following the sale. All of the accounts receivable as of December 31, 2011, relate to sales in the fourth quarter of 2011.

c. The cost of sales is expected to increase to 60 percent of sales in 2012. Inventory is purchased in the quarter of expected sale. Eighty percent of inventory purchases is paid for in the quarter of purchase and 20 percent is paid for in the quarter following purchase.

d. The accounts payable balance as of December 31, 2011, relates to inventory purchases made in the fourth quarter of 2011.

e. Selling, general, and administrative costs are expected to increase to $225,000 per quarter in 2012. Of this quarterly amount, $10,000 is depreciation expense related to the property, plant, and equipment.

f. The inventory balance at the end of 2012 is $400,000.

g. The company's tax rate is expected to be 40 percent.

Required

A. Prepare a budgeted income statement for 2012.

B. Prepare a budgeted balance sheet as of December 31, 2012.

37. Static vs. Flexible Budgets LO8

The static budget for the College Book Division of Chasse and Joos Publishers estimated a sales revenue of $10,000,000 on sales of 165,000 units. The variable production costs (cost of goods sold) were estimated at $4,125,000, or $25 per unit sold. Actual results for the company exceeded expectations, with revenue of over $11,000,000 on sales of 180,000 units. However, the production manager was disappointed to see that the actual variable production costs of $4,400,000 exceeded the costs in the static budget by $275,000. The production manager did not understand why his costs were so much higher than the budgeted amount. If anything, he thought that his division had been very efficient and that costs should have been lower than reflected in the budget.

Required

Explain why the production manager's actual costs exceeded the amount estimated in the static budget. Should the production division be disappointed with the results?

CASE

38. Comprehensive Budget Problem
LO2, 3, 4, 5, 6

Tina's Fine Juices is a bottler of orange juice located in the Northeast. The company produces bottled orange juice from fruit concentrate purchased from suppliers in Florida, Arizona, and California. The only ingredients in the juice are water and concentrate. The juice is blended, pasteurized, and bottled for sale in 12-ounce plastic bottles. The process is heavily automated and is centered on five machines that control the mixing and bottling of the juice. The amount of labor required is very small per bottle of juice. The average worker can process 10 bottles of juice per minute, or 600 bottles per hour. The juice is sold by a number of grocery stores under their store brand name and in smaller restaurants, delis, and bagel shops under the name of Tina's Fine Juices. Tina's has been in business for several years and uses a sophisticated sales forecasting model based on previous sales, expected changes in demand, and economic factors affecting the industry. Sales of juice are highly seasonal, peaking in the first quarter of the calendar year.

Forecasted sales for the last two months of 2012 and all of 2013 are as follows:

2012	Bottles
November	375,000
December	370,000
2013	
January	350,000
February	425,000
March	400,000
April	395,000
May	375,000
June	350,000
July	375,000
August	385,000
September	395,000
October	405,000
November	400,000
December	365,000

Following is some other information that relates to Tina's Fine Juices:

a. Juice is sold for $1.05 per 12-ounce bottle, in cartons that hold 50 bottles each.

b. Tina's Fine Juices tries to maintain at least 10 percent of the next month's estimated sales in inventory at the end of each month.

c. The company needs to prepare two purchases budgets: one for the concentrate used in its orange juice and one for the bottles that are purchased from an outside supplier. Tina's has determined that it takes 1 gallon of orange concentrate for every 32 bottles of finished product. Each gallon of concentrate costs $4.80. Tina's also requires 20 percent of next month's direct material needs to be on hand at the end of the budget period. Bottles can be purchased from an outside supplier for $0.10 each.

d. Factory workers are paid an average of $15 per hour, including fringe benefits and payroll taxes. If the production schedule doesn't allow for full utilization of the workers and machines, one or more workers are temporarily moved to another department.

e. Most of the production process is automated, the juice is mixed by machine, and machines do the bottling and packaging. Overhead costs are incurred almost entirely in the mixing and bottling process. Consequently, Tina's has chosen to use a plantwide cost driver (machine hours) to apply manufacturing overhead to products.

f. Variable overhead costs will be in direct proportion to the number of bottles of juice produced, but fixed overhead costs will remain constant, regardless of production. For budgeting purposes, Tina's separates variable overhead from fixed overhead and calculates a predetermined overhead rate for variable manufacturing overhead costs.

g. Variable overhead is estimated to be $438,000 for the year, and the production machines will run approximately 8,000 hours at the projected production volume for the year (4,775,000 bottles). Therefore, Tina's predetermined rate for variable overhead is $54.75 per machine hour ($438,000 ÷ 8,000 machine hours).

Tina's has also estimated fixed overhead to be $1,480,000 per year ($123,333 per month), of which $1,240,000 per year ($103,333 per month) is depreciation on existing property, plant, and equipment.

h. All of the company's sales are on account. On the basis of the company's experience in previous years, the company estimates that 50 percent of the sales each month will be paid for in the month of sale. The company also estimates that 35 percent of the month's sales will be collected in the month following sale and that 15 percent of each month's sales will be collected in the second month following sale.

i. Tina's has a policy of paying 50 percent of the direct material purchases in the month of purchase and the balance in the month after purchase. Overhead costs are also paid 50 percent in the month they are incurred and 50 percent in the next month.

j. Selling and administrative expenses are $100,000 per month and are paid in cash as they are incurred.

Required

A. Prepare a sales budget for the first quarter of 2013.

B. Prepare a production budget for the first quarter of 2013.

C. Prepare a purchases budget for the first quarter of 2013.

D. Prepare a direct labor budget for the first quarter of 2013.

E. Prepare an overhead budget for the first quarter of 2013.

F. Prepare cash receipts and disbursements budgets for the first quarter of 2013.

Variance Analysis—
A Tool for Cost Control and Performance Evaluation

Introduction

As discussed in the previous chapter, budgeting is a tool that managers use to plan and to make decisions. In this chapter, we expand our discussion of budgeting to include its use as a control tool.

Control involves the motivation and monitoring of employees and the evaluation of people and other resources used in the operations of the organization. The purpose of control is to make sure that the goals of the organization are being attained. Control includes the use of incentives and other rewards to motivate employees to accomplish an organization's goals, as well as mechanisms to detect and correct deviations from those goals.

A control mechanism is a little like a thermostat in your house. If you desire to keep your house at 70 degrees (the budgeted temperature), the thermostat continually measures the actual temperature in the room and compares the actual temperature with the budgeted temperature. If the actual temperature deviates from 70 degrees, the thermostat will signal the heating system to come on (if the actual temperature is less than 70 degrees) or will turn on the air-conditioning (if the temperature is above 70 degrees). Managers need a similar type of control system to control budgetary differences.

In business, control often involves the comparison of actual outcomes (cost of products, units sold, sales prices, and so on) with desired outcomes as stated in an organization's operating and strategic plans. Control decisions include questions of how to evaluate performance, what measures to use, and what types of incentives to use. At the end of an accounting period (month, quarter, year), managers can use the budget as a control tool by comparing budgeted sales, budgeted production, and budgeted manufacturing costs with actual sales, production, and manufacturing costs. These comparisons are typically made through a process called **variance analysis**.

Control Involves the motivation and monitoring of employees and the evaluation of people and other resources used in the operations of the organization.

Variance analysis Allows managers to see whether sales, production, and manufacturing costs are higher or lower than planned and, more important, *why* actual sales, production, and costs differ from those budgeted.

Variance analysis helps companies such as Corinne's Country Rockers control costs and evaluate performance.

Variance analysis allows managers to see whether sales, production, and manufacturing costs are higher or lower than planned and, more important, *why* actual sales, production, and costs differ from those budgeted.

The key to effective variance analysis is **management by exception**. Management by exception is the process of taking action only when actual results deviate significantly from planned results. The key term in this definition is *significantly*. Managers typically do not have the time to investigate every deviation from budget (nor would such investigations likely add value to the organization), so they should focus on material, or significant, differences. Such a focus allows managers to concentrate their energy where it is

Management by exception
The process of taking action only when actual results deviate significantly from planned results.

© Jill Lang/Shutterstock.com

needed and where it is likely to make a difference. The concept of materiality and its use in variance analysis is discussed in more depth later in the chapter.

LO1 **Standard Costing**

To facilitate the use of flexible budgeting for control purposes, it is helpful to examine the budget at the microlevel rather than the macrolevel—that is, to develop a budget for a single unit of a product or a service rather than for the company as a whole. A budget for a single unit of a product or a service is known as the **standard cost** of the product or service. Just as the cost of a product consists of three components—direct materials, direct labor, and manufacturing overhead—a standard cost will be developed for each component. In addition, each component consists of two separate standards—a standard quantity and a standard price. The **standard quantity** tells us the budgeted *amount* of materials, labor, and overhead in a product, whereas the **standard price** tells us the budgeted *price* of the materials, labor, or overhead for each unit (gallon, hour, and so on).

Standards can be determined in a couple of ways. Management can analyze historical cost and production data to determine how much materials and labor were used in each unit of product and how much the materials and labor cost. Likewise, management can look at historical data to determine the amount of overhead costs incurred in producing a certain number of units. For companies with a long history of producing the same product, historical data can be very useful in forecasting future prices and quantities. However, historical data must be used with caution and adjusted

> The type of standard (practical or ideal) chosen to evaluate performance can have significant effects on employee morale and behavior.

when necessary. For example, changes in product design or manufacturing processes can dramatically change both the amounts and the prices of materials, labor, and overhead.

Another method of setting standards is called **task analysis**. Task analysis examines the production process in detail, with an emphasis on determining what it *should* cost to produce a product, not what it cost last year. Task analysis typically involves the use of engineers who perform time-and-motion studies to determine how much material should be used in a product, how long it takes to perform certain labor tasks in manufacturing the product, how much electricity is consumed, and so on. Typically, some combination of task analysis and historical cost analysis will be used in determining standard costs.

Ideal versus Practical Standards

Because standard costs are used to evaluate performance, human behavior can influence how the standards are determined. Should standards be set so they are easy to attain or set so they can rarely be attained? An **ideal standard** is one that is attained only when near-perfect conditions are present. An ideal standard assumes that every aspect of the production process, from purchasing through shipment, is at peak efficiency. Some managers like ideal standards because they believe that employees will be motivated to achieve more when the goals are set very high. Others argue that employees are discouraged by unattainable standards. Employees may be motivated to cut corners, use less-than-optimum materials, or skimp on labor to achieve the standards. This type of behavior can lead to poor quality and an increase in defective units produced, which may cost the company more in the long run.

A **practical standard** should be attainable under normal, efficient operating conditions. Practical standards take into consideration that machines break down occasionally, that employees are not always perfect, that waste in materials does occur. Most managers would

Standard cost A budget for a single unit of product or service.

Standard quantity The budgeted amount of materials, labor, or overhead for each product.

Standard price The budgeted price of the materials, labor, or overhead for each unit.

Task analysis A method of setting standards that examines the production process in detail to determine what it should cost to produce a product.

Ideal standard A standard that is attained only when near-perfect conditions are present.

Practical standard A standard that should be attained under normal, efficient operating conditions.

agree that practical standards encourage employees to be more positive and productive.

Use of Standards by Nonmanufacturing Organizations

The use of standard costing applies to merchandising and service organizations as well. Just as **Panasonic** needs to determine how much it should cost to make a telephone, an automobile dealership needs to know how much it should cost to sell a car, the city of Atlanta needs to know how much it should cost to provide garbage pickup to a residence, and colleges and universities need to determine how much it should cost to provide an education to an incoming student. CPA firms have standards for the amount of time needed to prepare certain types of tax forms or returns, auto repair shops have standards for the time needed to make each repair, and airlines have standards for on-time departures. The use of standards is common in all types of businesses. For example, in the mid-1980s, **United Parcel Service** (UPS) developed standards for how fast drivers should walk to a customer's door (three feet per second) and how long it should take to handle a customer's package. More recently, managed health care companies have developed a standard amount of time for doctors seeing patients for particular ailments. An initial office visit might have a standard time of 20 minutes, whereas a full physical for a patient might have a standard time of 45 minutes.

LO2 Flexible Budgeting with Standard Costs

In Chapter 9, we introduced the concept of flexible budgeting, based on the actual volume of production rather than on the planned level of production. Flexible budgets based on standard costs are the centerpiece of effective variance analysis.

To illustrate the concept of flexible budgets, consider the case of Corinne's Country Rockers. Corinne's builds a high-quality rocking chair with a reputation for lasting a lifetime and also uses a unique (and patented) rocking mechanism. The chairs are sold directly by Corinne's through mail order and the Internet and have a retail price of $250 each. Corinne's produces each chair to order and has the capacity to produce 1,600 chairs per month. The standard quantity, standard price, and standard cost of direct materials, direct labor, and variable overhead in each chair are summarized in Exhibit 10-1. Estimated variable selling and administrative costs (per unit) and total fixed overhead and fixed selling and administrative costs are also provided.

A static budget based on estimated production and sales of 1,500 chairs is provided in Exhibit 10-2. In addition, a flexible budget based on the actual production and sale of 1,600 rockers is provided.

As you can see, the actual operating income for Corinne's is somewhere in the middle of that predicted by the static budget and the flexible budget. What does that

Exhibit 10-1 Standard Costs for Corinne's Country Rockers

	Standard Quantity	Standard Price	Standard Cost
Direct materials	20 linear feet of oak	$ 2 per foot	$ 40
Direct labor	5 labor hours	12 per hour	60
Variable overhead	5 labor hours	3 per hour	15
Total variable production costs			$ 115
Variable selling and administrative costs			25
Total variable costs			$ 140
Fixed overhead ($5,000 per month, or $15,000 per quarter)			$15,000
Fixed selling and administrative costs ($6,000 per month, or $18,000 per quarter)			18,000
Total fixed costs			$33,000

© Cengage Learning 2013

Exhibit 10-2 Static Budget, Flexible Budget, and Actual Results for Corinne's Country Rockers

	Static Budget	Flexible Budget	Actual Results
Units produced and sold	1,500	1,600	1,600
Sales revenue	$375,000	$400,000	$396,800
Variable manufacturing costs	−172,500	−184,000	−189,200
Variable selling and administrative costs	− 37,500	− 40,000	− 40,800
Contribution margin	$165,000	$176,000	$166,800
Fixed manufacturing costs	− 15,000	− 15,000	− 16,000
Fixed selling and administrative costs	− 18,000	− 18,000	− 16,000
Operating income	$132,000	$143,000	$134,800

© Cengage Learning 2013

mean? Unfortunately, not much! It means that Corinne's earned more than budgeted at the beginning of the year. But remember, the static budget was based on expected production and sales of 1,500 units. Corinne's ended up producing and selling 1,600 units. Comparing the static budget with the actual results is like comparing apples with oranges. It just does not make sense!

LO3 Flexible Budget Variance

Comparing the flexible budget amounts with the actual results shown in

Flexible budget variance The difference between the flexible budget operating income and actual operating income.

Exhibit 10-3 is more meaningful. Remember that the flexible budget was calculated on the basis of the actual production and sales of 1,600 units. It represents the amount of revenue and cost that Corinne's expected to incur during the first quarter for the actual number of units produced and sold. The difference between the flexible budget operating income and actual operating income is called the **flexible budget variance**. As shown in Exhibit 10-3, the flexible budget variance for Corinne's is $8,200. Because actual

Exhibit 10-3 The Flexible Budget Variance for Corinne's Country Rockers

	Flexible Budget	Flexible Budget Variance	Actual Results
Units produced and sold	1,600		1,600
Average sales price per unit	× $ 250		× $ 248
Sales revenue	$400,000	$3,200 unfavorable	$396,800
Variable manufacturing costs	− 184,000	5,200 unfavorable	− 189,200
Variable selling and administrative costs	− 40,000	800 unfavorable	− 40,800
Contribution margin	$176,000	9,200 unfavorable	$166,800
Fixed manufacturing costs	− 15,000	1,000 unfavorable	− 16,000
Fixed selling and administrative costs	− 18,000	2,000 favorable	− 16,000
Operating income	$143,000	$8,200 unfavorable	$134,800

© Cengage Learning 201

income is less than budgeted income, the variance is considered unfavorable.

However, we still do not have much information concerning exactly *why* operating income is $8,200 below budget. As shown in Exhibit 10-4, the unfavorable (U) flexible budget variance of $8,200 is caused by a combination of factors: a $3,200 unfavorable sales price variance, a $5,200 unfavorable variable manufacturing cost variance, a $1,000 unfavorable fixed manufacturing overhead spending variance, an $800 unfavorable variable selling and administrative cost variance, and a $2,000 favorable (F) fixed selling and administrative cost variance. These variances are discussed more fully in the pages that follow.

> *The flexible budget variance is the difference between the flexible budget operating income and the actual operating income.*

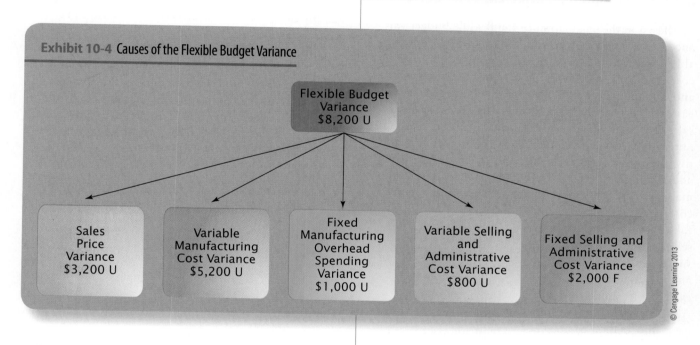

Exhibit 10-4 Causes of the Flexible Budget Variance

© Cengage Learning 2013

Sales Price Variance

The flexible budgeting process removes any differences, or variances, due to variations in production and sales volume. Therefore, any differences in sales revenue between the flexible budget and actual results must be caused by differences in the sales price.

The **sales price variance** is computed by comparing the actual sales price with the flexible budget sales price and multiplying their difference by the actual sales volume:

> Sales price = (Actual sales price − Expected sales price) ×
> variance　　Actual volume

Plugging in the numbers for Corinne's, we find that the sales price variance is as follows:

$$(\$248 - \$250) \times 1{,}600 = \$3{,}200 \text{ (unfavorable)}$$

The sales price variance can direct management's attention to a potential problem area. However, at this point, it is difficult to tell whether the unfavorable variance is the result of reducing the sales price of all rockers by $2 or perhaps the result of accepting a special order of 100 rockers at a price of $218 per chair.

> **Sales price variance** The difference between the actual sales price and the flexible budget sales price, times the actual sales volume.

Sales price variances result from charging sales prices that are different from those which were planned.

The variance simply points out that the actual sales price is different from the budgeted sales price. Management should investigate it further to determine its cause.

Selling and Administrative Expense Variance

As shown in the calculation of the flexible budget variance in Exhibit 10-3, Corinne's had an $800 unfavorable variance for variable selling and administrative costs and a $2,000 favorable variance for fixed selling and administrative costs. Variable selling and administrative costs include such things as commissions on sales, the cost of advertising brochures that are sent out with each chair purchased, the cost of administrative time to process each sale, and so on. Fixed selling and administrative costs include the salaries of the sales manager and personnel manager and such facility costs as rent and insurance. Like overhead variances, selling and administrative variances are difficult to analyze and interpret. However, companies utilizing ABC systems may have sufficient information to analyze portions of this variance in more detail. For example, Corinne's is interested in reducing the costs associated with processing telephone sales and has established a quantity standard for the time spent to process each call (6 minutes). Likewise, it has established a pricing standard for this activity, consisting of the salary costs incurred by sales representatives handling the call ($1 per call, based on a salary of $10 per hour) plus the direct costs of the toll-free line ($0.60 at $0.10 per minute). The actual costs incurred in handling sales calls can then be compared with the flexible budget amount, and price and usage variances can be calculated.

LO4 Variable Manufacturing Cost Variances

The flexible budget variance (see Exhibit 10-3) shows us that actual variable manufacturing costs were $5,200 higher than budgeted, but determining the true cause of that variance is a little more difficult. Did Corinne's spend too much on materials or use too much? Did the company incur more labor costs than usual, owing to paying a higher wage, or did it spend more time making each chair than budgeted? Did Corinne's spend more than budgeted on electricity, supplies, and other variable overhead or use more than budgeted? We simply do not know. In fact, the real reason may be a combination of any or all of the preceding.

To analyze the variable cost variances, we must step back and examine the flexible budget in more detail. Given the standard cost information provided in Exhibit 10-1, the flexible budget for variable manufacturing costs is as shown in Exhibit 10-5. More details concerning the actual variable manufacturing costs of $189,200 are also provided.

Exhibit 10-5 Variable Manufacturing Costs for Corinne's Country Rockers

	Flexible Budget	Actual Costs	Flexible Budget Variance
Direct materials	$ 64,000[1]	$ 63,840[4]	$ 160 F
Direct labor	96,000[2]	101,640[5]	5,640 U
Variable overhead	24,000[3]	23,720[6]	280 F
Total variable manufacturing costs	$184,000	$ 189,200	$5,200 U

[1]Flexible budget for direct materials = (20 feet per unit × 1,600 units) × $2 per unit = $64,000.
[2]Flexible budget for direct labor = (5 hours per unit × 1,600 units) × $12 per hour = $96,000.
[3]Flexible budget for variable overhead = (5 hours per unit × 1,600 units) × $3 per hour = $24,000.
[4]33,600 feet × $1.90 per foot = $63,840.
[5]8,400 hours × $12.10 per hour = $101,640.
[6]Actual variable overhead costs consist of the variable portion of utilities ($16,390), shop supplies and indirect materials ($4,140), and repairs and maintenance ($3,190).

The total variance for variable manufacturing costs is $5,200. Note that this dollar amount is the same as the flexible budget variance for variable manufacturing costs shown in Exhibit 10-3. Because actual costs are greater than budgeted, this variance is called "unfavorable" (indicated by the "U" following the amount in the last column of the table). Even though Corinne's actual expenditures for total variable production costs were greater than budgeted, Corinne's spent slightly less than the amount budgeted for direct materials and variable overhead but much more for direct labor.

Because actual costs for direct materials are less than the flexible budget amount, the $160 difference is "favorable." Although it is useful to know that we spent less than budgeted for direct materials, this type of analysis still does not tell us *why* Corinne's spent less. Did the company use less lumber than budgeted or pay less for each foot? To fully utilize the available information, we need to break down the total direct material variance presented earlier into its components and calculate both price and usage (quantity) variances.

We can examine the direct labor variance in the same way. Because actual labor costs are greater than the flexible budget amount, the variance is unfavorable. However, once again we do not really know *why* Corinne's spent more than budgeted. It could be because the company used more labor hours than budgeted or paid more for each hour of labor or some combination of the two. Further analysis is necessary to break down the total labor variance into its price and usage components and to fully understand the cause of the variances.

Analyzing variable overhead is much like analyzing direct materials and direct labor. Of course, direct materials and direct labor are also variable costs. Although we know that Corinne's spent less on variable overhead than budgeted (the variance is favorable), we do not know whether the price paid for electricity, supplies, and other variable overhead was less than budgeted or whether Corinne's used less.

As you will recall, rather than budget each individual overhead item, we prepared the flexible budget in Chapter 9 by combining all variable overhead costs and budgeting these separately from fixed overhead costs. The flexible budget for variable overhead for Corinne's was prepared by multiplying the predetermined overhead rate of $3 per direct labor hour by the number of direct labor hours expected to be incurred in producing 1,600 units (8,000 hours).

Although traditional variance analysis of variable overhead can help provide answers to questions about whether a company spent more or less or used more or less in total, it does not provide us with information concerning the components of overhead. In other words, traditional analysis does not tell us whether we spent more than budgeted on electricity or supplies; it just tells us that the overall amount of spending was higher than budgeted. Companies adopting activity-based costing to allocate overhead to products can extend variance analysis to look at the overhead costs associated with each activity and its associated cost driver. This analysis yields much more detailed information than is provided by traditional variance analysis.

The Variance Analysis Model

The next step in variance analysis is to break down the direct material, direct labor, and variable overhead variances into their components (a price variance and a usage, or quantity, variance), using the basic variance analysis model shown in Exhibit 10-6. The equations are as follows:

Price variance = Actual quantity (AQ) × [Actual price (AP) − Standard price (SP)]

Usage variance = Standard price (SP) × [Actual quantity (AQ) − Standard quantity (SQ)]

Exhibit 10-6 Basic Variance Analysis Model

AQ × AP (Actual Cost)

AQ × SP

SQ × SP (Flexible Budget Amount)

AQ (AP − SP) Price Variance

SP (AQ − SQ) Usage Variance

AQ = Actual Quantity or Actual Hours   AP = Actual Price or Actual Rate
SP = Standard Price or Standard Rate   SQ = Standard Quantity or Standard Hours

© Cengage Learning 2013

Whereas AQ, AP, and SP are self-explanatory, the calculation of SQ (standard quantity) needs to be explained a little. In Chapter 9, the flexible budget was prepared on the basis of the cost that should have been incurred to manufacture the actual number of units

produced. SQ is a simi-
lar concept. It is the standard (budgeted) quantity
of material or number
of hours that should be
incurred for the actual
level of production.

Price Variance As you
can see, the material
price variance is the difference between the ac-
tual quantity multiplied
by the actual price (AQ ×
AP) and the actual quan-
tity multiplied by the
standard price (AQ ×
SP). Simplifying, we have
(AQ × AP) − (AQ ×
SP) = AQ(AP − SP). In
other words, the price variance is simply the difference
in price multiplied by the actual quantity.

Usage Variance Likewise, the **usage variance** is the difference between the actual quantity multiplied by the
standard price (AQ × SP) and the standard quantity
multiplied by the standard price (SQ × SP). Simplifying, we have (AQ × SP) − (SQ × SP) = SP(AQ − SQ).
In other words, the usage variance is simply the difference in quantity multiplied by the standard price. The
variance model separates the overall flexible budget
variance (AQ × AP) − (SQ × SP) into two components—
one the result of paying more or less than budgeted
and the other the result of using more or less than
budgeted.

Exhibit 10-7 Analysis of Direct Material Variances

AQ × AP	AQ × SP	SQ × SP
33,600 × $1.90	33,600 × $2.00	32,000 × $2.00
= $63,840	= $67,200	(20 ft./unit × 1,600 units) × $2.00
		= $64,000

33,600 ($1.90 − $2.00)
AQ (AP − SP)
Price Variance
$3,360 F

$2.00 (33,600 − 32,000)
SP (AQ − SQ)
Usage Variance
$3,200 U

Total Direct Material Variance = $3,360 F + $3,200 U = $160 F
AQ = Actual Quantity   AP = Actual Price
SP = Standard Price   SQ = Standard Quantity

LO5 Direct Material Variances

Using the standard cost data for Corinne's Country Rockers provided in Exhibit 10-1 and the
breakdown of actual direct material costs shown in
Exhibit 10-5, we calculate direct material variances as
shown in Exhibit 10-7.

Price variance The difference between the actual
price and the standard price, times the actual volume
purchased.

Usage variance The difference between the actual quantity
and the standard quantity, times the standard price.

Direct Material Price Variance

The price variance is calculated by multiplying the actual amount of material purchased (33,600 feet) by the
difference in the actual price paid per foot ($1.90) and
the standard, or budgeted, price per foot ($2.00). This
variance of $3,360 is considered favorable because the
actual price was less than the budgeted price.

Direct Material Usage Variance

The usage variance for direct materials is found by multiplying the standard price by the difference in the actual quantity used and the standard quantity allowed.
Remember that the standard quantity allowed is the
amount of direct material that *should* have been used to
produce the actual output (the flexible budget amount).
In this case, the budget for materials is 20 feet of lumber
per chair. Corinne's actually produced 1,600 chairs during the quarter and should have used 32,000 feet of lumber (1,600 chairs × 20 feet per chair = 32,000 feet). The
variance of $3,200 is considered unfavorable because
the actual quantity of material used (33,600 feet) was
greater than the flexible budget amount (32,000 feet).

The total favorable variance of $160 for direct
materials can now be examined in more detail. It is
the sum of a favorable price variance of $3,360 and
an unfavorable usage variance of $3,200. Although
the overall direct material variance was quite small,
you can see that both the price variance and the usage
variance are quite large and just happen to offset each
other. Possible reasons for a favorable price variance

include taking advantage of unexpected quantity discounts or negotiating reduced prices with suppliers. However, favorable direct material price variances can also result from the purchase of low-quality materials. Unfavorable material usage variances can likewise be caused by a number of reasons: poorly trained workers, machine breakdowns, or perhaps even the use of low-quality materials if they result in more defective units, machine downtime, rework, and so on.

What are some possible reasons for an unfavorable direct material price variance and a favorable material usage variance? Unfavorable material price variances might result from rush orders (requiring faster delivery and higher prices), purchasing in small lot sizes (and not taking advantage of quantity discounts), and purchasing higher quality materials than budgeted. Favorable material usage variances are likely a result of highly efficient workers and well-maintained machinery and equipment.

Direct Material Variances When Amount Purchased Differs from Amount Used

If the amount of material purchased is not the same as the amount of material used in production, the variance model for materials must be modified slightly (see Exhibit 10-8). To isolate the variances as soon as possible, the price variance should be calculated by using the total amount of material purchased, whereas the usage variance should be calculated on the basis of the amount of material actually used in production. For example, if Corinne's purchases 35,000 feet of lumber

but uses only 33,600 feet, the price variance would be calculated as follows:

$$AQ_{purchased}(AP - SP)$$
$$= 35,000(\$1.90 - \$2.00) = \$3,500 \text{ F}$$

The usage variance is calculated as before; that is,

$$SP(AQ_{used} - SQ)$$
$$= \$2.00(33,600 - 32,000) = \$3,200 \text{ U}$$

Note that when the amount of material purchased is not equal to the amount of material used, the price and usage variances should not be added together to calculate the total direct material variance.

LO6 Direct Labor Variances

Direct labor variances are calculated with the same basic variance model used to calculate direct material variances. Because we are talking about labor instead of materials, we substitute rates for price (AR and SR instead of AP and SP) and hours for quantity (AH and SH instead of AQ and SQ). In addition, the direct labor usage variance is often referred to as an efficiency variance. Using the standard cost data for Corinne's Country Rockers provided in Exhibit 10-1 and the breakdown of actual

Exhibit 10-8 Analysis of Direct Material Variances When Quantity Purchased Differs from Quantity Used

| $AQ_{purchased} \times AP$ 35,000 × $1.90 = $66,500 | $AQ_{purchased} \times SP$ 35,000 × $2.00 = $70,000 | $AQ_{used} \times SP$ 33,600 × $2.00 = $67,200 | $SQ \times SP$ 32,000 × $2.00 = $64,000 |

35,000 ($1.90 – $2.00)
$AQ_{purchased}$ (AP – SP)
Price Variance
$3,500 F

$2.00 (33,600 – 32,000)
SP (AQ_{used} – SQ)
Usage Variance
$3,200 U

$AQ_{purchased}$ = Actual Quantity Purchased
SP = Standard Price
AQ_{used} = Actual Quantity Used

AP = Actual Price
SQ = Standard Quantity

© Cengage Learning 2013

Personnel managers and production managers are often responsible for direct labor variances.

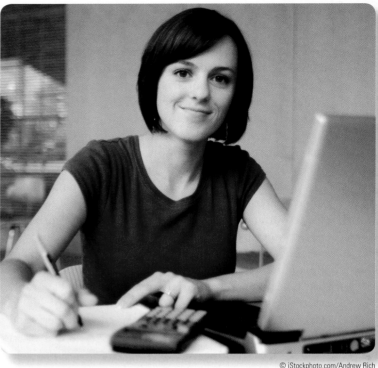

direct labor costs in Exhibit 10-5, we calculate direct labor variances as shown in Exhibit 10-9.

If we evaluate the two components of the direct labor variance, we see that most of the variance results from inefficiencies in the use of labor. Potential causes of an unfavorable direct labor efficiency variance include poorly trained workers, machine breakdowns, the use of poor quality raw materials (resulting in more time spent in production), or just general employee inefficiencies resulting from poor supervision. In this case, the unfavorable direct labor rate variance is small but still may be important. Potential causes of unfavorable direct labor rate variances include the use of workers paid at a rate higher than budgeted, unexpected increases in wages owing to union negotiations, and so on.

What are some possible reasons for favorable direct labor rate and efficiency variances? Hiring workers at a lower wage rate is one obvious reason for a favorable direct labor rate variance. However, that may be problematic if the workers are less skilled than required. By contrast, favorable labor efficiency variances most often result from using highly skilled workers. Obviously, there are trade-offs here. Paying higher wage rates can result in unfavorable labor rate variances and favorable labor efficiency variances, whereas paying lower wage

rates can result in favorable labor rate variances and unfavorable labor efficiency variances.

LO7 Variable Overhead Variances

With slight modifications, we can calculate variable overhead variances with the same variance model we used for direct material and direct labor variances. As with direct material and direct labor, (AQ × AP) is simply the actual cost incurred—in this case, the actual variable overhead costs. SR is the variable predetermined overhead rate (sometimes called SVR). Because variable overhead was estimated with direct labor used as the cost driver, AH is simply the actual number of labor hours incurred. Likewise, SH is

Exhibit 10-9 Direct Labor Variances

AH × AR 8,400 × $12.10 = $101,640		AH × SR 8,400 × $12.00 = $100,800		SH × SR 8,000 × $12.00 = $96,000

| | 8,400 ($12.10 − $12.00)
AH (AR − SR)
Rate Variance
$840 U | | $12 (8,400 − 8,000)
SR (AH − SH)
Efficiency Variance
$4,800 U | |

Total Direct Labor Variance = $840 U + $4,800 U = $5,640 U

AH = Actual Hours   AR = Actual Rate
SH = Standard Hours   SR = Standard Rate

> *The variable overhead efficiency variance does not measure the efficient use of overhead; instead, it measures the efficient use of the cost driver, or overhead allocation base, that appears in the flexible budget.*

the standard number of labor hours allowed for actual production. Consequently, SH × SVR is the amount of applied variable overhead.[1] The price variance is often called a variable overhead spending variance, and, like the labor usage variance, the usage variance for variable overhead is called an efficiency variance.

The variable overhead spending and efficiency variances are calculated as shown in Exhibit 10-10. What do these variances tell us? Whereas the price variance

variable overhead spending variance is a little different. A spending variance for variable overhead indicates, of course, that the actual price of variable overhead items, such as supplies, utilities, repairs, and maintenance, was more or less than the flexible budget amount, but it is also affected by excessive *usage* of overhead caused by inefficient operations or waste. For example, although the rates for electricity usage (charged by the utility) might be exactly as budgeted, excessive usage might result from poorly maintained equipment. Likewise, even if the price of supplies were lower than budgeted, excessive use of the supplies owing to waste could still result in an unfavorable variable overhead spending variance.

The variable overhead efficiency variance is also interpreted differently from the direct material and direct labor usage variances. It does not measure the efficient use of overhead at all; instead, it measures the efficient use of the cost driver, or overhead allocation base, that appears in the flexible budget. The efficiency variance has nothing to do with the efficient use of utilities, maintenance, and supplies. The efficiency variance shows only how efficiently the organization used the chosen base to apply overhead to the cost of product produced.

In the case of Corinne's Country Rockers, the favorable variable overhead spending variance tells us that Corinne's spent less than budgeted on the items included in the variable overhead portion of its flexible budget. Although this outcome might have resulted from paying less per kilowatt hour for electricity, it might also have resulted from using less electricity than expected. A detailed analysis of each line item would provide more information. The unfavorable variable overhead efficiency variance tells us simply that more *direct labor hours* were used than budgeted. It does not tell us anything about the efficient use of electricity, supplies, or repairs and maintenance.

The interpretation of variable overhead spending and efficiency variances is made difficult by the use of a single cost driver to apply variable overhead to products and services.

Exhibit 10-10 Variable Overhead Variances

Actual Variable Overhead Expense = $23,720

AH × SVR
8,400 × $3.00 = $25,200

SH × SVR
8,000 × $3.00 = $24,000

Actual – (AH × SVR)
$23,720 – (8,400 × $3.00)
Spending Variance
$1,480 F

SVR (AH – SH)
$3.00 (8,400 – 8,000)
Efficiency Variance
$1,200 U

Total Variable Overhead Variance = $1,480 F + 1,200 U = $280 F
AH = Actual Hours   SH = Standard Hours
SVR = Standard Variable Rate

© Cengage Learning 2013

for materials and the rate variance for labor tell us whether the price of materials and the rate for labor are more or less than budgeted, the interpretation of the

[1]Of course, overhead can be applied by using cost drivers other than direct labor. If overhead is applied on the basis of machine hours, AH is simply the actual number of machine hours used and SH is the budgeted number of machine hours allowed for actual production.

In sum, the total variable manufacturing cost variance of $5,200 that we saw in Exhibits 10-3 and 10-4 has now been broken down into six separate variances: two for direct materials, two for direct labor, and two for variable overhead (see Exhibit 10-11).

not depend on production volume, no activity levels are used in its calculation:

$$\text{Fixed overhead budget (spending) variance} = \text{Actual fixed overhead} - \text{Budgeted fixed overhead}$$

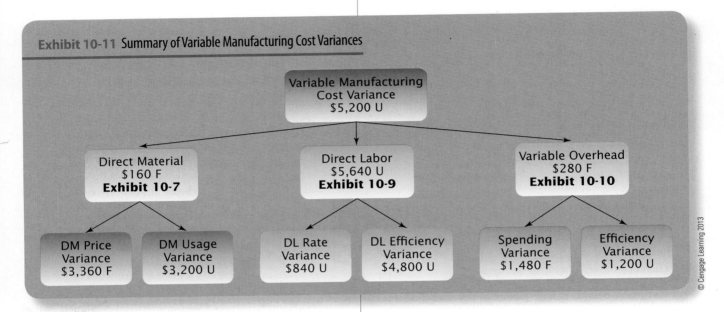

Exhibit 10-11 Summary of Variable Manufacturing Cost Variances

Variable Manufacturing Cost Variance
$5,200 U

Direct Material
$160 F
Exhibit 10-7

Direct Labor
$5,640 U
Exhibit 10-9

Variable Overhead
$280 F
Exhibit 10-10

DM Price Variance
$3,360 F

DM Usage Variance
$3,200 U

DL Rate Variance
$840 U

DL Efficiency Variance
$4,800 U

Spending Variance
$1,480 F

Efficiency Variance
$1,200 U

© Cengage Learning 2013

LO8 Fixed Overhead Variances

Corinne's fixed manufacturing overhead variance (see Exhibit 10-3) is $1,000 over budget ($16,000 actual costs, compared with the flexible budget amount of $15,000). Unlike variable overhead, fixed overhead (and other fixed costs) should not be affected when production increases or decreases. Consequently, the variance model used in analyzing variable costs (direct material, direct labor, and variable overhead) is not appropriate for analyzing the fixed overhead variance.

Fixed overhead variances consist of a budget variance and a volume variance. The **budget variance** (or spending variance) is simply the difference between the amount of fixed overhead actually incurred and the flexible budget amount. Because fixed overhead does

The **volume variance** is the difference between the flexible budget amount and the amount of fixed overhead *applied* to products. Overhead is applied by multiplying the predetermined overhead rate (for fixed overhead) by the number of standard hours (or budgeted hours) allowed to complete the actual units produced:

$$\text{Fixed overhead volume variance} = \text{Budgeted fixed overhead} - \text{Applied fixed overhead}$$

A company using variable (direct) costing rather than absorption (full) costing treats fixed overhead as a period cost and expenses it immediately (see Chapter 5). In these companies, there will not be a fixed overhead volume variance, because fixed overhead is not "applied" to products. It is simply expensed in the period incurred.

Fixed overhead variances for Corinne's Country Rockers are calculated in Exhibit 10-12. The predetermined fixed overhead rate is $2 per labor hour ($15,000 budgeted fixed overhead divided by 7,500 budgeted labor hours [1,500 budgeted units × 5 hours per unit]). Applied fixed overhead is $16,000 ($2 predetermined overhead rate × 8,000 hours [1,600 actual units × 5 hours per unit]).

The spending variance is unfavorable because Corinne's spent more on fixed overhead items than the

Budget variance The difference between the amount of fixed overhead actually incurred and the flexible budget amount; also known as the spending variance.

Volume variance The difference between the flexible budget amount and the fixed overhead applied to products.

Exhibit 10-12 Fixed Overhead Variances

Actual Fixed Overhead Expense = $16,000	Budgeted Fixed Overhead: 7,500 labor hours (1,500 chairs × 5 hours) × $2.00/hour = $15,000	Applied Fixed Overhead: 8,000 labor hours (1,600 chairs × 5 hours) × $2.00 = $16,000
	Budget (Spending) Variance $1,000 U	Volume Variance $1,000

© Cengage Learning 2013

> *The fixed overhead volume variance should not be interpreted either as favorable or unfavorable or as a measure of the efficient utilization of facilities.*

company had budgeted. As you can see, the volume variance is simply a result of Corinne's manufacturing more chairs than budgeted (1,600 instead of 1,500). Everything else in the comparison of budgeted and applied overhead is the same. The fixed overhead volume variance is calculated primarily as a method of reconciling the amount of overhead applied to products under an absorption-costing system with the amount of overhead actually incurred—and, consequently, the over- or underapplied overhead. The total amount of the variable overhead spending variance, variable overhead efficiency variance, fixed overhead spending variance, and fixed overhead volume variance will equal the company's over- or underapplied overhead for a period.

For Corinne's, manufacturing overhead was overapplied by $280 for the quarter. Actual overhead cost was $39,720 and consisted of variable overhead of $23,720 (Exhibit 10-10) and fixed overhead of $16,000 (Exhibit 10-12). Applied overhead was $40,000 and consisted of variable overhead of $24,000 (Exhibit 10-10) and fixed overhead of $16,000 (Exhibit 10-12). The $280 difference is the sum of Corinne's $1,480 favorable variable overhead spending variance, $1,200 unfavorable variable overhead efficiency variance, $1,000 unfavorable fixed overhead spending variance, and $1,000 fixed overhead volume variance.

The fixed overhead volume variance generally should not be interpreted as favorable or unfavorable and should not be interpreted as a measure of over- or underutilization of facilities. Either misinterpretation can be particularly problematic when the applied overhead is smaller than the budgeted amount (when a company produces fewer products than budgeted). Companies may reduce production for a number of reasons, including reduced demand for products and temporary material or labor shortages, among others.

A summary table of the variances discussed in this chapter, together with references and associated formulas, is shown in Exhibit 10-13.

Exhibit 10-13 Summary of Variances

Variance	Reference	Formula
Flexible Budget Variance	Exhibit 10-3; Page 212	Flexible Budget − Actual Results
Sales Price Variance	Exhibit 10-4; Page 213	(Actual − Expected Sales Price) × Actual Volume
Direct Material Price Variance	Exhibit 10-7; Page 216	Actual Quantity × (Actual Price − Standard Price)
Direct Material Usage Variance	Exhibit 10-7; Page 216	Standard Price × (Actual Quantity − Standard Quantity)
Direct Labor Rate Variance	Exhibit 10-9; Page 218	Actual Hours × (Actual Rate − Standard Rate)
Direct Labor Efficiency Variance	Exhibit 10-9; Page 218	Standard Rate × (Actual Hours − Standard Hours)
Variable Overhead Spending Variance	Exhibit 10-10; Page 219	Actual Overhead − (Actual Hours × Standard Variable Rate)
Variable Overhead Efficiency Variance	Exhibit 10-10; Page 219	Standard Variable Rate × (Actual Hours − Standard Hours)
Fixed Overhead Spending Variance	Exhibit 10-12; Page 221	Actual Fixed Overhard − Budgeted Fixed Overhead
Fixed Overhead Volume Variance	Exhibit 10-12; Page 221	Budgeted Fixed Overhead − Applied Overhead

© Cengage Learning 2013

LO9 Interpreting and Using Variance Analysis

Although standard costs and variance analysis can be useful to managers attempting to diagnose organizational performance, they are most effective in stable companies with mature production environments characterized by a heavy reliance on direct labor. They may not be much help, however, in rapidly changing companies, companies with flexible manufacturing systems (in which more than one product is manufactured on an assembly line), companies with heavily automated manufacturing processes, or companies that emphasize continuous improvement and the reduction of non-value-added activities in the production process. Although variance analysis may still be of value as a summary report for top management, it has a number of drawbacks when used in many modern manufacturing environments:

1. The information from variance analysis is likely to be too aggregated for operating managers to use. To be useful, material variances may need to be broken down into detail by specific product lines and even batches of product and labor variances may need to be calculated for specific manufacturing cells.

2. The information from variance analysis is not timely enough to be useful to managers. As product life cycles are reduced, timely reporting is even more critical than in the past.

3. Traditional variance analysis of variable and fixed overhead provides little useful information for managers.

4. Traditional variance analysis focuses on cost control instead of product quality, customer service, delivery time, and other nonfinancial measures of performance. These measures are discussed in more detail in Chapter 11.

Even in traditional and stable manufacturing environments, the effective use of variance analysis for control and performance purposes requires the proper application of "management by exception" and careful interpretation of variances (including understanding their causes).

> Management by exception is the key to effective variance analysis and involves taking action only when actual and planned results differ significantly.

Management by Exception

The proper application of "management by exception" requires an understanding that it is neither necessary nor desirable to investigate all variances. If you think about it, you will see that it is likely that actual costs will always deviate from budgeted costs to some extent. Utility prices are affected by the weather, and prices of raw materials can change suddenly owing to shortages, surpluses, or new sources of competing products. Unexpected machine breakdowns affect the amount of time workers spend manufacturing products. Even fixed costs can differ from budgeted costs when rent is unexpectedly increased, new equipment is purchased, or insurance rates go up. Because of these random fluctuations, managers should generally investigate variances (favorable or unfavorable) that are material in amount and outside a normal acceptable range. Traditionally, materiality thresholds were often based on absolute size (investigate everything over $1,000) or relative size (investigate everything over 10 percent of the budgeted amount) or some combination of the two. Today, companies are more likely to use statistical techniques and to investigate variances that fall outside a "normal" range of fluctuations. For example, companies may investigate variances that are more than two standard deviations from the mean. Regardless of materiality, trends in variances might also warrant investigation. For example, continually occurring and increasing material price variances might be vitally important to a restaurant regardless of their absolute size.

Interpreting Favorable and Unfavorable Variances

Although we have referred to variances as favorable or unfavorable, these designations should not necessarily be interpreted as good or bad. In order to interpret variances, the underlying cause must be determined.

For example, consider a manager who is investigating an unfavorable direct labor efficiency variance. Although, on the surface, the unfavorable variance would seem to indicate a problem in worker efficiency, the real problem may be the combination of a workforce that is fixed in the short run and a lack of sufficient orders to keep workers busy. Companies may be reluctant to lay off workers for short periods when demand is unexpectedly reduced or other production problems make it difficult to keep the workers fully employed. It may be costly to rehire workers or they may find other jobs. As discussed elsewhere, this problem often makes direct labor a fixed cost in the short run.

Likewise, an unfavorable direct material usage variance generally points to a problem in production. However, further analysis might reveal that usage was high because of an unusual number of defective parts and that the large number of defective parts was a result of the purchasing manager buying materials of inferior quality. This problem then becomes one of the purchasing manager buying inferior materials, not the production manager using excessive amounts of material. Note that in this case, even though the purchasing manager's action led to the unfavorable direct material usage variance, the material price variance itself would likely be favorable.

Identifying management's objectives is vitally important in deciding how to use and interpret variances. If the problem is one of insufficient orders and management is truly concerned about controlling costs, management must be careful not to use the direct labor efficiency variance for purposes of motivating and controlling the production supervisor. Although this conclusion may seem counterintuitive, put yourself in the shoes of the production supervisor. The production supervisor really has two options: either continue producing products to keep workers busy or have an unfavorable labor efficiency variance. But keeping workers busy has definite drawbacks. For example, building inventory levels is costly. Holding high levels of inventory results in additional costs of storage and insurance and can result in increased waste from theft and obsolescence.

In other situations, understanding whether the primary objective of management is cost control or producing a high-quality product is important. If cost control is paramount, an unfavorable direct material price variance might well be considered "bad"; however, if management's objective is to provide a high-quality product, an unfavorable material price variance might be acceptable if the higher price is necessary to obtain high-quality materials.

Once managers are sure of the root cause(s) of a variance and have considered their own objectives in utilizing variance analysis, they can intelligently consider options available to deal with the problem. For example, if management finds that an unfavorable direct labor efficiency variance is caused by a lack of customer orders and a workforce that is fixed in the short run, options may include accepting special orders, utilizing the workers in other areas, and utilizing the time to train workers or to repair machinery.

Behavioral Considerations

As you have seen throughout this chapter, the use of standard costs and variance analysis, although valuable for control and performance evaluation, can also cause dysfunctional behavior among employees and management. The use of ideal standards can cause resentment among managers who are continually faced with "unfavorable" variances. Some companies tie compensation to performance that is at least partly measured by variances. Even though this practice is likely to make managers aware of costs, it may have undesirable side effects. Too much emphasis on the direct material usage variance can compel production managers to increase production so as to appear efficient, causing inventories to rise above acceptable levels. By focusing on variances, a purchasing manager may be encouraged to purchase inferior products to make his or her performance appear better, even though the manager knows that the poor quality material will cause problems in the production area. It is important to understand the root causes of variances and to assign responsibility accordingly. It is also important to remember that variance analysis provides just one measure of performance. The uses of other financial and nonfinancial measures of performance are discussed in Chapter 11.

STUDY TOOLS 10

BRIEF EXERCISES

1. Standard Costing LO1

Review the following incomplete statements about standard costing and related issues.

a. A(n) _____ standard allows for normal and efficient operations and takes into consideration typical production problems.

b. A budget for a single unit of a product is referred to as a(n) _____.

c. Managers must compare actual and budgeted results to control operations. This comparison process is generally called _____.

d. The _____ indicates how much a company should generally pay for the materials, labor, or overhead for a single unit of product.

e. _____ is often the key to effective variance analysis.

Required

Complete the preceding incomplete statements with the correct term from the following list of terms provided (note that not all terms will be used): *variance analysis, ideal standard, practical standard, standard cost, standard price, management by exception, task analysis.*

2. Variable Manufacturing Cost Variances LO4, 5, 6

Companies incur a variety of variable manufacturing costs, including those related to direct materials and direct labor. The following statements relate to variable manufacturing cost variances.

a. Computing a price variance involves multiplying the difference in the actual quantity used and the standard quantity allowed by the actual price per unit.

b. Usage, or efficiency, variances are appropriately calculated for direct materials, but not for direct labor.

c. Traditional variance analysis is less informative than variance analysis conducted in an environment in which a company uses activity-based costing.

d. The price variance for direct materials is calculated as the difference between the actual price and the standard price, times the actual volume purchased.

e. Potential causes for an unfavorable direct labor variance include the use of higher paid workers than budgeted and unexpected increases in wage rates due to union negotiations.

Required

Indicate whether each of the preceding statements is true or false.

3. Overhead Variances LO7, 8

A company must understand overhead variances just as it does those related to direct labor and direct material. The following statements relate to overhead variances.

a. In the calculation of the variable overhead variance, the standard number of hours allowed for actual production multiplied by the variable predetermined overhead rate (i.e., SH × SVR) is the amount of actual variable overhead.

b. The variable overhead efficiency variance indicates how efficiently a company used the base chosen to apply overhead to the cost of a product.

c. Fixed overhead variances consist of a volume variance and a spending variance.

d. The fixed overhead volume variance can be interpreted as favorable or unfavorable just as any other variance can.

e. The fixed overhead volume variance is the difference between the budgeted fixed overhead and the applied fixed overhead.

Required

Indicate whether each of the preceding statements is true or false.

4. Using Variance Analysis LO9

Review the following incomplete statements about the use of variance analysis.

a. Variance analysis has a number of _____ when it is used in a modern manufacturing environment.

b. The focus of traditional variance analysis is _____ rather than on customer service, delivery time, and other nonfinancial measures.

c. Management by exception suggests that it is _____ necessary to investigate all variances.

d. _____ is a likely result of using ideal standards when managers continually face unfavorable variances.

e. In order to interpret variances, the _____ must be determined.

Required

Complete the preceding incomplete statements with the correct term from the following list of terms provided (note that not all terms will be used): *absolutely, advantages, competition, cost control, drawbacks, not, product quality, resentment, underlying cause.*

EXERCISES

5. Flexible Budget LO2

Gordon knits wool caps for sale at the local ski resorts. He prepared a budget for the production and sale of 150 wool caps. Unfortunately, Gordon fell ill with a bad case of the flu and was able to make and sell only 125 wool caps. Here is Gordon's budget:

Sales revenue	$1,500.00
Variable costs:	
Direct materials (yarn)	375.00
Direct labor	750.00
Commission to resort	112.50
Fixed costs	75.00
Net income	$ 187.50

Required

Prepare a flexible budget for Gordon based on the production and sale of 125 wool caps.

6. Flexible Budget Preparation LO2

Garcia and Buffet, a local CPA firm, has budgeted $100,000 in fixed expenses per month for the tax department. It has also budgeted variable costs of $5 per tax return prepared for supplies, $35 per return for labor, and $10 per return for computer time. The firm expects revenue from tax return preparation to be $300,000, based on 2,000 tax returns at $150 each. During the current month, 1,850 tax returns were actually prepared, at an average fee of $147 each. Actual variable costs were $9,100 for supplies, $65,000 for labor, and $18,000 for computer time. Actual fixed costs were $100,000.

Required

Prepare a flexible budget for the tax department of Garcia and Buffet for the current month.

7. Flexible Budget Variance LO3

Refer to the information in Exercise 6.

Required

Compute the flexible budget variance for Garcia and Buffet.

8. Sales Price Variance LO3

The Quick Brick Shop had an unfavorable sales price variance of $150. The budgeted selling price was $10 per unit and 50 bricks were sold.

Required

What was the actual selling price of Quick Brick's bricks?

9. Direct Materials Price and Usage Variances LO5

The Woods Enterprises prepared the following standard costs for the production of one stuffed bear:

Direct materials	1.5 pounds of stuffing @ $2 per lb
Direct labor	2 hours of assembly @ $15 per hr

Actual production costs for the production of 1,000 stuffed bears required 1,750 pounds of stuffing at a cost of $1.95 per pound and 1,950 labor hours at $15.25 per hour.

Required
A. Calculate the direct material price variance.
B. Calculate the direct material usage variance.

10. Direct Labor Rate and Efficiency Variances LO6

Refer to the information in Exercise 9.

Required
A. Calculate the direct labor rate variance.
B. Calculate the direct labor efficiency variance.

11. Direct Materials Price and Usage Variances LO5

Wheeler Corporation produces and sells special eyeglass straps for sporting enthusiasts. For the year, the company budgeted for production and sales of 1,200 straps. However, the company produced and sold just 1,100 straps. Each strap has a standard requiring one foot of material at a budgeted cost of $1.50 per foot and two hours of assembly time at a cost of $12 per hour. Actual costs for the production of 1,100 items were $1,435.50 for materials (990 feet at $1.45 per foot) and $29,161 for labor (2,420 hours at $12.05 per hour).

Required
A. Calculate the direct material price variance.
B. Calculate the direct material usage variance.

12. Labor Rate and Efficiency Variances LO6

Refer to the information in Exercise 11.

Required
A. Calculate the direct labor rate variance.
B. Calculate the direct labor efficiency variance.

13. Materials and Labor Variances LO5, 6

Last year, Vera Corporation budgeted for production and sales of 20,000 cloth handbags. Vera produced and sold 19,250 handbags. Each handbag has a standard requiring 4 feet of material at a budgeted cost of $2.50 per foot and 45 minutes of sewing time at a cost of $0.28 per minute. The handbags sell for $45.00. Actual costs for the production of 18,000 handbags were $201,600 for materials (80,000 feet at $2.52 per foot) and $260,400 for labor (868,000 minutes at $0.30 per minute).

Required
A. What is the handbag's direct material price variance?
B. What is the handbag's direct material usage variance?
C. What is the handbag's direct labor rate variance?
D. What is the handbag's direct labor efficiency variance?

14. Variable Overhead Spending and Efficiency Variances LO7

Bittermen Company, which uses standard costing, reported the following overhead information for the last quarter of the year:

Actual overhead incurred:	
Fixed	$10,500
Variable	66,810
Budgeted fixed overhead	11,000
Variable overhead rate per direct labor hour	5.00
Standard hours allowed for actual production	13,100
Actual labor hours used	13,000

Required
A. What is the variable overhead spending variance?
B. What is the variable overhead efficiency variance?

15. Variable Overhead Spending and Efficiency Variances LO7

Hennings Travel Company specializes in the production of travel items (e.g., clocks, personal care kits). The following data were prepared so that a variance analysis could be performed:

Forecast Data (Expected Capacity)	
Direct labor hours	40,000
Estimated overhead:	
Fixed	$16,000
Variable	$30,000

Actual Results	
Direct labor hours	37,200
Overhead:	
Fixed	$16,120
Variable	$28,060

The number of standard hours allowed for actual production was 37,000.

Required
A. Calculate the variable overhead spending variance.
B. Calculate the variable overhead efficiency variance.

16. Fixed Overhead Volume and Spending Variances LO8

Refer to the information in Exercise 15.

Required
A. Calculate the fixed overhead volume variance.
B. Calculate the fixed overhead spending variance.

17. Variable Overhead Spending and Efficiency Variances LO7

Simon Enterprises applies variable overhead at a rate of $1.50 per direct labor hour and fixed overhead at a rate of $1.75 per direct labor hour. The company budgets two direct labor hours for each of the 5,900 units that are scheduled for production. Last year, Simon incurred actual variable overhead totaling $18,750, and actual fixed overhead totaling $21,500, for the production of 6,000 units. In addition, 11,800 direct labor hours were actually incurred.

Required
A. Calculate the variable overhead efficiency variance.
B. Calculate the variable overhead spending variance.

18. Fixed Overhead Volume and Spending Variances LO8

Refer to the information in Exercise 17.

Required
A. Calculate the fixed overhead volume variance.
B. Calculate the fixed overhead spending variance.

19. Drawbacks of Variance Analysis LO9

Variance analysis allows managers to compare budgeted and actual performance so that necessary corrective steps can be taken. Frequently, the analysis helps managers identify operational inefficiencies and other areas that can be improved. Nonetheless, variance analysis does have several potential drawbacks.

Required
Describe the various drawbacks of variance analysis.

PROBLEMS

20. Standard Costing LO1

Petty Petroleum, Inc., uses various chemicals to manufacture its products. Variance data for last month for the three primary chemicals used in production are as follows (F indicates a favorable variance; U indicates an unfavorable variance):

	X42	AY8	9BZ
Material price variance	$ 84,000 F	$ 50,000 F	$ 42,000 U
Material usage variance	80,000 U	60,000 U	96,000 U
Total materials variance (net)	$ 4,000 F	$ 10,000 U	$138,000 U
Products requiring this chemical	200,000	220,000	250,000

The standard called for 1 pound of chemical for each product requiring the specific chemical. Because of falling prices in the chemical industry, Petty Petroleum generally paid less for chemicals last month than in previous months. Specifically, the average price paid was $0.40 per pound less than standard for chemical X42; it was $0.20 less for chemical AY8; and it was $0.14 greater for chemical 9BZ. All of the chemicals purchased last month were also used during the month.

Required
A. For chemical X42, calculate the number of pounds of material purchased, the standard cost per pound of material, and the total standard material cost.
B. For chemical AY8, calculate the number of pounds of material purchased, the standard cost per pound of material, and the total standard material cost.
C. For chemical 9BZ, calculate the number of pounds of material purchased, the standard cost per pound of material, and the total standard material cost.

21. Flexible Budget Variance LO2

Fort Worth Company is a printer and binder of specialized booklets and pamphlets. Last year, the company's sales manager estimated sales to be 10,000 booklets and pamphlets combined. The sales manager also estimated that the items would retail for approximately $10 each. Various production costs, including direct and indirect material, direct and indirect labor, and variable overhead, were estimated to total $50,000, while fixed costs were estimated to be $20,000.

During the year, Fort Worth's unit sales equaled its production of 12,000 units. Because of changing market conditions—specifically, competition—the average selling price fell to just $9.50 per unit. There were increased variable costs as well that resulted in average per-unit variable costs of $6. At the end of the year, the company's controller accumulated fixed costs and found them to be $21,000.

Required
Prepare a report to show the difference between the actual contribution margin and the budgeted contribution margin per the static budget. Then, compare the actual contribution margin and the budgeted contribution margin per the flexible budget.

22. Comprehensive Variance Analysis LO2, 3

Byrd Company is a manufacturer affiliated with the furniture industry. The company produces a wide variety of "hardware" component parts. Examples of products include drawer slides, hinges, door pulls and handles, springs, and locks. Dent Tripoli is the company's new chief financial officer. Dent is very concerned with providing the company's president and board of directors with accurate financial reports. He is concerned that the company's use of static budgeting does not convey a fair presentation of the company's performance. The following contribution margin format income statement reports the results of Byrd Company's operations for the last quarter of 2012:

Sales Revenues (400,000 units)		$2,440,000
Variable Costs		
Manufacturing	$1,060,000	
Marketing and administrative	748,000	1,808,000
Contribution margin		$ 632,000
Fixed Costs		
Manufacturing	$ 400,000	
Marketing and administrative	200,000	600,000
Operating profit		$ 32,000

Byrd's 2012 budgets were based on production and sales of 375,000 units at an average selling price of $6. At that volume, variable manufacturing costs were budgeted to be $2.50 per unit and variable marketing and administrative costs were budgeted to be $2.00 each. Had the company's actual performance equaled the budgeted performance, Byrd would have reported an operating profit of $62,500.

Required
A. On the basis of the information provided in the problem, re-create Byrd's 2012 static budget. Be sure to include a comparison between the static budget and the actual results for the year.
B. On the basis of the information provided in the problem, prepare a flexible budget for Byrd for 2012. Be sure to include a comparison between the flexible budget and the actual results. The comparison should report the flexible budget variance.
C. Calculate Byrd's sales price variance for 2012. Is the variance favorable or unfavorable?

23. Comprehensive Variance Analysis
LO3, 4, 5, 6

Timmer Bachman founded the Bachman Corporation over 25 years ago. The company's genesis was spurred by the unique climbing apparatus developed by Timmer, an avid mountaineer. Bachman Corporation has continued to produce that first product, but it has now diversified into other outdoor activity equipment as well. In fact, the vast majority of the company's revenues are now accounted for by sales of nonclimbing products. Timmer is considering whether his company should continue producing and selling some of its oldest products, all of which relate to mountain climbing.

To begin his decision-making process, Timmer has asked the company's controller, Marin Hennesy, to accumulate data on the original locking carabiner that set the company on its way. Accordingly, Marin accumulated the following data for last year:
- Budgeted production and sales: 5,000 carabiners.
- Actual production and sales: 6,000 carabiners.
- The standard for a carabiner requires 1.5 ounces of material at a budgeted cost of $1.52 per ounce and two hours of assembly and testing time at a cost of $12.50 per hour.
- The carabiner sells for $32 each.
- Actual production costs for the 6,000 carabiners totaled $12,900 for 8,600 ounces of materials and $161,700 for 13,200 labor hours.

Required
A. What was the budgeted contribution margin per carabiner?
B. What was the actual contribution margin per carabiner?
C. What was Bachman's flexible budget variance?
D. What was Bachman's direct material price variance?
E. What was Bachman's direct material usage variance?
F. What was Bachman's direct labor rate variance?
G. What was Bachman's direct labor efficiency variance?
H. What would the sales price variance be if each carabiner sold for $33?
I. On the basis of the available information, should Bachman continue making the carabiner?

24. Comprehensive Variance Analysis
LO3, 5, 6

Turner Corporation produces overdrive transmission parts for several small specialty automobile companies. Prior to founding the firm, Benson Turner, the company's president, had an illustrious stock-car-racing career. After several serious injuries, Benson's family convinced him that it was time to retire from the sport and pursue a calmer and safer line of work.

The company has been operating for just over five years and is beginning to show signs of significant growth. Benson is a planner, and he wants to get a handle on his manufacturing operations before the company's growth becomes his primary preoccupation. The company's plant manager and controller met last week to pull together information that they could present to Benson. Although the company produces over 150 different parts, the two of them thought that accumulating detailed data on one single typical part would be sufficient for the quickly called

meeting. As a consequence, the following data were captured for the last 12 months:
- Budgeted production and sales: 12,000 parts.
- Actual production and sales: 11,000 parts.
- Each part has a standard requiring 1 pound of material at a budgeted cost of $1.50 per pound.
- Each part has a standard requiring 20 minutes of assembly time at a cost of $0.25 per minute.
- The average actual wholesale price for each part is $8.
- Actual costs for the production of 11,000 parts were $17,094 for 11,100 pounds of material.
- Actual labor costs were $58,080 for 242,000 minutes of labor time.

Required
A. What was the budgeted contribution margin per part?
B. What was the actual contribution margin per part?
C. What was Turner's flexible budget variance?
D. What was Turner's direct material price variance?
E. What was Turner's direct material usage variance?
F. What was Turner's labor rate variance?
G. What was Turner's labor efficiency variance?

25. Material and Labor Variances: Solve for Missing Data LO5, 6

Sparky Electric produces a special type of grounded outlet. The outlet is used in areas where water is likely to be present, such as kitchens, bathrooms, outdoor work areas, porches, poolsides, and workshops. Sparky Electric has a policy to maintain as little inventory of Materials A and B as possible. For the quarter included in this analysis, there was no beginning or ending inventory of either material. Selected standard cost information is as follows:

Cost Standards		
Material A	2 pounds at $6.00 per pound	$12.00
Material B	3 gallons at $3.00 per gallon	9.00
Labor	4 hours at $3.20 per hour	12.80
Total standard unit cost		$33.80

The performance report for the third quarter of the year appears as follows (F indicates a favorable variance; U indicates an unfavorable variance):

Comparison of Actual and Standard			
	Actual	Standard	Total Variance
Material A	$37,515	$38,400	$ 885 F
Material B	30,195	28,800	1,395 U
Labor	39,525	40,960	1,435 F

Analysis of Variance			
	Usage	Price/Rate	Total Variance
Material A	$1,500 F	$ 615 U	$ 885 F
Material B	900 U	495 U	1,395 U
Labor	160 F	1,275 F	1,435 F

Required
A. How many units were produced during the quarter?
B. How many pounds of Material A were used during the quarter?
C. What was the actual price paid per pound for Material A during the quarter?
D. How many gallons of Material B were purchased during the quarter?
E. What was the actual price paid per gallon for Material B during the quarter?
F. How many actual labor hours were used during the quarter?
G. What was the actual wage rate per hour during the quarter?

26. Comprehensive Variance Analysis: Decision Focus LO5, 6, 7, 8

Small Tykes World Company mass-produces chairs for children. The chairs can be purchased in a variety of colors, but only one basic design. The chairs are wildly popular, especially with young, highly educated parents. The design is the key to the company's success, and there seems to be no end to the demand for Small Tykes's products. The following data were extracted from the company's standard cost sheet:

Plastic	10 pounds at $4.50 per pound
Molding	3 feet at $3.00 per foot
Direct labor	4 hours at $6.00 per hour
Variable overhead	$3 per direct labor hour
Fixed overhead	$55,000 per period

Transactions during the month of June were as follows:
- Small Tykes purchased plastic at $4.45 per pound and issued 185,000 pounds to production.
- Small Tykes purchased molding at $3.10 per foot and issued 50,000 feet to production.
- The direct labor payroll totaled $435,000 for 72,500 hours.
- Total overhead costs were $275,000, including $221,125 of variable overhead.
- Small Tykes produced 18,000 chairs during the month.

Required
A. Calculate all material, labor, variable overhead, and fixed overhead variances.
B. Interpret the material and labor variances. What do they indicate about the company's performance?
C. On the basis of your response to question B, what areas need to be investigated?
D. How could the company control or better manage its operations?
E. In your opinion, what are the best options? Why?

27. Variable and Fixed Overhead Variances LO7, 8

Surfs Up manufactures surfboards on the Big Island in Hawaii. The company's founder and world-famous surfer, Danny Kehono, has an accounting degree from Upper Island State University. He understands the importance of standards for production control and planning. The following standard costing data are available for the current period:

Actual fixed overhead	$ 10,500
Actual variable overhead	66,810
Budgeted fixed overhead	11,000
Variable overhead rate per labor hour	5.00
Fixed overhead rate per labor hour	0.80
Standard hours allowed for actual production	13,100
Actual labor hours used	13,000

Required

A. Calculate the variable overhead spending variance.
B. Calculate the variable overhead efficiency variance.
C. Calculate the fixed overhead spending variance.
D. Calculate the fixed overhead volume variance.

28. Variable and Fixed Overhead Variances LO1, 7, 8

Franklin Glass Works's production budget for the year ended November 30, 2012, was based on 200,000 units. Each unit requires two standard hours of labor for completion. Total overhead was budgeted at $900,000 for the year, and the fixed overhead rate was estimated to be $3 per unit. Both fixed and variable overhead are assigned to the product on the basis of direct labor hours. The actual data for the year ended November 30, 2012, are as follows:

Production in units	198,000
Labor hours	440,000
Variable overhead	$352,000
Fixed overhead	$575,000

Required

A. What are the total standard hours allowed for actual production for the year ended November 30, 2012?
B. What is Franklin's variable overhead efficiency variance?
C. What is Franklin's variable overhead spending variance?
D. What is Franklin's fixed overhead spending variance?
E. What is Franklin's fixed overhead volume variance?

CASE

29. Comprehensive Variance Analysis with Behavioral Issues LO1, 5, 6, 7, 8, 9

Jan Dan, Inc. (JDI), is a specialty frozen-food processor located in the southeastern United States. Since its founding in 1992, JDI has enjoyed a loyal local clientele that is willing to pay premium prices for the high-quality frozen foods it prepares from specialized recipes. In the past two years, the company experienced rapid sales growth in its operating region and had many inquiries about supplying its products on a national basis. To meet this growth, JDI expanded its processing capabilities, resulting in increased production and distribution costs. Moving onto the national scene also caused JDI to encounter pricing pressure from competitors outside its region.

Because JDI wants to continue expanding, Nick Guice, the company's chief executive officer, engaged a consulting firm to assist in determining JDI's best course of action. The consulting firm concluded that premium pricing is sustainable in some areas, but if sales growth is to be achieved, JDI must make price concessions in other areas. Also, to maintain profit margins, costs must be reduced and more tightly controlled. The consulting firm recommended the implementation of a standard cost system that would facilitate a flexible budgeting system to better accommodate the changes in demand that can be expected when serving an expanding market area.

Recently, Guice met with his management team and explained the consulting firm's recommendations. Guice then assigned the task of setting standards to his management team. After the management team discussed the situation with their respective staffs, the team met to review the matter.

Janie Morgan, purchasing manager, advised that meeting expanded production would necessitate obtaining basic food supplies from companies other than JDI's traditional sources. This in turn would entail increased raw material and shipping costs and might result in lower quality supplies. Consequently, these increased costs will need to be counterbalanced by reduced costs in the processing department if current cost levels are to be maintained or reduced.

Dan Walters, processing manager, suggested that the need to accelerate processing cycles to increase production, coupled with the possibility of receiving lower grade supplies, could be expected to result in poorer quality and a greater product rejection rate. Under these circumstances, per-unit labor utilization cannot be maintained or increased and forecasting future unit labor content becomes very difficult.

Corinne Kelly, production engineer, advised that if the equipment is not properly maintained and thoroughly cleaned at prescribed daily intervals, it can be anticipated that the quality and unique taste of the frozen-food product will be affected. Kent Jackson, vice president of sales, stated that if quality cannot be maintained, JDI cannot expect to increase sales to the levels projected.

When Guice was apprised of the problems enumerated by his management team, he advised the team members that if agreement could not be reached on appropriate standards, he would arrange to have the standards set by the consulting firm and everyone would have to live with the results.

Required

A. List the major advantages of using a standard cost system.
B. List disadvantages that can result from using a standard cost system.
C. Identify those who should participate in setting standards, and describe the benefits of their participation in the standard-setting process.
D. Explain the general features and characteristics associated with the introduction and operation of a standard cost system that make it an effective tool for cost control.
E. What could be the consequences if Nick Guice has the standards set by the consulting firm?
F. Explain what is meant by variance and variance analysis.
G. Discuss material variances and why they might occur at JDI.
H. Explain overhead variances in the context of this case. Include a discussion of variable and fixed overhead variances.

Decentralization,
Performance Evaluation, and the Balanced Scorecard

Introduction

As the CEO of a chain of local retail shoe stores, you would be responsible for all aspects of your company's performance, from purchasing shoes, to setting prices, to investing in new fixtures, or even to expanding operations by opening new stores. Consequently, your performance should be evaluated on the basis of all these factors: the costs incurred, the revenue generated, and the investment made in the company. Contrast the responsibilities of the CEO of the company to the responsibilities of a manager of a specific store. As the store manager, you are likely to have some authority over setting prices of shoes, but purchasing decisions are made for the entire chain. Likewise, although you are likely to have some responsibility for making improvements to your store, major renovations and expansions can be made only with the approval of the CEO. Obviously, it would not be fair to the store manager to evaluate his or her performance on the basis of the profit earned by the entire chain. In addition, it would probably not be appropriate to evaluate the store manager's performance on the basis of the profit of his or her store, because a major component of the costs (the cost of shoes sold) is out of the store manager's control. In general, managers should be held responsible for only those things over which they have control. The challenge for companies is to find tools that allow the evaluation of managers at all levels in the organization—from a plant manager in a factory, to the manager of a retail store, to the regional sales manager, to the CEO.

Learning Objectives

After studying the material in this chapter, you should be able to:

LO1 Describe the structure and management of decentralized organizations and evaluate the benefits and drawbacks of decentralization.

LO2 Evaluate how responsibility accounting is used to help manage a decentralized organization.

LO3 Define cost, revenue, profit, and investment centers and explain why managers of each must be evaluated differently.

LO4 Compute and interpret segment margin in an organization.

LO5 Compute, interpret, and compare return on investment (ROI) and residual income.

LO6 Describe the balanced scorecard and its key dimensions.

LO7 Define quality costs and explain the trade-offs among prevention costs, appraisal costs, internal failure costs, and external failure costs.

LO8 Recognize the importance of using incentives to motivate managers and discuss the advantages and disadvantages of using cash-based, stock-based, and other forms of managerial compensation.

LO1 Management of Decentralized Organizations

Decentralized organization
An organization in which decision-making authority is spread throughout the organization.

A **decentralized organization** is an organization in which decision-making authority is spread throughout the organization, as opposed to being confined to top-level management. When a few

Evaluating performance of a retail store requires a consideration of responsibility accounting.

© Neil Beckerman/Taxi/Getty Images

individuals at the top of an organization retain decision-making authority, the organization is referred to as centralized. In a decentralized environment, managers at various levels throughout the organization make key decisions about operations relating to their specific areas of responsibility. These areas are called segments. Segments can be branches, divisions, departments, or individual products. Any activity or part of the business for which a manager needs cost, revenue, or profit data can be considered a segment. Reporting financial and other information by segments is called segment reporting. This chapter discusses segment reporting and cost control and performance evaluation issues in segments of decentralized organizations.

Decentralization varies from organization to organization. Most organizations are decentralized to some degree. At one end of the spectrum, managers are given complete authority to make decisions at their level of operations. At the other extreme, managers have little, if any, authority to make decisions. Most firms fall somewhere in the middle.

Benefits of Decentralization

There are several benefits to decentralization:

- Decentralization fosters an environment of entrepreneurship and innovation.
- Generally, those closest to a problem are most familiar with the problem and its root causes. By pushing decision-making authority down to lower levels, managers most familiar with a problem have the opportunity to solve it.
- Top management has more time to devote to long-range strategic planning, as decentralization removes the responsibility for much of the day-to-day decision making.
- Studies have shown that managers allowed to make decisions in a decentralized environment have higher job satisfaction than do managers in centralized organizations.
- Managers who are given increased responsibility for decision making early in their careers generally become better managers because of the on-the-job training they receive. In other words, experience is the best teacher.
- Decisions are often made in a more timely fashion.

Drawbacks of Decentralization

However, there can be drawbacks as well:

- When decision-making authority is spread among too many managers, the company can lack focus.

> Decentralized organizations must have managers who are competent, are experienced, and have the authority required to make decisions.

Managers may become so concerned with their own areas of responsibility that they lose sight of the big picture. Because of this lack of focus on the company as a whole, managers may tend to make decisions benefiting their own segments, a practice that may not always be in the best interest of the company.

- Managers may not be adequately trained in decision making at the early stages of their careers. The costs of training managers can be high, and the potential costs of bad decisions while new managers are being trained should be considered.
- There may be a lack of coordination and communication between segments.
- Decentralization may make it difficult to share unique and innovative ideas.
- Decentralization may result in duplicative efforts and duplicative costs.

Decentralized organizations require well-developed and well-integrated information systems. The flow of information and open communication between

MAKING IT REAL

Decentralization at Johnson and Johnson

Although you may think of Johnson and Johnson (J&J) primarily as a consumer products company selling baby products and Band-Aids®, the company actually consists of three business segments: consumer products, medical devices and diagnostics, and—the largest of the three—pharmaceuticals. The company is highly decentralized, with over 200 operating companies.

And what are the primary benefits of the decentralization to J&J? Local managers that understand the marketplace, the opportunity to develop leaders, and innovation fostered across the company. The downside is the difficulty in achieving coordination: "trying to get people together and moving in the same direction" and getting people to go outside of their silos.

Source: "Johnson and Johnson CEO William Weldon: Leadership in a Decentralized Company," Interview with William Weldon, published online at http://knowledge.wharton.upenn.edu/article.cfm?articleid=2003, June 25, 2008.

divisions and upper and lower management is critical. This can be a problem for companies whose systems do not provide the kind of quantitative and qualitative information needed at the segment level. For that reason, the use of enterprise resource planning (ERP) systems has been particularly helpful in decentralized organizations.

LO2 Responsibility Accounting and Segment Reporting

The key to effective decision making in a decentralized organization is **responsibility accounting**: holding managers responsible for only those things under their control. In reality, the amount of control a manager has can vary greatly from situation to situation. For example, 75 percent of the shoes offered for sale at the shoe department of a store may be purchased by a regional purchasing manager in order to obtain quantity-purchase discounts from suppliers. Only 25 percent are purchased at the discretion of the individual store managers. In this case, because a local manager does not control the quantity or style of most of the shoes in his or her store or how much was paid for them, that manager should not be held responsible for the cost of shoes purchased and the profit earned on shoe sales in the store.

In the previous chapter, variance analysis was used to help evaluate the performance of managers by focusing on who had responsibility for a variance. Usage variances were typically the responsibility of production managers, and price variances were typically the responsibility of purchasing managers. However, as you will recall, general rules like this must be used with caution. For example, the purchasing manager might be responsible for a usage variance if low-quality materials contributed to excessive waste.

In decentralized organizations, detailed information is needed to evaluate the effectiveness of managerial decision making. Companywide budgets, cost standards, income statements, and so on are not sufficient to evaluate the performance of each of a company's segments. For example, overall financial statements generated for external reporting purposes would be of limited use in evaluating the performance of the managers of **Johnson and Johnson**'s 200 separate operating companies.

> The key to effective decision making in a decentralized organization is responsibility accounting: holding managers responsible for only those things under their control.

LO3 Cost, Revenue, Profit, and Investment Centers

Organizations typically identify the different segments, or levels of responsibility, as cost, revenue, profit, or investment centers and attach different levels of responsibility to each segment (see Exhibit 11-1).

Exhibit 11-1 Responsibility Levels at Cost, Revenue, Profit, and Investment Centers

Cost Center	Revenue Center	Profit Center	Investment Center
Responsible for costs only	Responsible for revenue only	Responsible for costs and revenues	Responsible for profit and investments in property, plant, & equipment

© Cengage Learning 2013

Cost Centers

A **cost center** manager has control over costs but not over revenue or capital investment (long-term purchasing) decisions. The purchasing manager of a store, the production manager for a particular type of DVD player, the maintenance manager in a hotel, and the human resources manager of a CPA firm would likely be considered managers of cost centers. The manager of a cost center should be evaluated on how well he or she controls costs in the respective segment. Consequently, performance

Responsibility accounting An accounting system that assigns responsibility to a manager for only those areas which are under that manager's control.

Cost center An organizational segment, or division, in which the manager has control over costs but not over revenue or investment decisions.

Businesses are often broken into cost, revenue, and profit centers as a means to evaluate managers' performance levels.

reports typically use variance analysis to focus on differences between budgeted and actual costs. A **performance report** provides key financial and nonfinancial measures of performance appropriate for a particular segment.

Revenue Centers

A **revenue center** manager has control over the generation of revenue but not costs. Examples include the sales manager of a retail store, the sales department of a production facility, and the reservation department of an airline. Performance reports of a revenue center often focus on sales price variances (discussed in Chapter 10).

Profit Centers

A **profit center** manager has control over both cost and revenue but not capital investment decisions. Although the purchasing manager of a retail store is a cost center manager, the overall manager of the store will probably be a profit center manager. Likewise, the manager of an entire product line in a factory, the manager of a particular location of a hotel chain, and the partner in charge of the tax department at a CPA firm would be considered

profit center managers. It is important to understand that profit center managers still do not have control over decisions to invest in and purchase new property, plant, and equipment. For example, the profit center managers described here could not make decisions to remodel a store, buy new manufacturing equipment, add a swimming pool to a hotel, or open a new office.

The manager of a profit center should be evaluated on both revenue generation and cost control. Consequently, performance reports typically focus on income measures, such as the overall flexible budget variance (discussed in Chapter 10). The flexible budget variance is the difference between the actual and budgeted operating income. However, using this measure to evaluate the performance of a manager of a profit center can be problematic when uncontrollable fixed costs are included in the analysis. Segment managers should be held responsible for only those costs under their control. Consequently, other measures of profit center performance, such as segment margin (discussed on page 238), are also commonly used.

Investment Centers

In addition to being responsible for a segment's revenue and expenses, an **investment center** manager is responsible for the amount of cash and other assets invested in generating the segment's income. An investment center is, in essence, a separate business with its own value chain. Consequently, investment centers are frequently referred to as **strategic business units (SBUs)**. An investment center manager is involved in decisions ranging from research and development, to production, to marketing and sales and customer service. Large international companies may have several core businesses operating as investment centers or SBUs.

Although the manager of an investment center can be evaluated with some of the same tools as profit

Performance report Provides key financial and nonfinancial measures of performance for a particular segment.

Revenue center An organizational segment, or division, in which the manager has control over revenue but not costs or investment decisions.

Profit center An organizational segment, or division, in which the manager has control over both costs and revenue but not investment decisions.

Investment center An organizational segment, or division, in which the manager has control over costs, revenue, and investment decisions.

Strategic business unit (SBU) Another term for investment center.

centers, the amount of assets or investment under the manager's control must also be considered. Measures of performance for investment centers are discussed later in the chapter.

LO4 Profit Center Performance and Segmented Income Statements

Segmented income statements calculate income for each major segment of an organization in addition to the company as a whole. Although it is usually easy to keep records of sales by segment, tracing costs to a particular segment and deciding how to treat costs that benefit more than one segment can be very difficult.

Variable costs are generally traced directly to a segment. Remember, variable costs vary in direct proportion to sales volume. Therefore, they can be allocated to a segment on the basis of sales volume.

Deciding which fixed costs to assign, or allocate, to a segment requires an analysis of the overall company and the individual areas of responsibility (segments) within an organization. **Segment costs** should include *all* costs attributable to that segment but *only* those costs that are actually caused by the segment. Fixed costs that can be easily and conveniently traced to a segment should obviously be assigned to that segment. The problem is that many fixed costs are indirect in nature. Should indirect fixed costs be allocated to segments? A good test for deciding whether to allocate indirect fixed costs is to determine whether the cost would be reduced or eliminated if the segment were eliminated. If the cost cannot be reduced or eliminated, it is referred to as a common cost. **Common costs** are indirect costs that are incurred to benefit more than one segment and that cannot be directly traced to a particular segment or allocated in a reasonable manner on the basis of what causes the cost to be incurred. In general, common costs should not be allocated to segments for purposes of performance evaluation.

For example, Camelback Mountain Community Bank (headquartered in Phoenix, Arizona) has six branches located in and around the Phoenix metropolitan area. One of those branches is located in Tempe. The Tempe branch incurs a fixed lease expense to rent the building in which the bank is located. Obviously, this lease expense is directly traceable to the individual branch (a segment) and should be allocated to that segment. However, if the lease expense is for the corporate headquarters building in Phoenix, the cost is an indirect one and probably should not be allocated to the Tempe branch. In this case, it is doubtful that the lease expense for the headquarters building would be reduced or eliminated if the Tempe branch were eliminated. Therefore, that expense is probably best treated as a common cost and should not be allocated to the segment. In practice, companies sometimes allocate common costs from headquarters to segments without using them for evaluation purposes. This practice has the advantage of making the segment manager aware that the cost is being incurred and that the cost must ultimately be paid for by revenue generated by the segment.

Other indirect costs can be allocated to a segment if there is a sufficient causal relationship between the cost and the segment. For example, all loan processing for Camelback Mountain Community Bank is done in the headquarters building in Phoenix. Although these costs (for credit checks, loan processing, staff salaries, and so on) may be difficult to trace directly to the Tempe branch, they can be allocated in a manner that reflects the cause of the costs (the number of loans processed, the dollar amount of the loans processed, and so on). In addition, it is reasonable to assume that at least some of the loan-processing costs would be reduced or eliminated if the branch were closed.

To allocate indirect costs, there should be a causal relationship between the allocation base and a segment's use of the common cost. Allocating costs by using an arbitrary allocation base is inappropriate. Although Camelback Mountain Community Bank could allocate the lease cost of the headquarters building to its branches on the basis of an allocation base, such as square footage or total deposits, such a base would be completely arbitrary. There is no causal relationship between the square footage or total deposits in a branch and the lease expense in the headquarters building. Arbitrary allocations like this may result in a profitable segment appearing unprofitable and may lead to less-than-optimal decisions concerning that segment.

Segmented income statements Reports that calculate income for each major segment of an organization in addition to the company as a whole.

Segment costs All costs attributable to a particular segment of an organization but only those costs that are actually caused by the segment.

Common costs Indirect costs that are incurred to benefit more than one segment and that cannot be directly traced to a particular segment or allocated in a reasonable manner.

Divisions

Garcia and Buffett is a full-service local CPA firm offering services in three departments: tax, audit, and consulting. The tax department is broken down into individual and business divisions. Garcia and Buffett has annual client billings of $1 million, with 50 percent generated from the tax department, 40 percent from the audit department, and the remaining 10 percent from the consulting department. The following table shows a segmented income statement broken down into three segments based on the three practice departments:

Segmented Income Statement

		(Segments Defined as Departments)		
	Total Firm	Tax Department	Audit Department	Consulting Department
Service revenue	$1,000,000	$500,000	$400,000	$100,000
Less: Variable expenses	400,000	200,000	160,000	40,000
Contribution margin	$ 600,000	$300,000	$240,000	$ 60,000
Less: Traceable fixed expenses	200,000	100,000	75,000	25,000
Segment margin	$ 400,000	$200,000	$165,000	$ 35,000
Less: Common fixed expenses	200,000			
Net income	$ 200,000			

The $100,000 of fixed costs traceable to the tax department include advertising geared specifically to the tax department, the salary of the tax manager, the costs of research material used in the tax library, and computer software used for tax preparation. Common fixed costs (for the firm as a whole) include the salaries of the managing partner of the firm, human resources manager, and receptionist and the depreciation of the office building.

In the table that follows, Garcia and Buffett goes a step further and provides a segmented income statement for the two divisions within the tax department. Note that the statements are based on the contribution margin format introduced in Chapter 6. The primary differences are the separation of fixed costs into traceable fixed costs and common fixed costs and the interim calculation of segment margin.

Segment margin The profit margin of a particular segment of an organization, typically the best measure of long-term profitability.

Evaluating investment centers requires focusing on the level of investment required in generating a segment's profit.

Segmented Income Statement

		(Segments Defined as Divisions)	
	Tax Department	Individual Tax Division	Business Tax Division
Service revenue	$500,000	$100,000	$400,000
Less: Variable expenses	200,000	80,000	120,000
Contribution margin	$300,000	$ 20,000	$280,000
Less: Traceable fixed expenses	80,000	30,000	50,000
Divisional segment margin	$220,000	$(10,000)	$230,000
Less: Common fixed expenses	20,000		
Departmental segment margin	$200,000		

Note that although $100,000 of fixed costs were traced to the tax department in the first table (when segments were defined as departments), only $80,000 are subsequently traced to the individual and business divisions; $20,000 of traceable costs have become common costs. In this case, the advertising costs for the tax division and the cost of research materials in the tax library cannot be traced directly to either the individual or the business division.

As discussed in Chapter 6, the contribution margin and the contribution margin ratio are primarily measures of short-run profitability, because they ignore fixed costs. The contribution margin ratio is used extensively in short-run decisions, such as CVP analysis and the evaluation of special orders. By contrast, the **segment margin** and segment margin ratio (segment margin/sales) are measures of long-term profitability and are more appropriate in addressing long-term decisions, such as whether to drop product lines.

In the case of Garcia and Buffett, the segment margin of the tax department is positive but the segment margin of the individual tax division is negative. In the long run, the individual tax division is not profitable. However, before the firm decides to eliminate the individual tax division, it should consider other factors (both quantitative and qualitative), including the impact on its highly profitable business tax division.

For example, it may be important for the firm to be perceived as a full-service firm to which owners of small businesses can come for help with all their tax and business problems. In addition, planning for a small business must often be integrated with planning for the individual owner of the business. For these reasons, the firm may decide to retain the division even if it has not been profitable. Accordingly, instead of eliminating the division, Garcia and Buffett may decide to focus on ways to make the division profitable through expanding the array of services offered to clients. For example, the firm may begin offering personal financial planning services to its clients to help them meet their overall financial goals.

LO5 Investment Centers and Measures of Performance

In addition to being responsible for a segment's revenue and expenses, an investment center manager is responsible for the amount of capital invested in generating the segment's income. Investment center managers can make capital-purchasing decisions, including decisions to remodel facilities, purchase new equipment, expand facilities, or add new locations. Investment centers are typically major divisions or branch operations of a company involved in all aspects of the value chain. In addition to using the approaches discussed earlier for cost and profit centers, evaluating investment centers requires focusing on the level of investment needed to generate a segment's profit. For this reason, performance reports focus on measures specifically developed for that purpose: return on investment and residual income.

Managers of investment centers are given complete control over all activities in their respective segments. Managers want to be associated with well-run, profitable divisions. Competition between investment center managers within an organization is sometimes intense. Because of compensation issues, such as year-end bonuses based on performance, managers of investment centers must also be evaluated. Although all the financial measures of performance used in evaluating the managers of cost, revenue, and profit centers apply to investment center managers, they are not sufficient.

To some extent, controlling costs and generating revenue is a function of the amount of assets under a manager's control. For example, if a manager had unlimited assets and resources, production costs could be reduced by buying the most efficient manufacturing equipment available. Likewise, sales might be maximized by additional spending on advertising. Very large companies typically have higher revenue and higher income than very small companies. However, the manager of an investment center should not be evaluated with respect to the amount of costs, revenue, and income generated without reference to the size of the investment center being managed and the assets under the manager's control.

Return on Investment

DuPont was the first major company in the United States to recognize that the performance of an investment center must consider the level of investment along with the income generated from that investment. **Return on investment (ROI)** measures the rate of return generated by an investment center's assets.

ROI can be a very simple concept. For example, if you invest $1,000 in a bank certificate of deposit for one year and receive $50 at the end of the year, your return on that investment is 5 percent ($50 ÷ $1,000). However, the calculation of return gets a little more complicated when the income is reinvested in another certificate, the amount of assets change, or costs are incurred to manage the money.

Margin and Turnover. In business, the calculation of ROI is generally broken down into two components: a measure of operating performance (called margin) and a measure of how effectively assets are used during a period (called asset turnover). **Margin** is found by dividing an investment center's net operating income by its sales. As such, it can be viewed as the profit that is earned on each dollar of sales. A margin of 10 percent indicates that 10 cents of every sales dollar is profit. **Asset turnover** is calculated by dividing an investment center's sales by its average operating assets during a period. It measures the sales that are generated for a given level of assets.

> **Return on investment (ROI)** Measures the rate of return generated by an investment center's assets.
>
> **Margin** For each sales dollar, the percentage that is recognized as net profit.
>
> **Asset turnover** The measure of activity used in the ROI calculation; it measures the sales that are generated for a given level of assets.

The formula for return on investment (ROI) is as follows:

$$\text{ROI} = \text{Margin} \times \text{Turnover}$$
$$\text{Margin} = \text{Net operating income} \div \text{Sales}$$
$$\text{Turnover} = \text{Sales} \div \text{Average operating assets}$$
$$\text{ROI} = \frac{\text{Net operating income}}{\text{Sales}} \times \frac{\text{Sales}}{\text{Average operating assets}}$$

or

$$\text{ROI} = \frac{\text{Net operating income}}{\text{Average operating assets}}$$

The elements composing ROI are shown in graphical form in Exhibit 11-2.

Exhibit 11-2 Elements of Return on Investment (ROI)

© Cengage Learning 2013

Net operating income Net income from operations before interest and taxes.

Operating assets Typically include cash, accounts receivable, inventory, and the property, plant, and equipment needed to operate a business.

Although various investment centers (including companies) may have similar ROIs, their margin and turnover may be very different. For example, a grocery store and a furniture store both have an ROI of 20 percent. However, the grocery store's ROI may be made up of a profit margin of $0.02 per dollar of product sold and a turnover of 10, whereas the furniture store may have a margin of $0.10 per dollar of product sold and a turnover of 2. In this case, the grocery store does not make much from each dollar of sales but generates a lot of sales for the amount of its assets. In contrast, the furniture store makes more from each sale but does not generate as many sales for the amount of assets under its control.

Net operating income is most frequently used as the measure of income in the ROI formula. **Net operating income** is a measure of operating performance and is defined as net income from operations before interest and taxes. Interest and taxes are typically omitted from the measure of income in the ROI calculation because they may not be controllable by the manager of the segment being evaluated.

Likewise, the most common measure of investment is average operating assets. **Operating assets** typically include cash, accounts receivable, inventory, and the property, plant, and equipment needed to operate a business. Land and other assets held for resale or assets that are idle (e.g., a plant that is not being used) are typically not included in operating assets. Because income is measured over time, assets are also generally measured as an average of beginning- and end-of-period numbers. By focusing on operating income and average operating assets, ROI attempts to isolate the financial performance of a company's core operations.

Whereas cash, accounts receivable, and inventory are generally easy to measure, the measurement of depreciable property, plant, and equipment for purposes of determining ROI poses some interesting questions.

Evaluating the performance of investment center managers is complex and often involves using measures such as ROI and residual income.

The use of net book value (the cost of the assets less accumulated depreciation) is consistent with the calculation of operating income (which includes depreciation expense) but can have some undesirable consequences. For example, as an asset ages, the net book value of the asset decreases. Using net book value can cause ROI to increase over time simply because of the reduction in book value of assets used in the calculation. The choice of depreciation method can also affect ROI calculations. Choosing an accelerated method over straight-line depreciation makes the book value of the asset decrease more rapidly, increasing ROI. Both of these factors may discourage managers from replacing old assets, such as manufacturing equipment. If managers are evaluated on the basis of ROI, they may be reluctant to replace aging machinery with a low book value with an expensive, but more efficient, piece of equipment.

The use of gross book value to measure operating assets eliminates the age of an asset as a factor in the ROI calculation, as well as any distortions that can be caused by the depreciation method chosen.

Example

To illustrate the use of ROI, consider the financial results for Big Al's Pizza Emporium (see Exhibit 11-3). Last year, Big Al's had average operating assets of $100,000, consisting of cash, accounts receivable, inventory, and furniture and equipment at book value. Big Al's sales for the year were $350,000 (consisting of $275,000 for 23,000 pizzas and $75,000 for drinks and other side orders). The ROI for Big Al's, using the net book value method, would be 17.5 percent, consisting of margin of 0.05 ($17,500 ÷ $350,000) and asset turnover of 3.5 ($350,000 ÷ $100,000).

Exhibit 11-3 ROI with Operating Assets of $100,000 and Sales of $350,000

Sales revenue	$350,000
Variable costs	250,000
Contribution margin	$100,000
Fixed costs	82,500
Net operating income	$ 17,500
Average operating assets	$100,000
ROI	$17,500 ÷ $100,000 = 17.5%

© Cengage Learning 2013

If Al would like to increase ROI, what are his options? In general, sales can be increased, operating expenses can be reduced, or the investment in operating assets can be reduced. The first two alternatives increase operating income, and the last option decreases net operating assets.

Increase Sales Volume or Sales Price. Sales revenue can be raised either by increasing sales volume without changing the sales price or by increasing the sales price without affecting volume. Remember that when sales volume increases, variable costs increase by the same proportional amount because variable costs stay the same per unit but increase in total as more units are sold. In addition, fixed costs remain the same. Thus, if sales volume increases by 5 percent (resulting in sales revenue of $367,500), income will increase by $5,000, to $22,500. As shown in Exhibit 11-4, ROI will increase correspondingly, to 22.5 percent.

Exhibit 11-4 ROI When Sales Increases to $367,500

Sales revenue	$367,500
Variable costs	262,500
Contribution margin	$105,000
Fixed costs	82,500
Net operating income	$ 22,500
Average operating assets	$100,000
ROI	$22,500 ÷ $100,000 = 22.5%

© Cengage Learning 2013

If Al just changes the price of his products, the analysis is a little different. Increasing sales prices (without a corresponding change in volume) does not affect variable costs or fixed costs. Thus, if revenue were increased by $17,500 because of a 5 percent increase in sales price, income would increase by the same $17,500. ROI would increase to 35 percent ($35,000 ÷ $100,000).

Decrease Operating Costs. ROI can also be increased by decreasing operating costs. The decrease in costs can be concentrated in variable or fixed costs or both. The key is that any decrease in operating costs will increase operating income and have a positive impact on ROI. In Exhibit 11-5, variable costs are reduced to $241,250 by using a different supplier for direct materials. Income increases by $8,750, resulting in an ROI of 26.25 percent.

Exhibit 11-5 ROI When Variable Costs Are Reduced to $241,250

Sales revenue	$350,000
Variable costs	241,250
Contribution margin	$108,750
Fixed costs	82,500
Net operating income	$ 26,250
Average operating assets	$100,000
ROI	$26,250 ÷ $100,000 = 26.25%

© Cengage Learning 2013

Decrease the Amount of Operating Assets. The third way to increase ROI is to decrease the amount invested in operating assets. Although this may be difficult to do in the short run with property, plant, and equipment, average operating assets can be decreased through better management of inventory. For example, let's assume that Big Al's reduces operating assets by 10 percent by reducing the amount of materials kept in inventory. As shown in Exhibit 11-6, reducing average operating assets to $90,000 will increase ROI to 19.44 percent.

Exhibit 11-6 ROI When Operating Assets Are Reduced to $90,000

Sales revenue	$350,000
Variable costs	250,000
Contribution margin	$100,000
Fixed costs	82,500
Net operating income	$ 17,500
Average operating assets	$ 90,000
ROI	$17,500 ÷ $90,000 = 19.44%

© Cengage Learning 2013

Residual income The amount of income earned in excess of a predetermined minimum rate of return on assets.

Residual Income

As an alternative to evaluating the manager of an investment center on the basis of ROI, the manager can be evaluated on the basis of the residual income generated by the investment center. **Residual income** is the amount of income earned in excess of a predetermined minimum rate of return on assets:

$$\text{Residual Income} = \text{Net operating income} - \left(\text{Average operating assets} \times \text{Minimum required rate of return} \right)$$

All other things being equal, the higher the residual income of an investment center, the better off the center will be. Referring back to the original scenario in Exhibit 11-3 (average operating assets of $100,000 and net operating income of $17,500), and assuming that Big Al's has a minimum required rate of return of 15 percent, we would calculate the residual income as follows:

$$\$17,500 - (\$100,000 \times 15\%) = \$2,500$$

If Big Al's increases sales to $367,500, net operating income increases to $22,500 and ROI increases to 22.5 percent (see Exhibit 11-4). Likewise, residual income will increase to $7,500:

$$\$22,500 - (\$100,000 \times 15\%) = \$7,500$$

If Big Al's decreases variable costs to $241,250, net operating income increases to $26,250 and ROI increases to 26.25 percent (see Exhibit 11-5). Under the new scenario, residual income would be $11,250:

$$\$26,250 - (\$100,000 \times 15\%) = \$11,250$$

ROI vs. Residual Income In some cases, using ROI to evaluate the performance of an investment center and its manager can cause problems. For example, Al recently opened a second location and hired a new manager to run the business at the original location. Because the new location is substantially larger than the original location, he wants to devote his full attention to the successful start-up of the new location.

Currently, ROI at the original location is 25 percent ($25,000 net operating income and average operating assets of $100,000). Big Al's goal and minimum acceptable return for both locations is to maintain an ROI of 15 percent. However, if the new manager is evaluated on the basis of the location's ROI, he may reject potential projects or investments that would be profitable (and earn a return greater than 15 percent) but would lower the location's overall ROI.

As an example, suppose the new manager is considering purchasing a new automated pizza oven that will reduce the time it takes to make a pizza and the electricity consumed. The equipment costs $15,000 and is expected to result in increased income of $3,200. Although the return on investment for this particular piece of equipment is over 21 percent ($3,200 ÷ $15,000), the manager is likely to reject the purchase because it will reduce his overall ROI from 25 percent ($25,000 ÷ $100,000) to 24.5 percent ($28,200 ÷ $115,000).

Note that using residual income avoids this problem. If the new manager has the opportunity to purchase a new pizza oven at a cost of $15,000 and expects that profits will increase by $3,200, using residual income to evaluate the new manager will encourage the manager to purchase the new oven. The residual income of the existing location will increase from $10,000 [$25,000 − ($100,000 × 15%)] to $10,950 [$28,200 − ($115,000 × 15%)].

However, residual income is not without its own problems. Because it is an absolute measure, it should not be used to compare the performance of investment centers of different sizes. For example, Big Al's new location is considerably larger than the existing location. As shown in Exhibit 11-7, average operating assets in the new location total $300,000, compared with $100,000 in the existing location.

Exhibit 11-7 Return on Investment and Residual Income

	Existing Location	New Location
Average operating assets	$100,000	$300,000
Minimum required return	15%	15%
Net operating income	$ 25,000	$ 70,000
Residual income	$ 10,000	$ 25,000
ROI	25%	23.3%

© Cengage Learning 2013

As demonstrated in Exhibit 11-7, the residual income of the new location (run by Al) is higher than the residual income of the existing location (run by the new manager). However, Al is not necessarily managing the new location better; it's just bigger. As you can see, the ROI of the new location is actually lower than the ROI

of the existing location. Which measure is better? Both are useful but often for different purposes. Residual income is more useful as a performance measure for a single investment center. By contrast, because ROI is independent of size, it is better suited as a comparative measure.

Decentralization and Performance Evaluation in a Multinational Company

Segments or divisions in a multinational company are often created along geographic lines. Frequently, U.S. companies have subsidiaries that operate in other countries. Sometimes these subsidiaries are involved in manufacturing, but in other cases they may be responsible for marketing or distributing products and services in foreign countries. These foreign divisions may operate as cost, profit, revenue, or investment centers.

When responsibility centers are located in more than one country, the management style and decision-making structures used by the companies and the methods of performance evaluation employed by the companies must take into account differences in economic, legal and political, educational, and cultural factors in the business environment of each country.

Economic factors include things like the stability of the economy, whether a country is experiencing high inflation, the strength of underlying capital markets, and the strength of the local currency. Legal and political factors include the degree of governmental control and regulation of business and the political stability of each country. Educational factors include the availability of an educated, adequately trained work force. Cultural factors may include things like attitudes toward authority, work ethic, and loyalty and commitment to employers by employees and to employees by employers. Because of the unique challenges facing multinational companies as a result of these factors, there are often clear advantages to decentralizing operations in a multinational company, including improving the quality and timeliness of decision making when done at the local level and minimizing social, cultural, political, and language barriers.

LO6 Performance Evaluation Using the Balanced Scorecard

Traditional accounting measures of performance that rely on historical financial data are of little use in making decisions concerning customer satisfaction,

The balanced scorecard approach integrates financial and nonfinancial performance measures.

quality issues, productivity, efficiency, and employee satisfaction. Managers also need timely information concerning the success or failure of new products or marketing campaigns and the success of programs designed to enhance customer value. The **balanced scorecard** approach to performance measurement uses a set of financial and nonfinancial measures that relate to the overall strategy of the organization. By integrating financial and nonfinancial performance measures, the balanced scorecard helps to keep management focused on all of a company's critical success factors, not just its financial ones. The balanced scorecard also helps to keep short-term operating performance in line with long-term strategy.

As shown in Exhibit 11-8, utilizing a balanced scorecard approach requires looking at performance from four different, but related, perspectives: financial, customer, internal business, and learning and growth.

Financial Perspective

The primary goal of every profit-making enterprise is to show a profit. Profit allows the enterprise to provide a return on investment (ROI) to investors, to repay creditors, and to adequately compensate management and employees. Critical success factors under this perspective include sales, costs, measures of profit such as operating income and segment margin, and measures of investment center performance such as ROI and residual income. However, under the balanced scorecard approach, financial performance is seen in the larger context of the company's overall goals and objectives relating to its customers and suppliers, internal processes, and employees.

Customer Perspective

Many successful businesses have found that focusing on customers and meeting or exceeding their needs is more important in the long run than simply focusing on financial measures of performance. After all, it is the customer who ultimately incurs the costs of producing products and contributes to a company's profits. Considering the customer perspective is therefore key to attaining the financial goals of a company. Critical success factors under this perspective are likely to include improving the quality of products and services, reducing delivery time, and increasing customer satisfaction. Measures of performance appropriate under this perspective include the number of warranty claims and returned products (for quality), customer response time and the percentage of on-time deliveries (for reducing delivery time), and customer complaints and repeat business (for customer satisfaction).

A second dimension of the customer perspective focuses on the critical success factors of increasing market share and penetrating new markets. Measures

Exhibit 11-8 The Balanced Scorecard Approach to Performance Measurement

Financial Perspective
How do we create value for our stakeholders?

Customer Perspective
How do customers view us?

Strategy

Internal Business Perspective
At what business processes must we excel?

Learning-and-Growth Perspective
How do we continue to improve, learn, and grow?

© Cengage Learning 2013

Balanced scorecard An approach to performance measurement that uses a set of financial and nonfinancial measures that relate to the overall strategy of the organization.

of performance appropriate for this dimension include market share, market saturation, customer loyalty, and new products introduced into the marketplace. Focusing on the customer perspective can result in impressive financial returns. For example, at **Ford**, a 1-percentage-point increase in customer loyalty results in significant increases in sales and profits.

Internal Business Perspective

The internal business perspective deals with objectives across the company's entire value chain: from research and development to post-sale customer service. It is linked to the financial perspective through its emphasis on improving the efficiency of manufacturing processes and to the customer perspective through its focus on improving processes and products to better meet customer needs. Every company will approach this perspective differently, because the processes that add value to products and services are likely to differ by company. However, critical success factors include productivity, manufacturing cycle time, throughput, and manufacturing cycle efficiency (MCE).

Productivity **Productivity** is a measure of the relationship between outputs and inputs. How many cars are produced per labor hour, how many loaves of bread are baked per bag of flour, how many calculators are produced per machine hour, how many customers are serviced per shift, and how many sales dollars are generated per full-time sales clerk are all measures of productivity.

Manufacturing Cycle Time and Throughput **Manufacturing cycle time** is the amount of time it takes to produce a defect-free unit of product from the time raw material is received until the product is ready to deliver to customers. In addition to actual processing time, cycle time includes time spent moving materials and products from one place to the next, time spent waiting for machine availability, and time spent inspecting materials and finished goods. The concept of manufacturing cycle time is directly related to velocity, or throughput. Whereas manufacturing cycle time is the time required to produce a unit of product, **throughput** refers to the number of defect-free units that can be made in a given period. The shorter the manufacturing cycle time, the greater is the throughput. Because manufacturing cycle time and throughput focus on the production of defect-free units, they are directly influenced by quality (see Exhibit 11-9). As such, you can view throughput and

manufacturing cycle time as directly related to quality and productivity measures.

Exhibit 11-9 High Quality Leads to Low Cycle Time and High Throughput

© Cengage Learning 2013

Manufacturing Cycle Efficiency (MCE) **MCE** is the value-added time in the production process divided by the total manufacturing cycle time:

$$MCE = \frac{\text{Value-added time}}{\text{Manufacturing cycle time}}$$

Value-added time includes time spent in the actual manufacturing of a product (machining, assembly, painting, and so on). Non-value-added time includes the time a product is waiting to move to the next step in the production process and the time spent moving the product to the next step. Manufacturing cycle efficiency is a key measure of performance that is directly related to the customer service perspective as well as to the internal business perspective. By increasing MCE, customer response time is reduced, and non-value-added activities are reduced.

Learning-and-Growth Perspective

The learning-and-growth perspective links the critical success factors in the other perspectives and ensures an environment that supports and allows the objectives of the other three perspectives to be achieved. If learning

> **Productivity** A measure of the relationship between outputs and inputs.
>
> **Manufacturing cycle time** The total time a product is in production, including process time, inspection time, wait time, and move time; cycle time includes both value-added and non-value-added time.
>
> **Throughput** The amount of product produced in a given amount of time, such as a day, week, or month.
>
> **Manufacturing cycle efficiency (MCE)** The value-added time in the production process divided by the throughput, or cycle time.

improves, internal business processes will improve, leading to increased customer value and satisfaction and, ultimately, to better financial performance. Critical success factors center on three areas. The first is the efficient and, effective, use of employees (employee empowerment). Measures include improving employee morale, increasing skill development, increasing employee satisfaction, reducing employee turnover, and increasing the participation of employees in the decision process. The second critical success factor is increasing information systems capabilities through improving the availability and timeliness of information. The third critical success factor involves measures of product innovation, such as increasing the number of new products, new patents, and so on. Exhibit 11-10 provides a summary of critical success factors within each of these perspectives.

companies do business. As a result, one of the critical success factors under the customer perspective of the balanced scorecard is increasing the quality of products and services. Quality is no longer just a buzzword, but a way of life. Managers have come to realize that improving quality increases sales through higher customer satisfaction and demand, reduces costs, and increases the long-term profitability of companies.

However, before we go any further, just what is meant by quality? Although you may "know it when you see it," most businesses describe **quality** as "meeting or exceeding customers' expectations." Of course, this criterion requires that a product perform as it is intended but also requires that a product be reliable and durable and that these features be provided at a competitive price.

Companies have focused on improving the quality of the products or services they sell through a variety of initiatives, such as Six Sigma, The Baldrige National

Exhibit 11-10 Critical Success Factors Related to the Four Perspectives of the Balanced Scorecard

Critical Success Factors	Perspectives of the Balanced Scorecard			
	Financial	Customer	Internal Business	Learning and Growth
Sales, costs, measures of profit (operating income, segment margin, etc.), ROI, residual income	X			
Quality		X	X	
Delivery time (customer response time)		X		
Customer satisfaction		X		
Market share		X		
New markets		X		
Productivity			X	
Manufacturing cycle time and throughput			X	
Manufacturing cycle efficiency (MCE)		X	X	
Employee empowerment				X
Information systems capabilities				X
Product innovation		X		X

© Cengage Learning 2013

LO7 Measuring and Controlling Quality Costs

Over the past 25 years or so, the demand by customers for quality products and services at affordable prices has drastically changed the way

Quality Usually defined as meeting or exceeding customers' expectations.

Quality Program, and the International Organization for Standardization (ISO) family of quality improvement standards. Six Sigma is a quality improvement initiative focused on product quality and process improvement, with the goal of limiting defective products to 3.4 per million. The Baldrige National Quality Program focuses on quality excellence for the entire organization, and ISO quality standards concentrate on fixing quality system problems. Although the details of these methods may differ, all focus on meeting or exceeding customer expectations, continuous improvement, and

Six Sigma at Caterpillar

© Matthew Lloyd/Bloomberg via Getty Images

At Caterpillar, Six Sigma is used throughout the company. Rather than applying Six Sigma only to its engineering and manufacturing activities, Caterpillar also utilizes it in its financial and human resource processes. For example, the company used Six Sigma to determine whether its benefits package was competitive with ones at other companies. The company has also taught its suppliers and dealers the benefits of Six Sigma, demonstrating the value of total quality management throughout the value chain.

Source: "How Caterpillar Uses 6 Sigma to Execute Strategy," by John Gillett, Ross Fink, and Nick Bevington, *Strategic Finance*, April 2010.

employee empowerment. Continuous improvement, an idea pioneered by **Toyota** in Japan, refers to a system of improvements based on a series of gradual and often small improvements rather than major changes requiring very large investments. Called **kaizen** in Japan, continuous improvement requires active participation by all of a company's employees—from the CEO to the worker on the assembly line. Everyone is responsible for continuous improvement.[1] Employee empowerment involves companies providing appropriate opportunities for training, skill development, and advancement so that employees can become active participants and active decision makers in an organization. As discussed earlier, empowering employees is a key dimension of the learning-and-growth perspective of the balanced scorecard.

While **Toyota** strives for kaizen, or continuous improvement, in its manufacturing processes, it also strives for **hejunka**, or standardization. Although standardization creates efficiencies and helps companies reduce product costs, it can backfire when quality issues arise. For example, **Toyota** used a common gas pedal design produced by the same company for eight of its models. When problems caused by "sticky" gas pedals resulted in recalls of millions of cars, sales of all eight vehicles were halted.[2]

Improving the quality of products and services is an important component of both the customer perspective and the internal business perspective of the balanced scorecard. From a customer perspective, one of the most important measures of quality is customer satisfaction and the number of customer complaints. If the number of meals returned to the kitchen is increasing, management should probably infer that customers are unhappy with the quality of the food. The number of warranty claims can also serve as a measure of quality. An increase in warranty work performed on a certain model of automobile indicates a potential problem with the production process and the quality of the car produced. However, poor quality is not the only explanation for increasing customer complaints or warranty claims. In addition, these measures are not perfect, in that customers do not always complain or return products when quality problems are evident. For example, restaurant patrons may not complain about subpar meals and customers may simply discard defective merchandise instead of returning it. Therefore, management must be careful to provide a mechanism to make it easy for customers to complain, easy for them to return defective products, and so on.

[1]In addition to encouraging quality improvements, kaizen techniques are used to continually reduce the cost of products and services in target costing.

[2]"How Lean Manufacturing can Backfire," by Daisuke Wakabayashi, *The Wall Street Journal*, January 30, 2010.

Kaizen A system of improvement based on a series of gradual and often small improvements.

Hejunka A system of standardizing manufacturing processes to improve efficiency.

Kaizen at Seattle Children's Hospital

To improve patient care and reduce costs, a continuous performance improvement (CPI) program at Seattle Children's Hospital examined every aspect of a patient's stay at the hospital from the time the patient arrived until he or she was discharged. More efficient scheduling of MRIs reduced the waiting time for nonemergency procedures from 25 days to just 2 days. In the psychiatric inpatient facility, scheduling postdischarge outpatient care as soon as patients entered the hospital (thereby ensuring that such care would be available at discharge) allowed the unit to cut the average hospital stay from 20 days to 10 days and to accommodate 50 percent more patients. Overall, the hospital has increased its capacity from 27,000 patients a year to 38,000 without adding beds and has reduced its costs per patient by 3.7 percent.

Source: "Factory Finesse, at the Hospital," by Julie Weed, *New York Times*, July 11, 2010.

From the internal business perspective, quality measures center on improving output yields, reducing defects in raw materials and finished products, and reducing downtime owing to quality problems. Ideally, defects are detected before they leave the factory and the manufacturing process is adapted accordingly. The amount of scrap can also indicate potential quality problems in the production process. Although a certain amount of scrap is acceptable and even necessary in most manufacturing environments, an excessive amount should raise a red flag because it indicates possible problems causing an increase in the number of defective units in the process.

The Costs of Quality

Improving quality can be expensive, requiring significant investments in training and infrastructure. In evaluating managers on the basis of quality initiatives, it is useful to have a framework for comparing the benefits of providing a high-quality product or service with the costs that result from poor quality. To facilitate this comparison, quality costs are typically classified into four general categories: (1) prevention costs, (2) appraisal costs, (3) internal failure costs, and (4) external failure costs. Examples of specific types of prevention, appraisal, internal failure, and external failure costs are shown in Exhibit 11-11.

Exhibit 11-11 Quality Costs

Prevention Costs	Appraisal (Detection) Costs	Internal Failure Costs	External Failure Costs
Design and engineering costs	Inspecting raw materials	Material, labor, and other manufacturing costs incurred in rework	Repairs made under warranty
Quality training	Testing goods during the production process	Scrap	Replacement of defective parts
Supervision	Final product testing and inspection	Spoilage	Product recalls
Quality improvement projects		Downtime	Liability costs from defective products
Training and technical support provided to suppliers		Design changes	Lost sales
		Reinspections	
		Disposal of defective products	

© Cengage Learning 2013

Prevention costs are incurred to prevent product failure. These costs are typically incurred early in the value chain and include design and engineering costs as well as training and supervision costs and the costs of quality improvement projects. If parts are purchased from an outside supplier, prevention costs may include the cost of providing training and technical support to the supplier in order to increase the quality of materials purchased. Prevention costs are incurred to eliminate quality problems before they occur. Most companies find that incurring prevention costs up front is less expensive in the long run than being subject to product failure costs.

Appraisal (detection) costs are incurred in inspecting, identifying, and isolating defective products and services before they reach the customer. These costs include the costs of inspecting raw materials, testing goods throughout the manufacturing process, and final product testing and inspection. In practice, it is very difficult to ensure quality through inspection. It is time consuming and costly to inspect every unit of product. Therefore, sampling is usually used to identify problems with the production process. However, sampling is certainly not foolproof and is not likely to catch all quality problems. In general, it is more effective to design quality into a product through prevention activities rather than to inspect quality into a product through appraisal activities.

If a product or a service is defective in any way or does not meet customer expectations, failure costs are incurred. **Internal failure costs** are incurred once the product is produced and then determined to be defective (through the appraisal process) but before it is sold to customers. Internal failure costs include the material, labor, and other manufacturing costs incurred in reworking defective products, as well as the costs of scrap and spoilage. Internal failure costs also include the costs of downtime caused by quality problems, design changes, and reinspections and retesting. On the one hand, if no defects exist, internal failure costs will be zero. On the other hand, a high level of internal failure costs should be an indication to management that more attention needs to be paid to preventing quality problems in order to eliminate or reduce the number of defective products during the production process.

External failure costs are incurred after a defective product is delivered to a customer. External failure costs include the costs of repairs made under warranty, the replacement of defective parts, and product

> The traditional view of quality costs is that total quality costs are minimized at some *acceptable level* of defects, whereas the contemporary view is that total quality costs are minimized at a *zero* defect level.

recalls (as in the automobile industry), as well as liability costs arising from legal actions against the seller and, eventually, lost sales. Although the costs of potential lawsuits and lost sales may be difficult to measure, the cost of external failures is likely to exceed other quality costs. Failure costs, both internal and external, are like bandages: They only address symptoms rather than fixing the underlying problem. When unhappy customers decide not to purchase products from a company because of quality problems, the domino effect can be devastating—particularly when safety is a concern.

Minimizing Quality Costs

Experts suggest that the total costs of quality should not exceed 2 to 4 percent of sales. The problem faced by management is to reduce the costs of quality while maintaining a high-quality product or service. The goal, of course, is to minimize all the quality costs. However, it may be prudent to increase expenditures in one or more areas in order to decrease other costs.

Prevention costs Costs incurred to prevent product failures typically related to design and engineering.

Appraisal (detection) costs Costs incurred to inspect finished products or products that are in the process of production.

Internal failure costs Costs incurred once the product is produced and then determined to be defective.

External failure costs Costs incurred when a defective product is delivered to a customer.

For example, as you have seen, external failure costs are serious and potentially devastating to companies. Both external and internal failure costs can be reduced (theoretically to zero) by paying more attention to quality issues early in the value chain. Products can be designed to emphasize quality and durability, suppliers can be certified, employees can be trained, and the manufacturing process can be improved to increase quality throughout the value chain. Increasing expenditures related to prevention and appraisal can result in significant overall cost savings in the long run. As you can see in Exhibit 11-12, the traditional view of managing total quality costs suggests that increasing prevention and appraisal costs will reduce defective units (and failure costs) but that there are trade-offs in doing so. The traditional view suggests that total quality costs are minimized at a level of product quality below 100 percent.

Exhibit 11-12 implies that total quality costs are minimized at a point less than that associated with zero defects. However, additional prevention and appraisal activities are likely to reduce defects even further. Should companies continue to incur prevention and appraisal costs beyond this point?

A more contemporary view of quality costs recognizes that a number of failure costs are difficult to measure. For example, poor quality can lead to lost sales. This outcome tends to increase the costs of external failures as the percentage of defective units increases. In addition, rather than continually increasing as quality improves (as in Exhibit 11-12), prevention and appraisal costs may actually decrease as a company nears a level of zero defects. As you can see in Exhibit 11-13, this approach implies that total quality costs are minimized at a level of zero defects.

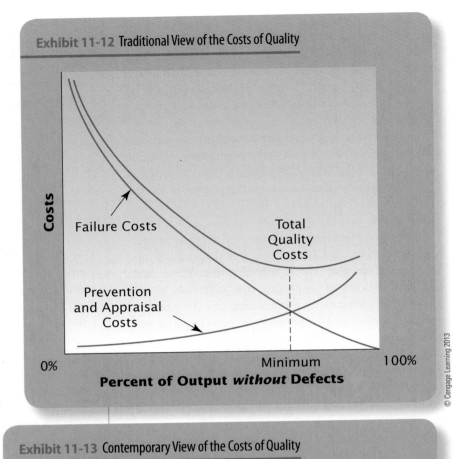

Exhibit 11-12 Traditional View of the Costs of Quality

Costs

Failure Costs

Total Quality Costs

Prevention and Appraisal Costs

0%　　　　　　　　　　　Minimum　　100%

Percent of Output *without* Defects

© Cengage Learning 2013

Exhibit 11-13 Contemporary View of the Costs of Quality

Costs

Total Quality Costs

Failure Costs

Prevention and Appraisal Costs

0%　Minimum　　　　　　　　　　100%

Percentage of Output *with* Defects

© Cengage Learning 2013

LO8 Performance and Management Compensation Decisions

In order to motivate managers and ensure goal congruence, the compensation of managers should be linked to performance and based on a combination of short-term and long-term goals.

Measuring the performance of a segment is not always the same as measuring the performance of the manager of that segment. For example, certain types of advertising might be specifically traced to a segment representing a geographic sales district (the Midwest or Southeast) or for a particular product. However, if advertising decisions and the advertising budget are controlled at the national level instead of by the segment manager, the cost of advertising should not be included in evaluating the performance of the segment manager. Likewise, although the segment manager's own salary or the property taxes paid by a segment are traceable to the segment, they are either controllable by others or not controllable at all. Measuring the performance of a manager should be based on variables that the manager controls. This approach, as mentioned earlier, is the goal of responsibility accounting.

In small companies that are owned and managed by the same person, motivating the owner–manager to do his or her best is usually not an issue. If the owner–manager works hard and the company is successful, the owner–manager directly reaps the benefits of the company's success and is rewarded through the receipt of salary or other forms of compensation from the company. Likewise, if the owner–manager does not manage the company well and the company fails, the owner–manager runs the risk of losing his or her entire investment in the company.

However, in most companies, owners hire managers to run the company for them. It is the owner's job to motivate managers in such a way that the managers make decisions and work to improve the performance of the company as a whole and hence maximize the owner's wealth, not just the individual manager's salary or other compensation. Accordingly, management compensation plans typically include incentives tied to company performance. The objective is to encourage goal congruence between the individual manager, on the one hand, and the company and its owners, on the other. Although tying executive compensation to corporate performance is a good idea from a managerial perspective, it also makes tax sense. Over a decade ago, Congress restricted the tax deduction of large publicly traded companies to $1 million of salary for the CEO and four other top executives—unless the compensation was related to company performance. However, if compensation was based on performance-related measures, an unlimited amount can be deducted.

The choice of the specific incentive structure is very important for both parties involved and can include cash compensation in the form of salary and bonuses, stock-based compensation in the form of stock options and restricted stock, and other noncash benefits and perquisites (often called perks).

Cash Compensation

Cash compensation can be paid in the form of salary or end-of-period bonuses. Many companies use a combination of the two in which a base salary is paid without regard to meeting individual or company performance criteria and bonuses are paid if managers meet or exceed established goals. For example, a manager may earn a base annual salary of $150,000 and a yearly bonus of $30,000 if the individual (or company) meets certain preestablished goals. Goals vary from company to company but might include individual measures such as meeting individual sales quotas, success in attracting and retaining key employees, attracting new customers, and so on. Bonuses may also be tied to companywide measures of performance such as ROI, residual income, increasing sales, or increasing net income by a certain dollar amount or percentage.

Tying bonuses to single measures of performance like income can be problematic. For example, a manager may increase income by putting off needed repairs and maintenance or may postpone the acquisition of new equipment (in order to keep depreciation low). As discussed in Chapter 5, if a company uses absorption costing to cost products, a manager may be able to increase income (at least in the short run) by increasing production.

CEO Compensation and Performance

Companies run by the best-paid CEOs generally deliver superior shareholder performance. A study of 127 CEOS at companies with annual revenues of $4 billion or more showed a strong correlation between corporate performance and total pay of their chief executive officer. However, three CEOs—those of Exelon Corp., Capital

One Financial Corp., and Lockheed Martin Co.—earned over $90 million in the last three years while their companies lost money. The study also uncovered a few bargains. CEOs of Owens-Illinois and AutoZone took home a modest $11.5 million and $9.5 million, respectively, while shareholders saw annual gains of close to 20 percent.

Source: "Measuring Bang for the Buck," by Scott Thurm, *The Wall Street Journal*, April 1, 2010.

Stock-Based Compensation

To encourage managers to take a longer term view, many companies provide compensation to top managers and executives in the form of stock-based compensation. The inclusion of stock in the management compensation package is designed to encourage goal congruence between the owners and management by making managers owners. One frequently used method of stock-based compensation is the granting of stock options to key employees.

A **stock option** is the right to buy a share of stock at a set price (called the option price or strike price) at some point in the future. For example, a company may give a manager an option to buy 1,000 shares of stock at a strike price of $15 per share. If the stock is currently selling for $10, the options are worthless. (A rational person would not pay $15 to exercise the option when the stock can be bought outright for $10.) However, if the stock price increases to $25 per share, the manager has the right to exercise the option and

purchase 1,000 shares for $15 per share. The value of the options increases as the stock price increases. This policy should encourage management to work hard to enhance the value of the stock over the long run. However, the use of stock options as compensation can result in short-term dysfunctional behavior if managers focus on increasing the share price in the short term rather than focus on the longer term success of the business. Stock options may have other disadvantages as well. From an individual manager's perspective, the stock price can vary with factors not subject to his or her control. Hence, a manager may not be rewarded even if his or her individual performance is very good.

A related method of stock-based compensation involves the use of **restricted stock**. With restricted stock compensation plans, a company makes outright transfers of company stock instead of stock options. However, the shares of stock come with restrictions. Frequently, in order to ultimately receive the stock, the manager has to stay with the company for a set length of time or meet established performance measures.

Noncash Benefits and Perks

Most management compensation plans include a variety of noncash benefits and perquisites. These may be club memberships, company cars, a corner office, and so on, depending on the desires of the particular manager. Such benefits and perks can be used to motivate managers to strive to attain the goals of the organization.

Stock option The right to buy a share of stock at a set price (called the option price or strike price) at some point in the future.

Restricted stock A form of management compensation in which employees receive shares of stock with restrictions such as requirements to stay with the company for a set length of time or requirements to meet established performance measures.

In the midst of the Great Recession of 2008–2009, a significant number of companies cut pay. In order to motivate and retain employees, companies resorted to other tools, including providing or enhancing career development opportunities, giving out noncash rewards, and offering recognition and flexibility options.[3]

Measuring and Rewarding Performance in a Multinational Environment

Like all organizations, companies that do business in more than one country must develop and use performance measures that provide incentives for managers to work toward the goals of the overall organization. However, what works as an incentive in one country may not work in another. Cultural differences may affect the desires and needs of managers in different countries. Attitudes toward work and leisure time vary in different countries. For example, German and French workers typically enjoy shorter workweeks than their American counterparts, in addition to having more vacation time and more holidays. The average worker in France gets 30 days of paid vacation. In Germany, the average worker gets 24 days off. In contrast, workers in Japan average 18 days and workers in the United States average only 10 vacation days per year. Some attribute the U.S. dominance in global markets to the American work ethic, which encourages and rewards hard work and risk taking.

As another example, in Japan employees are often evaluated as part of teams. Because many management control systems in the United States are designed around individual responsibility centers, developing and implementing measures evaluating team performance may be difficult for U.S. companies with operations in Japan.

As a final example, managers' sense of commitment and loyalty to their employers may vary from country to country. In Japan, companies have typically viewed their workers as permanent employees with opportunities for lifetime employment. This commitment on the part of the employer may result in a greater sense of loyalty by employees, who clearly have a vested interest in the long-run success of the company.

[3] "Firms Gingerly Rescind Salary Cuts," by Paul Glader, *The Wall Street Journal*, March 1, 2010.

STUDY TOOLS 11

Chapter review card

- ➲ Learning Objective and Key Concept Reviews
- ➲ Key Definitions and Formulas

Online (Located at www.cengagebrain.com)

- ➲ Flash Cards and Crossword Puzzles
- ➲ Games and Quizzes
- ➲ Herman Miller Video and E-Lectures
- ➲ Homework Assignments (as directed by your instructor)

BRIEF EXERCISES

1. Decentralized Organizations LO1

Decentralized organizations are characterized by decision-making authority being dispersed among many individuals as opposed to only a few individuals. The following statements relate to various aspects of decentralized organizations.

a. In a decentralized organization, managers are given responsibility for their specific areas, as well as for those of many other managers.

b. The tendency among modern organizations is to move toward more centralization.

c. Managers who are allowed to make decisions in a decentralized environment generally have higher job satisfaction than managers in a centralized environment.

d. A significant advantage of decentralization is the focus it introduces to a company's overall purpose and efforts.

e. Information systems play a critical role in decentralized organizations because of the need for data and information.

Required

Indicate whether each of the preceding statements is true or false.

2. Performance Measures and Centers LO2, 3

Organizations use a variety of performance measures to evaluate managers. Central to the idea of responsibility accounting is that performance measures are reflective of activities under a manager's influence and control. Organizations often identify different levels of responsibility and refer to these levels as segments. The following performance measures and reports are used to evaluate managers of various segments:

a. Return on investment
b. Cost budgets
c. Labor usage variance
d. Sales budget
e. Segment margin
f. Sales volume variance
g. Residual income
h. Overall flexible budget variance
i. Sales price variance

Required

For each performance measure and report listed, indicate which segment (cost center, revenue center, profit center, investment center) they would most likely be used to evaluate.

3. Profit Centers and Segmented Income Statements LO4

Profit center managers have more responsibility than cost center managers because profit center managers are expected not only to control costs, but also to generate revenues. The following partial statements describe several key terms and concepts related to profit centers.

a. _____ is a measure of long-term profitability that is appropriate in making long-term decisions, such as whether to add or drop a product or line of products.

b. _____ are costs that are incurred to benefit more than one segment and cannot be directly traced to a specific segment.

c. The income for each major segment of an organization is calculated on the _____.

d. _____ are those costs attributable to a particular segment and are actually caused by a specific segment.

Required

Complete the preceding incomplete statements with the correct term from the list of terms provided (note that not all terms will be used): *segment margin, segmented balance sheet, contribution margin, margin, united costs, segmented income statement, common costs, segment costs.*

4. ROI with Margin and Turnover and Residual Income LO5

Advanced Electronics has two separate, but related, divisions: digital video and analog video. The digital video division has sales of $800,000, net operating income of $80,000, and average operating assets of $1 million.

Required

A. What is the digital division's margin and turnover?
B. What is the ROI for the digital division?

5. Balanced Scorecard LO6

Review and complete the following incomplete statements about the use of the balanced scorecard.

a. The _____ perspective is captured in the ideal of being profit driven. Critical success factors under this perspective include sales and segment margin.

b. The number of defect-free units that can be made in a given period is referred to as _____.

c. A commonly used measure of the relationship between outputs and inputs is _____.

d. _____ is the perspective that links the critical success factors from the other perspectives in the balanced scorecard.

e. Manufacturing cycle efficiency is calculated by dividing _____ by the manufacturing cycle time.

Required

Complete the preceding incomplete statements with the correct term from the list of terms provided (note that not all terms will be used): *internal business, financial, value-added time, customer, learning and growth, defect-free production, throughput, productivity, production efficiency, non-value-added time.*

6. Quality Costs LO7

Following are partially completed statements that relate to quality and the costs of quality. Read each of the statements carefully.

a. _____ include(s) the cost of repairs made under warranty or the replacement of defective parts.

b. Costs incurred in reworking defective products and the costs of scrap and spoilage are referred to as _____.

c. Costs of inspecting, identifying, and isolating defective products before they reach the customer are called _____.

d. _____ is/are incurred to prevent product failures from occurring.

e. The _____ developed ISO 9000 as a set of guidelines for quality management.

f. Kaizen, also called _____, refers to a system of improvement based on a series of gradual and often small improvements.

Required

Complete each of the preceding partially completed statements by using one of the following terms: *appraisal costs, prevention costs, external failure costs, International Standards Organization, continuous improvement, internal failure costs.*

EXERCISES

7. Segmented Income Statement LO4

BTO, Inc., produces and sells two products: the X 100 and X 200. Revenue and cost information for the two products are as follows:

	X 100	X 200
Selling price per unit	$ 10.00	$ 27.00
Variable expenses per unit	4.30	19.00
Traceable fixed expenses per year	$142,000	$54,000

BTO's common fixed expenses total $125,000 per year. Last year, the company produced and sold 42,500 units of X 100 and 19,000 units of X 200.

Required

Prepare a segmented income statement, using the contribution format, for BTO.

8. Segment and Contribution Margin LO4

Paradise Burger Company makes two burgers, each in a separate division: cheeseburgers and chiliburgers. Segmented income statements for the most recent year are as follows:

	Cheeseburgers	Chiliburgers
Sales	$250,000	$600,000
Variable expenses	185,000	360,000
Contribution margin	$ 65,000	$240,000
Traceable fixed expenses	45,000	100,000
Segment margin	$ 20,000	$140,000

Paradise Burger's management is considering a special advertising campaign during broadcast coverage of a major sporting event. Management has determined that the $28,000 expense of the advertising campaign allows only one division to be featured. In-house marketing studies suggest that the campaign could increase sales of the cheeseburgers division by $100,000 or increase sales of the chiliburgers division by $75,000.

Required

Which product should be featured in the campaign? Why? Show computations to support your recommendation.

9. Segmented Income Statements LO4

Henrietta, Ltd., produces fine clothing for women. There are two primary divisions within the company: professional wear and formal wear. The following income statements were prepared for the divisions:

	Professional	Formal
Sales	$1,200,000	$1,750,000
Variable expenses	955,000	1,360,000
Contribution margin	$ 245,000	$ 390,000
Fixed expenses	115,000	175,000
Income	$ 130,000	$ 215,000

The income statements were prepared by an inexperienced staff accountant. Common fixed expenses of $50,000 were allocated to the two divisions as follows: 30 percent to professional wear and 70 percent to formal wear.

Required

Prepare new segmented income statements for Henrietta, Ltd., after removing the common fixed expenses.

10. ROI and Residual Income LO5

You are trying to determine which of two retail clothing stores would be a more beneficial investment to you. You have a minimum required rate of return of 7 percent and have collected the following information about the two stores:

	Company A	Company B
Sales	$800,000	$900,000
Net operating income	50,000	70,000
Average operating assets	500,000	800,000

Required

Calculate the ROI and residual income for each store. Explain the meaning of your calculations.

11. ROI and Margin LO5

Dinning Corporation has two divisions. In the most recent year, the Sintering Division reported sales of $150,000 and an asset turnover ratio of 3.0. The division's controller reported to headquarters that the rate of return on average invested assets was 18.0 percent.

Required

Calculate the percentage of net income to sales (i.e., the margin).

12. ROI and Asset Turnover LO5

Brew-Me-A-Cup is a new and growing chain of coffee shops. The company operates its business by using segments to control and manage operations. The most profitable division is the specialty drinks division. In the Hillsborough Avenue location, the division has sales of $600,000, net operating income of $15,000, and average operating assets of $1,200,000.

Required

What is the asset turnover for the specialty drinks division?

13. ROI with Margin and Turnover and Residual Income LO5

Comfortable Carpets manufactures and installs various types of carpets for its customers. Comfortable Carpets had sales of $1,200,000 for the year. The company also has net operating income of $300,000, and average operating assets of $1,500,000.

Required

A. What is Comfortable Carpets' margin and turnover for the year?
B. What is the ROI for the company?

14. ROI with Margin and Turnover and Residual Income LO5

Olive Patch Italian restaurant is divided into segments based on location. Its Capital Boulevard location in the eastern segment has sales of $600,000, net operating income of $60,000, and average operating assets of $800,000.

Required

A. What is Olive Patch's margin and turnover?
B. What is the ROI for Olive Patch?

15. ROI with Margin and Turnover and Residual Income LO5

There are two different hotel chains that you have identified as potential investment opportunities. You are looking for a minimum required rate of return of 8 percent. As a starting point, you have accumulated some basic information to calculate the return on investment and residual income:

	Hotel Aster	Hotel Bella
Sales	$10,000,000	$6,000,000
Net operating income	200,000	300,000
Average operating assets	2,000,000	3,000,000

Required

Calculate the ROI and residual income for each hotel. Explain the meaning of your calculations.

16. Residual Income LO5

Allied Electronics has a particular division that generates $3,000,000 in sales and operating income of $250,000 on average operating assets of $1,250,000. The company's management team has made it clear that division managers are expected to generate sufficient income to guarantee a minimum return of 10 percent.

Required

What is the division's residual income?

17. Net Operating Income and Residual Income LO5

Williamson Group operates a chain of bookstores. A recent business expansion plan resulted in the opening of more than 25 new stores. The Upland store has one feature that the Stowe store does not have: a small coffee shop. Early indications are that the coffee shop has driven up the location's revenues and profits. Operating data for two of these stores are as follows:

	Upland	Stowe
ROI	18.75%	14.0%
Net operating income	?	?
Minimum required return	15%	15%
Average operating assets	$200,000	$150,000
Residual income	?	?

Required

A. Calculate net operating income and residual income for each division.
B. Compare the two divisions, and discuss the usefulness of ROI and residual income for the purpose of comparing the divisions.

18. Dimensions of the Balanced Scorecard LO6

The balanced scorecard integrates financial and nonfinancial measures that relate to four perspectives: financial, customer, internal business, and learning and growth. This view of a company places emphasis on both financial and nonfinancial measures, because each contributes to the understanding of a company's performance.

Required

List two possible performance measures for each of the four perspectives included in the balanced scorecard.

19. Assessing Quality and Internal Business Perspective LO6

Improving the quality of products and services is an important component from both the customer perspective and the internal business perspective of the balanced scorecard.

Required

Discuss how quality can be assessed (i.e., measured) for the customer perspective and the internal business perspective. Use short and concise statements.

20. Quality Costs LO7

Tiffany Lamp Company produces stained-glass lamps that are appropriate for home and office use. The company expects sales to total approximately $50 million for the current year. Tiffany's management team has become increasingly concerned about a perception among some customers that quality is not particularly important to the company. Consequently, management recently implemented a quality improvement program and, after several months, accumulated the following data:

Warranty claims	$ 60,000
Rework costs	200,000
Quality training	305,000
Inspection of incoming materials	900,000
Statistical process control	400,000
Scrap costs	100,000
Product quality audits	250,000

Required
A. What are the total prevention costs?
B. What are the total appraisal costs?
C. What are the total internal failure costs?
D. What are the total external failure costs?
E. On the basis of your calculations, is there a reason for the perception that quality is not important to Tiffany Lamp Company? What is that reason?

21. Quality Costs LO7

No company can simply wish quality into being; rather, quality comes at a cost. Quality costs are often classified into four general categories: prevention costs, appraisal costs, internal failure costs, and external failure costs.

Required
Briefly describe each of the four general categories of quality costs, and provide several examples of costs that may be included in each category.

22. Quality Costs LO7

Timmer Meats is a large meat processor in the southeastern United States. The company's most recent year's sales totaled $50 million. Over the last several years, the company has had an unfortunate number of quality problems, which threaten its existence. Webb Timmer, the firm's president, asked the company's controller and quality control manager to accumulate data related to product quality. Those two individuals prepared the following data for Webb:

Warranty claims	$120,000
Food-poisoning liability lawsuits	200,000
Quality training	305,000
Inspection of incoming meat	900,000
Statistical process control	650,000
Spoilage and waste	900,000
Product quality audits	475,000

Required
A. Compute total prevention costs.
B. Compute total appraisal costs.
C. Compute total internal failure costs.
D. Compute total external failure costs.
E. Webb is considering spending more on inspections. What is the likely impact on other failure costs? What do you recommend?

23. Quality Costs LO7

Plum Republic is an upscale retail clothing store that sells clothes for professional working women. The store expects sales of $10 million for the year. Recently, Plum's customers have lodged complaints about the quality of the clothes and service received while shopping at the store. Consequently, management recently implemented a quality improvement program and accumulated the following data after several months:

Costs of returning poor quality clothes to manufacturers	$ 90,000
Employee training for buyers and salespeople	15,000
Inspections of new merchandise	30,000
Lost sales	100,000

Required
A. What are the total prevention costs?
B. What are the total appraisal costs?
C. What are the total internal failure costs?
D. What are the total external failure costs?

24. Quality Costs LO7

Crabby's Seafood Restaurant is a family-owned restaurant that has been around for many years and takes pride in its fresh fish and quality ingredients. However, over the past year, Crabby's has had increasing numbers of complaints from customers about the quality of the service received and the quality of the food served, and the company was even sued for food poisoning. Bill Crabby, the restaurant's owner, accumulated the following data related to the restaurant's product quality and service quality over the last year:

Costs of compensating customers for unsatisfactory meals	$ 7,000
Employee training for cooks and wait staff	15,000
Food-poisoning liability lawsuits	20,000
Cost of remaking entrees	10,000
Inspection of incoming ingredients	5,000
Spoilage and waste from discarding poor quality food	2,500
Lost sales	15,000

Required
A. Compute total prevention costs.
B. Compute total appraisal costs.
C. Compute total internal failure costs.
D. Compute total external failure costs.

25. Stock Options and Restricted Stock LO8

You recently spoke to a former classmate of yours who has worked for a start-up company since graduating from business school more than 10 years ago. She told you that she expects to receive some type of stock-based compensation in the near future. She has heard that she might receive stock options or a grant of restricted stock, but she is unsure of the difference.

Required

Explain to your friend the differences between stock options and grants of restricted stock.

PROBLEMS

26. Segment Margin and Contribution Margin LO4

Simon Hinson Company operates two divisions: Gordon and Ronin. A segmented income statement for the company's most recent year is as follows:

	Total Company	Gordon Division	Ronin Division
Sales	$850,000	$250,000	$600,000
Less: Variable expenses	505,000	145,000	360,000
Contribution margin	$345,000	$105,000	$240,000
Less: Traceable fixed costs	145,000	45,000	100,000
Division segment margin	$200,000	$ 60,000	$140,000
Less: Common fixed costs	130,000		
Net income	$ 70,000		

Required

A. If the Gordon Division increased its sales by $85,000 per year, how much would the company's net income change? Assume that all cost behavior patterns remained constant.
B. Assume that the Ronin Division increased sales by $100,000, the Gordon Division sales remained the same, and there was no change in fixed costs.
   1. Calculate the division segment margin for each division and the net income for the company as a whole.
   2. Calculate the segment margin ratios before and after these changes, and comment on the results. Explain the changes.
C. How do the sales increases and decreases affect the divisional contribution margin ratio and segment margin ratio?

27. ROI vs. Residual Income Using Different Asset Measures LO5

Top management is trying to determine a consistent, but fair, valuation system to use to evaluate each of its four divisions. This year's performance data are summarized as follows:

	Division			
	1	2	3	4
Operating income	$1,000	$1,200	$ 1,600	$1,600
Operating assets	4,000	6,000	15,000	8,000
Current liabilities	400	2,000	2,400	200

Required

A. Which division would earn a bonus if top management used ROI based on operating assets?
B. Which division would earn a bonus if top management used ROI based on operating assets minus current liabilities?
C. Which division would earn a bonus if top management calculated residual income on the basis of operating assets with a minimum return of 12 percent?
D. Which division would earn a bonus if top management calculated residual income on the basis of operating assets minus current liabilities with a minimum return of 12 percent?

28. ROI: Decision Focus LO5

You are the manager of a franchised operating division of the Sawyers Copy Company. Your company evaluates your division with the use of ROI, computed with end-of-year gross asset balances, and calculates manager bonuses on the basis of the percentage increase in ROI over the previous year. Your division has $9 million in assets. Your budgeted income statement for the fiscal year is as follows:

Sales	$16,500,000
Variable expenses	3,000,000
Contribution margin	$13,500,000
Fixed expenses	7,750,000
Depreciation expense	2,375,000
Division profit	$ 3,375,000

During the year, you consider buying a new copy machine for $4 million, enabling you to expand the output of your division and reduce operating costs. The copy machine would have no salvage value and would be depreciated over five years by straight-line depreciation. It will increase output by 10 percent while reducing fixed costs by $4 million. If you decide to purchase the copy machine, it will be installed in late December but will not be ready for use until the next year. As a result, no depreciation will be taken on it this year.

If you do buy the copy machine, you will have to dispose of the copy machine you are now using, which you just purchased during the current year. The old copy machine cost you $4 million but has no salvage value. Of the depreciation in the income statement, $1 million is for this machine. In the ROI calculations, the company includes any gains or losses from copy equipment disposal as part of the company's operating income.

Required

A. What is your division's ROI this year if you do not acquire the new machine?

B. What is your division's ROI this year if you do acquire the new copy machine?

C. What is your division's expected ROI for next year if the copy machine is acquired and meets expectations? Assume that unit costs and prices do not change.

D. As the manager, what action will you take and why?

29. ROI vs. Residual Income: Decision Focus LO5

Raddington Industries produces tool-and-die machinery for various manufacturers. Two years ago, the company expanded vertically by acquiring Regis Steel Company, one of its suppliers of alloy steel plates. In order to manage the two separate businesses, the operations of Regis Steel are reported separately as an investment center.

Raddington monitors its divisions on the basis of both unit contribution and return on average investment (ROI), with the investment defined as average operating assets used. Raddington has a policy of basing all employee bonuses on divisional ROI. All investments in operating assets are expected to earn a minimum return of 11 percent before income taxes.

Regis's cost of goods sold is considered to be entirely variable, whereas the division's administrative expenses are not dependent on volume. Selling expenses are a mixed cost, with 40 percent attributed to sales volume. Over the last two years, Regis's ROI has ranged from 11.8 percent to 14.7 percent. During the fiscal year ended November 30, 2012, Regis contemplated a capital acquisition with an estimated ROI of 11.5 percent; however, division management decided against the investment because it believed that the investment would decrease Regis's overall ROI.

The 2012 income statement for Regis is presented next. The division's operating assets were $15,750,000 on November 30, 2012, a 5 percent increase over the 2011 year-end balance.

Regis Steel Division Operating Statement For the Year Ended November 30, 2012 ($000 omitted)	
Sales revenue	$25,000
Cost of goods sold	16,500
Gross profit	$ 8,500
Administrative expenses	3,955
Selling expenses	2,700
Income from operations before income taxes	$ 1,845

Required

A. Calculate the unit contribution for Regis Steel Division if 1,484,000 units were produced and sold during the year ended November 30, 2012.

B. Calculate the return on investment (ROI) for Regis Steel Division for 2012.

C. Calculate the residual income, using the average operating assets employed, for 2012 for Regis Steel Division.

D. Explain why the management of Regis Steel Division would have been more likely to accept the contemplated acquisition if residual income rather than ROI were used as a performance measure.

E. Regis Steel Division is a separate investment center within Raddington Industries. Identify several items that Regis Steel should control if it is to be evaluated fairly by either the ROI or the residual income performance measure.

30. Quality Costing LO7

Rebecca's Pottery Loft makes a variety of handmade pottery items. She has asked for your advice on one of the items manufactured: a clay pelican. The following information is provided:

Number of defective pelicans	1,100
Number of pelicans returned	150
Number of pelicans reworked	200
Profit per defect-free pelican	$10.00
Processing cost of a returned pelican	$20.00
Profit per defective pelican	$ 5.00
Cost to rework defective pelican	$ 4.00
Total appraisal costs	$3,400
Total prevention costs	$6,000

Required

A. Calculate the total profits lost because Rebecca sold defective pelicans.

B. Calculate the rework cost.

C. Calculate the cost of processing customer returns.

D. Calculate the total failure cost.

E. Calculate the total quality cost.

31. Quality Costs Report LO7

Wailai Macadamia Confectioners is a maker of fine candies and chocolates. The company's founder believes that production has become less well controlled in recent months, resulting in a decrease in overall quality and a growing tide of customer dissatisfaction. Nimi Naoro, quality control manager, is also concerned, but she believes that the company is being sufficiently proactive to combat most quality concerns. She asks the controller to accumulate any data that might relate to the company's current quality control efforts. The following data are provided to Nimi:

Product refunds due to quality guarantee claims	$ 60,000
Product liability claim (one lawsuit that was settled)	100,000
Rework costs	300,000
Quality training	152,500
Inspection of incoming ingredients	450,000
Statistical process control	325,000
Spoilage of chocolates, candies, and ingredients	150,000
Product quality audits	237,500
Total annual sales	25,000,000

Required

Prepare a report that shows total prevention, appraisal, internal failure, and external failure costs. On the basis of the report, what recommendations would you make to the company? Be sure to consider the relation between quality costs and annual sales.

32. Quality Costs, Excel LO7

Tanner Leathers implemented a quality control and improvement program in 2012. The quality control manager, a daughter of the company's president, developed the following table, which shows the components of quality cost as a percentage of the company's sales for the last five years:

Year	Prevention	Detection	Internal Failure	External Failure
2012	3%	4%	9%	13%
2013	4	5	8	11
2014	5	6	6	8
2015	6	5	4	6
2016	7	2	1	2

Required

A. Prepare a graph that shows the trend for each quality cost category. To complete the graph in Excel, use the chart wizard and select "XY (scatter) graph with data points connected by lines" as the chart type. You should have one graph with four separate lines. Show the percentage of sales on the vertical axis and the year on the horizontal axis.
B. What does the graph tell you about the success of Tanner Leathers's quality program?

33. Forms of Management Compensation LO8

Watson Water Heaters (WWH) opened for business 30 years ago with fewer than 10 employees and with sales of just $500,000 in the first year of business. Today, the company has more than 1,000 employees and annual revenues of $450 million. The company's growth has caused management to begin considering how best to compensate employees. Historically, WWH has used a strictly cash-based compensation system. The company's chief executive officer, Will Harrell, and chief financial officer, Claire Greer, now believe that such a system is no longer feasible, primarily because they worry that it does not adequately motivate employees to think of the company's long-term interests. Will and Claire recently met with a compensation consultant to discuss new ways of compensating employees that may better link compensation and performance.

Required

A. Excluding cash compensation, what are the possible types of compensation that WWH may use?
B. What are the advantages and disadvantages of each type of compensation identified by you in question A?

C. Do you have a recommendation as to the types of compensation that would be most appropriate for WWH? What is the basis for your recommendation?

CASES

34. Comprehensive Responsibility Accounting, Segment Margin, and Management Compensation LO2, 4, 8

Gantry Manufacturing is a medium-sized organization with manufacturing facilities in seven locations around the southwestern United States. Of these facilities, Galveston and Amarillo are treated as profit centers, with local management exercising authority over manufacturing costs, certain nonmanufacturing costs (e.g., advertising at local minor league baseball stadiums, sponsoring local charity events), and sales revenue. The segment income statements that follow were prepared by facility-level accountants and were provided to the corporate office in Denver, Colorado, shortly after the end of this year's second quarter. Note that the statements are shown in parallel for convenience and are not intended to be combined for analysis purposes.

Segmented Income Statements Galveston and Amarillo Facilities For the Quarter Ending June 30, 2012		
	Galveston	**Amarillo**
Sales	$22,500,000	$18,450,000
Variable expenses	19,850,000	17,640,000
Contribution margin	$ 2,650,000	$ 810,000
Divisional fixed expenses	1,400,000	1,030,000
Segment margin	$ 1,250,000	$ (220,000)

The managers of these two facilities are former classmates at the University of Texas at Austin and routinely stay in touch with each other. Shortly after receiving the quarterly results from his accountant, the Amarillo manager, Jim Lowell, called his friend in Galveston to talk about the surprising loss shown on his facility's income statement. After a short conversation with the Galveston manager, Jim met with his accountant. He learned the following:

- A recent memo sent from the corporate controller to all facility controllers indicated that new manufacturing overhead rates should be used beginning May 1, 2012. The old rate was $2.80 per direct labor hour and the new rate is $3.25 per direct labor hour. The memo had a new policy statement attached to it asserting that individual manufacturing facilities could no longer establish individual overhead rates.
- An average of 210 employees worked 40 hours per week during the quarter. There were 13 weeks in the second quarter.

- Each division was required to record a onetime expense associated with ethics training for all new and current employees. The Amarillo facility received an expense allocation of $58,000. Sixty-five percent of the allocation is related to manufacturing employees, and the remainder is related to administrative employees.
- The corporate office also implemented a new policy related to certain divisional employees' retirement, insurance, and other benefits. In past years, all benefits were paid by the corporate office and were not allocated to local facilities. However, the company's new president believes that those costs are more properly reflected in the expenses of the individual facilities because they are incurred by local employees. In total, additional retirement and insurance expenses of $46,500 were incurred for each month during the quarter ended June 30, 2012. Thirty percent of the monthly expenses are related to manufacturing employees, and the remainder is related to administrative employees.

Jim was immediately frustrated by all that he learned from the accountant. Because his and other managers' bonuses depend on quarterly financial performance, he feels that the corporate memos unfairly reduce his division's profits. He asked his controller to prepare a revised income statement without the changes implemented by the corporate office during the quarter. Amarillo's revised income statement appeared as follows:

Segmented Income Statement Amarillo Facility For the Quarter Ending June 30, 2012 (Revised)	
Sales	$18,450,000
Variable expenses	17,511,310
Contribution margin	$ 938,690
Divisional fixed expenses	912,050
Segment margin	$ 26,640

Jim is not particularly pleased with the financial performance of his facility, preferring to report a small profit as opposed to a more significant loss. He now must decide how to communicate with the corporate office about this revised income statement. You should bear in mind that the corporate office only provides administrative services and does not manufacture goods; however, sales activities for five of the company's facilities are handled in the corporate office.

Required
A. Assist Jim by identifying reasons that support his desire that the Amarillo facility not be required to implement the changes made by the corporate office.
B. What are the implications of having the corporate office issue memos requiring the facilities to record certain expenses, given the company's bonus structure? How will the corporate office's new policy affect the facility management's motivation?

C. What are some of the possible bases that Gantry Manufacturing could use to allocate fixed expenses?

35. Comprehensive ROI: Decision Focus   LO5, 8

Elaine Shumate has been working for GSM, a pharmaceutical research company, for more than seven years. It is her first job since finishing her graduate work in molecular biology, and her performance evaluations have been exemplary. She has received increasing responsibility as opportunities have become available at GSM. Unfortunately, her knowledge and experience have not prepared her for the situation she currently faces. GSM has invested heavily in a molecular identification process (MIP) that the company's top management believes holds tremendous promise for the future. If all goes well, the company plans to patent the process and license it to large pharmaceutical companies for use in medication production. Elaine is the lead manager on MIP, and she is worried that the latest research results do not look as promising as earlier results. The vice president of research, Blake Walton, has asked Elaine to meet with him to discuss the results. After a brief discussion in the hallway, Blake suggests that Elaine take another look at the latest results. He doesn't believe that her interpretation of the data is correct.

In preparing for their meeting, she looks over the company's earlier cost estimates and operating income projections for the project. Records indicate that the estimated research-and-development costs are $140 million, and annual operating income is expected to be approximately $25 million. Given the latest results, MIP may have fewer applications in the pharmaceutical industry than originally believed.

Elaine speaks with Richard Lawrence, vice president of sales, to get an updated estimate of the potential market value for MIP. Richard suggests that MIP would likely generate operating income of just $17.5 million per year if the recent results hold up after further testing. Elaine knows that Blake is not going to be happy with this news. Blake is scheduled to meet with the company's board of directors next week to discuss the need for additional investment capital from venture capitalists in the next year and the company's plans for a public stock offering in the next several years. Elaine stands to benefit substantially from stock options if the company goes public. GSM's future may ride on the outcome of that meeting.

Required
A. What is the ROI for MIP, given the original estimates? What is the ROI if Richard Lawrence's new revenue projections are used?
B. Elaine feels pressure to deliver "good news" to Blake. What advice would you give to her? Given the possible personal financial rewards that Elaine may enjoy if GSM goes public, would your advice change?
C. What responsibilities does Elaine have to other GSM employees, the board of directors, and the venture capitalists?

Financial Statement
Analysis

Introduction

Decision makers need a variety of information in the decision-making process. Bankers and other lenders are interested in the ability of an organization to repay loans. Stockholders or potential stockholders are interested in earning a fair return on their investment. The management team of a company is concerned about these issues and more: the adequacy of cash flow to pay operating expenses, the efficient use of company resources, and ways to improve the overall performance of the company. Financial statement analysis is a useful tool for both external and internal users as they make decisions about a company or for a company.

LO1 Why Analyze Financial Statements?

The most compelling reason to analyze financial statements is simply that it provides useful information to supplement information directly furnished in financial statements. Ratio analysis offers additional information that enhances the decision-making ability of the users of the information. Although we will spend some time on the computation of various ratios, the most important aspect of the discussion is what the ratios mean and how to improve the performance of the organization by analyzing trends and changes in these ratios. In addition to showing how the company has performed in the past, financial ratios are very useful in predicting the future direction and financial position of organizations.

Limitations of Financial Statement Analysis

Financial statements are prepared with the use of generally accepted accounting principles (GAAP). However, GAAP allows financial statement preparers to use a variety of methods, estimates, and assumptions in their preparation. To properly prepare and interpret financial statement ratios, these methods, estimates, and assumptions must be considered. For example,

Learning Objectives

After studying the material in this chapter, you should be able to:

LO1 Explain why decision makers analyze financial statements and recognize the limitations of financial statement analysis.

LO2 Use comparative financial statements to analyze the performance of a company over time (horizontal analysis).

LO3 Prepare and use common-size financial statements to compare various financial statement items (vertical analysis).

LO4 Prepare and use liquidity ratios to analyze a company.

LO5 Prepare and use solvency ratios to analyze a company.

LO6 Prepare and use profitability ratios to analyze a company.

Inventory turnover is an important financial ratio for companies with large inventory balances.

inventory valuation methods include FIFO (first in, first out), LIFO (last in, first out), and other accepted cost flow assumptions. These methods affect the cost of inventory shown on the balance sheet. For example, a company using the LIFO method of inventory costing in a period of rising prices is always selling the most costly inventory purchased (the last inventory purchased is the first to be sold), whereas the inventory shown on the balance sheet is the oldest and least costly. As a result, inventory balances on the balance sheet may be very low and "undercosted" on the basis of today's prices. In

Ratio analysis provides additional information that enhances the decision-making ability of the users of the information.

© Katarzyna Gmitruk/Shutterstock.com

Rather than focus on a single ratio, decision makers need to evaluate a company by comparing ratios with those of previous years, with budgeted amounts, and with industry standards.

comparing companies, differences in accounting methods and cost flow assumptions need to be considered. If accounting methods or assumptions are changed from year to year, comparisons between years can be difficult.

Decision makers using financial statements and the resulting ratios should not place too much emphasis on any single ratio. Ratios must be looked at as a story that cannot be told without all the pieces. Ratios should be compared with previous years' results, with the budget for the current year, and with industry standards. Industry standards can be found in publications by Moody's and Standard & Poor's. These services provide up-to-date information on most industries and regions. Regional differences are very important factors in evaluating performance. In addition, owing to the size and complexity of many companies, industry standards are sometimes useful in evaluating single divisions of a business. For example, hotels that are affiliated with a casino are operated differently from hotels that are only in the hotel business. Rates for rooms are different, as are expectations, and the analysis of the financial ratios must be interpreted in light of these differences.

The Impact of Inflation on Financial Statement Analysis

Financial statements are prepared by using historical costs and are not adjusted for the effects of increasing prices. For example, although sales may have increased by 5 percent each year for the past five years, the impact of inflation on changing prices needs to be considered. If inflation averaged 3 percent annually over that same period, the real increase in sales dollars was only 2 percent. The impact of changing prices on long-term assets can be even more dramatic. Consider a building purchased 30 years ago for $100,000. If inflation averages 2.5 percent per year over the life of the building,

the market value of the building today will be more than double the historical cost used to record the building when purchased. To compound the problem, the building is likely to be almost fully depreciated, so the book value of the building may be very small.

LO2 Horizontal Analysis

Analyzing financial statements over time is called **horizontal analysis**. To demonstrate the concept of horizontal analysis, the financial statements for Robyn's Boutique are presented in Exhibit 12-1 and Exhibit 12-2.

Robyn's Boutique is a retail store specializing in children's clothes. The idea behind horizontal analysis is to analyze changes in accounts occurring between years. To facilitate this analysis, dollar changes and percentage changes in each item on the balance sheet are often provided. The percentage changes are over the previous year. In Exhibit 12-1, cash increased by $20,000, which is 18.2 percent of the 2011 balance ($20,000 ÷ $110,000).

Looking closely at the balance sheet for Robyn's Boutique, we see two accounts with large percentage changes between 2011 and 2012. Long-term investments have increased by 46.7 percent ($35,000 ÷ $75,000), and property and equipment have increased by 126.3 percent ($120,000 ÷ $95,000). Although increases like these are common in growing companies, analysts and others will likely be interested in how Robyn's paid for the acquisitions.

Changes in the income statement for Robyn's Boutique can be analyzed in a similar fashion. Sales increased by $50,000 (7.7 percent) from 2011 to 2012. On the surface, this would appear to be a positive sign. However, further analysis shows that the cost of goods sold increased by $45,000, or 9.9 percent, and total operating expenses increased by $28,750, or 27.6 percent. Although sales increased, expenses appear to be rising much faster than sales! Note that focusing on net income without looking at other changes in the income statement would be a mistake. Although net income was virtually unchanged from 2011 to 2012, operating income decreased by more than 26 percent.

Horizontal analysis of financial statements can and should include more than just 2 years of data. Many annual reports include, as supplemental information, up to 10 years of financial data. Using these supplemental reports, readers of financial statements can perform **trend analysis**. Decision makers can use trend analysis to build prediction models to forecast financial

Horizontal analysis An analysis of financial statements over time.

Trend analysis Horizontal analysis of multiple years of data.

Exhibit 12-1 Comparative Balance Sheets

	2012	2011	$ Change Increase (Decrease)	% Change Increase (Decrease)
Cash	$130,000	$110,000	$ 20,000	18.2%
Accounts receivable	130,000	120,000	10,000	8.3
Inventory	225,000	215,000	10,000	4.7
Prepaid insurance	25,000	30,000	(5,000)	(16.7)
Total current assets	$510,000	$475,000	$ 35,000	7.4
Long-term investments	110,000	75,000	35,000	46.7
Land	200,000	175,000	25,000	14.3
Property and equipment	215,000	95,000	120,000	126.3
Accumulated depreciation	(105,000)	(80,000)	(25,000)	(31.3)
Total assets	$930,000	$740,000	$190,000	25.7
Accounts payable	60,000	50,000	10,000	20.0
Payroll payable	10,000	8,000	2,000	25.0
Taxes payable	10,000	9,000	1,000	11.1
Total current liabilities	$ 80,000	$ 67,000	$ 13,000	19.4
Notes payable	100,000	80,000	20,000	25.0
Capital stock	500,000	400,000	100,000	25.0
Retained earnings	250,000	193,000	57,000	29.5
Total liabilities and stockholders' equity	$930,000	$740,000	$190,000	25.7

Exhibit 12-2 Comparative Statements of Income and Retained Earnings

	2012	2011	$ Change Increase (Decrease)	% Change Increase (Decrease)
Sales revenue	$700,000	$650,000	$ 50,000	7.7%
Cost of goods sold	500,000	455,000	45,000	9.9
Gross profit	$200,000	$195,000	$ 5,000	2.6
Payroll expense	$ 50,000	$ 42,250	$ 7,750	18.3
Insurance expense	30,000	29,000	1,000	3.4
Rent expense	18,000	18,000	—	—
Depreciation	35,000	15,000	20,000	133.3
Total expenses	$133,000	$104,250	$ 28,750	27.6
Operating Income	$ 67,000	$ 90,750	$(23,750)	(26.2)
Interest expense	$ (7,000)	$ (5,000)	$ (2,000)	40.0
Gain on vehicle sale	25,000	—	25,000	—
Loss on sale of securities	(25,000)	—	(25,000)	—
Interest revenue	75,000	50,000	25,000	50.0
Net income before interest and taxes	$135,000	$135,750	$ (750)	(0.06)
Tax	(40,000)	(40,250)	250	(0.06)
Net income	$ 95,000	$ 95,500	$ (500)	(0.05)
Dividends	(38,000)	(38,000)		
To retained earnings	$ 57,000	$ 57,500		
Retained earnings 1/1	193,000	136,000		
Retained earnings 12/31	$250,000	$193,500		

performance in the future. Trend analysis can also be used to identify problem areas by looking for sudden or abnormal changes in accounts.

Horizontal analysis can include the statement of cash flows (see Exhibit 12-3). Robyn's Boutique shows consistent and increasing cash flows from operations: $765,000 in 2012 and $690,000 in 2011. The company also shows an increase of $42,500, or 49.7 percent, in net cash provided by operating activities. These two changes indicate a good trend in cash flows from operating activities. Although the net increase in cash for

Exhibit 12-3 Comparative Statements of Cash Flow

	For the Years Ended December 31		$ Change	% Change
	2012	**2011**		
Cash Flows from Operating Activities				
Cash Receipts from				
Sales on account	$ 690,000	$ 640,000	$ 50,000	7.8%
Interest	75,000	50,000	25,000	50.0
Total cash receipts	$ 765,000	$ 690,000	$ 75,000	
Cash Payments for				
Inventory purchases	$ 500,000	$ 470,000	$ 30,000	6.4
Payroll	48,000	42,250	5,750	13.6
Insurance	25,000	29,000	(4,000)	(13.8)
Interest	7,000	5,000	2,000	40.0
Rent expense	18,000	18,000	—	—
Taxes	39,000	40,250	(1,250)	(3.1)
Total cash payments	$(637,000)	$(604,500)	$ 32,500	5.4
Net cash provided (used) by operating activities	$ 128,000	$ 85,500	$ 42,500	49.7
Cash Flows from Investing Activities				
Sale of note	$ 25,000	—	$ 25,000	—
Sale of vehicle	75,000	—	75,000	—
Purchase of equipment	(180,000)	$ (20,000)	(160,000)	800.0
Purchase of long-term investments	(85,000)	—	(85,000)	
Purchase of land	(5,000)	—	(5,000)	—
Net cash provided (used) by investing activities	$(170,000)	$ (20,000)	$(150,000)	750
Cash Flows from Financing Activities				
Issuance of stock	$ 100,000	—	$ 100,000	—
Payment of cash dividends	(38,000)	$ (38,000)	—	—
Net cash provided (used) by financing activities	$ 62,000	$ (38,000)	$ 100,000	263.2
Net increase in cash	$ 20,000	$ 27,500	$ (7,500)	(27.3)
Cash balance 1/1	110,000	82,500		
Cash balance 12/31	$ 130,000	$ 110,000		
Supplemental Schedule of Noncash Investing and Financing Activities				
Acquisition of land in exchange for note payable	$ 20,000	(2,000)		

2012 was less than the increase in 2011, the decrease can be easily explained by the additional cash used for investing activities in 2012.

LO3 Vertical Analysis

Vertical analysis compares financial statements of different companies and financial statements of the same company across time after controlling for differences in size. In comparing companies of different sizes, it is useful to standardize the statements. **Common-size financial statements** are statements in which all items have been restated as a percentage of a selected item on the statements. Common-size financial statements remove size as a relevant variable in ratio analysis and can be used to compare companies that make similar products and that are different in size (such as **Boeing** and **Cessna**, both aircraft manufacturers). They also can be used to compare the same company across years.

Common-size comparative balance sheets for Robyn's Boutique are shown in Exhibit 12-4. Note that all asset accounts are stated as a percentage of total assets. Similarly, all liability and stockholders' equity accounts are stated as a percentage of total liabilities and stockholders' equity.

> Vertical analysis uses common-size financial statements to remove size as a relevant variable in ratio analysis.

As mentioned earlier, there are two ways to use common-size financial statements. One is a comparison between years or over a number of years. The other is a comparison of similar companies of different sizes.

When comparing across years, analysts and other decision makers look for critical changes in the composition of accounts. One important measure from the balance sheet is working capital. **Working capital** is defined as the excess of current assets over current liabilities and is a measure of an entity's **liquidity**, or its ability to meet its immediate financial obligations. Robyn's Boutique had current assets and current liabilities in 2012 and 2011 as follows:

	2012	2011
Current assets	$510,000	$475,000
Current liabilities	(80,000)	(67,000)
Working capital	$430,000	$408,000

The amount of working capital has increased by $22,000 from 2011 to 2012, indicating that Robyn's has increased the amount of current assets available to pay current liabilities. However, without information concerning the makeup of working capital, the information is of limited use. If current assets consist primarily of inventory, the

Exhibit 12-4 Common-Size Comparative Balance Sheets

	2012	Percent	2011	Percent
Cash	$130,000	14.0%	$110,000	14.9%
Accounts receivable	130,000	14.0	120,000	16.2
Inventory	225,000	24.2	215,000	29.1
Prepaid insurance	25,000	2.7	30,000	4.1
Total current assets	$510,000	54.8%	$475,000	64.2%
Long-term investments	110,000	11.8	75,000	10.1
Land	200,000	21.5	175,000	23.6
Property and equipment	215,000	23.1	95,000	12.8
Accumulated depreciation	(105,000)	(11.3)	(80,000)	(10.8)
Total assets	$930,000	100%	$740,000	100%
Accounts payable	$ 60,000	6.5%	$ 50,000	6.8%
Payroll payable	10,000	1.1	8,000	1.1
Taxes payable	10,000	1.1	9,000	1.2
Total current liabilities	$ 80,000	8.7%	$ 67,000	9.1%
Notes payable	100,000	10.8	80,000	10.8
Capital stock	500,000	53.8	400,000	54.1
Retained earnings	250,000	26.9	193,000	26.1
Total liabilities and stockholders' equity	$930,000	100.0%	$740,000	100.0%

Common-size financial statements Statements in which all items have been restated as a percentage of a selected item on the statements.

Working capital The excess of current assets over current liabilities, which is a measure of an entity's liquidity.

Liquidity A measure of the ability of a company to meet its immediate financial obligations.

© Cengage Learning 2013

© Vasina Natalia/Shutterstock.com

company's liquidity could still be in jeopardy. In such a case, a slower conversion to cash would result than if current assets consisted primarily of accounts receivable.

Common-size comparative income statements for Robyn's Boutique are presented in Exhibit 12-5. The base on which all income statement accounts are compared is net sales, presented simply as sales revenue in Exhibit 12-5.

The common-size income statement points out some interesting, but small, changes between the two years presented. The gross profit percentage decreased from 30 percent to 28.6 percent. This is a closely watched ratio in many companies and industries.

An important use of common-size financial statements is to compare companies that are in similar lines of business but are of different sizes. The following table shows such a comparison:

Comparison of Robyn's Boutique and Competitor		
Account	**Robyn's**	**The Competitor**
	Percentage of Total Assets	**Percentage of Total Assets**
Cash	14.0%	17.0%
Inventory	24.0	20.0
Prepaids	2.7	3.4
Property and equipment (net)	33.3	39.5
Long-term investments	11.8	10.5
	Percentage of Liabilities and Equity	**Percentage of Liabilities and Equity**
Accounts payable	6.5%	8.5%
Income tax	1.1	2.0
Long-term debt	10.8	13.5
Cost of goods sold	71.4	65.0
Operating expense	19.0	23.5
Net income after tax	13.6	10.5

LO4 Ratio Analysis—Liquidity Ratios

Exhibit 12-5 Common-Size Comparative Income Statements

	2012	**Percent**	**2011**	**Percent**
Sales revenue	$700,000	100.0%	$650,000	100.0%
Cost of goods sold	500,000	71.4	455,000	70.0
Gross profit	$200,000	28.6%	$195,000	30.0%
Payroll expense	$ 50,000	7.1%	$ 42,250	6.0%
Insurance expense	30,000	4.3	29,000	4.5
Rent expense	18,000	2.6	18,000	2.8
Depreciation	35,000	5.0	15,000	2.3
Total expenses	$133,000	19.0%	$104,250	16.0%
Operating Income	$ 67,000	9.6%	$ 90,750	14.0%
Interest expense	$ (7,000)	(1.0)%	$ (5,000)	(0.8)%
Gain on vehicle sale	25,000	3.6	0	—
Loss on sale of securities	(25,000)	(3.6)	0	—
Interest revenue	75,000	10.7	50,000	7.7
Net income before interest and taxes	$135,000	19.3%	$135,750	20.9%
Tax expense	(40,000)	(5.7)	(40,250)	(6.2)
Net income	$ 95,000	13.6%	$ 95,500	14.7%

Current ratio A measure of an entity's liquidity; also known as working capital ratio.

© Cengage Learning 2013

Financial statement ratios simply refer to a relationship between two financial statement amounts stated as a percentage.

Current Ratio

The **current ratio**, or working capital ratio, is a measure of an entity's liquidity. The formula for the current ratio is as follows:

$$\text{Current ratio} = \frac{\text{Current assets}}{\text{Current liabilities}}$$

The current ratios for Robyn's Boutique for the past two years are as follows:

2012	2011
$\frac{\$510,000}{\$80,000} = 6.375$	$\frac{\$475,000}{\$67,000} = 7.090$

Liquidity ratios assess a company's ability to meet its short-term financial obligations.

What does this ratio tell us? In 2012, Robyn's Boutique had $6.38 of current assets for every dollar of current liabilities, and, in 2011, the boutique had $7.09 for every dollar of current liabilities. Although high current ratios would appear to be good (if you are a creditor of a company, a high current ratio indicates that you are more likely to be paid), a ratio that is very high may indicate that a company holds too much cash, accounts receivable, or inventory. Historically, a current ratio of 2.0 was considered good. However, many companies strive to maintain current ratios that are closer to 1.0. Internal managers look closely at the current ratio and its composition so that they can better control levels of current assets. As we have discussed elsewhere, holding inventory can be very costly for companies, and cash held in non-interest-bearing accounts might be more productively used elsewhere.

Quick Ratio

One way to reduce the concern over the composition of the current accounts when computing the current ratio is to use the quick ratio, or acid-test ratio. The **quick ratio** removes inventories and prepaid assets from the current asset amount used in the calculation of the current ratio. These current assets are considered the least liquid. The quick ratio formula is

$$\text{Quick ratio} = \frac{\text{Quick assets}}{\text{Current liabilities}}$$

Using the amounts from Robyn's Boutique, we can calculate the quick ratio as follows:

2012	2011
$\dfrac{\$260,000}{\$80,000} = 3.25$	$\dfrac{\$230,000}{\$67,000} = 3.433$

A quick ratio less than 1.0 should be of concern to both creditors and internal managers, as it indicates that liquid current assets are not sufficient to meet current obligations. Interestingly, Robyn's has unusually high quick ratios. High quick ratios may indicate other problems to management. Unless management has good reasons for holding excess cash (say, it is to be used for large purchases of property, plant, and equipment; future expansion; and so on), Robyn's should probably try to convert its excess cash into assets generating higher returns.

Ratio of Cash Flow from Operations to Current Liabilities

The current ratio and the quick ratio have two major weaknesses. The first is that all debt payments are made with cash, whereas current assets include noncash assets. The second is that both ratios focus on liquid and current assets at one point in time (the balance sheet date). However, cash, inventories, accounts receivable, and other current assets change over the course of the year. For these reasons, the amount of cash flow from operations (from the statement of cash flows) is sometimes

Quick ratio A stricter test of a company's ability to pay its current debts with highly liquid current assets.

used as the numerator in a ratio, with an average balance of current liabilities in the denominator:

$$\text{Ratio of cash flow from operations to current liabilities} = \frac{\text{Net cash provided by operating activities}}{\text{Average current liabilities}}$$

The computation of the 2011 ratio requires the 2010 end-of-year current liability balance. The December 31, 2010, balance sheet for Robyn's Boutique is shown in Exhibit 12-6.

Exhibit 12-6 Balance Sheet as of December 31, 2010

Cash	$ 95,000
Accounts receivable	105,000
Inventory	175,000
Prepaid insurance	25,000
Total current assets	$400,000
Long-term investments	$ 45,000
Land	175,000
Property and equipment	85,000
Accumulated depreciation	(60,000)
Total long-term assets	$245,000
Total assets	$645,000
Accounts payable	$ 35,000
Payroll payable	6,500
Income tax payable	7,000
Total current liabilities	$ 48,500
Notes payable	$ 70,000
Total liabilities	$118,500
Capital stock	$400,000
Retained earnings	126,500
Total stockholders' equity	$526,600
Total liabilities and stockholders' equity	$645,000

The ratios of cash flow from operations to current liabilities for Robyn's Boutique are as follows:

2012	2011
$\dfrac{\$128,000}{\left[\dfrac{(\$80,000 + \$67,000)}{2}\right]} = 1.74$	$\dfrac{\$85,500}{\left[\dfrac{(\$67,000 + \$48,500)}{2}\right]} = 1.48$

Accounts receivable turnover ratio One of the best measures of the efficiency of the collection process.

Robyn's is generating sufficient cash from operations to pay current obligations.

Accounts Receivable Analysis

The **accounts receivable turnover ratio** is one of the best measures of the efficiency of the collection process. Management's analysis of accounts receivable is very important in monitoring collection and credit-granting policies. The accounts receivable turnover ratio is

$$\text{Accounts receivable turnover ratio} = \frac{\text{Net credit sales}}{\text{Average accounts receivable}}$$

This ratio is known as an activity ratio, which means that it consists of an activity (sales) divided by a related base (accounts receivable). Using the accounts receivable balances in the 2010, 2011, and 2012 balance sheets (Exhibits 12-4 and 12-6), we calculate the ratios for Robyn's Boutique as follows:

2012	2011
$\dfrac{\$700,000}{\left[\dfrac{(\$120,000 + \$130,000)}{2}\right]} = 5.60$	$\dfrac{\$650,000}{\left[\dfrac{(\$105,000 + \$120,000)}{2}\right]} = 5.78$

These ratios tell us that, on average, Robyn's Boutique sold on account and subsequently collected accounts receivable almost six times during the year. To convert these amounts to a more understandable measure, consider this question: If you can do something almost six times in a year, how many days did it take you to do it once? The average number of days to collect a credit sale, computed as follows, measures this concept:

$$\text{Number of days sales in receivables} = \frac{\text{Number of days in the period}}{\text{Accounts receivable turnover}}$$

The calculations for Robyn's for 2011 and 2012 are as follows:

2012	2011
$\dfrac{365}{5.6} = 65.18 \text{ days}$	$\dfrac{365}{5.78} = 63.15 \text{ days}$

This ratio tells us that the average time to collect sales on account was 63.15 days in 2011 and 65.18 days in 2012. Is this amount of time to collect sales acceptable? That depends on the credit policy of the particular business and on industry standards. If the accounts are due in 30 days, a collection period in excess of 60 is not good. If the credit policy allows for 60 days, the collection period is in line with existing policy. Large retailers often have collection periods of less than one week.

The accounts receivable turnover ratio will have an impact on ROI and other measures of return on invested assets. One of the key components of ROI is turnover of assets. When turnover is increased, ROI and related measures will also increase.

Inventory Analysis

The analysis of inventory is similar to the analysis of accounts receivable. The first ratio is the **inventory turnover ratio**:

$$\text{Inventory turnover ratio} = \frac{\text{Cost of goods sold}}{\text{Average inventory}}$$

The inventory turnover ratios for Robyn's for 2011 and 2012 are as follows:

2012		2011	
$\dfrac{\$500,000}{\left[\dfrac{(\$215,000 + \$225,000)}{2}\right]}$	= 2.27	$\dfrac{\$455,000}{\left[\dfrac{(\$175,000 + \$215,000)}{2}\right]}$	= 2.33

These ratios tell us that, on average, Robyn's Boutique bought inventory and then subsequently sold it 2.33 and 2.27 times per year in 2011 and 2012, respectively. The value of the ratio for 2011 does not mean that every item in inventory was sold 2.33 times; instead, it means that the value of inventory was sold 2.33 times. Determining the appropriate level of inventory turnover is totally dependent on industry and company standards. Some businesses expect higher inventory turnover than others do. For example, a grocery store would expect inventory turnover of 50 or even 100 times per year. A bakery may expect inventory turnover as high as 200 because it would expect to sell all fresh baked goods the same day they are produced. At the other extreme, furniture stores may expect inventory turnover of only 1 or 2 per year. Retail clothing stores such as Robyn's Boutique should expect to turn over inventory much more frequently than 2 times per year; if not, this is a serious concern for management. Another way to look at inventory turnover is to calculate the number of days inventory is held before it is sold:

$$\text{Number of days inventory is held before sales} = \frac{\text{Number of days in the period}}{\text{Inventory turnover}}$$

On average, Robyn's held inventory for more than 150 days in both 2011 and 2012, calculated as follows:

2012	2011
$\dfrac{365}{2.27}$ = 160.79 days	$\dfrac{365}{2.33}$ = 156.65 days

Low turnover ratios and a correspondingly high number of days in which inventory is held for sale can direct management's attention toward a variety of problems. A large amount of obsolete inventory that is not being written off can adversely affect these ratios. Inventory turnover ratios can also indicate problems in the sales department or problems with the product, both of which can cause decreases in sales. As with accounts receivable turnover, if inventory turnover increases, ROI and other measures of return on invested assets will also increase.

Cash-to-Cash Operating Cycle Ratio

The **cash-to-cash operating cycle ratio** measures the length of time between the purchase of inventory and the eventual collection of cash from sales. To calculate this ratio, we combine two measures:

$$\text{Cash-to-cash operating cycle ratio} = \text{Number of days in inventory} + \text{Number of days in receivables}$$

Inventory turnover ratio A measure of the number of times the value of inventory is sold in one year.

Cash-to-cash operating cycle ratio A measure of the length of time between the purchase of inventory and the eventual collection of cash from sales.

The cash-to-cash operating cycle ratios for Robyn's Boutique are as follows:

2012	2011
160.79 + 65.18 = **225.97 days**	156.65 + 63.15 = **219.80 days**

On average, it took Robyn's 219.80 days in 2011 and 225.97 days in 2012 to turn purchased inventory into cash.

LO5 Ratio Analysis—Solvency Ratios

Solvency represents a company's ability to remain in business over the long term. Solvency is related to liquidity but differs with respect to the time frame. Liquidity measures the ability to pay short-term debt, whereas solvency measures the ability to stay financially healthy over the long run.

Debt-to-Equity Ratio

The main focus of solvency analysis is capital structure. Capital structure refers to the relationship between debt and stockholders' equity. The **debt-to-equity ratio** is as follows:

$$\text{Debt-to-equity ratio} = \frac{\text{Total liabilities}}{\text{Total stockholders' equity}}$$

Robyn's debt-to-equity ratios for 2011 and 2012 are as follows:

2012	2011
$\dfrac{\$180,000}{\$750,000}$ = **0.24 to 1**	$\dfrac{\$147,000}{\$593,000}$ = **0.25 to 1**

Debt-to-equity ratio A solvency measure focusing on the amount of capital provided by creditors.

Times interest earned A measure of the company's ability to meet current interest payments to creditors.

These ratios tell us that for every $1 of capital (capital stock and retained earnings), creditors provided 25 cents in 2011 and 24 cents in 2012. Low debt-to-equity ratios indicate a preference to raise funds through equity financing and a tendency to avoid the higher risk of debt financing. What is considered a good debt-to-equity ratio? As with all other ratios, this is dependent on the business, the industry, and other factors. Although a high debt-to-equity ratio may be of concern to creditors, it may be desirable and necessary for a new business to borrow money. The decision whether to capitalize a company with debt or with equity involves many variables, including the income tax impact of debt versus equity on both the corporation and its shareholders. If management borrows funds at 8 percent and earns a return on investment of 10 percent, the use of debt (leverage) is desirable. But it adds some risk, owing to the obligation to repay the debt and the interest on the debt. This level of risk can be measured by the next ratio, times interest earned.

Times-Interest-Earned Ratio

Times interest earned measures a company's ability to meet current interest payments to creditors by specifically measuring its ability to meet current-year interest payments out of current-year earnings:

$$\text{Times interest earned} = \frac{\text{Net income} + \text{Interest expense} + \text{Income tax}}{\text{Interest expense}}$$

Both interest expense and income tax expense are added back to net income because interest is deducted from net income to arrive at taxable income. This adjustment gives us a "purer" measure of income available to pay interest. The times-interest-earned ratio is especially important to bankers and other lenders. The ratios for times interest earned for Robyn's are as follows:

2012	2011
$\dfrac{(\$135,000 + \$7,000 + \$40,000)}{\$7,000}$ = **26.0 to 1**	$\dfrac{(\$135,750 + \$5,000 + \$40,250)}{\$5,000}$ = **36.2**

The ratios for Robyn's Boutique are very good. Robyn's could pay (from current earnings) the interest on debt 36 times in 2011 and 26 times in 2012.

Debt Service Coverage Ratio

Two major weaknesses are associated with the use of the times-interest-earned ratio as a measure of the ability to pay creditors. First, the ratio considers only interest expense. Yet management and other decision makers must also be concerned about the amount of principal that must be repaid on the currently maturing debt. Second, the ratio does not take into account any noncash adjustments to net income that arise because of accrual accounting. Accordingly, the **debt service coverage ratio** is used to measure the amount of cash generated from operating activities that is available to repay principal and interest in the upcoming year. That ratio is as follows:

$$\text{Debt service coverage ratio} = \frac{\text{Cash flow from operations before interest and taxes}}{\text{Interest and principal payments}}$$

Referring back to the comparative statement of cash flows, we can compute the ratios for Robyn's:

2012	2011
$\dfrac{(\$128,000 - \$7,000 - \$39,000)}{\$25,000} = 3.28$	$\dfrac{(\$85,500 - \$5,000 - \$40,250)}{\$5,000} = 1.61$

These ratios indicate that Robyn's generated $1.61 in cash for every $1 of interest and principal paid in 2011 and $3.28 for every $1 of interest and principal paid in 2012. The 2011 ratio is weak, but the improvement is dramatic.

Cash Flow from Operations to Capital Expenditures Ratio

The **ratio of cash flow from operations to capital expenditures** measures a company's ability to use cash from operations to finance its acquisitions of property, plant, and equipment. The ability to use cash from operations diminishes the need to acquire outside financing, such as debt. The ratio is computed as follows:

$$\text{Ratio of cash flow from operations to capital expenditures} = \frac{\text{Cash flow from operations} - \text{Total dividends paid}}{\text{Cash paid for acquisitions}}$$

Solvency ratios assess the extent to which a company must borrow money to operate the business and the amount of interest paid on that money.

The calculation of these ratios for Robyn's is as follows:

2012	2011
$\dfrac{(\$128,000 - \$38,000)}{\$105,000} = 0.86$	$\dfrac{(\$85,500 - \$38,000)}{\$20,000} = 2.38$

The ratio for 2011 tells us that Robyn's generated cash from operations approximately 2.4 times greater than what was needed for its acquisition of capital assets. The ratio for 2012 shows that Robyn's generated cash from operations to cover only 86 percent of the capital asset needs. Note that the amount used to compute the 2012 ratio was net assets acquired. Robyn's had acquired $180,000 of new assets but sold a vehicle for $75,000.

LO6 Ratio Analysis— Profitability Ratios

Another group of ratios of importance to decision makers consists of those ratios concerned with profitability analysis. Creditors are concerned with profitability because it indicates an ability to make required principal and interest payments. Stockholders are very interested in profitability because of related increases in stock prices or dividends paid to shareholders.

Debt service coverage ratio A measure of the amount of cash generated by operating activities that is available to repay principal and interest in the upcoming year.

Ratio of cash flow from operations to capital expenditures A measure of a company's ability to use cash flow from operations to finance the acquisition of property, plant, and equipment.

Managers are also concerned with profitability, as it is often related to performance evaluations and tangible rewards from bonus payments and other incentive compensation plans.

Return on Assets

Return ratios measure the relationship between a return and a specific investment made in the company by various groups of investors, creditors, and owners. **Return on assets (ROA)** considers the return to investors on all assets invested in the company. Because we are measuring a return to investors, net income is often adjusted by interest expense paid to creditors. The formula for the computation of return on assets is as follows:

$$ROA = \frac{\text{Net income} + \text{Interest expense (net of tax)}}{\text{Average total assets}}$$

Assuming a 30 percent tax rate, we calculate ROA as follows:

	2012	2011
Net income	$ 95,000	$ 95,500
Add back:		
Interest expense $7,000		$5,000
× (1 − Tax rate) × 0.70	4,900	× 0.70 3,500
Numerator:	$ 99,900	$ 99,000
Assets, beginning of year	$ 740,000	$ 645,000
+ Assets, end of year	930,000	740,000
= Total	$1,670,000	$1,385,000
Denominator: Average total assets	$\left(\frac{\$1,670,000}{2}\right) = \$835,000$	$\left(\frac{\$1,385,000}{2}\right) = \$692,500$
ROA	$\frac{\$99,900}{\$835,000} = 11.96\%$	$\frac{\$99,000}{\$692,500} = 14.30\%$

The interpretation of this ratio is based on (1) the company's required return on assets, (2) industry standards,

Profitability ratios provide measures of how effectively a company is using its assets.

and (3) trends. In this case, the decline in ROA is likely to be of concern to the owners of Robyn's Boutique.

Like return on investment, ROA can be broken down into margin and turnover components: return on sales and asset turnover. The two ratios are computed as follows:

$$\text{Return on sales} = \frac{\text{Net income} + \text{Interest expense (net of tax)}}{\text{Net sales}}$$

$$\text{Asset turnover ratio} = \frac{\text{Net sales}}{\text{Average total assets}}$$

The ratios for Robyn's are as follows:

	2012	2011
Return on sales	$\frac{\$99,900}{\$700,000} = 14.27\%$	$\frac{\$99,000}{\$650,000} = 15.23\%$
Asset turnover ratio	$\frac{\$700,000}{\$835,000} = 0.84 \text{ times}$	$\frac{\$650,000}{\$692,500} = 0.94 \text{ times}$

Both the return on sales (income generated as a percentage of sales) and the asset turnover ratio (sales generated as a percentage of assets) declined from 2011 to 2012. Of particular concern to management is the low asset turnover ratio.

Return on Common Stockholders' Equity

Return on common stockholders' equity (ROCSE) measures the return to common stockholders (net income reduced by preferred dividends) as a percentage of stockholders' equity:

$$ROCSE = \frac{\text{Net income} - \text{Preferred dividends}}{\text{Average common stockholders' equity}}$$

The ROCSE ratios for Robyn's are as follows:

	2012	2011
	$\frac{\$95,000}{\left[\frac{(\$593,000 + \$750,000)}{2}\right]} = 14.15\%$	$\frac{\$95,500}{\left[\frac{(\$526,500 + \$593,000)}{2}\right]} = 17.06\%$

Predicting Stock Performance with Financial Statement Analysis

A nalysts constantly strive to develop models using financial data to predict future stock performance. In a recent article published in *The Journal of Finance*, Long Chen and Lu Zhang improve on the classic capital asset pricing model (CAPM) and develop a model based on three simple factors: return on assets, changes in inventory divided by book value, and changes in capital expenditures divided by book value. The implication for investors? Focus on companies with a high return on assets, lean firms that sell their inventories quickly, and firms with limited growth in acquisitions of property, plant, and equipment.

Source: "A Better Measure," by Jack Hough, *Smart Money*, October 2009, and "A Better Three-Factor Model That Explains More Anomalies," by Long Chen and Lu Zhang, *The Journal of Finance*, Vol. LXV, No. 2, April 2010.

The ratios indicate that the common stockholders earned a 17 percent return in 2011 and will earn a 14 percent return in 2012. Adequacy of return on stockholders' equity depends on a number of factors, including the risk of the investment.

Earnings per Share

Current stockholders and potential investors use **earnings per share (EPS)** as a key measure of performance. In contrast to measures of net income, EPS can be used to compare the performance of companies of different size. However, it should be used with caution in comparing companies across different industries. EPS is calculated as follows:

$$EPS = \frac{\text{Net income} - \text{Preferred dividends}}{\text{Average number of common shares outstanding}}$$

The EPS for Robyn's is as follows:

	2012	2011
EPS	$EPS = \frac{\$95,000}{45,000} = 2.11$	$EPS = \frac{\$95,500}{40,000} = 2.39$

Robyn's Boutique has a $10-per-share par value, resulting in 40,000 shares outstanding in 2011. In 2012, the boutique sold another 10,000 shares for $100,000, so 50,000 shares were outstanding at the end of 2012. The average number of shares outstanding in 2012 was 45,000 ([40,000 + 50,000] ÷ 2).

Price Earnings Ratio

Earnings per share is a very important ratio for investors because of the relationship of earnings to dividends and the market price of a company's stock. Investors are also interested in the current price of a company's stock in comparison to its earnings. The **price–earnings (P/E) ratio** is computed as follows:

$$\text{Price–earnings ratio} = \frac{\text{Current market price}}{\text{EPS}}$$

Earnings per share (EPS) A key measure of performance that is often used to compare companies of different size.

Price–earnings (P/E) ratio A measure of the current price of a company's stock in comparison to its earnings. Theoretically, the P/E ratio tells us something about how investors think that a company's stock will perform in the future compared with other companies' stock.

Assuming that the current market price for Robyn's Boutique stock is $13 per share, we can compute the P/E ratio as follows:

2012	2011
$\frac{\$13}{\$2.11} = 6.16 \text{ to } 1$	$\frac{\$13}{\$2.39} = 5.44 \text{ to } 1$

Theoretically, a company's P/E ratio tells us how much an investor is willing to pay for the company's stock. If a stock has a P/E ratio of 15, it means that the stock is currently selling for 15 times the company's earnings. Although you might expect that the P/E ratio of one company would be about the same as the P/E ratio of another, in reality P/E ratios vary greatly from company to company and by industry. For example, as of May 16, 2011, the average P/E ratio for companies in the basic materials sector was 15.20.[1] However, looking more specifically at industries within the sector reveals that steel and iron companies had an average P/E ratio of 12.2 whereas oil and gas pipeline companies had an average P/E ratio of 41.2. At the same date, large automobile manufacturers had an average P/E ratio of 18.4, electric utilities an average P/E ratio of 19.2, and money center banks an average P/E ratio of 9.7. Thus, the P/E ratio is a reflection of an industry's growth prospects in addition to how optimistic investors are about the future of a particular company and its earnings. If a company has a P/E ratio that is higher than the industry average, it typically means that investors think that the company will outperform other companies in the industry. Similarly, if a company has a P/E ratio that is lower than the industry average, investors are generally pessimistic about the company's future prospects and earnings compared with those of other, similar companies.

[1] http://biz.yahoo.com/p/s_peed.html

STUDY TOOLS 12

Chapter review card

- ❍ Learning Objective and Key Concept Reviews
- ❍ Key Definitions and Formulas

Online (Located at www.cengagebrain.com)

- ❍ Flash Cards and Crossword Puzzles
- ❍ Games and Quizzes
- ❍ E-Lectures
- ❍ Homework Assignments (as directed by your instructor)

1. Analyzing Financial Statements LO1

Companies communicate a great deal of information in their financial statements. Analyzing the statements is a critical step in understanding companies' operations and performance. The following statements relate to the analysis of financial statements.

a. The use of generally accepted accounting principles eliminates variability in financial reporting by different companies so that financial statement analysis is easier to perform.

b. Financial statement analysis can be useful for predicting a company's future financial performance.

c. Decision makers should use a variety of financial statement ratios, rather than a single ratio, if they wish to understand a company.

d. One important tool to use in analyzing a set of financial statements is industry comparisons.

e. Inflation should be ignored in conducting financial statement analysis.

Required

Indicate whether each of the preceding statements is true or false.

2. Horizontal and Vertical Analysis
LO2, 3

Financial statement analysis can be performed in a variety of ways. The following statements relate to two of these ways: horizontal and vertical analysis.

a. Horizontal analysis should not include more than two years of data.

b. Only the balance sheet should be subjected to horizontal analysis.

c. A special type of horizontal analysis called trend analysis is useful for identifying patterns over long periods.

d. Vertical analysis controls for differences in company size, whereas horizontal analysis does not.

e. Common-size financial statements are statements for companies of approximately the same size and in the same industry.

f. Liquidity is a measure of a company's ability to meet its immediate financial obligations.

Required

Indicate whether each of the preceding statements is true or false.

3. Liquidity Ratios LO4

Financial statements of two competing companies report the following data (amounts in millions):

	Company A	Company B
Sales	$4,500	$2,700
Accounts receivable, January 1	3,000	1,950
Accounts receivable, December 31	1,500	600

Required

Compute the accounts receivable turnover for each company.

4. Solvency Ratios LO5

A company has the following financial statement data (in millions):

Accounts payable	$ 1,200
Notes payable	3,120
Capital stock	4,000
Retained earnings	14,000

Required

Compute the debt-to-equity ratio for the company.

5. Profitability Ratios LO6

A company has the following financial statement data (in millions):

Net income	$ 600
Average total assets	12,000
Interest expense (net of taxes)	240

Required

Compute the return on assets for the company.

EXERCISES

6. Return on Assets: Margin vs. Turnover LO3

Information taken from recent annual reports of two retailers follows (amounts in thousands). Dan's Duds and Handsome Hal's both sell men's clothing. The income tax rate is 34 percent.

	Dan's Duds	Handsome Hal's
Sales	$4,071	$20,649
Interest expense	64	136
Net income	245	837
Average total assets	2,061	5,746

Required

Indicate which of these companies is the discount store and which is the specialty retailer. Explain your answer.

7. Liquidity Ratios LO4

Annual reports of two manufacturing companies in the same industry reveal the following for a recent year (amounts in millions):

	Company 1	Company 2
Sales	$3,793	$3,671
Accounts receivable, January 1	219	505
Accounts receivable, December 31	275	537

Required

A. Compute the accounts receivable turnover for each company.
B. Compute the average number of days that accounts receivable are outstanding for each company.
C. Which of these two companies is managing its accounts receivable more efficiently?

8. Liquidity Ratios LO4

The following relates to the activities of a pharmaceutical company (amounts in millions):

	Year 1	Year 2	Year 3	Year 4
Sales	$3,271	$3,720	$3,644	$4,070
Cost of goods sold	1,175	1,346	1,303	1,337
Average inventory	662	694	655	645

Required

A. Compute the inventory turnover for each year.
B. Compute the average number of days that inventories were held each year.
C. Compute the ratio of cost of goods sold to sales, expressed as a percentage for each year.
D. How well has the company managed its inventories over the four years?

9. Solvency Ratio: Calculation of Debt-to-Equity Ratio LO5

Canopy Corporation rents out tents for large parties thrown for such things as graduations, weddings, and birthdays. Part of Canopy's financial statements for last year is as follows:

Accounts payable	$ 45,000	
Payroll payable	5,000	
Taxes payable	10,000	
Total current liabilities		$60,000
Notes payable		20,000
Total liabilities		$80,000
Capital stock	$250,000	
Retained earnings	100,000	
Total stockholders' equity		$350,000
Total liabilities and stockholders' equity		$430,000

Required

What is Canopy Corporation's debt-to-equity ratio?

10. Asset Turnover Ratio LO6

The following information relates to a manufacturer of CD players (amounts in millions):

	Year 1	Year 2	Year 3
Sales	$210	$538	$1,051
Average total assets	70	145	256
Net income	36	87	137

Required

A. Compute the asset turnover ratio for each year.
B. How well has the company managed its investment in plant assets over the three years?

11. Return on Assets: Margin vs. Turnover LO6

Information about two video game companies was recently taken from the companies' annual reports. Virtual Videos and Games Galore both have an income tax rate of 34 percent, and following is the information collected from the two stores (amounts in thousands):

	Virtual Videos	Games Galore
Sales	$15,134	$20,143
Interest expense	80	150
Net income	524	982
Average total assets	3,048	7,125

Required

Calculate the return on assets, return on sales, and asset turnover for both companies. What can you tell about each company on the basis of these ratios?

12. Profitability Ratios LO6

Recent annual reports of two beverage companies reveal the following financial information (in millions):

	Company 1	Company 2
Revenues	$8,338	$13,007
Interest expense	199	345
Net income	1,045	762
Average total assets	8,028	10,079

The income tax rate is 34 percent.

Required

A. Calculate the rate of return on assets for each company.
B. Break the rate of return on assets into return on sales and total asset turnover.
C. Comment on the relative profitability of the two companies.

13. Profitability Ratios LO6

Recent annual reports of two fast-food chains (Company 1 and Company 2) reveal the following financial information (in millions):

	Company 1	Company 2
Revenues	$3,043	$8,017
Interest expense	95	184
Net income	852	1,426
Average total assets	2,841	7,671

The income tax rate is 34 percent.

Required

A. Calculate the rate of return on assets for each company.
B. Break the rate of return on assets into return on sales and total asset turnover.
C. Comment on the relative profitability of the two companies.

14. Rate of Return: Comparison of Different Companies LO3, 6

The following data show five items from the financial statements of three companies for a recent year (amounts in millions):

	Company A	Company B	Company C
For the Year			
Revenues	$8,824	$9,000	$11,742
Income before interest and related taxes[1]	615	1,043	611
Net income to common shareholders[2]	477	974	503
Average during the Year			
Total assets	9,073	6,833	7,163
Common shareholders' equity	2,915	3,494	2,888

[1]Net income + Interest expense × (1 − tax rate)
[2]Net income − Preferred stock dividends

Required

A. Compute the rate of return on assets for each company. Separate the rate of return on assets into the return on sales and the asset turnover ratio.
B. The three companies are an airline, a pharmaceutical company, and a retail department store. Which of the companies are most likely to correspond to A, B, and C, respectively? What clues did you use in reaching your conclusions?

PROBLEMS

15. Ratio Analysis: Decision Focus LO1, 2, 4, 5, 6

Avantronics is a manufacturer of electronic components and accessories that has total assets of $20,000,000. Selected financial ratios for Avantronics and the industry averages for firms of similar size are as follows:

	Avantronics			Industry Average
	Year 1	Year 2	Year 3	
Current ratio	2.09	2.27	2.51	2.24
Quick ratio	1.15	1.12	1.19	1.22
Inventory turnover	2.40	2.18	2.02	3.50
Profit margin	0.14	0.15	0.17	0.11
Debt-to-equity ratio	0.24	0.37	0.44	0.35

Avantronics is being reviewed by several entities whose interests vary, and the company's financial ratios are a part of the data being considered. Each of the following parties must recommend an action based on its evaluation of Avantronics's financial position:

MidCoastal Bank. The bank is processing Avantronics's application for a new five-year term note. MidCoastal has been the banker for Avantronics for several years but must reevaluate the company's financial position for each major transaction.

Ozawa Company. Ozawa is a new supplier to Avantronics and must decide on the appropriate credit terms to extend to the company.

Drucker & Denon. A brokerage firm specializing in the stock of electronics firms that are sold over the counter, Drucker & Denon must decide whether it will include Avantronics in a new fund being established for sale to Drucker & Denon's clients.

Working Capital Management Committee. This is a committee of Avantronics's management personnel chaired by the chief operating officer. The committee is responsible for periodically reviewing the company's working-capital position, comparing actual data against budgets, and recommending changes in strategy as needed.

Required

A. Describe the analytical use of each of the five ratios presented in the chart.
B. For each of the four entities described, identify the financial ratios, from those ratios presented,

that would be most valuable as a basis for its decision regarding Avantronics.

C. Discuss what the financial ratios presented in the question reveal about Avantronics. Support your answer by citing specific ratio levels and trends, as well as the interrelationships among these ratios.

16. Horizontal Analysis LO2

Following are the income statements for Martha's Miscellaneous for Year 1 and Year 2:

Martha's Miscellaneous Comparative Statements of Income and Retained Earnings				
	Year 2	Year 1	$ Change	% Change
Sales revenue	$700,000	$650,000		
Cost of goods sold	500,000	455,000		
Gross profit	$200,000	$195,000		
Payroll expense	$ 50,000	$ 42,250		
Insurance expense	30,000	29,000		
Rent expense	18,000	18,000		
Depreciation	35,000	15,000		
Total expenses	$133,000	$104,250		
Operating income	$ 67,000	$ 90,750		
Interest expense	(7,000)	(5,000)		
Gain on vehicle sale	25,000	—		
Loss on sale of securities	(25,000)	—		
Interest revenue	75,000	50,000		
Net income before interest and taxes	$135,000	$135,750		
Income taxes	40,000	40,250		
Net income	$ 95,000	$ 95,500		
Dividends	38,000	38,000		
Total retained earnings	$ 57,000	$ 57,500		
Retained earnings, 1/1	193,500	136,000		
Retained earnings, 12/31	$250,500	$193,500		

Required

Complete the comparative income statement by computing dollar change ($ change) and percentage change (% change).

17. Common-Size Statements LO3

Following are the balance sheets for Howard's Hammocks for December 31, 2012, and 2011:

Howard's Hammocks Comparative Balance Sheets		
	2012	2011
Cash	$130,000	$110,000
Accounts receivable	130,000	120,000
Inventory	225,000	215,000
Prepaid insurance	25,000	30,000
Total current assets	$510,000	$475,000
Long-term investments	$110,000	$ 75,000
Land	200,000	175,000
Property and equipment	215,000	95,000
Accumulated depreciation	(105,000)	(80,000)
	$420,000	$265,000
Total assets	$930,000	$740,000
Accounts payable	$ 60,000	$ 50,000
Payroll payable	10,000	8,000
Taxes payable	10,000	9,000
Total current liabilities	$ 80,000	$ 67,000
Notes payable	100,000	80,000
Capital stock	500,000	400,000
Retained earnings	250,000	193,000
Total liabilities and stockholders' equity	$930,000	$740,000

Required

Using the preceding income statement figures, prepare common-size statements for 2012 and 2011.

18. Comprehensive Ratio Analysis LO4, 5, 6

The 2012 financial statements for the Griffin Company are as follows:

Griffin Company Statement of Financial Position		
	12/31/12	12/31/11
Assets		
Cash	$ 40,000	$ 10,000
Accounts receivable	30,000	55,000
Inventory	110,000	70,000
Property, plant, and equipment	250,000	257,000
Total assets	$430,000	$392,000
Liabilities and Stockholders' Equity		
Current liabilities	$ 60,000	$ 50,000
5% mortgage payable	120,000	162,000
Common stock (30,000 shares)	150,000	150,000
Retained earnings	100,000	30,000
Total liabilities and stockholders' equity	$430,000	$392,000

Griffin Company
Income Statement For the Year Ended December 31, 2012

Sales on account	$420,000
Less expenses:	
Cost of goods sold	$214,000
Salary expense	50,000
Depreciation expense	7,000
Interest expense	9,000
Total expenses	$280,000
Income before taxes	$140,000
Income tax expense (50%)	70,000
Net income	$ 70,000

Required

Compute the following ratios for the Griffin Company for the year ending December 31, 2012:
A. Profit margin ratio (before interest and taxes)
B. Total asset turnover
C. Rate of return on total assets
D. Rate of return on common stockholders' equity
E. Earnings per share of stock
F. Inventory turnover
G. Current ratio
H. Quick ratio
I. Accounts receivable turnover
J. Debt-to-equity ratio
K. Times interest earned

Income Statement for the Year Ended December 31 (in millions)

Net sales	$24.2	$24.5	$24.9
Cost of goods sold	(16.9)	(17.2)	(18.0)
Gross margin	$ 7.3	$ 7.3	$ 6.9
Selling and administrative expenses	(6.6)	(6.8)	(7.3)
Earnings (loss) before taxes	$ 0.7	$ 0.5	$(0.4)
Income taxes	(0.3)	(0.2)	0.2
Net income	$ 0.4	$ 0.3	$ (0.2)

Required

A. What is the rate of return on total assets for 2012?
B. What is the current ratio for 2012?
C. What is the quick (acid-test) ratio for 2012?
D. What is the profit margin for 2011?
E. What is the profit margin for 2012?
F. What is the inventory turnover for 2011?
G. What is the inventory turnover for 2012?
H. What is the rate of return on stockholders' equity for 2011?
I. What is the rate of return on stockholders' equity for 2012?
J. What is the debt-to-equity ratio for 2012?

19. Comprehensive Ratio Analysis LO4, 5, 6

Using the following financial statements for Eagle Company, compute the required ratios:

Eagle Company Balance Sheet as of December 31 (in millions)

	2010	2011	2012
Assets			
Cash	$ 2.6	$ 1.8	$ 1.6
Government securities	0.4	0.2	0.0
Accounts and notes receivable	8.0	8.5	8.5
Inventories	2.8	3.2	2.8
Prepaid assets	0.7	0.6	0.6
Total current assets	$14.5	$14.3	$13.5
Property, plant, and equipment (net)	4.3	5.4	5.9
Total assets	$18.8	$19.7	$19.4
Liabilities and Shareholders' Equity			
Notes payable	$ 3.2	$ 3.7	$ 4.2
Accounts payable	2.8	3.7	4.1
Accrued expenses	0.9	1.1	1.0
Total current liabilities	$ 6.9	$ 8.5	$ 9.3
Long-term debt, 6% interest	3.0	2.0	1.0
Total liabilities	$ 9.9	$10.5	$10.3
Shareholders' equity	8.9	9.2	9.1
Total liabilities and shareholders' equity	$18.8	$19.7	$19.4

The Statement of
Cash Flows

Learning Objectives

After studying the material in this chapter, you should be able to:

LO1 Recognize the purpose of a statement of cash flows and the activities making up a cash-flow statement.

LO2 Discuss the difference between the direct and the indirect methods of computing cash flow from operating activities.

LO3 Prepare a comprehensive statement of cash flows, using the direct and indirect methods.

Introduction

The statement of cash flows reports the impact of a firm's operating, investing, and financing activities on cash flows during the accounting period. Along with the balance sheet, the income statement, and the statement of changes in stockholders' equity, the statement is a required component of a company's external financial statements.

Users of financial statements have made the statement of cash flows one of the most important of the four required financial statements. Creditors that have loaned money to a corporation are concerned about the ability of an organization to repay its debts and meet its interest payments. Recognizing that accrual accounting may mask cash-flow problems, investors may use cash flow instead of or along with earnings per share as a measure of the financial health of a company.

However, it is interesting to note that the accounting profession has expressly forbidden reporting information on cash flow per share in external financial statements. The profession believes that this type of information is not an acceptable alternative to earnings per share as an indicator of company performance. As is the case in other areas of financial statement disclosures, there is disagreement on what is the most useful information to disclose in financial statements!

LO1 The Statement of Cash Flows

The main purpose of the statement of cash flows is to provide information to decision makers about a company's cash inflows and outflows during a certain period. The statement of cash flows provides information relating to the change in cash balances between two balance sheet dates. Balance sheets provide a "snapshot" of the financial position of a company at a particular point in time, whereas the statement of cash flows reports changes over time. The statement of cash flows should be viewed as an explanation of the changes to the cash balance reported on the balance sheet.

The statement of cash flows is viewed by many as the most important financial statement because it provides evidence of the company's ability to meet its short-term financial obligations.

Managing cash flow is critically important for most companies.

The statement of cash flows also discloses items that affect how the balance sheet changed but that don't show up in the income statement, such as issuance of stock or acquisitions of property, plant, and equipment.

The statement of cash flows summarizes and explains all major cash receipts (inflows) and cash payments (outflows) during the period in question and categorizes the changes as resulting from operating, investing, or financing activities (see Exhibit 13-1).

Operating Activities

Operating activities include acquiring and selling products in the normal course of business. Different types of businesses will have different transactions that are

> **Operating activities** Include acquiring and selling products in the normal course of business.

> The statement of cash flows reports all the major sources and uses of cash that result from different activities of the company.

Exhibit 13-1 A Summary of Activities Making Up a Cash-Flow Statement

Cash Flows from Operating Activities =	Cash received from the sale of goods or services and cash received from interest and dividends −	Cash paid for operating expenses, cash paid for interest on debt, and cash paid for taxes
Cash Flows from Investing Activities =	Cash received from the sale of investments and from the sale of property, plant, and equipment −	Cash paid for investments and for purchases of property, plant, and equipment
Cash Flows from Financing Activities =	Cash received from the sale of capital stock or the borrowing of funds −	Cash paid for dividends on stock or repayments of debt or reacquiring capital stock

© Cengage Learning 2013

included in cash flows from operating activities. Typical types of items reported as inflows in this section of the statement of cash flows are cash from sales to customers, cash collected from past sales that were made on credit, and interest and dividends received. Typical outflows of cash from operating activities are purchases of merchandise for sale, purchases of materials to manufacture products, payments for operating expenses, interest on debt, payments for services, and payments of taxes.

Investing activities Include the purchase and sale of property, plant, and equipment; the purchases and sales of securities; and loans made as investments.

Investing Activities

Cash flows from **investing activities** include cash inflows from the sale of property, plant, and equipment; the sale of securities (stocks and bonds) of other companies; and the receipt of loan payments. Cash outflows include the purchase of property, plant, and equipment; the purchase of securities; and making loans as investments. Loans directly related to the sale of products or services are likely classified as operating activities. The interest on loans included as an investing activity is also classified as a cash flow from operating activities.

MAKING IT REAL

How Much Cash Is Enough?

In response to the financial crisis and the tightening of the credit markets, the 500 largest U.S. companies are holding more cash than at any time in the last 40 years. As a percentage of total assets, cash holdings increased from 4.4 percent in 1989 to 9.8 percent in 2009. As of the end of

© Terri Miller/E-Visual Communications, Inc.

2010, Google held $35 billion in cash, cash equivalents, and marketable securities, up from $15.8 billion at the end of 2008. As the economy improves, the large cash balances provide companies with a war chest that can be used to fund acquisitions, restart hiring, and increase capital spending.

Source: "Jittery Companies Stash Cash," by Tom McGinty and Cari Tuna, *The Wall Street Journal*, November 3, 2009.

Financing Activities

Cash flows from **financing activities** include cash inflows from selling stock or from issuing bonds. Cash inflows from financing activities also include contributions from owners and borrowing from banks on a long-term basis. Cash outflows from financing activities include repayment of notes and bonds, cash payments to repurchase stock (Treasury stock), and payment of dividends. Once again, all interest payments are included in cash flows from operating activities.

As an example, consider Gordon, Inc., whose Consolidated Statements of Cash Flows are presented in Exhibit 13-2. Notice that the company had earnings of $212 million in 2011 and similarly positive earnings in the preceding two years. Now, look near the bottom of the statement to find the "Increase in cash and cash equivalents." In 2011, Gordon's cash increased by $217 million—more than the company's earnings of $212 million. How did this happen?

The answer is that the company generates and uses cash for different purposes. For example, the company's operations generated more cash than was needed to pay for operations. In fact, operations generated almost $500 million. What accounts for the difference? Look at the company's investing and financing activities. The company appears to have reinvested a large amount of cash in new equipment, facilities, and other investments. Similarly, Gordon was paying off liabilities and even paying dividends to the owners of the company's stock.

The Definition of Cash: Cash and Cash Equivalents

Before we begin our discussion of the preparation of the statement of cash flows, it is important to be specific about exactly what is meant by cash. Accounting standards define certain items as equivalent to cash and that are combined with cash on the balance sheet and the statement of cash flows.

Commercial paper (short-term notes issued by corporations), money market funds, and Treasury bills are examples of cash equivalents. A **cash equivalent** is an item that can be readily converted to a known amount of cash and that has an original maturity of three months or less to the investor. For example, a three-year Treasury bill purchased three years before maturity is not a cash equivalent, but if that same Treasury bill were purchased three months prior to maturity, it would be a cash equivalent.

An understanding of the effects of different types of transactions on a company's cash flows helps investors and other financial statement users recognize how a company is generating and using its cash.

Noncash Transactions

It is not uncommon for organizations to have exchange transactions that do not directly involve cash inflows or outflows but still warrant disclosure on a statement of cash flows. These transactions are primarily in the financing and investing areas. For example, if an exchange of stock were made for an asset, the transaction would require an accounting entry to record the issuance of the stock and the addition of the asset. This transaction would not directly affect cash flows. However, if the company sold the stock on the open market and then used the cash it received to purchase the asset, the transaction would directly affect cash and be shown on the statement of cash flows. The sale of stock would show up as an inflow in the financing activities section, and the purchase of the asset would show up as an offsetting outflow in the investing activities section of the statement of cash flows. The key point is that the form of the transaction differs between the two transactions (exchange versus sale and purchase), whereas the substance (or result) of the two transactions is the same. Both transactions result in the same impact on the financial statements. Because we are more concerned with the substance of accounting transactions and full disclosure to users of the information, generally accepted accounting principles require that any significant noncash transaction be reported either in a separate schedule or in a footnote to the financial statements.

Financing activities Include cash flows from selling or repurchasing capital stock, long-term borrowing, and contributions from owners.

Cash equivalent An item that can be readily converted to a known amount of cash and that has an original maturity of three months or less to the investor.

Exhibit 13-2 Consolidated Statements of Cash Flows (Gordon, Inc.)

Gordon, Inc., and Subsidiaries
Consolidated Statements of Cash Flows
Fiscal Years Ended in December
(Thousands of Dollars)

	2011	2010	2009
Cash flows from operating activities			
Net earnings	$212,075	$195,977	$157,664
Adjustments to reconcile net earnings with net cash provided by operating activities:			
Cumulative effect of accounting change, net of tax	—	—	17,351
Depreciation and amortization of plant and equipment	78,097	75,618	88,070
Other amortization	102,035	70,562	76,053
Loss on early extinguishment of debt	—	1,277	20,342
Loss on impairment of investment	—	8,988	—
Change in fair value of liabilities potentially settleable in common stock	(2,080)	(12,710)	13,630
Deferred income taxes	(24,032)	34,624	22,774
Compensation earned under restricted-stock programs	74	138	172
Change in operating assets and liabilities (other than cash and cash equivalents):			
Decrease (increase) in accounts receivable	39,341	75,590	(13,202)
Decrease (increase) in inventories	10,677	(15,838)	34,846
Decrease in prepaid expenses and other current assets	74,531	29,423	7,845
Increase (decrease) in accounts payable and accrued liabilities	33,211	(89,735)	16,707
Other, including long-term advances	(27,305)	(15,408)	11,903
Net cash provided by operating activities	$496,624	$358,506	$ 454,155
Cash flows from investing activities			
Additions to property, plant, and equipment	(70,584)	(79,239)	(63,070)
Investments and acquisitions, net of cash acquired	(79,179)	(9,824)	—
Proceeds from sale of property, plant, and equipment	33,083	4,309	4,570
Other	(3,991)	(213)	(6,379)
Net cash utilized by investing activities	$(120,671)	$ (84,967)	$ (64,879)
Cash flows from financing activities			
Repurchases and repayments of borrowings with original maturities of more than three months	(93,303)	(57,974)	(389,279)
Net repayments of other short-term borrowings	(3,685)	(6,598)	309
Purchase of common stock and other equity securities	(48,030)	—	(3,378)
Stock option transactions	45,278	25,836	39,892
Dividends paid	(58,901)	(37,088)	(20,851)
Net cash utilized by financing activities	$(158,641)	$ (75,824)	$(373,307)
Effect of exchange rate changes on cash	(46)	6,540	9,406
Increase in cash and cash equivalents	217,266	204,255	25,375
Cash and cash equivalents at beginning of year	725,002	520,747	495,372
Cash and cash equivalents at end of year	$ 942,268	$725,002	$ 520,747
Supplemental information			
Interest paid	$ 33,265	$ 35,781	$ 64,189
Income taxes paid	$ 32,962	$ 40,647	$ 28,354

© Cengage Learning 2013

Exactly What Is Cash?

Most of us think we have an understanding of what constitutes cash. Many companies report their cash as part of "Cash and cash equivalents" on the balance sheet. Accounting rules generally state that cash and cash equivalents include coins, currency, and short-term, highly liquid investments that are easily convertible into known amounts of cash and that mature in the near future

© macka/Shutterstock.com

(usually in three months or less). Changes in today's investment environment have caused a number of companies to begin investing in financial instruments that were not contemplated when the accounting rules describing cash equivalents were issued. As a consequence, companies are increasingly required to convince their financial statement auditors that their "cash" really is cash.

Source: Steven D. Jones, "Firms Ponder What Constitutes Cash," *The Wall Street Journal*, July 27, 2006, C3.

LO2 Direct Method vs. Indirect Method

Organizations use two methods (direct and indirect) to report cash flows from operating activities. The **direct method** reports major classes of gross cash receipts and payments. For example, the direct method would report cash collected from customers, cash paid for inventory, cash paid for salaries and wages, and so on. The **indirect method**, in comparison, starts with net income and then removes the effect of all noncash items resulting from accruals or from noncash expenses such as depreciation. In other words, the indirect method essentially converts the accrual-basis income statement to a cash-basis income statement by taking out noncash items such as depreciation and nonoperating items such as accruals.

In order to compare the two methods, consider the income statement and balance sheet that follows. The company began operations on January 1, 2011, with the owners investing $100,000 in cash. The financial statements for the year ending December 31, 2011, are as follows:

Income Statement For the Year Ended December 31, 2011	
Sales revenues	$800,000
Operating expenses	− 640,000
Income before tax	$160,000
Income tax expense	− 40,000
Net income	$120,000

Balance Sheet as of December 31, 2011			
Assets		**Liabilities and Stockholders' Equity**	
Cash	$150,000	Accounts payable	$ 60,000
Accounts receivable	130,000	Capital stock	100,000
		Retained earnings	120,000
Total assets	$280,000	Total liabilities and stockholders' equity	$280,000

Direct Method

With the direct method, each item on the income statement must be looked at to determine how much cash each of these activities either generated or used during the year. As an example, if all sales were for cash, cash collections from customers would be equal to sales revenue. However, if sales are made on account, sales revenue must be adjusted for changes in accounts receivable:

> Sales revenue + Beginning accounts receivable − Ending accounts receivable = Cash collections from customers

> **Direct method** Reports cash collected from customers and cash paid for inventory, salaries, wages, and so on.

> **Indirect method** Starts with net income and removes the impact of noncash items and accruals.

or

> Cash collections from customers = Sales
> ± Decrease (Increase) in accounts receivable

In this case, the company had a beginning accounts receivable balance of $0. The ending accounts receivable balance is $130,000, so cash collections from customers equal $670,000 ($800,000 + $0 − $130,000).

Applying the same concept, we see that if all operating expenses are paid in cash, cash outflows for operating expenses will equal $640,000. However, if some of the expenses are incurred on account, expenses must be adjusted for any changes in related accounts payable balances:

> Cash outflows for operating expenses = Operating expenses
> + Beginning accounts payable
> − Ending accounts payable

Therefore, the cash outflow from operating expenses is $580,000 ($640,000 + $0 − $60,000). Assuming that the company's tax payments are made in cash (note that there is no liability for taxes payable), we obtain the following cash flows from operating activities:

Cash Flows from Operating Activities (Direct Method)	
Cash collected from customers	$670,000
Cash payments for operating activities	(580,000)
Cash payments for taxes	(40,000)
Net cash inflow from operating activities	$ 50,000

Indirect Method

The indirect method of preparing the cash flows from operating activities starts with the net income for the period, which is $120,000. This amount is then adjusted to arrive at the amount of cash provided by operating activities. The first adjustment to net income will be the change in accounts receivable. In this case, the increase of $130,000 will be subtracted from revenue. The next adjustment will be for the increase in accounts payable ($60,000). The increase in accounts receivable means that some of the sales were not collected and thus did not result in cash flows. The increase in accounts payable means that current-period expenses were unpaid at the end of the period, decreasing cash outflow.

> *The only difference between the direct and indirect methods is in the presentation of the cash flows from operating activities. Cash flows from investing activities and cash flows from financing activities are calculated in exactly the same way.*

Under the indirect method, cash flows from operations are presented as follows:

Cash Flows from Operating Activities (Indirect Method)	
Net income	$120,000
Adjustments to Reconcile Net Income with Net Cash	
Increase in accounts receivable	(130,000)
Increase in accounts payable	60,000
Net cash inflow from operating activities	$ 50,000

Proponents of the direct method point to the straightforward presentation of the cash flows from operating activities and point out that anyone, even someone with no training in accounting, can very easily use this information in decision making. Proponents of the direct method also argue that the method provides more useful information for evaluating operating efficiency.

Supporters of the indirect method argue that it focuses attention on differences between the cash and accrual bases of accounting, a focus that is very important for decision making. They also point out that if the direct method is used, the indirect schedule must still be prepared. Consequently, more companies choose to report with the indirect method.

The Statement of Cash Flows and the Accounting Equation

The basic accounting equation, as presented in your financial accounting course, is

> Assets = Liabilities + Owners' equity

In more detail,

$$\text{Cash} + \text{NCCA} + \text{Long-term assets} = \text{Current liabilities}$$
$$+ \text{Long-term liabilities}$$
$$+ \text{Capital stock}$$
$$+ \text{Retained earnings (RE)}$$

NCCA = Noncash current assets

We can rearrange the equation so that cash is on the left side and all the other terms are on the right side:

$$\text{Cash} = \text{Current liabilities}$$
$$+ \text{Long-term liabilities}$$
$$+ \text{Capital stock}$$
$$+ \text{RE}$$
$$- \text{NCCA}$$
$$- \text{Long-term assets}$$

Using this equation, we see that any changes in cash (the left side of the equation) must be accompanied by a corresponding change on the right side of the equation. For example, the following table is illustrative:

Transaction	Activity	Left Side	Right Side
Collect accounts receivable	Operating	+ Cash	− NCCA
Prepay insurance	Operating	− Cash	+ NCCA
Collect customer's deposit	Operating	+ Cash	+ Current liabilities
Pay suppliers	Operating	− Cash	− Current liabilities
Make a cash sale	Operating	+ Cash	+ RE
Sell equipment	Investing	+ Cash	− Long-term assets
Buy equipment	Investing	− Cash	+ Long-term assets
Issue bonds	Financing	+ Cash	+ Long-term liabilities
Retire bonds	Financing	− Cash	− Long-term liabilities
Issue capital stock	Financing	+ Cash	+ Capital stock
Buy treasury stock	Financing	− Cash	− Capital stock
Pay dividends	Financing	− Cash	− Retained earnings

LO3 Preparing the Statement of Cash Flows

To prepare the statement of cash flows, we must gather appropriate information, which includes comparative balance sheets (last year's and this year's), the current income statement, and additional information needed to analyze noncash transactions. After gathering the preceding information, we must complete six steps in preparing the statement of cash flows:

1. Compute the net change in cash (increase or decrease)

2. Compute net cash provided or used by operating activities

3. Compute net cash provided or used by investing activities

4. Compute net cash provided or used by financing activities

5. Compute net cash flow by combining the results from operating, investing, and financing activities

6. Report any significant noncash investing and/or financing activities in a separate schedule or a footnote

As an example, consider the financial statements for Robyn's Boutique, which retails children's clothes:

Robyn's Boutique Income Statement For the Year Ended December 31, 2011		
Revenues and Gains		
Sales revenue	$700,000	
Interest income	75,000	
Gain on sale of vehicle	25,000	
Total revenues and gains		$800,000
Expenses and Losses		
Cost of goods sold	$500,000	
Payroll expense	50,000	
Insurance expense	30,000	
Interest expense	7,000	
Rent expense	18,000	
Depreciation	35,000	
Loss on sale of long-term investments	25,000	
Income tax expense	40,000	
Total expenses and losses		705,000
Net income		$ 95,000

Robyn's Boutique Comparative Balance Sheets		
	12/31/2011	12/31/2010
Cash	$130,000	$110,000
Accounts receivable	130,000	120,000
Inventory	225,000	215,000
Prepaid insurance	25,000	30,000
Total current assets	$510,000	$475,000
Long-term investments	$110,000	$ 75,000
Land	200,000	175,000
Property and equipment	215,000	95,000
Accumulated depreciation	(105,000)	(80,000)
Total long-term assets	$420,000	$265,000
Total assets	$930,000	$740,000
Accounts payable	$ 60,000	$ 50,000
Payroll payable	10,000	8,000
Income tax payable	10,000	9,000
Total current liabilities	$ 80,000	$ 67,000
Notes payable	400,000	380,000
Total liabilities	$480,000	$447,000
Capital stock	200,000	100,000
Retained earnings	250,000	193,000
Total liabilities and stockholders' equity	$930,000	$740,000

Additional information

1. Long-term investments were purchased for $85,000.

2. Long-term investments were sold for $25,000, with a book value of $50,000, resulting in a loss of $25,000.

3. Land was purchased for $25,000; $5,000 of the purchase price was paid in cash. The remaining $20,000 was borrowed from the seller.

4. Equipment was purchased for $180,000.

5. A vehicle with an original cost of $60,000 and a book value of $50,000 was sold for $75,000, resulting in a gain of $25,000.

6. Capital stock was issued for $100,000 in cash.

7. Dividends of $38,000 were paid.

Step 1: Compute the Net Change in Cash

The net change in cash, as shown on the balance sheet, is $20,000.

Step 2: Compute Net Cash Provided or Used by Operating Activities

Direct Method

Operating activities generating cash inflows for Robyn's Boutique include selling goods and services and collecting interest income. Sales revenue was reported as $700,000. However, we must consider the change in accounts receivable to determine how much cash was actually collected from sales. Using the formula on page 287, we find that cash collections are equal to $690,000 ($700,000 sales + $120,000 beginning accounts receivable − $130,000 ending accounts receivable). Interest income reported on the income statement is $75,000. How can we tell whether the entire $75,000 was collected in cash? In this case, because there is no "interest receivable" account on the balance sheet, the entire amount must have been collected in cash.

Operating activities that generate cash outflows include buying merchandise for resale to customers, making payments to employees, and making payments for other operating expenses, such as insurance, interest, rent, and taxes. The cost of goods sold is reported at $500,000. However, cash outflows for purchases of inventory may be different. To determine the amount of cash expended to purchase inventory, we must analyze changes in the inventory account as well as changes in accounts payable, because inventory purchases are normally made on credit. Using the cost-of-goods-sold model for a merchandising company developed in Chapter 2, we have

Beginning inventory + Cost of goods purchased = 10

Consequently,

Cost of goods purchased = Cost of goods sold
− Beginning inventory
+ Ending inventory

Therefore, the cost of goods purchased by Robyn's is $510,000 ($500,000 − $215,000 + $225,000). However, we still don't know whether all these purchases were in cash. Using the formula developed earlier for analyzing cash expenditures for operating expenses, we obtain

> Cash outflows for purchases = Cost of goods purchased
> + Beginning accounts payable
> − Ending accounts payable

Robyn's cash outflows for purchases equal $500,000 ($510,000 + $50,000 − $60,000).

Next, consider the payroll expense of $50,000. Once again, if any payroll expense is accrued at the end of the year for employees who are owed wages but not paid by year's end, the payroll expense must be adjusted for changes in payroll liabilities to determine the cash outflows for payroll. The formula is as follows:

> Cash outflows for payroll = Payroll expense
> + Beginning payroll payable
> − Ending payroll payable

Cash outflows for payroll are therefore $48,000 ($50,000 + $8,000 − $10,000).

Another way to look at the cash outflows for payroll is to assume that Robyn's paid the amount owed from last year ($8,000) plus all this year's expense ($50,000), except the amount owed at the end of the current year ($10,000)—in other words, $8,000 + $50,000 − $10,000 = $48,000.

The next item on the income statement is insurance expense. Although there are no liabilities for insurance at the end of 2010 or 2011, you will note that the balance sheet does include an asset called prepaid insurance, with a beginning-year balance of $30,000 and an ending-year balance of $25,000. The $30,000 beginning balance represents prepayments that were made in 2010 for insurance coverage provided in 2011. This $30,000 was expensed on the income statement in 2011 as insurance coverage provided for Robyn's Boutique. Likewise, the $25,000 prepaid balance at the end of 2011 represents cash outflows for insurance that occurred in 2011. This amount will be expensed on the income statement for the year ended December 31, 2012.

Cash outflows for interest expense and rent expense are equal to $7,000 and $18,000, respectively. Note that Robyn's must have paid for these items in cash because no related liabilities or assets appear on the balance sheet. Although Robyn's also reports a depreciation expense of $35,000, depreciation does not result in a cash outflow. The cash outflow occurs at the time the depreciable property is purchased and is shown in the investing activities section of the cash-flow statement. Finally, income tax expense is equal to $40,000. Adjusting for related increases in income tax liabilities on the balance sheet, we see that cash outflows for income taxes during the year must have been $39,000 ($40,000 income tax expense + Beginning income tax payable balance of $9,000 − Ending income tax payable balance of $10,000), as shown in the following financial statement:

Net Cash Flows from Operating Activities (Direct Method)	
Cash Receipts from	
Sales on account	$ 690,000
Interest	75,000
Cash Payments for	
Inventory purchases	(500,000)
Payroll	(48,000)
Insurance	(25,000)
Interest	(7,000)
Rent expense	(18,000)
Taxes	(39,000)
Net cash provided (used) by operating activities	$ 128,000

Indirect Method

The indirect method reconciles net income with net cash flow from operating activities by taking the income statement amounts of revenues and expenses and adjusting for changes in related noncash assets and liabilities:

> Net income
> + Increases in related liabilities
> + Decreases in related noncash assets
> − Increases in related noncash assets
> − Decreases in related liabilities
> = Cash flow from operating activities

> *In using the indirect method, increases (decreases) in asset (liability) accounts during the year must be deducted from net income. When asset (liability) accounts decrease (increase) during the year, the amount of decrease or increase must be added to net income in arriving at net cash provided by operating activities.*

Robyn's Boutique
Net Cash Flows from Operating Activities (Indirect Method)

Net income	$ 95,000
Adjustments to Reconcile Net Income with Net Cash Provided (Used) by Operating Activities	
Increase in accounts receivable	(10,000)
Increase in inventory	(10,000)
Decrease in prepaid insurance	5,000
Increase in accounts payable	10,000
Increase in payroll payable	2,000
Increase in income taxes payable	1,000
Gain on sale of vehicle	(25,000)
Loss on the sale of securities	25,000
Depreciation expense	35,000
Net cash provided (used) by operating activities	$128,000

Additions to Net Income	Deductions from Net Income
Decrease in accounts receivable	Increase in accounts receivable
Decrease in inventory	Increase in inventory
Decrease in prepaid assets	Increase in prepaid assets
Increase in accounts payable	Decrease in accounts payable
Increase in accrued liabilities	Decrease in accrued liabilities

In addition, gains (losses) on sales of assets and securities must be deducted from (added to) net income because these amounts are not operating cash flows. Although the cash received from the sale will affect cash flow, it will be reported in the investing activities section of the cash flow statement rather than in the operating activities section. Likewise, because depreciation expense does not affect cash flow, it must be added back to net income, via the indirect method.

With the indirect method, the net cash provided by the operating activities section of the cash flow statement for Robyn's Boutique would appear as follows:

Step 3: Compute Net Cash Provided or Used by Investing Activities

Investing activities for Robyn's Boutique include cash inflows from the sale of a vehicle and the sale of long-term investments and cash outflows for purchases of land, equipment, and long-term investments. As shown on the income statement, the sale of the vehicle (listed on the balance sheet as property and equipment) generated a gain of $25,000. However, the actual cash generated from the sale was the sales price of $75,000.

The vehicle that was sold had a book value of $50,000 and originally cost $60,000, meaning that accumulated depreciation was $10,000 ($60,000 − $50,000). Likewise, the sale of securities generates cash inflows equal to the amount of cash that was received ($25,000), not the loss on securities sold.

Long-term investments increased by $35,000 during the year (from $75,000 to $110,000). However, just looking at the net change in the accounts does not really tell the complete story of what happened. During the year, long-term investments were purchased for $85,000 cash (increasing the asset account by $85,000), and investments with a book value of $50,000 were sold.

Equipment was purchased for $180,000. Land was also purchased for $25,000. However, the land purchase was made by paying $5,000 in cash and borrowing the remaining $20,000 from the seller.

Net Cash Flows from Investing Activities

Cash Inflows from		
Sale of note	$ 25,000	
Sale of vehicle	75,000	
Cash Outflows for		
Purchase of long-term investments	(85,000)	
Purchase of equipment	(180,000)	
Purchase of land	(5,000)	
Net cash provided (used) by investing activities	$(170,000)	

The information on the acquisition of land in exchange for the note payable is disclosed on a supplemental schedule of noncash investing and financing activities as follows:

Supplemental Schedule of Noncash Investing and Financing Activities

Acquisition of land in exchange for note payable	$20,000

Step 4: Compute Net Cash Provided or Used by Financing Activities

Activities reported in this section include a $100,000 increase in capital stock and payment of dividends of $38,000:

Net Cash Flows from Financing Activities

Cash Inflows from	
Issuance of stock	$100,000
Cash Outflows for	
Payment of cash dividends	(38,000)
Net cash provided (used) by financing activities	$ 62,000

Step 5: Compute Net Cash Flow by Combining the Results from Operating, Investing, and Financing Activitiess

Combining all the information contained in the three schedules of operating, investing, and financing activities and adding the supplemental schedule, we can easily prepare the completed statement of cash flows for Robyn's Boutique for the year ended December 31, 2011.

Robyn's Boutique
Statement of Cash Flows (Direct Method)
For the Year Ended December 31, 2011

Cash Flows from Operating Activities		
Cash Receipts from		
Sales	$ 690,000	
Interest	75,000	
Total cash receipts		$ 765,000
Cash Payments for		
Inventory purchases	$ 500,000	
Payroll	48,000	
Insurance	25,000	
Interest	7,000	
Rent expense	18,000	
Taxes	39,000	
Total cash payments		$(637,000)
Net cash provided (used) by operating activities		$ 128,000
Cash Flows from Investing Activities		
Sale of securities	$ 25,000	
Sale of vehicle	75,000	
Purchase of equipment	(180,000)	
Purchase of long-term investments	(85,000)	
Purchase of land	(5,000)	
Net cash provided (used) by investing activities		$(170,000)
Cash Flows from Financing Activities		
Issuance of stock	$ 100,000	
Payment of cash dividends	(38,000)	
Net cash provided (used) by financing activities		$ 62,000
Net Increase in Cash		$ 20,000
Cash balance 12/31/09		110,000
Cash balance 12/31/10		$ 130,000

Step 6: Report Any Significant Noncash Investing or Financing Activities in a Separate Schedule or a Footnote

Supplemental Schedule of Noncash Investing and Financing Activities

Acquisition of land in exchange for note payable	$20,000

Chapter review card

➔ Learning Objective and Key Concept Reviews

➔ Key Definitions and Formulas

Online (Located at www.cengagebrain.com)

➔ Flash Cards and Crossword Puzzles

➔ Games and Quizzes

➔ E-Lectures

➔ Homework Assignments (as directed by your instructor)

BRIEF EXERCISES

1. Adjustments to Net Income via the Indirect Method: Operating Activities LO1

Tiffany Company uses the indirect method to prepare the operating activities section of the statement of cash flows. The following activities occurred during the year at Tiffany Company:

a. _____ Depreciation expense
b. _____ Gain on the sale of used delivery truck
c. _____ Bad-debt expense
d. _____ Increase in accounts payable
e. _____ Purchase of a new delivery truck
f. _____ Loss on retirement of bonds
g. _____ Increase in prepaid rent
h. _____ Decrease in inventory
i. _____ Increase in investments
j. _____ Amortization of patents

Required

For each of the preceding items, fill in the blank to indicate whether it would be added to net income (A), deducted from net income (D), or not reported in this section of the statement, under the indirect method (NR).

2. Investing vs. Financing Activities and Cash Equivalents LO1, 3

The following transactions occurred for a company during the year.

a. Purchased a six-month certificate of deposit
b. Purchased a 90-day Treasury bill
c. Issued 10,000 shares of common stock
d. Purchased 5,000 shares of stock of another company
e. Purchased 10,000 shares of its own stock to be held in the treasury
f. Invested $10,000 in a money market fund
g. Sold 1,500 shares of stock of another company
h. Purchased 10-year bonds of another company
i. Issued 20-year bonds
j. Repaid a nine-month bank note

Required

Using the following legend, indicate how each of the preceding transactions would be reported on the statement of cash flows:

II =	inflow from investing activities
OI =	outflow from investing activities
IF =	inflow from financing activities
OF =	outflow from financing activities
CE =	classified as a cash equivalent and included with cash for purposes of preparing the statement of cash flows

3. Operating, Investing, and Financing Activities LO1

The following transactions occurred for a company that uses the direct method to prepare its statement of cash flows.

a. _____ A company purchases its own common stock in the open market and immediately retires it.

b. _____ A company issues common stock in exchange for land.

c. _____ A six-month bank loan is obtained.

d. _____ Thirty-year bonds are issued.

e. _____ A customer pays the balance in an open account.

f. _____ Income taxes are paid.

g. _____ Cash sales are recorded.

h. _____ Cash dividends are declared and paid.

i. _____ A creditor is given common stock in exchange for a long-term note.

j. _____ A new piece of machinery is acquired for cash.

k. _____ Stock of another company is acquired as an investment.

l. _____ Interest is paid on a bank loan.

m. _____ Workers are paid for one week's wages.

Required

For each of the preceding transactions, fill in the blank to indicate whether it would appear in the operating activities section (O), in the investing activities section (I), or in the financing activities section (F). Put an (S) in the blank if the transaction does not affect cash but is reported in a supplemental schedule of noncash activities.

4. Accrual to Cash Conversions LO1, 2

Each of the following cases is an independent situation:

Case 1	
Accounts receivable, beginning balance	$250,000
Accounts receivable, ending balance	200,000
Credit sales for the year	275,000
Cash sales for the year	160,000
Uncollectible accounts written off	135,000
Total cash collections for the year	?
Case 2	
Inventory, beginning balance	$180,000
Inventory, ending balance	155,000
Accounts payable, beginning balance	125,000
Accounts payable, ending balance	115,000
Cost of goods sold	275,000
Cash payments for inventory (assume that all purchases are on account)	?

Case 3	
Prepaid insurance, beginning balance	$ 27,000
Prepaid insurance, ending balance	30,000
Insurance expense	25,000
Cash paid for new insurance	?
Case 4	
Interest payable, beginning balance	$105,000
Interest payable, ending balance	125,000
Interest expense	300,000
Cash payments for interest	?
Case 5	
Income taxes payable, beginning balance	$ 55,000
Income taxes payable, ending balance	75,000
Income tax expense	100,000
Cash payments for income taxes	?

Required

Determine the missing amount for each individual case.

5. Accrual to Cash: Direct Method LO2

Vardy Toys, Inc., prepays insurance on various policies in January of each year. The beginning balance in prepaid insurance was $12,500, and the ending balance was $10,000. The income statement reports insurance expense of $65,000.

Required

Under the direct method, what amount would appear for cash paid for insurance in the operating section of the statement of cash flows?

6. Accrual to Cash: Direct Method LO2

Williams Media, Inc.'s comparative balance sheets included accounts receivable of $100,000 on December 31, 2011, and $125,000 on December 31, 2012. Sales of consulting services reported by Williams Media on its 2012 income statement amounted to $2 million.

Required

What is the amount of cash collections that Williams Media should report in the operating section of its 2012 statement of cash flows, under the assumption that the direct method is used?

7. Accrual to Cash: Direct Method LO2

Workman-Smith Company's comparative balance sheets included inventory of $120,000 on December 31, 2011, and $110,000 on December 31, 2012. Workman-Smith's comparative balance sheets also included accounts payable of $60,000 on December 31, 2011, and $55,000 on December 31, 2012. Workman-Smith's accounts payable balances are composed solely of amounts due to suppliers for purchases of inventory. Cost of goods sold, as reported by Workman-Smith on its 2012 income statement, amounted to $850,000.

Required

What is the amount of cash payments for inventory that Workman-Smith should report in the operating activities section of its 2012 statement of cash flows, under the assumption that the direct method is used?

8. Impact of Cash and Stock Dividends LO1, 3

The account balances for the noncash current assets and current liabilities of Abraham Music Company are as follows:

	December 31	
	2011	2012
Dividends payable	$ 50,000	$ 40,000
Retained earnings	545,000	375,000

Other information for 2011:

a. Abraham reported $375,000 in net income for 2011.

b. The company declared and distributed a stock dividend of $85,000 during the year.

c. The company declared cash dividends at the end of each quarter and paid them within the first 30 days of the next quarter.

Required

A. Determine the amount of cash dividends paid during the year for presentation in the financing activities section of the statement of cash flows.

B. Should the stock dividend appear on a statement of cash flows? Explain your answer.

9. Investing Activities and Noncash Activities LO1, 3

Van Buren Company acquires a piece of land by signing a $100,000 promissory note and making a $30,000 down payment.

Required

How should this transaction be reported on the statement of cash flows?

10. Cash Equivalents and Investing Activities LO1, 3

Van Patten, Inc., made two purchases during September. One was a $25,000 certificate of deposit that matures in 90 days. The other was a $50,000 investment in Microsoft common stock that will be held indefinitely.

Required

How should each of these transactions be treated on the statement of cash flows?

11. Financing Activities LO1, 3

Walden Book Buyers buys 5,000 shares of its own common stock at $25 per share. The company purchases the shares as Treasury stock.

Required

How is this transaction reported on the statement of cash flows?

12. Investing Activities: Indirect Method LO1, 3

Washburn Delivery Company sold a company car for $12,000. Its original cost was $35,000, and the accumulated depreciation at the time of sale was $20,000.

Required

How does the transaction to record the sale appear on a statement of cash flows prepared with the indirect method?

13. Cash Equivalents LO1, 3

Whitney R.V.'s, Inc., has invested its excess cash in the following instruments during December 2011:

Certificate of deposit, due Jan. 31, 2012	$100,000
Certificate of deposit, due May 31, 2012	150,000
Investment in City of Portland bonds, due June 30, 2012	110,000
Investment in Sheetz, Inc., stock	125,000
A money market fund	225,000
90-day Treasury bills	125,000
Treasury note, due December 2012	200,000

Required

A. What should be included in cash equivalents at year-end 2011?

B. Where should the amount of cash equivalents be disclosed?

PROBLEMS

14. Adjustments to Income via the Indirect Method: Operating Activites LO1, 2, 3

The following account balances are for the noncash current assets and current liabilities of Wynn Bicycle Company at the end of 2011 and 2012.

	December 31	
	2011	2012
Accounts receivable	$ 4,000	$ 6,000
Inventory	30,000	20,000
Office supplies	5,000	8,000
Accounts payable	10,000	7,000
Salaries and wages payable	2,500	4,000
Interest payable	1,500	2,500
Income taxes payable	5,500	2,500

In addition, the income statement for 2012 is as follows:

Sales revenue	$110,000
Cost of goods sold	85,000
Gross profit	$ 25,000
General and administrative expense	$ 9,000
Depreciation expense	2,000
Income before interest and taxes	$ 14,000
Interest expense	2,000
Income before tax	$ 12,000
Income tax expense	4,800
Net income	$ 7,200

Required

A. Prepare the operating activities section of the statement of cash flows, using the indirect method.

B. What does the use of the direct method reveal about a company that the indirect method does not?

15. Impact of Operating and Investing Activities: Indirect Method LOI, 2, 3

The following account balances are taken from the records of Roadhouse Corporation for the past two years:

	December 31	
	2012	2011
Plant and equipment	$750,000	$500,000
Accumulated depreciation	160,000	200,000
Patents	92,000	80,000
Retained earnings	825,000	675,000

Other information available for 2012 is as follows:
a. Net income for the year was $200,000.
b. Depreciation expense on plant and equipment was $50,000.
c. Plant and equipment with an original cost of $150,000 was sold for $64,000. (You will need to determine the book value of the assets sold.)

d. Amortization expense on patents was $8,000.
e. Both new plant and equipment and patents were purchased for cash during the year.

Required

Indicate, with amounts, how all items related to these long-term assets would be reported in the 2012 statement of cash flows, including any adjustments in the operating activities section of the statement. Assume that Roadhouse Corp. uses the indirect method.

16. Operating Activities: Direct vs. Indirect Method LOI, 2, 3

The account balances for the noncash current assets of Allen Company are as follows:

	December 31	
	2011	2012
Accounts receivable	$ 45,000	$ 38,000
Inventory	40,000	50,000
Prepaid insurance	21,000	17,000
Total current assets	$106,000	$105,000

Net income for 2012 is $35,000. Depreciation expense is $22,000. Assume that all sales and all purchases are on account.

Required

A. Prepare the operating activities section of the statement of cash flows, using the indirect method. Explain why cash flow from operating activities is more or less than the net income for the period shown.

B. What additional information do you need to prepare the operating activities section of the statement of cash flows, using the direct method?

C. Explain the usefulness of each method for managerial decision making.

MAKING IT REAL!

ACCT2 will prepare you for the real world by showing you how accounting information is used to make business decisions.

Throughout the text, take a look at the Making it Real features that highlight everyday businesses.

GO ONLINE!
Visit CengageNOW™ for **ACCT2** at www.cengagebrain.com.

- A **new case**, the Daily Grind, puts you in the role of a managerial accountant as you apply the concepts and techniques you have learned to a small coffee shop.
- View 14 videos from the **Experience Accounting Video** series!

The brief **Experience Accounting Videos** demonstrate how today's companies fuel better business performance. Several of the companies featured include:

BP: Process Costing
Washburn Guitars: Job-Order Costing
Hard Rock Café: Capital Investments
Cold Stone Creamery: Activity-Based Costing
High Sierra: Budgets & Profit Planning
Boyne Resorts: Cost-Volume-Profit Analysis
Navistar: Relevant Costs
Zingerman's Deli: Cost Behavior

COLD STONE   HIGH SIERRA   Washburn

ACCT

Introduction

When decisions are affected by cash flows that are paid or received in different periods, it is necessary to adjust those cash flows for the time value of money (TVM). Because of our ability to earn interest on money invested, we would prefer to receive $1 today rather than a year from now. Likewise, we would prefer to pay $1 a year from now rather than today. A common technique used to adjust cash flows received or paid in different periods is to discount those cash flows by finding their present value. The **present value (PV)** of cash flows is the amount of future cash flows, discounted to their equivalent worth today. To fully understand the calculations involved in finding the present value of future cash flows, it is necessary to step back and examine the nature of interest and the calculation of interest received and paid. Interest is simply a payment made to use someone else's money. When you invest money in a bank account, the bank pays you interest for the use of your money for a certain length of time. Clearly, if you invest $100 and the bank pays you $106 at the end of the year, then you earned $6 of interest on your money (and 6 percent interest for the year).

Future Value

Mathematically, the relationship between your initial investment (present value), the amount in the bank at the end of the year (future value), and the interest rate (r) is as follows:

$$FV_{(Year\ 1)} = PV(1 + r)$$

In our example, $FV_{(Year\ 1)} = 100(1 + 0.06) = \$106$. If you leave your money in the bank for a second year, what happens? Will you earn an additional $6 of interest?

It depends on whether the bank pays you simple interest or compound interest. **Simple interest** is interest on the invested amount only, whereas **compound interest** is interest on the invested amount plus interest on previous interest earned but not withdrawn. Simple interest is sometimes computed on short-term investments and debts (i.e., those which are shorter than six months to a year). Compound interest is typically computed for financial arrangements longer than one year. We will assume that interest is compounded in all examples in this book. Extending the future-value formula to find the amount we have in the bank in two years gives us the formula

$$FV_{(Year\ 2)} = PV(1 + r)(1 + r)$$

or

$$FV_{(Year\ 2)} = PV(1 + r)^2$$

In our example, $FV_{(Year\ 2)} = 100(1 + 0.06)^2$, or $112.36. We earned $6.36 of interest in Year 2—$6 on our original $100 investment and $0.36 on the $6 of interest earned but not withdrawn in Year 1 ($6 × 0.06).

In this example, we have assumed that compounding is on an annual basis. Compounding can also be calculated semiannually, quarterly, monthly, daily, or even continually. Go back to our original $100 investment in the bank. If the bank pays 6 percent interest compounded semiannually instead of annually, we would have $106.09 after one year. Note that the interest rate is typically expressed as a percentage per year. We are really earning 3 percent for each semiannual period, not 6 percent. It

---

Present value (PV) The amount of future cash flows, discounted to their equivalent worth today.

Simple interest Interest on the invested amount only.

Compound interest Interest on the invested amount plus interest on previous interest earned but not withdrawn.

Exhibit A-1 The Impact of More Frequent Compounding on the Future Value of $100

Annual Compounding

$100.00   6% $106.00

0   1 year

Semiannual Compounding

$100.00   3% $103.00   3% $106.09

0   6 months   1 year

Monthly Compounding

$100.00 $100.50 $101.00 $101.51 $102.02 $102.53 $103.04 $103.55 $104.07 $104.59 $105.11 $105.64 $106.17

0.5%   0.5%   0.5%   0.5%   0.5%   0.5%   0.5%   0.5%   0.5%   0.5%   0.5%   0.5%

0   1   2   3   4   5   6   7   8   9   10   11   12 months

is usually easier to visualize the concept of interest rate compounding graphically, with the help of time lines. Exhibit A-1 graphically demonstrates the impact of annual, semiannual, and monthly compounding of the 6 percent annual rate on our original $100 investment.

Mathematically, our formula for future value can once again be modified slightly to account for interest rates compounded at different intervals. We have $FV_{(n \text{ periods in the future})} = PV(1 + r)^n$, where n is the number of compounding periods per year multiplied by the number of years and r is the annual interest rate divided by the number of compounding periods per year. Before the advent of handheld calculators and computers,

tables were developed to simplify the calculation of FV by providing values for $(1 + r)^n$ for several combinations of n and r. These tables are still commonly used, and an example is provided in Exhibit A-2. The factors in Exhibit A-2 are commonly referred to as cumulative factors (CF) and are simply calculations of $(1 + r)^n$ for various values of n and r.

Using this new terminology, we see that the future value formula is simply

$$FV_{(n \text{ periods in the future})} = PV(CF_{n,r})$$

Exhibit A-2 Future Value of $1

n/r	0.5%	1%	2%	3%	4%	5%	6%	7%	8%	10%	12%
1	1.0050	1.0100	1.0200	1.0300	1.0400	1.0500	1.0600	1.0700	1.0800	1.1000	1.1200
2	1.0100	1.0201	1.0404	1.0609	1.0816	1.1025	1.1236	1.1449	1.1664	1.2100	1.2544
3	1.0151	1.0303	1.0612	1.0927	1.1249	1.1576	1.1910	1.2250	1.2597	1.3310	1.4049
4	1.0202	1.0406	1.0824	1.1255	1.1699	1.2155	1.2625	1.3108	1.3605	1.4641	1.5735
5	1.0253	1.0510	1.1041	1.1593	1.2167	1.2763	1.3382	1.4026	1.4693	1.6105	1.7623
6	1.0304	1.0615	1.1262	1.1941	1.2653	1.3401	1.4185	1.5007	1.5869	1.7716	1.9738
7	1.0355	1.0721	1.1487	1.2299	1.3159	1.4071	1.5036	1.6058	1.7138	1.9487	2.2107
8	1.0407	1.0829	1.1717	1.2668	1.3686	1.4775	1.5938	1.7182	1.8509	2.1436	2.4760
9	1.0459	1.0937	1.1951	1.3048	1.4233	1.5513	1.6895	1.8385	1.9990	2.3579	2.7731
10	1.0511	1.1046	1.2190	1.3439	1.4802	1.6289	1.7908	1.9672	2.1589	2.5937	3.1058
11	1.0564	1.1157	1.2434	1.3842	1.5395	1.7103	1.8983	2.1049	2.3316	2.8531	3.4785
12	1.0617	1.1268	1.2682	1.4258	1.6010	1.7959	2.0122	2.2522	2.5182	3.1384	3.8960
24	1.1272	1.2697	1.6084	2.0328	2.5633	3.2251	4.0489	5.0724	6.3412	9.8497	15.1786
36	1.1967	1.4308	2.0399	2.8983	4.1039	5.7918	8.1473	11.4239	15.9682	30.9127	59.1356
48	1.2705	1.6122	2.5871	4.1323	6.5705	10.4013	16.3939	25.7289	40.2106	97.0172	230.3908

With 6 percent annual compounding, our $100 investment grows to

$$\$100(CF_{1,6\%}) = \$100(1.060) = \$106.00$$

With 6 percent semiannual compounding,

$$\$100(CF_{2,3\%}) = \$100(1.0609) = \$106.09$$

With 6 percent monthly compounding,

$$\$100(CF_{12,.5\%}) = \$100(1.0617) = \$106.17$$

Most financial calculators will compute future value after the user inputs data for present value, the annual interest rate, the number of compounding periods per year, and the number of years. For example, using a business calculator to compute the future value of $100.00 with 6 percent annual compounding requires the following steps:

Keys	Display	Description
1 P/YR	1.00	Sets compounding periods per year to 1 because interest is compounded annually
100 ± PV	–100.00	Stores the present value as a negative number
6.0 I/YR	6.0	Stores the annual interest rate
1 N	1	Sets the number of years or compounding periods to 1
FV	106.00	Calculates the future value

Calculating the future value of $100 with 6 percent monthly compounding simply requires changing both the compounding periods per year (P/YR) and the number of compounding periods (N) to 12:

Keys	Display	Description
12 P/YR	12	Sets compounding periods per year to 12
12 N	12	Sets the number of compounding periods to 12
FV	106.17	Calculates the future value

Exhibit A-3 Finding the Future Value by Using the FV Function in Excel

Likewise, many spreadsheet programs have built-in functions (formulas) that calculate future value. The Excel function called FV simply requires input of an interest rate (Rate), the number of compounding periods (Nper), and present value (Pv) in the following format: =FV(Rate, Nper, Pmt, Pv, Type).[1] Entries for Pmt and Type are not applicable to simple future-value problems. To calculate the future value of $100 in one year at 6 percent interest compounded monthly, enter =FV(.5%,12,−100). Excel returns a value of $106.17 (see Exhibit A-3).

Present Value

A present-value formula can be derived directly from the future-value formula. If

$$FV_{(n \text{ periods in the future})} = PV(1 + r)^n$$

then

$$PV = \frac{FV}{(1 + r)^n} \quad \text{or} \quad PV = FV\left(\frac{1}{(1 + r)^n}\right)$$

Just as a cumulative factor table was developed to calculate $(1 + r)^n$, present-value tables calculate $1 \div (1 + r)^n$

[1]Built-in functions can be accessed in Microsoft Excel by clicking on the Formula icon or the Insert Function icon and selecting or searching for the desired formula. Formulas for the time value of money are included in the Financial category of formulas.

Exhibit A-4 Present Value of $1

n/r	0.5%	1%	2%	3%	4%	5%	6%	7%	8%	10%	12%
1	0.9950	0.9901	0.9804	0.9709	0.9615	0.9524	0.9434	0.9346	0.9259	0.9091	0.8929
2	0.9901	0.9803	0.9612	0.9426	0.9246	0.9070	0.8900	0.8734	0.8573	0.8264	0.7972
3	0.9851	0.9706	0.9423	0.9151	0.8890	0.8638	0.8396	0.8163	0.7938	0.7513	0.7118
4	0.9802	0.9610	0.9238	0.8885	0.8548	0.8227	0.7921	0.7629	0.7350	0.6830	0.6355
5	0.9754	0.9515	0.9057	0.8626	0.8219	0.7835	0.7473	0.7130	0.6806	0.6209	0.5674
6	0.9705	0.9420	0.8880	0.8375	0.7903	0.7462	0.7050	0.6663	0.6302	0.5645	0.5066
7	0.9657	0.9327	0.8706	0.8131	0.7599	0.7107	0.6651	0.6227	0.5835	0.5132	0.4523
8	0.9609	0.9235	0.8535	0.7894	0.7307	0.6768	0.6274	0.5820	0.5403	0.4665	0.4039
9	0.9561	0.9143	0.8368	0.7664	0.7026	0.6446	0.5919	0.5439	0.5002	0.4241	0.3606
10	0.9513	0.9053	0.8203	0.7441	0.6756	0.6139	0.5584	0.5083	0.4632	0.3855	0.3220
11	0.9466	0.8963	0.8043	0.7224	0.6496	0.5847	0.5268	0.4751	0.4289	0.3505	0.2875
12	0.9419	0.8874	0.7885	0.7014	0.6246	0.5568	0.4970	0.4440	0.3971	0.3186	0.2567
24	0.8872	0.7876	0.6217	0.4919	0.3901	0.3101	0.2470	0.1971	0.1577	0.1015	0.0659
36	0.8356	0.6989	0.4902	0.3450	0.2437	0.1727	0.1227	0.0875	0.0626	0.0323	0.0169
48	0.7871	0.6203	0.3865	0.2420	0.1522	0.0961	0.0610	0.0389	0.0249	0.0103	0.0043

for various combinations of *n* and *r*. These factors are called discount factors, or DFs. An example of a DF table is provided in Exhibit A-4. Our PV formula can now be rewritten as follows:

$$PV = FV(DF_{n,r})$$

Now we are ready to calculate the present value of a future cash flow. For example, how much must be invested today at 8 percent compounded annually to have $1,000 in two years? Mathematically,

$$PV = \$1,000\left(\frac{1}{(1 \times 0.08)^2}\right) = \$857.34$$

or, if we use the DF table,

$$PV = \$1,000(DF_{2,.08}) = \$1,000(0.8573) = \$857.30 \text{ (rounded)}$$

Once again, the frequency of compounding affects our calculation. Just as more frequent compounding *increases* future values, increasing the frequency of compounding decreases present values. This effect is demonstrated in Exhibit A-5 for annual, semiannual, and quarterly compounding.

Exhibit A-5 The Impact of More Frequent Compounding on the Present Value of $1,000

Using a business calculator to compute present value is similar to using it to compute future value. For example, the present value of $1,000 received or paid in two years at 8 percent compounded quarterly requires the following steps:

Keys	Display	Description
4 [P/YR]	4.00	Sets the compounding periods per year to 4
1,000 [FV]	1000.00	Stores the future value as a positive number
8.0 [I/YR]	8.0	Stores the annual interest rate
8 [N]	8.0	Sets the number of compounding periods to 8
[PV]	−853.49	Calculates the present value

In Microsoft Excel, the built-in function is called PV and requires input of the applicable interest rate (Rate), number of compounding periods (Nper), and future value (Fv) in the format =PV(Rate, Nper, Pmt, Fv, Type). In the previous example, entering =PV(2%,8,−1000) returns a value of $853.49. Note once again that Pmt and Type are left blank in simple present-value problems, as they were in future-value calculations (see Exhibit A-6).

When FV and PV are known, either formula can be used to calculate one of the other variables in the equations (n or r). For example, if you know that your $100 bank deposit will be worth $200 in six years, what rate of interest, compounded annually, will you earn? Using the mathematical present-value formula, we have

$$PV = FV\left(\frac{1}{(1 + r)^n}\right) \quad \text{or} \quad \$100 = \$200\left(\frac{1}{(1 + r)^6}\right)$$

Simplifying by dividing each side by $100 gives $1 = 2 \div (1 + r)^6$, and multiplying each side by $(1 + r)^6$ simplifies the equation to $(1 + r)^6 = 2$. The value of r can be calculated by using a financial calculator or, mathematically, by using logarithmic functions.[2] In using a business calculator, the following steps are typical:

Keys	Display	Description
1 [P/YR]	1.00	Sets compounding periods per year to 1
200 [FV]	200	Stores the future value
100 [±][PV]	−100	Stores the present value as a negative number
2 [N]	2.0	Sets the number of compounding periods to 2
[I/YR]	0.122462	Calculates the annual interest rate

The tables can also be used to solve for n and r. Using our table formula, $PV = FV(DF_{n,r})$, we see that if $PV = 100$ and $FV = 200$, DF must be equal to 0.5. If we know that n is equal to 6, we can simply move across the table until we find a factor close to 0.5. The factor at 12 percent is 0.5066. If we examine the factors at both 10 percent (0.5645) and 14 percent (0.456), we can infer that the actual interest rate will be slightly higher than 12 percent. Our logarithmic calculation is 12.2462 percent. In Microsoft Excel, the RATE function requires input of Nper, Pv, and Fv in the following

Exhibit A-6 Finding the Present Value by Using the PV Function in Excel

Function Arguments [?][X]

PV

Rate	2%	= 0.02
Nper	8	= 8
Pmt		= number
Fv	-1000	= -1000
Type		= number

= 853.4903712

Returns the present value of an investment: the total amount that a series of future payments is worth now.

Fv is the future value, or a cash balance you want to attain after the last payment is made.

Formula result = $853.49

Help on this function   [OK] [Cancel]

[2] $(1 + r)^6 = 2$ can be rewritten in logarithmic form as $\log(1 + r)^6 = \log 2$, or $6 \log(1 + r) = \log 2$. Therefore, $\log(1 + r) = \log 2 \div 6$, which simplifies to $\log(1 + r) = 0.1155245$. Switching back to the equivalent exponential form, we have $e^{0.1155245} = (1 + r)$, $(1 + r) = 1.122462$, and $r = 0.122462$ (12.2462%).

Exhibit A-7 Finding the Interest Rate by Using the RATE Function in Excel

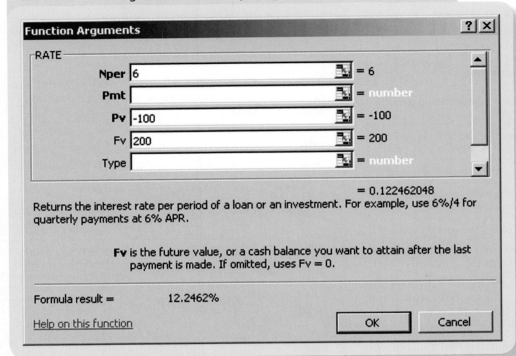

Function Arguments   `? X`

RATE

Nper `6`   = 6

Pmt `[                    ]`   = number

Pv `-100`   = -100

Fv `200`   = 200

Type `[                    ]`   = number

= 0.122462048

Returns the interest rate per period of a loan or an investment. For example, use 6%/4 for quarterly payments at 6% APR.

Fv is the future value, or a cash balance you want to attain after the last payment is made. If omitted, uses Fv = 0.

Formula result =   12.2462%

Help on this function   `OK`   `Cancel`

the DF formula, we see that DF must again be equal to 0.5. If r is known to be 12 percent, we simply move down the 12 percent column until we find a DF close to 0.5. Not surprisingly, we find a factor of 0.5066 for an n of 6. Examining the factors for an n of 5(0.5674) and 7(0.4523), we can infer that the actual time will be something slightly greater than 6 years. The NPER function in Microsoft Excel requires input of Rate, Pmt, Pv, Fv, and Type in the format =NPER(12%, −100, 200) and returns a value of 6.116 years. Note that Pv is entered as a negative amount, and that Pmt

format: =RATE(Nper, Pmt, Pv, Fv, Type, Guess). Because Excel uses an iterative trial-and-error method to calculate the interest rate, Guess provides a starting point. It is generally not necessary but may be required in complicated problems. Entering =RATE(6,−100,200) returns an interest rate of 12.2462 percent (see Exhibit A-7).

The calculation of n is done in a similar fashion. If we know that our investment earns 12 percent but do not know how long it will take for our $100 to grow to $200, then, mathematically, we have

$$PV = FV\left(\frac{1}{(1 + r)^n}\right)$$

or

$$\$100 = \$200\left(\frac{1}{(1 + 0.12)^n}\right)$$

Solving the equation by using logarithms or a financial calculator gives us an n of 6.116 years.[3] Using

and Type are not necessary, because this is essentially a present-value problem (see Exhibit A-8).

Exhibit A-8 Finding the Number of Periods by Using the NPER Function in Excel

Function Arguments   `? X`

NPER

Rate `12%`   = 0.12

Pmt `[                    ]`   = number

Pv `-100`   = -100

Fv `200`   = 200

Type `[                    ]`   = number

= 6.116255374

Returns the number of periods for an investment based on periodic, constant payments and a constant interest rate.

Fv is the future value, or a cash balance you want to attain after the last payment is made. If omitted, zero is used.

Formula result =   6.116

Help on this function   `OK`   `Cancel`

[3]Using a business calculator, we simply input 1 P/YR, 200 FV, 100 PV, and 12 I/YR and solve for n. Then we can rewrite $(1 + 0.12)^n = 2$ in logarithmic form as $\log(1 + 0.12)^n = \log 2$, or $n \log 1.12 = \log 2$. Therefore, $n = (\log 2) \div (\log 1.12) = 6.116$.

Annuities

An **annuity** is a series of cash flows of equal amount paid or received at regular intervals.[4] Common examples include mortgage and loan payments. The present value of an ordinary annuity (PVA) is the amount invested or borrowed today that will provide for a series of withdrawals or payments of equal amount for a set number of periods. Conceptually, the present value of an annuity is simply the sum of the present values of each withdrawal or payment. For example, the present value

The mathematical formula for PVA can be derived from the formula for PV and is equal to

$$PVA_{n,r} = R \left(\frac{1 - \dfrac{1}{(1 + r)^n}}{r} \right)$$

where R refers to the periodic payment or withdrawal (commonly called a *rent*). Calculated values for various combinations of n and r are provided in Exhibit A-9.

Exhibit A-9 Present Value of an Ordinary Annuity

n/r	0.50%	1%	2%	3%	4%	5%	6%	7%	8%	10%	12%
1	0.9950	0.9901	0.9804	0.9709	0.9615	0.9524	0.9434	0.9346	0.9259	0.9091	0.8929
2	1.9851	1.9704	1.9416	1.9135	1.8861	1.8594	1.8334	1.8080	1.7833	1.7355	1.6901
3	2.9702	2.9410	2.8839	2.8286	2.7751	2.7232	2.6730	2.6243	2.5771	2.4869	2.4018
4	3.9505	3.9020	3.8077	3.7171	3.6299	3.5460	3.4651	3.3872	3.3121	3.1699	3.0373
5	4.9259	4.8534	4.7135	4.5797	4.4518	4.3295	4.2124	4.1002	3.9927	3.7908	3.6048
6	5.8964	5.7955	5.6014	5.4172	5.2421	5.0757	4.9173	4.7665	4.6229	4.3553	4.1114
7	6.8621	6.7282	6.4720	6.2303	6.0021	5.7864	5.5824	5.3893	5.2064	4.8684	4.5638
8	7.8230	7.6517	7.3255	7.0197	6.7327	6.4632	6.2098	5.9713	5.7466	5.3349	4.9676
9	8.7791	8.5660	8.1622	7.7861	7.4353	7.1078	6.8017	6.5152	6.2469	5.7590	5.3282
10	9.7304	9.4713	8.9826	8.5302	8.1109	7.7217	7.3601	7.0236	6.7101	6.1446	5.6502
11	10.6770	10.3676	9.7868	9.2526	8.7605	8.3064	7.8869	7.4987	7.1390	6.4951	5.9377
12	11.6189	11.2551	10.5753	9.9540	9.3851	8.8633	8.3838	7.9427	7.5361	6.8137	6.1944
24	22.5629	21.2434	18.9139	16.9355	15.2470	13.7986	12.5504	11.4693	10.5288	8.9847	7.7843
36	32.8710	30.1075	25.4888	21.8323	18.9083	16.5469	14.6210	13.0352	11.7172	9.6765	8.1924
48	42.5803	37.9740	30.6731	25.2667	21.1951	18.0772	15.6500	13.7305	12.1891	9.8969	8.2972

of an annuity of $100 paid at the end of each of the next four years at an interest rate of 10 percent looks like this:

Although cumbersome, the present value of an annuity can be calculated by using the present-value table on page 302 (see Exhibit A-4) to find the present value of each $100 payment:

$$PVA = \$100(DF_{1,.10}) + \$100(DF_{2,.10}) + \$100(DF_{3,.10}) + \$100(DF_{4,.10})$$

$$= \$100(0.9091) + \$100(0.8264) + \$100(0.7513) + \$100(0.6830)$$

$$= \$316.98$$

The PVA formula can therefore be rewritten as follows:

$$PVA = R(DFA_{n,r})$$

As previously discussed, common examples of annuities are mortgages and loans. For example, say you are thinking about buying a new car. Your bank offers to loan you money at a special 6 percent rate compounded monthly for a 24-month term. If the maximum monthly payment you can afford is $399, how large a car loan can you get? In other words, what is the present value of a $399 annuity paid at the end of each of the next 24 months, assuming an interest rate of 6 percent compounded monthly? Using a time line, we see that the problem looks like this:

Annuity A series of cash flows of equal amount paid or received at regular intervals.

[4]An ordinary annuity is paid or received at the end of each period, whereas an annuity due is paid or received at the beginning of each period. In examples throughout this book, we will assume that the annuity is ordinary.

PVA $399 $399 $399 $399 $399 $399 $399 $399 $399 $399 $399 $399 $399 $399 $399 $399 $399 $399 $399 $399 $399 $399 $399 $399

| 0.5% | 0.5% | 0.5% | 0.5% | 0.5% | 0.5% | 0.5% | 0.5% | 0.5% | 0.5% | 0.5% | 0.5% | 0.5% | 0.5% | 0.5% | 0.5% | 0.5% | 0.5% | 0.5% | 0.5% | 0.5% | 0.5% | 0.5% | 0.5% |

0   24 months

Mathematically,

$$PVA_{24,.005} = 399\left(\dfrac{1 - \dfrac{1}{(1 + 0.5)^{24}}}{0.005}\right)$$

Using the DFA table, we have

$$PVA_{24,.005} = \$399(DFA_{24,.005}) = \$399(22.5629) = \$9{,}002.60$$
(rounded)

The following steps are common in using a business calculator:

Keys	Display	Description
12 [P/YR]	12.00	Sets periods per year
2×12 [N]	24.00	Stores number of periods in loan
0 [PV]	0	Stores the amount left to pay after 2 years
6 [I/YR]	6	Stores interest rate
399 [±] [PMT]	−399.00	Stores desired payment as a negative number
[PV]	9,002.58	Calculates the loan you can afford with a $399-per-month payment

In Microsoft Excel, the PV function is used to calculate the present value of an annuity, with additional entries for the payment amount (Pmt) and type of annuity (Type). The payment is entered as a negative number, and the annuity type is 0 for ordinary and 1 for an annuity due. The format is therefore PV(Rate, Nper, Pmt, Fv, Type). Entering =PV(.5%,24,−399,0,0) returns a value of $9,002.58 (see Exhibit A-10).

The PVA formula can also be used to calculate R, r, and n if the other variables are known. This is most easily accomplished by using the DFA table or a financial calculator. If the car you want to buy costs $20,000 and you can afford a $3,000 down payment (your loan balance is then $17,000), how much will your 36 monthly payments be, assuming that the bank charges you 6 percent interest compounded monthly?

Using the DFA table, we find that

$$PVA_{36,.005} = R(DFA_{36,.005})$$
$$\$17{,}000 = R(32.871)$$
$$R = \$517.17$$

The following steps are common in using a business calculator:

Keys	Display	Description
12 [P/YR]	12.00	Sets periods per year
3×12 [N]	36.00	Stores number of periods in loan
0 [PV]	0	Stores the amount left to pay after 3 years
6 [I/YR]	6	Stores interest rate
17,000 [PV]	17,000	Stores amount borrowed
[PMT]	−517.17	Calculates the monthly payment

In Microsoft Excel, the calculation is simply =PMT (.005,36,−17000,0,0) (see Exhibit A-11).

In a similar fashion, assume that a used-car dealer offers you a "special deal" in which you can borrow $12,000 with low monthly payments of $350 per month for 48 months. What rate of interest are you being charged in this case? Using the DFA table shows that

$$PVA_{48,.??} = \$350(DFA_{48,.??})$$
$$\$12{,}000 = 350(DFA_{48,.??})$$
$$DFA_{48,.??} = 34.2857$$

Looking at the row for an n of 48, we see that a DFA of 34.2857 is about halfway between an r of 1 percent and an r of 2 percent (closer to 1 percent), meaning that you are being charged an annual rate of almost 18 percent (1.5% × 12)—not such a good deal after all! Using a business calculator, observe the following:

Keys	Display	Description
12 [P/YR]	12.00	Sets periods per year
4×12 [N]	48.00	Stores number of periods in loan
0 [PV]	0	Stores the amount left to pay after 4 years
12,000 [PV]	12,000	Stores amount borrowed
350 [±] [PMT]	−350	Stores the monthly payment
[I/YR]	17.60	Calculates the annual interest rate

Exhibit A-10 Finding the Present Value of an Annuity
by Using the PV Function in Excel

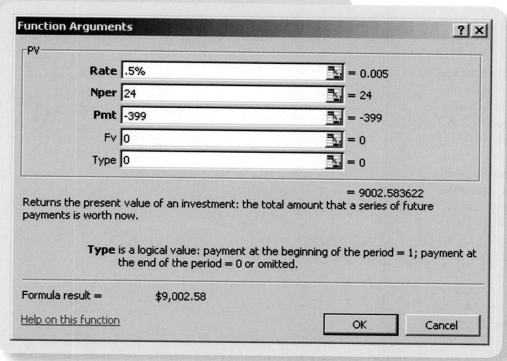

Function Arguments

PV

Rate	.5%		= 0.005
Nper	24		= 24
Pmt	-399		= -399
Fv	0		= 0
Type	0		= 0

= 9002.583622

Returns the present value of an investment: the total amount that a series of future payments is worth now.

Type is a logical value: payment at the beginning of the period = 1; payment at the end of the period = 0 or omitted.

Formula result = $9,002.58

Help on this function   OK   Cancel

Exhibit A-11 Finding the Payment by Using the PMT
Function in Excel

Function Arguments

PMT

Rate	.5%		= 0.005
Nper	36		= 36
Pv	-17000		= -17000
Fv	0		= 0
Type	0		= 0

= 517.1729367

Calculates the payment for a loan based on constant payments and a constant interest rate.

Type is a logical value: payment at the beginning of the period = 1; payment at the end of the period = 0 or omitted.

Formula result = $517.17

Help on this function   OK   Cancel

In Excel, =RATE(48, −350,12,000,0) generates a monthly rate of 1.4667 percent and an annual rate of 17.60 percent. The use of the RATE function requires that the payments be the same each period. Excel's IRR function is more flexible, allowing different payments. However, each payment has to be entered separately. For example, if the car is purchased for $17,000 with annual payments of $4,000, $5,000, $6,000, and $7,000 at the end of each of the next four years, the interest rate charged on the car loan can be calculated by using the IRR function (see Exhibit A-12). Excel also offers more sophisticated tools for calculating IRR when the schedule of cash flows is not periodic (XIRR) and when the user would like to input the rate of return on reinvested cash flows (MIRR).

Exhibit A-12 Finding the Interest Rate Using the IRR Function in Excel

ACCT

Appendix B
The Daily Grind[1]

Twelve months ago, David opened a coffee shop, The Daily Grind, in Mercy Hospital's former gift shop. David was confident that he had the knowledge to make a success of this new business. He produced a quality product that people needed, had priced the product to be very competitive, and had a great location in a high-traffic area of the hospital.

Material Costs

The Daily Grind uses a specialty brand of Kona coffee beans costing $8 per pound. Each pound of coffee beans produces 256 ounces of coffee. Coffee is sold in three sizes: a small cup holding 8 ounces, a medium cup holding 12 ounces, and a large cup holding 16 ounces.

The cups needed to serve the coffee cost $.05 for the small cup, $.06 for the medium cup, and $.07 for the large cup. Lids cost $.03 per cup and are the same regardless of cup size. Sleeves cost an additional $.04 per cup. On average, sugar and cream cost $.02 per cup for small cups, $.03 for medium cups, and $.04 for large cups.

Labor Costs

The Daily Grind is open 12 hours each day, 7 days a week (365 days per year), and is staffed with three employees during the morning shift (7:00–11:00), two employees from 11:00 until 3:00, and three employees from 3:00 to 7:00. Labor is a fixed cost, because the employees are paid regardless of whether coffee is sold. David worked 60 hours each week, on average, and was paid a salary of $30,000 during

the first year of operations. Fringe benefits for David, including health insurance and payroll taxes, accounted for an additional $10,000 of costs for the company. Part-time employees work an average of 24 hours each week and are paid $9 per hour. Payroll taxes and other costs average about $1.00 per hour for part-time employees. As shown in the following table, part-time employees worked from 656 hours to 727 hours each month:

Month	Part-time Employee Labor Hours
January	722 hours
February	656 hours
March	727 hours
April	705 hours
May	727 hours
June	705 hours
July	727 hours
August	727 hours
September	705 hours
October	727 hours
November	705 hours
December	727 hours

Overhead Costs

During the first year of operations, the hospital charged rent of $2,000 per month. As part of the rental cost, the hospital provided furniture and fixtures for the shop, as well as nightly cleaning services. David leased a drip coffeemaker, refrigerator, coffee grinder, scale, and cash register for $150 per month, total. David paid directly for his utilities (electricity and water). The costs of electricity include the costs of heating and cooling the shop. as well as the cost of running the electric appliances (refrigerator, coffeemaker, etc.).

[1]This comprehensive case includes topics and concepts covered in Chapters 1 through 6 of the book, including product costing, cost behavior, and cost-volume-profit analysis. The case also includes a writing requirement. Ideally, it would be assigned after completion of Chapter 6.

For the first 12 months of operations, utility expenses were as follows:

Month	Utility Expense
January	$472
February	$510
March	$524
April	$460
May	$440
June	$460
July	$452
August	$430
September	$535
October	$570
November	$580
December	$600
Total	$6033

Selling and Administrative Costs

David incurred $200 a month in accounting fees and spent $500 on various promotional and advertising materials during the year. He also paid $1,000 for liability insurance.

Sales Revenue

During the first year of operations, David set the shop's prices to be slightly lower than their competitors'. The Daily Grind sells a small cup of coffee for $1.25, a medium cup for $1.65, and a large cup for $1.95. Sales revenue was as follows:

Month	Sales in Cups of Coffee
January	9,300 cups*
February	9,800
March	10,850
April	9,500
May	9,300
June	9,000
July	8,800
August	8,600
September	11,000
October	11,620
November	12,000
December	12,400

*Coffee sales average 10% small cups (8 ounces), 50% medium cups (12 ounces), and 40% large cups (16 ounces).

Requirements

1. Calculate the cost of coffee beans per ounce of coffee sold.

2. Calculate the cost of cups, lids, sleeves, cream, and sugar per unit for small, medium, and large cups of coffee and in total.

3. Calculate the total labor costs for the year.

4. Prepare an income statement for The Daily Grind for the last year. You can assume that there are no inventories on hand at the end of the year. (All coffee and supplies purchased during the year are consumed.)

5. Determine whether the costs incurred by The Daily Grind are fixed, variable (with respect to number of cups of coffee sold), or mixed.

6. Use regression analysis and the high/low method to calculate the monthly fixed cost and the variable component of the utility expenses incurred by The Daily Grind. Use cups of coffee sold as the independent variable and utility expense as the dependent variable in your regression analysis. After calculating *both* numbers, round your final answers to two decimal places.

7. Compare the regression results with the high/low results. Which model would you suggest?

8. Calculate the contribution margin earned for each product (round to three decimal places) and the weighted-average contribution margin (round to four decimal places).

9. Assume the sales mix given in the problem. What is Daily Grind's break-even point in terms of the number of cups of coffee sold during the year?

10. David is contemplating adding a new 20-ounce product for the coming year and discontinuing sales of the small 8-ounce cup. The new cup, lid, and sleeve cost the same as the 16-ounce cup, but cream and sugar is expected to cost $.06 per cup instead of $.04 per cup. The new extra-large cup would be priced at $2.40. David anticipates that the new sales mix would be 50% for the 12-ounce cup, 30% for the 16-ounce cup, and 20% for the new 20-ounce cup. Assume that material, labor, and overhead costs remain the

same in the upcoming year. How would this change in sales mix affect the company's break-even point?

11. David would like to increase sales in the second year of operations so that he may raise his salary to $50,000 (not including $15,000 of fringe benefits) while reducing his workload to 40 hours per week with two paid weeks of vacation during the year. Reducing his workload will require increasing the number of hours worked by part-time employees by 1,080 hours per year. Assume the introduction of the extra-large cup and the new sales mix as discussed in requirement 10. What level of annual sales would be required in order for David to reach his goal?

12. Write a short memo to David and discuss whether you think he will be able to reach his goal during the second year of operations.

Index

A

ABC. *See* Activity-based costing (ABC)
Absorption (full) costing
    comparison of variable costing and, 104, 105–106
    defined, 104
    exh., 104
    production, sales, and income under, *exh.*, 106
Accounting
    comparison of financial and managerial, 4–9
    equation, statement of cash flows and, 288–289
    financial, 4
    managerial, 2–13
    responsibility, 235
Accounting information, 3–4
    contemporary view of, *exh.*, 4
    external and internal users of, *exh.*, 8
Accounting information system (AIS), 3–4
    defined, 3
Accounts receivable analysis, 270–271
Accounts receivable turnover ratio, 270–271
    defined, 270
Acid-test ratio, 269
Activities
    controlling, 6
    and cost drivers, *exh.*, 77
    defined, 76
    financing, 285
    identification of, 76–77, 80
    investing, 284
    making up cash flows statement, summary of, *exh.*, 284
    operating, 6, 283–284
    planning, 6
Activity-based costing (ABC), 74–84
    benefits and limitations of, 83–84
    cost comparison between traditional and, *exh.*, 82
    cost of units based on, *exh.*, 81
    defined, 76
    life insurance and, 78
    price comparison between traditional and, *exh.*, 82
    systems in nonmanufacturing environments, 77–78
    traditional overhead allocation and, 78–83

Activity ratio, 270
Actual costing, defined, 25
Advertising, increase, 125–126
Allocation
    of costs, identification of, 80–83
    defined, 45
    of service department costs to production departments, 60–62
American Red Cross, 2
Analysis of direct material variances, *exh.*, 216
Annuity, present value of (PVA), 163
Applied overhead, calculation of, *exh.*, 49
Appraisal (detection) costs
    defined, 249
    exh., 248
Asset turnover, defined, 239
Asset turnover ratio, return on assets and, 274
Assets
    operating, 240, 242
    return on, 274
Automating production processes, 165–166
AutoZone, Inc., 252

B

Balance sheet
    budgeted, *exh.*, 195
    common-size comparative, *exh.*, 267
    comparative, *exh.*, 265
    exh., 270
Balanced scorecard, 232–253
    approach to performance measurement, *exh.*, 244
    critical success factors related to four perspectives of, *exh.*, 246
    defined, 244
    performance evaluation using, 243–246
Batch-level costs, 76–78
    defined, 76
Behavior of fixed costs, *exh.*, 92
Behavior of variable costs, *exh.*, 94
Behavioral considerations, 223
Behavioral implications of budgeting, 181
Ben & Jerry's, 6, 47
Benefits
    of decentralization, 234
    and limitations of ABC, 83–84
    and perks, noncash, 252–253
Boeing Company, 267

IT'S ALL ABOUT
THE HOMEWORK!

CengageNOW™ is an **easy-to-use online resource** that helps you **study in less time** to **get the grade you want** – NOW.

CengageNOW™ is your online resource for ACCT2 and features:

- All end-of-chapter homework from the textbook written by the authors
- Additional hints and guidance during homework via enhanced feedback
- Interactive eBook
- Personalized Study Plan, including pre- and post-test assessments, videos, games, E-lectures, and more!

How to Register Your Access Code:

1. Launch a Web browser. Go to login.cengagebrain.com and click on "Create a New Account." Already have an account? Enter your email/password under "Log In."
2. Enter your access code in the field provided, exactly how it appears on your card.
3. New users: Enter your account information and click "Continue."
4. Record your email address and password below, and store it in a secure location for future visits.

[Email Address: _____]
[Password: _____]

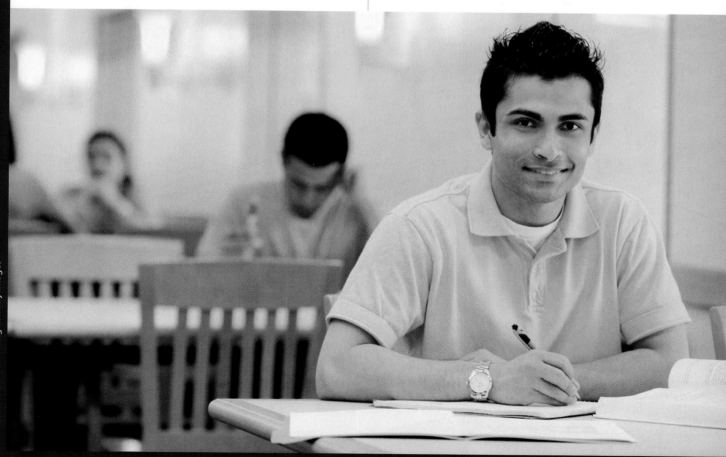

REVIEW!

ACCT2 puts a multitude of study aids at your fingertips. After reading the chapters, check out these resources for further help:

- **Review Cards,** found in the back of your book, include all learning objectives, key terms and definitions, and visual summaries for each chapter.

- **Online Printable Flash Cards** give you additional ways to check your comprehension of key accounting concepts.

- **Animations,** found in the **CengageNOW™** Personalized Study Plan, offer dynamic, visual examples based around key concepts. One example is the "Make-or-Buy Decision" based on Birdie Maker Golf Company in Chapter 7.

- **Interactive games** include Beat the Clock, a timed quiz for each chapter, and Quiz Bowl—a Jeopardy-style game that helps test your knowledge and understanding of the critical concepts within the chapter.

Find these and other great resources online as part of **CengageNOW™** for **ACCT2**.

Learning Objectives

LO1	Describe the contemporary view of accounting information systems and describe and give examples of financial and nonfinancial accounting information.	
LO2	Compare and contrast managerial accounting with financial accounting and distinguish between the information needs of external and internal users.	
LO3	Recognize the role of relevant factors in decision making.	
LO4	Understand sources of ethical issues in business and the importance of maintaining an ethical business environment.	

Key Concepts

Accounting information includes both financial and nonfinancial information used by decision makers.

Financial accounting information is focused on the information needs of external users, whereas managerial accounting information is focused on the information needs of internal users.

Sunk costs and future costs that do not differ among alternatives are not relevant. Opportunity costs, however, are relevant.

Establishing an ethical business environment encourages employees to act with integrity and conduct business in a fair and just manner.

Key Definitions

Accounting information system (AIS) A transaction-processing system that captures financial data resulting from accounting transactions within a company. (p. 3)

Controlling activities The motivation and monitoring of employees and the evaluation of people and other resources used in the operation of the organization. (p. 6)

Data Reports such as financial statements, customer lists, and inventory records. (p. 2)

Decision making The process of identifying alternative courses of action and selecting an appropriate alternative in a given decision-making situation. (p. 9)

Ethics programs Company programs or policies created for the express purpose of establishing and maintaining an ethical business environment. (p. 12)

External users Stockholders, potential investors, creditors, government taxing agencies, regulators, suppliers, customers, and others outside the company. (p. 5)

Finance function Responsible for managing the financial resources of the organization. (p. 7)

Financial accounting The area of accounting concerned primarily with the preparation and use of financial statements by creditors, investors, and other users outside the company. (p. 5)

Human resource function Concerned with the utilization of human resources to help an organization reach its goals. (p. 7)

Information Data that have been organized, processed, and summarized. (p. 2)

Internal users Individual employees, teams, departments, regions, top management, and others inside the company—often referred to as managers. (p. 6)

Knowledge Information that is shared and exploited so that it adds value to an organization. (p. 2)

Managerial accounting The area of accounting concerned primarily with generating financial and nonfinancial information for use by managers in their decision-making roles within a company. (p. 5)

Concept Questions

1. Discuss the relationships among data, information, and knowledge.

2. What is the primary purpose of financial accounting and of managerial accounting?

3. Define strategic and operational planning.

4. Briefly describe the role of the finance function within an organization.

5. Why has the role of the managerial accountant changed in recent years?

6. Define sunk costs and opportunity costs, and discuss their importance in decision making.

7. "Businesses must first do well before they can do good." Do you agree or disagree with the preceding statement? Why or why not?

Key Definitions (continued)

Marketing function Involved with the process of developing, pricing, promoting, and distributing goods and services sold to customers. (p. 7)

Operating activities The day-to-day operations of a business. (p. 6)

Operational planning The development of short-term objectives and goals (typically, those to be achieved in less than one year). (p. 6)

Operations and production function Produces the products or services that an organization sells to its customers. (p. 7)

Opportunity costs The benefits forgone by choosing one alternative over another. (p. 10)

Planning The development of both the short-term (operational) and long-term (strategic) objectives and goals of an organization and the identification of the resources needed to achieve them. (p. 6)

Relevant costs Costs which differ among alternatives. (p. 10)

Strategic planning Addresses long-term questions of how an organization positions and distinguishes itself from competitors. (p. 6)

Sunk costs Costs that have already been incurred. (p. 10)

Key Exhibits

Exhibit 1-1 A Contemporary View of Accounting Information

Accounting Information

- Traditional Financial Accounting Information
- Nonfinancial Information

Financial Information
- Assets
- Liabilities
- Revenues
- Gross margin
- Operating expenses

Other Quantitative Information
- Percentage of defects
- Number of customer complaints
- Warranty claims
- Units in inventory
- Budgeted hours

Qualitative Information
- Customer satisfaction
- Employee satisfaction
- Product or service quality
- Reputation

Exhibit 1-2 External and Internal Users of Accounting Information

	Users	Type of Accounting Information Needed	Source
External	Shareholders and creditors	Sales, gross profit, net income, cash flow, assets and liabilities, earnings per share, etc. Although such information is primarily financial, it may also include nonfinancial information (units in inventory). This information is often provided in summary form (for the company as a whole) and typically is historical in nature.	Annual reports, financial statements, and other available documents
External	Government agencies	Varies by agency but includes taxable income, sales, assets, comparisons of actual expenditures with budgets, etc. This information is usually provided for the company as a whole and is historical in nature. It can include both financial and nonfinancial information.	Tax returns and other reports
External	Customers and suppliers	Order status, shipping dates, inventory levels, etc. This information must be very detailed and timely to be useful.	Limited-access databases available to specific customers and suppliers
Internal	Marketing, operations and production, finance, and human resource managers	Timely and detailed information on sales and expenses, product costs, budgetary considerations, and measures of performance. Often includes nonfinancial data (direct labor hours, units to break even, etc.). Accounting information is frequently needed for segments of an organization and is more likely future oriented than historical.	Cost reports, budgets, and other internal documents

Exhibit 1-3 Relevant and Irrelevant Costs

Relevant Costs		Irrelevant Costs	
Future costs that differ among alternatives	Opportunity costs—benefits that are forgone by choosing one alternative over another	Future costs that do not differ among alternatives	Sunk costs—costs that have already been incurred

Learning Objectives

LO1	Describe basic production processes used by manufacturing companies.	
LO2	Identify the key characteristics and benefits of lean production and JIT manufacturing.	
LO3	Distinguish manufacturing costs from nonmanufacturing costs and classify manufacturing costs as direct materials, direct labor, or overhead.	
LO4	Diagram the flow of costs in manufacturing, merchandising, and service companies and calculate the cost of manufacturing or selling goods and services.	
LO5	Evaluate the impact of products costs and period costs on a company's income statement and balance sheet.	

Key Concepts

Production processes require the combination of raw materials, labor, and other items, such as electricity and supplies, to create finished goods.

Lean production and JIT provide many benefits, including improved production quality and reduced processing time.

Manufacturing costs are incurred in the production facility, whereas nonmanufacturing costs are incurred elsewhere in the company, such as in the marketing department.

Costs flow the same way that products flow through a production facility.

Product costs attach to the product and are expensed only when the product is sold, whereas period costs are expensed in the period in which they are incurred.

Key Definitions

Actual costing A product costing system in which actual overhead costs are entered directly into work in process. (p. 25)

Direct cost Costs that are directly attached to the finished product and can be conveniently traced to that product. (p. 21)

Direct labor Labor that can easily and conveniently be traced to particular products. (p. 21)

Direct materials Materials that can easily and conveniently be traced to the final product. (p. 21)

Finished-goods inventory Inventory of finished product waiting for sale and shipment to customers. (p. 18)

Indirect cost Costs that are attached to the product but cannot be conveniently traced to each separate product. (p. 21)

Indirect labor Labor used in the production of products but not directly traceable to the specific product. (p. 22)

Indirect materials Materials used in the production of products but not directly traceable to the specific product. (p. 22)

Just-in-time (JIT) manufacturing The philosophy of having raw materials arrive just in time to be used in production and for finished-goods inventory to be completed just in time to be shipped to customers. (p. 18)

Lean production A system focused on eliminating waste associated with holding more inventory than is required, making more product than is needed, overprocessing a product, moving products (and people) farther than is required, and waiting. (p. 18)

Manufacturing companies Companies that purchase raw materials from other companies and transform those raw materials into a finished product. (p. 16)

Manufacturing costs Costs incurred in the factory or plant to produce a product; typically consists of three elements: direct materials, direct labor, and manufacturing overhead. (p. 21)

Manufacturing overhead The cost of indirect materials and labor and any other expenses related to the production of products but not directly traceable to the specific product. (p. 22)

Concept Questions

1. What is the difference among raw materials inventory, WIP, and finished-goods inventory?

2. Why are traditional manufacturing systems sometimes called "push" systems of production whereas JIT systems are called "pull" systems?

3. Briefly describe a just-in-time manufacturing system.

4. What are some of the advantages of lean production and JIT manufacturing?

5. Describe how some of the principles of lean production might be applied to a bank.

6. Compare the terms *direct cost* and *indirect cost*.

7. Define the three components of manufacturing costs.

8. Define nonmanufacturing costs.

9. Briefly describe the flow of costs in a manufacturing company.

10. Are the terms *cost* and *expense* synonymous? Why or why not?

11. Compare product and period costs. Why is the designation important?

12. Why do companies need to determine accurate product costs?

Key Definitions (continued)

Merchandising companies Companies that sell products that someone else has manufactured. (p. 16)

Nonmanufacturing costs Costs that include selling and administrative costs. (p. 22)

Normal costing A product costing system in which estimated or predetermined overhead rates are used to apply overhead to work in process. (p. 25)

Period costs Costs that are expensed in the period incurred; attached to the period as opposed to the product. (p. 22)

Product costs Costs that attach to the products as they go through the manufacturing process; also called inventoriable costs. (p. 22)

Raw materials inventory Inventory of materials needed in the production process but not yet moved to the production area. (p. 18)

Service companies Companies that do not sell a tangible product as their primary business. (p. 16)

Work in process inventory (WIP) Inventory of unfinished product (in other words, what is left in the factory at the end of the period). (p. 18)

JOURNAL ENTRIES

A. Record the purchase of raw materials:

| Raw Materials Inventory | xxx | |
| Accounts Payable (or Cash) | | xxx |

B. Record the transfer of raw materials from raw materials inventory to WIP inventory:

| Work in Process Inventory | xxx | |
| Raw Materials Inventory | | xxx |

C. Record the incurrence of direct labor costs:

| Work in Process Inventory | xxx | |
| Salaries and Wages Payable (or Cash) | | xxx |

D. Record the incurrence of manufacturing overhead costs (under actual costing):

| Work in Process Inventory | xxx | |
| Accounts Payable (or Cash) | | xxx |

E. Record the transfer of finished goods from WIP to finished-goods inventory:

| Finished-Goods Inventory | xxx | |
| Work in Process Inventory | | xxx |

F. Record the cost of goods sold and the transfer of goods out of finished-goods inventory as the product is sold:

| Cost of Goods Sold | xxx | |
| Finished-Goods Inventory | | xxx |

Key Exhibits

Exhibit 2-3 Overview of Cost Flows in a Manufacturing Company

Exhibit 2-5 Cost Flows in Northern Lights Custom Cabinets

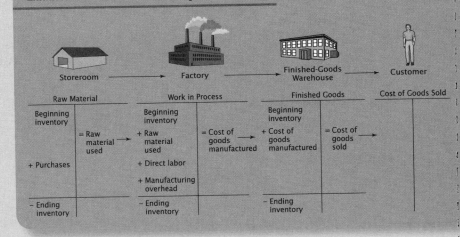

Exhibit 2-7 Income Statement for a Manufacturing Company

Sales		$XX
Cost of goods sold:		
Beginning finished-goods inventory	$XX	
Add: Cost of goods manufactured	XX	
Goods available for sale	$XX	
Deduct: Ending finished-goods inventory	$XX	$XX
Gross margin		$XX
Less: Selling and administrative expense		$XX
Net operating income		$XX

Exhibit 2-10 The Path to the Income Statement—Product and Period Costs

Visit **www.cengagebrain.com** for additional study tools!

review card

Learning Objectives		Key Concepts	Key Definitions
LO1	Contrast job costing, process costing, and operations costing and explain how they are used to accumulate, track, and assign product costs.	The type of costing system used depends upon the manufacturing process and the nature and availability of cost data.	**Allocation** The process of finding a logical method of assigning overhead costs to the products or services a company produces or provides. (p. 45)
LO2	Recognize issues related to the measurement of direct material and direct labor costs in job costing.	Direct material costs include the cost of the primary materials used in production, along with shipping costs and sales taxes. Direct labor cost are the wages paid to production workers, including fringe benefits (e.g., health insurance and retirement benefits).	**Cost drivers** Factors that cause, or drive, the incurrence of costs. (p. 45) **Cost pools** Groups of overhead costs that are similar; used to simplify the task of assigning costs to products with ABC costing. (p. 46)
LO3	Recognize issues related to the allocation of manufacturing overhead cost to products.	Overhead cannot be directly tracked to products and services but must instead be allocated with the use of cost drivers.	**Direct method** A method of allocating service department costs that allocates costs directly to production departments. (p. 60)
LO4	Explain the need for using predetermined overhead rates and calculate overhead applied to production.	In order to provide relevant information for decision making, overhead must often be estimated. Under normal costing, the cost of a product includes the actual amount of direct materials, the actual amount of direct labor, and an applied amount of manufacturing overhead.	**Equivalent units** The number of finished units that can be made from the materials, labor, and overhead included in partially completed units. (p. 51) **Fringe benefits** Payroll costs in addition to the basic hourly wage. (p. 44) **Idle time** Worker time that is not used in the production of the finished product. (p. 44)
LO5	Determine whether overhead has been over- or underapplied and demonstrate the alternative treatments of the over- or underapplied amount.	Overapplied and underapplied overhead may be allocated to WIP, finished goods, and costs of goods sold, or charged directly to cost of goods sold, depending upon the magnitude of the overapplied or underapplied amount.	**Job costing** A costing system that accumulates, tracks, and assigns costs for each job produced by a company. (p. 40) **Normal costing** A method of costing using an estimate of overhead and predetermined overhead rates instead of the actual amount of overhead. (p. 47)
LO6	Describe basic process costing and the calculation of equivalent units of production.	Process costing assigns costs to products as they pass through departments, rather than assigning costs to each individual product.	**Operations costing** A hybrid of job and process costing; used by companies that make products in batches. (p. 42) **Overapplied overhead** The amount of applied overhead in excess of actual overhead. (p. 48)
LO7	Compare and contrast the weighted-average and first-in, first-out (FIFO) methods of process costing and apply each step of the four-step process costing system under both methods.	The FIFO method assumes that all units in beginning WIP were the first units finished. The weighted-average method treats units in beginning WIP as though they were started in the current period.	**Overtime premium** An additional amount added to the basic hourly wage owing to overtime worked by the workers. (p. 44) **Predetermined overhead rates** Used to apply overhead to products; calculated by dividing the estimated overhead for a cost pool by the estimated units of the cost driver. (p. 48)
LO8	Allocate service department costs using the direct and step-down methods	The direct method allocates overhead costs only to production departments, while the step-down method allocates overhead costs to production and service departments.	**Process costing** A costing system that accumulates and tracks costs for each process performed and then assigns those costs equally to each unit produced. (p. 41)

Key Definitions (continued)

Production report Report that provides a summary of the units moving through a processing department during the period as well as a computation of equivalent units of production and the costs per equivalent unit. (p. 56)

Step-down or **sequential method** Recognizes that service departments consume resources of other service departments and allocates those costs to other service departments and then to production departments in a sequential fashion. (p. 60)

Underapplied overhead The amount of actual overhead in excess of applied overhead. (p. 48)

Concept Questions

1. Explain the importance of product cost information in the context of management decision making.

2. Briefly describe job costing and process costing. Give an example of the type of organization most likely to use job costing and an example of the type of organization most likely to use process costing.

3. What two components of product costs must be carefully measured and tracked when a company uses job costing?

4. Describe the basic elements of a job cost sheet.

5. Why is overhead difficult to track and allocate to products in a traditional manufacturing environment?

6. What should managers look for when trying to choose a cost driver for overhead costs?

7. When should a normalized (i.e., predetermined) overhead rate be used?

8. Why would a manager prefer one treatment for over-applied overhead to another?

9. Define the term *equivalent units of production*.

10. Why is the FIFO method preferred for calculating equivalent units and calculating unit costs?

Key Formulas

Overhead Rate	$\text{Overhead rate} = \dfrac{\text{Manufacturing overhead}}{\text{Cost driver}}$
Predetermined Overhead Rate	$\text{Predetermined overhead rate (for a cost pool)} = \dfrac{\text{Estimated overhead for the cost pool}}{\text{Estimated units of the cost driver}}$
Applied Overhead	$\text{Applied overhead} = \text{Predetermined overhead rate} \times \text{Actual units of cost driver}$

Equivalent Units of Production (FIFO)

Equivalent Units of Production = Equivalent units required to complete beginning inventory*
+ Units started and completed during the period
+ Equivalent units in ending inventory at the end of the period

*Units in beginning inventory × (100% − % completion of beginning inventory)

Equivalent Units of Production (Weighted Average)

Equivalent units of production = Units completely finished during the period and transferred to finished goods
+ Equivalent units in WIP inventory at the end of the period

Key Exhibit

Exhibit 3-1 Product Costing Systems

	Costing System		
	Job Costing	**Operations Costing**	**Process Costing**
Type of Product	Custom	Standardized within batches	Homogeneous
Examples	Construction, movie studios, hospitals, print shops, CPA and law firms	Automobile and clothing manufacturers	Beverages, oil refineries, paint, paper, rolled steel

THE FOUR STEPS OF BASIC PROCESS COSTING

1. Analyze physical flow of units and their associated costs.
2. Calculate equivalent units of production.
3. Calculate the cost per equivalent unit.
4. Allocate costs to the ending work in process and to finished goods.

reviewcard

Learning Objectives		Key Concepts	Key Definitions
LO1	Classify overhead costs as unit-, batch-, product-, or facility-level costs.	Activity-based costing allocates costs on the basis of activities that drive overhead, rather than using simple volume or unit-based measures.	**Activities** Procedures or processes that cause work to be accomplished. (p. 76) **Activity-based costing (ABC)** A system of allocating overhead costs that assumes that activities, not volume of production, cause overhead costs to be incurred. (p. 76)
LO2	Describe ABC and recognize typical activities and cost drivers in an ABC system.	Unit-level costs are incurred each time a unit is produced. Batch-level costs are incurred each time a batch of goods is produced. Product-level costs are incurred as needed to support the production of each type of product. Facility-level costs simply sustain a facility's general manufacturing process.	**Batch-level costs** Costs that are incurred each time a batch of goods is produced. (p. 76) **Diverse products** Products that consume resources in different proportions. (p. 84) **Facility-level costs** Costs that are incurred to sustain the overall manufacturing process. (p. 76)
LO3	Calculate the cost of a product by using ABC and compare traditional volume-based costing with ABC.	Although there are common activities that drive overhead costs, every company should evaluate its activities carefully. Volume-based costing systems often result in overcosting high-volume products and undercosting low-volume products. This cross subsidy is eliminated by the use of ABC.	**Product-level costs** Costs that are incurred as needed to support the production of each type of product. (p. 76) **Unit-level costs** Costs that are incurred each time a unit is produced. (p. 76)
LO4	Evaluate the benefits and limitations of ABC systems.	ABC systems generally improve the accuracy of cost data, but are often time consuming and expensive to develop.	

Concept Questions

1. Overhead costs are typically identified as belonging to one of four categories. List and briefly describe each category.

2. Define activity-based costing.

3. Identify and describe the two stages of cost allocation in an activity-based costing system.

4. Discuss the importance of choosing the right cost driver and the potential impact of choosing the wrong cost driver.

5. Why would a company that utilizes just-in-time techniques also wish to implement an activity-based costing system?

6. How can activity-based costing techniques be applied to selling and administration activities?

7. What are "cross subsidies between products" and how can they be controlled?

8. What are some of the benefits of activity-based costing systems?

9. What are some of the downsides of activity-based costing systems?

Key Exhibits

Exhibit 4-2 Overhead Costs and Cooper's Hierarchy

Unit-Level Costs

Supplies for factory

Depreciation of factory machinery

Energy costs for factory machinery

Repairs and maintenance of factory machinery

Batch-Level Costs

Salaries related to purchasing and receiving

Salaries related to moving material

Quality control costs

Depreciation of setup equipment

Product-Level Costs

Salaries of engineers

Depreciation of engineering equipment

Product development costs (testing)

Quality control costs

Facility-Level Costs

Depreciation of factory building or rent

Salary of plant manager

Insurance and taxes on factory building

Employee training

Exhibit 4-3 Activities and Cost Drivers

Activity	Level	Typical Cost Drivers
Repair and maintenance of factory equipment	Unit	Machine hours, labor hours, or number of units
Machining of products	Unit	Machine hours
Purchasing	Batch	Number of purchase orders or number of parts
Receiving	Batch	Amount of material or number of receipts
Setting up equipment	Batch	Number of setups
Product testing	Product	Number of change orders, number of tests, or hours of testing time
Engineering	Product	Number of engineering hours or number of products
Product design	Product	Number of new or revised products
Quality control	Unit, batch, product	Number of inspections, hours of inspection, or number of defective units

Activity-Based Costing

Allocating overhead to products under activity-based costing (ABC) can be explained as a four-step process:

Step 1: Identify activities. ABC costing allocates overhead to the activities that consume overhead costs. It forces a company to identify the activities necessary to make its product: order materials, make the product, inspect the product, pack and ship the product.

Step 2: Allocate the costs of the activities into activity cost pools. Assume that, for the first activity, the cost of ordering material is $80,000, including all expenses for the activity.

Step 3: Select an activity base. A means of allocating the cost of each activity to the product must be chosen. Assume that the purchasing department places 10,000 orders per year.

Step 4: Calculate an activity rate and allocate the costs to products.

Activity Rate: Cost to place an order = Activity cost pool/Activity Base = 80,000/10,000 = $8 per order.

If manufacturing a product causes the purchasing agent to place two orders for materials, the overhead cost allocated to that product as the result of ordering materials is $16 (2 × $8). Once this process is complete for the purchasing activity, the same steps must be taken for the remaining activities.

Learning Objectives

LO1	Describe the nature and behavior of fixed and variable costs.	
LO2	Use regression analysis and the high/low method to define and analyze mixed costs.	
LO3	Illustrate the impact of income taxes on costs and decision making.	
LO4	Identify the difference between variable costing and absorption costing.	
LO5	Identify the impact on the income statement of variable costing and absorption costing.	
LO6	Recognize the benefits of using variable costing for decision making.	

Key Concepts

Costs behave in predictable ways. Within the relevant range, fixed costs are constant in total and vary per unit, whereas variable costs vary in total and are constant per unit.

Mixed costs must be separated into fixed and variable cost components before their behavior can be understood.

Many operating costs are tax deductible and most revenues are taxable. Managers must consider the impact of taxes when making decisions.

The only difference between variable and absorption costing is in the treatment of fixed overhead.

Variable costing is consistent with CVP's focus on differentiating fixed and variable costs and provides useful decision-making information that is often not apparent with absorption costing.

Variable costing offers many benefits that focus on managerial performance and cost behavior.

Key Formulas

Variable Cost per Unit

$$\text{Variable cost per unit} = \frac{\text{Change in cost}}{\text{Change in volume}}$$

Total Overhead Cost

$$\text{Total overhead cost} = \text{Fixed cost} + (\text{Variable cost per unit} \times \text{volume})$$

After-Tax Cost

$$\text{After-tax cost} = \text{Pretax cost} \times (1 - \text{tax rate})$$

After-Tax Benefit

$$\text{After-tax benefit} = \text{Pretax receipts} \times (1 - \text{tax rate})$$

After-Tax Income

$$\text{After-tax income} = \text{Pretax income} \times (1 - \text{tax rate})$$

Key Definitions

Absorption (full) costing A method of costing in which product costs include the costs of direct materials, direct labor, and fixed and variable overhead; required for external financial statements and for income tax reporting. (p. 104)

Cost behavior How costs react to changes in production volume or other levels of activity. (p. 92)

Dependent variable The variable in regression analysis that is dependent on changes in the independent variable. (p. 98)

Fixed costs Costs that remain the same in total when production volume increases or decreases but that vary per unit. (p. 92)

Independent variable The variable in regression analysis that drives changes in the dependent variable. (p. 98)

Mixed costs Costs that include both a fixed and a variable component, making it difficult to predict the behavior of a mixed cost as production changes, unless the cost is first separated into its fixed and variable components. (p. 96)

R square (R^2) A measure of goodness of fit (how well the regression line "fits" the data). (p. 101)

Regression analysis The procedure that uses statistical methods (least squares regression) to fit a cost line (called a regression line) through a number of data points. (p. 97)

Relevant range The normal range of production that can be expected for a particular product and company. (p. 94)

Step costs Costs that vary with activity in steps and may look like and be treated as either variable costs or fixed costs; step costs are technically not fixed costs but may be treated as such if they remain constant within a relevant range of production. (p. 95)

Variable costs Costs that stay the same per unit, but change in total, as production volume increases or decreases. (p. 93)

Variable (direct) costing A method of costing in which product costs include the costs of direct materials, direct labor, and variable overhead; fixed overhead is treated as a period cost; variable costing is consistent with CVP's focus on cost behavior. (p. 104)

Concept Questions

1. Describe the behavior of direct material cost in total and per unit as production volume changes.

2. Describe the relevant range and how it relates to cost behavior.

3. How will fixed costs expressed on a per-unit basis react to a change in the level of activity?

4. Give the equation that best describes the fundamental relationship among total costs (TC), fixed costs (FC), and variable costs per unit (VC). Use TC, FC, and VC in formulating your answer.

5. Discuss the meaning of dependent and independent variables in regression analysis.

6. Discuss the meaning of R square in regression analysis. What does an R square of 1.00 mean?

7. Discuss situations in which the high/low method may provide inaccurate estimates of fixed and variable costs.

8. Why are fixed costs not relevant for most short-term decisions?

9. Compare and contrast the terms *relevant costs* and *irrelevant costs* as they pertain to decision making.

10. Discuss the impact of taxes on costs and how that impact affects decision making.

11. If production exceeds sales, which costing method will show higher net income? Why?

12. If sales exceed production, which costing method will show higher net income? Why?

13. How do the two costing methods differ when sales and production are equal? Why?

14. What is the primary difference between absorption costing and variable costing?

15. If a company uses absorption costing to prepare its financial statements, is it possible to increase net income without increasing sales or decreasing expenses? How?

16. How are fixed manufacturing overhead costs moved from one year to another under absorption costing?

17. Under absorption costing, how can net income increase without sales increasing?

18. How are selling and administrative costs treated under variable costing?

Key Exhibits

Exhibit 5-1 The Behavior of Fixed Costs

Fixed Cost in Total

Fixed Cost per Unit

Exhibit 5-2 The Behavior of Variable Costs

Variable Cost in Total

Variable Cost per Unit

Exhibit 5-13 Absorption and Variable Costing

Absorption Costing		Variable Costing	
Product Costs	**Period Costs**	**Product Costs**	**Period Costs**
Direct materials		Direct materials	
Direct labor	Selling, general, and administrative costs	Direct labor	Selling, general, and administrative costs
Variable overhead		Variable overhead	
Fixed overhead			**Fixed overhead**

Exhibit 5-14 Production, Sales, and Income Under Absorption Costing and Variable Costing

When Production = Sales   Absorption Income = Variable Income

When Production > Sales   Absorption Income > Variable Income

When Production < Sales   Absorption Income < Variable Income

Learning Objectives

LO1	Use the contribution margin in its various forms to determine the impact of changes in sales on income.	
LO2	Analyze what-if decisions by using CVP analysis.	
LO3	Compute a company's break-even point in single- and multiproduct environments.	
LO4	Analyze target profit before and after the impact of income tax.	
LO5	Compute a company's operating leverage and understand the relationship of leverage to cost structure.	

Key Concepts

LO1
The contribution margin income statement is structured to emphasize cost behavior as opposed to cost function.

For every unit (dollar) change in sales, contribution margin will increase or decrease by the contribution margin per unit multiplied by the increase or decrease in sales volume (dollars).

The contribution margin per unit and the contribution margin ratio will remain constant as long as sales vary in direct proportion to volume.

LO2
Managers must be careful to consider the implications of choices they make in what-if analyses because of the potential impact decisions may have on production cost or customer demand.

LO3
A thorough understanding of fixed and variable costs is necessary before a manager can calculate and understand a break-even analysis.

LO4
The payment of income taxes is an important variable in target profit and other CVP decisions if managers are to understand the bottom line effect of their decisions.

LO5
A company operating near the break-even point will have a high level of operating leverage, and income will be very sensitive to changes in sales volume.

Key Definitions

Break-even point The level of sales at which the contribution margin just covers fixed costs and income is equal to zero. (p. 126)

Contribution margin per unit The sales price per unit of product, less all variable costs to produce and sell the unit of product; used to calculate the change in contribution margin resulting from a change in unit sales. (p. 122)

Contribution margin ratio The contribution margin divided by sales; used to calculate the change in contribution margin resulting from a dollar change in sales. (p. 123)

Cost–volume–profit (CVP) analysis A tool that focuses on the relationships among a company's profits and (1) the prices of products or services, (2) the volume of products or services, (3) the per-unit variable costs, (4) the total fixed costs, and (5) the mix of products or services produced. (p. 120)

Gross profit The difference between sales and cost of goods sold. (p. 121)

Operating leverage The contribution margin divided by net income; used as an indicator of how sensitive net income is to a change in sales. (p. 130)

Concept Questions

1. Describe the primary difference between traditional income statements and contribution margin income statements.

2. What happens to the contribution margin when fixed expenses decrease and variable costs per unit remain constant?

3. Define the term *contribution margin*.

4. If the total contribution margin decreases by a given amount, what will be the effect on net operating income?

5. Describe the formula for computing the break-even point in sales dollars and units.

6. How might a company decrease its break-even point?

7. How do income taxes affect CVP computations?

8. As a company nears the break-even point, what happens to its operating leverage?

Key Formulas

Contribution Margin

$$\text{Contribution margin (per unit)} = \frac{\text{Contribution margin (in \$)}}{\text{Units sold}}$$

$$\text{Contribution margin ratio} = \frac{\text{Contribution margin (in \$)}}{\text{Sales (in \$)}}$$

Break-Even Point

$$\text{Break-even (units)} = \frac{\text{Fixed costs}}{\text{Contribution margin per unit}}$$

$$\text{Break-even (\$)} = \frac{\text{Fixed costs}}{\text{Contribution margin ratio}}$$

$$\text{Break-even (units) (with multiple products)} = \frac{\text{Fixed costs}}{\text{Weighted-average contribution margin per unit}}$$

Target Profit Analysis

$$\text{Sales volume (to reach a target profit before tax)} = \frac{[\text{Fixed costs} + \text{Target profit (before tax)}]}{\text{Contribution margin}}$$

$$\text{Sales volume (to reach target profit before tax) (with multiple products)} = \frac{[\text{Fixed costs} + \text{Target profit (before tax)}]}{\text{Weighted-average contribution margin per unit}}$$

Before-Tax Profit

$$\text{Before-tax profit} = \frac{\text{After-tax profit}}{(1 - \text{tax rate})}$$

Operating Leverage

$$\text{Operating leverage} = \frac{\text{Contribution margin}}{\text{Net operating income}}$$

Exhibit 6-1 Comparison of Income Statements

Traditional			Contribution Margin		
Sales		$1,000	Sales		$1,000
Less: Cost of goods sold:			Less: Variable costs:		
Variable costs	$350		Manufacturing costs	$350	
Fixed costs	150		S, G, & A costs	50	
Total cost of goods sold		500	Total variable costs		400
Gross profit		$ 500	Contribution margin		$ 600
Less: S, G, & A costs:			Less: Fixed costs:		
Variable costs	$ 50		Manufacturing costs	$150	
Fixed costs	250		S, G, & A costs	250	
Total S, G, & A costs		300	Total fixed costs		400
Net operating income		$ 200	Net operating income		$ 200

Learning Objectives	Key Concepts	Key Definitions
LO1 Analyze the pricing of a special order.	The price of a special order must be higher than the additional variable costs plus any opportunity costs incurred in accepting the special order.	**Bottlenecks** Production-process steps that limit throughput or the number of finished products that go through the production process. (p. 147)
LO2 Analyze a decision involving outsourcing labor or making or buying a component.	A product should continue to be made internally if the avoidable costs are less than the additional costs that will be incurred by buying or outsourcing.	**Constraint** A restriction that occurs when the capacity to manufacture a product or to provide a service is limited in some manner. (p. 146)
LO3 Analyze a decision dealing with adding or dropping a product, product line, or service.	A product should be dropped when the fixed costs that are avoided exceed the contribution margin that is lost.	**Make-or-buy decisions** Short-term decisions to outsource labor or to purchase components used in manufacturing from another company rather than to provide services or produce components internally. (p. 141)
LO4 Analyze a decision dealing with scarce or limited resources.	Resource utilization decisions hinge on an analysis of the contribution margin earned per unit of the limited resource. The goal is to maximize the contribution margin per unit of the limited resource.	**Resource utilization decision** A decision requiring an analysis of how best to use a resource that is available in limited supply. (p. 146)
LO5 Describe the theory of constraints and explain the importance of identifying bottlenecks in the production process.	Bottlenecks must be identified and managed if a business is to be successful in overcoming constraints.	**Special-order decisions** Short-run pricing decisions in which management must decide which sales price is appropriate when customers place orders that are different from those placed in the regular course of business (onetime sale to a foreign customer, etc.). (p. 138)
LO6 Analyze a decision dealing with selling a product or processing it further.	A product should be processed further if the additional revenue exceeds the additional cost of processing.	**Theory of constraints** A management tool for dealing with constraints; identifies and focuses on bottlenecks in the production process. (p. 147)
		Vertical integration Accomplished when a company is involved in multiple steps of the value chain. (p. 142)

Concept Questions

1. The production of a special order will increase income when the additional revenue from the special order is greater than what?

2. In considering a special order that will enable a company to make use of presently idle capacity, list the costs that would more than likely be relevant in the decision-making process.

3. What costs are usually relevant in a make-or-buy decision?

4. Name some qualitative factors that would cause a decision maker to favor the buy choice in a make-or-buy decision.

5. What are some of the disadvantages of outsourcing the production of a part?

6. In deciding whether to manufacture a part or to buy it from an outside supplier, name a cost that would not be relevant to that short-run decision.

7. The decision to drop a product line should be based on what factors?

8. What should be the goal of a manager who is faced with a limited-resource decision?

9. What steps should be taken in dealing with a production bottleneck?

10. What is the general rule of thumb that should be followed in making a decision whether to sell as is or process a particular product further?

Key Decision Rules

Special-Order Decision: The price of a special order must be higher than the additional variable costs plus any opportunity costs incurred in accepting the special order.

The Make-or-Buy Decision: A product should continue to be made internally if the avoidable costs are less than the additional costs that will be incurred by buying or outsourcing.

The Decision to Drop a Product or Service: A product should be dropped when the fixed costs that are avoided exceed the contribution margin that is lost.

Resource Utilization Decision: When faced with limited resources, a company will maximize profit by making the product with the highest contribution margin per unit of the limited resource.

The Decision to Sell or Process Further: A product should be processed further when the additional (incremental) revenue exceeds the additional (incremental) cost of processing

Exhibit 7-8 The Decision to Sell or Process Further

Learning Objectives	Key Concepts	Key Definitions
LO1 Use the NPV method to evaluate capital investment decisions.	Long-term investment decisions require a consideration of the time value of money. The time value of money is based on the concept that a dollar received today is worth more than a dollar received in the future. If the present value of cash inflows is greater than or equal to the present value of cash outflows (the NPV is greater than or equal to zero), then the investment provides a return at least equal to the discount rate (the minimum required rate of return) and the investment is acceptable.	**Capital investment decisions** Long-term decisions involving the purchase (or lease) of new machinery and equipment and the acquisition or expansion of facilities used in a business. (p. 160) **Cost of capital** What the firm would have to pay to borrow (issue bonds) or raise funds through equity (issue stock) in the financial marketplace. (p. 162) **Depreciation tax shield** The tax savings from depreciation. (p. 169) **Discount rate** Used as a hurdle rate, or minimum rate of return, in calculations of the time value of money; adjusted to reflect risk and uncertainty. (p. 162)
LO2 Use the IRR method to evaluate capital investment decisions.	The internal rate of return (IRR) is the actual yield, or return, earned by an investment.	**Internal rate of return (IRR)** The actual yield, or return, earned by an investment. (p. 163) **Net present value (NPV)** A technique for considering the time value of money whereby the present value of all cash inflows associated with a project is compared with the present value of all cash outflows. (p. 162)
LO3 Distinguish between screening and preference decisions and use the profitability index to evaluate preference decisions.	The profitability index is a valuable tool for making preference decisions because it can be used to compare projects that require investments of different amounts.	**Payback period** The length of time needed for a long-term project to recapture, or pay back, the initial investment. (p. 170) **Preference decisions** Decisions that involve choosing among alternatives. (p. 166)
LO4 Evaluate the impact of taxes on capital investment decisions.	Taxes are a major source of cash outflows for many companies and must be taken into consideration in calculations of the time value of money.	**Profitability index (PI)** Calculated by dividing the present value of cash inflows by the initial investment. (p. 167) **Screening decisions** Decisions about whether an investment meets a predetermined company standard. (p. 166)
LO5 Use the payback method to evaluate capital investment decisions, and discuss the limitations of the method.	The payback method can be useful as a quick approximation of the discounted cash flow methods when the cash flows follow similar patterns.	**Time value of money** The concept that a dollar received today is worth more than a dollar received in the future. (p. 160)

Concept Questions

1. Define the term *cost of capital*. How would cost of capital be used in an investment decision?

2. If the net present value of a proposed project is negative, then the actual rate of return is what?

3. For the internal rate of return to rank projects the same as net present value, which conditions must exist?

4. Describe the process in which the internal rate of return is used to accept or reject projects.

5. Define profitability index and discuss how it is used in capital investment decisions.

6. Compare screening decisions with preference decisions.

7. Explain the depreciation tax shield. Why should managers consider the tax shield in their decision-making process?

8. Define *payback period*. What are the primary advantages and disadvantages of the method?

Key Formulas

Present Value of an Annuity	$PVA = R(DFA_{n,r})$
Payback Period	$\text{Payback period} = \dfrac{\text{Original investment}}{\text{Change in volume}}$
Depreciation Tax Shield	$\text{Tax savings from depreciation} = \text{Depreciation expense} \times \text{Tax rate}$
Profitability Index	$\text{Profitability index} = \text{Present value of cash inflows}/\text{Initial investment}$
Net Present Value	$NPV = \text{Present value of cash inflows} - \text{present value of cash outflows}$

CAPITAL INVESTMENT DECISIONS

A. **Net Present Value (NPV):** considers the time value of money and requires the choice of a discount rate to be used.
   1. If NPV is = or > than zero, accept project.
   2. If NPV < than zero, reject project.

B. **Internal Rate of Return (IRR):** is the discount rate that makes NPV = 0 and is actual yield of return earned by an investment.
   1. If IRR is equal to or greater than cost of capital, accept project.
   2. If IRR is less than cost of capital, reject project.

C. **Payback Method:** ignores the time value of money and is valuable as approximation used in capital investment decisions.
   EXAMPLE

   $\text{Payback period} = \dfrac{\text{Original Investment}}{\text{Net Annual Cash Flows}}$

   By investing $50,000 to purchase a new delivery van, cash sales will increase by $14,000 annually for the next 6 years. The payback period is 3.57 years, or $50,000/$14,000.

Key Exhibit

Exhibit 8-4 Using NPV and IRR as Screening Tools

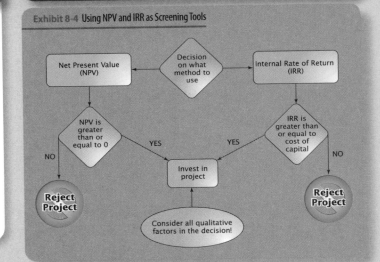

reviewcard
The Use of Budgets in Planning and Decision Making

Learning Objectives		Key Concepts	Key Definitions
LO1	Describe the budget development process, behavioral implications of budgeting, advantages of budgeting, and the master budget.	Budgets must start with a top-down strategic plan that guides and integrates the whole company and its individual budgets.	**Budgets** Plans dealing with the acquisition and use of resources over a specified period. (p. 178) **Cash disbursements budget** Used to project the amount of cash to be disbursed during the budget period. (p. 191) **Cash receipts budget** Used to project the amount of cash expected to be received from sales to customers and cash collections from customers. (p. 189) **Control** Involves ensuring that the objectives and goals developed by the organization are being attained; often involves a comparison of budgets with actual performance and the use of budgets for performance evaluation purposes. (p. 178) **Direct labor budget** Used to project the dollar amount of direct labor cost needed for production. (p. 187) **Flexible budgets** Budgets that take differences in spending owing to differences in volume out of the analysis by budgeting for labor (and other costs) on the basis of the *actual* number of units produced. (p. 196) **Manufacturing overhead budget** Used to project the dollar amount of manufacturing overhead needed for production. (p. 187) **Master budget** Consists of an interrelated set of budgets prepared by a business. (p. 182) **Material purchases budget** Used to project the dollar amount of raw materials purchased for production. (p. 185) **Operating budgets** Used to plan for the short term (typically one year or less). (p. 183) **Operating** Involves day-to-day decision making by managers, which is often facilitated by budgeting. (p. 178) **Participatory budgeting** A budgeting process that starts with departmental managers and flows up through middle management and then to top management. Each new level of management has responsibility for reviewing and negotiating any changes in the proposed budget. (p. 181)
LO2	Explain how managers develop a sales forecast and demonstrate the preparation of a sales budget.	Budgets are future oriented and make extensive use of estimates and forecasts.	
LO3	Prepare a production budget and recognize how it relates to the material purchases, direct labor, and manufacturing overhead budgets.	The sales forecast (budget) is the starting point in the production budget.	
LO4	Prepare budgets for material purchases, direct labor, manufacturing overhead, and selling and administrative expenses.	Preparing budgets for material purchases, direct labor, overhead, and selling and administrative expenses is critical because these budgets often require companies to commit to expenditures months in advance.	
LO5	Explain the importance of budgeting for cash and prepare a cash receipts budget, a cash disbursements budget, and a summary cash budget.	Accurate cash flow projections are critical if a company is to pay its employees, suppliers, and creditors on a timely basis.	
LO6	Prepare budgeted income statements and balance sheets and evaluate the importance of budgeted financial statements for decision making.	Preparing budgeted, or pro forma, financial statements allows managers to determine the effects of their budgeting decisions on the company's financial statements.	
LO7	Contrast budgeting in a manufacturing company with budgeting in a merchandising company and a service company.	A primary focus of budgeting in a service company is on labor (e.g., a time budget).	
LO8	Differentiate static budgets from flexible budgets.	Flexible budgets are based on the actual number of units produced rather than on the budgeted units of production.	

Key Definitions (continued)

Planning The cornerstone of good management; involves developing objectives and goals for the organization, as well as the actual preparation of budgets. (p. 178)

Pro forma financial statements Budgeted financial statements that sometimes are used for internal planning purposes but more often are used by external users. (p. 193)

Production budget Used to forecast how many units of product to produce in order to meet the sales projections. (p. 184)

Sales budget Used in planning the cash needs for manufacturing, merchandising, and service companies. (p. 182)

Sales forecast Combines with the sales budget to form the starting points in the preparation of production budgets for manufacturing companies, purchases budgets for merchandising companies, and labor budgets for service companies. (p. 182)

Static budgets Budgets that are set at the beginning of the period and remain constant throughout the budget period. (p. 196)

Summary cash budget Shows cash receipts and cash disbursements, along with any required borrowing or repayments made during the month. (p. 192)

Zero-based budgeting Requires managers to build budgets from the ground up each year. (p. 180)

BUDGETING

A. Uses of Budgets
1. **Planning:** developing objectives and goals.
2. **Operating:** making day-to-day management decisions.
3. **Control:** ensuring that objectives and goals are met, comparing actual with budget.

B. Advantages to Budgeting: include driving communication throughout organization, identifying bottlenecks and constraints, and defining standard of performance for evaluating future performance.

Concept Questions

1. What are some of the characteristics of a typical budget?
2. Using no amounts, outline a budget that you might employ in managing your personal finances.
3. Why is the sales budget the most important piece of the budgeting process?
4. List and describe some of the major factors and information sources typically used in sales forecasting.
5. What are the essential elements of a production budget?
6. Comment on the following statement: The materials, labor, and overhead budgets can be prepared before the production budget can.
7. What are several decisions that management can address by using the cash receipts budget?
8. Why is so much emphasis put on cash flow in the budgeting process?
9. Discuss ways that pro forma financial statements might be used both internally and externally.
10. Discuss why financial budgets for merchandising companies are different from those for manufacturing companies.
11. Discuss the difference between static and flexible budgets.

Key Formulas

Production Budget

$$
\begin{array}{l}
\quad \text{Sales forecast (in units)} \\
+ \text{ Desired ending inventory of finished goods} \\
\hline
= \text{ Total budgeted production needs} \\
- \text{ Beginning inventory of finished goods} \\
\hline
= \text{ Required production}
\end{array}
$$

Required production = Budgeted sales + (−) increase (decrease) in finished-goods inventory

Material Purchases Budget

$$
\begin{array}{l}
\quad \text{Raw materials needed to meet the required production budget} \\
+ \text{ Desired ending inventory of raw materials} \\
\hline
= \text{ Total raw materials needs} \\
- \text{ Beginning inventory of raw materials} \\
\hline
= \text{ Raw materials to be purchased}
\end{array}
$$

Summary Cash Budget

$$
\begin{array}{l}
\quad \text{Beginning cash balance} \\
+ \text{ Cash receipts} \\
\hline
= \text{ Total cash available} \\
- \text{ Cash disbursements} \\
\hline
= \text{ Cash balance before borrowing/repayment} \\
+/- \text{ Borrowing from/repayment of line of credit} \\
- \text{ Interest on line of credit} \\
\hline
= \text{ Ending cash balance}
\end{array}
$$

reviewcard

Learning Objectives	Key Concepts
LO1 Describe methods of determining standard costs and discuss the use of ideal versus practical standards.	The type of standard (practical or ideal) chosen to evaluate performance can have significant effects on employee morale and behavior.
LO2 Prepare a flexible budget using standard costs and contrast a flexible budget with a static budget.	Flexible budgets that are based on standard costs are the centerpiece of effective variance analysis.
LO3 Calculate a flexible budget variance and break it down into its components.	The flexible budget variance is the difference between the flexible budget operating income and the actual operating income.
LO4 Break down the variable manufacturing cost variance into direct material, direct labor, and variable overhead variances.	The variance analysis model, through the use of both price and usage variances, separates the overall flexible budget into two primary components.
LO5 Compute and interpret price and usage variances for direct materials.	Purchasing managers are often held responsible for price variances; production managers are held responsible for usage variances.
LO6 Compute and interpret rate and efficiency variances for direct labor.	Personnel and production managers are often responsible for direct labor variances.
LO7 Compute and interpret spending and efficiency variances for variable overhead.	The variable overhead efficiency variance does not measure the efficient use of overhead; instead, it measures the efficient use of the cost driver, or overhead allocation base, employed in the flexible budget.
LO8 Compute and interpret spending and volume variances for fixed overhead.	The fixed overhead volume variance should not be interpreted either as favorable or unfavorable or as a measure of the efficient utilization of facilities.
LO9 Analyze important considerations in using and interpreting variances, including the concept of management by exception.	Management by exception is the key to effective variance analysis and involves taking action only when actual and planned results differ significantly.

Key Definitions

Budget variance The difference between the amount of fixed overhead actually incurred and the flexible budget amount; also known as the spending variance. (p. 220)

Control Involves the motivation and monitoring of employees and the evaluation of people and other resources used in the operations of the organization. (p. 208)

Flexible budget variance The difference between the flexible budget operating income and actual operating income. (p. 212)

Ideal standard A standard that is attained only when near-perfect conditions are present. (p. 210)

Management by exception The process of taking action only when actual results deviate significantly from planned results. (p. 209)

Practical standard A standard that should be attained under normal, efficient operating conditions. (p. 210)

Price variance The difference between the actual price and the standard price, times the actual volume purchased. (p. 216)

Sales price variance The difference between the actual sales price and the flexible budget sales price, times the actual sales volume. (p. 213)

Standard cost A budget for a single unit of product or service. (p. 210)

Standard price The budgeted price of the materials, labor, or overhead for each unit. (p. 210)

Standard quantity The budgeted amount of materials, labor, or overhead for each product. (p. 210).

Task analysis A method of setting standards that also examines the production process in detail to determine what it should cost to produce a product. (p. 210)

Usage variance The difference between the actual quantity and the standard quantity, times the standard price. (p. 216)

Key Definitions (continued)

Variance analysis Allows managers to see whether sales, production, and manufacturing costs are higher or lower than planned and, more important, *why* actual sales, production, and costs differ from those budgeted. (p. 208)

Volume variance The difference between the flexible budget amount and the fixed overhead applied to products. (p. 220)

Concept Questions

1. Discuss ideal versus practical standards and how they might affect employee behavior.

2. What is the primary difference between a static budget and a flexible budget?

3. Discuss the value of a flexible budget to management decision making.

4. Which area of management would normally be responsible for sales price variances? Why?

5. How is the standard quantity (SQ) computed in the calculation of the direct material usage variance?

6. What is the focus of a usage variance?

7. What are some possible causes of an unfavorable direct labor efficiency variance?

8. What does a variable overhead efficiency variance tell management?

9. The predetermined fixed overhead application rate is a function of a predetermined "normal" activity level. If standard hours allowed for good output are equal to this predetermined activity level for a given period, what will the volume variance be?

10. Discuss the advantages and disadvantages of using "management by exception" techniques.

Key Formulas

Sales Price Variance

Sales price variance = (Actual − Expected sales price) × Actual volume

Generic Price Variance

$$\text{Generic price variance (DMPV, DLRV, and VOHSV)} = \text{Actual quantity (AQ)} \times [\text{Actual price (AP)} - \text{Standard price (SP)}]$$

Generic Usage Variance

$$\text{Generic usage variance (DMQV, DLUV, and VOHEV)} = \text{Standard price (SP)} \times [\text{Actual quantity (AQ)} - \text{Standard quantity (SQ)}]$$

Fixed Overhead Budget (Spending) Variance

$$\text{Fixed overhead budget (spending) variance} = \text{Actual fixed overhead} - \text{Budgeted fixed overhead}$$

Fixed Overhead Volume Variance

$$\text{Fixed overhead volume variance} = \text{Budgeted fixed overhead} - \text{Applied fixed overhead}$$

Flexible Budget Variance

Flexible budget variance = Flexible budget − Actual results

Key Exhibit

Exhibit 10-6 Basic Variance Analysis Model

AQ = Actual Quantity or Actual Hours AP = Actual Price or Actual Rate
SP = Standard Price or Standard Rate SQ = Standard Quantity or Standard Hours

Learning Objectives		Key Concepts	Key Definitions
LO1	Describe the structure and management of decentralized organizations and evaluate the benefits and drawbacks of decentralization.	Decentralized organizations must have managers who are competent, are experienced, and have the authority required to make decisions.	**Appraisal (detection) costs** Costs incurred to inspect finished products or products that are in the process of production. (p. 249)
LO2	Evaluate how responsibility accounting is used to help manage a decentralized organization.	The key to effective decision making in a decentralized organization is responsibility accounting: holding managers responsible for only those things under their control.	**Asset turnover** The measure of activity used in the ROI calculation; it measures the sales that are generated for a given level of assets. (p. 239)
LO3	Define cost, revenue, profit, and investment centers and explain why managers of each must be evaluated differently.	Businesses are often broken into cost, revenue, and profit centers as a means to evaluate managers' performance levels.	**Balanced scorecard** An approach to performance measurement that uses a set of financial and nonfinancial measures that relate to the overall strategy of the organization. (p. 244)
LO4	Compute and interpret segment margin in an organization.	Evaluating investment centers requires focusing on the level of investment required in generating a segment's profit.	**Common costs** Indirect costs that are incurred to benefit more than one segment and that cannot be directly traced to a particular segment or allocated in a reasonable manner. (p. 237)
LO5	Compute, interpret, and compare return on investment (ROI) and residual income.	Evaluating the performance of investment center managers is complex and often involves using measures such as ROI and residual income.	**Cost center** An organizational segment, or division, in which the manager has control over costs but not over revenue or investment decisions. (p. 235)
			Decentralized organization An organization in which decision-making authority is spread throughout the organization. (p. 232)
LO6	Describe the balanced scorecard and its key dimensions.	The balanced scorecard approach integrates financial and nonfinancial performance measures. The approach requires looking at performance from four different, but related, perspectives: financial, customer, internal business, and learning and growth.	**External failure costs** Costs incurred when a defective product is delivered to customer. (p. 249)
			Hejunka A system of standardizing manufacturing processes to improve efficiency. (p. 247)
			Internal failure costs Costs incurred once the product is produced and then determined to be defective. (p. 249)
			Investment center An organizational segment, or division, in which the manager has control over costs, revenue, and investment decisions. (p. 236)
			Kaizen A system of improvement based on a series of gradual and often small improvements. (p. 247)
LO7	Define quality costs and explain the trade-offs among prevention costs, appraisal costs, internal failure costs, and external failure costs.	The traditional view of quality costs is that total quality costs are minimized at some *acceptable level* of defects, while the contemporary view is that total quality costs are minimized at a *zero* defect level.	**Manufacturing cycle efficiency (MCE)** The value-added time in the production process divided by the throughput, or cycle time. (p. 245)
			Manufacturing cycle time The total time a product is in production, including process time, inspection time, wait time, and move time; cycle time includes both value added and non-value-added time. (p. 245)
LO8	Recognize the importance of using incentives to motivate managers and discuss the advantages and disadvantages of using cash-based, stock-based, and other forms of managerial compensation.	In order to motivate managers and ensure congruence of their goals, the compensation of managers should be linked to performance and based on a combination of short-term and long-term goals.	**Margin** For each sales dollar, the percentage that is recognized as net profit. (p. 239)
			Net operating income Net income from operations before interest and taxes. (p. 240)
			Operating assets Typically include cash, accounts receivable, inventory, and the property, plant, and equipment needed to operate a business. (p. 240)
			Performance report Provides key financial and nonfinancial measures of performance for a particular segment. (p. 236)

Key Definitions (continued)

Prevention costs Costs incurred to prevent product failures typically related to design and engineering. (p. 249)

Productivity A measure of the relationship between outputs and inputs. (p. 245)

Profit center An organizational segment, or division, in which the manager has control over both costs and revenue but not investment decisions. (p. 236)

Quality Usually defined as meeting or exceeding customers' expectations. (p. 246)

Residual income The amount of income earned in excess of a predetermined minimum level of return on assets. (p. 242)

Responsibility accounting An accounting system that assigns responsibility to a manager for only those areas which are under that manager's control. (p. 235)

Restricted stock A form of management compensation in which employees receive shares of stock with restrictions such as requirements to stay with the company for a set length of time or requirements to meet established performance measures. (p. 252)

Return on investment (ROI) Measures the rate of return generated by an investment center's assets. (p. 239)

Revenue center An organizational segment, or division, in which the manager has control over revenue but not costs or investment decisions. (p. 236)

Segment costs All costs attributable to a particular segment of an organization but only those costs that are actually caused by the segment. (p. 237)

Segment margin The profit margin of a particular segment of an organization, typically the best measure of long-term profitability. (p. 238)

Segmented income statements Reports that calculate income for each major segment of an organization in addition to the company as a whole. (p. 237)

Stock option The right to buy a share of stock at a set price (called the option price or strike price) at some point in the future. (p. 252)

Strategic business unit (SBU) Another term for investment center. (p. 236)

Throughput The amount of product produced in a given amount of time, such as a day, week, or month. (p. 245)

Concept Questions

1. Identify the advantages and disadvantages of decentralization.
2. What is responsibility accounting and what is its impact on decision making?
3. Define an investment center and explain how investment center managers might be evaluated.
4. Describe segment costs and compare them with common costs.
5. Define residual income and discuss how it compares with ROI.
6. When is ROI a more useful performance measure than residual income?
7. Describe a balanced scorecard and explain how it helps an organization meet its goals.
8. Discuss what is meant by quality in today's manufacturing environment.
9. Describe the two costs of controlling quality and the two costs of failing to control quality.
10. Why is noncash compensation important?

Key Formulas

ROI

$$ROI = Margin \times Turnover$$
$$Margin = Net\ operating\ income \div Sales$$
$$Turnover = Sales \div Average\ operating\ assets$$
$$ROI = \frac{Net\ operating\ income}{Sales} \times \frac{Sales}{Average\ operating\ assets}$$
$$ROI = \frac{Net\ operating\ income}{Average\ operating\ assets}$$

Residual Income

$$Residual\ income = Net\ operating\ income - \left(Average\ operating\ assets \times Minimum\ required\ rate\ of\ return \right)$$

BALANCED SCORECARD

Critical Success Factors
1. **Finance Perspective:** sales, ROI, and operating income.
2. **Customer Perspective:** reducing delivery time and increasing customer satisfaction.
3. **Internal Business Perspective:** productivity and manufacturing cycle time.
4. **Learning and Growth Perspective:** enhancing employee morale and reducing employee turnover.

Key Exhibit

Exhibit 11-11 Quality Costs

Prevention Costs	Appraisal (Detection) Costs	Internal Failure Costs	External Failure Costs
Design and engineering costs	Inspecting raw materials	Material, labor, and other manufacturing costs incurred in rework	Repairs made under warranty
Quality training	Testing goods during the production process	Scrap	Replacement of defective parts
Supervision	Final product testing and inspection	Spoilage	Product recalls
Quality improvement projects		Downtime	Liability costs from defective products
Training and technical support provided to suppliers		Design changes	Lost sales
		Reinspections	
		Disposal of defective products	

Learning Objectives	Key Concepts	Key Definitions
LO1 Explain why decision makers analyze financial statements and recognize the limitations of financial statement analysis.	Ratio analysis provides additional information that is necessary to enhance the decision-making ability of the users of the information. Rather than focus on a single ratio, decision makers need to evaluate a company by comparing ratios with those of previous years, with budgeted amounts, and with industry standards.	**Accounts receivable turnover ratio** One of the best measures of the efficiency of the collection process. (p. 270)
LO2 Use comparative financial statements to analyze the performance of a company over time (horizontal analysis).	Horizontal analysis is used to analyze changes in accounts occurring between years.	**Cash-to-cash operating cycle ratio** A measure of the length of time between the purchase of inventory and the eventual collection of cash from sales. (p. 271)
LO3 Prepare and use common-size financial statements to compare various financial statement items (vertical analysis).	Vertical analysis uses common-size financial statements to remove size as a relevant variable in ratio analysis. Ratio analysis is useful in assessing the impact of transactions on ROI, residual income, and other key measures of performance.	**Common-size financial statements** Statements in which all items have been restated as a percentage of a selected item on the statements. (p. 267)
LO4 Prepare and use liquidity ratios to analyze a company.	Liquidity ratios assess a company's ability to meet its short-term financial obligations.	**Current ratio** A measure of an entity's liquidity; also known as working capital ratio. (p. 268)
LO5 Prepare and use solvency ratios to analyze a company.	Solvency ratios assess the extent to which a company must borrow money to operate the business and how much interest is paid on that money.	**Debt service coverage ratio** A measure of the amount of cash generated by operating activities that is available to repay principal and interest in the upcoming year. (p. 273)
LO6 Prepare and use profitability ratios to analyze a company.	Profitability ratios provide measures of how effectively a company is using its assets.	**Debt-to-equity ratio** A solvency measure focusing on the amount of capital provided by creditors. (p. 272)

Earnings per share (EPS) A key measure of performance that is often used to compare companies of different size. (p. 275)

Horizontal analysis An analysis of financial statements over time. (p. 264)

Inventory turnover ratio A measure of the number of times the value of inventory is sold in one year. (p. 271)

Liquidity A measure of the ability of a company to meet its immediate financial obligations. (p. 267)

Price-earnings (P/E) ratio A measure of the current price of a company's stock in comparison to its earnings. Theoretically, the P/E ratio tells us something about how investors think that a company's stock will perform in the future compared with other companies' stock. (p. 275)

Quick ratio A stricter test of a company's ability to pay its current debts with highly liquid current assets. (p. 269)

Ratio of cash flow from operations to capital expenditures A measure of a company's ability to use cash flow from operations to finance the acquisition of property, plant, and equipment. (p. 273)

Key Definitions (continued)

Return on assets (ROA) A measure of return to investors on all assets invested in the company. (p. 274)

Return on common stockholders' equity (ROCSE) A measure of return to common stockholders as a percentage of stockholders' equity. (p. 274)

Times interest earned A measure of the company's ability to meet current interest payments to creditors. (p. 272)

Trend analysis Horizontal analysis of multiple years of data. (p. 264)

Working capital The excess of current assets over current liabilities, which is a measure of an entity's liquidity. (p. 267)

Concept Questions

1. Explain the purpose of financial statement analysis.
2. Explain the limitations of financial statement analysis.
3. Why would individuals want to perform a trend analysis?
4. Is it better to use more or fewer years when performing a trend analysis? Why?
5. Why are common-size financial statements useful?
6. Why should companies monitor their working capital?
7. What is the formula to compute accounts receivable turnover?
8. A company has a current ratio of 3 to 1 but would like to decrease the ratio. What types of options does it have to accomplish this task?
9. At the beginning of the year, the Golden Eagle Company had a current ratio of 2 to 1. What could Golden Eagle do to increase this ratio?
10. What does the debt-to-equity ratio tell about a company?
11. If sales are $475, beginning assets are $420, and ending assets are $480, what is the asset turnover ratio?

Key Formulas

Liquidity Ratios

$$\text{Current ratio} = \frac{\text{Current assets}}{\text{Current liabilities}}$$

$$\text{Quick ratio} = \frac{\text{Quick assets}}{\text{Current liabilities}}$$

$$\text{Cash flow from operations to current liabilities ratio} = \frac{\text{Net cash provided by operating activities}}{\text{Average current liabilities}}$$

Asset Management Ratios

$$\text{Accounts receivable turnover ratio} = \frac{\text{Net credit sales}}{\text{Average accounts receivable}}$$

$$\text{Number of days sales are in receivables} = \frac{\text{Number of days in the period}}{\text{Accounts receivable turnover}}$$

$$\text{Inventory turnover ratio} = \frac{\text{Cost of goods sold}}{\text{Average inventory}}$$

$$\text{Number of days inventory is held before sales} = \frac{\text{Number of days in the period}}{\text{Inventory turnover}}$$

$$\text{Cash-to-cash operating cycle ratio} = \text{Number of days in inventory} + \text{Number of days in receivables}$$

Solvency Ratios

$$\text{Debt-to-equity ratio} = \frac{\text{Total liabilities}}{\text{Total stockholders' equity}}$$

$$\text{Times interest earned} = \frac{\text{Net income} + \text{Interest expense} + \text{Income tax}}{\text{Interest expense}}$$

$$\text{Debt service coverage ratio} = \frac{\text{Cash flow from operations before interest and taxes}}{\text{Interest and principal payments}}$$

$$\text{Ratio of cash flow from operations to capital expenditures} = \frac{\text{Cash flow from operations} - \text{Total dividends paid}}{\text{Cash paid for acquisitions}}$$

Profitability Ratios

$$\text{ROA} = \frac{\text{Net income} + \text{Interest expense (net of tax)}}{\text{Average total assets}}$$

$$\text{Return on sales} = \frac{\text{Net income} + \text{Interest expense (net of tax)}}{\text{Net sales}}$$

$$\text{Asset turnover ratio} = \frac{\text{Net sales}}{\text{Average total assets}}$$

$$\text{ROCSE} = \frac{\text{Net income} - \text{Preferred dividends}}{\text{Average common stockholders' equity}}$$

$$\text{EPS} = \frac{\text{Net income} - \text{Preferred dividends}}{\text{Average number of common shares outstanding}}$$

$$\text{Price–earnings ratio} = \frac{\text{Current market price}}{\text{EPS}}$$

Learning Objectives	Key Concepts	Key Definitions
LO1 Recognize the purpose of a statement of cash flows and the activities making up a cash-flow statement.	The statement of cash flows is viewed by many as the most important financial statement because it provides evidence of the company's ability to meet its short-term financial obligations. The statement of cash flows reports all the major sources and uses of cash that result from different activities of the company. An understanding of the effects of different types of transactions on a company's cash flows helps investors and others recognize how a company is generating and using its cash.	**Cash equivalent** An item that can be readily converted to a known amount of cash and that has an original maturity of three months or less to the investor. (p. 285) **Direct method** Reports cash collected from customers and cash paid for inventory, salaries, wages, and so on. (p. 287) **Financing activities** Include cash flows from selling or repurchasing capital stock, long-term borrowing, and contributions from owners. (p. 285) **Indirect method** Starts with net income and removes the impact of noncash items and accruals. (p. 287) **Investing activities** Include the purchase and sale of property, plant, and equipment; the purchases and sales of securities; and loans made as investments. (p. 284) **Operating activities** Include acquiring and selling products in the normal course of business. (p. 283)
LO2 Discuss the difference between the direct and the indirect methods of computing cash flow from operating activities.	The only difference between the direct and indirect methods is in the presentation of the cash flows from operating activities. Cash flows from investing activities and cash flows from financing activities are calculated in exactly the same way.	
LO3 Prepare a comprehensive statement of cash flows, using the direct and indirect methods.	In using the indirect method, increases (decreases) in asset (liability) accounts during the year must be deducted from net income. When asset (liability) accounts decrease (increase) during the year, the amount of decrease or increase must be added to net income in arriving at net cash provided by operating activities.	

Concept Questions

1. What is the purpose of the statement of cash flows?

2. Discuss how the statement of cash flows differs from an income statement.

3. What is a cash equivalent? How is it used in the preparation of the statement of cash flows?

4. How is depreciation expense handled on the statement of cash flows?

5. Explain why, when a company uses the indirect method to prepare the operating activities section of the statement of cash flows, a decrease in a current asset is added back to net income.

6. "To prepare a statement of cash flows, all you have to do is compare the beginning and ending balances in cash on the balance sheet and compute the net inflow or outflow of cash." Do you agree with this statement? Why or why not?

7. "The statement of cash flows is the easiest of the basic financial statements to prepare because you know the answer before you start." Do you agree with this statement? Why or why not?

Key Formulas

Cash Collections from Customers

$$\text{Cash collections from customers} = \text{Sales revenue} + \text{Beginning accounts receivable} - \text{Ending accounts receivable}$$

$$\text{Cash collections from customers} = \text{Sales} \pm \text{Decrease (Increase) in accounts receivable}$$

Direct Method (Cash Flows from Operating Activities)

Direct method (cash flows from operating activities) = Cash receipts from:
  Cash sales
  + Collections of accounts receivable
  + Interest and dividends

Less:
Cash payments for:
  Operating expenses
  − Interest paid on debt
  − Taxes
  _____
  = Net cash provided (used) by operating activities

Indirect Method (Cash Flows from Operating Activities)

Indirect method (cash flows from operating activities) = Net income
  + Increases in related liabilities
  + Decreases in related noncash assets
  − Increases in related noncash assets
  − Decreases in related liabilities
  _____
  = Net cash provided (used) by operating activities

Additions to Net Income	Deductions from Net Income
Decrease in accounts receivable	Increase in accounts receivable
Decrease in inventory	Increase in inventory
Decrease in prepaid assets	Increase in prepaid assets
Increase in accounts payable	Decrease in accounts payable
Increase in accrued liabilities	Decrease in accrued liabilities

Key Exhibits

Exhibit 13-1 A Summary of Activities Making Up a Cash-Flow Statement

Cash Flows from Operating Activities	=	Cash received from the sale of goods or services and cash received from interest and dividends	−	Cash paid for operating expenses, cash paid for interest on debt, and cash paid for taxes
Cash Flows from Investing Activities	=	Cash received from the sale of investments and from the sale of property, plant, and equipment	−	Cash paid for investments and for purchases of property, plant, and equipment
Cash Flows from Financing Activities	=	Cash received from the sale of capital stock or the borrowing of funds	−	Cash paid for dividends on stock or repayments of debt or reacquiring capital stock

CengageNOW Student Study Tools Guide

What's Inside

ACCT has many resources to help you succeed in the course! See below for the valuable assets you will find in the Study Tools tab of CengageNOW.

Animations

Built from examples in selected chapters of the book, these animations bring the examples and underlying concepts to life. If you are a visual learner or you need some review on this particular topic, Animations will be a great resource for you.

Electures

Need something that will help you review concepts if you miss class or need additional help in an audio-visual format? These refreshers on the concepts for each chapter mirror the classroom experience and are PowerPoints with recorded audio walking you through concepts like a live lecture.

Crossword Puzzle

These fun puzzles help you review key vocabulary and definitions from the chapters.

PowerPoint Slides

These slides summarize key concepts and help you organize your review for enhanced understanding and exam and quiz prep.

Beat the Clock

This game quizzes you on important aspects of each chapter and helps you practice answering questions while the clock is ticking.

Quiz Bowl

This "Jeopardy-style" game is a fun way to review concepts and key terms. Regardless of whether you get the answer right or wrong, you will receive feedback on the correct answer so that you learn through the process.

Quizzing

Want to prep for your upcoming quiz or exam? Students often ask for practice with multiple-choice questions like those that often show up on tests and exams. Get used to answering multiple-choice accounting questions by quizzing yourself!

What's Inside

Using the *Personalized Study Plan* and *Interactive eBook*:
In addition to housing all of the study resources available to you, the *Study Tools* tab is where you will find access to your interactive eBook as well as your *Personalized Study Plan*. This card will explain how to use these powerful learning tools.

Using the Personalized Study Plan

First, take the Pre-Test.
While on the *Study Tools* tab, click on *Study Plan View* on the right to access the pre-test. This will help you gauge what you understand right now about chapter topics. When finished, view your graded pre-test & feedback by clicking on your score under *Result.* Click on *Home* to go back to the *Study Plan View*.

Next, view your Personalized Study Plan.
The *Personalized Study Plan* will suggest readings or study tools based on your pre-test results to help you focus your study. To access, click on *View* under the *Study Tools* column.

Finally, take the Post-Test and review your Revised Study Plan.
The post-test can be taken again and again until you have mastered the concepts. Click on the link to take the *Post-Test*. The personalized study plan will continue to revise based on your pre-test results.

Using Your Interactive eBook
ACCT offers a dynamic eBook that will help you interact with accounting content while on the go! Check out how you can read & study with your eBook.

Table of Contents:
Easily navigate to various chapters or to specific learning objectives within a chapter with the *Table of Contents* tab on the left.

Search:
Looking for all content related to a specific word or phrase? Use the *Search* bar to find all mentions of your search term throughout the eBook.

Index:
Another way to find exactly what you are looking for is to click on the *Index* tab, which will take you directly to the pages where a term or concept is covered.

Glossary:
To find the definition of a key term in the text, go straight to the *Glossary* or hover over the term in the text.

Notes:
As you move through the eBook, you can write notes to yourself next to certain parts of the text. Click on the *Add Notes* button at the top.

Highlights:
To highlight sections of text, click on the *Add Highlight* button at the top and drag your mouse over the section you want to highlight.

Notes & Highlights:
All of your notes and highlights are captured for you in one easy place under the *Notes & Highlights* tab. Use this as your "virtual study guide" to focus on what you have deemed the most important parts of the chapter.

Present Value of $1 Due in n Periods

$$\text{Factor} = \frac{1}{(1 + r)^n}$$

_r_

Periods	1%	2%	3%	4%	5%	6%	7%	8%	9%	10%	12%	14%	15%	16%	18%	20%	24%
1	0.9901	0.9804	0.9709	0.9615	0.9524	0.9434	0.9346	0.9259	0.9174	0.9091	0.8929	0.8772	0.8696	0.8621	0.8475	0.8333	0.8065
2	0.9803	0.9612	0.9426	0.9426	0.9070	0.8900	0.8734	0.8573	0.8417	0.8264	0.7972	0.7695	0.7561	0.7432	0.7182	0.6944	0.6504
3	0.9706	0.9423	0.9151	0.8890	0.8638	0.8396	0.8163	0.7938	0.7722	0.7513	0.7118	0.6750	0.6575	0.6407	0.6086	0.5787	0.5245
4	0.9610	0.9238	0.8885	0.8548	0.8227	0.7921	0.7629	0.7350	0.7084	0.6830	0.6355	0.5921	0.5718	0.5523	0.5158	0.4823	0.4230
5	0.9515	0.9057	0.8626	0.8219	0.7835	0.7473	0.7130	0.6806	0.6499	0.6209	0.5674	0.5194	0.4972	0.4761	0.43731	0.4019	0.3411
6	0.9420	0.8880	0.8375	0.7903	0.7462	0.7050	0.6663	0.6302	0.5963	0.5645	0.5066	0.4556	0.4323	0.4104	0.3704	0.3349	0.2751
7	0.9327	0.8706	0.8131	0.7599	0.7107	0.6651	0.6227	0.5835	0.5470	0.5132	0.4523	0.3996	0.3759	0.3538	0.3139	0.2791	0.2218
8	0.9235	0.8535	0.7894	0.7307	0.6768	0.6274	0.5820	0.5403	0.5019	0.4665	0.4039	0.3506	0.3269	0.3050	0.2660	0.2326	0.1789
9	0.9143	0.8368	0.7664	0.7026	0.6446	0.5919	0.5439	0.5002	0.4604	0.4241	0.3606	0.3075	0.2843	0.2630	0.2255	0.1938	0.1443
10	0.9053	0.8203	0.7441	0.6756	0.6139	0.5584	0.5083	0.4632	0.4224	0.3855	0.3220	0.2697	0.2472	0.2267	0.1911	0.1615	0.1164
11	0.8963	0.8043	0.7224	0.6496	0.5847	0.5268	0.4751	0.4289	0.3875	0.3505	0.2875	0.2366	0.2149	0.1954	0.1619	0.1346	0.0938
12	0.8874	0.7885	0.7014	0.6246	0.5568	0.4970	0.4440	0.3971	0.3555	0.3186	0.2567	0.2076	0.1869	0.1685	0.1372	0.1122	0.0757
13	0.8787	0.7730	0.6810	0.6006	0.5303	0.4688	0.4150	0.3677	0.3262	0.2897	0.2292	0.1821	0.1625	0.1452	0.1163	0.0935	0.0610
14	0.8700	0.7579	0.6611	0.5775	0.5051	0.4423	0.3878	0.3405	0.2992	0.2633	0.2046	0.1597	0.1413	0.1252	0.0985	0.0779	0.0492
15	0.8613	0.7430	0.6419	0.5553	0.4810	0.4173	0.3624	0.3152	0.2745	0.2394	0.1827	0.1401	0.1229	0.1079	0.0835	0.0649	0.0397
16	0.8528	0.7284	0.6232	0.5339	0.4581	0.3936	0.3387	0.2919	0.2519	0.2176	0.1631	0.1229	0.1069	0.0930	0.0708	0.0541	0.0320
17	0.8444	0.7142	0.6050	0.5134	0.4363	0.3714	0.3166	0.2703	0.2311	0.1978	0.1456	0.1078	0.0929	0.0802	0.0600	0.0451	0.0258
18	0.8360	0.7002	0.5874	0.4936	0.4155	0.3503	0.2959	0.2502	0.2120	0.1799	0.1300	0.0946	0.0808	0.0691	0.0508	0.0376	0.0208
19	0.8277	0.6864	0.5703	0.4746	0.3957	0.3305	0.2765	0.2317	0.1945	0.1635	0.1161	0.0829	0.0703	0.0596	0.0431	0.0313	0.0168
20	0.8195	0.6730	0.5537	0.4564	0.3769	0.3118	0.2584	0.2145	0.1784	0.1486	0.1037	0.0728	0.0611	0.0514	0.0365	0.0261	0.0135
21	0.8114	0.6598	0.5375	0.4388	0.3589	0.2942	0.2415	0.1987	0.1637	0.1351	0.0926	0.0638	0.0531	0.0443	0.0309	0.0217	0.0109
22	0.8034	0.6468	0.5219	0.4220	0.3418	0.2775	0.2257	0.1839	0.1502	0.1228	0.0826	0.0560	0.0462	0.0382	0.0262	0.0181	0.0088
23	0.7954	0.6342	0.5067	0.4057	0.3256	0.2618	0.2109	0.1703	0.1378	0.1117	0.0738	0.0491	0.0402	0.0329	0.0222	0.0151	0.0071
24	0.7876	0.6217	0.4919	0.3901	0.3101	0.2470	0.1971	0.1577	0.1264	0.1015	0.0659	0.0431	0.0349	0.0284	0.0188	0.0126	0.0057
25	0.7798	0.6095	0.4776	0.3751	0.2953	0.2330	0.1842	0.1460	0.1160	0.0923	0.0588	0.0378	0.0304	0.0245	0.0160	0.0105	0.0046
26	0.7720	0.5976	0.4637	0.3607	0.2812	0.2198	0.1722	0.1352	0.1064	0.0839	0.0525	0.0331	0.0264	0.0211	0.0135	0.0087	0.0037
27	0.7644	0.5859	0.4502	0.3468	0.2678	0.2074	0.1609	0.1252	0.0976	0.0763	0.0469	0.0291	0.0230	0.0182	0.0115	0.0073	0.0030
28	0.7568	0.5744	0.4371	0.3335	0.2551	0.1956	0.1504	0.1159	0.0895	0.0693	0.0419	0.0255	0.0200	0.0157	0.0097	0.0061	0.0024
29	0.7493	0.5631	0.4243	0.3207	0.2429	0.1846	0.1406	0.1073	0.0822	0.0630	0.0374	0.0224	0.0174	0.0135	0.0082	0.0051	0.0020
30	0.7419	0.5521	0.4120	0.3083	0.2314	0.1741	0.1314	0.0994	0.0754	0.0573	0.0334	0.0196	0.0151	0.0116	0.0070	0.0042	0.0016

Present Value of an Annuity of $1 per Period

$$\text{Factor} = \frac{1 - \dfrac{1}{(1 + r)^n}}{r}$$

Periods	1%	2%	3%	4%	5%	6%	7%	8%	9%	10%	12%	14%	15%	16%	18%	20%	24%
1	0.9901	0.9804	0.9709	0.9615	0.9524	0.9434	0.9346	0.9259	0.9174	0.9091	0.8929	0.8772	0.8696	0.8621	0.8475	0.8333	0.8065
2	1.9704	1.9416	1.9135	1.8861	1.8594	1.8334	1.8080	1.7833	1.7591	1.7355	1.6901	1.6467	1.6257	1.6052	1.5656	1.5278	1.4568
3	2.9410	2.8839	2.8286	2.7751	2.7232	2.6730	2.6243	2.5771	2.5313	2.4869	2.4018	2.3216	2.2832	2.2459	2.1743	2.1065	1.9813
4	3.9020	3.8077	3.7171	3.6299	3.5460	3.4651	3.3872	3.3121	3.2397	3.1699	3.0373	2.9137	2.8550	2.7982	2.6901	2.5887	2.4043
5	4.8534	4.7135	4.5797	4.4518	4.3295	4.2124	4.1002	3.9927	3.8897	3.7908	3.6048	3.4331	3.3522	3.2743	3.1272	2.9906	2.7454
6	5.7955	5.6014	5.4172	5.2421	5.0757	4.9173	4.7665	4.6229	4.4859	4.3553	4.1114	3.8887	3.7845	3.6847	3.4976	3.3255	3.0205
7	6.7282	6.4720	6.2303	6.0021	5.7864	5.5824	5.3893	5.2064	5.0330	4.8684	4.5638	4.2883	4.1604	4.0386	3.8115	3.6046	3.2423
8	7.6517	7.3255	7.0197	6.7327	6.4632	6.2098	5.9713	5.7466	5.5348	5.3349	4.9676	4.6389	4.4873	4.3436	4.0776	3.8372	3.4212
9	8.5660	8.1622	7.7861	7.4353	7.1078	6.8017	6.5152	6.2469	5.9952	5.7590	5.3282	4.9464	4.7716	4.6065	4.3030	4.0310	3.5655
10	9.4713	8.9826	8.5302	8.1109	7.7217	7.3601	7.0236	6.7101	6.4177	6.1446	5.6502	5.2161	5.0188	4.8332	4.4941	4.1925	3.6819
11	10.3676	9.7868	9.2526	8.7605	8.3064	7.8869	7.4987	7.1390	6.8052	6.4951	5.9377	5.4527	5.2337	5.0286	4.6560	4.3271	3.7757
12	11.2551	10.5753	9.9540	9.3851	8.8633	8.3838	7.9427	7.5361	7.1607	6.8137	6.1944	5.6603	5.4206	5.1971	4.7932	4.4392	3.8514
13	12.1337	11.3484	10.6350	9.9856	9.3936	8.8527	8.3577	7.9038	7.4869	7.1034	6.4235	5.8424	5.5831	5.3423	4.9095	4.5327	3.9124
14	13.0037	12.1062	11.2961	10.5631	9.8986	9.2950	8.7455	8.2442	7.7862	7.3667	6.6283	6.0021	5.7245	5.4675	5.0081	4.6106	3.9616
15	13.8651	12.8493	11.9379	11.1184	10.3797	9.7122	9.1079	8.5595	8.0607	7.6061	6.8109	6.1422	5.8474	5.5755	5.0916	4.6755	4.0013
16	14.7179	13.5777	12.5611	11.6523	10.8378	10.1059	9.4466	8.8514	8.3126	7.8237	6.9740	6.2651	5.9542	5.6685	5.1624	4.7296	4.0333
17	15.5623	14.2919	13.1661	12.1657	11.2741	10.4773	9.7632	9.1216	8.5436	8.0216	7.1196	6.3729	6.0472	5.7487	5.2223	4.7746	4.0591
18	16.3983	14.9920	13.7535	12.6593	11.6896	10.8276	10.0591	9.3719	8.7556	8.2014	7.2497	6.4674	6.1280	5.8178	5.2732	4.8122	4.0799
19	17.2260	15.6785	14.3238	13.1339	12.0853	11.1581	10.3356	9.6036	8.9501	8.3649	7.3658	6.5504	6.1982	5.8775	5.3162	4.8435	4.0967
20	18.0456	16.3514	14.8775	13.5903	12.4622	11.4699	10.5940	9.8181	9.1285	8.5136	7.4694	6.6231	6.2593	5.9288	5.3527	4.8696	4.1103
21	18.8570	17.0112	15.4150	14.0292	12.8212	11.7641	10.8355	10.0168	9.2922	8.6487	7.5620	6.6870	6.3125	5.9731	5.3837	4.8913	4.1212
22	19.6604	17.6580	15.9369	14.4511	13.1630	12.0416	11.0612	10.2007	9.4424	8.7715	7.6446	6.7429	6.3587	6.0113	5.4099	4.9094	4.1300
23	20.4558	18.2922	16.4436	14.8568	13.4886	12.3034	11.2722	10.3711	9.5802	8.8832	7.7184	6.7921	6.3988	6.0442	5.4321	4.9245	4.1371
24	21.2434	18.9139	16.9355	15.2470	13.7986	12.5504	11.4693	10.5288	9.7066	8.9847	7.7843	6.8351	6.4338	6.0726	5.4509	4.9371	4.1428
25	22.0232	19.5235	17.4131	15.6221	14.0939	12.7834	11.6536	10.6748	9.8226	9.0770	7.8431	6.8729	6.4641	6.0971	5.4669	4.9476	4.1474
26	22.7952	20.1210	17.8768	15.9828	14.3752	13.0032	11.8258	10.8100	9.9290	9.1609	7.8957	6.9061	6.4906	6.1182	5.4804	4.9563	4.1511
27	23.5596	20.7069	18.3270	16.3296	14.6430	13.2105	11.9867	10.9352	10.0266	9.2372	7.9426	6.9352	6.5135	6.1364	5.4919	4.9636	4.1542
28	24.3164	21.2813	18.7641	16.6631	14.8981	13.4062	12.1371	11.0511	10.1161	9.3066	7.9844	6.9607	6.5335	6.1520	5.5016	4.9697	4.1566
29	25.0658	21.8444	19.1885	16.9837	15.1411	13.5907	12.2777	11.1584	10.1983	9.3696	8.0218	6.9830	6.5509	6.1656	5.5098	4.9747	4.1585
30	25.8077	22.3965	19.6004	17.2920	15.3725	13.7648	12.4090	11.2578	10.2737	9.4269	8.0552	7.0027	6.5660	6.1772	5.5168	4.9789	4.1601

r

Notes

Notes